Marriage and Family in the Modern World

A BOOK OF READINGS

Ruth Shonle Cavan

Mary Ashby Cheek Professor of Sociology, Rockford College

THOMAS Y. CROWELL COMPANY   New York

Established 1834

Library of Congress Catalog Card Number: 60-6058

Designed by Edwin H. Kaplin

Manufactured in the United States of America
by the Vail-Ballou Press, Inc., Binghamton, N.Y.

Preface

THE PURPOSE of this book of Readings is to place in the hands of college students and other readers a carefully selected collection of articles and excerpts from books which contribute to the understanding of marriage and family living. The book is planned primarily for the course in preparation for marriage and family living, and secondarily for the course in sociology of the family. The approach is what is termed functional, that is, the articles are interpretative and often include applications to specific situations. Therefore the advanced student, the researcher, and the professor interested in the testing of new theories and the use of intricate research methods may find little that contributes to his work. However, the student bent on guidance in marriage and family living, the teacher of the marriage and family life courses, and the general reader should find the book understandable and useful. Although deeper meaning may be given to some of the articles by background preparation in sociology, psychology, or biology, genuine appreciation of the articles is not dependent upon such preparation.

The 93 articles are organized into 25 chapters. The first four chapters give the setting for the study of marriage and family life in the United States: the significance of marriage socially, personally, and biologically; the entire family life cycle, a few segments of which this book emphasizes; a brief historical perspective from colonial families to the family of the future; and a contrast with marriage in three contemporary cultures. Chapters 5 through 10 begin with a discussion of differences between men and women and traverse the subjects of dating, engagement, love, intimacies, and legal regulations. Chapters 11 through 19 deal with husband and wife in the experience of marriage, beginning with when to marry and covering roles, finances, problems mild and serious, and disintegration and readjustment. Chapters 20 through 23 deal with parents and children. Chapter 20 contains five nontechnical articles on subjects of heredity and is followed by discussions of the first baby, relations between parents and children, and some serious adjustment problems that a minority of children face. Chapter 24 is devoted to in-laws and grandparents. Chapter 25 presents discussion groups and marriage counseling as aids to successful marriage.

The book covers the subjects included in most textbooks in the marriage field. It extends beyond in the sociological material in the first four chapters, some of the biological material, and more than average attention to men as earners and fathers. The hard problems of marriage that come to a minority of couples (alcoholism, divorce) or that may come only once in a lifetime (bereavement) have not been bypassed, although it is often easier to overlook them in a field of study that is generally optimistic.

In selecting nontechnical articles, the policy followed was that the articles should be authoritative but written in nontechnical language and uncomplicated style. Sometimes it was possible to use articles or chapters from books written by professionals for professionals. It was discovered, however, that many specialists who contribute terse theoretical or research articles to the outstanding professional journals also contribute interpretative articles based upon their research to other types of journals and to magazines. These interpretative articles have been used extensively. A second source of articles was those written by professional magazine writers and journalists who have double specialization, in writing and in some field of knowledge (e.g., the family or biological science) and who put scientific knowledge into nontechnical language for the general reading public. Finally an occasional popular article that seemed to add insight and zest was included.

One difficulty of readings books is that the great number of authors included prevents the reader from coming into rapport with them, as he may do with the single author of a book. To overcome this difficulty, a brief biographical note gives salient facts about each author so that the reader may feel that he is being addressed by a person and not merely by a name.

Finally, to increase the usefulness of the book a chart has been placed in the appendix listing the chief texts in marriage preparation and the family by chapter and citing appropriate articles in the Readings by number. With this system the instructor may easily refer students to the articles that may clarify or amplify any specific chapter in the text being used.

The editor wishes to thank the many colleagues who gave helpful written or verbal suggestions or who gave permission to reprint articles and consented to revisions of articles. The book has been made possible also by the generous willingness of many publishers to have articles or parts of books reprinted.

Ruth Shonle Cavan

Rockford, Illinois
January, 1960

Contents

PREFACE

THE PURPOSE of this book of readings is to place in the hands of college students and other readers a carefully selected collection of articles and excerpts from books that contribute to the understanding of marriage and family living. The volume is planned for courses in preparation for marriage, family living, and sociology of the family. The articles tend to be interpretative and often include applications to specific situations; therefore, the advanced student, the researcher, and the professor interested in the testing of new theories and the use of intricate research methods may find little that contributes to his work. However, the student bent on guidance in marriage and family living or an understanding of the sociology of the family, the teacher of the appropriate courses, and the general reader should find the book understandable and useful. Although deeper meaning may be given to some of the articles by background preparation in sociology, psychology, or biology, genuine appreciation of the articles is not dependent upon such preparation.

The seventy-eight articles are organized into twenty-two chapters. The first four chapters give the setting for the study of marriage and family life in the United States: the significance of marriage socially, personally, and biologically; the family life cycle; a brief historical perspective from colonial families to the family of the future; and a contrast with marriage in three contemporary cultures. Chapters 5 through 10 begin with a discussion of differences between men and women and traverse the subjects of dating, engagement, love, intimacies, unmarried parents, and legal regulations. Chapters 11 through 15 deal with husband and wife in the experience of marriage, covering husband-wife interaction, employment roles, finances, the nuclear family and the kinship web, and the middle and later years. Chapters 16 and 17 are concerned with stresses, conflict, divorce, and re-adjustment. Chapters 18 through 21 focus on parents and children, answering a number of questions on the first baby, heredity, and parent-child relationships. Finally, Chapter 22 presents discussion groups and counseling as aids to successful marriage.

Marriage and Family in the Modern World covers the subjects included in most textbooks on marriage and the family. More than average attention is given to men as earners and fathers. The difficult problems of marriage that come to a minority of couples (alcoholism, divorce) or that may come only once in a lifetime (bereavement) have not been bypassed, although it is often easier to overlook them in a field of study that is generally optimistic.

In selecting nontechnical articles, the policy followed was that the articles should be authoritative but written in nontechnical language and uncomplicated style. Sometimes it was possible to use articles or chapters from books written by professionals for professionals. It was discovered, moreover, that many specialists who contribute terse theoretical or research articles to the outstanding professional journals also contribute interpretative articles based upon their research to other types of journals and to magazines. These interpretative articles have been used extensively. A second source of articles was those written by professional magazine writers and journalists who have double specialization, in writing and in some field of knowledge (for example, the family or biological science) and who put scientific knowledge into nontechnical language for the general reading public.

One difficulty of readings books is that the great number of authors included prevents the reader from coming into rapport with them, as he may do with the single author of a book. To overcome this difficulty, a brief biographical note gives salient facts about each author so that the reader may feel that he is being addressed by a person and not merely by a name.

Finally, to increase the usefulness of the book a chart has been placed in the appendix listing recent texts in marriage preparation and the family by chapter and citing appropriate articles in the readings by number. With this system the instructor may easily refer students to the articles that may clarify or amplify any specific chapter in the text being used.

The editor wishes to thank the many colleagues who gave helpful written or verbal suggestions or who gave permission to reprint articles and consented to revisions of articles. The book has been made possible also by the generous willingness of many publishers to have articles or parts of books reprinted.

DeKalb, Illinois   RUTH SHONLE CAVAN
January, 1965

CHAPTER 1

Significance of Marriage and the Family Today

1 · What Strong Family Life Means to Our Society *

KIMBALL YOUNG

In the midst of the many books and articles that cast doubt upon the value of the family, it is refreshing to find this article which extols the limited though fundamenal values of the family both to society and to the family members. Realistic rather than idealistic, the article briefly outlines recent changes in the family as a springboard for discussion of developments such as the importance of employment of the mother, for children as well as for the bank account; or the pulls away from and back to the home of public commercial recreation, radio, and television. The effects of crises—from depression to divorce—are suggested. The author concludes that the family must seek reorganization—not by turning back to the past, but by facing the present and future and making use of scientific findings on what makes for successful family life.

THE FAMILY as a group of interacting individuals fulfils certain basic functions. First of all it provides the biological means of perpetuating the race. Second, it acts as the chief agency in the socialization of the new generation; that is, it conveys to the growing boy or girl the fundamentals of the cul-

* Social Casework, 34 (October, 1953), 323–329; also published under the title "Family Life in Our Society," The Social Welfare Forum (1953), 158–170. Reprinted by permission of Social Casework and the National Conference on Social Welfare, respectively, and the author.

The author, who is Chairman of the Department of Sociology, Northwestern University, received the degree of Doctor of Philosophy (in psychology) at Leland Stanford University. He is widely known for his textbooks in social psychology and sociology. He is author of a study of the historical Mormon family, entitled Isn't One Wife Enough?

ture of a given society, its customs, traditions, skills, and moral values. These are necessary to enable the new member to play his role as a participant in society.

Yet the family is more than the means of reproducing the species and of training the offspring for their place in the world. As a functioning group, the family provides its members with a number of basic satisfactions. Among others are the outlets of love between the spouses, of love between the parents and children, and finally love between or among the children themselves. Such affectional expression has been long regarded as important for the emotional development of the individual. Then, too, the home normally gives the child some sense of economic stability.

Yet there are some situations in family life marked by competition and, under severe stress, by conflict. Interpersonal opposition is quite as normal in group life as are co-operation and mutual aid. The husband and wife may differ over entertainment, over who shall be their friends, over expenditures, about the way to bring up children, and a variety of other things. A parent may fall into strong conflict with an adolescent son or daughter regarding dating, staying out late at night, and various other matters. Moreover, in sibling rivalry, which is present in one form or another in practically all families, we find various oppositional attitudes developing.

In short, the family is, as C. H. Cooley long ago remarked, our primary human grouping. It is primary in the sense of being the basis of the reproduction and socialization of the next generation by the previous one. It is also the initial proving ground of co-operative and oppositional habits bound up with satisfying needs for affection, security, and status. Yet historically the family has been even more than this. It has had important economic, protective, religious, and recreational functions as well. In fact, to understand many of its present dilemmas, we must review briefly some of the striking changes that have taken place in family life in the last fifty or one hundred years.

Changes in Structure and Function

One obvious fact is the steady decline in family size. At the time of our first census, in 1790, the average number of persons per family was 5.7. One hundred years later it was 4.9. By 1940 the average size of the American family had fallen to 3.8; and today it is around 3.6. It is estimated that by 1980 the average American family will consist of 3.1 persons. Since the two parents are a constant factor in the size of the normal family, it is clear that the number of children has grown steadily less. In the interval from the first census to 1940, the average number of children per family declined from 3.2 to 1.2.

Changes in the family size, of course, are related to other factors. Among these are childless marriages. The extent of this is evident in the fact that 15 per cent of the American women who marry bear no children. The second factor is that of the aging population. In other words we have an increasing fraction of families in which there are no minor children. In the third place there is an increase in the average span of life between marriage and the birth of the first child. And fourth, there is a general decline in the rate of population growth. On this last point, Paul C. Glick writes: "Because of the steady fall in family size, the population has always tended to increase at a slower rate than the number of families. For example, there are now [in 1940] 175 per cent more families than in 1890, but the population has grown by only 110 per cent. Between . . . [1940] and 1980 the number of families is expected to increase approximately 40 per cent, while the population is augmented by only 16 per cent." [1]

A number of important shifts in the nature of the family functions have also occurred. There are modifications in the importance of the family as an economic unit, changes in the educative or training function, in its protective aspects, in religious training, and with regard to recreation.

The shifts in the household as an economic unit are most noteworthy. Today the money wage of the chief breadwinner is the principal source of family support. Even in our rural areas there has been a shift to more individualized economic functions. Another measure of changes in household economy is the decrease in the amount of time women spend in baking bread, laundering, canning fruits and vegetables, and making clothes. The increase in the number of restaurants and lunchrooms reflects, in part, the disappearance of formerly accepted household duties. So, too, there has been a steady increase in the use of power machinery in the home, such as vacuum cleaners, mechanical dishwashers, power laundry units, and the like.

One of the most striking reflections of this whole matter is the increase in the number of women, especially married women, who are gainfully employed outside the home. For the age group 14 years and up, of the 62,-234,000 gainfully employed persons, nearly 19,000,000 are women. Of this latter number one-half are married. That is, there are nearly 10,000,000 married women in the nation's labor force. However, it is interesting to note that five-sixths of these have no young dependent children or children of school age only. The proportion of married women among all women gainfully employed has steadily risen. For example, in 1890 there were just over half a million married women in the labor force, and they made up only 14 per cent of all women employed at that time.

Another important shift has been in the educative functions of the family.

---

[1] Paul C. Glick, "Family Trends in the United States, 1890 to 1940," *American Sociological Review*, Vol. VII, No. 4 (1942), p. 506.

For thousands of years the family was the fundamental or basic educative agency *vis-à-vis* the rising new generation. In recent times these functions have more and more been taken over by other agencies. A significant illustration is the rise of the nursery school. Some years ago I was talking about the whole matter of child training to a group of P.T.A. women. In the discussion period one mother raised some serious objections to the setting up of a nursery school in that community. With considerable emotion she spoke of the fact that the nursery school was robbing the cradle and making women unhappy because they did not have their children at home to pour out their affections on. This sentimental woman little realized that the nursery school arose because of certain shifts in family function. It was not set up by enterprising educators to rob the home of its basic functions. In terms of the metaphor, she had the cart before the horse.

An older institution, but one that is growing, is the kindergarten, which serves to take over some of the socialization of children at an early age. For a long time, of course, the elementary and the high schools have absorbed important educative functions, both formal and informal. The high value attributed to education in this country is shown by the fact that in 1951, of the 21,000,000 persons in the age group of 5 to 13 years, 90 per cent were in school. For the ages 14 to 19 years, 77 per cent of the 6,312,000 in this age bracket were in school. Never in the history of the world has it been possible for so many individuals of the adolescent years to be relieved of the obligation to work in order to spend their time in the preparation for later life.

Other changes in family functions concern protective operations. In many areas of social control civil officials have long since taken over the protective functions of the home. In the same way religious training has moved more and more out of the home into the hands of formal religious organizations. The Sunday school and like agencies illustrate clearly the fact that religious and moral training, which for hundreds of years was given by the parents, has now been taken over by institutions outside the home.

By the same token recreation, once centered in the family, has in large part departed from the home to other places. The commercialization of pleasure is clearly indicated in the whole development of the motion picture industry, the radio, and more recently television. In this country there are nearly 20,000 movie houses with a seating capacity of just under 12,-000,000 individuals. There is probably a weekly attendance of something between 50 and 60 million individuals, a considerable decline from former high attendance estimated to be around 75 million. In recent years, of course, we have seen the radio, and latterly television, come to compete with the motion picture for entertainment and education. For example, in October, 1952, there were about 110,000,000 radio sets in this country.

There were over 46,000,000 American homes with radios; 25,000,000 automobiles had radios. Today there are something on the order of 21,000,000 television sets in American homes.

Whereas the motion picture has tended to take individuals out of the home, it has been argued in some quarters that radio, and especially now television, has tended to restore some home-centered recreation. Just what this means in terms of bolstering traditional family function is hard to say. Certainly radio and television programs have on occasion—though how much we do not know—tended to set up certain kinds of conflict situations as when Junior wants to see Hopalong Cassidy and the parents want to hear the news or listen to a concert. Be this as it may, we are at a loss to know at this time how much television and radio have modified the earlier general drift of recreation out of the home.

A basic principle regarding social change that I should like to stress is exemplified in the saying, "We cannot go back to the old." There is an irreversibility in any basic institutional change. This fact is often neglected or ignored by sentimental reformers and the "do-gooders" who wish somehow to restore the good old days. But a directional drift in social change cannot be altered. I do not mean to deny the facts of social causation. Whatever happens in the future will, of course, be affected by what has happened in the past. What I am saying is that there is no evidence that we can restore something that has already passed away.

Family Crises

Let us now examine some of the important crises that family members face today. We begin by noting what may happen between husband and wife. First, let us look at the shattering effects of the shifts in the conception that each person has of the other. On the one hand, every individual carries a self-image of himself, which may serve as an ideal and as a basis for his actual operations. Sometimes the behavior of the individual is quite different from that of his self-image; but nevertheless the self-image becomes an important element in the personality. Then, too, there is always the image of the other person. For example, the marriage partner carries an image of his spouse; that is, a picture in his mind of how the other individual operates. The individual's self-image and his image of his spouse are important factors in their reaching successful, mutual adjustment. Under stress and strain of family life, these images break down. For example, in the humdrum routines of day-by-day living, under difficult conditions such as economic hardship, the idealism of the romantic courtship may give way to a somewhat drab conception of each other. Also, shock may be precipitated by the discovery of a certain amount of previous concealment. The shock reaction may be related to such things as discovering that the age alleged by one is not really the true fact, that certain relatives have suffered mental breakdowns or have been in prison, that the income actualities of the spouse have been concealed, or to such things as a prior marriage or physical defects that first come to light after the wedding. Sometimes, too, religious differences may not have been settled before marriage. Differences in the educational level may also make for trouble. In professional circles an early marriage may break up later because the husband goes on to better his professional status by continuing education whereas the wife does not follow suit. Later serious conflict in terms of educational status and mutual understanding may arise. So, too, disagreement regarding friends and forms of recreation may also arise to harass a couple.

An external element that influences family life is the business cycle. A prolonged business depression, for example, may gravely reduce the living standards of large numbers of families. On the human side, this may bring about a change in family roles. It is not uncommon, when the husband is out of a job, for the wife to become the chief wage earner. Such a change may alter her relationship to the other family members. In particular the reduction of the husband's and father's status may prove to be a severe blow to his ego.

A prolonged depression may act to shift the support of the family from a wage earner to state agencies of some kind. In the old days, relatives would often rally to help a family member in economic distress. Now families turn to the government for aid. Such practice illustrates a new device to maintain the family as well as a definite shift in social values. In fact, families on relief may come, in time, to expect some kind of governmental subsidy if not complete support.

In a study made by Cavan and Ranck [2] of a hundred families during the depression they discovered, among other things, that well-organized families faced up to the depression with far less severe consequences than did those that were already disorganized, that they reacted to the depression in much the same way as they had to other crises, and that the period of unadjustment or disorganization, which was characterized by emotional strain in the early stages of the depression, was usually followed by a period of readjustment or a drift to outright maladjustment. These findings suggest that families, like individuals, vary in their breaking point. That is, families differ in their capacity to face up to serious trouble.

War is another external crisis that affects family life. In the first place the military may put the principal breadwinner into the armed services,

[2] Ruth S. Cavan and Katherine H. Ranck, *The Family and the Depression*, University of Chicago Press, Chicago, 1938.

thus altering the family in many ways. War also frequently means that both single and married women go into factories to help in the war effort. Again the effects of this on the whole family are varied. Several studies, made abroad, on the effects of war experiences upon children, have established that anxiety, loneliness, loss of intimate contact, and other features appear when children are separated from their parents under conditions of evacuation.

More common problems which the family may have to face are the death or desertion of a spouse or parent. But the most widely discussed problem of family breakdown is that of divorce. In the United States, the divorce rate has gone up over 250 per cent in the last forty years. Shortly after World War II the rate was about one divorce to three marriages; today, there is about one divorce to every four and one-half marriages. Although the statistics show that for every five couples getting married one is divorced, we must remember that we have a very high rate of remarriage. Hence, the divorce rate is not an entirely adequate measure of disorganization. Moreover, there are various differentials in divorce. For example, in 1951 the major proportion of divorced persons lived in urban areas; in the rural farm areas the relative percentage of divorced persons was very much lower. Divorce is probably a function of industrialization and urbanization.

Divorce, of course, does not always represent a crisis. Where there have been years of separation, the divorce is frequently but the final indication of a family breakdown which had, in fact, taken place long before. Then, too, divorces following forced marriages seldom show any marked emotional involvement and hence do not constitute any problem of readjustment.

Nevertheless, in most instances a divorce does constitute a crisis. Despite the fact that divorces are much more common now than formerly a great deal of guilt and shame continue to be associated with this form of family disruption. The breakup of long-established relationships means that each partner may have to seek new friends or move away to take a new job. On the other hand, much can be said for programs of reconciliation; some couples do remarry and make a go of it later.

The time element is an important factor in divorce. If a marriage lasts five years, the chances are pretty high that it will persist. The great majority of divorces today occur in the first few years of married life.

Stabilizing Factors

Let us now examine some of the factors that make for family stability. The old bases of family integration have largely disappeared, especially in urban families. A good many of the old rituals, the old values, have gone and they cannot be restored. Standard institutional blueprints as to how one should behave in the face of family crises are lacking.

Today the most important single need for the modern family is that of adaptability. In order to survive it must develop new resources to meet recurrent crises. Two approaches to the problems of family continuity and reorganization are indicated. The first is to check the tendencies of disorganization in given families and to reshape the family life by redefining the attitudes and values of the husband, the wife, the parents in relation to the children, and the children to each other and to their parents. The second is to develop a new concept or idea of the family which will influence all families.

Certainly new agencies to strengthen the family are emerging. We cannot go back to the old traditional patterns. As indicated earlier there is an irreversibility in institutional change. The suggestions of Zimmerman and Sorokin that we should return to the older practices and moral values are probably quite out of the question.[3] We have no evidence from history that we ran reverse social trends in the way they suggest. Rather, as Burgess and Locke have pointed out, we are probably moving in the direction of what they call a companionship family. They describe this type of family as follows:

> The form of the family that appears to be emerging in modern society may be called the companionship family because of its emphasis upon intimate interpersonal association as its primary function. Other characteristics of the companionship family are: the giving and receiving of affection; the assumption of equality of husband and wife; democracy in family decisions, with a voice and a vote by the children; the personality development of its members as a family objective; freedom of self-expression which is consistent with family unity; and the expectation that the greatest happiness is to be found in the family.[4]

In our current efforts to stabilize and strengthen the family, several new developments have taken place. One is illustrated by the rise of such an organization as the Planned Parenthood Federation. The organization of groups to foster the planning of children reflects not only a growing rational view of marriage and family life in some circles but the belief that "by taking thought" we can control frequency of pregnancies and births, do much regarding prenatal and postnatal care of mothers and infants, and otherwise influence the birth rate and improve a baby's chances of healthy survival.

---

[3] See Carle C. Zimmerman, *Family and Civilization*, Harper and Brothers, New York, 1947; Pitirim A. Sorokin, *The Crisis of Our Age*, E. P. Dutton and Company, New York, 1941.
[4] Ernest W. Burgess and Harvey J. Locke, *The Family, From Institution to Companionship* (2d ed.), American Book Company, New York, 1953, p. 651.

Although there is opposition to it on the part of certain organizations that oppose contraception, there is little doubt that in the long run this kind of agency will make its influence felt.

At the educational level, many courses dealing with marriage and the family have been developed. These are designed to give advice to young people about the basic problems of family adjustment. Some are given at the high-school level and many experts in this field feel that the high-school age is the most appropriate time for these educational programs. The bulk of high-school graduates marry fairly soon after graduation and only a small fraction of them go on to college.

The topics covered in these courses range from the biological aspects of sex behavior with reference to marriage, to all kinds of matters involving psychological and social interaction of spouses, and of parents and children. Sometimes one wonders just how effective such courses are. It is difficult to give more than the most general advice to large groups. On the other hand, young people may be helped to understand their own emotions and their own problems through discussion and with the help of reading and direction from others. Certainly there is no evidence of harm coming from such courses and the information given may help in orienting the young man or woman to a more realistic conduct in engagement and marriage.

The development of marriage counseling on an individual basis is probably a far more effective and important service. The profession of marriage counselor has spread considerably, especially in our urban centers. Sometimes this work is done by voluntary agencies, such as family service agencies, which provide counseling without cost or with little expense to the clients. In other instances, a professional clinic for marriage counseling is set up and charges are made sufficient to support the counselors. Then, too, counseling is done by ministers and teachers as a part of their particular work.

The application of measures to predict marital success or failure may be very helpful to the marriage counselor. On the basis of various research studies, tables of expectancy of degrees of success or failure have been worked out. These tables, of course, will not specify that Richard Roe should or should not wed Daisy Doe, nor having married her how successful the match will be. But it will tell Richard or Daisy that, given a certain score on the scale of marital adjustment, his or her chances are thus and so that the marriage will be all right or go on the rocks.[5]

These studies have shown, moreover, that some human experiences are more important than others as predictive items in a scale. Both premarital

---

[5] See Ernest W. Burgess and Leonard S. Cottrell, Jr., *Predicting Success or Failure in Marriage*, Prentice-Hall, New York, 1939, p. 284.

and postmarital elements have been examined by various investigators. For premarital background, such elements as a high degree of happiness in the marriage of the parents, happy childhood of spouses, prolonged attendance at Sunday school, number of years of schooling, and marriage at a later rather than a younger age have been shown to be significantly correlated with success in marriage. Direct factors in marital adjustment itself are shown to be personality characteristics, cultural backgrounds, social participation, sexual adaptability, and others.

Approached from the negative standpoint the following six psychological elements have been shown to make for unhappiness in marriage: (1) unhappy disposition as indicated in tendency to pessimism; (2) such neurotic expressions as being grouchy or touchy, easily hurt, full of self-pity, and "bothered by useless thoughts"; (3) overbearing determination to have one's own way regardless of the feelings of others; (4) hypercritical and inconsiderate attitudes toward others; (5) on the part of the husband, lack of self-confidence; and (6) self-sufficiency, that is, ability to handle difficulties alone without carrying them to others. Of course, it is the combination of these six or some fraction of them that is basic in predicting the chances of success or failure, and again it is the group average, not the individual prediction, with which we are concerned.[6]

Cultural differences also have bearing. For example, the social status of the husband is more important than that of the wife. In our society, the cultural definition holds that a man may marry below his economic and social station but not a woman. On the other hand such differences as variation in amount of education or differences in religious affiliations have, in some studies, been shown to be of less importance. Level of education of the spouses' parents is important; and some studies show that mixed marriages of certain religious affiliates are less satisfactory than marriage within one's own faith. The significance of this latter factor depends very largely on the nature and degree of "emancipation" of the spouses from traditional religious views and practices.

Several measures of social participation are used in the various scales for getting at marital adjustment. Among other items found significant for success in marriage are these: (1) frequent attendance at Sunday school and church services; (2) having a wide circle of friends; (3) high level of education; (4) wide participation in social organizations of the community; and (5) residence in neighborhoods of single-family dwellings.

With regard to economic matters, Burgess and Cottrell found these, on the whole, to be less important than had been assumed at the outset of

---

[6] For a summary of various studies on marital adjustment, see Ernest W. Burgess and Harvey J. Locke, *op. cit.*, Chapters 14 and 15.

their investigation. Yet several items were found to be significantly associated with good marital adjustment: (1) stable occupations giving moderate economic status and security, and associated with superior education and stable personality; (2) moderate income at time of marriage, rather than a low or a high income; (3) for wife, if gainfully employed prior to marriage, such vocations as domestic service, professional, skilled, or office work; (4) regular work record; and (5) bank savings before marriage.

The data on the much-discussed importance of sex in marital adjustment bring out some interesting facts. Burgess and Cottrell hold that the sex factors are secondary to those of personality and cultural background. As Burgess and Locke put it in discussing this matter: "With the majority of couples, problems of sexual adjustment in marriage appear to be a resultant not so much of biological factors as of psychological characteristics and of cultural conditioning of attitudes toward sex." [7]

Other studies have shown that sex instruction in childhood is significantly related to later marital adjustment. Terman, on the basis of a large number of items dealing with sexual matters, concluded that only two of his list were statistically significant with regard to marital happiness. These were similarity of sexual drives of the spouses, and what he calls the "orgasm capacity" of the wife.[8]

It must be recalled that the bulk of these results comes from studies made of middle-class, white, American families and a few comparable studies of middle-class families in Sweden. We have little or no adequate data on these matters for the upper and top-elite class or for the lower class in our own or other societies.

On the broad front, we may look for a considerable amount of modification of the older patterns of courtship and marriage and in the maintenance of the family. The extreme romantic patterns of the past will probably have to be modified if the modern family is to become more stable. There is no doubt that part of the difficulty in the modern family is that young people begin with high romantic ideals only to find later that they have to face up to certain kinds of realities not in the rosy romance pattern they imagined. In other words, we should move in a direction of more realistic understanding of human interrelationships. This is not to say that love should disappear from marriage but rather that it must be qualified by a certain amount of day-by-day realism. It is upon this particular point that Burgess and Locke have made their strong plea for what they call companionship. This would mean that the family as a group of interacting individuals would be concerned not only with reproduction and child training

---

[7] *Ibid.*, p. 437.
[8] Lewis M. Terman and others, *Psychological Factors in Marital Happiness*, McGraw-Hill Book Company, New York, 1938, pp. 373–376.

but with the interactions in which there would be emotional security, mutual respect, and a good deal of comradeship outside the strictly sexual and affectional relations usually associated with marriage. In particular, this is important because the older functions of the economic, protective, religious, and recreational sort have gone from the family and are not likely to return. This means that some new values, attitudes, and habits will have to be built up if the family is to remain a stable agency in the future as it has been in the past.

2 · The Family as a Unity of Interacting Personalities *

ERNEST W. BURGESS

The family has been studied from many points of view—legal, ethical, economic, and in its historical and institutional aspects. In the 1920's—a period of postwar adjustment to change, rapid technological expansion and high prosperity, not unlike the past decade—the family came in for criticism and new examination. Into this confused state of thinking, the article here reprinted came as the crystallization of many lines of thought, to serve as the starting point for a new approach to thinking and research that is still central in our concept of family life. In his search for a central theme, Dr. Burgess, sociologist famed for his interest in family life, collected from diverse sources and from family histories of students a vast array of material on the family. His study of this material led to his now classic formulation of the family as a unity of interacting personalities.

In READING these cases, reflecting upon them, and seeking to analyze them, certain facts began to emerge and finally to crystallize in rather clear form.

* Family (now Social Casework), 7 (March, 1926), selections from pages 3–6. Reprinted by permission of the publisher and the author.
The author, whose degree of Doctor of Philosophy is from the University of Chicago, for many years has been an outstanding leader in formulating new approaches to study of the family, in carrying out research especially in prediction of successful adjustment in engagement and marriage, and in stimulating many others to engage in research. He is coauthor of Predicting Success or Failure in Marriage, Engagement and Marriage, and The Family from Institution to Companionship, a contributor to many books, and the author of dozens of articles. He was chairman of the Department of Sociology, The University of Chicago, at the time of his retirement; since then he has turned his attention to research on adjustment to retirement.

The first was that in spite of the undoubtedly great differences between individual families or between family life in various cultural groups, there was a family type in general. In the last analysis, the essential characteristics of the family were found to be everywhere the same. And what are these characteristics? The whole body of familial sentiments which naturally and inevitably grow out of and maintain the relationships of husband and wife and parents and children. The rôle of the mother, for instance, we immediately recognize as basically the same, despite the apparent superficial differences in the care of children among Eskimos, Turks, or Englishmen.

My next discovery was a sudden perception of the tremendous difference between the modern family and the family of the past. How many of us realize how modern a phenomenon is the small family of father, mother, and children emancipated from the control of the wider kinship group of grandparents, uncles, aunts, and cousins? Do we perceive that it is to be found as a typical specimen perhaps only in cities, and particularly in the urbanized areas of our very largest American cities? The small family group in apartment houses or residential hotels is, no doubt, the most notorious illustration of effectual detachment from the claims of kinship. The absence in the city home of "the spare bedroom," that famous institution of the country-side, serves as a convenient defense against invading relatives.

At the same time, the family in modern life is undergoing changes and modifications which can hardly be appreciated or understood except in the perspective of the past or by an opportunity for comparison with a contemporary organization of the large family in process of disintegration, such as China affords. But, as the large family was organized in the interests of the older generation to resist change, and so to perpetuate the family pattern, the modern family is exposed to change since it begins in a certain sense anew with every marriage and is thus at the mercy of the new romantic notions of the younger generation.

In contrasting the small family of these city areas with the kinship or large family group—whether in ancient Israel, Greece, or Rome, or in contemporary India, Japan, or China, or even with the large peasant family of Poland or Russia, or with the kinship clans of American rural communities—differences are at once apparent. The large family group tends in every culture to be impressed in one standardized form; while within the same culture the small family tends to exhibit a variety of patterns. Already in American society are to be found the following patterns classified by size of family: the childless family or the so-called "companionate"; the one-child family; the two-child family; the family with three or more children. And these are not merely biological or economic classes, they are in large part determined by custom, or by new fashions in the folkways. Dr. Mowrer [1] has even classified areas of the city by types of family life, the non-family areas with their Hobohemian and Bohemian centers; areas of the so-called emancipated family in the rooming-house regions; the patriarchal family areas of the immigrant colonies; the equalitarian family areas of apartment house districts; and finally, in the so-called dormitory suburbs that new type of family where the husband leaves for down-town before the children are awake and returns after they are asleep, the modern matri-archal family, or perhaps more accurately, the matricentric family. This correlation between cultural areas of the city and types of family life is no fortuitous coincidence. It suggests the ways in which family life is related to the ecology of the city. The pattern of family life develops under certain life conditions and thrives only in conformity with the folkways and mores of the local community.

Next I found peculiarly revealing a classification of families by the pattern of personal relationships between husband and wife and parents and children. Two contrasted patterns soon presented themselves: the highly integrated family and the unintegrated or loosely integrated family. These in turn might be subdivided into several varieties. Upon analysis it was found that the highly integrated family possessed one or more of the following traits: elaborate ritual, rigorous discipline, sentimental inter-dependence; stimulating co-operative activities or objectives; while the unintegrated or loosely integrated family had little or no ritual, exerted slight control either through discipline or sentimental attachment and its members were only in small degree unified by common family aims to which individual purposes were subordinated. The typical orthodox Jewish family has in marked degree all the traits that are positive for the highly integrated family. The Puritan family, stigmatized by the younger generation as the Puritanical family, is a conspicuous illustration of in-tegration through the characteristics of rigorous discipline and dominant family objectives.

This study of the patterns of personal relationships in family life led directly to the conception of the family as a unity of interacting persons. By a unity of interacting personalities is meant a living, changing, growing thing. I was about to call it a superpersonality. At any rate the actual unity of family life has its existence not in any legal conception, nor in any formal contract, but in the interaction of its members. For the family does not depend for its survival on the harmonious relations of its members, nor does it necessarily disintegrate as a result of conflicts between its members.

---

[1] Mowrer, Ernest R.: *Family Disorganization* (to be published) [Chicago: University of Chicago Press, 1927].

The family lives as long as interaction is taking place and only dies when it ceases.

. . . .

The family is even more than an interaction of personalities. In this interaction, the family develops a conception of itself. When this conception of familial relations is recognized by the community, the family acquires an institutional character. This is what is meant by the family as a social institution. A family that had no conception of its rôle in the community, or of the responsibilities of its individual members would not be an institution, perhaps not even a family. It is just these natural relationships of family life, the obligations and responsibilities spontaneously assumed in family interaction, which the community seeks first through custom and then through law to define, to make contractual, and to enforce. But everywhere, and always, by those who are dealing with problems of family life it is paramount to recognize that the family as a reality exists in the interaction of its members and not in the formalities of the law with its stipulations of rights and duties.

Often too the family is thought of as a mere collection of interacting individuals rather than a unity of interacting persons. Herein lies the value for research of the technical distinction, made by Professor Park, between the individual and the person.

> The person is an individual who has status. We come into the world as individuals. We acquire status, and become persons. Status means position in society. The individual inevitably has some status in every social group of which he is a member. In a given group the status of every member is determined by his relation to every other member of that group. The individual's self-consciousness—his conception of his rôle in society, his "self," is based on his status in the social group or groups of which he is a member.[2]

This definition of the person as an individual with status has thrown a flood of light upon family interaction. The members of the family do react to each other as individuals and that is important. But they react to each other as persons and that is also important. For every person has, with more or less awareness, a conception of his rôle, not only in society, but in all groups of which he is a member. Not only does the person have a lively conception of his own rôle in the family, but he has a sense of the rôles of all the other members of the family and notions of what family life is or ought to be. The rôles of the good father, the good mother, and the good child enter powerfully in determining the conception which each member holds of his place in the world of family life.

---

[2] Park, R. E., and Burgess, E. W.: *Introduction to the Science of Sociology*, page 55.

In a stable, homogeneous society, ideas of family life and the rôles of its different members are relatively fixed and constant. In a changing society composed of heterogeneous elements, familial attitudes are almost inevitably in a state of flux. Instead of a common pattern of family life intrenched in tradition and crushing out all impulse to variation by the sheer weight of universal conformity, our American society presents what at first sight seems to be a chaotic conglomeration of every conceivable pattern of family organization and disorganization, from the patriarchal kinship groups of our Southern Mountain highlands to the free unions of our Greenwich Villages. Hardly a day passes but the public is shocked and outraged by some new form of wild and reckless behavior, particularly of youth in revolt no longer regulated by customary controls.

But these random and aimless variations away from the basic pattern of family life are not, as some believe, an indication of the future of family life and sexual relationships. They are only the symptoms in the present, as in similar times in the past, that society is undergoing change. When an equilibrium is re-established a new pattern of family life will emerge, better adapted to the new situation, but only a different variety of the old familiar pattern of personal relationships in the family.

3 · Universal Biological Features of the Family *

WESTON LA BARRE

One way to view the family is as the natural result of the biological features of man, woman, and child which make each dependent upon the others. The following brief selection from a longer article prepared for social workers singles out the biological aspects that necessitate some type of family life throughout the entire human race. This approach to the family does not negate the importance of cultural or interpersonal aspects, but puts a firm floor under them in the biological make-up of man himself.

---

* "Appraising Today's Pressures on Family Living," Social Casework, 32 (February, 1951), 54–55. Reprinted by permission of the publisher and the author.

The author, now Professor of Anthropology at Duke University, received his degree of Doctor of Philosophy from Yale University. His early interest in the use and effect of peyote (a drug) among Indians, which led to the publication of The Peyote Cult, has continued, but has not limited him. He has applied his anthropological knowledge to analyses of the family, child training, and personality development. His writings include many book reviews, articles in professional journals, and chapters in books. He is also the author of The Human Animal.

Permanent Features of the Family

So far this discussion has been in terms of the vicissitudes and changeable contingencies of the family. What of the inner strengths of the family? What of the universal and indestructible features of the family? What are the permanencies upon which sound family casework can build? Here the anthropologist is able to give a firm reassurance, based scientifically upon his long perspective of many societies and cultures.

For one thing, the family is a universal human phenomenon, both inclusively and exclusively. Every human group known to us, past and present, has the basic family unit of organization; and, more than that, our species, Homo sapiens, is the unique animal which has a fully familial kind of societality. In fact, I believe that it is uniquely the *biological* nature of human nature to be familial in its structure. The universality of the human family is based upon unchangeable *biological* grounds, not upon shifting cultural or moral grounds. This is not to say that locally we cannot have considerable differences in the *form of marriage*—polygyny, polyandry, and the like —but these local phrasings of the *form* of marriage never can and never do impugn the basic biological *norm* which the *family* constitutes.

In these days of rapid change in institutions, I think it is well to emphasize the permanency of the family in our very biological nature. Anthropologists so often talk about the divergencies of cultural institutions that it is often forgotten that the anthropologist also has the responsibility to discern beneath all these the basic and universal character of human nature. Family casework is *not* building its house upon the sand of a merely temporary institution. Family casework is *not* just another aspect of "bourgeois decadence," attempting vainly to breast the wave of the future.

The family, just because it is a human universal, is too easily taken for granted. As a matter of fact, the usual mammalian "family" consists only in the mother and her young and entirely lacks the social or the legal or the moral father. The human trinity of mother-child-and-father is a new kind of biological association among animals. Each member of this trinity shows in his or her very anatomy and physiology the accommodations made to membership in the symbiotic trinity. The human female has specialized in sexual dimorphism, with an ample pelvis obviously related to the bearing of big-brained human young. The human infant, also, has specialized, so to speak, in *infantilism*. No other animal is so specialized in this fashion; no other animal commits so much of the newborn infant to brain—fully one-seventh of the total birth-weight in humans—and so little to an immature undeveloped body, which is almost an afterthought in a newborn baby. The only so-called "instincts" a baby is born with—the sucking reflex and the grasping reflex—are precisely those that adapt him to *infancy*, and not to an early or an immediate adult functioning. With a large brain and without such instincts, the human animal above all others is adapted to learning, and it is particularly in this feature that an additional importance of the family as a conditioner of the infant emerges. We make human beings whatever familial and social and cultural conditionings make them. If the human female is in a sense the domesticate shaped by the male and by the infant, the infant is just as much a domesticate shaped by the mother and the father. Similarly, the human male has his own biological modifications; it is clear that the human male everywhere forms somewhat permanent associations with a female or females, not because of cultural compulsions, but because, biologically speaking, he wants to: Homo sapiens is conspicuous for his non-seasonal permanent sexual drive, which conduces to the formation of the permanent human family groupings.

For the rest, it is perfectly clear anthropologically that we are human because of our peculiar traits as an animal species. The complex, briefly, is something like this: Uniquely bipedal walking, with the weight on two instead of four limbs, requires a more massive, larger pelvis; a more capacious pelvis is the enabling factor behind the bigger-skulled human birth, with more commitment relatively to brain than to body. But since the big-brained, largely instinctless human infant is physically so immature in his body, the female must also specialize in mammalian nurture and nutrition. On the other hand, female and infant could hardly specialize so far respectively in maternity and infancy unless they were protected by the specialized male, with his larger bones and muscles, and the like. And the male would not have increased his attendance upon the dependent mother-child unit in a permanent fashion, unless he had a permanent sexual interest in the female which bound him to it. The male uses the family for his instinctual purposes, but the family also uses him. For the rest, we have language only because we are *social* animals who live together in the relatively stable, relatively permanent, emotionally close-knit units which alone would facilitate the rise of such symbolic systems as language and culture. The kind of animal the human infant is also clearly facilitates its *learning* a culture, since it is not equipped with a full set of adult-animal instinctual responses. The child is a learning animal, hence one capable of being enculturated or socialized to a given culture, and this capability has meaning primarily in terms of human familial societality.

I consider these biological facts reassuring rather than alarming, since they indicate that the permanence of the human family is something we need not worry about; indeed we shall have the family so long as human beings are around, and our major concern is literally whether or not there will be human beings around, not whether they will be familial animals. Thus, a casework based upon a preservation of the integrities of the human family seems to me to be based on the hard rock of human biology. The family is as fundamental as our specialized human anatomy and physiology; we could not change our propensity to be familial animals even if we imagined we wanted to. We shall always live in family constellations and we need waste no anxiety when calamity howlers proclaim that the family as such is irrevocably disintegrating.

4 · *Marriage as a Status-Achieving Device* *

JAMES H. S. BOSSARD

In this article the author moves away from the idea of basic functions and relationships, as discussed in the first part of this chapter, and analyzes an auxiliary function of the family, very dominant in the American scene—marriage as a means of increasing personal and social status. In a society acutely conscious of personal status and motivated by the desire for upward mobility, the author has put his finger on a significant aspect of marriage. He believes that marriage is a status-achieving device partly because in the United States formally organized ways of gaining status are not well developed; through marriage, the person may work individually for a gain in status.

IN A status-changing society such as ours,[1] great emphasis comes to be placed upon the mechanism by which status is determined. Social scientists, chiefly sociologists and anthropologists, have emphasized thus far mostly the processes and factors in the ascription of status, with relatively little attention to the ways in which status may be achieved. Yet in a mobile

* *Sociology and Social Research,* 29 (September–October, 1944), 3–10. Reprinted by permission of the editor and the author.

The author has long been associated with the University of Pennsylvania, from which he received his degree of Doctor of Philosophy and where he is now Professor of Sociology and William T. Carter Professor of Child Development as well as Director of the William T. Carter Foundation for Child Development. He is also Professor of Sociology at the University's Medical School. He has been active in research and writing for many years and among other books is author or coauthor of the following: *Toward Family Stability, Ritual in Family Living, Parent and Child, The Large Family System, One Marriage—Two Faiths,* and *Why Marriages Go Wrong.*

[1] For ideas included in this article, I am indebted to Mrs. Marjorie Chavenelle, of the staff of the William T. Carter Foundation.

and fluid society, it is the achieved statuses and the devices by which they are obtained that become important. The purpose of this article is to present a conception of marriage as a status-achieving device, with the further insistence that such a concept is of value for an understanding of marriage and its problems as well as of the status system of our society.

Perhaps the clearest illustration of the status possibilities of marriage is to be found in those marriages which are obviously of the status-raising kind. Innumerable heroines of humbler status who have married the prince dot the literature of the past. In more contemporary times, the show girl who marries the banana king's heir or the screen star who invades the social four hundred is of the same kind. It fact, success in the artist world is one of the most promising short cuts which are open, especially to women who wish to consummate status-raising marriages. Particularly has this been true since the 1920's, when fortunes have come to be amassed and popular favor has been won, not so much by persons who developed our natural resources as by those who have entertained us. Witness the creation of Cafe Society, that peculiar form of the so-called elite in which the higher your status the less you have to do with cafes. Cafe Society has been defined as a mixture of producing artists, easy money, and old social names, with publicity as its foundation.[2]

Again, the utilization of marriage as a status-raising device constitutes a distinctive phase of minority group relationships. Here, too, marriage is a short cut to escape from a lower status, to some extent for one's self and even more so for one's children. Direct evidence supporting this statement can be found in a recent study of Jewish-Gentile intermarriage in Chicago. Slotkin identified eight different types of persons among those intermarrying. Of these, at least two types, the rebellious and the marginal, are personality types whose intermarriage is apt to reflect the effort to raise status by marrying out of the minority group status. Slotkin definitely refers to this in his description of the marginal type. "Marginal people," he writes, "sometimes amalgamate with members of the dominant group in order to increase their own status or that of their offspring." [3] My own studies of nationality and nativity as factors in marriage selection confirm the basic importance of group distinctions, the summary table of 68,196 marriages in New York state in 1936 having all the precision of a status-rating time table.[4] Marriage is life's most intimate relationship, and acceptance on this basis by a group of higher social prestige is the essence of status achieve-

---

[2] "Cafe Society," *Fortune Magazine*, New York, December, 1937, p. 127 ff.

[3] J. S. Slotkin, "Jewish-Gentile Intermarriage in Chicago," *The Sociological Review*, February, 1942, p. 38.

[4] "Nationality and Nativity as Factors in Marriage," *The Sociological Review*, December, 1939, p. 796.

ment. Similar in implication are Whyte's studies of Italian attitudes on the sex code.

> In the social and ethnic group category, the most desirable woman for non-marital sex relations is the girl of old American-stock background, preferably blonde, who has a higher status than the corner-boy.[5]

Crises, either societal or personal, tend to account for another type of status-raising marriages. As an illustration of the first instance were many depression marriages. Studies of depression and predepression marriage rates in Philadelphia revealed that, although the marriage rate for Phila-delphia as a whole fell during the depression years, it actually rose among certain groups and in certain areas of the city. This rise occurred primarily in the lowest income groups, and in the areas where the lowest planes of living prevailed. The interpretation advanced is that in this socioeconomic class and type area it is marriage, rather than any given plane of living, that is the status-conferring condition. This would be particularly true of those elements whose religious traditions and teachings emphasize marriage as a form of life completion.[6]

An instance of the role of personal crises can be found in the men who are pulled precipitantly from civilian life and placed in the rank of pri-vates in a huge military organization. For many men this involves, among other things, a sudden change in status. As privates in the army, they are the underdogs. They take orders and are directed hither and yon. They do menial work. They falter in the learning of a new occupation. Whatever else happens in a confused and frustrating world, one can at least get mar-ried. The civilian job may be gone, the sergeant may bellow, life may be hard and its margins may be narrow, but there is one place where every man may be a king. You can have your own family. At least the little woman will look up to you. You can regain your sense of status by getting married. Thus conceived for their compensatory status-achieving results, many war-time marriages become intelligible, perhaps for the first time.

While these more spectacular instances serve as illustrations of the status-raising implications of marriage, we are concerned here primarily with marriage as a status-achieving device in terms of social process. There fol-low herewith six aspects of its operation in our status system.

1. To marry is to gain status in your family. "Emma is now married." "John has a family of his own." These are sentences that carry a world of meaning in most families, the weight of that world varying on the

---

[5] William Foote Whyte, "A Slum Sex Code," *American Journal of Sociology*, Chicago, July, 1943, p. 28.

[6] Bossard, "Depression and Pre-depression Marriage Rates: A Philadelphia Study," *The Sociological Review*, October, 1937, p. 695.

basis of family and group values and traditions. Over against these positive expressions are the implications in such thinly veiled questions as: "Doesn't Helen have a boy friend? How old is she getting to be?" "Isn't John thinking of getting a wife?" Who has not sensed the uncertainty and even anxiety in many families when the children pass a given year and remain unmarried? Who has not seen the problem of the "thirtyish" unmarried son or daughter and the family machinations, subtle and less so, to help them meet effective matrimonial temptation? Somehow the status of the whole family seems to be at stake. To all such, marriage is the answer. No more hints from relatives; no more prods from parents: the thing is done. The newly married have gained the same status as the manipulator and the prodder.

2. To marry is to gain status in your job or profession. We prefer the doctor who is married. Certain fields of specialized medical practice would not be considered proper for bachelor physicians, unless perhaps in the impersonal setting of a very large city. The preacher needs to take a wife. In fact, the appointment or selection of young pastors may be contingent, in many communities, upon their approaching marriage. The wisdom of a married professor is more mature. In sociology, for example, it is now opportune for him to give certain courses. A married case worker, many board members will think, has more insight into family problems. When you are a "Mrs.," you can work more appropriately with children, or be a counselor, or do personnel work, because now you *understand*. Being married, you are more deserving of promotion. You are a more responsible employee. You are supposed to be more settled in your habits. You can be used more appropriately in supervisory and administrative jobs.

3. To marry is to gain status in the community. A community is, from one point of view, a confederation of families. This is perhaps most true in suburban and rural communities, and least so in the transitory neighborhoods of large cities. To marry is to be admitted to this confederation. As a husband, you have given a token of stability and intent. As a wife, you are eligible now for admission into various groups of women in the community and can share their communal interests. You have a home, and a husband. Parenthood is now in order for both husband and wife or is already here: they have a stake in the community. Often home ownership comes to reinforce the existing status. One is now a married person—of substance.

4. Marriage confers status within the circle of one's friends. Almost immediately after marriage, verbal references to this change of status appear. "Oh, he's married now." "He is a married man." "Yes, she's been married since last summer." "You see, I'm married now and don't date anymore." "He's been hooked." Whether the superficial implication is one

of prestige, regret, pride, or condolence, the basic meaning of all such remarks is that of the achievement of a new status.

Marriage is, to many of one's unmarried friends, the answer to all problems, the status which changes the viewpoint toward all things. The sophistication of the married state is appealing. Then, too, the aureole of parenthood has come, or looms. Whatever one's trials or worries, marriage tends to be regarded as the solution. Says an epileptic:

> Saturday I was going to call on some friends and felt it coming on. The doctor said I should sit down, but you hate to sit down on the street. And I fell. A lady was passing by. She stopped and helped me, and when I came around they drove me home. There are a lot of nice people in this world. I want to tell you one thing—but I see you are. I was going to say: For God's sake, get married.[7]

To one's married friends, marriage is the common password. You are one of us now. Welcome into the fraternity. Now you can be told. Now we can talk freely to you. "We're all married here." You understand our problems and interests. It is no longer necessary to temper conversation to the unmarried lamb. When invited out socially, it is no longer necessary to worry about a willing and acceptable partner. You are now a reliable "twosome" for social purposes.

5. Marriage affects financial or economic status. To marry with an eye to financial security is, of course, an age-old practice. Security is but another name for status. Once this motive was attributed chiefly to women. This sex preponderance was natural at a time when women had no economic opportunities save as they were attached to family units. Today, with increasing employment opportunities outside the home open to women, this motive in their marriages may be less operative, but it still remains of considerable importance. The complement of its declining importance for women may be its increasing role with men. A working wife is an asset. It means two wage earners in the family. Furthermore, there is the security which inheres in the possibility of a working wife, even if she is not now employed. During the depression this twofold reliance proved a savior for many families.

6. Marriage gives a new status in regard to the problems of life. If it be argued at once that marriage does not solve problems but often increases and complicates them, there still remains the fact of a new orientation toward them. To keep this in mind enables one at times to assess the complaints of wives and husbands, and even parents, at their true worth. For many wives, complaint of their husbands is but disguised boasting. "My

---

[7] From the files of the William T. Carter Foundation, University of Pennsylvania.

husband neglects me," she says. The general and superficial interpretation of this is to underscore the word *neglects*. Actually, the words that should be emphasized are *my husband*. The inexperienced (and unmarried?) case worker is apt to lose sight of this fact. Actually the complaint is an unconscious compensatory declaration of status, half in tears and half in pride. She *is* neglected, but it is by *her husband*, not by an uncertain boy friend. Surgical operations and husbands are the twin satisfactions of many women, albeit both of a certain incisive nature. Similarly, the girl who is constantly threatening to leave her husband is often close kin to the butler who is always giving notice—neither has any intention of doing so. Or, the deserted wife who is always "taking back" her husband, who stays up most of the night to wash and iron his shirt so that he may look well when he appears in court the next morning on a charge of desertion and non-support, is but reasserting her status as a wife. Nor should these illustrations be selected wholly from one sex. The husband who refers to his "ball and chain" is often but calling spectacular attention to his blonde wife, whom he is proud enough to own. The man who cannot "get out" at night because of his jealous wife is boasting more often than not of *his* attractiveness rather than of *her* jealousy. Most parents, I am convinced after years of observation, who complain habitually about their children do so, at least in some measure, to call attention to themselves as parents.

The motives that lead to marriage are many and varied. They are not usually given adequate consideration in the study of marriage. In any realistic approach to the family, however, marriage must be recognized as a status-achieving device. Recognition of this fact makes for a better understanding of marital relationships and family problems. Marriage, to be sure, has always been utilized as a status-achieving device, but its importance as such clearly is greater in a society where status changes occur with great frequency and status-achieving devices are at a marked premium. In fact, it is not unreasonable to conclude that the status-achieving value of marriage is one of the reasons for the relatively high percentage of the American population, ten years of age and over, that is or has been married. It seems equally obvious that the relative ease and popular acceptance of divorce increase the use of marriage as a status-achieving device. One can marry, achieve the status, and then make further arrangements. At least, one has been married.

5 · No World for a Single *

MARTIN PANZER

> Having viewed marriage and the family in terms of its social and personal advantages, the reader may now look at the desirability of marriage through the laments of those who have not married.

A FEW WEEKS ago, I casually suggested to my wife, "Let's eat out tonight." Before I could turn around, she had the two children dressed and we were on our way.

We found the restaurant crowded, with a line of would-be diners waiting to be seated. At the head of the line was a friend of ours, a bachelor who lived down the street.

The hostess held up her hand and signaled for three. A family group ahead of us went to the table. Then there was a call for four, another call for three, a call for two and then, finally, a call for four again. That was us.

But our bachelor friend was still at the head of the line, waiting for a signal for a single. "Been waiting long?" I asked as we passed him.

"Yes," he said in a resigned voice, "I always wait a long time. This is no world for a single."

That situation has long been known to people who live alone, but is rarely realized by those living in groups. Take our bachelor friend, for instance. When he does get a table, everyone connected with the restaurant seems to resent it.

The hostess is upset because when only one person occupies a table, part of the restaurant space goes to waste and profit is lost. The waiter is unhappy because he knows he can't get more than one tip from that table. Hence, it is not an overstatement to say that the best service is not reserved for singles.

When singles go to the grocer or butcher, the clerks seem to look the other way. They are usually the last ones served because they buy small

* *Coronet*, 37 (April, 1955), 32–34. Reprinted from *Coronet*, April, 1955, © 1955 by Esquire, Inc., with permission of the publisher.

The author assembled his material by observation and conversations with unmarried people. He has written other magazine articles and a number of books, usually with a humorous touch. Several of these deal with family situations; for instance, *Father Knows Better*, a humorous book on bringing up a baby, and *Watch Out Europe, Here We Come*, an account of a tour through Europe with his wife and children.

quantities and the tradespeople reserve their best and most attentive manner for those who buy for families. And they get inferior merchandise, like the wilted lettuce, that married people wouldn't accept.

"When I finally do get the stuff home," a single, middle-aged lady of our acquaintance says, "my troubles really begin. If I want to prepare soup, I have to open a can made for two or three persons. Two-thirds of it goes to waste because I never like to eat it after it's been a day or two in the refrigerator."

Then there's the matter of bread. When bread is bought for a group, it goes fast and is eaten fresh. Singles seldom get the full benefit of a loaf, because, by the time it's half-finished, the rest is too stale to eat. The same with a quart of milk. And the upshot is that a single spends as much to feed himself as it would cost to feed a small family.

A bachelor friend complains, too, that it costs him more to maintain his apartment than it costs a family to live in a similar apartment. The rent is the same. But he has to tip the service people more because he requires more service. He is never home during the day and everything that is delivered has to be handled by the doorman, the porter and the elevator man. He has to have more maid and cleaning service than family people.

"It's no joke," he says. "And because I'm a bachelor 'with no one to support or worry about,' every time a relative needs help he comes to me. I do help, whenever I can. Comes tax time, however, do I get any credit? Can I claim any additional dependency exemptions? Not on your life."

"Then there's the telephone, utilities, garage and all that. Every item costs me alone as much as it would cost a whole family."

Service and cost are not the only disadvantages to living alone. A girl who likes to call herself a lady-bachelor tells me that she is far more restricted in her normal activities than are any of the family groups in her city apartment house.

"You have no idea how self-conscious a person gets living alone," she says. "The single occupant is the mystery person in every apartment house. Whenever a man visits me, everyone, including the service people, looks askance.

"The most innocent things breed suspicions. I wouldn't dare, for instance, to go to an apartment on another floor, because it would start all sorts of rumors. And yet the married women in the building visit each other freely, and there is no gossip about it."

For a bachelor, the entertainment problem is a very real one. He can be as certain as he is of death and taxes that every time he is invited to a party at the home of a married friend, there will be a girl planted there as a possible wife.

"I'd like to go to just one party to have fun," one wailed. "Just one party where I could be myself and not a potential husband. Why is it that married people can't rest as long as there is someone in sight who isn't married?"

Another thing is the difficulty of returning hospitality. Without a woman around the house, he feels silly serving sandwiches and tea. To add to the unfairness, since he is usually entertained by families of two or more persons, he has to entertain a like number in return.

And there are times when the single literally gets shoved around—on trains, in theaters, at lunch counters. The world seems to be annoyed at his taking up room, so the single finds himself being nudged and hears the old familiar, "Would you mind moving over so we can have two together?" or "Would you slide down to the end to make room for three?"

There comes a time in the life of every single, no matter how courteous or well-bred he may be, when he rebels and turns on a startled world with a firm "No!"

It is in periods of sickness, however, that the single most wishes he were not alone. Then, even mild illnesses become major problems. Family people have loved ones to wait on them hand and foot when they are under the weather. But the single has to drag himself about, even for a drink of water.

The only way he can get the care he needs is to hire a nurse or go to a hospital. Since people don't usually hire nurses or go to hospitals for minor ailments, the singles usually suffer as much from them as others do from much more serious illnesses.

Yes, indeed, the world isn't made for singles. The world is made for sharing with others, and the only thing you can't share is loneliness.

CHAPTER 2:

The Family Life Cycle

---

6 · Stages of the Family Life Cycle *

RUTH SHONLE CAVAN

When life is full of many interests and activities, it is all but impossible not
to become absorbed in the present. These are the best years, we think; the
past fades into insignificance; the future has not yet arrived. Of the past
we say, "it's all water under the bridge," and of the years to come, "let the
future take care of itself." But of course the present never stands alone; no
one period of life is detached from what has gone before or what will come
after. Life is all of a piece—a long river of experience that begins at birth,
already loaded with heredity from the past of the family, that flows on until
the end of life, passing along in its turn hereditary factors and learned values
to younger lives in the earlier stages of the process of living.

---

* This article is based on Robert J. Havighurst, *Human Development and Education*
(New York: Longmans, Green & Company, Inc., 1953), Evelyn Millis Duvall's book
Family Development (Philadelphia: J. B. Lippincott Company, 1957) and her article
"Implications for Education through the Family Life Cycle," *Marriage and Family
Living*, 20 (1958), 334–342, and the author's own book, *The American Family*
(New York: Thomas Y. Crowell Company, 1953).

The author is editor of this book of readings and author of numerous books and
articles dealing with various aspects of the family, including two texts, *The American
Family* and *American Marriage*. Her degree of Doctor of Philosophy is from the University of Chicago and she is Professor of Sociology at Rockford College.

Robert J. Havighurst received the degree of Doctor of Philosophy from Ohio State
University. He is Professor of Education at the University of Chicago. He is author
or coauthor of numerous books and articles an educational subjects and on adjustment
to old age.

Evelyn Millis Duvall, who received her degree of Doctor of Philosophy from the
University of Chicago, has held professional positions with the Association for Family
Living, Chicago, and the National Council on Family Relations. She is now a Family
Life Consultant who devotes much of her time to conducting workshops, lecturing,
and writing. Among her many publications are *Family Living, Facts of Life and Love
for Teenagers, When You Marry* (coauthor), *In-laws Pro and Con*, and *Family Development*.

28

It is often possible and practical to select one or two phases or stages of life and study them intensively. That is really what this book does. Most of the articles deal with the years shortly before or soon after marriage. So that perspective will not be lost, it seems wise to emphasize the on-flowing quality of life, whether of the individual or of the family. Dating, courtship, marriage, and early family building are part of the life span that appeal as being dramatically important to individuals and society. They are but one segment of the whole of life.

THE IDEA of the unbroken flow of a person's life from birth through childhood, adolescence, adulthood, and old age is a fairly familiar one. Any one of us can look backward at the stages we have passed through, assess our present stage, and from our observation of those around us anticipate the stages to come. All in all, eight or nine stages can readily be distinguished during one person's life. These stages can be thought of in terms of his individual development, as Robert J. Havighurst has presented them, or in terms of his family relationships, as Evelyn Millis Duvall has emphasized. Each person has his own life, but for most people personal development is closely linked to family life. The discussion that follows merges the Havighurst and Duvall approaches.

Family and Individual Developmental Stages

Prior to marriage, husband and wife have passed through the developmental stages of infancy, early and middle childhood, and adolescence, living with the family into which they were born, sometimes referred to as the family of orientation. Since these stages are discussed under family stages 2, 3, 4, 5, and 6 in terms of the children of our hypothetical couple, they are omitted here.

1. The Beginning Family

With marriage, a man (average age, twenty-three) and a woman (average age, twenty) change their family relationships. If they have been living with their parents, or in close relationship to them, they have usually thought of themselves and been considered by others as members of their fathers' families. With marriage, the two individuals, previously members of two separate family units, loosen these early bonds and join together to begin the task of building a unique family life, according to their own ideals and to fit their needs. Dr. Duvall refers to this newly married couple as a beginning family.

Husband and wife draw on earlier family experiences and on the general cultural expectations and values for family life, but the particular combination of factors and the special points of emphasis are their own. If this beginning of family life is strongly structured, the couple will be ready for the next stage.

In this developmental stage the young husband is often confronted with a number of tasks, overlapping in time or closely following one another: training for and establishing himself in an occupation, fulfilling his military service requirements, and learning to fit into his domestic roles. The wife also has her tasks in learning to manage a household and gaining experience as a hostess. Often she aids in financing a home; 60 per cent of new wives are employed. Together, husband and wife adjust conflicting roles and interests and develop compatible intimate relationships.

2. The Childbearing Family

The beginning family typically shifts into the childbearing family (sometimes called the family of procreation) during the second year of marriage. In many ways the change is not abrupt, for the roles of new parents gradually develop during the months of pregnancy. Nevertheless the actual physical arrival in the family of a live baby with its own demands changes the marriage relationship. The new roles of mother and father are added to the earlier roles of wife and husband. The wife may also exchange a previous role as employed woman for the combined role of homemaker, mother, and soon nursery school teacher, all in her own home. Only 13 per cent of mothers of preschool children are employed.

The husband, as father, may think first in terms of added financial burdens, especially if his wife previously was employed. He must develop a new sense of responsibility. He also must allow time in his schedule to spend with his wife, who may be more dependent upon him than before for companionship. Typically he also wants free time to spend with his child.

Together husband and wife need to reach common goals for their children and to agree on methods of child rearing. They need to build up their social life and their intimate personal life, both of which may have been subordinated to the needs of the wife and new baby.

Usually, other children are soon added to the first-born, with the last child being born when the mother is about twenty-six and the father about twenty-nine years old.

Not only has the family passed into a new developmental stage, but each baby in turn has its own developmental tasks to accomplish. Although the baby is unaware of "tasks," he is most happy when able to try out and put to use his developing abilities. During the first two years of life the baby typically learns the rudiments of handling various physiological processes, such as when and where to sleep, how to eat in a way suitable to his age, the routine of elimination, coordination of muscles, walking, and talking. He begins to learn how to adjust to other people and how to maintain some simple forms of self control; he begins, also, to recognize himself as a distinct personality.

3. The Family with Preschool Children

As husband and wife learn to accept each new pregnancy and birth with confidence, their attention is focused on the development of the older children. The family with preschool children refers to the family whose oldest child is approaching the age of six. Typically, younger children have been born—in fact the family may be complete. Although at first glance it may seem that each child simply brings a repetition of the parents' first-child adjustment, actually with each child the situation changes for everyone. Parents repeat their care of the infant with each child—but each child has his own individual characteristics. At the same time, they must also keep advancing with the oldest child into his new stages of growth. Responsibilities increase, more money and a larger house are needed, more household tasks must be done. The father and mother are now threatened with the possibility of losing their marriage in family life. The mother, especially, may become almost completely absorbed in keeping her home running and personally caring for her children.

The older children, aged four to six, are no longer infants; they have passed into the recognizable stage of early childhood. They are able to manage their bodies and their conversation with a fair degree of adequacy. They can accept limited responsibilities not only for themselves but for tasks around the house. They know what they want and are able to express themselves in demanding fulfillment; at the same time they can delay fulfillment a moderate length of time. They are able to learn a moderate degree of self control and how to manage limited independence. Conscience, or a sense of right and wrong, begins to develop as they internalize their parents' values.

4. The Family with School Children

Soon the family has developed into the family with children in school, between the ages of six and thirteen. Littler ones may still be preschoolers. The parents are in their thirties. This is the stage at which parents must begin to let go of their children. They are aided by the school, which takes the children many hours each day. Soon Scouts and other organizations claim them for outings and camping trips. Nevertheless the parents are usually pretty well submerged in family life and in trying to meet the needs of rapidly growing children. They have little privacy or time for themselves. Family life has become a complex set of interrelationships as each child strives for physical and mental space in which to develop.

The child is now in middle childhood, which carries him through the elementary school years. Most of his associates are of his own age and sex, and it is important that he learn how to adjust well to them. His abilities from earlier years continue to develop; he also has new tasks in development. As he becomes more aware of himself, he formulates attitudes toward himself as a boy or a girl. The acceptance of a masculine or feminine self conception and role is important as a forerunner to later adolescent development. He is also becoming accustomed to organized groups and to cooperation with adults other than his parents.

5. The Family with Teen-agers

By the time the parents are in the middle or late thirties, their family life changes sharply. The elementary school child has given way to the high-school teen-ager, whose interests change almost overnight as he enters into an entirely new world and feels the impact of new cultural expectations. For approximately seven years parents go through a period fraught with anxiety for their children and insecurity for themselves, as the children more and more turn toward their peers for life satisfactions. The mother often begins to change her pattern of life, seeking part- or full-time employment; 40 per cent of mothers between ages thirty and forty are employed. Expenses increase rapidly and her earnings help to ease the burden on the father and to provide children and adults with additional opportunities or luxuries that they crave. The center of family life is still primarily in the children.

Although teen-agers still have some of their closest ties with their own age-sex group, they are becoming aware of the opposite sex. One of the developmental tasks of the teen years is to learn to adapt to the opposite sex; mixed groups increase in number. Girls learn to look upon themselves and other girls as potential women; and boys see themselves and other boys as fast developing into men. Sexual attraction between boys and girls must be admitted and managed within the scope of social conventions. With mixed-group activities comes a new type of social life, with the need to learn social skills—how to dance, carry on a conversation, and play social games. Other group skills are also learned through committees and the planning and carrying out of school, church, or club projects. Independence from parents increases. Toward the end of the teen period comes a definite interest in marriage as a foreseeable part of future life.

6. The Family as a Launching Center

This is the name given by Dr. Duvall to the family whose children are leaving home to attend college, find employment in some other community, or marry. The parents themselves are entering middle age; the marriage of the last child typically finds the mother in the late forties, the father entering the fifties. The father is probably nearing the peak of his earning power and of his influence in the community. The specter of retirement and old age has not yet appeared. As the mother loses status in the family with the departure of children, she seeks and gains status in the community or through employment. Nevertheless, she sometimes feels lost, unwanted, as though the most significant part of her life had ended. The impersonal success on the job or some board or committee does not seem to compensate for the warm, personal relationship she once had with her children. She also often is experiencing the menopause, which may be a symbol of loss of youthfulness that she finds hard to accept. The father also has adjustments to make, not only to the removal of his children but also to his wife's new role as an independent employed woman. He may have to accept less catering to his individual wishes and may feel he should assume new obligations at home to prevent overburdening of his wife. An important task for both husband and wife is to rethink their philosophy of life and search for new values to carry them into middle age.

Children have completed the transition from adolescence into young adulthood. For a time the young person becomes more or less detached from his family group. He is able to act with a high degree of independence as an individual. Unless he is in college, he loses contact with his age group, a contact that has carried him along all through school, and he becomes an adult among adults of all ages. He no longer gains status from his family connections in the same degree as earlier in his life. This is the period when he must prove himself on his own merits. For the young man, settling into an occupation is all important; finding a mate and marrying is highly significant. The girl looks upon work as temporary and actively though modestly works on the problem of finding a husband. Both young men and women sometimes doubt their ability to select the proper mates for themselves and seek books, lectures, and courses on preparation for marriage. Young men also must adjust to military service and adjust this service to their other major interests of vocation and marriage.

It may be said that this period from approximately eighteen to twenty-five is probably the most significant in the lives of most people. Childhood is definitely and conclusively left behind and adulthood is embraced in all phases of life. The development that began with conception has now found fruition in adult life; the pattern set at this time tends to color the remainder of life, although the person does not stand still in his development.

7. The Family in the Middle Years

Husband and wife are in their fifties and early sixties. Their children have left home. They are again a couple, again primarily husband and wife and secondarily father and mother. This is the period for mending fences of communication and joint living which may have become ragged or even damaged in the busy years of child rearing. In one sense this phase is a renewal of the early married years, as the couple again seek a new personal adjustment. It differs, however, as it is based on years of experience together and the memories of their joint enterprise in rearing a family. They must put these experiences away as memories and turn to their future as a couple, a future of some twelve to fifteen years before death begins to create a significant number of widows or widowers.

Husband and wife must adjust to declining sexual interests and some loss of physical vigor and youthful appearance on both sides. The way is open, however, for growth of personal companionship.

During middle age, the couple usually become grandparents. They step into new roles, different from the roles of parents. The roles must be learned and must not be allowed to intrude on the parental roles of the parents of their grandchildren, for in our society each parent-child combination must be allowed its own freedom to develop. The middle-aged couple are now in the position that their parents were when they were in stages 2 and 3 of family development.

The married children now have their own homes, their own family life. They are becoming parents and entering upon stages 2, 3, and 4, through which their parents passed some twenty-five to thirty years earlier; these stages have already been described above.

8. The Aging Family

This stage is usually thought of as beginning with retirement and lasting until the death of both husband and wife. The couple have already adjusted to the independence of their married children and are well versed in the arts of grandparenthood. The early part of the aging period is dominated by adjustment to retirement, which typically brings both lowered income and decline in social status.

The later part of the period is marked by physical and sometimes mental decline and eventually by the death of either husband or wife; typically the husband dies first and an elderly widow must adjust to a single life after forty or more years as one of a married couple. If the wife dies first, the widower has the adjustment to make. The remaining one has the difficult task of becoming accepted into other groups at a time of life when adaptation is difficult.

The married children are now themselves middle-aged; their children are adolescent or marrying and having children, and another swing of the life cycle has begun. Their attention now comes back to their aging parents with concern for their welfare. Sometimes the aging parents, especially a widowed mother, joins them in their home, but often the bond is the one of maintaining a helpful friendship with a parent in his or her own home.

In time, the married children themselves pass into the old-age stage of the cycle and in their turn look to their children for security and love. Thus the never-ending cycle of family life moves through the generations.

Overlapping Stages

The preceding discussion is highly simplified. Families with three or four children, especially if they are widely spaced, typically are in several phases of family development at one time. From the point of view of the oldest child the family may be one with teen-agers; but the youngest child may demand that the family still adjust to the preschooler.

This dual process may place additional strains on the family and between the members since the needs of the teen-ager may conflict with those of the young child. The parents are caught between the needs of the two and somehow must help each child to satisfy his needs. From another point of view, however, the slow movement from stage to stage may help the family. Perhaps the tensions would be even greater if the family had to move abruptly from one stage to another, a situation which could happen only if a family consisted simply of twins or triplets, or in lesser degree in the case of one child. As it is, the family "learns" on the oldest child and then more confidently and with more composure accepts the developing needs of each succeeding child and the changes in their own family and personal relationships. As Dr. Duvall phrases the situation in *Family Development* (pages 9–10):

> We see a family being pushed out into new unknowns in its experience as its oldest child becomes a preschooler, goes to school, gets into the teens, and finally leaves for a life of his own. As younger children come along, they arrive in a family already somewhat familiar with these normal events and stages of children's growth through the induction given by the eldest.

Developmental Tasks

In the passage of person or family from one stage to another certain general trends may be noticed. At each stage, individual or family, young person or old, is faced with certain developmental tasks. A developmental task, according to Havighurst, who is referring to the individual, "is a task which arises at or about a certain period in the life of the individual, successful achievement of which leads to his happiness and to success with later tasks, while failure leads to unhappiness in the individual, disapproval by society, and difficulty with later tasks." Dr. Duvall adopts this definition and applies it to family life.

Thus a developmental task, well done, produces a well-adjusted individual or family for the present and creates the competence for moving on to the next stage and achieving success there also. Each stage of development rests on the stage that has preceded. Successful childhood rests on successful development in infancy, adolescence on childhood, early adulthood on adolescence, and so on. If the person fails to accomplish adequately the tasks of any one stage, he is hampered in achieving success in the next stage, and the next. In either individual or family, it is not possible to ignore some stages as unimportant and to feel that only certain stages are significant. Each stage, its tasks well achieved, brings immediate reward and also lays the foundation for success in the next stage. Conversely, failure at any one stage brings immediate unhappiness or dissatisfaction and makes success at later stages difficult.

The developmental tasks of any one stage rest on three factors, according to Havighurst and Duvall. The basic factor is the person's physical readiness for a particular function. A baby cannot learn to talk, walk, or control elimination until mind and body have matured to the place where these things are possible for him. The older boy or girl cannot become a parent until sex organs mature. At the other end of life, when physical and mental powers are declining, the developmental tasks are to adjust to lessened capacities. The time comes when the athlete can no longer play successfully with or against younger people; there comes a time when the scholar cannot read without glasses, grasp difficult concepts readily, nor originate new concepts. Thus for the first part of life the person's powers are expanding and his tasks are concerned with learning to use these expanding powers successfully. During the latter part of life, powers are contracting and the person's task is to conserve and learn to live successfully with his lessening powers.

A second, strong factor in development is the expectations of the society in which the person lives as to what form development should take, and what the specific tasks should be. Children become able to learn to talk between the ages of one and two. They are expected to learn at this time; parents become greatly concerned if their children do not begin to talk at this age; they encourage, coax, and praise. The child of five or six is able to take care of his bodily needs and to endure separation from his mother. Therefore social expectation is that he will enter school and be successful in school life. Older children and parents help to prepare the child for school, and if he does not enter school as expected, parents are called to account. Sometimes the expectations of society are that the child will not immediately make use of his growing powers but will control and restrain them, fitting them into a larger pattern of life. The adolescent is not expected to use his sexual powers but quite conversely to refrain from using them until other cultural expectations have been met—education, personal maturity, and economic competence.

Third is the factor of personal aspirations and values. These are closely related to the first two factors, but in time become a motivating force in their own right. The youth makes his own choice of occupation and young men and women choose whom they will marry. Each person develops his own scale of values and philosophy of life.

Recurrent Tasks

Another important point developed by Havighurst is that certain tasks are learned once and for all, but other tasks recur at different levels of maturity or development. Getting along with other people is an important task that recurs in different forms at different stages. The child of six to ten years is expected to get along with age mates of his own sex. In adolescence, boys and girls are expected to learn how to get along with each other, without however abandoning their previous ability to get along with their own sex. In adulthood, both sexes are expected to learn to cooperate for impersonal purposes and projects. And in old age people are expected to learn to associate with other old people. Thus each stage of development adds a new type of association to those learned before, but at no point is the early learning lost or unneeded.

Other tasks are accomplished only once in a lifetime. Talking and walking are illustrations. The person may increase his capacity for talking and walking and apply the skills in various ways, but the actual physical skills do not need to be learned more than once.

The Continuity of Family Life

An individual is born and dies; but if we think in terms of family, there is no beginning and no end, unless, in some given generation, there are no descendants. Even though one given couple have no children, the family in a larger sense does not die, since married brothers or sisters of the couple may have children who carry on the family inheritance and culture. People who have pride in the idea of family continuity sometimes take great pains to maintain a record of the family tree which traces the generations back for hundreds of years, without a break in continuity. The family continuity is most clear in societies in which the different generations continue to live in the same community, perhaps even in the same household. In old China, such a living arrangement was the accepted thing: each son brought his wife into his father's household and reared his children there as part of a large family group. In time, when the father died, the eldest son became head of the family, or perhaps the brothers separated, each brother to become head of a branch family that continued on down through the generations.

In the United States we often lose this sense of continuity, since at marriage each couple tends to splinter off from the parental families and to set up an independent and autonomous household, sometimes many miles distant from either set of parents.

Nevertheless, family continuity continues in a biological sense. If families of different generations maintain close contact, the continuity also usually incorporates family traditions, values, and customs. In spite of the high degree of mobility in this country, members of many families do remain in close contact with each other. Dr. Duvall reports the following figures, credited to Robert O. Blood, Jr., sociologist, based on a study of Detroit, Michigan, an industrial city where one would expect to find a high degree of mobility. Among 731 Detroit families, 89 per cent had relatives living in the metropolitan area of Detroit. Among these Detroit families, intrafamily visiting was frequent: 29 per cent visited daily, 37 per cent weekly, 20 per cent monthly, and 13 per cent yearly.

Whenever we talk about the developmental stages of an individual family, we are simply dipping into the continuous stream of family life and lifting out a small segment of the total, the experiences of one couple. Stretching out behind them is the family of their parents and grandparents, and reaching into the future is the family of their children and grandchildren. Since couples now tend to marry in the late teens and early twenties and have children before they are thirty, there is a lag of about twenty-five years between equivalent stages of two generations. When one couple are in the twenties, their parents are middle-aged, and the members of the next generation are being born. When the couple are passing into old age, the second generation is middle-aged and the third generation is already leaving home to start yet another generation. Thus there is no end to the continuous flow of family life.

7 · *The American Husband* *

METROPOLITAN LIFE INSURANCE COMPANY

For the reader who likes his facts in figures, this article and the one that follows picture precisely the present status of the American husband and wife: where they live and with whom, relative ages of husband and wife, number of children, and employment.

Tracing through the changes with increasing age for either husband or wife provides a picture of the family life cycle, with the small percentage of men and women married in the age group between fourteen and twenty-four, the peak of marriage in mid-maturity, and the decline in old age as husband or wife dies. The very young marrieds may live with relatives but the separate household, once achieved, tends to be retained into old age. Children under eighteen are a customary part of the household until the parents are middle-aged, when the number of childless households rapidly increases. In these age-by-age comparisons made possible by the two tables, one sees the supporting facts for the descriptive statement in the first article in this chapter.

THE TYPICAL American male is married at a relatively early age, establishes a household soon after marriage, and bears the responsibility for raising a family during most of his working life. Data on the characteristics of husbands in the United States are shown in the accompanying table; only those members of the Armed Forces who live off post or with their families on post are included in the figures, which means that the majority of married men in military service are excluded.

A large proportion of our married men are relatively young; over one quarter are under 35 years of age and an additional quarter are at ages 35–44. At the same time, the number at ages 65 and over is close to 4.4 million, or about 11 percent of the total, and is growing rapidly.

More than nine out of every 10 husbands maintain a household for their family. The others are nearly equally divided between those who live with their wife in a household not their own and those who live apart from their spouse under a variety of housing arrangements. Many of the couples doubling up are young newlyweds who share the living quarters

---

* *Statistical Bulletin*, Metropolitan Life Insurance Company, 37 (April, 1956), 4–6. Reprinted by permission of the editor of the *Bulletin*.

Characteristics of Husbands* in the United States, April 1955

Characteristic	Age of Husband, in Years					
	14 and over	14–24	25–34	35–44	45–64	65 and over
Husbands—number in thousands	39,125	2,205	8,886	9,782	13,865	4,387
—percent distribution	100.0	5.6	22.7	25.0	35.5	11.2
—percent of all men in age group	69.9	21.1	76.8	88.3	84.7	67.3
Residence—percent	100.0	100.0	100.0	100.0	100.0	100.0
Urban	64.6	67.9	64.9	63.9	65.8	60.0
Rural nonfarm	22.6	22.0	26.2	23.7	19.9	21.8
Rural farm	12.8	10.1	8.9	12.4	14.3	18.2
Family status—percent	100.0	100.0	100.0	100.0	100.0	100.0
Living with wife, in	96.0	96.4	96.3	96.6	95.3	96.2
Own household	92.7	82.0	91.8	94.1	93.8	93.2
Relative's household	3.0	13.3	4.2	2.0	1.3	2.8
Nonrelative's household	.3	1.1	.3	.5	.2	.2
Not living with wife	4.0	3.6	3.7	3.4	4.7	3.8
Separated because of marital discord	1.9	2.3	2.0	1.7	2.0	1.8
Living apart for other reasons	2.1	1.3	1.7	1.7	2.7	2.0
Age of wife †—percent	100.0	100.0	100.0	100.0	100.0	100.0
14–24 years	11.4	88.6	24.1	1.5	.1	.1
25–34 years	27.0	11.0	70.8	34.2	2.4	.2
35–44 years	24.9	.4	4.9	60.4	25.9	1.4
45–64 years	29.8	—	.2	3.9	69.8	42.5
65 years and over	6.9	—	—	—	1.8	55.8
Number of own children under 18 years of age †—percent	100.0	100.0	100.0	100.0	100.0	100.0
No children	44.3	38.8	20.0	20.6	62.4	95.4
One child	21.0	37.9	27.8	22.6	18.2	2.9
Two children	18.1	15.6	28.9	26.8	10.3	.8
Three children	9.5	5.8	15.2	16.1	4.5	.6
Four children or more	7.1	1.9	8.1	13.9	4.6	.3
Own children under age 18 per 100 husbands	120	96	170	192	74	8
Labor force participation						
Living with wife—percent	100.0	100.0	100.0		100.0	100.0
Husband only in labor force	64.6	67.1	71.3		64.3	35.9
Husband and wife in labor force	26.1	27.8	27.5		29.5	8.3
Wife only in labor force	1.7	3.1	.5		1.7	5.6
Neither in labor force	7.6	2.0	.7		4.5	50.2

* Civilian population and members of the Armed Forces who live off post or with their families on post.
† Data relate to husbands living with wife in April 1953.
Source of basic data: Various reports and unpublished data from the Bureau of the Census.

of their parents or other relatives until they can establish their own home. Doubled-up families have declined steadily from almost 9 percent of all married couples in 1947 to only 3½ percent in 1955. Favorable economic conditions and the increasing availability of new dwelling units have undoubtedly enabled many of these families to acquire their own home.

Currently, four fifths of the families where the husband is aged 25–34 have at least one young child, and nearly one quarter have three or more children. The relatively large families are even more common where the husband is in the age group 35–44. After his 45th birthday, families generally decrease in size as an increasing number of children marry or leave home for other reasons. But even at this period of life, American couples still have nearly 10 million of their children under age 18 living with them. Many of these families, in addition, provide for older children who are not yet self-supporting as well as for related children from broken homes.

About 95 percent of all married men under age 65 are in the labor force. The proportion is still above one half for several years after age 65, but diminishes rapidly thereafter. In most families the husband is the sole breadwinner. However, an increasing proportion of wives are working— many in part-time or intermittent employment—in order to supplement the family income. Currently, in more than one fourth of all families, both spouses are in the labor force.

8 · The American Wife *

METROPOLITAN LIFE INSURANCE COMPANY

The statistical facts about the American wife confirm those just given about the husband. The number of children that the wife has and her position in the labor force are of special interest in showing some of her responsibilities.

THE PATTERN of family life in the United States has changed markedly since World War II. The married population has risen to a record high, the birth rate is at the highest level in a generation, and more wives than ever before are actively participating in the economic life of the country.

Married women in our population numbered not far from 40 million in April 1954, a gain of 9¾ million since 1940 and of more than 2⅓ million

* *Statistical Bulletin*, Metropolitan Life Insurance Company, 36 (October, 1955), 1–3. Reprinted by permission of the editor of the *Bulletin*.

Characteristics of Wives in the United States, April 1954

Characteristic	Age of Wife, in Years					
	14 and over	14–24	25–34	35–44	45–64	65 and over
Wives—number in thousands	39,869	4,479	10,660	9,819	12,208	2,703
—percent of all women in age group	67.0	37.6	86.7	85.8	73.7	36.9
Age of husband *—percent	100.0	100.0	100.0	100.0	100.0	100.0
14–24 years	5.8	45.0	2.4	.1	—	—
25–34 years	24.4	51.6	63.8	4.8	.2	.1
35–44 years	24.2	3.2	30.6	58.8	3.2	.1
45–64 years	34.4	.2	3.1	35.7	80.7	8.9
65 years and over	11.2	—	.1	.6	15.9	90.9
Year of marriage †—percent	100.0	100.0	100.0	100.0	100.0	100.0
1952–April 1953	3.9	21.4	2.9	1.2	.8	.4
1950–1951	7.6	37.4	7.4	3.0	1.3	.9
1945–1949	20.5	39.5	43.6	10.8	3.9	2.1
1940–1944	15.1	1.7	34.1	17.3	4.5	2.0
1930–1939	22.1	—	12.0	56.7	15.9	2.7
Before 1930	30.8	—	—	11.0	73.6	91.9
Family status—percent	100.0	100.0	100.0	100.0	100.0	100.0
Living with husband, in	93.7	87.8	94.1	94.4	94.4	95.6
Own household	90.0	77.6	90.0	92.0	92.4	91.6
Relative's household	3.3	9.5	3.8	1.9	1.5	3.9
Nonrelative's household	.4	.7	.3	.5	.5	.1
Not living with husband	6.3	12.2	5.9	5.6	5.6	4.4
Husband in Armed Forces	1.1	6.3	1.0	.4	.1	—
Separated because of marital discord	2.8	3.3	2.8	3.1	2.9	1.4
Living apart for other reasons	2.4	2.6	2.1	2.1	2.6	3.0
Number of own children under 18 years of age *—percent ‡	100.0	100.0	100.0	100.0	100.0	100.0
No children	44.3	28.6	22.1	36.0	66.3	92.3
One child	21.0	32.1	26.1	21.2	16.0	4.3
Two children	18.1	22.8	27.3	20.8	9.3	1.7
Three children	9.5	11.0	14.9	11.8	4.2	1.0
Four children or more	7.1	5.5	9.6	10.2	4.2	.7
Own children under age 18 per 100 wives	120	137	172	147	68	14
Labor force participation †—percent	100.0	100.0	100.0	100.0	100.0	100.0
Living with husband						
Husband only in labor force	62.9	65.1	69.2	63.3	62.1	36.9
Husband and wife in labor force	23.1	23.1	23.6	30.5	21.0	3.6
Wife only in labor force	1.2	.8	.4	.8	2.4	1.6
Neither in labor force	6.9	.7	.8	1.0	9.3	52.1

Characteristic	Age of Wife, in Years					
	14 and over	14–24	25–34	35–44	45–64	65 and over
Not living with husband						
Wife in labor force	2.8	4.8	3.0	2.5	2.6	.7
Wife not in labor force	3.1	5.5	3.0	1.9	2.6	5.1
Residence—percent	100.0	100.0	100.0	100.0	100.0	100.0
Urban	65.3	60.0	65.6	67.6	65.4	64.0
Rural nonfarm	22.0	26.8	24.3	20.5	19.9	20.5
Rural farm	12.7	13.2	10.1	11.9	14.7	15.5

* Data relate to wives living with husband in April 1953.
† Data relate to married persons in April 1953.
‡ Estimated by the Statistical Bureau, Metropolitan Life Insurance Company.
Source of basic data: Various reports and unpublished data from the Bureau of the Census.

since 1950. According to present indications, they may total nearly 42½ million by 1960.

Most American wives are relatively young, as the table . . . shows; almost two fifths are under age 35 and an additional one fourth are in the age group 35–44. This situation reflects our tradition of early marriage as well as the upsurge in marriages during and immediately after World War II. In fact, almost one half of all the wives in our country have married since 1940. At the other extreme, there are now more than 2.7 million married women at ages 65 and over; nine tenths of them have been married a quarter century or more.

In the great majority of families the wife is somewhat younger than her husband, but in about one eighth of the families she is older than her spouse. More than half the married women under 25 years of age have husbands who are 25 or older. Less than 2½ percent of the wives at ages 25–34 are married to men under age 25.

The typical wife lives with her husband in a household of their own; this is the situation in nine tenths of the families. A considerable proportion of the couples who share the living quarters of relatives or others are young people—about one third of these wives are under 25 years of age. Only about 6 percent of all married women live apart from their husbands, and in most of these cases it is not because of marital discord. Many husbands are away from home in civilian employment; about 446,000 are in the Armed Forces, a large number having married shortly before or soon after entering military service.

More than one half of all married couples have young children living with them. Nearly four fifths of the families in which the wife is aged 25–34 have at least one child in their care. Many married women past midlife are still responsible for bringing up children; this is the case for one third of the wives at ages 45–64. Although the proportion decreases at the older ages, even families where the wife is 65 or older have more than ⅓ million of their children under 18 years of age living with them. In addition, a large number of grandchildren and other relatives are found in such families, often because the youngsters have lost one or both natural parents. Many middle-aged couples also provide for their own or related children who are past age 18, but who are not yet self-supporting.

Although the majority of husbands still bear the sole responsibility for supporting their family, an increasing number of wives are in gainful employment. Currently, about 10.7 million married women—27 percent of the total—are in the labor force. It has long been customary for young wives to work until the baby came, but recently more and more of them are returning to the labor market after the children grow up. Thus, about one third of all wives at ages 35–44 now work outside the home; the proportion is one fourth for those in the age range 45–64. The fact that about two out of every three married women live in urban areas enables many to take advantage of employment opportunities in industry.

A large proportion of employed wives work part time or intermittently. Their earnings are nevertheless an appreciable contribution toward the family budget. Under the circumstances it is not surprising that large numbers of women purchase Life insurance to protect their dependents and to build a savings fund. The total amount of Life insurance in force on the lives of women in the United States now exceeds $50 billion and is rising rapidly.

9 · The Ebb and Flow of Finances in the Family Life Cycle *

HOWARD F. BIGELOW

Income and the demands made upon income fall into a pattern with the increasing and then declining power of the husband to earn, and the increasing and then declining size of family. Unfortunately, affluence in money and affluence in children do not always coincide. Professor Bigelow's article

---

* "What Are Usual Family Patterns?" *Journal of Home Economics*, 42 (1950), 27–29; also, copyright, 1953, by J. B. Lippincott Company. Reprinted by permission of the publishers and the author.

The author, an economist, holds the Master of Arts degree from Harvard University and is now Professor of Economics at West Michigan College. He is the author of *Family Finance* and of contributions in this field to various books and journals.

is explicit in tracing the changing financial demands from marriage to old age. It may provide a very realistic look into the future for those planning marriage.

A FAMILY's financial situation in any given stage of the family life cycle depends in large part on what it has accomplished or failed to accomplish in earlier stages. Many of a family's most difficult financial problems are due to the fact that for one reason or another—sometimes lack of knowledge, sometimes circumstances beyond its control—it has been unable in an earlier stage of the family cycle to make proper provision for some one or more of the family's wants. In one case, a severe depression wipes out the savings a family had been setting aside for the children's education. In another, war interrupts a young man's education and delays for several years his establishment in his profession. Another family, in the preschool and elementary stage, buys too expensive a house, drives too big a car, saves too little money, and is faced with the necessity for financial retrenchment if the boys or girls are to go to college. Families can work out their financial problems more intelligently if they have clearly in mind the usual wants for which a family must provide during each stage of the family life cycle.

The classic pattern runs something like this. In the courtship stage, man and girl complete school and their trade or professional training. The man gets a job, buys a car, a portable radio, some life insurance, and puts some money in the bank. The girl usually works for a while after she finishes school, spends plenty on clothes, buys a few things to make her room attractive, takes out a little life insurance, and puts a little money in the bank.

As soon as the man is earning enough to be "able to support a family," they are married and enter the next stage, establishing the family. Their friends provide them with many bits of household equipment as wedding presents. They buy the rest of the furnishings they need to start housekeeping and either rent an apartment or a small house, or, if they are permanently located and the husband's savings adequate, they make a down payment on a home. They set up their establishment, living well within their income, keeping up their insurance, and adding to their cash savings. Looking forward to the child-bearing and preschool period, they take out hospital insurance. Food and clothing expenses are usually low, and recreation moderate. The big items are furniture and furnishings, in some cases the payments on the home, and—most important of all—plenty of cash savings for emergency reserves and for working capital.

In the child-bearing and preschool stage, food and clothing expenses continue reasonably low. If the family has been living in a rented apartment, it may be necessary to move to a house where children are permitted, preferably near a good elementary school. The big outlays are for medical care and for household help, if domestic service is available, and otherwise for the equivalent in baby sitters, labor-saving equipment, and commercial services. During this stage, expenditures should be concentrated on items which will save the mother's time and energy. Expenditures for recreation are usually low, but enough should be provided for recreation outside the home to insure her getting adequate relief from the constant care of small children. And as the years go by, there will be expenditures for toys and backyard play equipment.

During the elementary school stage, there are no outstanding items of expenditure. The cost of food and clothing increases gradually. Medical expenditures may increase for a time early in the elementary school stage, when the oldest of the children comes home from school with the usual series of children's communicable diseases. But medical expenses are usually low for the balance of this period. There are gradually increasing expenditures for school books and supplies. About the time he starts school, each child should be given a small allowance, and the amount should be increased gradually as he shows he is learning how to use his money effectively. The one item which is most often overlooked is adequate addition to the family's savings in a form which will be available for use later in the high school and college period.

In the high school stage, expenses of all sorts increase rapidly. Adolescent boys and girls have voracious appetites. Clothes assume a new importance. They must be selected with careful attention to fashion and to other social values. There must be additions to the children's allowances to cover school lunches, carfare, and tickets to games and school social functions. During the high school period, the emphasis should be upon expenditures which are important for the children's social development. Even though the children earn most of their spending money, few families can save much during these years. Many must draw on savings.

If the children can live at home, the college stage is not very different from the high school stage, except that it is more expensive. If they go away to college, substantial increases in cash outlay are required, for board and room and travel to and from school as well as larger allowances for incidentals. This is a time when most families, especially those with more than one child in college, find it necessary to draw on their savings to finance a substantial part of the college expenses.

When the children's formal schooling is completed, at the end of high school, college, or advanced professional training, the family usually assumes that its financial responsibility for the children is at an end. In many cases this is so. Often, however, they can make more satisfactory vocational adjustment if they know that they can fall back on their family for financial assistance, should the first job prove to be one with little or no future, should an excellent opportunity to get valuable work experience pay less than a living wage during the learning period, or should they need more money than they have been able to save in order to move to a new job with better prospects for promotion.

During the period of vocational adjustment, wise counsel and moral support is as important as financial aid. Many families advance funds during this period with the understanding that the money is to be repaid later. They believe the boys and girls should learn to pay their own way. But they also know that there are times when family funds make it possible for young people to take advantage of opportunities which would not be open if they had to depend solely on their own resources.

When the children finally are on their own, a period of financial recovery follows. Current expenses are low. Savings again have a prominent place in financial planning. The first concern of most families during this period is to rebuild depleted inventories, and then to accumulate funds to draw upon during the retirement period.

If they have borrowed on their home or on their life insurance to finance the children's education, their first cash savings go to paying off these loans. If the old home is too large to suit their needs, too run down, or too heavily mortgaged, they may decide to trade it for a small, conveniently located, modern home. Or they may divide it into apartments, which will provide them with suitable housing and some cash income in their declining years.

The extent to which the family will be able to take life a little more easily or to participate more actively in social and community affairs, and the degree to which they must concentrate on savings in anticipation of the retirement period will depend in part on the earning power of the husband, in part on the family's current financial status, and in part on eligibility for social security or other pension payments. If the available pension provides retirement income only during the husband's lifetime, he must provide from family savings for his wife's needs, should she survive him. But even though the family must make substantial savings in anticipation of retirement, it is equally important during this stage, especially for the husband, to develop some avocational interests with which to occupy himself after he has retired from active employment.

The family has a number of financial adjustments to make at the beginning of the retirement period. At this time most families find themselves with a sharply lowered income. The opportunity for continued savings is usually at an end. At the same time, there is no longer need of insurance against loss of earned income. Yet parents want to leave as much as possible in the way of an estate to their children. They must decide whether it will be better to use part of their savings to continue to pay premiums on life insurance or to cash in most of their policies and use the proceeds to purchase joint and survivor annuities to supplement their retirement income so that they can keep the family's investments intact to leave to their children.

During the retirement stage, current expenses are usually moderate. There should be provision for travel, recreation, and various avocational activities. Medical expenses are somewhat unpredictable but tend to increase during later years. The family should keep its hospital insurance in force. Adequate provision for personal service in case of disabling illness is the single item which may run very high in retired families.

Of course, financial planning involves consideration of income as well as expenditures. The classic pattern assumes that while the wife may work for a time before marriage, after marriage the husband should earn the income and the wife should devote her entire time to housekeeping and home management. Since the war, as a method of adapting to interrupted education and delayed vocational adjustment, there has come into use another method of financing marriage.

In the postwar-modern pattern, when they reach the usual chronological age, the man and girl are married. They share both the earning and the housework. They rent their shelter, at first only housekeeping rooms or a very small furnished apartment. They live simply, saving as much as possible of the wife's earnings, and sometimes a substantial part of the husband's earnings as well. In many cases, they complete their education and pay off their school debts. As soon as they are able to find a suitable place and buy some furniture, they move to a small house or a larger partly furnished apartment. At the beginning of the child-bearing period, they must adjust to living on the husband's income alone. If the wife becomes pregnant before they have completed their savings program, they may find it necessary to buy the house and furnishings—and the baby, too—on the installment plan.

Whether the wife returns to gainful employment for a time after the baby is born depends in part on her training and earning power, in part on her preference, and in part on the demand for her services. Usually, however, she will work only occasionally, if at all, during the preschool years. She may earn a little money from time to time, as occasion offers, during the elementary school period. She will give serious consideration to the desirability of working full time to ease the financial pressure while the children are in high school and college. She will work during the recovery period only if she prefers gainful employment to enlarged participation in social activities and community affairs.

It is possible in a short article to give only a general outline of the problems a family faces in each stage of the family cycle. The particular style which families follow in their planning—the classic, the postwar-modern, or any of the many variations of each of these—will depend in part on their temperament and preference, in part on necessity, and in part on current fashions in family finance.

10 · Housing and the Family Life Cycle *

TESSIE AGAN

The tangible impact on its environment of the family as it moves through the stages of the family life cycle is evident in the difference in housing needs of a newly married couple, a "launching" family, and an old-age family. Imagination, ingenuity, and adaptability on the part of the family lead to remodeling or to moving at strategic points in the changing cycle. However the needs for differences in the physical layout of the house may be met, the flow of family life continues unbroken.

THE REQUIREMENTS for a family dwelling change during the life of the family. These changes in housing requirements, moreover, parallel changes in the family life pattern. Members of the family undergo physical and mental changes; financial stability varies; children are born, grow up, and leave home; interests change; family members form different concepts of life in general. These and other changes affect family life from its beginning to the end.

Although such changes occur from week to week and from month to month, in some periods of family life there are similarities, and between some periods there are decided differences. These periods were considered by the National Conference on Family Life as the beginning family, the expanding family, the launching family, the middle-life family, and the old-age family.

Each period in the family life cycle has its set of circumstances which pose their own unique problems. Aside from the challenging problems of human relations and of the financial and other management of the home, there is also the problem of use of the present dwelling to the best ad-

* *Journal of Home Economics*, 42 (1950), 351–354. Reprinted by permission of the publisher and the author.

The author, who holds the Master of Science degree from Kansas State College, is Associate Professor of Family Economics at this College. She is author of numerous articles on housing planned for family needs and of the college text *The House*.

vantage as a background for family life or the choice of another house. For either choice, it is necessary to understand the functions required of the dwelling to carry on all the activities of the family members and to be able to interpret house design in terms of the ease with which these activities can be carried on.

The design of the house in terms of the functions for which it serves as a background is only now emerging from a prescientific basis. The recent studies on family activities and housing preferences made on a regional basis and sponsored by the Bureau of Human Nutrition and Home Economics, as well as the interest of sociologists and others in family life programs, are providing means for a more scientific planning. When we have fuller knowledge of the habits of different families and their ease or difficulties in adjusting to various types of dwellings at different periods of family life, we shall be in a better position to determine exactly characteristics of adequate house design.

The house, in whatever form it is, is the center of family life. It must provide space for group and individual activities of the family such as recreation, reading, and shared experience among family members. It must afford facilities for the withdrawal of individuals for study, rest, or thinking during periods of family activity; for sleeping and personal hygiene, including the needs of infants, the aged, or others with special requirements. It must make easy such service activities as food preparation, the serving of meals, dishwashing, laundering, and housecleaning. It must make available space for children's play and for hobbies of adults and children. It must provide for the arrangement and storage of articles required for all these activities.

The design of any family dwelling should facilitate these essential activities, foster harmonious family life, and minister to the privacy and integrity of the individuals living in it. Yet withal, it should not be too large nor costly for the scale of living of its occupants.

Because of the fixity of its location, the intricacy of its mechanical installations, its bulk, and the multiplicity of its functions, the family dwelling is an exceedingly complex structure. And it is the variety of functions at any period of the family life cycle, as well as the changing set of functions with each new period, which contributes to the complexity.

Added to these complexities is the problem of acquiring a suitable dwelling at a time when the national supply, both on rental and home ownership bases, is notably short for those in the moderate or lower income brackets. This problem is especially difficult because housing requirements begin to increase before the family has attained its full economic capacity, and other changes in requirements occur when economic capacity is on the wane.

The Beginning Family

Fortunately, the requirements made of a dwelling for a beginning family are relatively simple.

Characteristics. Husband and wife alone make up the family. They are learning to know each other and how to live with each other. Both are learning how to interpret their place in an adult community. They are not yet established financially. The husband may not be launched on a lifework, for he may still be in college. The wife may be employed part or full time to supplement income, or she may also be in college. The wife is learning or perfecting techniques of food preparation and home management. Entertaining at home is likely to be for a few other couples for a meal or games.

Housing Requirements. They need inexpensive private quarters, usually rented and located where they can assume their full share of individual family responsibility and develop responsible independence. Two or three rooms, including living room, bedroom, and kitchen, with bathroom and closet space, constitute a comfortable minimum. Meals are served in living room or kitchen. Owned equipment and furnishings should be the best they can afford but kept to a minimum at first.

Efficiently arranged, well-equipped work centers help the wife establish good techniques and reduce the time she will need to spend in caring for the home.

The Expanding Family

Statistics show that the family begins to expand in approximately one to three years after marriage and continues for several years until the last child is born, which may be when the first child is from five to twelve years old. About half the men marry when they are 25, and about half the women marry at 23. The first child arrives in about a year after marriage, the second child in two years more, and the third in another two years. The coming of infants and the growth and development of children bring many changes in the pattern of life for the family and the requirements made of the family dwelling.

Characteristics. Infants and young children are included in the family. The children are at habit-forming and experimental stages physically, mentally, and socially. They want to run, to climb, to make noise, to eat, as well as to engage in creative activities such as painting, reading, watching adults, making floor projects, make-believe games, and theatricals, showing collections, and practicing music. Preparing simple but special diets, providing clean clothes, giving baths, and supervising toilet, sleep, and play are important service activities of the mother for the infant and young children. The husband is developing his business or profession. Finances are more certain but still not bountiful. His time at home is devoted to reading, odd jobs for the home, and life with his family. His only times for enjoying children are at meals and during evenings and holidays. Entertainment is likely to be dinners or games for other families or relatives. The family may need to entertain people important to the husband's business or profession. Children's parties, both planned and spontaneous, must not be forgotten.

Housing Requirements. More space is needed. Probably a house is taken to provide outside space for the children. A bedroom is needed for each two children of the same sex or each separate child of opposite sex. A playroom-bedroom 11 feet by 12 feet is large enough for now and later permits sleeping and dressing besides storage space for toys and room for rumpus activities. Controlled temperatures and proper illumination are important. The work area is the important hub of the house. The kitchen, laundry, bath, and bedrooms for children are best if adjacent or readily accessible. The kitchen should be large enough to provide efficient work centers, space for a high chair in work centers, play space for children within sight indoors and out, space for the recital of the day's events by husband and children, and space for informal meals. Finishes should be scar- and water-resistant. Probably meal serving space will be desired separate from living room and in addition to kitchen. Working heights in kitchen and bath should allow the wife to lift weights without strain.

A place is needed where the adults can relax or receive their guests and a place for the children—space large enough to entertain both adults and children.

The Launching Family

The next important change in family life which affects its housing requirements comes when one or more of the children have reached adolescence. The home has been regarded as the launching place from which sons and daughters may find a mate and discover their lifework or major interests.

Characteristics. Adolescent youth and young adults are included in the family. Children are at the most restless and boisterous period of life, early adolescence. Each is interested in the opposite sex, as well as being clannish with his or her own sex. They want to withdraw from adults and be secretive. Both sexes are usually involved in many social activities. Personal appearance is important with both sexes. Girls want exclusive use of the social area. All want to eat between meals. The husband is well established in his business or profession, if he is going to be. He may have civic and recreational interests. The drain on financial resources is severe. The wife is counselor and adviser to the children, as well as hostess and general supervisor of family social life. Preparing wholesome and hearty food, providing clean clothes for daily and special occasions, and maintaining attractive living quarters are her service contributions to the family.

Housing Requirements. Bedrooms, living rooms, bathrooms with suitable furnishings, and private traffic-ways become important to younger members. The family may seek another house or remodel the old one if owned. The young people have bedrooms alone or share with another of the same sex and of near their own age. Much storage space for clothes is needed. Facilities to display collections without adult interference may be wanted. Living rooms should be well furnished and available to the young women and their friends. Sturdy but attractive recreation rooms are enjoyed. Competition for bathrooms becomes acute. At this period, it is well to have a separate living room space for the nonadolescent family members. The husband may want a quiet place to study, bring his own friends, or retire with his wife from the activity of the children.

Work areas should be convenient so that work connected with care of the family can be done with as little effort as possible.

The Middle-Age Family

About 25 years after the beginning of the family, the older children have left the family home for careers or homes of their own. Within a few years, all have departed. The parents are probably between 45 and 50 years old. About half the families can count on about 11 more years together. The average wife usually lives 13 years after her husband's death. The average husband, in the family where the wife dies prematurely, survives six years. Very few young couples have adult relatives in their home, but from the age of 45 onward about half of the couples have. About an eighth of these are married sons or daughters and their spouses.

Characteristics. The husband and the wife are now alone. Employed children may return for holidays or vacation. The grandchildren may come with parents or alone for short or long visits. Older relatives of the husband or wife or the married children and their spouses, either for short periods or permanently, may now be included. The wife is still vigorous in mind and body, although both she and her husband may be somewhat slowed down by chronic ailments. They are able to develop new interests in social and community affairs. She may work outside the home or resume her career. The husband is at the peak of his profession or business and needs this period to prepare for the approaching period of decreased earnings.

Housing Requirements. The same house which served the launching family is usable, for sons and daughters and their offspring come to fill it on occasions. Storage space may be needed for the many possessions of employed but unmarried sons or daughters away from home.

Enlarged social activities of the wife make redecoration or remodeling desired. Remodeling may involve an apartment made in the house for use of married children or for rental. Work centers may be modernized to reduce labor and allow time for new activities or work. Family reunion meals and more entertainment make a large serving area with its furnishings desirable. Quiet sleeping rooms and a bath downstairs with controlled temperatures may be desirable if older relatives are present.

The Old-Age Family

Retirement from business or the professions comes to men at about 65 or 70 years of age. Old age is coming if it has not already arrived. Statistics show increasing numbers of people with expectancy of ten or more years in this age group. Over half of aged people continue in private homes of their own, and all wish to continue as long as possible.

Characteristics. The husband and wife may be together, or either may be alone. Income has likely been reduced. Strength, vigor, and the tempo of their lives are decreased. Chronic ailments may be common. An attendant may be required in later years. They want to keep favorite items of furniture and have many keepsakes. They need to have outdoor exercise.

Housing Requirements. They likely would prefer to maintain their own home as long as possible, but they may decide that smaller quarters like those with which they started are suitable. If an apartment was made in the house during the middle-life period, they may take it and use the large part of the house as an income producing unit, if needed.

The location of any living arrangement is best if near old friends, close relatives, and within walking distance of shops and church. Quarters on the ground floor equipped with laborsaving devices and with storage for belongings between shoulder and hip height help them to do their own work. Adequate, glareless illumination and draftless warmth for comfort are needed.

From these descriptions it is apparent that it is difficult for the average family to occupy the same dwelling throughout all the periods of its life cycle, although some houses are so well planned that this is possible. Basic implications in the choice of features desirable in the dwelling for any period are fundamental needs, interests, activities, and financial status of the specific family concerned.

11 · Increased Chances for a Golden Wedding *

METROPOLITAN LIFE INSURANCE COMPANY

The old fairy tales ended, "and they were married and lived happily forever after." Year by year, the "forever after" part of marriage has been becoming more and more true, as medical science pushes the life expectancy to an ever greater number of years. The statistical table is worth pondering even though it requires careful study for an understanding. The reader may find his or her place on the table for 1955 and then discover the chances in a thousand of reaching the tenth anniversary, the silver wedding, and the golden wedding day according to whether husband and wife are the same age, or the wife younger or older. The younger the couple are at marriage, naturally, the greater the chance of reaching the golden wedding. For example, the boy of seventeen who marries a girl four years younger has the best chance of all of celebrating the golden wedding. But one should hasten to add that other complications may beset such a youthful marriage. A comparison may be made between the figures for the chances of the newly married in 1955 and those for 1900–1902, which show the chances that the grandparents had to survive together until the golden wedding day.

Although the last years of the family life cycle are almost inevitably spent alone by husband or wife (since few couples die at or near the same time), nevertheless, the average couple marrying now will spend many more years together than was true of any average couple in the past.

THE CONTINUING decline in mortality since the turn of the century has increased markedly the chances that a bride and groom will celebrate a 50th wedding anniversary. For the typical young couple now entering marriage, the likelihood that both will survive to the golden anniversary is more than twice what it was for the average couple of a half century ago. Thus, for the man aged 21 who marries a girl four years younger than himself, the chances are 419 in 1,000—more than 2 out of 5—that both will survive through the next 50 years, according to mortality conditions for the white

---

* *Statistical Bulletin*, Metropolitan Life Insurance Company, 38 (November, 1957), 1–3. Reprinted by permission of the editor of the *Bulletin*.

Chances in 1,000 of Joint Survival for 10, 25, or 50 Years
White Males and White Females, United States, 1955 and 1900–02

Age of Male	Years of Joint Survival								
	10	25	50	10	25	50	10	25	50
	Female four years younger			Female same age as male			Female two years older		
					1955				
17	978	932	539	977	927	501	977	923	476
19	977	924	480	977	918	438	976	913	413
21	977	914	419	976	906	375	976	901	350
23	977	902	357	976	892	314	975	886	289
25	976	886	296	975	875	254	973	867	228
27	974	867	237	972	853	195	971	845	170
29	971	843	181	968	827	142	966	817	120
31	967	815	131	963	797	97	960	785	79
33	961	783	88	956	762	61	953	749	47
35	953	746	55	947	723	34	944	707	25
37	943	704	32	937	678	18	933	660	12
39	932	658	17	924	627	9	919	607	6
					1900–02				
17	899	699	267	887	683	235	882	675	216
19	887	681	229	877	666	197	873	659	179
21	878	664	192	869	650	161	865	643	144
23	870	648	157	862	634	127	859	627	111
25	862	631	123	856	617	96	853	609	82
27	855	614	92	849	598	68	846	588	56
29	847	594	65	842	576	45	839	564	36
31	840	571	42	835	550	28	832	536	21
33	833	545	26	828	520	15	824	504	11
35	825	515	14	820	487	8	816	470	5
37	817	482	7	810	451	3	805	432	2
39	807	445	3	798	411	1	792	390	1

population of the United States in 1955; the corresponding chances were only 192 in 1,000, according to the mortality prevailing in 1900–02. For the groom of 25 with a bride of 21 the chances of joint survival for a half century are 296 per 1,000, compared with 123 in the earlier period.

The probabilities of joint survival for 10, 25, or 50 years for couples of various ages are shown in the table . . . . As the figures indicate, the prospects of a golden wedding are bright for young couples, but decrease rapidly with advance in age at marriage. For example, when the groom and bride are both 17 years of age, the chances are 1 in 2; when both are 25 at marriage, the chances drop to 1 in 4, and decrease further to about 1 in 10 at age 31. In cases of relatively late marriage—at ages 39 or later —the chances of joint survival for 50 years are less than 1 in 100.

The outlook for celebrating a silver anniversary has also increased greatly during recent decades. A very high proportion of young brides and grooms can look forward to that happy event. The chances are now 9 in 10 for grooms up to age 23 who take a bride four years younger, and also for grooms up to age 21 if their bride is of the same age or as much as two years older. Even for men who marry as late as age 35, the chances of a 25th wedding anniversary are better than 7 in 10. As is evident from the table, this is more favorable than the comparable chances for teenagers who married around 1900.

The typical American bridal couple today is almost certain to survive to its 10th wedding anniversary. For example, the chances are about 98 in 100 for men and women who marry in their early twenties, or one eighth greater than they were a half century ago. Even for brides and grooms in their late 30's, the chances of celebrating a 10th anniversary are greater than 90 in 100.

Our country has reaped many social and economic benefits from the marked improvement in survival at the younger and middle ages. Prominent among these has been an increase in the stability of family life by postponing widowhood to the older ages and by markedly reducing the burden of orphanhood. Although the risk of family disruption by premature death has been greatly lessened, it is still a contingency which every family must face. In order to mitigate the economic losses entailed by death, more than 115,000,000 people in the United States and Canada own Life insurance in legal reserve companies.

CHAPTER 3:

From Colonial Family to the Family of the Future

12 · The Changing American Family *

ERNEST W. BURGESS

The family is subject not only to changes of the family life cycle but also to pressures from the technological advances of our society. A series of changes that has almost run its course is from farm to city to suburb.

The following descriptions should be read not merely for their interest but in the light of their relationship to their rural or urban environment. The colonial family was necessarily well organized and the form of organization it took was the traditional patriarchal form. The rural colonial family was not only a social group but a work group as well. As does a small business, the farm had a manager (the father), a foreman (the mother), and workers of various degrees of skill (relatives and children). In semi-isolation, it had to depend upon itself for most of its needs; it had to be resourceful, loyal, helpful to all its members. The farm family of the early 1900's was still family-centered but it depended to some extent upon community facilities and therefore did not need to be so rigidly organized. In the 1920's the city family was often the rural or small-town family transplanted to the city, breathless in its effort to swing into the rapid and uneven pace of the many streams of city life. By 1960 there are more special services to help city families and a pattern of city living has begun to develop. The finger of concern now points to the suburban family.

THE MOST evident and perhaps the most fundamental change that has taken place in American family life is the emergence of what may be called

* *Religious Education*, 23 (May, 1928), selections from pages 408–411. Published by The Religious Education Association, New York 25, New York. Reprinted by permission of the publisher and the author.
The author's background is given in connection with article 2.

the urban family. It is different in many striking ways from the traditional American family which is characteristically rural. The changes in the American family caused by the transition from the rural to the urban environment may be seen in a comparison of three families (1) a colonial American family; (2) a rural family before the [first] World War; and (3) an ultra-modern urban family.

The colonial American family was of the patriarchal type. The following case of the Lay family stands for what might be termed a survival of or a reversion to this large patriarchal type of family like that of the Hebrew patriarchs or that still found in China, Japan and India. Almost every American rural community has a large family group more or less resembling the Lay family:

Mr. and Mrs. Lay were pioneer farmers in an area of virgin forest. The draining of the water made the swamp district available for agriculture. The deep black soil once drained of the excess water proved to possess almost inexhaustible fertility. The land now became valuable. And Mr. Lay gradually acquired the status of a well-to-do, prosperous farmer.

The family increased in numbers. Five sons and two daughters were born to Mr. and Mrs. Lay. As soon as the boys and girls were able, they were called upon to do their share of the farm work. With the increase of labor resources a large acreage became possible. The draining of the land provided this increased acreage. With the increase and growth of the children the additional labor was provided. They made that farm blossom like a garden. It is true the schooling facilities were meagre, and the school attendance was sadly curtailed because of the necessary work on the farm, but the cultivation of the farm was deemed of greater importance than the cultivation of the mind.

From the very beginning Mr. Lay considered himself as the ruling spirit of the family group. The farm was his, and the income was his to control. All moneys received, even that from the sale of poultry and dairy products, passed into the family treasury, that was absolutely controlled by the father. Nothing was bought without his consent and approval. He ruled absolutely from barn to kitchen. He was not tyrannical nor harsh in the execution of his authority. His despotism was of a benevolent kind, but he demanded recognition of his authority as something self-evident, and the family submitted to it in the like spirit.

There was some kind of social life in which the family participated. Every Sunday morning the entire family attended church. The drive to town was an event in their life. After church the afternoon was spent visiting their relatives. Or possibly the relatives would accompany them to their home. In later years, after the children had established their own homes, the entire family would meet either at the homes of the parents or at one of the children's homes for a Sunday afternoon reunion. As the family constituted a large group, this resulted in limiting the circle of their social intercourse to the family circle. The group thus became an inner group of prime importance.

As the boys married, it became evident that additional farm lands must be secured to provide the family with their means of livelihood. It is needless to state that the prospective bride was always thoroughly inspected and her virtues, particularly her capacity for work and willingness to save money, discussed before permission to marry was given by the father. No son married without the father's consent. But once the permission to marry was granted, the father set out to acquire a farm for the young couple, where they might reside. But the farm remained the father's property and the young people were considered his tenants. They were permitted to enjoy larger liberties, but in matters pertaining to the cultivation of the farm, the purchase of farm equipment, and of livestock, the father always had control. No calf was ever purchased or sold without his consent. Every little detail, such as planning the cultivation of the land, the sowing of a particular kind of wheat or other grain, was left to the father. He was the head of the group, and his will ruled supreme. The fact that the father possessed good judgment and business ability, and that his advice was always good, and the other fact that his authority was not wielded in a tyrannical manner, brought about a willingness on the part of the sons to continue their submission to this head of the family government.

This case brings out vividly the dominating control of the husband and father as the head of the family, a power that recalls that of the *pater familias* in the large Roman household or resembles that of the house manager or the head of the large patriarchal Chinese family. This case may be regarded as extreme because the title to all the property is held by the father and because he exercises the deciding voice in the marriage of his children. The entire social life of its members is concentrated in the family and in the wider kinship circle. In fact, the will of each individual is definitely subordinate to the family interests as embodied in the will of its dominating head.

The A family is a more typical representative of the rural family of [about 1900], in the generation before the automobile and the [first] World War.

The A family had five children, James, 19, Albert, 16, Carrie, 14, Aileen, 12, and Edmund, 2. They lived on a farm of four hundred acres four miles from Chermont. They attended a country school two miles from home.

The boys always worked for their father and the girls helped their mother. Once in a while Carrie worked for Mrs. B., who lived about two miles away. This was when her mother did not need her. Carrie was allowed to keep her money but was expected to get her clothes with it.

Mr. A. gave the boys their spending money each week.

The friends of the family were the C., B., P., M., L. and K. families.

These families often had dances at their respective homes and all the family attended and danced.

Albert, Carrie, and Aileen always asked their parents if they might go to a skating party, box social or to the large town to corn palace. Mr. and Mrs. A. let them go but not very often for they thought it was best for them to stay at home and not start running around too young. You always found all the family at home or else all away to visit some neighbor.

When Albert, Carrie, and Aileen started to go with girls and boys they first went with school mates whom they had known many years. Carrie was married to a neighbor boy and they went to live on a near-by farm. Albert married a Chermont girl and went to live on a farm about ten miles from home. Aileen was married to a neighbor boy whom she had known since childhood.

While the old type of patriarchal domination is absent from the A. family, the central place of the family in the life of its members is most evident. The family is both an economic and a social unity.

A day in the life of a city family [in the 1920's] presents a thought provoking contrast to the two types of rural families.

Mr. Jay is awakened at 7 o'clock, and dresses quietly in the bathroom in order not to awaken his sleeping wife. He eats breakfast alone, with his newspaper, and leaves the house at 8 o'clock without a member of his family. Mrs. Jay never awakens before 8:30 or 9, and then has her coffee in bed. The two children, James, aged 17, and Julia, aged 12, eat breakfast at 8:10, and leave for school at 8:30. If it is a rainy morning the limousine takes them after it returns from taking their father to his office. They seldom say good-bye to their mother as she is usually asleep.

Mrs. Jay, in negligée, commences with the cook, and does the ordering for the day, over the telephone. She never goes to market. After giving the two servants their directions for the day's work, she looks after her bills or writes letters at her desk.

If she has not a luncheon engagement, or some shopping downtown, she has an engagement for the afternoon—cards, or calling, or a concert or matinee. She is usually dressing for dinner when her husband returns from work. She languidly asks him about his business and receives monosyllabic replies. He is vice-president of a large bond house and is very busy in his office all day.

Dinner is at seven, and the children do most of the talking. In the evening, Mr. Jay either goes to the club to play cards or goes to the theatre or to a party with his wife. They have many wealthy friends who entertain a great deal. During the ride home and while they are going to bed they are too tired to talk much.

James goes to high school. After he has deposited his books in his locker, he runs to his class room, bluffs through the morning classes, chats with the girls and "fellows" between classes, and eats lunch with the "gang." His lunch usually consists of three sandwiches and a cream puff, which are eaten on the street. After his afternoon classes, he either goes to the movies or plays baseball in the yard of one of his friends. He returns in time for supper, after which he pretends to study until his parents have gone out. Then he, too, goes out.

Julia, aged 12, goes to a private school for girls. The work is not strenuous and she has plenty of time to scribble notes to the girl on her left and whisper. She takes English, arithmetic, French, reading, geography, and sewing. At 10:30, hot chocolate is served; at 12:30, a hot luncheon is given to the pupils. School is out at 2, and Julia hurries home for her music lesson or to practice piano. Twice a week she is tutored in arithmetic, because she is backward. If several of her girl friends interrupt her practicing, they make fudge and giggle. Julia seldom goes outdoors except for her walk from school.

After she has washed and dressed for dinner, and eaten with her parents, she studies or reads "The Little Colonel Books," and telephones to all her little friends whom she has seen during the day. She retires at 9:30, and usually keeps her light burning in order to read in bed. She seldom receives a good-night kiss from her parents. Her companionship with her brother is very slight, as they quarrel continually. He delights in teasing her.

Altogether, the home life of this family is very neglected. The four members only meet together once during the day, at dinner. They all tell what they have done during the day, but they scarcely know each other. If Julia enters her mother's room, she usually is told, "Go away, dear, I'm dressing now." James does not approach his father much except to ask for some new article or funds with which to buy it. Mr. Jay is usually too busy reading or dressing to do anything but grant his son's request.

The children have practically no home life, nor connection with their parents. They are quite independent. Mrs. Jay takes little interest in her husband's work, and he cares not at all for her social interests during the day. His cards and his business occupy him completely.

This not altogether sympathetic account of the external behavior of the different members of the Jay family introduces us to many, if not all, of the changes which urban life has wrought in the rural pattern of the traditional American family. First of all, the urban family no longer possesses the economic unity of its agricultural prototype. In the rural family even today all its members are united by the roles which they play in a common economic enterprise of which the husband and the father is the manager. In the city the husband's business tends to be remote not only spacially, but also as in this case, spiritually from the others in the family. The wife has become a woman of leisure and the two children are unencumbered by the necessity of performing any household tasks.

Added to this lack of economic unity is the absence of social unity in this family. The dinner at night is the only meal that brings together all the members of the family. The independence of each individual is so well nigh complete that the question may well be raised, "what is keeping the family together."

The objection may be raised that this is an extreme case of family life in the urban environment. That charge is no doubt quite true. But the point is that this extreme case, just because it is unusual, causes us to realize the nature and intensity of certain forces that are changing family life under city conditions.

13 · Family in the New Suburb *

RUTH SHONLE CAVAN

By 1950 a new trend in urban growth was noticeable—the suburban and fringe areas around cities were growing more rapidly than the inner cities, while rural areas continued to decline in population. The colonial farm, the modern farm, and the great urban centers had each molded the basic American family to fit its own opportunities and limitations. Family specialists are asking, "is the suburb also creating a new type of family?"

THE MOST distinctive type of suburb, often referred to as the "new" suburb, is built in a hurry by one or a few building corporations, rather than slowly, as the older suburbs were built, by private owners, house by house, with each house suited to the needs of the owner. In each new suburb, house style and price are markedly uniform. If one house in a given suburb has a carport with sundeck, the chances are high that most houses will have them. If the three-paneled picture window appears in one house, it will characterize the entire suburb. Often one house plan is basic: it is reversed left for right, it is varied as to trim and color of paint, but basically the plan is used throughout the development. One suburb will run to frame houses, another to brick. But regardless of style or material, each house has its own lawn and back yard, and dead end and curving streets are popular.

---

* Comments based on observations in suburbs and on a wide variety of readings including the following: William M. Dobriner, editor, *The Suburban Community* (New York: G. P. Putnam's Sons, 1958), pp. 147–164; Sidonie M. Gruenberg, "The Challenge of the New Suburbs," *Marriage and Family Living*, 17 (May, 1955), 133–137; E. G. Jaco and Ivan Belknap, "Is a New Family Form Emerging in the Urban Fringe?" *American Sociological Review*, 18 (October, 1953), 551–557; John Keats, *The Crack in the Picture Window* (Boston: Houghton Mifflin Company, 1957); and John R. Seeley, Alexander Sim, and E. W. Loosley, *Crestwood Heights* (New York: Basic Books, Inc., 1956), Chapter 7.
A brief biographical sketch of the author appears with article 6.

The uniformity of construction accounts for the first characteristic of the suburban family. Each suburb is designed for and appeals to but one income level—lower middle, or upper middle, or upper class income. Often the builders and the first residents emphasize that renters or buyers should belong to one race, religious group, or ethnic group. Thus there tends to be marked uniformity of background among the families in each suburb. The families may tend to become restricted in their appreciation for families unlike themselves.

Since the large yards give considerable running space, the new suburb appeals to married couples with young children. It is possible to go up and down the streets and see dozens of children under the age of twelve but no adolescents. The suburban family is definitely child-centered. Parents are deeply concerned about the health, recreation, and education of their children. Rearing well-balanced and well-educated children is a primary value toward which the parents strive. Family activities tend to be home-centered. The new house into which the family moves suggests many possibilities for further development—adding a patio for outdoor cooking and eating, creating a breezeway between house and garage, or converting the garage into a recreation room; improving the lawn and planting flower and vegetable gardens, or building sand boxes and swings. These activities bring the family together in projects that tie the family to the house and yard.

In early evening and week ends in summer men exchange business suits for slacks or shorts. They mow, trim, sprinkle; they compare notes on effectiveness of fertilizers and sprays. Children mill about and tumble on the damp grass. Mothers sit on the patios or gather in little clusters, ignoring the wails of babies already put to bed. Expeditions away from home usually include the entire family with children, dogs, and even cats crowded into the rear seat of car or station wagon. In a community with few teen-agers, baby sitters are hard to find; expense is also to be considered by families still making monthly payments on house, car, refrigerator, freezer, automatic washing machine and dryer, and other costly equipment.

Since the husband usually works in the city and is absent all day, the women have heavy responsibilities in addition to managing their children and normal housework. In an emergency they cannot call an apartment superintendent as they could in the city; they must locate the proper re-pairman or make their own household repairs. They are often active in the affairs of the community, sitting on boards and committees that frequently substitute for formal government in the first years of a suburb's existence. In the present stage of growth of the new suburbs few wives work, but as the youngest child reaches school age many probably will find employment.

The point has been made by some writers that the suburban husband is torn between two roles. His basic role is played in his occupation. At the same time his wife and the community expect much more of him in the way of small construction projects, care of grounds, and family activities than is expected of city husbands. Not all husbands enjoy the full round of the suburban activities; or some may feel that some of the time would be better spent on their jobs, where pressures are also placed on them to improve themselves and to advance in their status and responsibilities.

In comparison with the rural and the urban families, the new suburban family is kin to both. It enjoys the family-centered activities, outdoor life, and informality that we associate with rural living. At the same time the links with the city are strong. The city is the source of income. Many suburban shopping centers are built around branches of inner-city stores which offer the suburban wife the latest in smart apparel and household furnishings. If the family has previously lived in the city, the husband and wife may miss many of the cultural opportunities and diversions of the city. Thus some families move to the suburbs on a trial basis and after a period of time return to the city.

Among families that like suburban life, their stay in any one suburb may be limited. Husbands who are financially successful move their families to other suburbs of higher income level and a more costly standard of living.

In time, the uniformity of the new suburbs will tend to disappear. Children will grow into college age and leave. Their parents may return to city apartment life. Families of many types will be likely to fill the vacancies and the new suburb will begin to resemble any urban residential area. But at present the new suburb is where one is most likely to find the middle or upper class family with children, whose financial roots are in the inner city, but whose family values are child- and home-centered.

14 · Technology and the Future of the Family *

MEYER F. NIMKOFF

Many brides and grooms would like to peer into the future and see what is in store for them as a married couple. This article will not help the individual couple to foresee their future, but it does lay bare some of the changes that are in store for families in general because of technological devices and scientific discoveries. The author, a specialist in this field, does not try to predict what new and as yet unknown discoveries will be made; he contents himself with a logical analysis of the probable effect on the family of inventions and discoveries already in existence but only beginning to touch the family, such as the full impact of television, artificial insemination, or improved knowledge of interpersonal relations.

THE DISCUSSION that follows will not deal with the family of the future but only with the probable influence of inventions and discoveries on the family, which is the subject of this chapter. The family in the future will be influenced by forces other than those of inventions and discoveries . . . . The approach, moreover, will not be in terms of the probable influences of particular innovations, for these are too numerous to detail; and to treat them separately would not be profitable, for . . . it is generally the convergence of many innovations on a given aspect of family life that is effective and not the influence of separate innovations. It will be more profitable, therefore, for us to consider certain important aspects of family life, recent major changes in the family, and ask how clusters of innovations are likely to affect these items in the future. Since the further ahead we try to look, the more uncertain the prognostication, we shall limit ourselves to the next twenty to fifty years, more or less. Since there is a time lag between the introduction of an innovation and the full effects that

---

* From *Technology and Social Change*, by Francis R. Allen, Hornell Hart, Delbert C. Miller, William F. Ogburn, and Meyer F. Nimkoff (New York: Appleton-Century-Crofts, Inc., 1957), pp. 316–322. Reprinted by permission of Appleton-Century-Crofts, Inc.
The author, who received his degree of Doctor of Philosophy from the University of Southern California, is chairman of the Sociology Department of Florida State University. He is active in many professional societies, has been editor of the journal *Marriage and Family Living*, is the author of a college textbook *Marriage and the Family*, and coauthor of a text *Sociology* and of the book from which the present selection is taken.

flow from it, it is highly probable that most of the changes in the family in the near future will result from inventions and discoveries that are already in existence or that are imminent.

The discussion of the future effects of innovations will be divided into two parts, the first having to do with the effects of technology and the second with the effects of scientific discoveries. This is done not just as a matter of convenience because of pedagogical reasons but, as will be shown later, because of a significant difference in the aspects of family life which these two types of innovation influence.

Less Production at Home. The key to the family of the present is the decline of economic production in the home because of the rise of industrial production. It is therefore appropriate to ask what the future is likely to hold for the family in the way of production. It was steam power that moved production from the household to the factory, for the home was too small to house the steam engine and steel tools and, later, the assembly line. Since that time, electricity has become available and electricity can be run into a house through a wire. But, despite electricity, it is not expected that production will return to the home, because the home cannot compete with the economy of mass production. The net effect expected of technological innovations is that the departure of a few existing productive functions, like sewing, may be delayed and still fewer new ones added. The manufacture of ice in the mechanical refrigerator is about the only new productive function that has been recently added to the home.

Less Preparation of Food at Home. With less food grown at home, and fewer objects made at home, there is considerably more purchasing of goods by members of families than formerly, especially by women. It is expected that there will be less preparation of food at home in the future because of more processing away from home, in the form of frozen, condensed, and precooked foods. Vitamins, amino acids, and minerals will be purchased in larger quantities as supplements to the diet. The mechanical refrigerator, the deep freezer, the pressure cooker, and later the electronic stove will simplify the preparation of food.

The loss of economic production by the home has led to the loss by the family of much of its authority over its members. The family with the patriarch, who, as head of the family enterprise, ruled over its members, is a thing of the past and there is no prospect of its return.

Increasing Attractiveness of Homes. The heating of homes, with which man has had long experience, has been greatly improved by central heating, insulation, and thermostatic controls. A more recent innovation is the cooling of homes in hot weather. The knowledge exists of ways to regulate the air as to the amount of moisture, dust, mold, and pollen. At a price, practically any type of climate can be created indoors. Increasingly it will be possible to provide the kind of indoor environment desired. Furnishings using light metals, plastics, glass, and other new materials will make the interior more comfortable and, in the view of many, more attractive.

The house will especially be a place of increasing recreation, made possible mainly because of electricity. There are already the radio, television, high-fidelity phonograph, tape recorder, micro-film and micro-card viewers, photographic equipment, and workshops of considerable variety. The television set will make of the home a combined motion picture theater and legitimate theater. It appears to reduce the time spent in other ways, as in conversation between family members. It will require other adjustments in household activities on the part of viewers. But the television set is well adapted to the home.

That there will be more recreation and education for family members is indicated by two additional trends, the one toward fewer working hours and the other toward more income. The median family income in the United States in 1949 was about $3,000. In 1900 it was about $1,500 in 1950 dollars. In the first half of the twentieth century, then, the real income of American families doubled. It is estimated that before the end of the twentieth century the median family income will double again, and will be about $6,000 in 1950 dollars.[1] This gain is expected (unless prevented by destructive wars or other causes) mainly because of the increased productivity of new machines.

The increasing comfort and recreation in the home does not guarantee more happiness or family accord. The divorce rate has been rising in most countries despite increasing comfort, leisure time, and play activities.

Redistribution of Population. The trend has been for fewer families to remain on farms and for families to increase greatly in the environs of cities, that is, in towns, villages, and small cities located near large cities, as well as in the fringes and suburbs of the cities. The population of cities has also increased, but at a lesser rate. It is expected that these trends will continue in the near future.

The effect of this redistribution of population is to accentuate different types of families. There are families with more children on the fringes of cities, more middle-aged families in the cities, as well as more older persons and more divorced, separated, and never-married persons.

Scientific Discoveries and the Future of the Family

Technological developments during the past century, ushering in our urban civilization, have diminished the power of the family as an institution,

---

[1] W. F. Ogburn, "Technology and the Standard of Living in the United States," *American Journal of Sociology,* Vol. LX, No. 4 (January, 1955), pp. 380–386.

while increasing the power of industry and government. The economic functions of production have been largely transferred from the home, as have also many of the protective functions and educational functions. Recreational activities in the home have been increasing because of the electrical inventions.

The functions remaining in the home are sex and procreation, and the provision of affection and companionship between mates, between parents and children, and among the children themselves. The preschool education of children also remains in the home. Since this is essentially a training of personality and character, we may say that the principal functions of the modern family are the personality functions.

Scientific discoveries relating to the family are significant because they affect mainly the personality functions of the family, whereas the technological innovations affect mainly the economic functions. The effect of technology on personality is largely indirect, via the changed economic and correlated functions, whereas the effect of scientific discoveries on personality is direct and therefore, all else being equal, more potent.

Conception Control and Fewer Children. Over the past century, the trend in the birth rate in the United States has been downward, and this trend is associated with the spread of birth control. Contraceptive methods now available are highly effective when properly used but are expensive and inconvenient. There is therefore a considerable demand for less expensive and more acceptable methods. One approach is improvements in contraceptive gels, using readily available, cheap ingredients like flour and salt. A newer approach is the physiological, in contradistinction to the mechanical and chemical, utilizing a variety of methods. One objective is to produce cheap and harmless antifertility compounds which can be added to the diet. But even if no new methods of control are introduced, the extension of present methods to populations in the open country, low-income groups, and certain religious groups which in the past have resisted birth control will result in a decline in the birth rate. It is expected that the drop in the birth rate will be especially marked in farm families in the future, what with the spread of farm machinery as well as birth control, although the birth rate on farms is likely to remain higher than in the cities. The differential in fertility between socioeconomic classes is also expected to be narrowed.

Fertility Promotion, Artificial Insemination, and the Preservation of Germ Cells. The spread of birth control will mean an increase in the number of wanted children. It will also entail an increase in the number of voluntarily childless couples, although the number will probably not be great, since married couples characteristically use contraception to limit and space their children rather than to remain altogether childless.

Methods are also being developed to promote fertility, which means that in the future there will be fewer couples who are involuntarily childless. Artificial insemination has been used for some time to promote fertility with semen contributed either by the husband or by a donor. A more recent development is the use of frozen semen. In 1953, three women were inseminated by physicians with semen that had been preserved for a time in the frozen state.[2] They conceived and gave birth to normal babies. If, as seems likely, semen can be preserved indefinitely without losing the fertilizing capacity, a number of interesting new possibilities are opened up. For instance, it will be possible to extend fatherhood beyond the life of the father, if his semen is preserved, and his wife is still living and able and willing to have children.

Procreation is a highly intimate function, into which even the long arm of the law is not allowed to intrude. Biological discoveries like these indicated above are therefore likely to be considered revolutionary. Artificial insemination with donor semen represents a transfer, in part, of the reproductive function from the family to an outside source. This has hitherto not been countenanced, and it will be interesting to see how the law comes to define artificial semination with donor semen. Artificial insemination, using stored semen from men with superior heredity, may lead to a renewed emphasis on eugenics by those who attach special significance to the influence of heredity. Also the separation of the physiological and psychological aspects of sex, already enhanced by birth control practices, is further emphasized by artificial insemination. These changes have the effect of raising the status of women who in addition to being regarded as the bearers of children are seen as contributors in other ways to their own happiness and the happiness of their husbands.

A *Longer and Healthier Married Life for More Old People.* The lower birth rate and the larger expectation of life has resulted in a larger percentage of old people in our nation, and the proportion is expected to increase. On the basis of 1949 vital statistics, white women in the United States had an average life expectancy in 1951 of 71.5 years, white men 65 years, 11 months, whereas it is estimated that a woman born in 1970 can expect to live 80 years, a man 74 years.[3] At the same time, they should be stronger, more alert, and more vigorous; and the creeping deterioration of old age should be retarded. New hormonal therapy, for instance, holds promise of modification of socio-sexual behavior. It restores virility to some persons and moderates changes in middle life.[4] A suitable diet helps to postpone aging and debilitating symptoms. The diet includes certain vitamins in heavy doses and emphasizes proteins, with the male hormone,

---

[2] R. G. Bunge, M.D., and associates of the University of Iowa Medical School.
[3] Harold F. Dorn, reported in *Science News Letter*, October 27, 1951, p. 261.
[4] *Science News Letter*, September 22, 1951, p. 178.

testosterone, given to help assimilate the protein; and other hormones given to help utilize sugars and starches.

Anticipated effects on family life are economic and psychological. On the economic side, better health and more physical vigor at an advanced age may mean reduced medical costs and a larger period of self-support for persons of advanced age. On the other hand, increased longevity may result in an increased period of outside support, if the aged are economically dependent. On the psychological side, more grandchildren are likely to have the opportunity to know their grandparents, with a resulting increase in family continuity. More couples will celebrate their golden wedding anniversary and experience a longer period together without children, after their children have grown up and left home.

More Knowledge About Interpersonal Relations. The personality functions of the family are concerned with affectionate relationships and companionship between (*a*) husbands and wives, (*b*) parents and children, and (*c*) brothers and sisters. It is expected that in the future there will be more knowledge which will contribute to harmonious and effective relationships between these members of families.

One area in which progress is likely to be made is our understanding of sex and its contribution to family welfare. A goal in marriage is mutuality in affectional and sexual response of husband and wife. In the past, mates have been hampered in achieving this goal by inaccurate ideas regarding women's sexual nature and the effects of repression on personality. Still to be unraveled are the ramifications of the relationship of sex and the sentiments, that is, precisely how sex is related to affection, and especially love of a spiritual nature. Also in need of fuller exploration is the relation of sex to happiness and the contribution that technique in sex relations may make to marital adjustment.

Research has shown that sex is a function of the total personality, and inquiry therefore leads at once from sex to the psychological factors in marital compatibility. Among the personality traits which research has shown to be conducive to marital maladjustment are emotional immaturity, narcissism, self-centeredness, inferiority feelings, rebelliousness, aggressivenesss, emotional fixation on parents, extreme dominance, guilt feelings, marked insecurity, and nervousness. These findings came from studies made by psychoanalysts and others working with individual cases, as well as by sociologists and psychologists using questionnaire and interview methods with groups of married couples. The association of the traits studied with marital happiness or unhappiness has not been high, perhaps in part because in the samples used individuals with extreme deviant traits were rare, and because the methods of research were deficient. In the future it is likely that there will be research using larger and more representative samples;

partial correlation and factor analysis instead of zero-order correlation: combinations of traits instead of single traits; and pairing of traits in husband and wife. Such research should contribute new knowledge regarding the factors involved in marital adjustment. In addition, prediction tests, when greatly improved, may be used in mate selection. There is, of course, the question as to how much use will be made of such tests. If the well-adjusted persons in larger numbers marry well-adjusted persons, then more of the poorly-adjusted will marry other poorly-adjusted individuals or not marry at all. The result, however, would be to increase the proportion of harmonious marriages. For if there were, say, 100 well-adjusted men and women and 100 poorly-adjusted men and women and they were to intermarry, the result in general would be less satisfactory than if the well adjusted were to marry within their own group.

If the emotional core of personality is mainly established during the early years of life, then the most effective preparation for marriage takes place during early childhood. The problem of wholesome personality in adults becomes the problem of proper child guidance. In rearing normal children, research has shown the importance of proper doses of affection; discipline that is administered with moderation, uniformity, and understanding; identification with the parent of the same sex for the purpose of normal sex-typing; confidences and congenial shared activities between parents and children.

In these areas and allied areas, having to do with interpersonal relations as they bear on the family, research is being carried on with increasing skill, resources, and vigor. Important advances in our knowledge are certain, and the demand for such knowledge will lead to its dissemination and use. It is hoped that as a result we shall have more success in eradicating undesirable personality traits and in avoiding them altogether.

15 · Bringing the House Up to Date *

JAY DOBLIN

The technological changes that rush at us with such rapidity are sometimes frightening as they threaten to upset the old, accustomed ways. Mr. Doblin,

* "House Planning for Young Families," National Parent-Teacher, 52 (February, 1958), 19–22. Reprinted by permission of the publisher and the author.
   The author, a graduate of Pratt Institute, is director of the Institute of Design established in Chicago by the world-famous Moholy-Nagy and now a part of the Illinois Institute of Technology. Mr. Doblin is a director and past president of the American Society of Industrial Designers.

however, sees in these changes the means to a more efficient, comfortable, and attractive type of home.

WHERE WILL you and your family be living ten years from now? If you're like a good many other young American families, you'll be somewhere else. More and more, Americans tend to be footloose, to move from house to house and from town to town. Sometimes it's a business opportunity that beckons. Sometimes it's better schools for the children or sunnier scenes for them to grow up in. And often there are economic changes in the life of the home owner. The young married man starts off in what might be called a bare minimum house. As his earnings increase (not to mention the size of his family), he moves into new and larger quarters.

For this new freedom of movement we have willingly given up the old dream of stability. That stability used to be symbolized by the family homestead—the house that took years to plan and save for, the house where the children were born and married, and which was passed on to the next generation as a precious heritage. Tomorrow the free-as-the-air spirit may be symbolized by a new and totally different kind of housing.

Families will live in two types of dwelling. One will be large, widely spaced, landscaped apartment buildings—whole communities of them in and around big cities. Usually such communities will have their own shopping centers, services, and recreation areas. The other type of dwelling will be a one-family unit—a house. This house, according to designers, will be built not to preserve but to use up, not to hoard but to spend. Instead of feeling anchored for life to a single home, the family of tomorrow will turn in its house for a new one every few years, to take care of its changing needs.

But will people be able to afford a new house as often as that? Why not? For the house of the future will be economical to build and maintain. Most of the parts will be manufactured in large factories and simply fastened together at the site. As builders and owners of "prefabs" know, this method is much less expensive than building a house from scratch.

Is there a "house of the future" ahead for *your* family? Yes, say designers in the most advanced schools of design and architecture. In ten years the new types of houses will be as popular as ranch homes are today and will be priced within the range of middle-income families. If that is true, what will the house of the future mean to your family's growth and comfort and happiness?

You can guess a little about that from the appearance of the houses, which will be warm, beautiful, and colorful but at the same time will suggest strength and personality. You will have your choice of many widely different styles, for even though the houses are mass produced they will vary greatly in design—far more, in fact, than do the houses of today.

Perhaps you will choose a domed house, a tent-like style, or a box of clear material that will permit the family to live outdoors inside an enclosure. In some localities this transparent home may have a natural floor of grass or stone, and there may be plants and trees inside as well as outside. For privacy and protection from the sun, the house could have double walls, and smoke or liquid could be passed between them.

Or you may prefer another type of house that you can assemble by buying ready-made rooms and coupling them together. You can easily enlarge this house at any time by just adding a new roof section. What a boon such flexibility would be! Suppose you need a nursery or a guest room for short-term use. You will be able to rent one and attach it to the house for as long as you need it—and then return it to the supplier.

Instead of buying appliances for your house-ten-years-from-now, you will buy a complete kitchen and complete bathrooms, one for each member of the family. (No longer will Father stand steaming outside the bathroom door, while Daughter is primping for her latest beau!) These rooms will be moved into place in a single section and will simply be hooked up, without any of the hand fitting that we require today for plumbing and wiring. Another big economy!

But won't utilities and plumbing be needed for the house of the future? Not necessarily, say the designers. A small generator will supply electricity for heat, light, and air-conditioning. Water will be condensed out of the air by your air-conditioning system and then stored, used, distilled, purified, and reused. By adding appropriate scents, you may live in a simulated atmosphere of balmy Bermuda, vigorous Maine, or any other climate that is to your liking.

Another thing you will find you can largely get along without is doors. In their place, you will have baffled entrances, which will prevent transmission of sight or sound—a welcome provision for privacy. Teen-agers can play the latest hi-fi recordings without deafening the rest of the family or interfering with Mother's or Dad's quieter pastimes. The few doors that are needed will be without knobs, locks, or keys. They will open by radio signal.

Cleaning your house of the future? A minor chore that won't call for brooms, mops—or that well-nigh extinct household helper, the cleaning woman. You will have a new type of vacuum cleaner that will be centrally located and will have outlets in each room. But you won't use it often, because the house will be pressurized and the air filtered.

Furniture will have damage-proof finishes, to protect it against scars, scratches, and burns. Nor will the children track in dirt, because the entries to the house will be self-cleaning. Clothing, shoes, and fabrics will all resist soil and dust better than those we have now, and they will be kept spotless by means of daily automatic cleaning in special closets.

Light Housekeeping

Will our ideas about interior decoration change? Of course that depends to some extent on individual tastes. Mostly, colors and textures will be warm and natural. You won't use much shiny metal or hard, cold finishes. An effect of luxury will be obtained by using elegant detail, art, and natural planting. Much of the decorating will be done with light. Walls, ceilings, and furnishings may be impregnated with fluorescent pigments. Any object or area you choose can be selected to glow and provide general lighting, and in any color. Scenes can be projected on the walls to make the rooms look larger and to give all sorts of decorative effects. You can even project three-dimensional scenes and figures that will appear actually to occupy space within the room. Your lamps can be wireless. Sensitive static switches will turn on lights ahead of you as you go from room to room.

What kind of furniture will be appropriate in such a house? For one thing, you will want it to be light in weight so that it can easily be rearranged and stored. Then, too, it will be built to collapse and stack. Chairs and sofas will be powered by canned pressure for raising, lowering, and reclining. Chairs shaped to fit the body will follow the movements of the sitter so as to prevent the fatigue that comes from remaining in one position. For all its functional quality, this furniture won't seem objectionably mechanical or cold, since beauty of design and traditional details will be skillfully built in.

Where You Come to Rest

Some of the most revolutionary changes will center around the bedroom. Your bedroom in the house of the future will be more truly a place to rest in than any sleeping room you have ever known. Bedclothes will be unnecessary, because rooms will be kept at the proper temperature and so will the mattress itself. You will be persuaded into sleep by soothing tones and by projection of restful colors and regular patterns. While you sleep, your bed can move constantly so as to exercise and stimulate your body.

Are you one of those people who hate to make beds and who couldn't miter the corners on a sheet if their lives depended on it? Take hope. In the house of the future you will never have any beds to make. There will be no bedclothes except the mattress cover, and this will be dry-cleaned and sterilized each day when the bed is folded into its sealed niche.

A concealed bathroom will open off of each bedroom. It won't be much like the tile and chrome baths we now know. Instead, it will be finished in a soft, resilient, nonskid material that will be warm and completely safe.

"His" and "Hers" towels can be discarded, for drying after the bath will be by heated, dehydrated air.

Closets will change from the present door-closed alcove to a column—square or circular—in the room. The walls of the column will retract into the floor and ceiling to expose all sides of the contents for easy access. When closed, these closets will clean your clothes by means of chemicals and supersonics.

You won't have to press garments, for new materials and finishes will make such care unnecessary. Clothing will be wired and heated in the winter like an electric blanket, so that there will be no need for cumbersome outer garments or seasonal changes of clothing. You won't have to worry about the children becoming either chilled or overheated.

Meals with Punch

What about meals in the house-ten-years-away? Are we going to learn to live without eating? Far from it. You will probably serve one of two types of meals. The first type will be something like the kind now used in aircraft, where sixty or more persons can be served simultaneously from a kitchen about the size of an average closet. Such utility meals will be every bit as tasty as are carefully prepared ones today. And they will bring you a wider variety of foods—Hawaiian poi, Scottish grouse, master pieces of cookery from many countries of the world. The plates will be completely prepared, loaded and ready to be used. They will be automatically delivered through an induction cooker that will cook them instantly. The finished courses will then be delivered to the dining area. Soiled dishes will be placed in a machine, where they will be cleaned and sorted. From the machine they will be picked up and returned to the factory for reloading.

Is this method of preparing meals too depersonalized to please your family? Then you may like the second type of meals, which are only a little more trouble but are under the control of the cook. For these you will have in the kitchen a bank of semi-prepared ingredients. You will prepare a menu listing the foods and quantities needed for a particular meal by means of a punch card. At the correct time, the foods will be dispensed from the food bank in wall or basement. The amount used will be recorded for replacement by a supplier, who will reload the unit from outside the house. The foods you "ordered" by means of the menu card will be placed in receptacles to be cooked. The punched menu card will then again take over to cook the foods at proper temperatures and for the correct length of time. You yourself will add the seasoning and further control the cooking.

All these conveniences are going to give you much more time to spend with your family. The breadwinner of the household will have more leisure, too, for he as well as you will benefit from technological advances that will shorten his working hours. With all this new leisure time, it is logical that the most treasured, as well as the most costly, areas of your home will be devoted to personal pursuits.

The recreation area will provide space and equipment for educational activities and hobbies such as music, horticulture, research projects in science, and arts and crafts.

Probably you and other American families will spend a good deal of time on hobbies. Indeed, if present trends continue there is every evidence that hobbies will be taken more and more seriously. They may even become a second profession or a money-making venture, and hobbyists of the future may well bring about genuine scientific and cultural advances. Botany and biology, music and painting and craft work—these pursuits will be carried on at home by housewives and businessmen alike. At surprisingly low cost you may have a gymnasium, including a swimming pool and sunroom.

Outside the recreation area proper, each room in your house may contain a device that will bring into the home whatever reading material, TV shows, and educational courses you wish. Through this device, too, you may request services from which your choice of music, books, and motion pictures can be obtained.

As a matter of fact we are even now rapidly approaching the time when we cannot depend on the education most of us have had to give us the information necessary for carrying on our daily lives and businesses. In your house of tomorrow, then, you will probably find it necessary to do a good bit of studying on your own. Just learning to understand the equipment being used in your everyday life will require some "boning up," in addition to keeping in touch with advances being made all around you in fields other than those you are most concerned with.

Such, in briefest summary, is the house of tomorrow that designers are planning for the young and growing families of today. Do some of the plans seem a bit farfetched? Well, frozen foods and television would have seemed quite mad to your parents when *they* were young marrieds. All the ideas presented here are based on facts well known to scientists. Many of the items described are already taking shape on the drawing boards of industrial designers. Some of them are being readied for production, and a few are available today.

Does it sound as if there would be too many and too complicated devices in your house of the future? You needn't worry. The trend will be toward simplified operation of all devices in the home. Science-fiction-type cartoons to the contrary, you won't have to deal with elaborate panel boards covered with mysterious buttons. Instead, there will be whole systems of operation that are completely unobtrusive, invisible, and noiseless. The mechanics of living will take their rightful place in the background, not the foreground, of the world of the future.

Picture Window on the Future

If the designers are right, we shall be living in this new world in about ten years. That is how long it will take to get the new homes and furnishings into production and introduce them to families that are looking for a place to settle down in—before taking flight for somewhere else.

One thing seems clear: The house of the future will reflect the tempo and the temper of the future. It will usher in an entirely new way of living. What will this new way of living mean to you and your family? Will it mean less tension, more beauty, more leisure, better health for mind and body, closer family ties, a finer opportunity for children to laugh and learn and grow?

Of course, in predicting the future, even the near future, the seer never sees enough. Yet it is our hope that all these forthcoming developments will lead to a happier existence for all mankind.

16 · Automation and the Family *

IRMA H. GROSS

This article also looks to the future to gauge the effect of automation on family living. Incorporated into household devices, automation makes for less drudgery, more efficiency; in its industrial aspects it will indirectly affect the family, for one thing, in making possible increased leisure. Automation is with us and Dr. Gross raises many questions and provides some answers.

WHEN NEW OR accelerated forces are at work in the world, it behooves those of us who are concerned with families to think of those forces in connection with homes and the people in those homes. Automation is such a force.

* *Journal of Home Economics*, 49 (April, 1957), 259–262. Reprinted by permission of the publisher and the author.

The author, with the degree of Doctor of Philosophy from the University of Chicago, is head of the Department of Home Management and Child Development of Michigan State University. She is active in organizations concerned with various phases of family life, contributes to several journals, and is coauthor of *Home Management in Theory and Practice* and *Management for Modern Families*.

The first question to be asked is, "Just what is automation?" It is a word that is much bandied about nowadays but is probably not accurately understood. The word itself is not even 10 years old, and people do not quite agree on its exact meaning. One definition is "The use of machines to run machines." There have been machines for at least 200 years. The first industrial revolution, which occurred at about the time of the American revolution, was so called because it was based upon the use of power machines to take the place of the human hand. Automation has been compared to a second revolution and even to a third or a fourth if electric power and mass production brought intermediate revolutions. But whether it is the second or the third or the fourth revolution, automation unquestionably is a revolution, because it combines various activities which formerly were not combined. It substitutes a mechanical device for the eye and the hand.

One of the striking parts of automation is what is called the "feed back." To illustrate, let us use that familiar mechanism the thermostat. All of us are familiar with heat-control devices and accept them unquestioningly; but, as a matter of fact, a heat-control device substitutes for eye, brain, and hand. It poses a question, answers it, and acts upon the answer. Earlier machines asked no questions; they simply did what the hand bade them do. This feed-back apparatus not only asks the question, "Is it too hot?" but it acts upon the answer. If the answer is yes, it proceeds to apply energy in such fashion that the source of heat is turned off. If the answer is no, it does not inaugurate any action, and the heat continues. This, then, is one of the marvels of automation—feeding back information to a machine and then enabling that machine to act upon that information.

In addition to this capacity for feed back or along with it, automation can link a series of activities—not merely carry out one activity. It may also revolutionize and probably is revolutionizing certain mechanical aspects of office work. At present, some insurance companies and banks are using it to carry out their bookkeeping activities.

So much then for what automation is; now as to its relationship to the home, both at present and projected into the future.

At present, there are certain common applications of automation that are so accepted we hardly think of applying the new name to them. The thermostat is an example. We are accustomed to thermostatic arrangements in many activities of homemaking: thermostatic control in ovens, in surface units, in pans. We are also accustomed to linked series of activities, for example, record changers that carry out several operations in sequence, or the automatic washer that carries through a fairly long sequence of activities without the human brain and hand between each two.

Startling but less common applications of automation to the home include "pushbutton houses" [1]—where there is considerable remote control of various activities. For instance, from a central spot, one can regulate the heat in any room, adjust awnings, water a plant, sprinkle the lawn, turn lights on and off in distant parts of the house or garage—even start the breakfast coffee in the kitchen while the breakfaster is still in bed.

A different example of automation in a household activity is what might be called "taping" a cake.[2] By use of a standard magnetic tape recorder, with a playback machine, it is possible to measure, combine, and mix ingredients for a cake in proper sequence. The instrument is connected by wiring to electronic relays that control glass tubes housing the cake ingredients and also control a household electric mixer. Speed is one of the exciting parts of this taping of a cake. The control board is first set with the amount of each ingredient needed, and that activity takes 90 seconds. Then there is "play back" in which the ingredients are selected in correct sequence and mixed, and that again takes 90 seconds, or three minutes in all.

Future Possibilities

Let us now project ourselves into the future for a few possibilities and limitations of automation in the home. Let us look at its results in two different ways: first, its effect on the material physical home and the activities that go on there as a setting for family life and second its influence upon the family members themselves, their roles and relationships.

A startling effect upon the physical aspects of homemaking is that in the foreseeable future drudgery in the home can disappear. When it will disappear is another matter and will be dependent upon economic status, geographical location, and stage of the family life cycle. Economic status will make a great deal of difference in the time of disappearance, because automation and the machines that it brings are expensive items; the same is true of geographical location, which in its turn is a strong factor in, or strongly linked with, the economic factor. The stage in the family life cycle is a less predictable factor. Automation can do away with drudgery for the young married woman without children and also for women whose families are older or perhaps gone from the home; but when there are little children in the home, automation is not the full answer to the elimination of hard physical work. We have no machines that will lift, carry, and work with little children, nor have we anything that can counteract the influence on work of the starting and stopping of activities which the presence of little children forces.

---

[1] Boone, A. R. Push-button paradise. *Pop. Sci.* 165 (Nov. 1954), pp. 147–149; and Thomas, E. Sensitive house. *Popular Mechanics Mag.*, 101 (Jan. 1954), p. 148.
[2] Mix your cake with magnetic tape. *Sci. Digest* 37 (Feb. 1955), p. 74.

There are, however, some activities in the home which could be handled by automation—perhaps. One such time-consuming and sometimes frustrating activity is the assembling of all the various items that go into preparing and serving a meal. Assembling and disassembling are two of the activities that are difficult for automation to take over even in the factory, and those are two activities that are very important in the household. Today many foods can be bought partially or fully prepared, but we still have to get them home, get them off the shelves, get them heated and cut or divided or put onto something and then onto a serving surface. Even a simple meal includes a good many different items to be thus handled.

An activity that most homemakers would yield up gladly to automation is the keeping of household accounts. Conceivably the keeping of household records could be taken over by automation. Such taking over, however, poses a very important question in connection with automation in the home. Will it be too expensive to use? Machines that take over office work in large companies cost millions of dollars. Now individual homes are and will probably remain small scale, and, even assuming that an apparatus could be invented for carrying out certain household activities, the question will always be, can any or enough homes afford the device to warrant putting it on the market?

For a factory to use automation there must be continuous production around the clock. It is not possible to turn the system on and off as one can operate separate machines or series of machines. If even the known pieces of equipment for the home, such as kitchen and laundry appliances, are to be produced in automated factories, it is essential that they be continuously produced. That in its turn means a continuous demand for new equipment and also the development of an organized markct for second-hand items.[3] It has been suggested that, to insure a continuous flow in the foreseeable future, homemakers may obtain their kitchen appliances on loan or rent. A five-year rental and service policy may take the place of outright purchase and ownership of specific pieces of equipment. We shall have to rethink our views about ownership of household equipment. Will it be a wrench to do so?

Effect on Standards of Living

It is well to speculate on the effects of automation on standards of living. Without question, it will raise standards of living. Every revolution, whether political or industrial, has been undertaken for just that purpose, and every successful revolution has actually brought that to pass. There will be more

---

[3] Drucker, P. F. The promise of automation. *Harper's Mag.*, 210 (April 1955), p. 43.

things available at a lower cost. Along with these more things at lower cost, there will be lessened consumption differences between socioeconomic classes. We are accustomed now to these lessened consumption differences in relation to much modern equipment. For example, refrigerators in different price ranges differ little in efficiency, only in convenience and size. We expect and get a good refrigerator in the lower priced models. Now, with this higher standard of living in the sense that more people will have more things, there will undoubtedly come greater emphasis on material things. Families will be encouraged to want more and more things in order to keep automation going. There would need to be continuous demand for items produced through automation.

Influence on People

Let us now turn to the influence of automation on the family and its members. Its direct influence will probably be very slight, its indirect influence far-reaching. To begin with, we must recognize that people change very slowly. What we have and what we work with can change at lightning speed, but we ourselves are not so sensitive to outside influences. We stay very much as we were. That point was brought home to the author in the report of a Minnesota study [4] of high school girls and boys in a small community. Their attitudes on 22 items concerned with the family were compared, 1939 against 1952. It is startling, but perhaps reassuring, to find that their attitudes had changed in a statistically significant manner on only one attitude and that only for the girls. The girls showed a decrease in the sense of obligation to the family. But on many other attitudes—for example, that one owes greatest obligation to his family, or that the home is a pleasant place in which to be—there were no significant differences over the 13-year period. Of course, this is only one small bit of research evidence, but there is general agreement that people do not change very rapidly. It is fair then to believe that "not a great deal of importance attaches to the increase in the comforts and conveniences of the home for changes in the family" [5] and to minimize the direct effects of automation on family members.

We must, therefore, look for indirect effects of automation on family members, their roles and relationships. Of these a few can be foreseen. Both labor and management recognize that fewer people will be needed in un-skilled and semi-skilled factory jobs as automation proceeds. Also fewer

[4] Ramsey, C. E., and Nelson, L. Change in values and attitudes toward the family. *Am. Sociol. Rev.*, 21 (Oct. 1956), pp. 605–609.
[5] Ogburn, W. F., and Nimkoff, M. *Technology and the Changing Family*. Boston: Houghton Mifflin Company, 1955, p. 278.

and fewer people will be needed in office work as automation takes over. Let us look at these two statements in relation to the opportunities for women, especially married women, to work outside of the home. We know that when jobs get scarce women lose them first, and, of the women, married women lose them soonest. In the short-run effects of automation it is conceivable then that women, married women especially, may have fewer opportunities to work outside of the home. A large proportion of all working women are in factory or office work. At present, about one out of every four married women has a paid job outside of the home. Of married women in the labor force in 1950, 23 per cent were operatives and another 23 per cent were in clerical occupations. Adding those two percentages includes nearly half of all married women gainfully employed, and thus their employment presumably may be lessened. The question immediately arises how, at least in the short run, will families buy the products of automation when so many of them today are basing their buying plans on two incomes? This statement is especially true of newly founded families.

Another indirect result of automation on family members stems from the shorter hours of work for persons in factories and activities that use automation. In addition to the fact that fewer women may work outside of the home, at least for a while, there is no doubt but that the men will be back in the home for longer periods of the day and more days of the week than at present. Hence, the father may become a much more vital part of the family circle than he was able to be at the time when he was out of the home long hours. He may come to be a much more vital influence on his children's lives.

The position of the wife in the family may be affected by her decreasing importance in physical production in the home. "Pride in being known as a good housekeeper was once great. If wives lose the art of cooking, less value may attach to it." [6] This trend is, of course, nothing new but it may be accelerated. However, as the role of producer of physical things in the home becomes less important, the managerial role of the homemaker will become of greater importance. Increasing need of persons in management is stressed in discussing the influence on labor in factories where automation enters. It should be equally true in the home. Those of us who are concerned with home economics must not only stress the managerial role of homemakers but help women to understand what is meant by that role and to value it more highly than at present. [7]

Perhaps the major indirect effect of automation on all family members will be the providing of additional leisure. It is said that we will have

[6] *Ibid.*, p. 287.
[7] Van Bortel, D. G., and Gross, I. H. A comparison of home management in two socioeconomic groups. Tech. Bull. 240, Mich. Agr. Expt. Sta., 1954.

twice as much free time in the future as our grandparents had in the past. We, therefore, will have an increasing amount of time under individual control, and new thinking about leisure time will be forced upon us. Unquestionably there will at first be boredom and dissatisfaction in its use, but eventually the use of leisure must become a satisfying experience. Fundamentally, to make it such, it will be necessary to attack the prevailing philosophy of leisure.[8] In the past, values were related to work. Work was considered the only truly valuable activity to give meaning to life and to enforce discipline in individual lives. Leisure was desirable as it was used to renew vigor for work. We have no means of measuring the value of leisure in itself as we have the means of measuring the value of work. For instance, we rely very heavily on the dollar value of our labor to gauge its importance. We give some lip service to all work as being of equal value, but there is certainly a feeling that those forms of work which give a higher dollar result are of special value. No such thing can be said about the uses of leisure. There are no concrete measures of its results to the individual using it or to anybody. We can, however, go back to the Greek word for leisure for a clue as to how it may profitably be used. The Greeks used the word *schole* for "leisure." That is the root of the English word "school." One sees immediately the linkage between leisure and learning. The vital question is, "Are we capable of developing a culture that does not depend upon work to give meaning to our lives." [9]

To summarize briefly: automation will favorably affect the physical home to the point that much if not most of the drudgery may be eliminated and an even greater measure of material comforts than now provided. People in the home will be affected both by what they do in the home and by the fact that they will have more time presumably together because of the increase in leisure.

In conclusion, a word of appraisal of automation and its effects on the family is in order. There is, of course, no use to sigh for the good old days; yet it is equally dangerous to accept blindly every change as something desirable; and also there is great value in thinking through ahead of time the changes that will probably be forced upon us. We have survived other gifts which seemed doubtful at the time they were given. For example, when the work period was cut from 12 hours and 7 days in the steel industry, a skilled steel worker upheld the long work period on the basis that "it kept the men out of mischief." Now many years later "it would be difficult to prove that drunkenness and debauchery are any more prevalent

---

[8] Carr, A. L. Automation—substitute for God?—I. *Christian Century*, 73 (May 30, 1956), pp. 666–667.
[9] Bendiner, R. The age of the thinking robot, and what it will mean to us. *Reporter*, 12, No. 7 (April 7, 1955), p. 18.

[than earlier]." [10] We certainly do not deplore the fact that women no longer age prematurely from overwork and heavy responsibilities. Many material things we accept gladly—for example, plumbing. Not many of us would want to go back to the good old days when we did not have it. It is important, however, to emphasize the need of critical judgment in our personal lives and in our family situations in the matter of developing and recognizing scales of values applicable to new conditions. Here is a place where we need the help of our churches along with that of our schools. In the final analysis "the achievements and the promise of technology must be examined and weighed in the moral balance." [11]

17 · Cultural Change and Mental Health *

JULES HENRY

The author draws a rather gloomy picture, as he admits, of the effect of change in generating a general condition of anxiety among Americans. His approach is in contrast to the earlier discussions which have detailed the advantages of technological changes. Dr. Henry calls for widespread mental hygiene education, with the family as the center for its practice.

WHEN WE look at a frank and objective description of another culture we sometimes ask ourselves, "How do people ever manage to live in it?" Whether it be strife-torn Greece or Rome, the humiliating misery of the Chukchee of Siberia or the degradation of the slums of Dickens' London, the question is often, "How did people manage to live in it?" And the implied second question is, "Without going mad?" To these questions anthropology returns the answer that people live in it because they have no place else to go, and that though populations do not become psychotic they do suffer severely emotionally.

* *Mental Hygiene*, 41 (July, 1957), 323–326. Reprinted by permission of the publisher and the author.
   The author is Professor of Anthropology at Washington University, St. Louis. He has the degree of Doctor of Philosophy from Columbia University. His work has taken him to Mexico. His present interests include social organization and personality and the structure and function of therapy groups. He has been active on the board of directors, the editorial board, and various committees of the American Orthopsychiatric Association and has been connected with several children's clinics.
[10] Soule, G. *Time for Living*. New York: Viking Press, 1955, p. 131.
[11] Adams, J. D. Speaking of books. *N. Y. Times Book Rev. Section* (Nov. 18, 1956), p. 2.

In the anxious and impulse-ridden America of today, then, the issue for mental health as a public health problem is not so much the treatment of diagnosed cases, but rather the prophylaxis of mass suffering.

In contemporary America no program of mental health can ignore the following facts: (1) the rapid growth of industry, population and metropolitan regions; (2) the increased use of automation; (3) the shift from superego to id-values. Since this is a forum devoted to exploring the causes and control of mental illness I shall devote no time to the cheerier aspects of the three facts but concentrate rather on their darker side.

Among the consequences of the growth of industry which are relevant to mental health are the following: (1) increasing pressure on small business; (2) increasing masses of anonymous workers; (3) destruction of the human habitat through industrial land use, stream pollution and exhaustion of water resources; (4) astronomical expenditures for advertising; (5) attraction into the labor force of more and more women; (6) rises in wages and consumer expenditures, sometimes called the rising standard of living, but which, as time passes, becomes a rising standard of luxury; (7) increase in the rate of industrial obsolescence.

These changes have the following effects:

(1) The small business man's struggle to survive becomes harder and he works and worries more and more for small returns. In these circumstances his family must bear the burden of his increasing anxiety.

(2) Since the mass of industrial employees work at jobs in which they feel insignificant and emotionally unrewarded, they plunge into impulse release when they check out. In contemporary America this means making great demands on wife and children for affection, approval and support.

(3) The destruction of the human habitat—the disappearance of wooded areas and stream pollution—deprives people of recreational facilities out of doors and throws them more and more on their own emotional resources and on those of their families and friends.

(4) Expenditures for advertising, estimated at $10,000,000,000 in 1956 and destined to increase rapidly in the future, increase the yearning for consumer goods, travel and commercial recreation, with consequent emphasis on release of impulse in all directions. This is advertising's contribution to the era of the id—of impulse release and fun. Meanwhile the distortion of values introduced into the communications channels by advertising has consequences which must be presumed to be important; otherwise the advertisers would not keep it up.

(5) The attraction of more and more women into the labor force naturally raises important questions in regard to the emotional life of the family. It means that just at that era of our civilization when the family needs her

most, mummie is going to be around less. This fact must be confronted, however, not by attempting to turn the clock back but by learning how to handle the new emotional situation. It means specifically that the emotional problems of the family can no longer be largely mother's concern but must be managed by the entire family.

(6) The rise in the standard of living has created a population with a strong drive toward obtaining the symbols of that rising standard: hard goods and a good time. This too has helped usher in the era of the id—of impulse release and fun.

(7) The snowballing increase in the rate of obsolescence of the instruments of technology means a corresponding speeding up of the obsolescence of occupations: the worker trained to one occupational category today has no guarantee that he will not be obsolete five years hence.

In general, the vast changes that are taking place within the structure of American society and economy add to the uncertainty of life and create continuous waves of anxiety.

The growth of our population results in increasing crowding and, in an intensely motorized public, will for a long time to come sustain a mounting accident rate. Americans have always been extremely sensitive to crowding and though, as compared to Europeans and Asiatics, they really do not know what crowding is like, they fly at the slightest sign of it. The consequent mobility will bring an even greater disruption in personal life than in the past.

Increase in population is already creating local problems in water supply and waste disposal and in strain on other usually adequate public facilities such as schools, public health systems and police. The flight of population outward from the city brings the social conflicts of the center into the suburbs and brings into suburban communities problems in social stratification that did not exist there previously.

Destruction of the human habitat is a consequence of population expansion as much as it is of industrial expansion, for the necessary homes, schools, roads and service facilities eat up the land. Consequent on this is the disappearance of wooded and other recreational areas and the frantic efforts of outlying municipalities to wall themselves off from change, with a resulting irritation in groups who feel themselves discriminated against.

The growth of metropolitan regions creates administrative problems of a new order, and as the metropolitan areas move toward consolidation their financial burdens increase, with a consequent need to rework the tax structure in order to accommodate new problems. The issue here is that administrative transformation at the metropolitan level changes the character of the administration of health programs, constantly changing *the administra-*

tive focus of health as the region changes. At the same time the rapid growth of suburbs creates budgetary problems they previously did not have. In these circumstances mental health programs easily become stepchildren, and the actual burden of management is thrown upon the family.

Finally, with respect to automation, the simplification and integration of continuous machine operations removes the worker even further from contact with the product on which he works, and in many cases will make it impossible for him even to stay awake at his job, [let alone] become involved in it. Work will become merely a vague sense of nausea, indistinguishable from a hangover.

On the positive side there is the expectation that there will be a great increase in leisure time which will be devoted to intellectual activities. Since, however, the majority even of those in the most favorable circumstances have never devoted themselves to intellectual pursuits, it is unlikely that it will occur now. Furthermore, because of the increasing emphasis on the expression of id-impulses and because of tensions brought about by the massive social changes, it is unlikely that much impulse will be sublimated in painting, music, reading and other gentlemanly interests. Rather, one can expect more of a Roman holiday—increased attendance at games, prizefights, burlesque, movies and TV; more picnics, barbecues and excursions.

Let us stop here a moment to consider the human context of the changes of which I speak. All of them take place among a people who have learned, in a liberal democracy, to expect government to take more and more responsibility for their problems and who will never be satisfied, for dissatisfaction is the essence of American democracy. In a sense the only reason local governments have been able to get away with totally inadequate provision for mental health is the ignorance of the citizens. When the public really learns about mental health—what it means and has meant to them and how they were deprived of help—they will feel they have been cheated.

In view of the fact that I have defined the problem of mental health today as a problem not of cases but of a *chronically suffering population*, what are the measures to be taken to relieve it?

In answer to this question I propose that beginning at puberty our citizens begin to receive instruction in the handling of each other's problems. The American family is the place where all the tensions generated by social change come to a focus and it is there that the problems must be resolved. We know enough now about emotional suffering to be able to say that it is a family epidemic. In these circumstances, the malady being widespread in a population approaching 200,000,000, its control cannot be handed over to outside agencies but must be treated by the family itself. School children have been taught physical hygiene; they can be educated to understand themselves and one another, which is mental hygiene, so that when they have families they will know what to do. Mental hygiene education must be given by specially trained personnel as part of the school curriculum beginning in junior high school and continuing through high school and into college. The curriculum would include reading, lectures and group discussion. It is the cream of the jest that knowledge of the outer world should be specifically provided for and communicated to children by trained persons while understanding of the inner world is left to chance. We have forgotten Socrates' admonition that the essence of knowledge is self-understanding.

In the past even the best school programs in mental health have been oriented toward case-finding and treatment. The essential issue, however, is that the management of tensions that disrupt life is a population problem and not merely a case problem and must be handled by public health methods that meet the tension at its source and handle the pathogenic vector directly. The place to begin to handle it is where it is—in children, where the necessary compulsion can be used. Public emotional illness is private menace and there is no more reason for making prophylaxis for emotional illness voluntary than there is for making vaccination or sanitary garbage disposal voluntary. Train our children in mental hygiene so that they will grow up to be understanding husbands, wives and parents who will cooperate with one another in the mutual management of family emotional problems. Train our children in human understanding so that America will assume a revolutionary kind of leadership among nations —a leadership of human international understanding. This alone is the true pathway to peace.

CHAPTER 4:

Courtship and Marriage in Other Countries

18 · The French Family: A Private Social World *

RHODA METRAUX AND MARGARET MEAD

Each society—each culture—produces its own peculiar form of family life. The American family, as shown in the last chapter, has had to make rapid adaptations from rural to urban to suburban living, and from hand labor to technological devices. Looseness of relationships, adaptability, and sometimes disorganization mark the American family. In France, the family clings more closely to traditions. It is distinguished by permanence, loyalty, and privacy of family life. This highly perceptive discussion by two anthropologists interprets the French family of today to American readers, who, when they travel in Europe, often complain of the difficulty of learning what family life means to the French.

THE FRENCHMAN at home is *chez-soi*, in his own place. For the French, *le foyer* is *un petit bien complet, un petit bien indépendant*—a small pos-

* Reprinted from *Themes in French Culture: A Preface to a Study of French Community* by Rhoda Metraux and Margaret Mead (Hoover Institute Studies, Series D: Communities, No. 1), selections from pages 1, 2, 3, and 5, with the permission of the publishers, Stanford University Press. Copyright 1954 by the Board of Trustees of Leland Stanford Junior University.

Rhoda Metraux holds the degree of Doctor of Philosophy (anthropology) from Columbia University. She has had extensive research experience in different parts of the world. Her present interests are in the cultures of the Caribbean area and the contemporary cultures of France, Germany, China, and the United States.

Margaret Mead, anthropologist, holds the degree of Doctor of Philosophy from Columbia University, and is a member of the professional staff of the American Museum of Natural History. Although her interests and professional connections are extensive, her anthropological field work has centered on the peoples of the Pacific Islands. Among her books that are of special interest to students of marriage and family living are *Coming of Age in Samoa, Growing Up in New Guinea*, and *Male and Female*. Other books and articles cover a wider range.

session, complete and independent. But *bien* means not only possession or, more specifically, a piece of property; it also conveys, among other meanings, those of comfort, excellence, and well-being, all of which—together with the idea of its privacy and autonomy—combine in the feeling about *le foyer*.

The term is an untranslatable one; to render it inadequately as *house* or *home* or *family*, with the connotations these words have for Americans, is to distort the total meaning which *le foyer* has for those who belong to it. It is a truism that this is a little used word in French daily conversation and, from one point of view, a discussion of French family life is itself an anomaly. For, generally speaking, this is a subject which in its intimate details is reserved to those close to the family and, as an entity, to formal, even solemn public occasions.

.   .   .   .

The arrangement of French dwellings conveys something of the distance between the world without and the world within the *foyer*. One need only recall houses in provincial France where a high wall, enclosing the garden or the court behind or the plot of land around the house, shuts out too-curious neighbors and passers-by; where a bell on garden gate or door rings, perhaps automatically, to announce each person—stranger or member of the family—who approaches; where every footfall around the house sounds on gravel. Or one may visualize the urban apartment building where the incomer must first pass the sharp scrutiny of the *concierge* [attendant or house superintendent] next to the entrance before proceeding, up briefly lighted stairs, to the door of his destination. Designs of nineteenth-century luxury apartments in Paris provide another, although somewhat different, image of the privacy of the *foyer*. Here each apartment occupies an entire floor of a building which also, on the first two floors, houses a business establishment and, in the attics, has rooms for servants and poor tenants. The close proximity of these unrelated worlds implies the detachment of each from the other. The specific image alters from one type of house, from one region of France to another. Common to them is the sense of the boundary set, the protection against possible intrusion. Not everyone, by any means, owns a house, a garden, or a plot of land; on the contrary, housing is a major problem in France today (including both the provision of housing in crowded cities and the utilization of antiquated housing in provincial towns). But ownership—and the maintenance of privacy and independent security—is something which the adult desires and expects: a home is inherited, bought or worked towards for eventual retirement, ideally, though it may not be attained in fact.

The household, established at marriage, is intended to have permanence. The furniture and appliances that are then installed are meant to last not until a change in fashion but throughout a lifetime. For the home, however agreeable, is arranged neither for extensive display nor as a meeting place with outsiders, but chiefly to please the taste and to suit the convenience of those who live in it. However, the house (or the apartment) is not in itself the *foyer*. In its figurative sense—and this is the way in which it is most commonly used—*le foyer* refers to a group of people—a married couple and their children—who live together in a fixed place and form a closed circle.

.   .   .   .

Of these circles [all types of social groups], the family—especially the *foyer*—is the most self-contained and enduring in that family relationships are regarded as all but indestructible and the individual's obligations to and benefits from the immediate family continue throughout life. For the child (especially the girl) who has grown up and become independent, the door to the parental home remains "always open"; reciprocally, parents feel that they have a continuing right to participate in major decisions made by their grown children that may affect the larger family. Parents and children have a mutual responsibility for each other's well-being that is reflected in legal arrangements about inheritance and the care of the indigent; parents cannot disinherit children nor can children disclaim responsibility for the care of elderly or ailing parents. Yet, ideally, reciprocity consists not in making return gifts for what has been received, but in protecting what one has and passing on to the next generation what one has received and cared for. Thus, the past is continually made part of the present and the *foyer*, like other social circles, is not isolated but is one of an interlocking series.

The larger family (*la famille, les parents*)—including grandparents, parents' siblings, cousins, and so on, as well as those who have married in —is regarded as having unity as it also has extension in time. But in fact, when "the family" is referred to, it is usually the members of the *foyer* and the closest, most congenial relatives and those from whom one expects to inherit (or to whom one expects to bequeath) who are meant. The household itself reflects something of this larger family with its extension over time. Describing what she misses in the American family, a young war-bride writes:

> One doesn't find that good French family tradition; the habits, the reminders (*souvenirs*), the family pictures, the family house and furniture. The family in the United States is in the present. In France, it is in the present, but in the past and future also.

The traditional symbol of the unity of the larger family and its exclusiveness is the *conseil de famille* (family council), which links together the several related *foyers*. Meeting formally or informally, this group may act for its members and in certain situations can be a legally responsible intermediary between the family and the rest of the world. Here the individual may ask advice from or may be called upon to give account to members of his family acting in concert.

. . . .

The *foyer* that is established at marriage is, ideally, autonomous. The fact that actual independence may be postponed or renounced until the death of the parents (as when a peasant son continues to live with his own family in his parental *foyer*) does not detract from this conception, as it concerns the intimate relationships of husband and wife and children to one another.

. . . .

Parents welcome children warmly and responsibly. With their birth, the human plan of the *foyer* is realized. Yet, though desired and loved, the child is regarded as a heavy charge upon its parents, for its upbringing requires foresight and long years of patient effort. Men and women alike stress the vital importance of bringing up the child properly (*élever l'enfant proprement*); they point out, besides, that all parents, according to their means, want to do well (*faire quelque chose de bien*) for each child. Consequently, people feel one should be able to decide upon the number of children one wishes to have and—though informants are quick to point out that they themselves know of large families—the general expectation is that the family will remain small.

19 · Social Life and Courtship in a French Village *

LAURENCE WYLIE

In contrast to the generalized account of the French family given in the preceding selection, this selection gives a first-hand intimate view of adolescence, courtship, and marriage roles as found in a typical village in

---

* Reprinted by permission of the publishers from Laurence Wylie, *Village in the Vaucluse* (Cambridge, Mass.: Harvard University Press, Copyright 1957, by The President and Fellows of Harvard College), selections from pages 99, 102, 103, 110, 111, 124–127.

The author, who received the degree of Doctor of Philosophy from Brown University, is Chairman of the Romance Language Department, Haverford College. He is especially interested in French community studies and in French literature as a vehicle of French culture.

Southern France. Dr. Wylie, his wife, and two sons, aged three and five, spent the year of 1950–1951 living on neighborly terms in a commune of about two thousand people, called Peyrane. He mingled with the villagers in their public life and his children played with the French children and attended the village school; in time he was invited into the homes. The commune is an old one. In the village are predominantly artisans, industrial miners, and tradesmen; small farmers nearby are also part of the commune.

Points to notice in contrast to our culture are the expectation that each boy or girl will begin to support himself upon leaving school, the close financial and personal control by the parents, and the relative freedom allowed the adolescent boys before marriage. The roles of married life are in contrast to this freedom; responsibilities of husband and wife are firmly fixed and enforced by public opinion.

FOR THE CHILDREN who are not sufficiently intelligent or ambitious to go away to school, life suddenly becomes enjoyable and simple after they have reached the age of fourteen. They are no longer children. They are young people, and only two things are expected of the young people of Peyrane: to support themselves and to have a good time. They will have no other obligations until they become sufficiently *sérieux* [mature] to settle down and establish a household of their own. The five or ten years between school and marriage are relatively free, free of the harsh discipline of school which the young people have left behind them, free of the family responsibilities they will eventually have thrust upon them. This is the period of life which the people of Peyrane call "the happiest years of one's existence."

·   ·   ·   ·   ·   ·   ·   ·   ·

[The boys work with their fathers—on the family farm, in the father's store, or in the nearby ocher mines if the father is a miner.]

It is usual for adolescent girls in Peyrane to have a job, although often it is only a temporary arrangement to support themselves until they are married. Of course, they do not all seek a paying job. Their first duty is to their mother. If she needs help at home, the daughter will stay with her and share the household tasks and the woman's work on the farm. This work is considered especially appropriate, since by helping run the household, a girl is preparing for her future adult role. [The daughters of wealthy fathers may take lessons, for example, sewing or hairdressing, instead of working.]

·   ·   ·   ·   ·   ·   ·   ·   ·

Of course, the children who take lessons earn no money. Neither do the boys who work on the farms with their father or the girls who work at home with their mother. But their financial situation is no different from that of the children who work for wages, since wages for adolescents are not given to the children but to their parents. Although adolescents are considered mature enough to earn money, they are not sufficiently *sérieux* to be entrusted with the money they earn.

No matter whether they work for the parents or work for wages, all adolescents are faced with the same situation: they have no money of their own. If their earnings are more than enough for their support, the excess goes not to them but to the household.

On the other hand, a father is duty bound to give his adolescent children enough money so that they may have a good time. Not only do adolescents expect spending money, but society demands that a father be generous with them. The niggardly father is criticized. . . . [The people of Peyrane] believe it to be the right of a young person to have a good time. More than that, they believe it is the *duty* of a young person to have a good time. And it is the duty of their parents not only to tolerate, but to abet their adolescent children in the quest for pleasure. An adult who has in some way been deprived of pleasure during his adolescent years is considered to a degree an incomplete person. He is looked upon with pity, or even with suspicion.

. . . .

[With release from school, young people enter into adult recreational activities. Girls join the women in their groups where work and talk are combined and boys begin to go to the café where the men congregate and to play cards with the men. Boys and girls participate in dances held in Peyrane and in neighboring villages. As a rule they do not attend the dances in pairs: the boys come together and the girls are brought in small groups by a father or older brother. They return home in the same way. The parents of one girl in Peyrane were criticized for permitting their daughter to ride to a neighboring village on the back of her fiancé's motorcycle; even though engaged, the couple should have been chaperoned. At the dance, boys congregate on one side of the room, girls on the other; but after a while they begin to dance. At intervals they visit the café to sit around the tables, talking and laughing, and drinking in moderation.]

The amusement the young people are most enthusiastic about, after dancing, is taking a *promenade*. A *promenade* is so vague and formless that it can be defined only as "an occasion on which people go somewhere for recreational purposes only." It may be a short walk through the village, a picnic in the woods, or a long anticipated trip to the top of Mont Ventoux. It may be made by a family group to celebrate a first communion, by a group of girls to see the annual parade at Apt, or by a boy and girl in love. Even a single person walking in what seems to be an aimless manner may be said to be taking a *promenade*.

.   .   .   .

The dances, the *promenades*, and the usual forms of adult recreational activity are supposed to offer adolescent girls adequate opportunities to have a good time. A well-behaved girl will not seek others, and most of the girls seem content. . . . As they get older they can expect suitors to call in the evening.

Boys are expected to seek wilder forms of amusement.

.   .   .   .

By the time young people are ready to marry they are acquainted with other young people from the whole area of the Apt Basin and even from more distant parts of the département. Family connections, visits, *promenades*, and above all the dances which they have attended have enlarged their circle of acquaintances beyond the limits of Peyrane.

.   .   .   .

When a young man decides he would like to marry a certain girl, his behavior makes his intentions obvious. At dances she is his only partner and he tries to keep other men from dancing with her. He tries to be with the girl on *promenades*. He drops into her home frequently, sometimes bringing a bottle of his sparkling wine. After a while the visits become so much a part of the family routine that he is almost accepted as a member of the family. In most families he is allowed to take the girl to a dance without a chaperone. He may take her on his motorcycle to visit relatives in a neighboring hamlet. The girl's family makes a point of retiring a little earlier than usual so that the young people may be alone.

After a few months the young man surprises no one when he asks the girl to marry him. If she consents, it is traditional for him to ask her father officially for his consent. This is legally necessary if the young people are minors. Family approval is not hard to obtain if it is evident that two conditions are fulfilled.

The first condition is that the couple should be in love. . . . The other important condition is that both the young man and the young woman should be *sérieux*. *Sérieux* means several things in this context. A serious husband or a serious wife is first of all faithful. A man who might "run after other women" or a woman who might be capable of "making horns grow on her husband's brow" is not serious. The most disgraceful thing that can happen to a person is for one's spouse to be so flagrantly unfaithful that the infidelity becomes generally known in the village.

Seriousness implies more than fidelity, however. A serious husband will try to earn as much money as the family needs to live "decently." He will not drink immoderately or spend too much time playing cards or boules. He will supplement his income by cultivating a garden. He will live so that he will be loved and respected by his wife and children.

A serious wife will be a hardworking, reasonable, and moderate woman. She will keep her house neat. She will feed and clothe the family economically and well. She will be on good terms with her neighbors but will not spend too much time gossiping. She will know how to stretch a hundred-franc note without having the reputation for being stingy. She will supplement her husband's income by making clothes, raising chickens and rabbits. If the need for money is desperate she will even take over the arduous task of raising silkworms or working in the grape harvest, without neglecting her regular household duties. She will not object if her husband goes to the café so long as he does not spend too much money or drink too much or come home too late for meals. She will not even object if he is moderately immoderate—that is, if now and then he goes on a bit of a binge. She will keep the children from running the streets when they are young and she will keep them clean. She will teach them good manners and will encourage them to love and fear their father. She may expect her husband to coöperate in disciplining the children, but except on rare occasions she may not ask him to spend his free time taking care of the children.

There are other qualities besides "seriousness" that one welcomes in a prospective son- or daughter-in-law. Since marriage brings the families of both spouses into close contact it would be preferable that the two families be compatible with each other, so that neither will be ashamed of the other or awed by it. Then there is the matter of money. Everyone says that it is stupid to marry for money, but when conversation falls on a particular ménage it becomes obvious that people do associate the question of money with the question of marriage.

20 · The Changing Moslem Family of the Middle East *

DOROTHY FAHS BECK

Moslemism is more than a religion; it is an entire cultural pattern, very different in values and customs from the Christian or Hebraic cultures. Although contact with the West has begun to crack the hard shell of the Moslem culture, much of the old remains. Spotted unevenly throughout the Arab nations of the Middle East one finds remnants of the older ways: the families of great wealth, with numerous wives and servants catering to the prestige and comfort of the male head of the household; the patriarchal family organization; the low social status of women; and, paralleling these households of wealth, the abject poverty of large segments of the population. Where the older culture remains, contacts with the West have sometimes simply added expensive cars and private planes to the possessions of the wealthy. But in many Middle Eastern countries, more fundamental changes have occurred and continue to occur: women are no longer forced by their families or public opinion to wear the veil; the harem is declining or has disappeared; women may hold jobs and vote. The changes have come unevenly to different countries or within the same country, where the cities tend to follow western ways but the villages still follow traditional Moslem ways. Turkey is the most completely westernized; Saudi Arabia the least. The Moslem religion is still the prevalent religion throughout.

In her article, based on first-hand experience and on reading, Dr. Beck does not confine herself to one country but gives a panoramic view of the Moslem family of the present in the midst of change. It is well to remember that the old patterns existed for many centuries and that men and women accepted and adapted to them without protest until the social and economic conditions of the countries began to change as a result of increased contacts with the western world. Note also in Dr. Beck's article that the change

* *Marriage and Family Living*, 19 (November, 1957), selections from pages 340–344. By permission of the publisher and the author.

The author, whose degree of Doctor of Philosophy (sociology) was granted by Columbia University, has carried out numerous statistical research projects in the medical field. She holds the position of Director of Research, Family Service Association of America. Most of her writings reflect her statistical research. A year spent in the Middle East as Assistant Professor of Biostatistics at the American University of Beirut and in travel plus library research netted a long article on the Moslem family, from which the present selections have been made.

creates strains in family relationships. The change-over to the western style of marriage is not complete; the framework of the older Moslem marriage is often poorly concealed beneath new western customs.

THE REMARKABLE change of Moslem family living patterns which has been accomplished in recent decades is perhaps best symbolized by the lifting of the veil that for more than a thousand years has held the Middle Eastern women in seclusion. While the veils used in different countries have varied in detail, they have all accomplished the same purpose, namely the hiding of the hair and usually also the face, and the prevention of any feminine appeal in public. Until the last three decades, the veil was worn almost universally by middle and upper class women throughout the area and has been an essential badge of social status and morality. To have said that a woman was without a veil was to have said she was "without shame."

· · · · · · · · ·

A second major technic for the seclusion of women is also passing, namely the harem, or "hareem" as it is called in the Near East. While I had always associated this term with polygyny, it is primarily used to mean either the separate quarters for women within the household or the women and children themselves thus held in seclusion. Every device was used to keep these family members hidden. Windows were covered with fancy but concealing carved wood latticework. Shades were drawn. Gardens were protected from the view of neighbors by high outer walls or the house structure itself. Only women, children, the husband, close relatives, blind men, and eunuchs were permitted to enter. Since even men servants were excluded, small boys provided the major link with the outside world.

· · · · · · · · ·

Today the harem is fast passing with the veil. The modern Moslem man of means builds himself a western-style house without separate quarters for the women. He shares his open balcony with his wife on a summer evening and when he goes out, she sometimes accompanies him. When he entertains at home, she joins the circle. The new homes have no carved wooden latticework in the windows and only in Iran, Iraq, and Afghanistan do they still build an outer wall for each compound to hide the family from view.

· · · · · · · · ·

This increased freedom for interpersonal contact, together with the impact of mass communication from the West, has placed a heavy strain on the old mores prohibiting premarital courtship. According to Moslem tradition, it was the parents' responsibility to arrange before they died a suitable match for each child. To avoid any moral slips, the Islamic norms provided for child betrothals and early marriage, especially for the girl. A suitable partner for a girl was defined as a man of Moslem faith who could maintain or enhance her social and economic status. Age and compatibility were ignored. Kinship marriages were common, cousins being especially preferred. The choice was entirely in the parents' hands and the well-bred girl was expected neither to offer objections to their choice nor to see her future mate prior to the final ceremony.

With the impact of higher education for women and contact with the Western pattern, this ethic is also changing. Both the age of betrothal and the age of women at marriage are rising, especially among the well-to-do where educational demands interfere with early marriage. The modern family now consults the children about the choice of spouse and the more daring children may themselves suggest the partner and ask their parents to arrange a contract.

.   .   .   .

If she does marry, the modern woman may find it very difficult to play her role in the patriarchal family where the husband or his father has unlimited authority. From the first, she will be expected to join the groom's extended and often quite large family household where she will share a communal living and a common purse. Her status will become that of junior assistant to her mother-in-law who will continue to direct the household chores. The young brides of an earlier era accepted this status as a matter of course, but with the trend toward the education of women and a later age at marriage, the older girls with modern notions from school sometimes have a difficult time adjusting to the ways and direction of their mothers-in-law. In time the more modern educated couples often break away from these larger family units and establish independent homes. When this happens, it is likely to be considered a reflection on the family. Separate units within the same compound are sometimes tried as a compromise. Few escape a period of dominance by a generation conditioned to the old family pattern.

In addition to adjusting to a new husband and a strange house full of new relatives, the young wife must worry about how to stay married. Moslem law permits the man to divorce his wife at will merely by pronouncing the words, "I divorce you," three times, preferably on separate occasions. The woman, except in Turkey where Swiss law has replaced Moslem law, cannot divorce her husband unless this right has been specified in the original marriage contract.

.   .   .   .

The third major threat to the security of the Moslem wife is the chance that her husband may tire of her and take a second, permanent or temporary wife. The Qur'an [Koran] says: ". . . marry of the women who seem good to you two or three or four, and if ye fear that ye cannot do justice then one . . ." (IV, 3). This requirement that justice be done to all wives has usually been interpreted as requiring that the husband provide each wife with a separate household of equal comfort to that of the other wives and clothes and food of comparable quality. In the agricultural village the extra wife paid her way with her extra pair of hands, but in the city an extra wife was never a luxury a poor man could afford. Even among the rich, polygyny was not typical. Now it is declining in repute also among the urban wealthy and is only a small factor in the total picture. It is forbidden in Turkey and characterizes only about 2 per cent of the marriages in Egypt at any one time. The figure for Iraq is 9 per cent, while in Saudi Arabia it is much higher.

21 · *Persian Courtship and Wedding* *

NAJMEH NAJAFI, AS TOLD TO HELEN HINCKLEY

The description of a typical Persian courtship and a Persian wedding shows that although the rituals are different from our own and the roles of husband and wife in contrast to those of Americans, nevertheless the girl enters marriage with all the eagerness and anticipation of an American bride. Marriage gives the girl prestige and carries both bride and groom into the adult world.

The author, Najmeh Najafi, grew up during a period of great change, when Persia became Iran, the veil for women was abolished legally by the reformer Reza Shah, and women gained the privilege of meeting in such public places as tearooms and westernized stores. She notes, however, that the old, conservative families clung to the old ways and tended to seclude their women. Her own family life began under the old ways. Her mother, at the age of twelve, married a man of forty, and bore him eight children, of whom

---

* Najmeh Najafi, as told to Helen Hinckley, *Persia Is My Heart* (New York: Harper and Brothers, 1953), selections from pages 87–90, 92–93, and 120–124. Copyright 1953 by Najmeh Najafi and Helen Hinckley Jones. Reprinted by permission of the publisher.

The author is a native of Persia (now Iran) who studied at Pasadena City College, California. She is the author also of *Reveille for a Persian Village*, written with Helen Hinckley.

the author was the youngest. An older sister married when thirteen and had her first child the following year. At this time, women still wore the veil when they went out, and the only places for women to go were the church and the community bathhouse, which served as a kind of social club where women met to discuss, gossip, and predict who the next bride would be.

IN THE CITY bathhouse and in the bathhouse of the village, the conversation is the same. Always in the minds of the women there is a lively interest in the young girls. For the women are the suitors of Persia. When a young girl leaves her tray to go into the hot pool or to dip screaming into the adjacent cold pool, many eyes will follow her. The girl does not mind. She knows that the place that a woman must occupy in her country is at best beloved doll to her husband and respected mother to her children.

.   .   .   .

It is the custom for the mother, with as many female relatives as care to make the call, to send a servant ahead to announce that she is making a call, object matrimony for her son. She goes into the house. The call is a polite one, but all eyes are open. The girl knows the eyes are upon her and she feels her knees knocking together, her smile made of cardboard on her face, her hands trembling. For this call she has prepared herself without make-up. Make-up might hide a blemish which the mother must see if she is not to be deceived.

.   .   .   .

If the suitors are pleased with the girl, with her accomplishments, with the wealth and position of her family, next time, very soon, the prospective groom will visit, too. The man will be older than the girl, maybe five years or so. Or maybe he will be a middle-aged or even an old man, looking for a wife to take the place of one lost by death or to add to his harem.

.   .   .   .

Reza Shah made a law forbidding child marriages. The girl, according to law, must be sixteen. But still many girls marry at eleven, twelve, thirteen.

.   .   .   .

Wives are not purchased in Persia as some people believe. Nevertheless, a wife from the highest class is worth at least five thousand dollars in gifts.

After the call by the female relatives, after the boy (or man) has visited the home and has said that he is satisfied, then the parents of both the boy and the girl get together to talk about the dowry of the girl, the gifts of the boy, the wedding, the ceremony, other matters.

The first gift of the groom's parents to the bride will be, most likely, a diamond ring. If the parents can afford it, the stone will be enormous. It reflects the position of the family. After this will come the handwritten, beautifully illuminated copy of the Koran. This too is a very expensive gift. Later there will be such gifts as silver candlesticks done with the care and creative precision of the Persian artisan, silver mirror, lacquered chests— the gifts are reflections of the artistic culture of Persia.

For two or three months, maybe even for a year the bride will remain in the home of her mother getting her dowry arranged. In my country this is a happy time in the girl's life and in the mother's too, when the two work together for the life-long happiness of the girl.

. . . .

[The author visits a girl friend, Shikuh, who is soon to be married.]
Shikuh's girl friends in Kasvin came very early and we began to sew. We cut and made the white wedding dress, the slips, the brassieres, all of the dainty things the bride would need.

. . . .

Four days seemed like one day. The next day we went to the public bath, fifteen laughing, merry girls. All day we spent in the bath. There was a special expert to pluck our eyebrows, treat our lashes, there was the shampoo, the soothing rub with the bath mitten, the steaming that makes one clean clear to the inside, the plunge in the hot water and the sharp chill of the cold water as we went shrieking into it for only a moment.

During the last part of the bath there had been a band of musicians playing outside the bathhouse. Our instruments are different from yours, but there are strings and drums and cymbals. As we came out the village people and the people of Kasvin threw flowers and little white candies on the street in front of Shikuh's feet.

The next night two mullahs [interpreters of the Islamic faith] came for the marriage ceremony. In my country there are mullahs of different prices. If you are wealthy you may buy the best mullah for the occasion. If you are not, poor mullahs will marry you as tightly.

. . . .

In Moslem weddings the bride, dressed in white and with a veil over her face, sits alone in a room close to the court, and close to the room for the women. She sits on the floor on a special piece of finest Persian pure silk with maybe threads of real metal worked into the design. Behind her is a mirror and tall candelabra. At each side there is a long piece of bread almost like a rug. You don't have anything in America like these very long pieces of flat bread, square at one end, the other end pointed. Into the bread, in beautiful Persian design, is placed colored incense for future burning.

Outside the door of the bridechamber the two mullahs stand one on each side, reading from the Koran. Two times the bride must not answer the questions of the mullah. At this time it is the custom of the boy's mother to bring a gift of gold to show that she is willing. Hoseh's [the groom] mother is dead so a kinswoman brings the golden bracelets. Now Shikuh answers "Yes," and there is a squeal from all the women at the celebration and a great clapping of hands from everyone. Two women of the family—women who have been especially happy in their lives—come and stand before the incense-covered bread. One has two cubes of sugar between her palms. As she rolls her palms together a thin stream of sugar falls upon the floor. The bride will be sweet to her husband. It is the best quality in women in my country. The other woman has needle and thread. She sews while she says she is closing the mouth of the new relatives.

In Persia the boy takes the bride to the home of his mother. Shikuh would go to the home of Hoseh. There are many who whisper that Shikuh is fortunate to be at once mistress of her house. It is hard, sometimes, for the young girl to go to the home of the mother-in-law, especially if there are other sons and their wives already in the home.

Then the groom is led into the bride's room and the two are left behind a drawn curtain while the mullahs make the marriage papers. One is for the parents of the girl, one for the parents of the boy.

[However, the bride does not immediately go to the home of her new husband. For several months she continues to live with her parents; she prepares her dowry and is instructed by her mother on the duties and responsibilities of a Moslem wife. Finally the day comes for her to leave her parents' home. Porters carry the dowry to the home of the groom, which will become her new home. Then the groom and his kinsmen come to accompany the bride to the new home; her parents may not go with her, as they cannot enter into her new life.]

22 · *Marriage and the Family in Korea* *

UN SUN SONG

In Korea, as in France, the Moslem countries, and the United States, marriage is important to the bride and groom, their families, and the society. As is marriage in each of the other countries, Korean marriage is colored by religious concepts—in this case, by Confucianism. Korean society is also undergoing change, which touches courtship and marriage. Dr. Song, a sociologist from Korea, points out the old customs, some of the changes, and the values of marriage.

IT HAS BEEN said that in order to understand a people you must first understand their family system. Especially in the case of Korea is this true, since every facet of life revolves around the family and the relations between its members. In the Western world, and especially the United States, love is the motivating force which leads to marriage. In Korea this ideal of romantic love is less evident; the most important reason for marriage in Korea is to continue the family line. To have a son who will continue the family name and reverence the family ancestors is the goal of every Korean, a fact which helps to explain the importance of the male in our culture.

Mate Selection and Courtship

Although the Western influence has brought about some variations in the old patterns of culture, it is the traditional customs which are still observed by the greater part of the people. Most Americans are usually surprised to learn that in Korea we have no "dating" custom such as there is in their country. Of course, this stems from the fact that romantic love does not determine marriages. In fact, there is an old proverb which says that, "Love does not always lead to marriage, but marriage often leads to love." The statement that we have no dating custom invariably elicits the question: "Well, how do boys and girls get to know each other well enough

* *Korean Survey*, 7 (April, 1958), 4–6, 12. Reprinted by permission of the publisher and the author.
The author, who was born in Seoul, Korea, received her college education in Tokyo and her graduate training in the United States, where she received the degree of Doctor of Philosophy (sociology) from the University of Maryland in 1958. She has since been engaged in research for a book on Korea.

to get married?" The answer is that they don't—at least not as well as the American girls and boys do. Although there are increasing numbers of so-called "love matches" to be found in Korea (since 1945), these are often frowned upon by the more tradition-minded elders. But this is getting somewhat ahead of the story. Let us take a look at the customs of an earlier day.

From the time that a child was born in Korea the parents were concerned about finding a mate for him or her. Although sometimes a child was "engaged" at a very young age this custom has passed away. Today, by the time the daughter is about eighteen and the son is twenty-two, the parents probably have already picked out some mate for them. It is interesting to note that the future spouse's family background and name is much more important than whether or not he is wealthy. Naturally, every family is anxious to get the best possible match for their children, but if it is a question of whether to marry a person with excellent family background and little money or poor family background and much money, they will choose the good family background.

Aside from family background, there are traditionally several other things which will determine whether or not a couple should be married. To begin with, there is a taboo which prohibits two families with the same surname and genealogy from marrying among themselves. In addition, the signs of the zodiac were consulted and the year, month, day, and hour of the couple's birth dates were compared and if they were found to be harmonious it was a good omen that the marriage should take place.

After the parents have chosen some likely candidates they show their son or daughter several pictures of them. The children are usually given an opportunity to pass judgment on whether or not they like the looks of the spouse-to-be, and choose the one they would like to marry. Then the parents make arrangements for their children to meet. Usually it is the girl's parents who send an "invitation" to the boy's family. Although in some cases this is the first time that the boy and girl have ever met, it often happens that they have gone to school together or were neighbors. At this formal meeting the two young people have a chance for a brief conversation and can learn something about each other. If the boy and girl want to know each other better, they may, with the approval of both families, see each other more often. In general, however, the couple will become engaged after the first meeting and will marry as soon as possible, usually as soon as the girl's trousseau is ready. The interval between the first meeting and the wedding ceremony may be anywhere from several weeks to six months or more.

It often happens that if the parents are unsuccessful in finding a suitable mate for their child, they consult a *chung-mai*, or professional matchmaker. This marriage broker is usually a widow who is well acquainted with a number of families; or it may be an old and respected member of the community, one's employer, or a person of influence or position. They all fulfill the same function, however, in that they seek to find the most eligible mate for their client or friend. If the *chung-mai* is professional, then it is customary to give her some kind of reward for her services. She receives commissions of money or gifts from both the families, which are given according to their financial situation. It is said that if a *chung-mai* succeeded in finding a good wife for a rich man's son, she would have no worries for the rest of her life.

Going back somewhat to the engagement period, one might ask just what the young couple may do while they are waiting for their marriage day. Well, here again there is much variation from place to place and from time to time. Generally speaking, the husband-to-be may visit his fiancee at her home, where they may talk to each other, have dinner together, or play cards with each other under the strict eye of some third party. This is a custom which is not unfamiliar in Spain, where the *duenna* acts as chaperone for the young people. If the couple would like to go out for a walk there is usually someone following them not far behind; or if they want to go to a movie they are chaperoned by some member of the family.

During this brief engagement period the girl's family is busily preparing her trousseau, and she is brushing up on her housekeeping. She is taught to take over such duties as cooking, sewing, and home management. Usually this is not too difficult for her, since she has been helping her mother keep house since she was very young. The mother, female relatives and friends, meanwhile, are preparing the things that she will need in order to set up housekeeping—kitchen utensils, furniture, and clothes or fabrics. This is a very expensive undertaking for the bride's family, especially if there is more than one daughter. In fact, Koreans have a proverb: "No thief attempts to rob the house of a man who has three daughters."

But when the time for the wedding finally arrives it is a time of great rejoicing. In fact, the marriage is probably the most important celebration in Korea. The traditional wedding ceremony is filled with color and symbolism and ritual, but the Western influence has been introducing many Christian aspects to the marriage until today many people have a Christian religious marriage. In any case, whether the ceremony itself is traditional or modern, it is always followed by a sumptuous feast to which many guests are invited. Everyone enjoys going to a wedding feast because there is such a variety of tasty delicacies—several meat dishes including beef, pork, and chicken; fish, both smoked and dried; fruits, pastries, and candies; vegetables and rice; and, of course, plenty of wine. The number and variety of dishes varies with the financial status of each family, but it is said that some rich families often have between sixty and seventy-five dishes at one feast.

If their families are well-to-do, the bride and groom may decide to go on a honeymoon to the famous hot springs at Onyang or Paikchon. If they decide not to go on a honeymoon then the couple will settle down to live with the parents of the husband, for according to tradition it is the responsibility of the son to live with his parents and take care of them in their old age. Although this custom is not practiced extensively among modern families, it is still prevalent among the majority of people and will probably reflect the ancient concept of filial piety for years to come, in spite of the passing of many folkways in the face of growing modernization and secularization.

The Korean Family

The traditional Korean family, as it exists in the rural areas of Korea, is patriarchal and monogamous. The key figure in the household is the patriarch, the oldest male member, in most cases. It is he who manages the family affairs. Insofar as ritual is concerned, the patriarch is the priest in the family worship, the breadwinner of the family, and, consequently, it is he who regulates the income of the family. The word of the patriarch is law. His decisions must be accepted by the other members of the family.

As a result of the patriarch's supervision of family members, he represents the family as a group to the outside world. The family's social status can be no higher than that of the father. The entire life of the family is subordinated to the wishes and desires of the patriarch; however, the attitude and behavior of the patriarch is seldom determined by self interest or concern. Rather he is controlled by the institutional demands of the family.

The key element in the relationship between the patriarch and his wife is just as Confucius decreed it should be thousands of years ago: respect. Their relationship must be harmonious; the husband is active and the wife is passive—he is like a needle and she like the thread. He is heaven; she is earth. All these analogies point out that each of them has a specific role to fulfill and that the one cannot fulfill the role of the other. Nor do the husband and wife show their affection toward each other in the presence of their children or friends. There is no kissing custom in Korea—this is strictly a Western innovation—therefore husbands don't kiss their wives. Or if they do, they don't do it where other people might see them and make fun of them. Public opinion is a very strong means of social control in Korea!

Although there are modern exceptions to the rule, women are supposed to walk behind their husbands, not beside them, when they are out in public. Formerly, whenever the men went out to some party or special dinner they would not take their wives, for in Korea there was a special class of female entertainer, the *kisaeng*, who would dance and sing for the guests. Even inside the home the traditional attitude of the husband is that a man should not work in the kitchen because it is beneath his dignity. But here again there are many husbands, who, when there are no outsiders around, will help their wives with the cooking and washing the dishes. Some men will not admit it, but they actually *enjoy* cooking.

The relationship of the husband and wife is expressed also in the language. When they speak to each other they may use the somewhat affectionate term, *yobo*. Most important, however, they may not call each other by their first name! This would be a most serious and insulting thing to do. Instead, they use many different terms such as *pakkan-yangpan* (husband), *uri chuin* (my master), *chip-e saram* (person of the house), *anhai* (wife). More common in the husband-wife interaction is the use of the term *aigi aboji* (father of the child) or *aigi omoni* (mother of the child) to refer to the husband or the wife. Also the name of the child may be used, for example, *Poktong-ui-aboji* meaning Poktong's father. Another interesting fact about the Korean husband-wife relationship is that when they marry, the wife keeps her maiden surname. Thus, if Kim Soon Hi marries a man named Lee, she is still referred to as Kim Soon Hi. If you wanted to call her "Mrs. Lee," you would have to say the equivalent of "Mr. Lee's Wife."

Sociologically speaking, the Korean family is parent-child centered rather than husband-wife centered, as most Western families are today. It is this parent-child relationship, more specifically the father-son relationship, which is the key to the understanding of the Korean family system. The importance of a son in the family can be readily understood in view of the Korean attitude toward ancestor reverence and ancestral tablets in continuing the family line, and "face," an attitude which is strengthened through the teachings of Confucianism. Only through a son can there be a continuation of the family line. Girls will marry into some other families and will no longer be considered members of their true family. In this social context lies the strong preference for male children rather than female. Nevertheless, Koreans would prefer to have daughters than to have no children at all. Another practical reason for the preference of a son is, of course, that sons are better able to work on the farms and can provide for the sustenance of the aged parents.

The father's attitude toward his children is an interesting one. He must always try to be very dignified, so that the children will show him the proper respect; therefore he is not too affectionate toward them, even though he loves them very much. There is no concept in Korea that the father is the "boy's best friend." It is the father's job to discipline the children. Sometimes he spanks them if he thinks it is necessary or makes them go to bed without eating their supper. When they speak to their father, they must use a respectful form of language. (Korean language is based upon a system of polite forms, some very polite and others less polite, being used between very close friends.) If a child ever used other than the honorific level to his father, he would expect to be punished very quickly. Korean children respect and fear their fathers and it is rare to find children who are hard to handle.

If we compare the parents to the human body, the father is the head and the mother is the heart. It is she who takes care of the food and clothing for the family. As all of the father's activity is carried on outside the home, the mother works inside the home. She works from dawn to dusk just managing the home. She can not go to bed until the father has gone, and she must get up before him in the morning. You will never find a Korean wife making her husband prepare his own breakfast before going to work.

Mother must do the thousand and one little things which often go unnoticed—things like remembering all the relatives' birthdays—so she doesn't go out very often. Therefore, she often asks her husband on some family occasion to invite their friends to the house and she prepares a big meal and spends the whole day chatting and gossiping with her friends.

Until quite recently the Korean wife did not work outside the home to earn money even if she was able to do so. It was considered a disgrace for such a thing to happen and the father would lose "face" among his friends and neighbors. Girls were trained to be good wives and mothers—not to be office girls. Boys are brought up so that they might become responsible husbands and fathers in the future. Today, as far as the girls are concerned, however, this old attitude is losing ground and many young girls and wives have found it necessary to seek work in offices and factories of the large cities in order to meet the demands of a war-shattered economy.

In most other ways, though, Korea retains the old customs. This helps to explain why there is very little divorce in Korea. In our culture divorce carries a stigma which is greater than in most Western countries, so couples are less inclined to seek a divorce as a solution to their problems. But, on the other hand, there is less reason to need a divorce because of the very nature of the roles of the husband and wife. The husband knows what is expected of him and he knows that no one will try to take over his duties unless he gives his permission. The wife is brought up to respect her husband and love her children. There is no conflict as to whether a woman should turn to a career or to housekeeping. The culture solves that problem. In the Western world there are many role conflicts between husband and wife, and the value of individualism de-emphasizes the importance of the family group. In Korea the men are supposed to be authoritarian and active while women are taught to be submissive and passive. Men and women cooperate in order to bring up their children and continue the family name.

The importance of a son to continue the family name helps to explain one of the ancient institutions which has recently been abolished, that is, concubinage. In the old days when a wife was barren the husband had the right to take a concubine in order to have a son. If the concubine had a son he would become the legal heir and she would receive much prestige. Even so, the wife's position would not be endangered, for she was still the wife and no one could take over her position.

I mentioned earlier that the patriarch was the authority in the family. This is quite true, but as he gets older he becomes more of a figurehead and it is the wife who has the greatest influence. Usually the patriarch knows that his wife is assuming more and more responsibility, but he lets her gradually take over more of his duties. If the wife has several sons it is easier for her to gain more power in the household because she already has a great deal of prestige. It often happens that the wife is able to make herself the real authority in the family without the husband's knowing or realizing it. In other words, the husband *thinks* he is the authority, but the wife *knows* that she is. This is one of the most important secrets for a happy marriage in Korea.

And when the couple is old they may expect that their children (the eldest son in particular) will take care of them for the rest of their lives. So old age, in Korea, becomes a time, not of worry and anxiety, but of peace and happiness, the aged parents secure in the knowledge that they have done their part in continuing the family line and contributing respectable citizens to their society.

CHAPTER 5:

Differences between
Men and Women

23 · Why Women Live Longer than Men *

SELIG GREENBERG

One of the mysteries of the normal life expectancy is that the average length
of life of women is at least six years longer than that of men. One result of
this difference is that many more women than men lose their marriage partners by death. Under present conditions, middle and old age bring widowhood to many women, who then must adjust to a single and often lonely
existence after the partnership of marriage. The period of widowhood is
prolonged because of the custom of women marrying men who are several
years older than themselves.

Mr. Greenberg examines first physical and then social reasons that contribute to the shorter lives of men. At the end of his article he suggests two
unconventional solutions to the prevalence of widowhood. In this connection, see article 30.

FOR SOME time now American women have been gaining on the men—at
least in numbers. Back in 1930, the men in this country outnumbered the
women by about a million and a half. Today the women hold a lead of
about the same size, and the Census Bureau is predicting that by 1975 they
will be ahead of the men by perhaps as many as 3,600,000.

One explanation is the decline in immigration, which at one time brought
millions of single men into the country. Another—and more significant—
is that American females have developed a habit of outliving the men; and

---

* *Harper's Magazine*, 215 (October, 1957), 70–73. Reprinted by permission of the
author.
The author has been on the staff of the Providence, Rhode Island, *Journal-Bulletin*
since he graduated from Brown University. He specializes in articles on medical science.

recent figures indicate that the gap between the life span of the sexes is widening steadily.

For example, at the turn of the century, the average American woman lived two years and ten months longer than the average man. Today she is outliving him by more than six years. If she is typical, she will not die until she is a little over seventy-three years and six months old—which gives her the longest life expectancy of any women in the world.

The men in her family, however, can expect to last only a few months past sixty-seven. The men of seven other countries do better than that—Dutchmen, Israelis, Norwegians, Swedes, New Zealanders, Danes, and Britons, in that order. At birth a boy in Holland can look forward to outliving the average American boy by more than three years. Furthermore, the older the American grows, the worse his prospects look. By the time he is forty, his life expectancy is poorer than that of the men of fifteen other nations; and at fifty his chances of living another ten years are 24 per cent less than they would be if he were an Italian and 55 per cent less than if he were a Swede.

These facts foreshadow some interesting changes in American society —in our courting and marriage habits, family life, the job market, and even politics. But before we try to figure out what is likely to happen as a result of the growing surplus of women, it might be well to look at two other questions:

(1) Why do women—traditionally regarded as the weaker sex—live so much longer than men?

(2) Why has their life expectancy increased so much more than that of American males during the past few decades?

The answer to the first is easy, if not very flattering to the male ego. Except for their greater muscular strength—which is no longer the asset it was in the Good Old Days of sweaty physical toil and hand-to-hand combat—men actually are the *weaker* sex. In most species, the female outlives the male. Among humans, nature compensates for this by arranging to have 105 boys born for every 100 girls. The proportion of male babies conceived is even larger than this, but their greater vulnerability makes its appearance even before birth. More boy babies fail to come to full term and are lost through miscarriages. The ratio of boys born with congenital malformations is also larger.

Even the normal boy baby has a physiological disadvantage, compared to the normal girl baby, from the very start. A girl is born with two complete X-chromosomes—the minute hereditary particles that substantially influence the fate of the organism—while boys have only one. As she grows older, she has a higher count of white blood cells which help to combat infections. And a woman's glandular system is superior to a man's. Her thyroid is larger, and her pituitary—the master gland which controls the body's over-all hormone productions—enlarges during pregnancy and remains somewhat larger from then on. This bolsters the performance of her adrenal glands, enabling her to resist stress more effectively; it keeps her blood pressure at a lower level and gives her greater tolerance for fatigue and illness. The female sex hormones apparently protect their owner against arterial disorders by helping to keep down the fat content of the blood. This may account for the fact that hardening of the arteries and subsequent heart disease are comparatively rare among women until after the menopause when the output of ovarian hormones drops off sharply.

The death rate is higher for males in every age group; but particularly in early adulthood and middle age. The initial male superiority in numbers lasts through the age of twenty-four. From that point on, the females in any given generation pull ahead, and their plurality gets progressively larger with the years. Last year there were 103.9 boys for every 100 girls in the age group under eighteen in the United States. In the eighteen to twenty-four category, males still predominated slightly. But in the twenty-five to forty-four group there were only 96.6 men for every 100 women, and in the sixty-five plus category, 85.7.

The Built-in Medicine Chest

Biologists reason that women's physiological advantages are nature's way of ensuring that the race will be carried on. A pregnant woman needs special reserves of strength. Her heart, for example, must be strong enough to meet both the ordinary needs of her own body and those of the developing fetus. Her lungs must supply her blood with extra oxygen. Every organ in her body must be able to work at a higher pitch. Because of this, one authority claims, women are provided with "better internal medicine chests" than men.

In any case, almost every disease kills more men than women. The only exceptions are diabetes and what the professionals call sex-specific conditions—like childbirth and cancer of the breast and genital organs. But diabetes, while it cannot be cured, is now relatively easy to control; in the last two decades alone deaths of mothers during childbirth have been slashed from eighty-five to five for every 10,000 live births; and encouraging progress has been made in the cancer field.

Here, too, women are doing better than men. Not only is the mortality rate from all forms of cancer about 5 per cent higher for men; the female cancer rate has been gradually declining while the male rate has remained static in some forms of the disease and risen in others. The over-all cancer mortality rate among women has dropped 10 per cent in the past fifteen years. In the same period, male fatalities from cancer of the lung and respiratory system have nearly tripled. One explanation may be that female cancers are usually easier to detect, more accessible, and more amenable to treatment; another possibility is that women are more apt to seek prompt medical advice when they discover any suspicious symptoms.

Nevertheless, the cancer picture is only one part of a larger picture which follows the same pattern. Although there are now about 1,500,000 more women than men in the United States, 200,000 more men than women have died annually in recent years. Diseases of the heart, blood vessels, and kidneys are about two and a half times more prevalent among men than women in the middle-aged group and account for well over 100,000 more male than female deaths each year. The male death rate from arteriosclerotic heart diseases is some 75 per cent higher than the female.

So we come to our second question: Why is the difference between the life spans of the sexes becoming wider in this country? The answer to this is hard to document, for it involves many intangibles. But I believe that, in addition to their biological superiority, women are psychologically better able to adapt themselves to the strains of our highly competitive society —that it is, in effect, easier to be a woman than a man in mid-twentieth century America.

The Pace That Kills

It is fashionable these days to say that American men are dying prematurely because they drive themselves beyond endurance to get things for their women. This broad and pat generalization can be neither proved nor disproved. What can be proved is that the modern American man is subject to a multitude of special pressures and frustrations, and that there has been a fundamental change in his position in society. Yet society still expects him to be the strong, silent male of tradition, above the temper tantrums and tears with which women help to dissipate and relieve their tensions. Since he has been trained to believe that it is unmanly to be too vocal about his feelings, the man tends to bury them as much as he can.

Medical authorities suspect that the damaging effect of such inhibition may be one reason why five times as many men as women die of stomach and duodenal ulcers which are attributable, at least in part, to excessive tension. And three times as many men as women commit suicide every year. (It must be said that more women *try* to kill themselves, but a large proportion of them bungle the job—either because they are less efficient than men, or because they never really meant to go through with it.)

In the decades which have marked women's increasing life expectancy, there has been a significant shift in the pattern of the American family —a shift which includes new concepts of the husband-wife relationship, the raising of children, and the management of the home. All these things, combined with the competitiveness of American life, have undermined the American man's sense of security. No longer king of the roost, the undisputed authority in his own house, he is ridden with anxieties, and some of the strongest are fears of sexual inadequacy.

It has become generally accepted in our society that the wife is expected to receive as well as give pleasure in sexual intercourse. While this frequently makes for a more deeply satisfying relationship, it is also apt to put a strain on the man, for whom sexual performance has always been something of a testing and a challenge. As he grows older, the inevitable decline in his potency can become a source of deep-seated insecurity. In other societies, where age increased rather than decreased social prestige and where the man's position in the community as well as the home was stable, the falling off of sexual powers did not represent so grave a threat to self-esteem. But since America has never developed these comforting traditions, too many of our men feel compelled to prove themselves as they age by increased activity in other spheres, often to the detriment of their physical and emotional health.

Compare this with the situation facing modern American women. They have been liberated both from the Victorian taboos regarding sex and from most of the perils of childbirth. The vast majority of them have also come to accept the planning of families so that there are very few women today, as there were in the past, who are exhausted by child-bearing before thirty.

It would be fatuous to deny that women, too, are confronted with difficult problems of adjustment, especially in regard to their still shifting position in our society. But on the whole they have things a whole lot easier than their mates. Ironically, man-made mores, stemming from the days when women were still in short supply in this country, are at least partially responsible. An American woman still expects—and generally receives—from the men around her certain considerations which, while they flatter the man's vanity, also put an added strain on him.

Far more than men, women are able to set their own pace. It is acceptable for them either to remain at home—where mechanical appliances and the easy availability of processed foods have vastly lightened the burden of housekeeping—or to take a job. And even when they work they are usually spared the grinding pressure to get to the top of the ladder which bears upon most men. Moreover, a woman who is taking care of a house is pretty sure to get a full daily quota of regular exercise, while her husband leads an essentially sedentary life and sometimes kills himself by sporadic bouts of strenuous physical activity. Then, too, as she grows older, a woman can taper off her work gradually; but her husband, in whom the whole aging process starts later, is apt to be brought suddenly face to face with the devastating jolt of retirement.

Women to Burn?

Whatever the causes, there are at present no signs that the trend in the life expectancy of the sexes will change—and the repercussions of a growing majority of women upon our society are certain to be formidable. Inevitably, the influence of women on social and political action will grow; they will control more and more of the nation's wealth (a sizable proportion of it is already in their hands); and they will invade the job market in greater and greater numbers, out of both economic and psychological necessity.

At present there are 7,600,000 widows in the United States, a good proportion of them in their early fifties and many in a precarious economic position. Even those who are financially comfortable face years of loneliness and frustration, and their chances of remarriage—never very strong —are growing steadily slimmer as the male deficit increases. For many of these women, a job may provide at least a partial solution. But we will still be faced with the rising number of women over sixty-five. The Census Bureau predicts that this group of women over the retirement age will climb at the rate of about two million per decade.

We may also expect that the surplus of women of marriageable age, not yet too serious, will begin to soar, and that it will become harder and harder for a girl to marry if she has not done so by a fairly early age. What the effect of more spinsterhood will be upon our morals and how great a threat it will present to the monogamous marriage system is hard to say, but we will undoubtedly be hearing more about it. Already a Tennessee state senator has introduced a bill to legalize polygamy as a means of alleviating the surplus of women, and Dr. Marion Langer, a sociologist specializing in marriage counseling, recently advised girls not to worry about cradle-snatching.

The best way to avoid being widowed, she suggested, is to "marry a man five, six, or even seven years your junior." She conceded, however, that under existing conditions a girl might have a hard time snaring a younger man and concluded by saying that our society has only two possible solutions to the mounting man shortage—polygamy or finding some way to lengthen man's life expectancy.

It is unlikely that we will ever adopt her first alternative. But her second involves almost as radical a modification in our mores and way of life. The male would have to jettison his cult of manliness and abandon his illusion of biological superiority. And the female would have to give up her demand for special consideration and accept the responsibilities of her greater stamina. The shock of both egos might be severe. All the same it is a possibility worth trying—for the sake of both men and women.

24 · The Private Worlds of Men and Women *

AMERICAN INSTITUTE OF FAMILY RELATIONS

Men and women differ not only physically and in the social stresses to which they are subjected but also in their modes of thought, interests, and customary activities. Understanding of these worlds and tolerance of them are essential to successful marriage adjustment.

IN LARGE and important areas of life, men and women have entirely different standards of value—or else they are not good specimens of their own sex. They do not speak the same language. Note, for instance, how often women use the adjective "little" as compared with its use by men. Sociologist James H. S. Bossard remarks, "This sex distinction is evident at every turn—in the words used, habits of exclamation, intensity of expression, and stock phrases, as well as the subjects discussed. The child learns early and is constantly reminded that there is prestige in learning the sex-appropriate forms of expression."

In short, boys and girls spend the first 10 or 15 years of their lives in relatively distinct social worlds. In marriage these two worlds have to be fused, in part, and much of the difficulty of marital adjustment grows out of the difficulty of this fusion, and frequent failure in it. This point is developed in sociologist E. E. LeMasters' new college textbook, *Modern Courtship and Marriage*,[1] more fully than in any other recent treatise.

Not only are there almost entirely different sexual worlds for males and females in our culture, Dr. LeMasters insists, but there are many male worlds into which a female can hardly enter. What he calls tavern society is basically a male world—the world of the Elks, Moose, Masons, American

---

* *Family Life*, 18 (October, 1957), 1–3. Reprinted by permission of the publisher, The American Institute of Family Relations.

This article is based in large part on a discussion by E. E. LeMasters in his book, *Modern Courtship and Marriage*. Dr. LeMasters, who holds the degree of Doctor of Philosophy from Ohio State University, is Professor of Sociology at Beloit College. He is the author of a number of professional articles on marriage and the family and of the textbook, *Modern Courtship and Marriage*.

[1] (New York: Macmillan Company, 1957.)

Legion and other veterans' organizations, of the luncheon clubs, athletic clubs, hunting clubs, and the like. "It is unwise for women approaching marriage to conclude that male society is now completely open to them, or to condemn their husbands for wanting to participate in the man's world, as he has been accustomed to doing since he can remember."

Hardly any women have a realistic understanding of what it means to participate for several years in the armed forces, as most men have done. The world of sports participation is foreign to women, and so on. The world of business, into which so many millions of women have now entered, is still essentially a man's world, and such an expression as "Business is business" is as foreign to women's basic way of thinking as the expression, "I haven't a thing to wear" is foreign to men's.

Now, how can a wife adjust herself to these facts? First, says Dr. Le-Masters, by respecting the man's world and realizing that she can never be fully admitted to it; then by a determination to understand it as far as she can; and finally by accepting the way of life of *her own* sex instead of trying to repudiate it and make an imitation man out of herself (Alfred Adler's *masculine protest*), an ambition in which she can never succeed.

On the other hand, men will have to try to understand (or accept resignedly if they can not understand) the separate world of women. This centers largely in clothes, and growing partly out of this is a difference in ideas about the value of money. It involves the matter of diet, which becomes an obsession with so many women. But there are many more deeply-rooted differences, associated with the constitutional differences between the sexes. "The average wife seems to need a good cry every so often," Dr. LeMasters observes; and the husband need not necessarily feel like a guilty brute to think that he has precipitated these tears.

Religion means more to women than to men. So do children: "married couples sometimes develop basic conflicts related to this intense preoccupation of the mother with her children. The husband with his outside work and interests may feel that his wife is becoming a slave to the children, which to some extent she usually is. The wife, on the other hand, may decide that her husband isn't interested in the children." It is useless for a woman to ask a potential husband whether he likes children, the author insists; of course he does,—if he doesn't have to take care of them. There is, he admits, a "marginal man" who has been domesticated. He is not a full-fledged member of the Male Society, but prefers to enjoy his leisure with his wife. He will spend his spare time tinkering around the house. If he goes hunting or fishing, he may take his wife with him. Such men, the author asserts, "may not scale the heights of economic success as well as their more masculine brothers, but for many women they make ideal husbands."

Excessive use of alcohol is more a masculine than a feminine pattern in our society, and men should remember that habits which "the gang" may tolerate, will be offensive to their wives. But some other supposed differences do not appeal to Dr. LeMasters as being well-founded. He doubts if wives have any more tendency to worry than do their husbands nowadays, nor that they have as much greater craving for security as is commonly imputed to them. But he thinks there is an important difference in their attitudes toward their own background families, which may be the cause of much conflict in marriage. Men are largely emancipated from their fathers and mothers, while women are always daughters who remain closer to their parents. There is certainly some truth in this; on the other hand several recent studies have pointed to the boy, overprotected by "Mom," as a serious source of difficulty in marriage.

Summarizing, Dr. LeMasters argues that it is important for each sex to accept the other as a distinct social group, and to recognize its right to be different.

25 · Difference in Attitude toward Love and Sex *

PERCIVAL M. SYMONDS

Dr. Symonds, an educational psychologist, points out that either love or sex may be overvalued, but that it is men who typically overvalue sex and women who overvalue love. Here again is a difference in attitudes between men and women which, misunderstood, may easily lead to tensions in courtship or marriage.

Overvaluation of Love and Sex

By Men. While love tends in our present civilization to be overvalued and sex to be undervalued, in certain individuals this is not true. Some men, for instance, tend to place too strong a value on sex. To them sex

---

* Percival M. Symonds, *The Dynamics of Human Adjustment* (New York: D. Appleton-Century Company, 1946), pp. 559–560. Reprinted by permission of Appleton-Century-Crofts, Inc.

The author has the degree of Doctor of Philosophy from Columbia University, where he is a professor in Teachers College. His special fields of interest include dynamic psychology, psychology of personality and character, and parent-child relationships. Among the books that he has written in these fields are *Diagnosing Personality and Conduct, Psychology of Parent-Child Relationships, The Ego and the Self,* and *Dynamics of Psychotherapy.*

is the most exciting and important thing in the world; everything is measured in terms of its contribution to sex needs. A man may overvalue sex as a way of meeting certain anxieties and of contributing in a neurotic way to the satisfaction of other needs. First of all there is the fear many men have of not being normal, particularly of not being sexually virile. This probably is a final repository of earlier anxieties which have settled on a concern over sexual adequacy. One may suspect that the man who overvalues sex is struggling with more pervasive doubts as to his adequacy as a person. The man who overvalues sex has strong needs to surpass his male rivals. Perhaps he has had these exaggerated rivalries as a boy, and they may go back to his original rivalry with his father. The sexually ardent man is attempting to restore his wounded self-esteem. He wants to prove that he can attract women and to dispel doubts as to any weakness that he may have in this direction.

In a more specific sense, sex may be overvalued because of specific early experiences. The boy who has been sexually stimulated or seduced as an infant may be made by such experiences to have an increased need for such pleasures, particularly when he feels they are to be denied.

By Women. Women in particular are inclined to set a high premium on love experiences, and while they may also overvalue sex, the sexual aspects typically play a lesser role. The woman for whom love experiences have an exaggerated significance perhaps doubts her own love qualities. Frequently she is attempting to surpass female rivals and to prove to herself that she is more attractive and more to be desired than others in her circle. This, too, goes back to a rivalry with sisters or, in the first instance, with the mother.

Women seek love experiences for the restoration of wounded self-esteem. Love serves as a compensation for the inferior sex role they are forced to play. Since a woman does not play the aggressive sex role, she has to prove that she can attract men. Horney [1] emphasizes the need of some women to be constantly surrounded by men and build themselves an entourage as protection against the anxieties their own feelings of inferiority arouse. Another explanation sometimes adduced for the overvaluation of love by women is the fact that they have been commonly denied other pleasures and satisfactions granted to men. In the Victorian era the compartmentalization of life allotted few other interests to women than love, whereas men had the whole range of life's interests from which to draw.

Women as well as men may have been overstimulated in early child-

---

[1] Horney, Karen, "The Overevaluation of Love," *Psychoanalytic Quarterly,* 3 (1934), 605–638.

hood, and these early experiences may have forced love and sex relations to assume a place of large importance.

A little girl, for instance, who was forced by her parents to sing and dance in a tavern and was fondled by the rough visitors may have developed a taste for sensuous experiences which afterward when repressed contributed to the development of a chronic depression arising from persistent guilt.

CHAPTER 6:

Dating and Selection of a Mate

---

26 · Dating in High School and College *

RUTH SHONLE CAVAN

Dating is sometimes thought of as the beginning of courtship, and for some people it may be. But many boys and girls now begin to date while still almost children, and for them dating has—and should have—other meanings. In a well-organized progression from childhood to adulthood, courtship should closely precede marriage, being separated from it only by an engagement period. We might say that a logical sequence would be dating in the early and mid-teens, courtship in the late teens and early twenties, followed by engagement which would terminate in marriage in the early twenties (for girls) and middle twenties (for men).

Some of the characteristics of dating are given in this article as reported by students in one college. The author supplements with information from other studies and interprets the meaning of the facts secured through questionnaire surveys.

IN ORDER to obtain a close-up view of dating, the writer and three senior women [1] at a college here called Alpha College made a questionnaire survey in the fall of 1958, just prior to the Thanksgiving holiday. Alpha is a privately supported liberal arts college of approximately 420 undergraduate students, almost evenly divided between men and women. Located in the Middle West, it is typical in many ways of other small colleges in this part of the United States. The findings from the survey are similar to the results of studies made elsewhere.

---

* A biographical note on the author is given in Chapter 2, article 6.
[1] The three seniors were Mary West Foster, Brenda Peters, and Lucretia Stephens. They administered the questionnaire and made the basic tabulations and some of the interpretations. Further tabulations and interpretations have been provided by the author.

The students came primarily from middle western towns and small cities. Of those participating in the survey, only 3 per cent came from farm families. A limited variety of social class levels was represented, as judged from the occupations of the fathers. Unskilled or semiskilled occupations accounted for only 3 per cent. Occupations usually associated with middle-class status were well represented: skilled crafts and trades, 21 per cent; foremen, supervisors, and others in positions of responsibility but not in white collar positions, 11 per cent; responsible white collar positions (accountants, insurance salesmen, and so forth), 15 per cent; business proprietors and managers, usually of small or moderate concerns, 19 per cent; and professional men, 16 per cent. Twelve per cent of the students gave no reply or stated that their fathers were dead. A minority of students in Alpha College come from upper-class families, but it was not possible to distinguish them by the data secured in the survey. All foreign students were excluded, as well as those who were married.

Although Alpha is now an independent college, it was established by a Protestant denomination. Its origin is perhaps reflected in the fact that three-fourths of the students in the survey were Protestant. Sixteen per cent were Catholic, many coming from the large segments of Catholic population in the city where Alpha is located. Less than 2 per cent were Jewish. The remainder, 9 per cent, stated that they had no religion, vaguely said "other" than the above classification, or gave no reply.

The survey, then, represents primarily middle west, middle-class, Protestant young people, drawn from villages and cities of various sizes.

The survey is based on 146 schedules from men, representing 66.4 per cent of all men undergraduates, and 143 schedules from women, representing 72.6 per cent.

Background of High-School Dating

For most students, college dating rests upon some dating experience in high school and for a few on a still longer span of dating.

Dating for the Majority. By the time Alpha students were in seventh grade, a minority had begun to date: 19 per cent of the men and 16 per cent of the women. Sometime during the ninth grade, half of each sex had become involved in dating. The tenth grade introduced many more to the dating stage of adolescence, bringing the total who had begun to date to 69 per cent of the boys and 74 per cent of the girls. Seventeen per cent of the boys and 12 per cent of the girls began to date in the last two years of high school. Thus entrance to college found only 8 per cent of both boys and girls who had not begun to date; another 6 per cent of each group failed to reply to the question, perhaps because they did not want to admit that they had not dated in high school. If we make this assumption, then 14 per cent of students entered Alpha College without dating experience. Both these students and the very early daters who began to date by seventh grade were the minorities, the exceptions. The general pattern was to begin dating between grades eight and eleven.

'Some students who had begun to date in junior or senior high school did not maintain the practice throughout high school, or dated only irregularly, as shown by a question regarding type of dating in the senior year of high school. Among those who dated in the senior year, playing the field (or intermittent dating) was the dominant pattern. Sixty-one per cent of boys and 57 per cent of girls played the field; the remainder steady-dated.

What Is Learned in High-School Dating. The Alpha survey did not query students as to what they felt they had learned from high-school dating. However, from other sources we know that at its best teen-age dating serves certain important functions in preparing boys and girls for adulthood and wise choice of a marriage partner; when unregulated, it can lead boys and girls into difficult situations.

Robert J. Havighurst, a specialist in human development, has classified the learning needs of adolescents into the following types:

1. Achieving new and more mature relations with age-mates of both sexes
2. Achieving a masculine or feminine social role
3. Accepting one's physique and using the body effectively
4. Achieving emotional independence of parents and other adults
5. Achieving assurance of economic independence
6. Selecting and preparing for an occupation
7. Preparing for marriage and family life
8. Developing intellectual skills and concepts necessary for civic competence
9. Desiring and achieving socially responsible behavior
10. Acquiring a set of values and an ethical system as a guide to behavior [2]

Of this list, dating can make a contribution to all except items 5, 6, and 8. Far from being only a social activity, teen-age dating opens the way to development of masculine and feminine concepts of self, gives practice in talking to and carrying on activities jointly with members of the opposite sex, and is an excellent field in which to develop responsible independence from parents.

However, other studies show that some adolescents are not able to make use of dating for their own personal development but are carried away by the emotional reactions and attachments that come with dating. Some rush

---

[2] Robert J. Havighurst, *Human Development and Education* (New York: Longmans, Green & Company, 1953), pp. 111–158.

into early marriage on the crest of a wave of romanticism, regardless of whether they are economically and educationally prepared for adulthood and the responsibilities of marriage. Some girls find themselves pregnant without even a hurried marriage. Other young people, although they do not marry during high school, are in love or engaged when they graduate and perhaps turn aside from the college education they had previously planned in order to work for a year or two and then marry. Still others enter college burdened with emotional attachments to someone from whom they are separated by many miles without possibility of dates.

Fragility of High-School Dating. For many students high-school dating is a matter of going steady with one person for a few weeks or months and then "breaking up" and forming another alliance. Among Freshmen at Alpha, queried in late November, 29 per cent had broken a previous relationship, in almost all cases steady dating. The hit-or-miss relationship of playing the field was not included. Two-thirds of the breaks had come within the previous six months, that is, between graduation from high school and the first major college holiday—Thanksgiving.

Values of High-School Dating. Possibilities for personal growth toward maturity and the acquisition of responsible social relationships may be found through high-school dating. But they are not automatically inherent in dating. Dating may also lead to complicated emotional problems. Much depends upon how the boy or girl views dating and how he chooses to use it. One thing that is certain is that high-school dating involves many changes of partners.

College Dating

College dating is similar in many ways to high-school dating. It differs in one important aspect—sometime during the college years young people arrive at the age when marriage seems desirable and suitable.

Transition to College Dating. Although Freshman women at Alpha College often seemed worried about finding dates, the survey shows that during the first ten weeks of the Freshman year, most students, both men and women, were dating. Of the 70 Freshman men answering the question about their current type of dating, 4 per cent said they had never dated,[3] 7 per cent that they were not dating at the time of the survey, and 89 per cent that they were engaged in some type of dating. The majority, 56 per cent, were playing the field; 23 per cent were going steady, and 10 per cent were pinned or engaged. Among the 68 Freshman girls, 1 per cent had never

---

[3] The percentages who had never dated given earlier refer to students from all four college classes, the present figures to Freshmen only.

dated, 12 per cent were not dating at the time of the survey, 69 per cent were playing the field, 12 per cent were going steady, and 6 per cent were pinned or engaged. Although there was little difference in percentage of boys and girls who were dating, many more girls than boys had not advanced beyond playing the field.

Some further analysis showed that more men than women students lived in the city in which Alpha is located and apparently carried over into their college years steady-dating relationships with town girl friends who were not necessarily attending college. Some of the concern of Freshman girls over their inability to establish dating relationships probably arose from this fact. With almost equal numbers of boys and girls in college, the continuation by boys of town dating created an imbalance and a shortage of college men for dates.

During the four college years some changes occurred in the dating pattern. Playing the field and going steady decreased to some extent; being pinned or engaged tended to increase. Nevertheless, the dominant pattern throughout was playing the field, and in every class from Freshman to Senior small percentages had never dated or were not dating at the time of the survey.

Although it is usually thought that girls strive to become engaged by the time they graduate from college, the survey shows that slightly more women than men had trouble finding dating partners and slightly more men than women were pinned or engaged at the time of the survey. One possible reason has already been mentioned: more men than women students lived in the college city and hence had opportunity for wider contacts; they were not limited as many women students seemed to be to contacts made on the campus. There are other probable reasons. First, the classification by occupations of the fathers showed that slightly more men than women had fathers in the ranks of the skilled trades; slightly more women than men had fathers who were professional men, proprietors, or managers. The men students were moving into the social status of the fathers of the girls, but were still thought of in terms of their fathers' occupations rather than of their own future ones. And girls as a rule prefer to date someone of their own or a higher social status. Second, men and women did not fall in equal proportions into the two major religious groups, Protestant and Catholic. From studies in other colleges and universities it is known that many students desire not only to marry but to date persons of their own religious background. Third, other studies have shown that the most favorable ratio of the sexes for dating by women is to have a reasonable excess of men. At Alpha men and women were almost equal in number at the time of the survey. Sometimes a nearby men's college will alleviate a shortage of men but such a college was not available. Although no one of these factors was conspicuous at Alpha College, each was unfavorable for dating by women.

Where Dating Partners Were Met. For both men and women, the most favorable places to become acquainted were, in order of frequency of mention, the class room, social events, the student union, and church. Girls found that employment created some opportunities for dates; men did not find employment an easy avenue, perhaps because the part-time employment of men students tends to be heavy work carried out among men, whereas girls often have sales or office jobs that bring them into contact with men whom they regard as desirable dates. Interest groups, committees, the favorite student hangout in town, and blind dating provided some dates but no one of these accounted for a large proportion. In general, by far the largest proportion of dates grew out of contacts easily available to all students and socially approved by students and deans. However, in spite of the apparent openness of opportunities for contacts, a fourth of the total body of women participating in the survey and slightly over a fifth of the men felt that there were inadequate opportunities to meet future dating partners. The suggestion may be made that the difficulty may not be the simple lack of opportunity to make contacts but perhaps some difficulty in meeting the exact type of person students desired to date in terms of social class or religion, or some deficiency on the part of the student in making friendly contacts and developing a potential dating situation.

What Dating Partners Do. Attending motion pictures was the most popular form of date at Alpha College, a fourth of both men and women having checked it as one of the things they did most often. Surveys in other colleges also indicate the popularity of motion pictures. College dances, a favorite also in other colleges, came second for men and third for women, with parties in someone's home as third and second respectively for men and women. Auto riding was also popular as a pastime.

The comments of a senior woman on the favorite types of dates reveal some probable reasons for their popularity.

> Movies are an available activity that a couple may attend without careful planning, and they do not require group participation. They are a means of receiving entertainment without giving entertainment.
>
> School dances are attended by a high percentage [17 per cent] of women because they are not dependent on local men for dates; they may invite partners from other campuses or from their home town or accept a blind date. Also, school dances are a publicized school interest; participation is thus stimulated.
>
> The town offers little commercial entertainment for students other than movies and bowling alleys. A city ordinance prohibits dancing in an establish-

ment that sells intoxicating beverages. Therefore dancing must be carried on either at school-sponsored functions or in private homes.[4]

A larger number of underclass women than of upperclass women attend parties in homes. This may indicate that the men whom underclass women date have more interests in common and are more interested in group activities—or that they have less money for dates than do the men dated by upperclass women.

How Many Dates. The most common frequency of dating was once or twice a week. More men than women dated in this pattern: 46 per cent of men and 37 per cent of women. The second most common frequency of dates was once or twice a month, with about a fifth of both men and women indicating that this was their most common dating pattern. Approximately 18 per cent of both men and women dated more than twice a week. Twenty-three per cent of women but only 17 per cent of men dated less than once a month or had not dated at all in college. The tendency of women to date less than men has already been discussed.

Studies in other colleges also show that the most frequent occurrence of dates is once or twice a week. Usually, however, larger percentages of students date more frequently and fewer date only at weekly intervals than at Alpha College. The comment might be made that students who attend college primarily for social life and husband-hunting or wife-finding prefer institutions with the tradition of frequent dating; but it is also true that students who regard college as a unique adventure in education may find constant dating an obstacle to their primary goal.

Relative Status of Partners. Each student was asked several questions under the heading, "Please check the qualities that you would like to find in husband or wife." We have no way of knowing to what extent their replies will actually influence their marriages (few of the students were engaged), but they do indicate certain preconceived ideas about suitable partners, for dating perhaps as well as for marriage.

Men preferred mates (and no doubt dates) who were younger than themselves, according to the replies of 53 per cent; their second most frequent choice, made by 30 per cent, was for a mate the same age as themselves; 5 per cent specified an older mate and 12 per cent did not reply. the preferences of women students did not coordinate well with those of the men. Seventy-seven per cent of the women desired a man older than themselves, only 15 per cent husbands of the same age, and 1 per cent

---

[4] A number of clubs in the city each year sponsor dances to which tickets are sold to nonmembers. Many churches have young people's recreation of various types. It is perhaps indicative of the schism between students and townspeople that students are unaware of these off-campus opportunities or do not feel free to attend.

younger husbands; 7 per cent did not reply. When these choices are applied to dating, they suggest that Freshman girls would look longingly at upperclass men, some of whom would be happy to date them. Upperclass girls would have to bide their time until they could meet men already graduated from college. Although upperclass men would often be content to date underclass women, a third would prefer girls of their own age. Freshman men desiring a more youthful partner would be at a disadvantage unless they turned to high-school girls. Some of the tabulations made by college class suggest that these handicaps related to age preferences exist, but the numbers in each class are too small for exact analysis.

In general, men preferred mates with the same amount of education that they had. This was the choice of 81 per cent; 7 per cent would prefer less well educated mates, and 3 per cent ones with better education; 9 per cent did not reply. Women, however, leaned toward a husband with more education, this being the preference of almost two-thirds of the women, with no woman wanting a husband with less education. Approximately a third preferred a mate with the same amount of education. Seven per cent of the women made no reply. Again there is lack of coordination between what men and women want in a mate.

Preference for degree of intelligence followed the same pattern as did preference in educational status. Almost 80 per cent of the men preferred a mate with the same intellectual power as themselves. Women were more evenly divided between choice of a mate with more intelligence than their own and with the same degree of intelligence. A few men and women expressed no preference.

Women are commonly thought to be eager for equality with men. But the preferences of Alpha students show that men lean more toward equality than women and that women tend to desire a status subordinate to their husbands. Some women, of course, desire equality and it may be hoped that they will find dating partners and mates with similar desires for equality. We may also hope that girls desiring to be subordinate will find husbands who wish to be superior to their wives. But the matching is not likely to come out evenly, according to the percentages. Some equality-minded men are going to have to select mates from the subordinate-minded women.

The differences in preferences raise some interesting speculations. Are young men shifting from their traditional superior status because they realize that economically they need the help of an intelligent, well-educated, and mature mate? Are some girls shrinking from accepting the degree of responsibility implied? Are men looking for intellectual companionship in their wives? Do men anticipate extended military service in the future which would remove them from their families and place responsibility temporarily in the hands of their wives, who would need to be well equipped to handle it? Are girls hesitant to face the reality of such a future? Or are men less traditional in attitude than women—more willing to give up their old prerogatives, whereas many women still cling to the traditional desire to be sheltered? To these questions the survey does not supply an answer.

Changing Dating Partners

Playing the field involves ephemeral relationships. It implies that each date fulfills itself and leaves no obligations. If the two people happen to want to date again, they are free to do so. However, if they did not enjoy the first date they need never date again. Or they may like variety in dating and go from partner to partner, usually within a restricted social circle, off and on dating an earlier partner. Change of partners then is part of the game of playing the field. The skills involved do not pertain to holding fast to one partner, but to having enough potential partners always to be reasonably sure of a date for at least the major social events and preferably for the weekly movie date as well.

Steady dating, pinning, and engagements are more stable relationships, each with certain obligations of loyalty between the partners and personal consideration for each other's well-being. The relationship is usually well known to parents and friends. Hence a break is likely to be more or less disconcerting. If the break is mutually agreed upon, the chagrin may be slight; nevertheless there is likely to be some feeling of letdown. If the break is at the hands of one partner and not desired by the other, the "jilted" one may feel inferior and rejected. Friends must be told and may take sides, condemning one and admiring the other. Unattached persons may move in quickly to capture the attention of one of the recently detached persons.

Such breaking of steady dating is common practice. For example, a study of serious dating at the University of Wisconsin showed that half of the students had gone with two or more steady partners—and the number no doubt increased before marriage was reached.[5]

Frequent reshuffling of partners takes place even at the engagement stage. A study of 1000 engagements made in the late 1930's showed that at the time of the study 24 per cent of the men and 36 per cent of the women had previously been engaged to some other partner.[6] In addition, 15 per

[5] R. D. Herman, "The 'Going Steady' Complex: A Re-examination," *Marriage and Family Living*, 17 (1955), 36–40.

[6] Ernest W. Burgess and Paul Wallin, *Engagement and Marriage* (J. B. Lippincott Company, 1953), p. 273.

cent of the couples later broke the engagements in which they were partners at the time of the study.

Among the students surveyed at Alpha College, 52 per cent of the
men and 51 per cent of the women had broken one or more dating relationships. The students were queried specifically only about the last break.
Of these, 87 per cent were steady dating, 6 per cent were pinning, and 7
per cent were engagements.

Recovery from Broken Relationships. Theoretically, good recovery would
be characterized by a more or less neutral attitude toward the former partner, with retention of neither love nor violent dislike. Neutral feelings
would open the way for the person to develop affection for a new partner
unhampered by a residue of emotion from a relationship that had ended.
Such a neutral state was reached by 78 per cent of the girls and 83 per cent
of the men, sometimes within a month after the break occurred. These
students were roughly divided into three groups, who "felt some attraction,"
were indifferent to the past partner, or had fallen in love with someone
else. Men were slightly more likely than girls to feel some attraction but
the difference was slight. In contrast were the 10 or 11 per cent who still
loved the former partner and the 6 or 7 per cent who disliked or alternately
liked and disliked the ex-partner. Even after the lapse of six or seven months,
some young people felt they still loved the former companion.

The Course of Steady Dating. Following a technique used earlier by
Professors Kirkpatrick and Caplow,[7] we gave Alpha students an opportunity to check a small graph showing the trend of their affairs of the heart
from beginning to end, or of drawing on a blank grid their own personal
pattern of emotional reactions.

The Kirkpatrick-Caplow study was made in 1940 with 141 men and 258
women at the University of Minnesota and covered all broken love affairs.
The Alpha study applied only to the most recent broken affair, chiefly
steady dating. Most of the Minnesota students began their love affairs
from a feeling of indifference or mild attraction, built up their feelings
to a point of deep attraction or love which lasted a long or short period of
time, and then experienced a decline in feeling to approximately the same
level of feeling at which the relationship began. Seventy-six per cent of
the male love affairs and 68 per cent of the love affairs of women fell into
this pattern, giving an indication of good recovery. The remainder of the
affairs carried the students through slashing ups and downs in feeling, some-

---

[7] Clifford Kirkpatrick and Theodore Caplow, "Emotional Trends in the Courtship
Experience of College Students as Expressed by Graphs with Some Observations on
Methodological Implications," *American Sociological Review*, 10 (October, 1945), 619–
626.

times repeatedly from love to dislike, or ended with the student still loving or having grown to hate the partner.

Alpha students, reporting on their last break only, fitted into this pattern of going from indifference or mild attraction to deep attraction or love and back to relative indifference in only 47 per cent of the dating affairs of the men and 51 per cent of those of the women. While most of the others began with indifference or attraction they went through violent alternations of love and indifference or dislike or ended with strong feelings of love or dislike. Nevertheless, as already stated, about four-fifths of the students quieted their feelings within a few months of the break.

Practical Suggestions for the Dating Student

On the basis of the foregoing survey of one college and some comparisons with similar surveys, what generalizations seem safe to make; what practical suggestions may students find useful?

1. In view of the high percentage of students who enter college with three or more years of dating experience, students who did not settle firmly into dating during high school may wish to give some thought to reasons why they did not follow the common pattern. This question is pertinent in view of the part dating plays in mate selection and the tendency in the United States to marry young. Were the nondaters so completely devoted to studying that they seemed to have no time for social affairs? Although an occasional scholarly student does so devote himself, often the absorption in studying arises as a defense against excessive shyness or helps the student avoid acknowledging that he has some personality qualities that prevent popularity. Review of his personal traits is a good thing for the nondater.

The desire to date should not lead a student into a frantic and direct effort to get a date. Since dating is a social engagement, the handicap is probably some simple one that may be interfering with all kinds of social relationships. The girl who seems never to be invited on a date and the boy who cannot bring himself to invite a girl—or who is always turned down—would be well advised to examine his personal skills for attracting and making friends. When these personal qualities and skills are in good order, making friends and securing dates may follow without much difficulty.

2. The heavy dater may face other problems. Excessive dating may be a "flight from reality" as much as excessive studying. Through constant dating the student may avoid the onerous tasks of writing a term paper, pre-

paring daily assignments, carrying part-time work, serving on committees, and so forth. Each student reaches a point when the time spent in dating interferes with the primary objectives of college. These objectives are the development of the mind and the acquisition of the best of world culture. During the college years the student should also complete his growth into adult responsibilities, which usually involves devotion of a considerable amount of time to campus committees and boards. Excessive dating should not be allowed to interfere with education and development toward adulthood.

3. Dating is sometimes difficult or unsatisfactory because of the make-up of the student body. A number of these characteristics and their effect on dating have been discussed. Students often desire to date only those of their own religious faith, nationality, or social class level. Either they do not enjoy people who are different from themselves or they fear they may fall in love and do not want to marry outside their familiar groups. It is true that studies show that marriages between people of like religious and cultural backgrounds have a somewhat better chance of success than marriages that bring into the home wide differences that must be reconciled. However, a distinction exists between social dating and courtship. Mingling with those of other backgrounds may widen one's cultural knowledge and enrich one's appreciation for elements of culture not found within one's own groups.

4. Girls who wish to be subordinate to their future husbands should review the implications of such a marriage, as should men who wish a wife subordinate to themselves. The general trend for many years has been toward equality of opportunity between men and women in all areas, education, occupations, control of property, right to vote, with some exceptions right to hold public office, and others. It is true that not all women have used these opportunities to the fullest. In marriage as judged by age, amount of education, and degree of intelligence approximately a third to a half of women students desire to be subordinate to their husbands.

For many reasons women should not seek to shelter themselves behind their husbands. Men are not always at hand to stand between their wives and the realities of life. At present compulsory military service removes many young men for a few years. In time of war men are removed for longer periods of time, during which their wives must carry the full burden of family management and child rearing, often under the tension of fear for the husband's safety. A second reason is that on the average women live longer than men. The protected woman is poorly equipped to face the adjustment to widowhood. A third reason is that married women now form the only untapped labor pool in the United States. Expansion of industry as well as increased production if required for military needs must depend more and more on married women as workers. At work, women must stand on their own merits and cannot depend upon their husbands to shelter them. Looking to the type of marriage needed now and in the near future, young men and women alike need to revise their conceptions of relative status of husband and wife based on age, education, and intelligence.

5. Both men and women college students need to develop skills for ending dating relationships as painlessly as possible for themselves and their partners. Many dating relationships are entered into on a more or less temporary basis for the summer only or for the current school year. Pinning also sometimes has a temporary quality, applying only to the periods when college is in session but not applying to vacations when the two are separated and must be free to date others or forego most social life. Even engagements are often treated as a trial period for deciding whether the two are sufficiently compatible for marriage. These shifting relationships are a way of sifting or screening partners until the "right" one is found. The fact that the partner may be changed is also a safeguard against premature falling in love, development of intense emotional attachments, and possibly hasty marriages. A succession of partners is also a way to tide one over until the time comes educationally and financially for marriage.

Some safeguards against devastating emotional reactions when steady dating ends may be suggested:

Acceptance of the relationship as of a temporary nature and retention of fluid social contacts outside the dating relationship so that the whole of one's social life is not tied up with the dating partner. The wider contacts will tend to spread one's interests and also make transition to a new dating partner easier when the first relationship begins to wear thin.

Avoidance of falling in love until signs of love are evident in the partner and also until the time approaches when marriage may be considered as a sensible reality. Our philosophy of romantic love as the only basis for marriage sometimes leads unsophisticated young people into frantic love affairs with the wrong type of person for successful marriage or at a time when youthfulness, incomplete education, and lack of finances make marriage a very precarious procedure.

Watchfulness for signs of restlessness in oneself or one's partner and acceptance of this indication that it is time to allow the relationship to fade out, preferably by mutual agreement. Continued love or strong dislike after the dating has ended are not only uncomfortable but also signs that the function of steady dating has not been grasped by the person. Indifference or mild attraction (impersonal friendliness) are more appropriate.

As a final note, dating, which developed without planning or guidance as a form of social life for young people, now can be manipulated and used to accomplish important steps in the process of maturing as well as to work one's way through the group of possible partners to find the compatible one for marriage. This conception of dating may not sound romantic, but it is conducive to successful choice of a mate.

27 · Boys, Some of You Rate Low at Dance, So the Girls Report *

MOLLY POTKIN

What impression do teenage daters make on their companions? To find out, Molly, who writes the teen column for the Chicago Sunday *Tribune*, queried high-school girls on their opinion of boys. This article and the one that follows show the efforts of boys and girls in the early dating stages to find out what is acceptable to their partners. They are overly concerned with establishing their dating status and hence are often awkward, backward, or forward in their behavior. In time they will learn how to handle their bodies and their emotions and will become comfortable and agreeable partners. Most college students have passed through this stage, but some still find dating an ordeal.

To ENCOURAGE the social graces, the female sophomores at Tuley High gave a dance in the school gymnasium for the male sophomores. The girls prepared the food, arranged for the music, got the room in order and did all the things considered proper for a school dance. The dance was a success and out of it came these reports on the types of boys seen at high school dances:

1. *The determined dancer.* He's like a bull in a china shop. Dances as if he's driving a truck. Pushes his 105-pound partner around as if she's a Notre Dame tackle. Heaven help her if she resists. Eventually winds up with his

---

* Chicago Sunday *Tribune* (June 1, 1958), Part 7, p. 5. Reprinted by permission of the author.

The writer of this humorous but pointed account is a Chicagoan who works primarily with and for children and adolescents. Starting as an artist she branched off into creating and drawing puzzles for children and in time became writer of the teen column of the Chicago Sunday *Tribune*. She has run artcraft classes at different teen clubs and has worked as a volunteer for several institutions for children.

partner as the only couple on the floor, the others having left before they were knocked down.

2. *The hungry dancer.* Enters the room, looks around, makes sure he sees all the girls, waits till the music starts, then casually sneaks over to the buffet table. Stays there for the better part of the evening (and the food), then strolls over to the girls to thank them for a wonderful time, assuring them he loves dances and would like to be invited again.

3. *The dance enthusiast.* He really loves dances. *Always* goes to dances. Would rather dance than eat—and does just that. He's on the floor from the moment the music starts until the last note. He's going to dance if it kills him (or his partner). Doesn't even stop for a coke. When he sees the tired, dreamy-eyed look of his partner, he knows it's one of contentment, and murmurs happily: "Isn't dancing fun?"

4. *The singer.* Loves dancing because he's so fond of music, and lets you know it. Starts humming at first, then singing words to the songs. Becomes progressively louder until you suddenly find yourself dancing to the music he's singing rather than to what the orchestra is playing (they're seldom the same tune).

5. *The show-off.* Knows all the latest jitterbug steps and does them (even if his partner doesn't). Never tires. He must get *all* his exercise this way. Some day he'll probably be a professional dancer because he gets plenty of exercise now by winding up as a solo. (The girl got tired long ago.)

6. *The conversational ball of fire.* Behaves as though he hasn't seen you in months and keeps talking while dancing. Wants to know what you've been doing the last few weeks—in detail. If you discourage this talk, he'll tell you what *he's* been doing.

7. *The beginner.* Explains that he doesn't often go to dances, but as long as he's here he may as well do it right, so he asks you to teach him the different steps—right on the dance floor. (When he learns to dance he'll invariably take every other girl except you to a dance.)

28 · *Hey, Girls! Look at How the Fellows Rate You* *

MOLLY POTKIN

Girls are not the only ones who rate their dates. The boys of a large Chicago high school were able to place their girl friends into seven categories.

* Chicago Sunday *Tribune* (April 6, 1958), Part 7, p. 5. Reprinted by permission of the author.
Information on the author may be found in connection with the preceding article.

HERE they are:

1. *The possessive female.* Superintends a quick reshuffling of your necktie, hair, and so forth, when you call for her. Decides, when she's altered your appearance, that you're ready to go out with her. At the dance or party she treats you like a yo-yo. She sends you over to talk to people—and yanks you back before you can even say hello.

She suggests that you might want to dance with her girl friend, but when you try to, you find that you can't break the half-nelson she's held on you all evening. You belong to her—brother! Invariably, on the way home she'll ask you why you don't mingle with other people at a party.

2. *The "naive" one.* Sweet and simple—O, yeah? Can't do a thing herself, not even walk a block. So you find yourself in a cab. You make all the decisions and, of course, any restaurant is all right with her. She just hasn't been around enough to know what to suggest.

You suddenly find that the headwaiter at the expensive eating place (how you got there you'll *never* know) calls her by her first name. After she's through ordering you're lucky to have bus fare left. And when you get her home—she coyly shuts the door in your face, to the soulful tune of—"It's been fun—let's do it again."

3. *The social one.* Spends the entire evening at the party talking to her girl friends—and wants you standing in attendance every minute. If you dare leave for a moment she sulks. If you dance with another girl, because your date is too busy to dance with you, she's already looking for someone else to take her home because she's *never* been so insulted in all her life.

4. *The social one (type B).* Also spends the entire evening at the party talking to her girl friends, only she's nice—she turns you loose first. By the time the party is over she can't even remember who her escort was. You have to reintroduce yourself—jog her memory a bit—and all the way home she tells you how she's enjoyed the evening with you.

5. *The femme fatale.* This gal is really a menace. Very attractive. Dresses beautifully and with much more flash than any other girl at the party (she makes sure of it). As soon as you get to the party, she goes to work—seeing how many men she can gather around her at one time. Presently you find yourself playing three-fourths of a ghost with five unescorted girls. Usually the words you select have to do with mayhem and gentle arts of destruction.

6. *The cautious one.* She trusts no man. When you're driving she sits so far away from you that you fear she's going to fall between the seat and the door. (You'll notice that this type always keeps one hand on the door handle when she's in a car with you.) She's "on guard" every minute. If you innocently raise your hand—maybe to scratch your ear or adjust your hat, her arms shoot up in front of her "on defense."

Always manages to bring a third (or fourth, fifth, or sixth) person along so that any "liberty" you might try to take is forestalled by a battery of chaperons. By the time the evening is over and you've said good night, without even a handshake at the door, you're beginning to wonder if maybe you shouldn't turn yourself in to the police as a criminal type.

7. *The sophisticate.* Quite a "comedown," she lets you know, to go out on this date with you. Nothing you do or suggest measures up to her past performances. But she goes to the party with you—and of course, eats more, dances more, and has a better time than anyone else. On the way home she lets you know what a meager and unsatisfactory evening it really was.

8. *The "honest" one.* A real gabber—and the things she says: "I'm only going out with you because my boy friend is at Fort Lewis and I won't see him till December." This loyalty doesn't interfere with her letting you spend all your money on her.

She's also the type who tells you about her hundreds of dates, including visits to the Pump Room, the Well, the Watering Trough and I suppose any other spot where your spirits can be thoroughly dampened. She'll also tell you about the school's football hero who spent the evening at her house last night, neglecting to add that he was visiting her brother.

29 · Do "Opposites Attract" or Does "Like Marry Like"? *

THOMAS AND VIRGINIA KTSANES

This article will require and merits very careful reading. In the preliminary paragraphs the authors discuss what is known about similarity (homogamy)

* From "The Theory of Complementary Needs in Mate-Selection," by Thomas and Virginia Ktsanes, pp. 435–453 of *Selected Studies in Marriage and the Family* by Robert F. Winch and Robert McGinnis (Editors). Reprinted by permission of Henry Holt and Company, Inc., Copyright 1953.

The theory of complementary needs was first set forth by Robert F. Winch. Dr. Winch, whose Doctor of Philosophy degree is from the University of Chicago, is Professor of Sociology at Northwestern University. For a number of years he has carried on careful research on the basic factors that operate in mate selection. His latest publication in this field is a book entitled *Mate Selection*. He is also author of *The Modern Family*.

Thomas Ktsanes received the degree of Doctor of Philosophy from Northwestern University and is now Associate Professor of Sociology at Tulane University; Virginia Ktsanes has the degree of Master of Arts from Northwestern University. Both the Ktsanes were associated with Professor Winch in the study of complementary needs from its beginning and carried out the interviewing of the men and women who were the subjects of the study. They are coauthors of a number of articles in professional sociological journals.

between husband and wife. They show that people tend to marry those with the same or similar occupational, educational, economic, and religious backgrounds. For a further discussion of religious likeness, see article 60, where students' opinions on interfaith marriages are given in detail. Homogamy, even when it exists, does not account for the individual choice. It simply defines the group within which each person will seek for a mate on personal grounds.

The main part of this article is a discussion of one important factor in the personal choice of a mate. The hypothesis is set forth that people love, and tend to marry, those who fulfill their needs. The perfect love match would be one in which each fulfilled the needs of the other while at the same time having his own needs fulfilled by the other. It follows that people, perhaps unconsciously, tend to fall in love with and marry those who gratify their needs. Research carried out after this article was written confirmed this hypothesis in part—mutual need gratification was one among other factors operating in mate selection.

The article ends with a long case, carefully analyzed to show how a husband and wife met each other's needs, while at the same time receiving satisfaction for their own needs.

Who Marries Whom?

The question of "who marries whom" is one which has aroused "common sense" as well as scientific interest. The common sense answer is paradoxical, for while everyone knows that "like marries like" and that "birds of a feather flock together," it is also equally clear that "opposites attract." As is frequently the case in folk wisdom, both assertions are probably true depending upon the characteristics considered. If by "like" one means similarity in regard to a variety of social characteristics such as ethnic origin, religion, occupation, residential location, and social status, then indeed the view that mates tend to be similar seems correct. If, on the other hand, "like" is used to denote similarity in a variety of psychological attitudes, traits, tendencies, or needs, then the situation is by no means clear. This being the case, it is in order to take a brief look at some studies which have attempted to answer the question of the degree to which homogamy or heterogamy prevails in marital choice. The tendency of persons to select mates who have certain characteristics similar to their own is called homogamy or assortative mating. Conversely, heterogamy refers to the selection of mates who are opposite or are merely different. We shall begin with a brief review of the research literature on homogamy. Later we shall present the theory of complementary needs as a special type of heterogamy.

Homogamy in Social Characteristics. Interest in the problem of assortative mating is probably an analogical extension out of the field of biology where for lower animals there seems to be a trend toward similarity in size and vitality. On the human level also there is some slight evidence for homogamy in physical characteristics.[1] With human beings, however, physical similarity has not been the principal concern. Most work on assortative mating has concerned a variety of social characteristics. We shall now briefly examine some of this evidence.

In an early study by Marvin [2] it was noted that there was a greater than chance tendency for marriages to occur between persons with similar occupations. More recently Centers [3] has pointed out that there tend to be no wide differences in the occupational statuses of spouses. Burgess and Wallin [4] have shown that there is homogamy in educational level. Further, basing their conclusions on the ratings by the couple of the social status of their parents and on their report of the present income of their fathers, Burgess and Wallin state ". . . it is clear that there is a considerable excess over chance for young people to fall in love and become engaged to those in the same social and economic class." [5] Kennedy [6] has indicated that there is a strong trend toward homogamy in regard to religious affiliation and a tendency, though less marked, toward homogamy in ethnic origin.

Bossard,[7] in a study repeated by subsequent researchers, showed that people usually select their mates from those who live nearby. In Bossard's classic study more than half of the marriages in his sample were between persons living within twenty blocks of each other. However, the effect of this factor of mere spatial propinquity must not be over-emphasized for it overlaps with the factors discussed before. The various ecological areas of the city are characterized by heavy concentrations of certain socioeconomic classes, ethnic and religious groups; and these groups as noted above tend to be endogamous.[8]

---

[1] In Mary Schooley, "Personality Resemblance Among Married Couples," *Journal of Abnormal and Social Psychology*, 31 (1936), 340–47, some low positive correlations were found to exist between mates on height, weight, visual acuity, and appearance.

[2] Donald Marvin, "Occupational Propinquity as a Factor in Marriage Selection," *Journal of the American Statistical Association*, 16 (1918–19), 131–50.

[3] Richard Centers, "Marital Selection and Occupational Strata," *American Journal of Sociology*, 54 (1949), 530–35.

[4] E. W. Burgess and Paul Wallin, "Homogamy in Social Characteristics," *American Journal of Sociology*, 49 (1943), 109–24.

[5] *Ibid.*, p. 114.

[6] R. J. R. Kennedy, "Single or Triple Melting-Pot? Intermarriage Trends in New Haven, 1870–1950," *American Journal of Sociology*, 63 (1952), 56–59.

[7] J. H. S. Bossard, "Residential Propinquity as a Factor in Marriage Selection," *American Journal of Sociology*, 38 (1932), 219–24.

[8] Endogamy refers to marriage within the group.

In summary, the studies reviewed indicate that persons who marry tend to be similar in regard to a variety of characteristics such as social class, ethnic background, educational level, religion, occupation, and area of residence. However, these findings actually bear little direct relationship to our problem. They are of some interest in that they give us a notion of the limits within which another principle of selection may operate. As we interpret them, these factors tend to define a field of eligibles from which a mate may be selected on psychological grounds.

Homogamy in Psychological Characteristics. Psychological characteristics which have been studied with respect to homogamy include a long and varied list. Characteristics investigated by means of "paper-and-pencil" personality inventories include neuroticism, dominance, self-sufficiency, etc. One early study [9] found moderately high correlations between mates on neurotic tendency and dominance. Burgess and Wallin [10] in their more recent study of 1000 engaged couples found homogamy in regard to a few traits. Their correlations, however, were of a rather low order and are therefore not too convincing. In regard to various "content" attitudes, *e. g.,* religious and political attitudes, there is some evidence for similarity.[11] These similarities, however, may have developed after marriage. The results in this area are thus considerably short of being definitive. Stagner in reviewing the studies on homogamy in psychological characteristics has pointed out that correlations indicating similarity are higher with respect to intellectual, interest, and attitude scores, but that measures of temperament do not show this tendency as clearly.[12] The measures of temperament referred to by Stagner are those estimates of various traits such as dominance, self-sufficiency, etc., which are arrived at by means of paper-and-pencil tests. Confidence in paper-and-pencil tests is vitiated by the fact that subjects can "fake" their responses and thereby create what they regard as favorable impressions.[13] When we try to get behind the picture of personality which the subject wants us to accept, and more particularly, when we want to understand a subject's motivational patterns of which he may be only partially aware, we find no systematic research on the question

---

[9] E. L. Hoffeditz, "Personality Resemblances Among Married Couples," *Journal of Abnormal and Social Psychology,* 5 (1934), 214–27.

[10] E. W. Burgess and Paul Wallin, "Homogamy in Personality Characteristics," *Journal of Abnormal and Social Psychology,* 39 (1944), 475–81.

[11] T. M. Newcomb and G. Svehla, "Intra-family Relationships in Attitude," *Sociometry,* 1 (1937), 180–205.

[12] Ross Stagner, *Psychology of Personality,* New York, McGraw-Hill, 1948, p. 387.

[13] *Cf.* Albert Ellis, "The Validity of Marriage Prediction Tests" [in Robert F. Winch and Robert McGinnis (eds.), *Selected Studies in Marriage and the Family,* New York, Holt, 1953], pp. 494–95.

of homogamous *vs.* heterogamous mate-selection.[14] In the absence of experimental evidence various writers have been theorizing on this problem.

Toward a More Adequate Theory

Ideas about types of harmonic intermeshing of needs have been suggested by various theorists and researchers. Many of these owe a debt to Freud, who made a distinction between "anaclitic" and "narcissistic" love.[15] By the anaclitic type Freud meant a love which was expressed in attitudes of self-derogation and reverential admiration toward the love-object. In this type of love one is dependent on the loved one toward whom he can express his need to revere and admire. Narcissistic love is essentially self-love but the narcissist has a great need to be admired by others as well as by himself. Thus in his formulation of the narcissistic-anaclitic typology, Freud posited a type of complementary relationship, *i.e.*, the dependent person who has the need to revere and admire and is attracted to the narcissistic person who has a great need to be admired and receive adulation.

Following the suggestion that persons with complementary psychic make-ups are attracted to each other, several psychoanalysts have proposed that matching occurs between those who are complementarily neurotic.[16] According to this hypothesis, for example, a dependent male with unresolved emotional ties to his mother would be attracted to an aggressive and dominant woman burdened with conflicts over her sex role. As a general theory of mate-selection, however, this literature is inadequate because the writers have explained attraction only in terms of the highly individualized neurotic patterns of their patients. What we are seeking is a theory which will be generally applicable, not merely to Freud's anaclitic and narcissistic types of persons, not merely to dependent people who marry nurturant people, not merely to neurotics, but to all kinds of personalities.

Gray[17] has used a broader approach to this problem. He hypothesized

[14] A few individual cases have been reported at this "deep" level of analysis, but they have been neurotic patients and the authors' reports have lacked experimental control. *Cf., e.g.,* C. P. Oberndorf, "Psychoanalysis of Married Couples," *Psychoanalytic Review*, 25 (1938), 453–57.

[15] Sigmund Freud, "On Narcissism: An Introduction," in *Collected Papers*, vol. 4, London, Hogarth, 1925, pp. 30–59.

[16] *Cf., e.g.,* C. P. Oberndorf, *op. cit.*; Edmund Bergler, *Unhappy Marriage and Divorce*, New York, International Universities Press, 1946; and Bela Mittleman, "Complementary Neurotic Reactions in Intimate Relationships," *Psychoanalytic Quarterly*, 13 (1944), 479–91.

[17] *Cf., e.g.,* H. Gray, "Psychological Types in Married People," *Journal of Social Psychology*, 29 (1949), 189–200; and "Jung's Psychological Types in Men and Women," *Stanford Medical Bulletin*, 6 (1948), 29–36.

that mate-selection would be complementary with respect to the types of personality formulated by Jung (extrovert-introvert, etc.) His empirical findings, however, were not convincing.[18]

Other theorists have tried to identify various motivation-linked aspects of interaction. Bernard, for example, suggests various dimensions of love.[19] She notes the usual dimension of dominance and also dwells upon the desire for response or acceptance and on the differential ability of persons to "give" as she calls it. As we shall see later, these are similar to some of the "needs" in our conceptual scheme. Bernard did not systematically state that attraction occurred between persons who were complementary in regard to these dimensions. Others, however, have come very close to this notion. Ohmann [20] stated this idea by saying that we are attracted to those who complete us psychologically. We seek in a mate those qualities which we do not possess.

Taking leads from all of the foregoing, Winch attempted to pull them together. He began by defining love in terms of needs:

> Love is the positive emotion experienced by one person (the person loving, or the lover) in an interpersonal relationship in which the second person (the person loved, or love-object) either (a) meets certain important needs of the first, or (b) manifests or appears (to the first) to manifest personal attributes (e.g., beauty, skills, or status) highly prized by the first, or both.[21]

Then he hypothesized that mate-selection would take place according to what he called the theory of complementary needs:

> In mate-selection each individual seeks within his or her field of eligibles for that person who gives the greatest promise of providing him or her with maximum need gratification.[22]

Perhaps this can be phrased more simply by hypothesizing that the personality needs of marriage partners tend to be complementary rather than similar. Two points require further clarification: (a) What are personality needs and which needs are germane to our problem? and (b) What exactly is meant by the term "complementary"?

---

[18] Winch applied tests of significance to some of Gray's data. These tests showed that the selection of mates in terms of Jung's types was not significantly greater than might have been expected by chance.

[19] Jessie Bernard, *American Family Behavior*, New York, Harper and Brothers, 1942, pp. 435–56.

[20] Oliver Ohmann, "The Psychology of Attraction," in Helen Jordan (*ed.*), *You and Marriage*, New York, Wiley, 1942, chap. 2.

[21] Robert F. Winch, *The Modern Family*, New York, Holt, 1951, p. 333.

[22] *Ibid.*, p. 406. In the phrase "field of eligibles" Winch takes account of the previously noted homogamy with respect to such social characteristics as race, religion, and social class.

Needs. One can think of the term "need" as meaning a goal-oriented drive. Goal in this sense refers not only to such things as material objects and status in the social structure but more particularly to such things as the quality and kind of response desired in interpersonal situations. Examples of the latter are the desire to give help or adulation to others, the desire to take care of others, the desire to control, etc. When these goals are attained, the need is gratified. However, gratification is a dynamic process, and a need once gratified does not cease to function. Patterns of behavior which are tension-reducing tend rather to be reinforced. In a marriage, for example, a woman who finds in her interaction with her spouse gratification for a need to control will continue to want to control him. One further characteristic of needs should be noted. Needs function at both the conscious and unconscious levels. A person may be conscious, partly conscious, or not at all conscious of the goals he desires.

Henry A. Murray has defined "need" in a more formal way:

> A need is a construct . . . which stands for a force . . . which organizes perception, apperception, intellection, conation, and action in such a way as to transform in a certain direction an existing, unsatisfying situation.[23]

Further, he has elaborated an extensive list of emotional needs. However, because Murray's list is so detailed, we found it necessary to depart from it in a number of ways. The following list of needs [24] is nevertheless based upon Murray's scheme.

Needs

n Abasement [25]	To accept or invite blame, criticism or punishment. To blame or harm the self.
n Achievement	To work diligently to create something and/or to emulate others.
n Approach	To draw near and enjoy interaction with another person or persons.
n Autonomy	To get rid of the constraint of other persons. To avoid or escape from domination. To be unattached and independent.
n Deference	To admire and praise a person.
n Dominance	To influence and control the behavior of others.
n Hostility	To fight, injure, or kill others.
n Nurturance	To give sympathy and aid to a weak, helpless, ill, or dejected person or animal.

---

[23] H. A. Murray, *et al.*, *Explorations in Personality*, New York, Oxford University Press, pp. 123–24.
[24] R. F. Winch, *op. cit.*, pp. 408–409.
[25] The notation "n" before the name of a variable is used as a shorthand form for the term "need," and where it is found on following pages, that is what it represents.

Needs (*continued*)

n Recognition	To excite the admiration and approval of others.
n Sex	To develop an erotic relationship and engage in sexual relations.
n Status Aspiration	To desire a socio-economic status considerably higher than one has. (A special case of achievement.)
n Status Striving	To work diligently to alter one's socio-economic status. (A special case of achievement.)
n Succorance	To be helped by a sympathetic person. To be nursed, loved, protected, indulged.

General Traits

Anxiety	Fear, conscious or unconscious, of harm or misfortune arising from the hostility of others and/or social reaction to one's own behavior.
Emotionality	The show of affect in behavior.
Vicariousness	The gratification of a need derived from the perception that another person is deriving gratification.

A study to test this theory has been undertaken with a group of middle-class subjects. Because striving for upward mobility (or higher socio-economic status) is so central to the middle-class value system, it was decided to include two variables pertaining to status.

Complementariness. To explain this theory let us imagine two persons, A and B, interacting with each other. Let us assume that both are deriving gratification from this interaction. Then the interactional sequence will be in accordance with the theory of complementary needs if:

1. the need or needs in A which are being gratified are *different* from the *need* or needs being gratified in B; *or*
2. the needs or needs in A which are being gratified are very *different* in *intensity* from the same needs in B which are also being gratified.

An example of (1) is found in the case of a person desirous of attention and recognition (n Recognition) who finds gratification in relationship with a person who tends to bestow admiration on the former (n Deference). Alternative (2) is illustrated in the interaction between a person who wants others to do his bidding (high n Dominance) and one lacking the ability to handle his environment who is looking for someone to tell him what to do (low n Dominance). It will be recognized that this definition of complementariness embraces two forms of heterogamy.

Points Requiring Further Elaboration. At present the theory of complementary needs is a hypothesis enunciating a general principle of mate selection when both spouses are given some freedom of choice. (It is clear that the theory would not be applicable under such a system of arranged marriages as has been traditional in Japan.[26]) This principle is now under empirical investigation, but the results of this study will not be available for some time.*

There are a few points to be noted about the theory before the results of the research are known. First, although marriage is viewed as a major source of gratification, it is a matter of common observation that most married people derive gratification from social interaction with other persons as well as with their respective spouses. To the degree that this is true it is not necessary to hypothesize that marriage partners will be totally complementary in their need-patterns. The theory also hypothesizes, however, that if there is not a minimum degree of complementariness in the need patterns of the two persons, they will tend to regard the relationship as unsatisfactory. Their dissatisfaction would probably be registered as follows. Either the relationship would be broken during the dating or engagement periods, or if the couple should be married, their marriage would have more than the average probability of ending in divorce.

At this time the minimum degree of complementariness, referred to in the above paragraph, is unknown, and some criteria are required concerning the number of needs sufficient to hold a relationship together. Other questions which may be raised but which cannot yet be answered are as follows:

First, can matching which occurs only on one need in each spouse hold the marriage together? It seems logically possible that only one need of each member of the couple might be met in a relationship. This need, however, might be so important that it would set the tone of the whole relationship.

Second, when a person exhibits two needs which are in conflict, for which of these needs is gratification sought in marriage? For example, in the case of a woman who is upwardly mobile and is also very dominant, does she marry an aggressive type male who will get for her the status she desires but who will not submit to her domination, or does she marry a dependent male who will give in to her but who lacks the initiative to

---

* [*Editor's note.* The research carried out by Professor Winch and his associates on mate-selection among twenty-five couples is reported in full in Robert F. Winch, *Mate-Selection* (New York: Harper & Brothers, 1958). Of the research, Winch concludes: ". . . it is my interpretation that the bulk of the evidence supports the general hypothesis of complementary needs in mate-selection, and I accept the hypothesis with the tentativeness usual in any scientific conclusion" (p. 119). He continues that not all variations in mate selection are accounted for by complementariness but that this factor seems to be one of the determinants among middle-class urban groups in the United States.]

[26] [Omitted]

achieve status? It would be interesting to determine how frequently this type of problem is resolved by the individual's directing one need towards the marital partner and the other towards interaction with other persons. On the other hand, it may be that many persons with this type of conflict never achieve a satisfactory solution and that hence the intrapsychic conflict becomes a source of conflict in marital interaction.

Third, in persons who show a marked disparity between needs which are expressed overtly (or directly) and those which are expressed covertly (or indirectly), on which level does matching occur? Persons may behave overtly in a fashion quite different from, or even opposite to, their more basic wishes. We all have known insecure persons whose bold and aggressive exterior is an attempt to convince themselves and others that they are really unafraid. In this situation it may be that matching at the covert level would be more important than at the overt level, but this we do not know as yet.

Illustration of the Theory

To illustrate the theory of complementary needs we have chosen a case from a sample of middle-class married couples and have attempted to show how these two partners complement each other need-wise. It will be noted that in this case the male shows some dependent trends. We do not feel that this case is atypical of our middle-class sample. Dependent needs in the personality of the middle-class male are probably more frequent than is popularly supposed.[27] It is to be emphasized that the man and wife discussed here are a normally functioning couple.

The Case of Anne and Frank Hamilton.[28] Before we can understand how

---

[27] For further elaboration on this point, *cf.*, for example, Arnold Green, "The Middle Class Male Child and Neurosis," *American Sociological Review*, 11 (1946), 31–41; and Talcott Parsons, *The Social System*, Glencoe, Ill., The Free Press, 1951, esp. pp. 262–69.

[28] This case represents one of those being studied in a project under the direction of Dr. Robert F. Winch at Northwestern University. This investigation is supported by a research grant, MH-439, from the National Institute of Mental Health, U.S. Public Health Service.

The material upon which the case analysis was done consists of a case-history type interview, Thematic Apperception Test protocols, and a second type of interview designed to get at the more behavioral aspects of personality. The full case analysis was made by the research staff of this project which consists of Dr. Winch, Mrs. Sandra K. Oreck, Dr. Oliver J. B. Kerner, and the authors of this article. The present report is a synopsis of their findings, which cannot be presented in their entirety because the analysis runs to about two hundred pages of manuscript. Much of the documentation for generalizations must be omitted. All names and identifying characteristics have been changed in order to preserve the anonymity of the couple without impairing the crucial facts of the case. It is our desire to present the case as simply as possible for the purpose of illustrating the theory.

individual needs function for mutual gratification in a marital relationship, it is first necessary to present the personalities involved. We shall consider first the wife and then the husband before we attempt to understand their relationship to each other.

Anne Hamilton is best described in build as "hefty." Her outstanding features facially are her large mouth and rather prominent teeth. That her mouth is so noticeable the interviewer attributes to the fact that "it never seems to be still." She talks loud and fast. She punctuates her words by dramatic use of her hands and facial expressions. Even when she is listening, her face does not relax. She smiles broadly or raises her eyebrows or in some other way responds aggressively to what is said.

Anne's energy is also evident in her capacity to work. To finish college in three years, she carried extra courses each term and still sailed through her undergraduate work. She earned most of the money to pay her college expenses even though her family was able and willing to pay them. But she just liked to keep busy, so not only did she work and keep up her grade average, but she also held responsible positions in numerous extra-curricular affairs. She was so efficient in getting ads for the school yearbook that for the first time that publication had a financial surplus.

Going along with this terrific need to achieve, there is a high need to dominate others, which Anne describes as "a certain element of bossiness in me." She feels that her way of doing things is best and she wants people to do things "in the manner I so designate." [29]

She does not like to be "stepped on" nor does she admire people who can be pushed around. Such people she cannot respect. "People that I cannot look up to, I have a tendency to shove out of my way or to trample on, just shove, push." Thus we see in Anne little need to feel sympathy for other persons (n Nurturance) but rather a hostile attitude towards them.

She tends to be critical of other people and apparently because of this she has encountered some difficulty in forming close friendships. She says that people usually like her if they can overcome their first impression which frequently is one of antagonism. She says on this point, "I'm very quick spoken and rarely stop to think that I may be hurting somebody's feelings or that they are not going to take it just the way I meant it." But she needs people and she wants them to like her.

The competitiveness and the need to manipulate people undoubtedly indicate compensatory behavior for feelings of insecurity at some level. There is some evidence to indicate that these feelings stem from her doubts about her being a feminine person. She tends to be jealous of pretty

---

[29] Shortly we shall note that this domination of others occurred very early in her life in her relationship to her parents and other members of the household.

women. She is contemptuous towards them when their attractiveness and "poise" win them positions of prestige which they are not equipped to handle because of a lack of the "executive ability" that she possesses. All her life she states that she wanted to be like her mother who is pretty and sweet and "gives a lot, perhaps too much." She feels, however, that she has not succeeded in becoming this sort of woman. She regards herself as a person who is "quick, uneven-tempered and impatient, ambitious . . . ready to tell others how to do things." Evidence that she rejects this "masculine" component in her personality is her view that she would not want a daughter to be like herself, but "more like Mother."

The postulation of such a conflict helps to explain why Anne did not continue with her career plans. She took a master's degree in advertising the year following her undergraduate work. She then set out to make a career in this field, but there were no jobs immediately available. Employers did not want college graduates who had their own bright ideas about the business, and, according to her account, they were unwilling to employ her for menial jobs which she was willing to take because they felt she was too intelligent and soon would become disinterested.

At this point Anne's career drive began to fluctuate. She took a job in an office. While there and while formally engaged to another man, she met Frank. She and Frank were married six months after their meeting, and they moved to a city where she had obtained a good job and where he enrolled in college. At the end of a year she became pregnant and stopped working for a while. By the third month of her pregnancy, however, she became bored with "sitting around home" and took a job as a waitress, much against the doctor's orders. She lost the child three months later. She stated that she wanted the child very badly and that she was broken up over her loss. This wish would be consistent with the feminine desire to be a "mother." In addition to the conscious desire to be feminine, it seems probable that she had an unconscious wish to abort and to deny willingness to play a feminine (maternal) role.

Perhaps if we look into Anne's background for a moment we can see more clearly the circumstances which led to the development of her pattern of aggressive behavior and the confusion over appropriate sex-role behavior.

Anne was the only child in a family of four adults. Her father was a self-made man, one who built up a trucking business to the point where it netted him an income of around $700 monthly even during the depression years. She describes him as being a short man, one who was hot-tempered and stubborn. He was 30 when Anne was born and her mother was only 18. The mother is described as being even-tempered, calm, and dependent. The third adult was Anne's maternal grandmother who came to live with the family shortly after Anne was born. She managed the house and Anne's mother and apparently Anne's father as well. Anne says her grandmother often warned the father against his outbreaks of wrath in front of the child. The grandmother brought with her one of her sons who was about the age of Anne's father and who was similar to Anne's mother in temperament. He was very good to Anne and gave her everything she wanted. He married for the first time and left the household when he was 50 years old.

Anne was the center of attention for these four persons. What she could not get from one, she could get from another. This pattern of relationships was conducive to her manipulation of persons and the need for recognition from them which we have noted earlier.

Grounds for the competitiveness may also be found in this network of relationships. Anne's mother was very young and still dependent upon her mother who looked upon Anne as "her youngest child." Thus the relationship between mother and daughter resembled sibling rivalry, not only for the "mutual mother's" love but for the husband-father's love as well. Here were two bases for Anne to dislike her mother, but her mother was such a sweet young thing that she never gave Anne any rationalization for hating her. This left Anne with an unexpressed hostility which apparently has been partially sublimated into an achievement drive and partially displaced onto "feminine" women like her mother. Her mother was better looking than she, so Anne could not compete with her on these grounds but had to seek other means of achieving superiority.

To strive in an aggressive manner was satisfactory in another way too because the father, who wanted a son, approved of such behavior in his little tomboy. Further, grandmother was a model of aggressive behavior. Anne's gratifying relationship with her fostered an identification. The aggressive pattern was fairly well set by the time Anne reached adolescence as is evident in her report that, in junior high school, teachers commented on it. One teacher advised her to change her ways or she would never get a husband. Father also changed his mind about what he wanted and began to look upon her as "feminine" and wanted her to become dependent on him while she was in college. These undoubtedly are the sources of some of the ambivalence we note in her picture, especially concerning career and motherhood.

Although she had doubts about her "feminine appeal," Anne apparently had little trouble in finding dating relationships. Though she confesses she was not the most popular girl on campus and that her weekend calendar was not always filled, she dated from the time she first entered high school. She had only one serious relationship before meeting Frank. This was an engagement to a man described as "suave and smooth . . . and with nice manners." It apparently was a stormy affair, off and on several times. The engagement was broken finally over the issue of whether or not there should be a formal wedding. Anne wanted one, but her fiancé's family did not.

Frank is unlike Anne in many ways. Whereas she gets much gratification from work and positions of responsibility, he much prefers just loafing and being with people. He is now in college, at Anne's request, and very much looks forward to the time when he will be through. College is just a means to an end for him; the less work he has to do to get through, the happier he will be. He wants the degree, however, because it will facilitate his getting a good job. He looks to the job to bring him status and prestige and to provide a large income so that he can buy sporty cars and a big house. Nevertheless, he does not like to work for such a position and is just as content if someone gets it for him.

Frank likes people and he gets along with them very well. It is important to him that they like him and give him attention. He loves to talk and to joke, and generally he is successful in winning friends. "I'm an easy person to get along with . . . I do a fair job of amusing people although I feel that people don't regard me as entirely full of nonsense." His physical appearance contributes to his acceptability for he is a good-looking man, tall and slightly heavy. His build is somewhat athletic but his muscles seem to lack the firmness and tonus of a well-developed athlete. He is light-hearted, pleasure-oriented, and loves to eat.[30]

To achieve acceptance Frank relates to people in a deferent manner. He consciously admires and accepts his allies almost uncritically. He shows no tendency to control them nor to compel them to do what he wants; in other words, he reveals no need to dominate. Though he likes very much to have the spotlight himself, he is willing to share it with others and even to concede it without resentment to people who are better attention-getters than he. He tends to establish friendships with such persons and to identify with them. Thus he receives vicarious gratification for his own need for recognition. This is illustrated in the fact that he joined the fraternity to which most of the "big wheels" on campus belonged though he himself was not a big wheel. Merely through association he felt he was able to share in their glory.

---

[30] In terms of the Freudian stages of development, this aspect of his personality would place him at the "oral" stage, the stage at which the infant, for example, does little more than *receive* love, care, and attention from the mother. The passive-dependent trends which we note in Frank's personality are considered the psychological counterparts of this stage of development. We shall note, however, that this characteristic is by no means the whole picture and that he is considerably more active than is implied for this stage.

It is interesting to note that Frank does not limit his struggle for recognition to a few fields or a select group of persons as mature adults generally do. He is almost child-like in his willingness to perform. Once when drunk, he paid the singer in a night club twenty-five dollars to let him sing with her in front of the microphone. He still wears the badge that he received when he was deputized a sheriff for a week in his home-town. The importance of this incident was shown when Frank flipped his lapel so the interviewer could see the badge.

In addition to recognition, Frank seems to want love and affection. He tells that he was the "mascot" of a sorority at the first college he attended, and he was chosen "king of the prom" one season. If he feels blue, which he says is rare, he can be cheered by having women, peers or the mothers of peers, tell him how handsome he is.

Apparently since high school Frank always got along well with women because he always had a girl. He tended to date one girl at a time and to go with her pretty "seriously." He expected the same of her, and as a result most of these relationships broke up by his becoming jealous when the girl would date another fellow. He became jealous he says because he wanted "all her attention." The girls he dated were all short and very attractive. They conformed to his "ideal" of "one other fellows thought highly of, a popular girl in other words." Apparently a girl of this type brought vicarious recognition to Frank in the same manner as did the "big wheels" in the fraternity.

Now let us consider Frank's background. Frank was the third son in a family of four boys, all of whom were born during a period of eight years. His father, who was 57 when Frank was born, was a successful salesman until the depression. After losing everything in the depression, the father stopped working. The major burden of supporting the family then fell upon his mother who was about 28 years younger than the father. In time this responsibility was shared by the oldest son. The mother was a petite and good-looking woman.[31] She was a very hard-working, efficient sort of person who, besides working at a full-time job, kept her house, herself, and her sons immaculately neat and also found time to participate in a few club activities. She had considerably more education than her husband in that she had a B.A. degree whereas he completed only the eighth grade. Frank remembers her as being undemonstrative in her affections and as a reasonably impartial judge in the children's quarrels but with a tendency to side with the underdog. Frank had little to say about his father's personality. Though the man had died only two years before the

---

[31] It will be recalled that the girls he dated were of similar stature.

interview, Frank gave the impression that his father had participated little in family affairs. Frank's few descriptive comments portrayed an opinionated man, harsh in his judgments.

Among the seemingly more important aspects of this family is the absence of daughters. Having two sons already, both parents had desired that the next children be girls. Indeed Frank can remember the time when his mother gave him a girl's haircut. It would appear therefore that this attitude on the part of his parents, and especially his mother, laid the groundwork for the passive-dependent trends we have noted in his personality. It seems logical that Frank wanted the love and attention that is given to the baby. At the age of two years, however, he could no longer be gratified in these desires because of the arrival of the fourth and final brother. It appears that Frank resented this brother greatly. In one two-hour interview he mentioned both of the older brothers but not this one. Undoubtedly as a consequence of this situation Frank has developed a fear of rejection to which he has responded by always doing what is expected of him and by endeavoring to please people in order not to be rejected by them. Frank did not react to his feelings of rejection by rebellion. Perhaps this was because the mother never actually rejected him; she just did not give him all the affection he desired. To avoid losing what he did receive and to try to get more he reacted by being a "good boy."

But Frank was not a sissy in the common use of the term. He was interested in athletics and became captain of his high school football team. He liked mechanics and cars. Currently he is studying mechanical engineering and hopes someday to become a salesman for some large engineering firm.[32]

These masculine interests are very important for understanding Frank's personality. We have shown the tendency towards dependency in his personality which culturally is considered "feminine." Generally, males in our culture who tend to be passive experience some conflict if they are not able to live up to the cultural imperatives that they be assertive and "masculine." Frank shows little anxiety on this score, however, and appears to be very well adjusted. His not having developed a conflict on this score may be due to his having achieved such successful identification with male authority figures that he consciously never questions his "maleness."

Undoubtedly, the oldest brother is a significant figure in understanding these identifications with males. Very early this brother became a counsellor to the mother. Frank felt ambivalent towards him. He was jealous because this brother played such an important role with the mother. On

---

[32] It is not surprising that Frank wants to become a salesman because he enjoys so much talking with people and feels certain that he is able to get along with them well.

the other hand, if he hated his brother, then the mother would reject him completely; but if he were like his brother, he would get his mother's attention and at the same time establish a good relationship with the brother, who was moderately successful in his own business and popular with people. Thus, the brother became an ego-model for him and at the same time was a person who could meet some of Frank's dependent needs.

Thus, we now see Frank as an amiable, non-anxious person who does not have a great deal of ambition but who has the knack of relating himself to people who can do things for him.

Up to this point we have attempted to describe both Anne and Frank with very little reference to each other. Now we shall discuss their case with relation to complementary need theory.

Frank says that he was attracted to Anne because "she's probably the smartest woman I've run into, and I admired her a great deal I think before I truly loved her." On the other hand, Anne admired his easy-going manner and his ability to get along with people. Knowing what we do about each of them individually, we can see in these two remarks alone some ground for their complementary matching. First of all, we have pointed out that Anne has had some difficulty in getting along with people and that she would like to be able to do so more easily. Frank's ability to attract friends and to keep them facilitates Anne's social relationships in that he attracts their mutual friends. For Frank, Anne's initiative and her ability to attain the financial and other goals she sets for herself complements his lack of drive. The question is open, however, whether or not this particular pattern of interaction which is now mutually gratifying will continue to be so if Frank becomes a successful salesman.

In their interaction with each other we note that Anne has the authority. She handles their finances, and she decided that he should go back to school. As we have seen, this is the way she likes to do things and we have also noted that Frank shows little need to dominate and he accedes quite willingly to her plans.

Anne tends to be a very emotional person who is easily aroused and upset. At such times Frank's calm and easy-going manner is consoling to her. He has a good shoulder to cry on and he is willing to listen to her problems. She feels that he is helping to calm her down.

About the only thing that disturbs Anne about Frank's personality is that he does not have as much ambition as she would like to see. Indeed she has been somewhat bothered by his rather lethargic attitude towards school work. She would prefer to see him as excited about it as she has always been, but she feels that she is learning to accept this attitude that graduation is the important thing and that the level of one's performance in school is soon forgotten.

Occasionally Frank is a little perturbed by Anne for sometimes he is embarrassed when she pushes ahead in a crowd and drags him along with her, but he goes along and says nothing about it. Undoubtedly he is ambivalent about her aggressiveness. On the one hand, her behavior and her drive facilitate the realization of such desires as the new car which they recently bought. On the other hand, Frank fears that the same aspects of Anne's personality may put him in a position of stepping on other people which might result in their rejecting him. However, this aggressiveness does not constitute one of the things he would change about her if he could push a button to change anything. He would want to modify only her quick temper and her heaviness.

Anne is very different from the girls that Frank dated. The other girls were like his mother in physical characteristics in that they were all short and attractive. Anne has none of these physical characteristics, but does resemble Frank's mother in her efficiency. Although very different from Anne's father, Frank tends to be more like Anne's uncle and Anne's mother who are calm, easy-going, and dependent.

Both Anne and Frank desire considerable recognition from other people. Frank is attentive to Anne and considerate of her. She undoubtedly regards his submissiveness to her as admiration. Anne does not pay as much attention to Frank as he would like. It would seem that although Frank would like more in the way of demonstrated "hero-worship," he does not feel too deprived because she facilitates his getting the symbols (e.g., the new sports car) which enable him to attract attention from other persons.

There is one other thing about Frank which Anne finds gratifying and which is worthy of mention here. Frank's attractive appearance and engaging manner enable Anne to compete successfully on a feminine basis with other women. Although this appeal on his part is gratifying to her in one sense, in another sense it threatens her. She mentioned that she is jealous if he pays too much attention to other women at parties. He also becomes jealous when she has occasion to lunch with another man. This mutual jealousy is understandable in terms of the marked need for recognition which each of them exhibits. On Frank's part, it undoubtedly is a manifestation of his fear of rejection; and from Anne's point of view, the insecurity stems from doubts about her feminine ability "to hold a man."

The complementariness that is described in this couple can be summarized generally as a case of a passive-dependent male finding gratification in relationship with a striving, aggressive woman (and vice versa). Indeed, they are not complementary on all counts, e.g., neither is willing to surrender his own desire for recognition in favor of the other. However, it would seem that the mutual choice that has been made satisfies the major, predominating trends within the personalities of each other.

30 · Should Men Marry Older Women? *

ALBERT ELLIS, WITH LESTER DAVID

Public opinion holds definite ideas about the relative age of husband and wife—the husband should be older. Is this idea simply tradition and custom? Or are there sound reasons for it? This article reviews the situation pro and con and comes to an interesting conclusion.

THERE IS a surprising and little-noted trend in this country that would make Grandpa and Grandma raise their eyebrows more than a little.

One in every seven new husbands is younger than his bride.

And of this group nearly half of the husbands are younger than their brides by three years or more.

Almost as many more are the same age. The two groups together add up to a quarter of the nation's marrying couples.

In Victorian days, it wasn't rare for a man to take a bride ten or even 20 years younger than himself. How things have changed! And the trend seems to be continuing, according to latest census figures.

Well, what about it? Is it good or bad? Are we throwing away a wise piece of folklore, or merely ridding ourselves of the deadening weight of tradition? My own reaction is—hooray! I think at long last we are on the way to eradicating a foolish taboo, one as outdated as the hard and fast rule of the past that no nice girl works.

---

* Reprinted from *This Week* Magazine (July 6, 1958), pp. 8–9. Copyright 1958 by the United Newspapers Magazine Corporation. Reprinted by permission of the publisher and the authors.
Dr. Ellis is a clinical psychologist who now carries on psychotherapy and marriage counseling independently, after having had experience with several kinds of institutions. He holds the degree of Doctor of Philosophy from Columbia University. His professional writings deal primarily with problems of sex, love, marriage, and family relations. He has written *The Folklore of Sex* and *The American Sexual Tragedy* and many professional articles; he has also edited several books in his field of interest.
Mr. David, who has the Master of Arts degree from Columbia University, is a journalist who specializes in articles on marriage and family relations. He has lectured on magazine writing in this area at New York University and The New School for Social Research. His many articles appear in nationally known magazines.

And I am not the only one who thinks so. At least a half dozen famous sociologists, following intensive investigations, have discovered that these marriages are often the happiest.

Dr. Judson T. Landis, of the University of California, studied 4,000 couples and found the lowest divorce rates among marriages in which the wife was older! Dr. Harvey J. Locke, of the University of Southern California, reports that age difference is not a major factor in good marital adjustment. And the late Dr. Lewis M. Terman, of Stanford University, went so far as to assert, on the basis of his investigations, that the happiest wives married men four to ten years younger.

Despite all this, many young people continue to be influenced by tradition and prejudice. I know one young man who broke up with his fiancée after two years because she was 34 and he 27. He finally decided the social pressures would be too much for him.

Obviously, this man should neither marry nor date older women if the age factor bothers him. But what bothers me is why the difference should matter to anybody in the first place.

Why does it, actually? Just suppose you were one of a couple planning a marriage in which the bride was older than the groom. Let's see how the commonest arguments against your plans would stack up:

1. *Other People Will Scoff*. Valid, but can be overcome. Many persons will look askance and remarks along the lines of "She's robbing the cradle" will be made. The man won't escape being talked about either. He'll be accused of immaturity in comments such as: "He doesn't want a wife, he needs a second mother." The woman, too, can expect the parlor psychiatrists to diagnose her motives: "She didn't marry him for love, it's just her mothering instinct."

However, as the marriage proves itself, the whispers will fade and most people will simply get used to it.

2. *When She Gets Older, He Will Start Roaming*. Very little validity. In most cases if a man is going to be unfaithful he will be—regardless of his wife's age. He may offer her age as a reason to himself, but it's only camouflage. If she were younger and prettier, he'd find another excuse.

If a deeply satisfying relationship is built up through the years, instead of crumbling as time goes on, it can grow stronger.

3. *Her Sex Desires Will Wane before His*. Completely invalid. Studies by the Kinsey Institute, confirmed by other researchers, prove conclusively that a woman's sexual interest continues virtually unabated until the 60's.

4. *Girls Mature Earlier and Need Older Men*. Invalid. During the teens, girls are often more mature, but in the twenties, the gap between the sexes vanishes.

5. *Friends of the Couple Will be of Different Ages.* Valid. A five or six-year gap could produce some noticeable effects. For instance, a 33-year-old teacher had difficulty adjusting to a marriage with an accountant of 26 for this reason.

Her friends, averaging 35, were mainly interested in their pre-teen children's problems, schools and running suburban homes. His friends were either unmarried or had much younger children, and the talk was still about formulas, nursery school, and the plan to buy a house.

There can be trouble if friends don't mesh, but time brings adjustment. After all, there's much less difference in outlook between 35 and 45 than between 25 and 35.

6. *He'd Be More Active, She'd Prefer a Quiet Life.* Not valid unless the age gap is extremely large. A few extra years do not put a wife in the rocking-chair class.

Thus, although some reasonable objections are apparent, the majority of arguments against reversing "tradition" wither when analyzed closely.

On the other hand, there are a number of decided advantages for both parties. Let's start with women:

A significant benefit which marriage with a younger man offers is the lessened likelihood of prolonged widowhood. According to life-expectancy tables, even if a man and wife were the same age on their wedding day, she would face an average of 5.5 years without him. These could be made fewer or even eliminated entirely, depending on the age balance at marriage.

Even more important, eradication of the taboo would offer many who face lifelong spinsterhood a second chance at finding husbands. Currently, there are about 1,200,000 single women in the U.S. between 30 and 44 who have never wed. The likelihood that they ever will is estimated at less than ten per cent, chiefly because the pool of available men diminishes sharply. There are plenty of single males, though, in younger age groups.

A third advantage for women lies in this simple but significant fact: A younger man can have a hard day at the office and still say to his wife: "Let's do something tonight." Often, only an act of Congress can budge an older man from his easy chair in the evening.

Finally, a younger man is less habit-hardened than a bachelor of some years' standing. The latter would tend to insist that married life conform to his old living patterns, while the former can change his ways readily and make a smoother adjustment to marriage.

Now how about the advantages to the men?

First, things will be easier for them. Let's be practical and let's be honest: No marriage counselor in his right mind would say that money doesn't matter in a marriage. It does! A woman better established financially can ease those early struggling years.

I am not in the least advocating that a young man turn to an older woman solely because of her job and bank balance. I'm a strong champion of love as a foundation-stone for marriage, but if a bride can help the family financially at the start, a great many problems will be solved even before they arise. Love is important, but it's also important to be realistic. I may believe in love, but I am a realist, too.

From this point stems another advantage for men. Many put off marriage because they can't afford a wife and family. If they turn their eyes to older women, the economic barrier may be eliminated. Thus instead of remaining single until they get on their feet, they can wed and enjoy more years of married life.

Finally, a man who picks an older woman usually selects her for solid wifely virtues and not because he is entranced by moonlight and roses. A more mature woman has lived long enough to be aware of life's everyday realities. She won't storm off to Mother quite so readily because married life didn't turn out as it was in her dreams or on television.

Add it all up and the conviction hardens: There is no sense in this unwritten law and it ought to be repealed. I am not saying all men should henceforth take unto themselves older brides—frankly, I myself did not. I am saying that a man should marry the woman he loves, and a few years plus or minus should make not one jot of difference in his mind, in her mind, in anyone's mind.

CHAPTER 7:

Broken Engagements and Delayed Marriages

31 · Factors in Broken Engagements *

ERNEST W. BURGESS AND PAUL WALLIN

Engagement is no longer considered the certain prelude to marriage. It has come to be considered, the authors say, "as the last stage in the selection process leading to the choice of a mate." The exclusive relationship of engagement is the last testing ground for the compatibility needed for marriage. Many engagements do not survive this last crucial test. Among one thousand engaged couples studied by Professors Burgess and Wallin, 24 per cent of the men and 36 per cent of the women reported that they had broken prior engagements; before the study closed, another 15 per cent of the couples had broken the engagements that they were partners in when the study began.

When the authors compared broken with unbroken engagements they found that they did not represent completely different types of relationships. However, the broken engagements more often than the unbroken ones were characterized by infrequent demonstration of affection, lack of confidence in the happiness of the marriage, short period of acquaintance, small amount of time spent together, parental disapproval, difference in religious affiliation, infrequent church attendance, disagreement on activities, desire to "be on

* Ernest W. Burgess and Paul Wallin, *Engagement and Marriage* (Philadelphia: J. B. Lippincott Company, 1953), pp. 273–282 and 297–300. Copyright, 1953, by J. B. Lippincott Company. Reprinted by permission of the publisher.

A biographical sketch of Ernest W. Burgess is given with article 2.

Paul Wallin, Professor of Sociology at Stanford University, received the degree of Doctor of Philosophy from the University of Chicago.

Engagement and Marriage is the report of an extensive study of one thousand engaged couples.

the go," and failure to avoid arguments. These characteristics are perhaps symptoms of underlying personality traits or lack of compatibility.

From interviews, the researchers isolated five factors in broken engagements which are discussed and illustrated in the first part of the following excerpt. The latter part details the process by which engagements are broken.

MANY CONCRETE explanations are given by young people for broken engagements, such as falling in love with another person, interference of the man or woman's mother, loss of interest, religious differences, or cultural conflicts. These, however, are frequently surface manifestations of more fundamental factors which need more intensive study than has as yet been given them.

The above, and other alleged "causes" of broken engagements, can be classified in five categories: (1) slight emotional attachment, (2) separation, (3) parental opposition, (4) cultural divergences, and (5) personality problems.

Slight Emotional Attachment

One or both parties to an engagement, as evident from case studies of broken engagements, may be in love to a slight or small degree if at all. Occasionally an engaged person is doubtful if he is in love, as in the following instance:

> Joan thinks she was very indifferent about her engagement to Frank. It did not impress her at all. She thinks now that she had no business ever to get engaged to him and that she is better off that the engagement is broken.

More often the youth has honestly believed himself to be in love only to realize later that his feelings were not deeply involved.

> Their real quarrels were about Ann being friendly with the men she knew before she became engaged. Her fiancé thought she should stop seeing them. She did not go out with them and could not see why he was so jealous of her. She did not consider that she gave him any reason to be jealous. The engagement was broken when she was nineteen. She thinks now she was too young to know what it was all about, and did not take it seriously enough.

A girl or youth may enter an engagement half-heartedly, not being too sure of keeping it.

> I never could get enthusiastic about the wedding because I felt that it would never take place. I never made any plans because I could not see myself married to Joe. Once during the engagement I danced with some friends when we were out together and Joe got angry. I had no respect for his

opinions. I had compared him often with other men whom I met and he did not stack up very well. I felt sorry for him but that was all I felt.

Sometimes, the couple have been thrown together by circumstances, as during a summer vacation, without the presence of other eligible young people. Or, as in the following case, they kept company and were finally engaged as the result of the college dating and rating system which often emphasizes superficial characteristics like popularity and appearance rather than vital common interests and complementary personality needs.

We were both the most popular in school for two years. I played football. She was vice-president of the class. We were both leaders in our respective groups. We took class after class together. My fraternity and her club had our marriage planned.

When the couple are held together only by a slight emotional attachment, the relation may easily be broken if one of them falls deeply in love with someone else. Of course, as seen in two of the above cases, one member of the couple may be more involved than the other.

Separation

Separation may be regarded as a special case of slight emotional involvement because it leads to the breaking of many engagements where love was not strong enough to hold the couple together.

But separation leads not only to the termination of relations based on a slight degree of emotional attachment. It also may result in the breakup of a certain proportion of engagements where there may have been rather strong mutual attraction. This takes place particularly among couples who have difficulty in maintaining their relationship by correspondence. One or the other is likely to drift into keeping company with a person who becomes a more emotionally significant object than the absent fiancé.

When I met George at college I did not know about the girl back home. He did not tell me about her until after he let me know he loved me. I insisted that he write her breaking off the relation before we became engaged.

In other cases there has been insufficient association to establish a vital relationship. The effect of the separation of the couple from each other is illustrated in the case of Mr. A who lived in New York nearly a thousand miles away from his fiancée Miss N. In their nine months of acquaintance they were together two months before their engagement and only a total of five weeks afterwards.

John used to write a letter each day. Then he wrote less often. He says that he just got tired of writing. There was never a quarrel. We just separated.

When he was writing less often I became emotionally upset for two months or more. It was quite a blow to me. Later he was very anxious to renew our correspondence. I did not want to be hurt again. Whether I got over it completely, I don't know. I don't think I ever want to be engaged to him again.

Parental Opposition

Parents take a keen interest in the love affairs of their children. But the mores sanction arrangements for marriage by young people without parental interference. Consequently children tend to resent any direct control exerted by parents over pairing and engagement. In a study by Bates,[1] sons report that parental influence was brought to bear upon their courtship by fathers in 49.1 per cent and by mothers in 79.4 per cent of cases. Daughters stated that they had experienced more or less pressure by fathers in 68.7 per cent and by mothers in 97.1 per cent of the cases. Direct participation of parents was characterized by their children as generally moderate. In one-fifth of the cases extreme pressure by parents was reported. A very high proportion of elopements were by children of parents of this type. Parents with serious personality problems were those most likely to interfere arbitrarily in the love affairs of their children.

Parental influence may be exerted in favor of one suitor or in opposition to another. In general, parents tend to apply standards in which the economic and social status of the young man and his present or prospective earning ability are given the highest weight. They are likely to ignore or minimize considerations of romance and of compatibility of personality and of interests.

Parental influence on courtship and engagement may be direct or indirect, overt or subtle. A mother may openly oppose and criticize the defects in each girl in whom her son becomes interested. Or a mother who is ill or dependent upon a daughter may influence her, out of considerations of duty, to delay and postpone marriage until the young man breaks the engagement. Frequently, but not always, the son or daughter goes ahead with plans for the wedding in spite of the open disapproval of the parents.

The more intelligent parent is likely to be more subtle and often more effective in preventing a marriage. The wealthy father, disapproving of his prospective son-in-law, may take his daughter on a European trip, or plan for her to meet more "eligible" young men. The mother, instead of outwardly opposing her son's selection of a wife on the ground of her lower-class origin, may invite her to week-end events where her lack of social accomplishments is made evident to all, including her son. In the

---

[1] Alan Bates, "Parental Roles in Courtship," *Social Forces*, 20, 1942, pp. 483–486.

following case the girl's mother puts pressure upon her to become better acquainted with her fiancé.

> We were to be married in the fall and my mother insisted that I spend the summer visiting him in order to find out what he was like before we got married. By the end of the summer when I returned to the city I was sure we would never marry.

The parental expectation may be that the future son- or daughter-in-law will become a part of the family. This may be perceived and objected to by the prospective family newcomer.

> Tom was completely dominated by his mother. Both let me understand that she would live with us. It was not necessary, but he could not say "no" to her. So I broke the engagement.

> To be frank, I am glad my engagement went on the rocks. The trouble was that I was marrying the family, not the girl.

Cultural Divergences

The term "cultural divergences" as used here covers a wide range of social differences. It includes differences in family background, in social class, in attitudes to the conventions, in habits such as drinking and smoking, and in interests, values, and ideals.

The cultural differences which most frequently lead to broken engagements are those involving religion, nationality stock, region of the country, rural-urban origin, and attitudes to sex, race, and interests and ideals.

In many engagements the initial interest of one or both has been on a superficial basis such as physical attraction, the personal prestige of the other, or association through the chance or romantic circumstances of propinquity. Or, as frequently happens, the couple were first attracted to each other by the novelty of their differences in cultural background.

Whatever the cause of their original interest in each other, cultural divergences often lead to difficulties in adjustment. The following case illustrates both the superficial nature of the mutual attraction which first brought the couple together and the cultural conflict which led to the break in the relationship.

> We had little in common. Oh yes, we went to dances and movies together, to picnics and different sports and parties, but that was only entertainment. Intellectually we were worlds apart. I was interested in good books. Tom was only interested in how well he could play golf.

One is most acutely conscious of cultural divergence in a group of intimate friends. This leads to a reappraisal of the relation as in the next case.

He had always irritated her when they were with friends. His talk was so ponderous, he had such difficulty expressing himself and formulating his ideas. He was always dragging in highly intellectual subjects like semantics. "He never understood my jokes or allusions to literature or current slang. He was just dumb."

Conflicts which sometimes break up an engagement are those arising out of religious differences. The most obvious of these are when the couple are of different religious faiths as in Protestant-Catholic or Protestant-Jewish unions. Sometimes even more important are differences in religious interest and devotion as in the following broken engagement:

We had planned to be married in June. In May a shower was given for me, I bought a wedding dress and arrangements were made for a home wedding. We would have been married except that he began asking why we had to go to church Sunday mornings, the only morning we have? I think he would have liked it just as well if we had gone into the country and enjoyed the beauty. I agree with him perfectly but I thoroughly enjoy going to church. I don't go to church because someone says I must. I find it inspiring and it helps to make me a more cheerful person. I have never felt that it was keeping me from doing something that I would rather be doing. I just feel that he doesn't feel that way. He started to argue the point and tried to convince me that I shouldn't go to church Sunday mornings. Then he began talking very peculiarly about how he was on one side of the fence and I was on the other and couldn't I see that that was the case. So I began to think that religion was going to be an issue. I don't think any marriage can be successful where there is any issue that big.

Occasionally the cultural roots of the conflict are below the surface. In the following case the young man, according to his ex-fiancée's account, seemed determined to be the dominating one in the relationship, a role which she apparently did not concede.

He was rather quiet. You had to get to know him before he'd open up. He was pretty set in some of his ideas. We used to fight all the time. We used to call it the Saturday-night session: that's when it usually happened. I think most of all he was afraid I was having my way too much.

This disagreement over the dominating role may be interpreted, of course, as due to personality conflict rather than cultural conflict since either factor, or both, may be involved.

Important divergences in values and interests may not be recognized until after engagement. The intimacy of this relationship gives an opportunity to discover if the couple have ideals and goals in life which will make for harmony or disharmony in marriage.

She had one trait I did not like and that was her social ambition. She was interested in people for the sake of social aims. Her friends respected her very highly and thought she was a sincere, warm person. But I think she made friendships more of a business than she needed to.

Personality Problems

The terms "compatibility" and "incompatibility" are in popular use as an explanation of successful and unsuccessful personality adjustment in engagement and marriage. Where all other factors are favorable—common interests, similarity in cultural backgrounds, congruent ideals and values—the couple may still have difficulties because of conflicts in temperament and personality traits.

First, there are persons with major personality problems which render them prone to break engagements. Men who are overly dependent upon their mothers, promiscuous in sexual relations, fearful of assuming marital responsibilities, or content with the irresponsibility and freedom of the bachelor state, may enter into, but often break, engagements.

Similarly, young women appear more likely to break engagements if they have idealized their fathers or have been attached to them to an extreme degree, if they are fearful of the physical aspects of marriage, or if their standards of mate selection are higher than the qualifications of their fiancés.

These and other attitudes may be symptomatic of underlying personality problems, such as feelings of inferiority, emotional insecurity, emotional instability, and emotional and social immaturity, which may have origins in the childhood family relationships of the person. The experience of a discordant home environment in childhood seems in some of the cases interviewed to be associated with the tendency to break engagements.

In my interviews on broken engagements one factor has appeared frequently in a variety of forms which seems to be related, at least in part, to the breaking of the association in a large proportion of cases. This factor is the presence of a major personality problem in one or both of the partners to the engagement. A "major personality problem" is a problem important enough to color all social action undertaken by that individual. This usually manifests itself in some attempted behavior adaptation caused by consciously or unconsciously felt insecurity—generally emotional insecurity.

A home environment which was markedly discordant for one reason or another seemed to be the most important cause of a major personality problem leading to the breaking of an engagement. A broken home, either through divorce or separation, not death; a home where the mother and father went their separate ways either with or without antagonism; a home where both mother and father were too concerned with their own affairs to bother with the children—either because of economic or temperamental difficulties—or a home where the children were taught to despise one parent, these were the types of discordant homes which have seemed to exert a significant influence in the formation of these personality problems.[2]

Since in our culture the engagement period is considered the final test of compatibility, the broken engagement is the recognition by one or both members of the couple of their lack of suitability. Incompatibility may take one or more of the following forms.

Incompatibility of temperament refers to clashes arising from the basic mood of the person. Two high-strung and tense individuals are likely to find difficulties in adjustment. So also are two people who are moody and pessimistic in their outlook on life. More often, one member of the couple has a temper or is emotionally unstable. Quarreling in the engagement period is the most frequent indication of temperamental incompatibility.

Jim had very much of a temper and was constantly at me whenever he wanted me to do something I didn't want to do. He liked to have his way all the time. In an effort to get this he would become very emotional and demonstrative. It made me sort of disgusted. We never quarreled before the engagement, but sometimes during the engagement. This was because of his gambling and his jealousy.

Every once in a while I used to break my engagement to Ned. I don't know why I did it. I would break it and make it up again. I think it gave me the jitters. I suppose it was just general emotional instability. I always wanted to marry him. The situations were not important to me; I can't even remember. I certainly was nasty. I would tell him I was not engaged. I used to get exasperated with Ned at times. Let me think. Most arguments we have had have been over subjects of a theoretical nature. We had no great disagreements but we were able to manufacture some. I don't remember anything over which we broke the engagement last summer.

Unsatisfied personality need is another source of incompatibility. The girl may wish for demonstration of affection and frequent verbal expressions of love which her fiancé does not supply. Or he may find that she does not give him the encouragement, understanding, and sympathy which he needs.

I did not measure our relations so much in terms of love as practical reality. Most important, she didn't understand me very well or my aims in life and what I hoped to achieve. She did not understand my intellectual interests, for example, my interest in religious theory. She was more of a motherly type of girl. She would make an excellent mother.

---

[2] Unpublished paper by Charlotte A. Cooper.

Unsatisfied personality need emphasizes two facts. First, liking is not the same as loving a person. There is a difference between love and friendship. Second, a sudden infatuation may represent only congeniality and not any emotional interdependence of the two, as is illustrated by the following case.

> Well, he was just nice, real nice. The moment you met him you could tell he was just a swell person inside. About the third date, we had it all planned what we were going to do. Real fast and sudden. We had "now this is the real feeling." But it didn't last. I think if it had, the same thing would happen as before—the same sweet boy, but I'd get bored again.

The parental personality pattern which each member of a couple unconsciously seeks in the other may not match sufficiently to insure the happiness of the union. One requirement of a satisfying interpersonal adjustment appears to be that the love object have those personality characteristics of the parent of the opposite sex which had affectional significance for the person as a child. Concretely, this means that a young man will tend to fall in love and be emotionally satisfied with a girl who possesses those personality traits that were important to him as a child in his response relation to his mother. Conversely, a girl finds herself emotionally drawn to a young man who manifests in his association with her the traits which had meaning in her earlier relationships with her father.

In the following case the girl fell in love with a young man who looked like her father but who, as she found later, did not have his characteristics. The young man resented her efforts to change his traits to be more like those she admired in her father. Each recognizes the fact in their separate statements:

> Any time you are second choice to the girl's father! It doesn't click. She was always measuring me up to him and comparing me to him. When I marry I'm not going to be a person for her to make over to be her old man.

> Frank looked something like my father used to look, but my present fiancé acts more like him. He is very competent just as my father.

Frequently in the engagement period one member of the couple finds that the other one, who is entirely satisfied with the relationship, does not meet his or her personality needs.

> Mr. A fell deeply in love with Joan who had some of his mother's outstanding personality traits. But she broke their private understanding to be married as soon as she knew him better. She was greatly attached to her father who was an aggressive masculine type. She found that Mr. A needed emotional support and said, "He wanted someone to lean on, but I wanted a husband I could lean on."

The *career interest* of either the man or girl may be a decisive factor in the breaking of the affectional association. This is particularly true of young people entering or even in training for a profession. The ministerial student develops a conception of the characteristics appropriate for a pastor's wife. If he perceives that his fiancée falls short of these he begins to think about breaking the engagement especially if he becomes interested in a girl who corresponds to his ideal of a life companion. A somewhat parallel example is the girl who is engaged to a young man before he decides on the career of a minister. Previously she had pictured herself as the wife of a successful businessman. She finds she is unable to readjust to her conception of the role of a pastor's wife.

Frequently, other related factors enter into this type of broken engagement. The young man, beginning his professional career or preparing for it, enters a new social world. He finds that his ideas and values are changing, sometimes in ways that conflict with those of his fiancée. While he has been growing intellectually and socially she may have been vegetating in an unstimulating environment.

An illustration of this pattern of the disruption of an engagement may be taken from the profession of medicine. The medical student after his formal training is required to complete an interneship in a hospital. Restricted in his social contacts, he falls in love and becomes engaged to a nurse who, besides her nurse's training, has had only a high school education. Her family background is of a lower social class than his. They have a common interest in medicine but in little else. He may realize before marriage that she will be unable to participate in other areas of his activities.

These different factors or conditions in broken engagements—slight emotional attachment, separation, parental opposition, cultural divergences, and personality problems—are seldom present independent of each other. Generally, two or more of them operate in conjunction. A given case of a broken engagement should be intensively studied to determine the actual interplay of factors which leads one or both members of a couple to seek the termination of their association.

.   .   .   .

Breaking the Engagement

Two different techniques may be used by the person who wishes to end the engagement. One is the sharp complete break; the other is the tapering-off procedure. The advantage of the immediate clean break inheres in its aboveboard character; there is none of the camouflage of feelings of the cooling-off technique. Its disadvantage is the emotional shock to the jilted person and all the aggressive behavior it may set off. In our group of broken engagements there was no instance of the classic case where the rejected suitor kills the girl and then commits suicide in accordance with the frustration-aggression theory of directing hostility first outwardly and then toward oneself.

The advantage of the tapering-off procedure is that the rejected person, realizing gradually the defection of the other, is somewhat prepared and suffers less severe emotional turmoil and acute distress. Its disadvantage is that he may continue to hope against hope and so take a longer time to make an emotional readjustment and be psychologically ready to enter into a new relationship.

.   .   .   .

The final break often occurs on the initiative of one member of the couple. The typical situation is that one wants the break and the other does not. Sometimes it comes as a "bolt out of the blue" to the jilted one. He has been oblivious, or so he claims, to the attitudes and intention of the other.

.   .   .   .

Reaction to the Broken Engagement

To the "jilted" person the broken engagement occasions an emotional crisis in something like direct proportion to its unexpectedness. The rejected individual is in a turmoil of conflicting impulses, feelings, and questionings. He is possessed by accusations against the errant lover about the reasons for the other's unaccountable and outrageous behavior, duplicity, and lack of frankness; by self-examination for failure in the engagement; and by real or imagined deficiencies. He considers any and all possible means of reestablishing the relationship. He may run the gamut of emotions from fantastic hope to deepest despair. He shrinks from the ordeal of meeting and informing relatives and friends. To himself and later to others he depreciates the qualities of his former inamorata, stressing defects where formerly he had seen only virtues. He may even reach the conclusion that she is morally irresponsible, mentally deranged, and may wonder why he had ever been attracted to her. A little later in a reversal of feeling he may affirm to himself and to others his willingness to forgive all if only she will consent to resume the relationship. Then his love, turning to hate, may lead to thoughts and threats of murder of the former loved one and even, in rare instances, to the act itself. Or he may contemplate, or attempt, or sometimes actually commit suicide. Literature includes instances of the murder of the loved one by the rejected suitor, followed by his suicide.

Later, however, the rejected person regains his emotional balance and when interviewed some months afterwards generally gives a less emotional account of the break.

.   .   .   .

Time, the comforting counsel of friends, the routine of life, new interests, and especially the formation of another attachment, gradually heal the injuries caused by the emotional wounding. Later, the person tends to minimize the degree of stress and strain experienced and to express satisfaction that the break occurred.

.   .   .   .

Engagement on the Rebound

Some persons pass rapidly from the emotional crisis of a broken engagement (or from an unsatisfactory love affair which has not reached this stage) to a new emotional involvement. This is particularly the case with persons with major personality problems, especially those with a history of rejections in family relationships in childhood. Even when there has been no childhood rejection, the need for emotional expression may impel the person into another close affectional relationship. Another contributing and sometimes decisive factor is the strength of the urge to regain status in one's intimate group of young people. These and other influences result in engagements and often marriages on the emotional rebound without the person making the discriminating choice he otherwise would be disposed to make.

Our engagement was a rebound from an unhappy romance that I was trying to get over. The boy I had been going with suddenly married someone else and it upset me very much. I never felt that this second engagement would end in a marriage.

The following is a generalized case indicating some of the typical features in a group of instances of engagements on the rebound from a broken engagement.

Polly was the pretty, charming, and intelligent daughter of a professional man of moderate means. She was pledged by one of the better sororities on entering a coeducational college. She was dated by several of the leading men of the campus and in her junior year was engaged to a young man who was able and ambitious. At the beginning of the second semester of the senior year he broke the engagement and before the school year was over the Sunday newspaper announced his engagement to the daughter of one of the wealthy and prominent families of the nearby metropolitan city. During the summer in her home town Polly met a high school acquaintance who had dropped his course in his high school sophomore year. She had previously paid little attention to him because he lived "across the tracks." But he was devoted and sympathetic and promised to go ahead with his education. They were engaged and married within a few months of the date of her former fiancé's wedding. After marriage, Polly soon realized that she and her husband were misfits psychologically, that they had no common interests, and that he had no serious intention of completing high school and preparing himself for a trade or profession. The situation became unbearable to both of them; she returned home and later secured a divorce.

32 · *Breaking an Engagement by Mutual Consent* *

BETTINA LOOMIS

On the surface, breaking an engagement by mutual consent seems a relatively painless way to end a relationship that has become unsatisfactory. The article that follows gives a fictional account of what may lie back of a newspaper announcement that "The engagement of Miss Katherine Anne Mason and Mr. Stephen Howard has been broken by mutual consent." The article also has some suggestions for helping the jilted partner to restore emotional equilibrium.

WHEN STEVE sat miserably in your living room and told you that it was all over, that he couldn't go through with it, that the wedding in October and the honeymoon in the Poconos and life together were just not going to be, you felt practically nothing. You heard yourself saying, "Of course. I understand. It's all right."

But now as you read the newspaper announcement, with its meaningless, face-saving phrase "by mutual consent," you know it isn't all right at all. Aching and desolate, you force yourself to look ahead to an endless string of days and nights without Steve. How can you face them?

Well, nobody can tell you it's going to be easy, because it isn't. Eventually you'll get over it—but not before you've seen a good many sleepless midnights and awakened a good many mornings to the awful realization that the nightmare is true. There will be times when the telephone rings and your heart leaps with hope, only to sink again because you know it

---

* "Brides and Brides-to-Be: . . . By Mutual Consent," *Good Housekeeping*, 139 (August, 1954), 38. Reprinted by permission of The Hearst Corporation. This article was written by a staff member.

can't be Steve. And other times when it's all you can do not to call him just to hear his voice.

There's nothing you can do to prevent these times of bitter unhappiness. But there *are* some things you can do to speed your recovery and to insure that not *all* the hours ahead will be hours of misery.

You can go away. Anywhere. The heroines of Victorian novels were shipped off to Europe for a year to cure their broken hearts. And while a year in Europe is probably far out of range, the principle is still a sound one. First, it removes you from a scene laden with memories. Second, it makes you *do* something, not just sit in your room and brood. So force yourself to make the effort. Visit a cousin in another town. Ask your mother to go with you on a motor trip. Induce a friend to join you on a bus or train excursion. Even a week or two away will help.

You can accept "unwanted" help from your family and friends. Your father, who loves nothing better than an evening at home watching television, suddenly develops a most uncharacteristic desire to go to the movies. You know he simply thinks that you should "get out." And so you should. You don't want to, but go anyway. You will probably discover at some point in the evening that for 20 consecutive minutes you haven't thought about Steve. A couple down the block invites you for dinner. You're sure the invitation is prompted by pity. Why not call it sympathy instead and accept? Get all dressed up, take them a bottle of wine or a bunch of daffodils, make a fuss over their baby. They'll really enjoy their guest, but much more important, you'll have taken the first step in reinstating yourself in the society from which you now feel so removed.

You can give your emotions occasional release. In the very beginning you may find that you have to hold yourself in strict check for fear of going to pieces. But after the first shock has subsided, it's a good idea—once in a while—to let off steam. Etiquette books imply that you should *never* say a word about what happened. But that isn't quite realistic. Of course you shouldn't regale casual friends with the details of your unhappiness, or weep on the shoulders of acquaintances. But you will *have* to do some talking and probably even a bit of crying, and we don't think your mother or a really good friend is going to think any the less of you if you do.

Explore some new activity, but do it with a group. People will be your most effective therapy. So sign up for that course in ceramics or join a Great Books group. And *make* yourself attend the first few meetings. After that it won't take as much effort.

Don't avoid men. Whether or not you think you want a new beau, you'll probably find yourself going to considerable lengths to avoid dates. When Marian invites you to dinner and tells you a chap from John's office is going to be there, you'll be tempted to beg off. When Frannie calls to say her date has a friend and why don't you all go dancing, you suddenly find you're catching a cold. What's the matter? Well, the matter is that because Steve rejected you, you think other men are going to too. But do a bit of reasoning with yourself. Tell yourself that the young man of the evening is neither going to reject you nor fall in love with you on one date. All he wants is the company of an agreeable young woman.

The going will be slow. There will be little spurts of progress followed by periods of setback. Sometimes you'll think your sadness is never going to leave you. But almost without your being aware of it, it will recede. Presently you'll discover that you've waked up every morning for a week without once feeling black depression. And then one evening you'll meet a young man who's so nice you're genuinely glad when he asks for a date.

Maybe you two will fall in love; maybe you won't. That's not the important point. The point is that you've been through your bad time and now it's over. And perhaps it wasn't all wasted. Perhaps you can now face life with a bit more character than if it had never happened.

33 · *How to Untie an Old Beau* *

BETTINA LOOMIS

In contrast to the preceding article, in this fictional account the man is the one who is jilted. The article concentrates on how the ex-fiancée can help him restore his self-esteem and emotional balance.

THROUGHOUT the last two years of college you were Sam's girl. You wore his fraternity pin, went to picnics and parties and Saturday-night movies with him; people took to linking your names as though they were hyphenated. You weren't exactly engaged, but when you thought of being married it was always to Sam.

Then Roger came along, and practically from the first moment you knew this was it. He knew too. So presently, as gently and kindly as you could, you told Sam.

After the first shock of agonized disbelief, Sam took it very well. He didn't pretend that it didn't hurt him but said Roger seemed like a swell guy. He said he hoped you'd be happy. He said he guessed he'd get over it.

---

* "Brides and Brides-to-Be: How to Untie an Old Beau," *Good Housekeeping*, 138 (June, 1954), 38. Reprinted by permission of The Hearst Corporation.
The article was written by a staff member.

But he hasn't.

You and Roger have been engaged for three months now—and it's evident to everybody that Sam is still carrying a torch for you. Your friends (who are naturally Sam's friends too) report that he goes everywhere stag, that when they round up new girls for him to meet he is polite but uninterested. When you run into him at the bowling alley or in the drugstore, you can feel his eyes following you. And then one Saturday afternoon you answer the doorbell and find that it's Sam. How do you behave?

It's Your Move

Well, that depends on the kind of man Sam is *and* the kind of man Roger is. If, although it's unlikely, Sam is the sort who might just possibly make a scene, now or ever, or might conceivably do anything to embarrass or discredit either you or Roger, this is the moment to make it clear that you two can have no further relationship at all. And by the same token, though it's even more unlikely, if Roger is inclined to be jealous, apt to feel either hurt or angry if you don't put Sam entirely out of your life, you must take the same course of action. In either case you needn't be rude to get your point across. After you and Sam have exchanged the usual "How are you" and "You're looking well," you can simply say, "Sam, I'm sorry I can't ask you in, but I'm dashing to the hairdresser." And if he doesn't accept that as rejection and offers to drive you there, you can make your position even clearer by saying, "I'm afraid someone might misunderstand." And that's that for Sam. You may have turned him into an enemy, you've certainly turned him into a stranger, but he *is* out of your life.

However, the chances are that Sam is not a scene maker and Roger is not jealousy-ridden. And in that case we think it would be both kinder and more sensible if, when Sam appears at the door, you summon all your poise and treat him exactly as you would treat any friend.

Checkmate

With just the same amount (no more, no less) of enthusiasm with which you'd welcome any other classmate, invite him in. Offer him a Coke. Inquire about a mutual friend. Show him the very funny cartoon in a current magazine. Report the latest news from your brother in Japan. But whatever you talk about, keep it casual.

Don't drag Roger into every third sentence. Sam *knows* you're engaged. There's no need to twist the knife. On the other hand, don't ever let the conversation take a nostalgic, it-might-have-been tack. If he recalls, tenderly, a day he spent with you at a remote beach, head him off quickly with,

"Yes, it was a perfectly lovely place. Some day this summer a bunch of us should really drive out there." Sam won't stay long. Obviously he called on an emotional impulse. But in the face of your impersonal friendliness, the emotion will subside quickly. Even so, as he says good-by, he may want to leave a door open for himself and so ask, "May I see you again?"

Now steer a middle course. It isn't necessary to put him off completely, and on the other hand it isn't wise to leap in with an invitation to dinner next Tuesday. "You'll be at the Martins' party a week from Saturday, won't you?" or "When we're settled, we hope to be at home every Sunday," are much better ways of indicating that Sam may see you, of course, but you won't make a *date* with him.

You probably won't have to go through this performance more than once or twice. Very soon Sam will realize exactly how things stand and will probably simply stop calling. But he'll leave with his dignity intact.

Winner's Reward

Why, you may wonder, if Sam is going to drift away anyway, should you go through these strained interviews? Well, there are several reasons why all of you—Sam, you, and Roger—will be happier if you use a bit of diplomacy. First, if you, in effect, shut the door in Sam's face you make *all* future meetings awkward. The three of you live in the same town, have the same friends, go to the same places. Do you really want to pass without speaking in the streets, to make people feel they can't have you to the same parties? Isn't it going to seem juvenile after you're married if Roger can't go on a fishing trip, or Sam has to turn down a college reunion, because the other will be present?

Secondly, Sam has paid you the tribute of loving you. Now he's engaged in the very painful business of falling out of love. Secure in your new love, can't you spare half an hour or so to help him? Delicately handled, these visits with you can have a tapering-off effect. And eventually, when Sam is back on an even keel, you may even find that you two can be friends.

Most important, this is not an etiquette-book exercise; this is a problem in adult human relations. And we think that by solving it with patience, discretion, and kindness, you prove that you're well equipped to lead a good, entirely grown-up life.

34 · Women and Single Life *

RUTH REED

Interviews with three hundred mature single women form the basis for Dr. Reed's interpretation of the life of the single woman. The marriage probabilities of women decline rapidly after age twenty-five and after age thirty the probability of marriage is slight. Dr. Reed first raises the question: why do some women not marry? The following is a summary of her answer:

1. Men and women are not evenly distributed over the United States. Men predominate in some areas, women in others. Job opportunities draw men to one part of the country or to certain types of cities, and women to other regions or cities. In general there are more women than men in cities, while the reverse is true in rural areas.

2. Women working in cities are often living away from home and find it hard to make social contacts without the aid of family or relatives.

3. The struggle of many young women to better themselves economically often absorbs a disproportionate amount of time and energy that otherwise might be directed toward social life; also, economic success may bring with it upward mobility out of the family and social groups in which they were reared. They then lose their normal contacts for courtship and marriage.

4. Girls who attend educational institutions in which students and teachers are predominantly feminine become habituated to a manless society. Sometimes their training develops in them traits that are not attractive to men nor suited to marriage.

5. Some men prefer to marry women who have less education than themselves. Thus, although more men receive higher education than women, some of the better-educated women are not chosen for marriage. The earlier tendency of some well-educated women to scorn the idea of marriage has now changed—young college-educated women know that they wish to be married.

6. Some women devote themselves to their parents, especially if they have been indoctrinated with a sense of duty to care for their parents or to repay the cost of their college education.

7. Some single women said that during their marriageable years they had

---

* Ruth Reed, *The Single Woman* (New York: The Macmillan Company, 1942), summary of pages 4–35 and selections from pages 68–75 and 92–95.
The author holds the degree of Doctor of Philosophy from Columbia University and is Professor of Social Research at Catholic University.

held such romantic views of marriage that they could not accept the attentions of the average young man. Some had been disappointed in love and romantically clung to the idea that they could not love again.

8. A few women become so absorbed in their occupations that they are unwilling to make any adjustments in order to marry.

The above are the reasons why three hundred women did not marry, as they related them to Dr. Reed. If there were deeper psychological reasons in some cases, they were not revealed.

From the interviews and her own perception, Dr. Reed arrives at a statement of how life can be satisfying to the single woman.

A Basis of Understanding

A home life which gives her the rest, the relaxation and the personal satisfactions that she needs is basically helpful to the single woman in getting on with people outside the home. But the determining consideration is, of course, the type of person that she is herself, the kind of womanly character that she has been able to achieve. The single woman at her best, characterized by broad interests and tolerant sympathy, a deep understanding and acceptance of human nature in all its aspects, humor, kindness, and an absence of pettiness in dealing with others, relates herself easily and happily to her associates in business and in her personal and social life. If it is remarked that such personalities are by no means common, this is readily admitted, for the achievement of a full maturity at any level is rare in human annals. But the fact that single women of this type were encountered with such frequency among the women with whom we talked in the course of this study indicates that the development of a well-poised, womanly character and of a deep personal happiness is not only a plausible goal for single women but one which has been achieved by many of them.

In the achievement of a personal integration and security which made satisfactory relations with others possible, it was remarked that the possession of a set of beliefs and convictions superior to mere social conventions and prejudices was a powerful stabilizing force. A philosophy which merely turned the single woman in upon herself and which was expressed in a series of practices focused upon the individual performing them seemed not to have a beneficial effect either upon her personal character and happiness or upon her relationships with others. But a way of looking at things which seemed to anchor the individual more securely to the good, the beautiful and the true appeared to give her a center of gravity in a deeper world and make her less subject to the petty disturbances and annoyances of everyday life. For it is obvious that until she has made her peace with herself, until she has been able to look at things as they are and see some meaning in them in relation to a larger whole, until then the basis of her equilibrium is so precarious that she will not be able to escape from her own problems to any interest in others or any concern for their welfare. And as long as her chief concern is with her own personal problems and her own welfare, she is as unhappy and as frustrated as any other self-centered egotist.

A fundamental point of departure seems to lie in her ability and her willingness to accept herself as an individual and as a single woman. Until she can do this, her attitude toward herself and toward others is wavering and uncertain, her position lacks clarity and honesty, and her dealings with others lack that degree of consistency and dependability which is necessary to any happy relationship.

The single woman, in accepting herself as a single woman, does not, in so doing, turn her back upon marriage, renounce happiness or make noble gestures of resignation or grief. She simply looks at the facts as they are. First, marriages of women over thirty are very rare; if a woman is not married by the time that she is thirty, it is extremely unlikely that she will ever marry. Most women before the age of thirty expect that they will marry, and their attitude toward themselves, toward others, and toward all that they do is colored by that expectation. The average unmarried girl under thirty expects that the pattern of her mature life will be that of the married woman; her thoughts and actions are oriented toward that goal. This orientation toward marriage is so strong in a few single women that they will not accept any other pattern of life as a possible one for themselves even when it is clear that they are not going to be married. They become frustrated, embittered old maids. There are also some women who are sure from a relatively early age that they are not going to be married; they are not the "marrying kind" either because of their lack of interest in marriage or because their childhood experiences of home life have conditioned them against marriage. These women adjust to single life without a struggle. But for the average single woman the realization that she is not going to marry grows gradually as does her acceptance of the fact. And as she accepts the fact that she is not going to marry she begins to orient herself toward the life of the single woman and to prepare herself to achieve the happiness, the success, the recognition, and the full life of adult womanhood which it is possible for the single woman to achieve in our democratic society. This acceptance of the content and values of the single, adult womanhood does not in any way preclude marriage should a change in circumstances occur. In fact, such an attitude may even lead in that direction, for the single woman with a sound realistic approach to the business of living, who makes a happy and contented life for herself, is a far more likely matrimonial prospect than the one who merely waits for a suitor to appear or for "something wonderful to happen."

Getting On with the Majority

This being willing to think of herself as permanently single proved to have some surprising components when we talked with single women about it. For they had apparently adjusted more easily and readily to the realities of the single woman's life than they had to other people's opinion of the single life for women and their estimate of its values. Like any other minority group single women find themselves under the necessity of adjusting to the majority opinion of it with its mingled components of insight and misconception. For the single woman not only has a life which is different in range and content from the lives of other women but she is likely to have that life misunderstood and its content and value questioned. It is obvious to the majority that the single woman lacks the development that comes from wifehood and motherhood but they do not always understand that she has found development and happiness along other lines and that the pattern of her life, while different from theirs, may have those elements of personal achievement and association which give her the realization of success and happiness. Some married women, of course, do have this realization, particularly the college-bred women and those who have worked before marriage, but most of them do not, and they imagine that the life of the woman who has remained single is like their own life before they were married, which was essentially a waiting period. This may have been a gay and exciting period and one happily remembered, but it contained nevertheless the element of waiting, with painful moments of doubt and uncertainty. Now the old maid is one who has continued to wait, whose dreams and hopes of marriage have lessened with the years or have changed to disappointment and bitterness. Some people think of all single women as old maids, although in the course of our study we found very few of them. For most of our adult single women had set aside their ideas of marriage or had relegated them to a quite minor position in life. They had turned their thoughts and energies toward being adult, single women. As a consequence they were not old maids, but adult women, single women, with a wide variety of interests and achievments. A great many people realize this, but a large number of them do not, and they feel sorry for all single women.

Now some single women are unduly conscious of this fact and sensitive about it. In a few sensitive souls it may even create a feeling of inferiority. The single woman who has achieved success and happiness is little conscious of it and when she has it brought to her attention she views it good humoredly. But a single woman who has not entered fully and wholeheartedly into the business of living, who still sits moping on the side lines may become concerned and unhappy about what some people think of her status and of the life she has been able to make for herself. One woman complained, "At best the single woman's life is a sublimation, a compensation. No substitution can be entirely satisfactory."

She had overlooked the fact that no one's life is entirely satisfactory and that sublimation and compensatory activities are necessary in any life in order to achieve even moderate happiness. Then, too, woman's nature is variable and for some of them marriage may require more compensatory activities than the single life and as much conscious effort. It is for this reason that the married woman's attitude toward the single woman is often one of mingled envy and contempt. She may despise the single woman because she has not married and envy her for the more personal development and achievement which she has and for her greater independence in some matters of choice. The single woman, on the other hand, while she prizes her independence, may imagine that marriage has, *ipso facto*, made the married woman happy. The married woman often overlooks the fact that the independence of the individual in contemporary life is restricted in all circumstances; and the single woman ignores the fact that marriage does not make a woman a happy woman. It merely makes her a married woman who, like the single woman, has a chance to achieve happiness if she makes the most of her opportunities.

.   .   .   .

The Will to Love

"Not to love is not to live" is an old proverb which has rich meaning for the single woman. For the person who does not love lives a life so meager and so attenuated that it is impossible to think of happiness as one of its attributes. Love has been so often associated with married happiness that many people think of the single life as a life without love. This is not true, however, unless the single woman wills it so, but the love life which characterizes the normal single state differs both in range and tone from the love of married people. For married love is closely centered upon one person, it is a "fixation"; it is intense; it is highly personal; and it drives toward possession of the loved one. But the love of the single person is more diffuse in nature; it has something of a detached and impersonal element about it; it is general rather than personal in tone; and it does not desire possession. The life of the single woman is not without personal attachments of course. She has the same love of parents, of brothers and sisters, of kin, and of friends as all people do, but the love which characterizes the maturity of her single life and which constitutes its warp and woof is the love for the many, who to her usually stand for some one aspect of the common good. With many this love is associated with work, but with others it is not. The best nurses have a deep love of their work; artists have it, teachers, social workers and others. Some single women do not achieve it, because they fear sentimentality, possessiveness, and other hampering aspects of a highly fixated love. But the single woman who has not been afraid to love knows that her love must be a disciplined, directed love which leads to a conscientious and well-rendered service, but that it must not be a love which indulges in sentiment, which demands a response in kind, or which drives toward possession. This love, when disciplined and enlightened, is a powerful socializing and developing force which has an important effect upon our culture and institutions. It may supplement the love which children receive in families and aid them in their development to adult life; it may steady the wavering adolescent in a way which he cannot accept from family love; and it may give the sick a detached, impersonal but devoted service when ministrations from family members would prove disturbing. It is the type of love which prevents professional services from becoming dead, cold matters of routine for it injects into them something of the warmth and spirit of neighborly friendliness without making any claim of neighborliness in return. It prevents hospitals from becoming formidable machines of routine and efficiency and it removes the cold blight from the social services without injecting the hampering elements of sentimentality into them. It represents a deep love and respect for human beings and their essential rights and it is motivated and colored and sustained by a drive to attain the good, the beautiful, and the true and to make these values live in human lives.

It may be said that some married women have this faculty of general love and it is evident that some of them do. But the average woman who has a husband and children develops a deep love for them which may strengthen her capacity for love but which tends to narrow its scope to members of her own family circle as long as their need of her is direct and immediate. Some married men also have this general love and some of them who do are good husbands and fathers. But it is often remarked, too, that men whose devotion to the general welfare is intense have a tendency to overlook the deeper and more personal needs of members of their family.

This general love, which many single women have, does not preclude, of course, devotion to friends and other forms of personal love. On the contrary, a general and diffused love helps the single woman to canalize her more personal loves and attachments into sanctioned forms and to keep them happy and wholesome. It preserves, too, the balance and tone of her emotional life and relieves her of much of that tedium and pettiness which is the plague of the feminine world. Such a general love should not be confused with the aggressive egotism of some exponents of isms and fads. For general love is not a self-centered or self-seeking love, it is outgoing in nature and it finds its most normal expression in an impersonal but interested and devoted service to others.

CHAPTER 8:

Love

35 · Role of Love in Human Development *

DANIEL A. PRESCOTT

Love is an emotion that almost everyone experiences in many different forms. Because love does take different forms it is hard to define. Dr. Prescott quotes what a number of different persons have to say about love and then presents his own analysis of the nature of love and its role in human development. He does not view loving or being loved as independent experiences but as two sides of one coin. The combined experience enriches life and facilitates adjustment.

THIS PAPER will address itself to three questions: (1) Is love a reality or a delusive romantic construct of our culture? (2) If love *is* a reality, what is its nature? (3) If love *is* a reality, what is its role in human development? In preparing this paper, I examined several dozen books in human development, educational psychology, cultural anthropology and sociology, psychiatry, and biography. In the majority of books in human development and educational psychology the word love did not occur. When it did occur, it was used without definition for the most part. I feel that if love is a reality, we need seriously and scientifically to study its influence on human lives and to learn what conditions are favorable to its enhancement and fulfillment. If it is not a reality, we shall need to study the reasons for the emergence of so strong a myth, so frustrating an aspiration, so delusive a

---

* *Journal of Home Economics*, 44 (March, 1952), 173–176. Reprinted by permission of the publisher and the author.

The author, whose degree of Doctor of Education is from Harvard University, is Professor of Education and Director of the Institute for Child Study at the University of Maryland. He is active in national and international educational organizations. He has contributed articles to professional journals and is the author of a number of books in education, including *The Child in the Education Process*.

pretention. There is a remarkably small amount of scientific material now available about it.

A very brief review of the ideas found in the books examined comes first. Breckenridge and Vincent,[1] Strang,[2] and Barker, Kounin and Wright [3] all mention love as a reality. The general idea expressed is that love markedly influences behavior, development, and adjustment. One notes a vagueness about the nature of love as a positive force and finds much more specificity about the negative effects of lack of love and of inappropriate use of love relationships. Kluckhohn and Murray [4] give a great amount of material about sexual behavior and about family processes but no discussion of love as such.

James Plant [5] clearly regards love as a reality but does not define it. Love affords children a basic security, a sure feeling of belonging, he says. Insecure, unloved children show anxious, panicky symptoms that contrast with the aggressive overcompensation of inadequate children. He shows that confusion about their security often arises as children try to meet the learning and behavioral demands set for them by the authority of their parents and of society and again as they struggle for independence.

Harry Stack Sullivan [6] defines love: "When the satisfaction or the security of another person becomes as significant to one as is one's own security, then the state of love exists."

Overstreet [7] says,

> The love of a person implies not the possession of that person but the affirmation of that person. It means granting him gladly the full right to his unique humanhood. One does not truly love a person and yet seek to enslave him—by law, or by bonds of dependence and possessiveness. Whenever we experience a genuine love we are moved by the transforming experience toward a capacity for good will.

Fromm [8] coins the term "productive love" because the word love as popularly used is so ambiguous. The essence of love, he contends, is the same

[1] Breckenridge, Marian E., and Vincent, Elizabeth L. *Child Development*. Philadelphia: W. B. Saunders Company, 1943.

[2] Strang, Ruth. *Introduction to Child Study*. New York: The Macmillan Company, 1951.

[3] Barker, Roger G., Kounin, Jacob S., and Wright, Herbert F. *Child Behavior and Development*. New York: The McGraw-Hill Book Company, 1943.

[4] Kluckhohn, Clyde, and Murray, Henry A. *Personality in Nature, Society and Culture*. New York: Alfred A. Knopf, 1948.

[5] Plant, James. *The Envelope*. New York: The Commonwealth Fund, 1950.

[6] Sullivan, Harry Stack. *Conceptions of Modern Psychiatry*. Washington, D.C.: William Alanson White Psychiatric Foundation, 1947.

[7] Overstreet, Harry. *The Mature Mind*. New York: W. W. Norton & Company, Inc., 1949.

[8] Fromm, Erich. *Man for Himself*. New York: Rinehart & Co., Inc., 1947.

whether it is the mother's love for a child, our love for man, or the erotic love between two individuals. Certain basic elements are characteristic of all forms of productive love. They are: care, responsibility, respect, and knowledge. He says,

Care and responsibility denote that love is an activity, not a passion . . . the essence of love is to labor for something, to make something grow. . . . Without respect for and knowledge of the beloved person love deteriorates into domination and possessiveness. Respect . . . denotes the ability to see a person as he is, to be aware of his individuality and uniqueness. . . . Love is the expression of intimacy between two human beings under the condition of the preservation of each other's integrity. . . . To love one person productively means to be related to his human core, to him as representing mankind.

Fromm also contends that love of others and of ourselves are not alternatives,

The affirmation of one's own life, happiness, growth and freedom is rooted in one's capacity to love. . . . If an individual is able to love productively he loves himself too. . . . Selfishness and self-love, far from being identical, are actually opposites. . . . The selfish person does not love himself too much but too little, in fact he hates himself. . . . He is necessarily unhappy and anxiously concerned to snatch from life the satisfactions which he blocks himself from attaining. . . .

The recurring mention in the literature of the relatedness of love for self (self-respect), love for other individuals, and love for mankind led me to examine biographies and writings of three men who have lived lives of great devotion to mankind: Kagawa, Gandhi, and Albert Schweitzer. Kagawa [9] says,

Love awakens all that it touches . . . creation is the art of life pursued for love. . . . Love is the true nature of God. . . . In social life human beings meet and love one another through a material medium. . . . Love spins garments for itself out of matter . . . through love economic life appears as the content of the spiritual. . . . Real reconstruction of society can be accomplished only through the operation of education through love. . . . If we view economics so, the study of it changes into a science of love. . . . Art must create externally beautiful objects and internally it is itself love.

The practical social and political application of love has worked several miracles in India during our times. Gandhi [10] said,

---

[9] Kagawa, Toyokiko. *Meditations*. New York: Harper & Brothers, 1950.
[10] Fischer, Louis. *The Life of Mahatma Gandhi*. New York: Harper & Brothers, 1950.

To be truly non-violent I must love my adversary and pray for him even when he hits me. . . . We may attack measures and systems. We may not, we must not attack men. Imperfect ourselves, we must be tender towards others . . . forgiveness is more manly than punishment.

Gandhi contended that God is love and can be known only through action. "Faith does not permit of telling. It has to be lived and then it is self-propagating."

Albert Schweitzer [11] is another extraordinary international figure who has accomplished the apparently impossible during the past 50 years. He has tremendous reverence for life and respect for the dignity of all human beings and believes that love is the great force of the universe. He says,

By the spirit of the age the man of to-day is forced into skepticism about his own thinking in order to make him receptive to truth which comes to him from authority . . . [but] it is only by confidence in our ability to reach truth by our own individual thinking that we are capable of accepting truth from outside. . . . Man must bring himself into a spiritual relation to the world and become one with it. . . . Beginning to think about life and the world leads a man directly and almost irresistibly to reverence for life . . . the idea of love is the spiritual beam of light which reaches us from the Infinite . . . in God, the great first cause, the will-to-create and the will-to-love are one. . . . In knowledge of spiritual existence in God through love he [man] possesses the one thing needful.

Each of these three men was a man of action who accomplished the seemingly impossible during his lifetime in the first half of this our twentieth century. Each affirmed that love was a central dynamic in his accomplishment, love of other individuals, love of mankind, and love of God. Theirs certainly was "productive love." We may, therefore, regard our first question as answered in the affirmative. Love does exist. It is a potent reality.

The Nature of Love

Now what about the nature of love? On the basis of this little research, I have developed a number of theses about love. They will be presented with brief mention of the degree to which they seem to be supported by ideas in the material already cited.

1. *Love involves more or less empathy with the loved one.* A person who loves actually enters into the feeling of, and so shares intimately

---

[11] Schweitzer, Albert. *Out of My Life and Thought.* New York: Henry Holt & Co., 1949.

the experiences of, the loved one and the effects of experiences upon the loved one. Sullivan indicates something of how this comes about: [12]

> If another person matters as much to you as you do yourself, it is quite possible to talk to this person as you have never talked to anyone before. The freedom which comes . . . permits nuances of meaning, permits investigation without fear of rebuff which greatly augments the consensual validation of all sorts of things.

2. *One who loves is deeply concerned for the welfare, happiness, and development of the loved one.* This concern is so deep as to become one of the major values in the organized personality or "self" structure of the loving person. All sources studied seem to agree on this proposition. It is especially validated by the lives of Kagawa, Gandhi, and Schweitzer. Each of them has shown by his actions that he values the human beings whom he serves not only as much as he values himself but even more.

3. *One who loves finds pleasure in making his resources available to the loved one,* to be used by the latter to enhance his welfare, happiness, and development. Strength, time, money, mind—indeed all resources—are happily proffered for the use of the loved one. This implies that a loving person acts with and on behalf of the loved one whenever his resources permit and the action is desired by the loved one. The loving person is not merely deeply concerned about the welfare, happiness, and development of the beloved; he *does* something to enhance them whenever possible. All sources seem to agree on this proposition, too.

4. *On the one hand the loving person seeks a maximum of participation in the activities that contribute to the welfare, happiness, and development of the loved one.* On the other hand, the loving one accepts fully the uniqueness and individuality of the loved one and accords him freedom to experience, to act, and to become what he desires. This thesis is agreed to by nearly all of our sources.

5. *Love is most readily and usually achieved within the family circle but can be extended to include many other individuals, or categories of people, or all of humanity.* For Schweitzer it also includes all living things and the Creative Force of the universe—God. In the same way a person can advantageously experience love from a limitless number of other human beings and living things. Of course, genuine full love is hard to achieve even with a few persons, as several of our sources pointed out. But this is not proof that with greater scientific understanding of its processes we cannot create conditions that will favor its broadening.

6. *The good effects of love are not limited to the loved one but promote*

---

[12] Sullivan, Harry Stack. *Op. cit.*, p. 20.

the happiness and further development of the loving one as well. Love is not altruistic, self-sacrificing, and limiting for the one who loves. On the contrary, it is a reciprocal dynamic which greatly enriches the lives of both. This idea is not too clearly stated in a number of our sources but seems implied where not stated in nearly all.

7. *Love is not rooted primarily in sexual dynamics or hormonal drives,* although it may well have large erotic components whether between parents and children, between children, or between adults. Fromm seems to support this position when he says that the essence of productive love is the same no matter who is concerned.

8. *Love affords many individuals fundamental insights into and basic relationships to humanity and to the Forces that organize and guide the universe.* It gives many persons a basic orientation in the universe and among mankind. It can become the basis for faith in God. I was surprised to find support for this thesis from all sources. For example, Plant affirms that [13] "from early adolescence on the Church gives a great many children a sense of belongingness which has greater continuity and certainty for the individual than anything provided by his parents." The other sources also intimated that love is a great aid in the developmental tasks of orienting the self toward the rest of mankind and within the universe toward God.

These eight theses, I hope, may be of some aid in analyzing the nature of love and the processes by which it develops. Admittedly they represent only a first and faltering attempt. But if they are sufficient to focus more scientific attention and research on love, the purposes of this paper will have been accomplished.

The Roles of Love in Human Development

Now we address ourselves to the third question. Since love does exist, it potentially can become a reality in the life of every human being. Then, if our theses regarding the nature of love are true, what roles can love play in human development? This question will be answered during the next decade, I hope, by a whole series of researches. The findings should fill many monographs and some books. In the meantime, I should like to propose a series of hypotheses as to the probable findings of these researches, in the hope of suggesting profitable research leads.

The first hypothesis is that being loved can afford any human being a much needed basic security. To feel that one is deeply valued because one is, rather than because of the way one behaves or looks, is to feel fundamentally at home whenever one can be with the person who loves one so. From

---

[13] Plant, James. *Op. cit.,* p. 26.

earliest infancy to most advanced age this feeling of being deeply valued is an important precondition to meeting life's challenges and expectations, to doing one's best without unhealthy stress.

The second hypothesis is that being loved makes it possible to learn to love oneself and others. The capacity of infants for empathy, before language development makes more explicit communication possible, permits the feeling of the nature of love very early in life. The closeness of mutual understanding among preadolescent peers makes its joyous expansion natural. The hormonal creation of unrest in the presence of peers of the opposite sex pushes its further development until it is stilled by intimate sexual sharing of vivid life in marriage. The mystery and the creative fulfillment that come with the first baby begin a cycle of nurturance and guidance of a rapidly developing new personality that brings tremendous fulfillment through the years. But this wonderful growth and enrichment of life by love seems possible only to those who first were loved by others. Indeed we suspect that a person who has never been loved cannot fully respect and love himself but must always restlessly be reassuring himself as to his fundamental worth.

Our third hypothesis is that being loved and loving others facilitates winning belonging in groups. Of course, winning roles in group activities requires that the individual have knowledge and skills that are valuable in carrying on the activities of the group. Of course, conformity to group customs and codes is necessary to group belonging, and being loved contributes to none of these. But being secure through love and being able to give love, favors personality characteristics that are easy and attractive in group situations. Such a child or youth has no reason to lord it over others, to be aggressive and hostile, or to be shy and withdrawing. Such children do not need constantly to climb in status by calling attention to the failure and inadequacy of others.

A fourth hypothesis is that being loved and loving in return facilitates identifications with parents, relatives, teachers, and peers by which the culture is internalized more readily and organizing attitudes and values are established easily. When one feels loved and loves in return, it is easy to learn that which is expected; it is easy to believe that which one's objects of love believe and to aspire in the directions encouraged by one's objects of identification. The unloved child feels so much insecurity that he scarcely dares try his wings in learning. Or he is so full of hostility that he tends to reject what he is told and to refuse to meet the expectancies that face him, as a way of demonstrating his power to himself. Obviously the readiness of loving persons to provide meaningful experiences and to aid them in the learning process are further facilitations that give great advantages to loved children.

Our fifth hypothesis is that being loved and loving facilitates adjustment to situations that involve strong unpleasant emotions. When a loved child fails at something, the failure does not cut so deep as to make him doubt his basic worth because he is still secure in that love relationship. Consequently he is more easily reassured and encouraged to try again and again. In contrast, the unloved child who fails is in double jeopardy. To his insecurity is added the feeling of inadequacy, and the world looks blacker and blacker. When a loved child is frightened, he can literally or figuratively take the hand of the person who loves him, approach and examine the terrifying situation, learn its true dimensions, and more readily find the courage to face it. But terror to the unloved child is unfaceable and overwhelming. Punishments, penalties, and the demands of authority are bearable for loved children because they do not imply rejection or fundamental lack of worth. Consequently they are analyzable by the loved child, who more easily can perceive their meaning and take them in stride. But to the unloved child these things may be taken as indicators of personal rejection or of unfavorable status. Resentment, rebellion against authority, hostility against peers who seem more favored, or fundamental doubts of own worth ensue.

All of our hypotheses about the role of love in human development show it as a powerful facilitator of wholesome and full self-realization. As Bruno Bettelheim has so ably pointed out, *Love Is Not Enough* to cure badly maladjusted children. But it surely is a great aid to their adjustment and, best of all, it is a great preventive of maladjustment for the children who are fortunate enough to feel it constantly as they face their evolving developmental tasks.

36 · Love *

NELSON N. FOOTE

The author begins his article by calling attention to our ambivalent or contradictory feelings about love: fear of being hurt or of seeming sentimental on the one hand and deep craving for love on the other. The true meaning

* Abridged from *Psychiatry*, 1953, 16:245–251, with permission of the author and The William Alanson White Psychiatric Foundation, Inc. Copyright, 1953, by The William Alanson White Psychiatric Foundation, Inc.

The author, formerly Director of the Family Study Center and Assistant Professor at the University of Chicago, is now associated with the Marketing Services of General Electric Company. His degree of Doctor of Philosophy is from Cornell University. His interests are in industrial sociology, social psychology, and family relations. He is coauthor of *Identity and Interpersonal Competence* and various articles on family life.

of love is concealed by our inability to accept it matter-of-factly. He defines love as "that relationship between one person and another which is most conducive to the optimal development of both." The remainder of the article is an elaboration of this definition.

THE TITLE of this paper has provoked comments from friends and acquaintances ever since it was publicly announced. If those comments are classified according to the attitudes they express, they appear to fall into four rough categories: *cynical, joking, sentimental,* and *matter-of-fact.* Comments falling into the fourth category were least frequent, totaling three cases out of perhaps twenty. Of these three persons, two pointed out to me that love is not considered a proper subject for academic discourse: one claimed that the title would draw only a group of moralistic or sentimental listeners, lacking in scientific motive; the other claimed that the regular academics would be scornful unless I devised a more pompous and wordy title. The third merely made the cryptic remark that it takes courage to speak on this subject. This paper is aimed at drawing scientific attention to a matter-of-fact attitude toward love. Serious matter-of-factness toward love is a minority point of view even among professed social scientists. Indeed, one gains some introductory illumination of the subject from recognizing that the first three categories of comments are far more representative of the common approach to love.

Ambivalence

Cynicism, joking, and sentimentality alike bespeak a fundamental ambivalence toward love. Cynicism is the attitude of a person who is afraid that he will become the victim of illusions—illusions which he believes exist, entrap others, and are dangerous to himself. He hungers and thirsts for beliefs he can trust, but he never finds any that he can trust. Joking is the classical symptom by which the field ethnologist identifies status relationships that evoke conflicting emotions. And sentimentality is of course the lavish counterfeiting of genuine emotion that occurs when genuine emotion is deemed appropriate in a particular social situation but is not forthcoming spontaneously.

Freud believed that ambivalence was characteristic of all human love, and he also appeared to believe that the characteristic complement of love was hate. There is much truth in what he says, but at the present time some refinement and qualification are required. In general, the appearance of ambivalence in love relationships is probably peculiar to our own highly competitive society and may not be characteristic of other times and places. To suggest that it may happily be made to disappear in our own time is the only preachment I would proffer in this paper.

To understand how ambivalence toward love may diminish and disappear requires more precise analysis than is implied by the simple concept of ambivalence as the concurrence of love and hate. In a competitive society, as Bacon long ago pointed out, "he that hath wife and children hath given hostages to fortune." One who entrusts himself fully to another may find his credulity and kindness exploited. His love may be rejected or betrayed. To expose oneself to another is to run the risk of getting hurt. It may take only foolhardiness, among specialists in human development, to talk about love, but it does take courage to love in a society like our own. Many dare not try; they fear involvement. In short, fear rather than hate appears to be the original rival of love in the ambivalent situations that one encounters daily.

To be sure, when the fear seems justified by some act of the other, then the sense of betrayal is keen, and hostility is at once engendered. Several years ago I formed a habit of collecting clippings about domestic crimes in which wives, husbands, and children burned, poisoned, shot, and butchered each other. These clippings mounted so fast that I soon had a manila folder full of them. . . . Aggression against the other is always potential in love relationships, but it forms a secondary and conditional phase; the fear of being hurt oneself is primary and continuous. Yet to the extent that one is withheld from entering into love relationships by fear of being hurt, he is deprived of love and may crave it all the more.

This unrequited craving for love, in a society which demands the seal of love upon most interpersonal relations, leads not only to the characteristic expressions of cynicism, joking, and sentimentality, but also to a kind of self-renewing vicious circle. The signs of love are demanded, disbelieved, and demanded again. The oftener they are required, the oftener they are simulated; the more often they are distrusted, the more often further reassurance is demanded—until it is a wonder that any sound currency for conducting valid exchanges remains in use at all. The inflation of amatory declaration in this country has regularly puzzled foreign visitors. Fortunately some Americans do develop a keen and insistent ear for the real article, whereby they can detect it beneath the babble of spurious affirmations. The honored heroes of our best fiction are those who can with relentless accuracy distinguish true from false in this shadowy realm; they are sparing in terms of endearment to the point of taciturnity.

Competence

A matter-of-fact approach to the study of love requires a redefinition and even some reconceptualization of its nature.

. . . .

Love is that relationship between one person and another which is most conducive to the optimal development of both. This optimal development is to be measured practically in the growth of competence in interpersonal relations.

.   .   .   .

If by definition we love most those to whose development we contribute most, whether wittingly or unwittingly, such a definition has specific virtues over the popular conception of love as a fluctuating emotion which can only to a degree be stabilized by ritual or pretense. Rather, love is to be known by its works. The familiar emotions may be evoked intermittently by the works of love; there is nothing drab about the joys of receiving the actual evidence of love as against merely its verbal affirmation; but the more important point is that the growth of love can thus be charted as a developing process, progressive fruition of which is more to be desired than attainment and fixation of a particular state of emotional response. From this viewpoint, one values another not only for what he is at the moment but for his potentialities of development, and these are necessarily assessed longitudinally and not by comparison shopping. One commits himself to another not on the basis of romantic, forced illusions, but of real possibilities which can emerge with proper cultivation. Trust and appreciation accumulate through proven results as indexed in mutual personal development.

Audience

I want to turn now to the question of the precise delineation of the relationship of lover to loved one—parent and child, husband and wife, friend and friend—which is most conducive to the optimal development of each. A beginning toward the precise characterization of the ideal form of this relationship can be made by likening it to the relationship of artist and audience. There are of course all kinds of artists and all kinds of audiences. But almost every artist is acutely conscious of the bearing of his audience upon his performance and development as an artist. To attain an audience that is critical but appreciative, objective but hopeful, and neither patronizing nor condemnatory nor sentimentally adulatory, is the ideal his experience leads him toward. This ideal audience expects from him a performance as good or better than he has given before; it expects him to work hard for it. But it is identified with the artist, and sympathetic in an informed, understanding way. Thus it never unrealistically demands that he exceed his powers, achieve a result he never aimed for, or be something he is not. Best of all is the audience that clearly differentiates between the artist and the work of art, judging the latter as a finished product but the former as a never-fully-disclosed realm of potential productivity. Such an audience is only disappointed when its favored artist does less than his best.

Everyone knows the prodigies of creativity which are occasionally unleashed when a person discovers and is discovered by the perfect critic. Many a person can look back upon an incident in his school career when a sensitive teacher recognized at the critical moment an emerging talent and thereby permanently exalted his conception of himself and his capabilities. These are the moments of love in its sublime power to move. Such incidents are the imputed reference when a husband speaks of his wife as his "best friend and critic," although the phrase has become shopworn through sentimental usage. To be critical is thus to be neither hypercritical nor hypocritical. To achieve the delicate adjustment which is required means that criticism itself must become almost an art. Many a great artist has been intimately associated with a great critic.

The ideal audience, however, is often found among those with whom the artist tends to compare himself in measuring his own worth, as in the case of his fellow students. For it is never quite as positive a stimulus for the artist to have his creative productions praised by a teacher or master, as it is for him to have them praised by those who are themselves his potential emulators and who know intimately what these creative productions cost the artist.

Thus the relationship most conducive to development may be further described as one of social equality and of reciprocity. It cannot be a relationship of superiority and subordination. Nor can it even be the relationship of counselor and client, contrary to some present-day currents of thought, for even the most nondirective counselor-client relationship is unequal and unilateral. It is worth while to glance still more closely at what social equality and reciprocity mean between two persons.

Somewhere Durkheim contends that equality is indispensable if genuine discussion is to occur between persons; Simmel has made the same point with reference to the occurrence of sociability.[1] Discussion and sociability are two of the activities indispensable to carrying on the dialectic of creation and criticism from which comes personal development. By equality, however, is not meant sameness; quite the contrary. Let us take parents and children as the most obvious case where the persons involved are never—unless perhaps in the case of twins—of the same age or powers. The practice of equality may be exhibited by sharing alike in certain valued experiences and by such devices as taking turns—things that are familiar to everyone who ever had brothers or sisters. But obviously it would be

---

[1] Kurt H. Wolff (ed.), *The Sociology of Georg Simmel*; Glencoe, Ill., Free Press, 1950; pp. 47–49.

ruinous for parents to insist that each child reach the same standard of performance. Rather, each is expected by a loving parent to move toward a standard which is reasonable for a person of his capacities. Moreover, the most important expression of the kind of equality I am defining lies in the conception of each child as *ultimately incommensurable with any other*. He may be compared quantitatively to another child in this or that respect, but as a whole person he is unique. Also, as a whole person he is such a pregnant complex, such a rich array of potentialities, that the loving parent can always find some respects in which each child does excel. By developing these special talents or virtues, each child can outshine the others on his own grounds; the competition which is so threatening and destructive when all are judged by a single standard loses its force when each child is judged by his own.

The parent does not have to determine arbitrarily the line of development for which each child is best disposed; he has only to observe attentively the outcome of the child's own search for the notion of his particular talents which is most satisfying and promising, and then to ratify, as only a sympathetic audience can, the correctness of the discovery made. To do otherwise is to be as disruptive of orderly and optimal development as is the patron who tells the artist what he is to create. Wholeness and individuality, integrity and autonomy, are inseparable.

Reciprocity is perhaps a peculiar kind of equality, but so peculiar that it needs careful analysis. Malinowski [2] has analyzed its ubiquitous function in regulating primitive social organization. Someone of equal genius, I hope, will someday set forth in full the way it works throughout interpersonal relations. In the many books and articles on child development, reciprocity rarely gets the attention due it in terms of the scope of its influence. The child who is denied the opportunity to reciprocate according to his powers the favors conferred upon him by his parents is thwarted in the growth of those powers. Many people have no doubt witnessed the crushing effect upon a child of having a parent ignore or disparage a gift which the child has made and tendered him. Conversely, when a child has labored unstintingly to produce some offering and the parent accepts it with honest gratitude and praise, the delight of the child is sometimes almost physically convulsive.

I cannot resist mentioning the first party which my seven-year-old daughter threw for her parents. It consisted only of two pieces of pastry taken secretly from the refrigerator, a small table cloth and napkins spread carefully on her own little table, two cups of milk, and of course two chairs. It was entirely her own idea, and from a realistic point of view it was rather

---

[2] Bronislaw Malinowski, *Argonauts of the Western Pacific*; New York, Dutton, 1950.

inappropriate, since we had only finished dinner half an hour before. She did not sit down with us after inviting our presence, but stood there giggling and squirming in ecstasy as we thanked her and praised her cooking. She has already learned the role of hostess and fancies grander successes in the future.

To deny a person opportunities for reciprocating is to forestall his respect for himself, to keep him dependent and inferior. This is one point where resentment of do-gooders arises. A person may garner flattery by surrounding himself with dependents, but flattery can hardly match the satisfaction of contributing to the growth of others by stimulating their achievement of autonomy and equality. In fact, the person who insists upon the expression of affection from dependents whom he cannot let go may not be autonomous himself—as in the case of overprotective parents. On the other hand, the encouragement of reciprocation by those of lesser powers is about as strong a medicine for stimulating their growth as is likely to be found. In competition, as studies on recreation show, stimulation is maximal when rivals are equally matched. Equality and reciprocity are not static concepts; it is hierarchy and unilateralism which are static and which hinder development.

Self-Transcendence

Any present-day scholar would be loath to say that the impulse to explore and develop individuality is natural, in the sense of being an inborn imperative. On the other hand, it is certainly an almost universal discovery that development of one's powers is the primary value in life, since these powers are the instruments which provide access to all other values. If a person is permitted freedom to play and is stimulated by a loving audience, he moves on not merely from one requisite developmental task to another, but toward self-chosen goals which are not requisite but are autonomously affirmed.

. . . .

Art, however, is not play, any more than it is work. It is an activity of intense seriousness and concentration, although it excites joy of a kind and degree which is neither an illusion nor a joking matter nor a hypocrisy. Perhaps art could be called the serious form of play. Both work and play at their best become art. In the best art, the artist performs at the limit of his capacities. By performing at the limit of his capacities, he continually transcends the limits of those capacities. That is, he goes beyond the point he had previously reached in the development of his capacities.

. . . .

This conception of love as the interpersonal conditions optimal for self-transcendence is a hard doctrine from which many will shrink, because it puts the claim of love to the test of the results produced. It should have a cauterizing effect upon the sentimentality and falsehood by which a parent can protest that he loves a child while frustrating his development. Likewise it implies a conception of marriage, in which the success of the marriage is judged by the degree to which each partner contributes reciprocally to the continuous development of the other.

37 · Expressions of Love *

PERCIVAL M. SYMONDS

In the first part of the selection, Dr. Symonds cautions that sexual expression and love, although they have much in common, are not identical. Sex, in a narrow sense, is physical; love, however, implies esteem of another's personality. The interweaving of sex and love is carefully analyzed. Love may also be expressed through friendship and cooperation.

Sex: Sex and Love Not Identical

The infrequent mention of sex in the foregoing discussion may seem to a number of persons to be strange inasmuch as love and sex are so commonly bracketed in most persons' minds. Love is almost universally used as a term to denote sex. When one picks up a book entitled The Art of Love, he expects to find a treatise on sex. Psychoanalysis in its early formulations was severely criticized because it was thought to overemphasize sex and to interpret all neurotic states as due to aberrations of the sexual impulse. It is true that psychoanalytic theory, being based mainly on extensive studies of neurotic persons, has failed to provide a wholly adequate analysis of love, which is in the main a characteristic of normal and stable individuals.

It is an interesting fact, however, that only recently in the history of the human race has love been considered an aspect of sexual activity. One does not speak of love in connection with the sexual activity of lower animals, and primitive man by no means linked love and sex together as

---

* Percival M. Symonds, The Dynamics of Human Adjustment (D. Appleton-Century Company, 1946), pp. 547–550. Reprinted by permission of Appleton-Century-Crofts, Inc.

A short biographical note on the author will be found with selection 25.

one and the same thing. Anthropological studies of primitive cultures will show that every conceivable emotional relationship can accompany sexual relations. For instance, Margaret Mead [1] in studying a New Guinea tribe found that a man gives all of his affection to his sister and that his relations with his wife are to a high degree impersonal and even antagonistic.[2]

Even in civilized countries where marriage is arranged between two children by their parents, the marriage is not based on love but becomes an economic and social transaction between families. Love may develop in the marriage relationship, but sex is not accompanied by love at the start. Indeed, romantic love as we know it in our own society has had a late historical development. What seems so important and inevitable is simply a product of our own culture. It is our way of conceiving sex.

Freud [3] has referred to love as "aim inhibited sex"; that is, he thinks of love as the tender feelings that one has left after sex has been inhibited. Sex, which was originally present, has been subtracted from these tender feelings. A libidinal concept of love was necessary for Freud because he saw pleasure or sex as the grand-swell out of which all the more mature emotions emerged. Freud's concept, however, fails to comprehend the dynamic character of love, for he attempted to fit it too narrowly into his libido theory. As we are discussing love in this chapter, it is more a function of the personality and its adjustments to the people who are part of its world than it is a function of sex.

But Sex and Love Have Much in Common

Physiologically, love and sex have much in common. They both represent the operation of the parasympathetic nervous system. The preparatory stages of sexual excitement, including tumescence and a turgid condition of the genital organs, represent a discharge of the parasympathetic. We

---

[1] *Growing Up in New Guinea* (New York: William Morrow and Company, Inc., 1930).

[2] "A man gives the allegiance of dependence to his father, occasionally to his mother, mutual affection and feeling of reciprocity and co-operativeness to his sister, playfulness and easy give and take to his female cross cousin, anxious, solicitous, sedulous care to his children. For his wife he reserves—what? Unrelieved by romantic fictions or conventions of wooing, untouched by tenderness, unbulwarked by co-operativeness and good feeling as between partners, unhelped by playfulness, preliminary play or intimacy, sex is conceived as something bad, inherently shameful, something to be relegated to the darkness of night. . . . Married women are said to derive only pain from intercourse until after they have borne a child."

[3] *Group Psychology and the Analysis of the Ego*, International Psychoanalytical Library, No. 6 (London: The Hogarth Press, 1922; first published in German, 1921).

Civilization and Its Discontents. International Psychoanalytical Library, No. 17 (London: The Hogarth Press, 1929).

have also seen that in a more general sense the discharge of the parasympathetic represents an essential condition for the expression of love. Both love and sex represent muscular relaxation, and freedom from inhibition and fear. They both represent pleasurable excitement. Both represent an outgoingness. Indeed, sex as a basic drive which demands the response of another person for its relief and satisfaction becomes a prime setting for the development of love. However, love must not be confused with sexual expression. There may be love of food and adventure in just as real and passionate a sense as the love which accompanies sex. On the other hand, sex must not be thought of too narrowly as the relief of physical tension. Indeed, most writers on sex would insist that the forepleasure and the personal relationship are important factors in the consummation of sexual pleasure. In this sense sexual love involves a confluence of two separate streams of expression and feeling, one purely physical, the other, emotional, based on human relationships. As these two come together, they result in a more profound and exalted experience than any other expression of love. Indeed, sexual expression depends for its highest satisfaction not only on the adequacy of the physical act but also on many other factors, just as the pleasures of eating are enhanced by refined appointments and entertaining company. The expectations of the culture determine in a large measure the quality of sexual expression. What custom permits and expects sets the stage for the quality of sexual pleasure. The vitality of the two partners also plays its part. The sexual temperaments of the man and woman as determined by their erotic experiences in infancy also determine the quality of sexual experience. Current discussions of sex put major emphasis on the adequacy of the sex act itself, but this is only one of a number of factors and not necessarily the most important one which contribute to the total satisfaction in sexual relations.

Sex in its narrow aspects is physical. Love implies, on the other hand, the esteem and recognition of another individual as a separate personality. For the most complete sexual relationships other persons must be acknowledged in a double way, first as persons and second as carriers of sex activities.

A disputed point for which conflicting arguments and evidence have been advanced is whether love or friendship must rest on a sensual and even a sexual basis. Some have asserted that any human relationship is to a degree sensual and ultimately will be found to invoke to some small degree an element of sex. One investigator [4] who collected many diaries and letters

---

[4] Iovetz-Tereschenko, N. M., *Friendship—Love in Adolescence* (London: George Allen and Unwin, 1936).

of adolescents believes that he has evidence to support the view that the feelings and expressions of friendship are different from, if not opposed to, those of sex. One cannot, perhaps, take a dogmatic position with regard to this issue at the present time, and it is not very important to do so. The fact of the matter is that even if there is a minute sensual basis to the most platonic friendships, it may be so minute as to be relatively unimportant. One knows, for instance, that there is moisture in unseasoned wood, because it will warp. However, in discussing wood the fact that it contains moisture within its pores would be a relatively unimportant characteristic.[5] There is a basic difference between sex and love in this respect. Sensual pleasure becomes extinguished when satisfied, whereas love continues unabated, indeed, is enhanced the more satisfaction a person derives from another. Actually, the satisfaction of the physical needs of sex occupies only a small, though necessary, part of life; whereas the emotional needs are all-embracing. To go back to Maslow's hierarchy of drives referred to in Chapter II, "Drive," the physical needs of sex are basic.[*] Generally they demand first satisfaction, but, unlike hunger, they can be widely displaced and sublimated. When the physical needs are met, the stage is set for the gratification of higher needs of safety, affection, recognition and self-realization.

Sex is one form of joint sharing and activity through which love may be expressed. Indeed, it is the most complete union and sharing of which men and women are capable. It represents the highest degree of intimacy; but it has been emphasized time and again that sex must not be thought of in its narrow physical aspects but in the whole circle of relationships, experiences, and responsibilities which accompany it.

Christian civilization, strangely enough, is opposed to sexuality while at the same time it endorses love. This inconsistent attitude makes all persons in our culture to a degree impotent and frigid. Love could receive a more widespread and deeper expression if society could take a less restrictive attitude toward sex.

Friendship

This long passage on the relation between love and sex would make it seem that sex is the only form of expression of object love. While it does occupy an important place, it is by no means the only form of expression.

---

[5] Illustration from conversation with Theodor Reik.

[*] [Editor's note. Maslow gives five levels of needs as follows: first, the basic physiological needs of hunger, sex, and so on; second, the needs of safety from external dangers; third, the need for love; fourth, the need for esteem; fifth, the need for self-realization. Gratification of the lower levels frees a person for the higher social needs. A. H. Maslow, "A Theory of Human Motivation," Psychological Review, 50 (1943), 370–396.]

Indeed, friendship in which the sexual element is minimized or missing can serve as the expression of love quite as effectively as though sex expression were present. Friends can have many bases for common interests, common pursuits, for sharing and helping one another, all of which foster love and serve as its expression. Reik points out that in friendship there is less overestimation of the object, less idealization, and a less intense possessiveness. Friendship usually involves certain qualities of the person and not the whole person himself. Reik sees the relationship in friendship as one of equality, but Fromm makes this equality a requisite of love. In friendship each of the two individuals keeps a stronger separate identity.

Cooperation

Love finds its social expression through various forms of cooperation. One of these is in the various modes of sharing. Husband and wife will find that love is enhanced to the degree in which they can share together in family life either their work or their play. A person feels that he is loved by another when he is invited to do intimate things. Sitting down to eat together is one form of intimacy and a valuable expression of love. The give and take of conversation is another form of sharing. One may give to another person his thoughts and feelings. To amuse him, to inspire him, to encourage him by the capacity to listen and to receive from the other person expresses fondness fully as much as the capacity to give. One must be ready to share grief as well as pleasure; and until one has shared hardships and trials, perhaps the bonds of love are not welded in their closest form. It is possible to establish love on a basis of interests as well as sex.

Helping another person and giving freely of one's time, energy, and wealth is another way of expressing love. The neglect of another person and the refusal to assist him is universally accepted as a refusal of love.

Exchanging gifts becomes an important token of love. A gift is a sign that the recipient is love-worthy. One gives freely objects such as food, toys, or clothing; his service or time; or erotic satisfaction only to a person whom he likes or admires.

Love also expresses itself through gentleness. The lover is considerate, is not brusque or importunate, and shows a quiet consideration of the other person.

Hart[6] has prepared the following tests of romantic love. (1) There is greater happiness in the presence of the loved partner than of any other

---

[6] Hornell Hart, *Personality and the Family* (Boston: D. C. Heath and Company, 1941), pp. 170ff.

person (this assumes a love that is exclusive and reciprocal). (2) There is a sense of unrest and dissatisfaction when they are separated. (3) The lovers find a wealth of things to say to each other. (4) There is an eagerness to share experiences. (5) Each is eager to give full consideration to his partner's opinions, judgments, and interest. (6) Plans and interests keep organizing themselves around the partner. (7) The lover takes pride in his partner. (8) He is eager for the success of his partner.

Probably the best description of how love is expressed was given by Paul in the passage from Corinthians.

> Love suffereth long, and is kind; love envieth not; love vaunteth not itself, is not puffed up, doth not behave itself unseemly, seeketh not her own, is not provoked; taketh not account of evil; rejoiceth not in unrighteousness, but rejoiceth with the truth; beareth all things, believeth all things, hopeth all things, endureth all things. (I Corinthians, 13:4–7)

38 · The Dialogue of Courtship in Popular Songs *

DONALD HORTON

A discussion of love would not be complete without the inclusion of romantic love. Perhaps nowhere are the symbols and expressions of romantic love more vividly displayed than in popular songs. In this article the author has effectively arranged the popular songs of 1955 into a sequence of four dramatic acts and fourteen scenes, carrying the lovers from courtship through the honeymoon to conflict and parting. Although the popular songs of the 1960's may differ from those of 1955, they undoubtedly could be arranged into a similar dramatic sequence. The function of the songs is analyzed in the latter part of the selection.

AMERICAN popular songs are frequently written in the mode of direct address, of intimate conversation, in which the speaker and the person spoken to are identified as "I" and "you." In some the "I" is identified as masculine or feminine, while in others no clues to the sex of the speaker are given, and the same verses could be used by either sex in addressing the other. The relationships described or implied in the lyrics are those of dating and court-

* American Journal of Sociology, 62 (May, 1957), 569–578. Reprinted by permission of the publisher and the author; most footnotes deleted with permission.

The author holds the degree of Doctor of Philosophy (anthropology) from Yale University. He is Research Associate at the Bank Street College of Education and has published in professional journals.

ship. Some merely express an attitude or sentiment of the speaker toward the one addressed. More often the content is an appeal, request, demand, complaint, or reproach, soliciting response, as though the songs were fragments of dialogue. Musical comedies, motion pictures, and television programs such as "Your Hit Parade" regularly dramatize them as intimate conversations between lovers.

We might surmise, then, that the popular song provides a conventional conversational language for use in dating and courtship, one whose highly stylized and repetitious rhetorical forms and symbols are confined to the expression and manipulation of a narrow range of values. The questions asked here are: What can be said in this language? To what situations is it appropriate? What relationships between speaker and others are recognized in it? With what problems of social interaction can it deal?

The important role of language in motivating and directing social interaction has been discussed by numerous social psychologists whose empirical studies have, however, been few in number. The present paper is intended as a discussion of the social-psychological functions of language as found in popular song lyrics but also as a contribution to the analysis of other forms of art, both popular and sophisticated. The data are verses published in the June, 1955, issues of four periodicals devoted to song lyrics: *Hit Parader*, *Song Hits Magazine*, *Country Song Roundup*, and *Rhythm and Blues*. The four magazines contained 290 lyrics, but with some duplication; a net total of 235 differnt lyrics constituted the material for analysis. Of these, 196 (83.4 per cent) are conversational songs about love. The various phases or stages of the love relationship represented in them may be arranged as "scenes" in a drama of courtship.

The Drama of Courtship

Prologue: Wishing and Dreaming. A few songs belong to what might be called a prologue to the drama; they voice the anticipations of youngsters who have not yet begun to take part in love affairs. "Someone To Watch Over Me" is a girl's prayer for a lover ("I hope that he'll turn out to be someone to watch over me"); in a complementary song, "A Girl To Love," the boy may sing, "Here I wait with open arms for a girl to love." Two of the lyrics seem to represent lines to be said by a more experienced actor to a reluctant neophyte. A girl may quote from "Dance with Me Henry" (subtitled "The Wallflower"), "Hey baby, what do I have to do to make a hit with you?" and advise the timid boy to "get the lead out of your feet," for, "If you don't start trying, / You're gonna end up crying." In the other the boy who knows from experience tells the one who does not: "If you ain't lovin' then you ain't livin'." To the prologue belong also some general recommendations of the state of love: "When You Are in Love" ("When you are in love / You will discover a wonderland") and "Cherry Pink and Apple Blossom White" ("It's cherry pink and apple blossom white / When your true lover comes your way").

Act I: Courtship. We might expect a boy and girl on first meeting to go through a period of friendship preceding love; but such a stage is not provided for in our songs, or at least there is no characteristic dialogue for it. The more aggressive of the two prospective lovers is provided with gambits for winning the reluctant other which might be called the "direct," the "sweet," and the "desperate" approaches. No doubt one might be used successfully without the others, but in the hypothetical drama they are successive scenes.

In Scene 1 the direct approach is provided with words like "Oh, what I'd give for a moment or two, / Under the bridges of Paris with you" ("Under the Bridges of Paris") or "I'd love to gain complete control of you, and handle even the heart and soul of you" ("All of You"). For the brash and boisterous there is "Here Comes All My Love," in which the lover can say: "You been teasin' long enough—now I'm gonna call your bluff," or "Main Event," which says: "Now that we've done a little fancy dancin', / Sparred with each other to our heart's content, / If you intend to do some real romancin' (Boing), / Let's get to the main event."

We may doubt that this kind of attack is often successful. At any rate, the current crop of songs provides the sweet dialogue of Scene 2, in which the lover makes some show of devotion and offers simple declarations of love in a variety of dialects: "I love you, / For sentimental reasons" ("I Love You"); "I love you more than Jambalaya Creole shrimp and crawfish pie" ("I Love You More and More"); and "Honey Bunch, I go for you" ("Honey Bunch"). The lover's demands may be excessively modest: "A little love that slowly grows and grows / . . . That's all I want from you" ("That's All I Want from You"). He asks for a return of love ("Do, do, do what your heart says, / Love me as I love you" ["Do, Do, Do"]) but may accept a policy of gradualism ("Little by little our dreams will come true" [*ibid.*]) and patience ("Someday you may love me the way I love you" ["It's Your Life"]).

When neither simple appeal nor gentle persuasion wins, the heroic and desperate songs of Scene 3 are available. In the language provided here the lover may plead, "How can I make you love me, / What can I say or do?" ("How Can I"), or "Your love is all I'm needing, / Why can't you hear my pleading?" ("Your Love"). If these supplications fail, he may make heroic promises: "For you my love I'd do most anything" ("For You My Love"); "I would laugh, I would cry, / For your love I'd gladly die" ("Sweet Brown-eyed Baby"). He may humble himself with "I'm just a fool, / A fool in love with you" ("Earth Angel"); "I confess pretty baby 'cause I'm just a fool for you" ("I Confess"). Reaching the depths of self-pity and self-humiliation, he may cry, "Bring me tears, bring me pain, / Fill my days with never-ending rain, / But bring me your love" ("Bring Me Your Love"); or "Treat me like a fool, / Treat me mean and cruel, / But love me" ("Love Me").

Before the beloved yields to these entreaties, he (or more probably she) may ask, in Scene 4, further reassurances and commitments. The developing love relationship may seem dangerous and overwhelming: "First you think it's fun to try to kiss and run, / But each time you do, then love comes running after you . . . / That's why I tried to run away, / Fly with panic in my heart" ("Boomerang"). Are the lover's avowals genuine? Can he be intrusted with love? Will the new relationship be founded on mutual respect and mutual obligations? "Are you in love with me honestly, honestly? . . . / Is this dream a perfect dream that we can share? / Is it love or is it just a love affair?" ("Honestly"); "If I give to you my kisses, / I've got to know that you know how to handle it. . . . / Whatever we arrange, / Let's make it a fair exchange" ("Fair Exchange"); "Darling, say that you'll be true, / Let each kiss express, / Just how much I mean to you" ("Fill My Heart with Happiness"); "Handle me with gentleness and say you'll leave me never" ("Softly, Softly"). The lover who cannot give these assurances is resisted: "Please stay away from my heart, / And please don't let me love you, / 'Cause I know you'll be untrue" ("Please Don't Let Me Love You"). Marriage or the promise of marriage may be added as a condition to these questions and pleadings, although only two songs in the present collection go so far: "You gotta walk me, walk me, walk me down that well-known aisle" ("D'ja Hear What I Say"); and "If I'm only dreaming, you'll make those dreams come true, / On the day I'm hearing wedding bells, / Walking down the aisle with you" ("Wedding Bells").

The ritual responses to these demands are provided in songs like "Pledging My Love" ("Forever my darling, / My love will be true") and "I'm Sincere" ("I'm sincere when I cry that I'll love you 'til I die"). Fidelity is sworn in such words as "Never will my lips be for any one but you" ("You're the Heart That Loves Me"), and considerateness is promised in "I'd never forgive myself / If I ever made you cry" ("I'd Never Forgive Myself"). In the song "Are You Mine?" a section of dialogue has alternate lines for the boy and the girl: "[Boy] Are you mine? [Girl] Yes, I am. [Boy] All the time? [Girl] Yes, I am. [Boy] Mine alone? [Girl] Yes, sirree. [Boy] All my own? [Girl] Yes, sirree." Only one song provides a specific answer on the marriage question: "So, baby, if you'll just tell me you want me to, / I'll book a weddin' for me and you" ("I've Been Thinking").

It is quite possible, of course, that the actors may go through this drama more than once. The same lyrics, read with different overtones and connotations, may serve at different (should we say "higher" or "lower"?) levels of experience. The metaphors of "heart," "love's wonderland," "make your dreams come true," "make you mine," and so on are serviceably ambiguous to confound the censors. In the songs themselves, however, references to prior loves or conflicts between a new love and an old are scarce. It is perhaps in Scene 4, the scene of appeals, promises, reassurances, and final commitments, that we should note the songs in which a struggle of loyalties is expressed. In "Make Believe" the lover sings: "You belong to another . . . / I belong to someone too, / But they can't seem to see / That our love has to be. / We'll make believe 'till / We can make it come true." In "Conscience" the conflict is more agonizing: "Conscience, keeper of my heart . . . / Let me live and let me love . . . / Please don't treat a love like ours / As just an evil thing. . . . / Will I choose the one I love / Or the one I'm tied to?" If this conflict is resolved, then the songs of pledge and counterpledge quoted above may be invoked.

In Scene 5 one of the lovers is becoming impatient. Mere acknowledgments, mere kisses, are not enough. "How long must I wait for you, / To do what I ask you to, / Baby, how long?" ("How Long Must I Wait"); and "Let's stay home tonight . . . / There's a message in your eyes and if I'm right, / Let's stay home tonight" ("Let's Stay Home Tonight"). To these urgencies the other may respond with some anxiety: "Your love's like quicksand, I'm sinking deeper by the hour. / I'm up to my heart, I'm helpless in your power" ("Quicksand"); or can warn himself (herself) with "Look out, little fool, you're not wise, not wise to love so completely, / Or fall for the look in her [his] eyes" ("Danger, Heartbreak Ahead"). The other may reply: "Come a little closer, don't have no fear. . . . I heard what you told me, / Heard what you said. / Don't worry, my pretty, won't lose my head." The timid, yielding, might whisper: "Take my all, darling, do, / But don't unless you love me too, / There's no right way to do me wrong" ("There's No Right Way To Do Me Wrong"); while the bold, putting all fears behind, might say: "Starting with the 'A, B, C' of it, / Right down to the 'X, Y, Z' of it, / Help me solve the mystery of it, / Teach me tonight" ("Teach Me Tonight").

Act II: The Honeymoon. "The first thing I want in the morning, and the last thing I want at night, / Is Yoo-hoo, baby" ("My Heart's Delight") sings the intoxicated lover in Scene 1 of Act II; "You sweet as honey that comes from a bee, / You precious as an apple that comes from a tree" ("Nothing Sweet as You"). This is the honeymoon period whose songs describe the exhilaration of mutual (and perhaps fulfilled) love: "Tweedle tweedle tweedle dee, I'm as happy as can be" ("Tweedle Dee"); "Baby when you hold me in your arms I feel better all over" ("Feel Better All Over"). The lover is by turns boastful ("I got a sweetie way over town, / He's so good to me . . . / I feel so proud walkin' by his side, / Couldn't get a better man, / No matter how hard I tried" ["I Got a Sweetie"]) or humble ("I will pray to every star above; / And give them thanks for you / And drink a toast to love" ["A Toast to Lovers"]) or astonished ("I found out since we've been kissin', / All the things I've been missin', / The wilder your heart beats, / The sweeter you love" ["The Wilder Your Heart Beats"]). Here is the appropriate place for the old favorite, "Carolina in the Morning": [1] "No-one could be sweeter / Than my sweetie when I meet her in the morning. . . . / Nothing could be finer / Than to be in Carolina in the morning."

If this happiness is troubled, it is only by a doubt that anything so wonderful could be real, "If you are but a dream, I hope I never waken" ("If You Are But a Dream"), and by the pain of parting at night, for these lovers are not yet legally married: "Please don't say goodnight to me so soon, / Hold me close some more, / That's what arms are for" ("Please Don't Go So Soon"). Even in this euphoric stage only one song refers to marriage: "I'm so happy, so happy, / This is my wedding day" ("My Wedding Day").

Act III: The Downward Course of Love. The first uncertainties may occur in the new relationship if the lovers are temporarily separated, an event not unlikely among youngsters who do not yet control their own lives. Scene 1 provides for simple loneliness: "There's a hope in my heart that you'll soon be with me" ("The Sand and the Sea"); but loneliness may be touched with anxiety: "I've hungered for your touch a long lonely time . . . / And time can do so much. / Are you still mine?" ("Unchained Melody"); "Don't forget how much I love you . . . / And tho' other eyes may shine, / Tie a string around your heart, / Ev'ry moment we're apart" ("Don't Forget"); "I can't stay away like this, / I'm afraid that you'll get careless, and someone will steal a kiss" ("I Can't Stand It Any Longer").

In Scene 2 forces hostile to love's happiness appear. Parents may intervene: "My mother, she is scoldin' me / Because I love you so" ("Oh, Mother Dear"). Jealousy, even jealousy of past loves, may arise: "How important can it be / That I've tasted other lips?" ("How Important Can It Be?"). Malicious talk is a danger: "Don't listen to gossip whatever you do, / It's usually lies that you'll hear, / What they say about me they say about you, / So kiss me and dry up your tears" ("Gossip"). The lover may be unfaithful or simply unkind: "Give me your love instead of all those heartaches

---

[1] Originally copyrighted in 1922 but reprinted in *Hit Parader.*

. . . why must you make me cry?" ("Give Me Your Love"); "Mama he treats me badly" ("He Treats Your Daughter Mean"); and, as one of the partners begins to "cool" (for whatever reasons), the other instantly detects it: "A heart may be fickle, / And words may deceive . . . / But kisses don't lie / . . . I know you are changing, that I'm losing you . . . / You don't want to hurt me, / But kisses don't lie" ("Kisses Don't Lie").

The answer to infidelities and unkindness is the threat of leaving (Scene 3) and the offending lover's remorse. "Maybe when I've said my last goodbye, / Your anxious heart will cry and cry" ("Anxious Heart"); "If you can't be true, I'm gonna fall out of love with you" ("I'm Gonna Fall Out of Love with You"); "If you can't give me half the love / That I've been giving you, / You'd better hold me tighter dear / 'Cause I'll go slipping through" ("Butterfingers"); and, finally: "Nobody loves me, / Nobody seems to care. / I'm going to pack my suitcase, / Movin' on down the line" ("Everyday I Have the Blues"). In reply to such threats, one may plead inexperience, as in "Give a Fool a Chance" ("If I make you cry at times, / If I tell a lie at times, / It's my first romance, / Give a fool a chance"), or simply, as in "One Mistake," beg for pity ("Oh, oh baby, why don't you forgive and forget, / Or will I have to spend the rest of my life / Paying for my one mistake?").

Now the final parting occurs, Scene 5 furnishing the melancholy dialogue: "One more kiss before I leave you . . . / You have caused a lot of trouble. / Darling, you have broke my heart" ("Don't This Road Look Rough and Rocky"); "I thought our love was here to stay / And now you tell me / That you don't love me, / And you must go, / And you must go" ("Is It True— Is It True"). The deserted lover may plead, "Why don't you reconsider, baby" ("Reconsider, Baby"), and the other may reply, "Let me go, let me go" ("Let Me Go, Lover"). The braver course is to say: "I'll step aside . . . / Your happiness means everything to me. / I'll step aside just for your sake, / Altho my heart will surely break" ("I'll Step Aside"), or "I'm losing you and it's grieving me, / But I'll say 'Goodbye' with a smile" ("No Tears, No Regrets").

Act IV: All Alone. "Time goes by and I still love you" ("Time Goes By") is the new motif. "Ever since my baby's been gone, I sure have a hard time living alone" ("Ever Since My Baby's Been Gone"). The forsaken lover still loves and dreams of persuading the other to come back. He may appeal to her pity for his miserable state: "Can't eat no more and my clothes don't fit right . . . / Since you left me baby / Can't sleep no more at night" ("Carry On"); "Since you've gone from me dear / And we've lost the flame, / Tears fall like rain on my window pane. / Please come back, all my dreams are in tatters" ("Parade of Broken Hearts"). To appeals for pity he may add apologies: "I made a horrible mistake / To ever try a new romance, / And now my heart will surely break / Unless you give me one more chance" ("Change of Heart"); "Thoughtlessly I know I hurt you" ("In the Year You've Been Gone"); "I guess I took that gal of mine / For granted too darn long" ("I Gotta Go Get My Baby"). Or, while blaming the other, he may forgive: "I gave you my heart / And carelessly, you broke it so carelessly . . . [yet] / If you'd call again, I'd give my all again" ("Foolishly"); "It may sound silly, / For me to say this, / After the way you broke my heart, / But I still love you . . . / It may sound silly, / But if you 'phoned me and asked forgiveness for doing me wrong . . . / I'd be waiting with open arms" ("It May Sound Silly"). But love, broken, is not easily mended. There are few lyrics for answering these appeals, unless, perhaps, some of the business of Act I may be repeated, with demands for new reassurances and new pledges. There is one song, however, giving an answer in the negative: "Don't ask me while we dance / To start a new romance, / I just can't take the chance, / No, not again" ("No, Not Again").

Scene 2 opens a prospect of hopeless love. The abandoned one no longer thinks of winning back the other: "There goes my heart, / There goes the one I love, / There goes the girl I wasn't worthy of . . . / There goes somebody else in place of me" ("There Goes My Heart"); "I'll keep remembering forever and ever, I'll love you dear / As long as I live" ("As Long as I Live"). The symbol of unrequited love appears to be the faded rose petal: "Now our love is a mem'ry / Where it's gone nobody knows, / But I'll hold so dear as a souvenir / Just a petal from a faded rose" ("A Petal from a Faded Rose").

Some actors in Scene 2 are less stoical and more given to tears: "To-morrow I'll be twice as blue, / Because I'm still in love with you" ("To-morrow's Just Another Day To Cry"); "When a romance sours, / Smiles are just a lie. / Play me hearts and flowers, / And let me cry" ("Play Me Hearts and Flowers"); or, still more forlornly, "Where does a broken heart go when it dies of pain? / Is there a heaven for broken hearts? / Will it live again?" ("Where Does a Broken Heart Go?").

A bitter dialogue is available as an alternative conclusion of Scene 2 in phrases such as, "I trusted you, believed your lies" ("Unsuspecting Heart"). The other is cruel, unfeeling, selfish: "To each new love a lot of pain is all you'll ever bring, / Because to you one broken heart just doesn't mean a thing" ("One Broken Heart Don't Mean a Thing"). In "Why Should I Cry Over You?" the forsaken one says, "All my love was a waste of time" and ends, with a touch of malice, "Someday your heart will be broken like mine, / So why should I cry over you?" In "I Hope" this uncharitable wish is expressed: "If another fool is blinded by a lie, I hope this time it's you."

In Scene 3, the lover, having thrown off the old love, may face the future with "My baby don't love me no more," but ending with the lines, "Somehow I'll find me a baby new, / And maybe I'll pick on you, / You'll hear me knocking at your door, / 'Cause my baby don't love me no more" ("No More"); or "You done messed around until I've found myself somebody new" ("All Gone"); or, finally, celebrate a new freedom by singing, "Let me be among the crowd, / I like the way I'm living now, / Untied, untied, untied" ("Untied").

.   .   .   .

Functions of the Song Language

The Dialectic of Courtship. It is striking that in so large a number of instances the dialogue reflects discordances in the relative positions of the lovers in the "career" of love and provides appeals by the one to bring the other "into step." In the earlier scenes of the drama, one lover is characteristically "ahead" in moving toward increasing intimacy and commitment while the other lags behind. Both parties to this changing and tense relationship are provided with an appropriate rhetoric—the one with devices of persuasion and reassurance, the other with ways of saying, "Go slow. I'm not ready. I'm not sure." In the later scenes, one is typically moving away from the relationship, while the other tries to restore it. There is a lexicon of appeals, promises, self-defenses, and self-accusations for the one; a lexicon of reproaches, refusals, and forgiveness for the other. Only in the "Honeymoon" period of Act II is untroubled mutual acceptance expressed. The drama reflects the dialectical progression of a complex and difficult relationship, and this is undoubtedly the character of romantic love generally and of adolescent love in particular. Not only are those involved developing at different rates and often making conflicting demands upon each other but their mutual adjustment is also subject to environmental difficulties and pressures. However stereotyped and sometimes ludicrous the song may be, it is functionally adapted to this phase of adolescent experience.

Vicarious Discourse. One would not suppose that young people carry on extensive colloquies in verse, although casual observation confirms the fact that they do murmur the lyrics of the songs to which they are dancing and repeat lines or phrases of songs in teasing and joking at social gatherings. In a culture in which skill in the verbal expression of profound feelings is not a general trait and in which people become embarrassed and inarticulate when speaking of their love for each other, a conventional, public impersonal love poetry may be a useful—indeed, a necessary—alternative. It is not essential that such a language be used in direct discourse, for, if two people listen together to the words sung by someone else, they may understand them as a vicarious conversation. By the merest gestures it can be made clear that one is identified with the speaker, and the other with the one addressed. This is undoubtedly one of the chief functions of the professional singer, whose audience of lovers finds in him their mutual messenger.

For the young adolescent, the neophyte in the drama of courtship, everything lies in the future; and in the popular songs of the day he or she finds a conventionalized panorama of future possibilities. These include standard situations and contingencies and the dialogue expressing appropriate standard attitudes and sentiments, for both one's own sex and the opposite sex as well. They offer the opportunity to experiment in imagination with the roles one will have to play in the future and the reciprocal roles that will, or should be, played by the as-yet-unknown others of the drama. Again, it may be the function of the popular singer, in dramatizing these songs, to show the appropriate gestures, tone of voice, emotional expression—in short, the stage directions—for transforming mere verse into personal expression. The singer is at the same time available as an object of vicarious identification or as a fancied partner with whom in imagination the relationships and emotions of the future may be anticipated.

The Self as Lover. As the youngster progresses in age and experience, he moves through the successive stages of the drama, finding that in each new situation the dialogue once practiced in play now can be said in earnest. At the same time, the songs appropriate to the stages already passed will have acquired the private meanings of personal history. When the cycle has been completed, the whole of this symbolic universe will have been reinterpreted, its meaning "reduced" from an abstract, conventional possibility to a concrete, completed personal experience. In the course of this continuous translation of cultural patterns of rhetoric into personal expression, the songs, like other formulas of personal communication, may promote a sense of identity.

The adolescent, especially, is preoccupied with the ceaseless construction and reconstruction of conceptions of who and what he is. He must not only learn the specifications of numerous interacting and reciprocal roles but come to identify some roles as his own. The working-out of a socially valid and personally satisfactory conception of himself and his role in relation to the opposite sex is one of his most urgent and difficult tasks, at least in contemporary America, where so much of the responsibility for this phase of development is left to the young people themselves, aided by their cynical and somewhat predatory allies of the mass media. If television, motion pictures, and popular literature demonstrate and name the roles he may properly assume, the popular songs provide a language appropriate to such an identity.

CHAPTER 9:

Intimacies before Marriage

39 · Attitudes of College Students toward Premarital Sex Experience *

ALFRED J. PRINCE AND GORDON SHIPMAN

The studies of sexual experiences of men and women made by Professor A. C. Kinsey and his associates startled the nation by the reportedly high proportion of men and women who had had premarital sex experience. The following article by two professors in a midwestern city does not purport to give over-all statistics. It does, however, give the attitudes of a limited group of college men and women toward premarital intimacies, the reasons why they participated or refrained, and their later reactions.

THE MAJOR purpose of this study [1] was to find what attitudes young people—students attending a state university in the Midwest, in particular—hold toward premarital sex relations. More specifically, the study was designed to seek answers to the following questions: (1) What are the attitudes of young people toward premarital sex relations with their anticipated marital partners and with others? (2) Are the expressed attitudes of

* *Coordinator,* 6 (June, 1958), 57–60. Reprinted by permission of the editor and the authors.

Alfred J. Prince holds the Master of Arts degree from the University of Idaho and the degree of Master of Science in Social Work from Our Lady of the Lake College. He is Assistant Professor of Social Work and Sociology at the University of Wisconsin–Milwaukee. His special interests are counseling, interfaith marriages, courtship behavior, and social work.

Gordon Shipman obtained the degree of Doctor of Philosophy from the University of Wisconsin. He is Chairman of the Department of Sociology and Anthropology at the University of Wisconsin–Milwaukee. His special professional interests are criminology, juvenile delinquency, marriage, and the family.

[1] The authors wish to express their appreciation to their colleague, Dr. Donald Everson, for his careful reading of the manuscript and helpful suggestions.

young people toward premarital sex relations influenced by their having had this experience? (3) What motivates young people in having premarital sex relations? (4) What effect does premarital sexual intercourse have on a couple's relationship? (5) What are the reasons young people give for refraining from premarital relations?

The data presented were obtained by an anonymous questionnaire given to unmarried students enrolled in introductory and advanced courses in sociology and social work at the University of Wisconsin–Milwaukee in the fall semester of 1957. The questionnaire was given to 182 students in a regular class session. To assure anonymity, each student was instructed to deposit his questionnaire in a sealed box provided for this purpose. The questionnaire was completed by all of the students, 60 men and 122 women.

The students ranged in age from 17 to 30, with an average age of 20.5; the men were on the average about 11 months older than the women.

Almost one-third of the students reported having premarital sex relations. One-half of the men and almost one-fifth of the women said they had engaged in premarital sex intercourse.

Analyses of the data on the courtship status of the students at the time of their premarital sex experience showed that the women had had premarital sex relations only with men with whom they were going steady or to whom they were engaged at the time. The respective percentages were 82 and 18. In contrast, only slightly more than half of the men who reported having premarital sex intercourse said the girls they had relations with were their "steady" (36 per cent) or engagement partners (18 per cent). These percentages would seem to indicate that women, more so than men, tend to limit their premarital sex experience to their anticipated marital partners.[2]

Analyses of the data showed that the women had gone steady on an average of 14 months (range: 4 to 30 months) at the time they first engaged in premarital sexual intercourse. The men had gone steady for less than half that time or an average of 6.5 months (range: 2 to 12 months) before they engaged in premarital relations. The average length of engagement at first occurrence of premarital sex intercourse was 7.5 months for both sexes.

The incidence of premarital sex intercourse was higher for students who attended church infrequently, whatever their religious affiliation, than for students who attended regularly. Of those who attended church less than once a month, over 60 per cent had engaged in premarital sexual relations.

---

[2] For a review of past studies on the incidence of premarital sex intercourse with future marital partners and others, see Ernest W. Burgess, and Paul Wallin, *Engagement and Marriage*. New York: J. B. Lippincott, 1953, pp. 322–330.

In contrast, of those who attended one to four times a month or more, less than 19 per cent reported having had premarital sex experience.

Incidence of premarital sex intercourse showed no significant relationship to ordinal position in the family or to source of sex information.

Respondents checked on the average, three major sources of sex information. Most frequently mentioned by both sexes were: (1) "books, pamphlets, and other reading material" (2) "friends and playmates" and (3) "parent of the same sex" in that order.[3]

The question arises: Are young people who engage in premarital relations more likely to evaluate their early sex education as "inadequate" than those who do not? Our data showed no apparent relationship. However, it was noteworthy that almost 40 per cent of the students in our sample felt that their sex education had been inadequate. For example, one student wrote:

> As a child and teen-ager, my sex education was far from adequate. I had little or no knowledge of conception, intercourse, or birth. Only in the last two years have I gained any real knowledge.

Another commented:

> My first explanation of sex frightened me; and I wasn't entirely straightened out on the subject until about seven years later. I knew no one who could sensibly answer my questions or wanted to. The subject has always been rather hushed up or laughed at in our family.

Another wrote:

> My parents never really gave me any sex information, yet they expected me to know about sex. I got my information from a home nursing and child care course and books. These sources, I feel, are not enough.

The respondents were asked the question: What motivates young people in having premarital sex relations? The reasons most frequently given by the men were: (1) satisfaction of sexual desire (35 per cent), (2) love and fact that person was also anticipated marital partner (22 per cent), (3) curiosity (14 per cent) and (4) heavy petting (13 per cent). One student wrote:

> It was a common desire and need for each other. We plan to marry in the future anyhow and felt the frustration of putting it off was not worth the effort. This was the first time for both of us.

Another commented:

---

[3] In answer to the question, "In your opinion, from what source should one receive most of his sex information?" the overwhelming majority of the students wrote "one's parents."

Being a male from a not too good neighborhood, I was at a young age under the impression that it was the thing to do. Ridicule if I didn't have a sex experience was probably the reason for the first few sex experiences I had.

One man stated he was motivated, in part, by a "fear of impotency." He wrote:

I wanted to because of a strong fear of impotency—that partly and partly because I merely desired to and partly to achieve some culmination or plateau as it were to the relationship.

The reasons most frequently given by the women were: (1) love and fact that person was also anticipated marital partner (50 per cent), (2) wish to satisfy partner (14 per cent), (3) heavy petting (12 per cent) and (4) fear of losing partner if did not cooperate (10 per cent). One woman wrote:

When I look back, I think it might have been because of a fear of losing the fellow I was going with. He was the first boy I really fell in love with. (This happened during the last semester of my last year in high school). Maybe I let it happen in hope he would fall in love with me as much as I fell for him.

This same woman added:

In more ways than one I am sorry we are having relations. It's just that now we do have plans for marriage and it's difficult to stop.

She concluded by stating:

Sometimes I would just like to be able to talk with someone very confidentially about premarital relations. Some people say it is right and others not. It can really mix you up!

Another commented:

What motivated me was what I thought was love. Also curiosity and desire were runner-ups. After two and a half years, your steady gets sick and tired of hearing you say no, and you get kind of tired of refusing.

Another wrote:

Before I started going with my present boyfriend, I had never had any sex experience of any kind (no petting either). It was quite a shock when petting started and I found I hadn't the will power to fight it. I never felt so helpless in my life. My boyfriend said since it made me so unhappy we would stop petting—there was so much conflict in me that at times I would cry. But neither of us could control ourselves and eventually the petting led to intercourse. Today, when couples can go out unchaperoned, problems of this sort develop. My only thought is that I don't get pregnant and lose all the faith people have in me.

What effect does premarital sex intercourse have on a couple's relationship? As seen in Table 1, half of the students felt that the experience had strengthened their relationship. The percentages for the men and women were 46 and 55 per cent respectively.

TABLE 1: Judgment of 30 Men and 22 Women as to the Effect of Premarital Sex Experience on Their Relationship

Effect of Premarital Intercourse	Men Per Cent	Women Per Cent
Strengthened relationship	46	55
Weakened relationship	7	19
Was factor in subsequent breakup of relationship	7	13
Had no effect on relationship	40	13
Total	100	100

Roughly one woman in five reported that premarital sexual intercourse had weakened the relationship. Slightly more than one woman in seven felt that the experience was a major factor in their subsequent break-up with their partners.

Forty per cent of the men, in contrast to 13 per cent of the women, reported that the experience had had little or no effect on their relationship.

TABLE 2: Percentages of 30 Men and 100 Women Giving Various Reasons for Not Having Engaged in Premarital Sex Relations *

Reason	Men Per Cent	Women Per Cent
Religious beliefs	27	40
I want to wait until married	17	19
Family training	10	14
Fear of pregnancy	7	12
Fear of losing partner's respect	7	12
Fear of losing self-respect	7	10
Fear of hurting parent's feelings	7	9
Conditions did not permit	3	—
Other	13	4
No reason given	13	3

* Percentages total more than 100 because some students gave more than one reason.

Of continued interest to investigators of our sexual mores are the reasons why young people, women in particular, refrain from premarital sex intercourse. Table 2 shows the percentages of men and women in our study giving the indicated reason for having refrained from premarital relations.[4]

It will be seen that over half (59 per cent) of the women gave as their reason for refraining from premarital sex experience "religious beliefs" or "I want to wait until married." Men who had refrained from premarital sex relations also gave these as the most common reasons for their chastity (44 per cent).

The excerpts presented below express in their own words why young people in our study were refraining from premarital sex relations.

MAN: First, unless you feel that the girl is really the one you want, you would feel committed to her and breaking off the relationship would be difficult, to say the least. Second, there are only several years that you pass through in which you are interested in sexual relations for the personal thrill alone and if you mature you will later become more objective.

WOMAN: I know it is wrong and I know if I allowed myself to do it my future husband would wonder about my past. I want him to respect me—how could he if I allowed that! I think since the sexual relationship is supposed to be so beautiful, it should be saved for marriage. This is a good reason in itself. Assuming, however, we left all other reasons behind, I do not want to get pregnant.

MAN: Although I have more than enough desire, it appears that I have a moral "mental block" and therefore I've never lost control of myself. I am engaged and the temptation seems great. But I don't think I shall have any difficulty waiting because both of us want our marriage to start right, without any guilt feelings.

WOMAN: I believe sexual relations should take place only inside the bonds of marriage and I think couples should not use the excuses of "love" or a "long period of time until marriage is possible" for engaging in sexual relations.

Attitudes to premarital sex relations will vary, of course, depending on the type of relationship with the other person. In the present study, therefore, an attempt was made to ascertain students' attitudes to premarital intercourse specifically with a prostitute, a pickup, a casual friend, a close friend, and anticipated marital partner. The findings of this study are presented in Table 3.

---

[4] See also, Burgess and Wallin, *op. cit.*, p. 344; Lemo D. Rockwood, and Mary E. N. Ford, *Youth, Marriage and Parenthood*. New York: John Wiley & Sons, 1945, p. 53; and Judson T. Landis and Mary G. Landis, *Building a Successful Marriage* (2nd Ed.). New York: Prentice-Hall, 1953, p. 135.

TABLE 3: Attitudes of 60 Men and 122 Women to Premarital Sex Relations Depending on Type of Relationship with Other Person

Would you object to having premarital sex relations with:	Students Who Had Premarital Relations Per Cent *		Students Who Had Not Had Premarital Relations Per Cent	
Men (N = 60)	Men (N = 30)		Men (N = 30)	
	Yes	No	Yes	No
a prostitute?	53	43	73	23.
a pickup?	33	60	73	23
a casual friend?	40	57	73	23
a close friend?	47	50	70	27
your "steady"?	30	66	63	33
your engagement partner?	17	77	47	53
Women (N = 122)	Women (N = 22)		Women (N = 100)	
	Yes	No	Yes	No
a prostitute?	—	—	—	—
a pickup?	100	—	95	5
a casual friend?	100	—	96	4
a close friend?	95	—	95	5
your "steady"?	64	36	91	8
your engagement partner?	45	55	76	19

* Percentages will not equal 100 because the "no responses" have been omitted.

Men were found to be more liberal than women in their attitudes to premarital sex relations with future spouses and others.

The data presented in Table 3 indicate also that the expressed attitudes of respondents seem to be influenced by their having had premarital sex experience. That is to say, students who had premarital sex experience appeared less likely to object to having relations with their future marriage partners and others than those who had not had premarital experience.

At the same time, it was noteworthy that almost two-thirds (64 per cent) of the women who had premarital sex intercourse would object to having sex relations with their "steady" and almost half (45 per cent) would object to having relations with their engagement partner. The corresponding percentages for the men were 30 and 17 per cent. It would appear, therefore, that many of the respondents who had engaged in premarital sex relations—women, in particular—regretted having done so. For example, one woman wrote:

I had sexual relations only once—it left me with a feeling of disgust. I received no enjoyment or thrill whatsoever. It didn't bring us any closer (we had already made plans for marriage). The effect was quite bad on both of us. For some time I cried continuously and avoided seeing him. I think he was glad I did avoid seeing him.

This same woman added:

I certainly can't find any justification for premarital sex experience at all!

Another woman who had engaged in sex relations with her "steady" wrote:

On my part, my sexual experiences were mistakes or failings. I do not intend to repeat these mistakes (Our relationship was later broken) . . . I believe that marriage is built on respect and love, so I will try very hard to win both from my future husband.

Another commented:

As far as I am concerned, I'm sorry I ever made my mistake and wish it had not happened. We're both trying to make up for it now.

One woman who had sex intercourse with her engagement partner wrote:

"Never again!" She then added: "It is hard to wait for so long, but then it's worth it to wait. Oh, I don't know, I wish I did!"

Another wrote:

After having one sexual experience, I feel that any relations outside of marriage should be strictly taboo because 8 times out of 10 something that is or was a beautiful partnership ends in disaster.

A man wrote:

At present, I am engaged but will not have any relations with her now because I know it is morally wrong and would like to wait for our marriage before having any relations. The girl I am engaged to at present is the one I had relations with but we both have a different outlook now and know we were wrong for doing it.

The final excerpt was written by a young man. He wrote:

In my case, the initial wonderful satisfaction of sex relations came before marriage. I feel that ideally it is best to wait until you are married. And if we were to begin again, I would definitely wait until marriage.

In conclusion, a recapitulation of the findings of this study shows the following:

(1) Almost one-third of the respondents in our sample reported having premarital sex relations. Half of the men and almost one-fifth of the women said they had engaged in premarital sexual intercourse.

(2) Women, more so than men, tended to limit their premarital sex experience to their anticipated marital partners.

(3) The average length of engagement at first occurrence of premarital sex intercourse was 7.5 months for both sexes.

(4) The incidence of premarital sex intercourse was higher for students who attended church infrequently, whatever their religious affiliation, than for those who attended regularly.

(5) Incidence of premarital sex intercourse showed no significant relationship to ordinal position in the family or to source of sex information.

(6) The reasons most frequently given by the men for engaging in premarital sex relations were: 1) satisfaction of sexual desire, 2) love and fact that person was also anticipated marital partner, 3) curiosity and 4) heavy petting, in that order.

(7) The reasons most frequently given by the women were: 1) love and fact that person was also anticipated marital partner, 2) wish to satisfy partner, 3) heavy petting and 4) fear of losing partner if did not cooperate, in that order.

(8) Half of the respondents who had engaged in premarital sex relations felt that the experience had strengthened their relationship.

(9) Slightly more than one woman in seven felt that the experience was a major factor in their subsequent break-up with their partners.

(10) Forty per cent of the men, in contrast to 13 per cent of the women, reported that the experience had had little or no effect on their relationship.

(11) Over half of the women gave as their reason for refraining from premarital sex experience "religious beliefs" or "I want to wait until married." Men who had refrained from premarital sex relations also gave these as the most common reasons for their chastity.

(12) Men appeared more liberal than women in their attitudes to premarital sex relations with future spouses and others.

(13) The expressed attitudes of respondents toward premarital sex relations seem to be associated with having had premarital sex experience.

(14) Lastly, although one third of the respondents in our study had engaged in premarital sex intercourse, many of them, women in particular, regretted having done so.

40 · Premarital Sex Relations: The Problem and Its Implications *

LESTER A. KIRKENDALL

Sometimes too great concentration on premarital sex relations as a moral issue or a practical problem obscures the fact that sex relations are only one part of a wider field of interpersonal relationships between men and women. Dr. Kirkendall places premarital sex relations in this wider context and evaluates them in terms of their effect on the couple and the relationship between them.

A SHARP controversy over acceptable premarital sex standards is developing. There is an increasing amount of discussion in newspapers and magazines in which various attitudes toward premarital intercourse are examined, supported, and attacked. Responsible leaders in all walks of life, including religion, are being engaged in the debate. To say that we are facing a penetrating and persistent challenge to conventional sex standards in both theory and practice seems no exaggeration. Since sex is involved, discussion is certain to produce strong and highly emotional reactions immediately. Yet we need to be creative and honest in our thinking, something which is very difficult when we are fearful and as beguiled by sex as we are.

This issue is raised even more sharply by data from the two Kinsey Reports which indicate that about half of the American women and even a larger proportion of American men have experienced premarital intercourse. They also indicate that so far as young women are concerned premarital intercourse is becoming an increasingly acceptable pattern.

Anyone who works closely with young people on their problems of love, mate selection, and family relationships knows that premarital standards are of vital concern to young people and their parents. Minister-counselors, teachers, and other youth workers face this issue. Knowing there is an issue is one thing; being of real help to perplexed individuals is another. I plan to outline an approach which has been very helpful to me in teaching

* *Pastoral Psychology*, 7 (April, 1956), 46–53. Reprinted by permission of the editor and the author.

The author, with the degree of Doctor of Philosophy from Columbia University, is Professor of Family Life at Oregon State College. In addition to holding several earlier teaching positions, he was formerly Director of the Association for Family Living, Chicago. He has written numerous cogent articles on sex education and is coauthor of *A Syllabus and Reading Guide for Courses in Marriage and Family Relations*.

and counseling on premarital sex problems, and which may be equally helpful to others. I regard it only as an approach. Much study and thought are still needed before conclusive answers are reached.

We make a mistake by considering the issue as first and primarily one of sex. Is not the problem at heart one of human interrelationships rather than one of sex? We would do better to be concerned with how our behavior can improve the quality of human interrelationships than to concentrate on whether a certain sexual act has or has not occurred.

To find ways of working together with trust and understanding is the paramount problem of our age. That applies to all aspects of living—to international relations as well as to male-female associations, to racial and labor relations, to parent-child relationships, to people in their personal, face-to-face associations, and in their relationships to all mankind. Our central concern should be for insuring the kind of experiences which make people now and in the long run more able to work together with trust, understanding, and sympathetic appreciation for others. Conduct which divides people, which creates suspicion, distrust, and an incapacity to work together with trust and understanding is socially undesirable and immoral. Sex standards and conduct need to be developed and judged in accordance with this principle. If we agree, instead of deploring sex, we find ourselves engaged in trying to understand how it may be used for the strengthening of personal and group interrelationships.

This point of view, to be helpful, must be genuinely accepted. The improvement of human interrelationships must be our first and sincere concern. Some persons have seemingly accepted this approach, but have then proceeded to use it to prove that some particular standard of sexual behavior should obtain. Their emotional involvement prevents objective analysis.

Premarital intercourse is certain to have a bearing, one way or another, on interrelationships. Sex is too intimately a part of our emotional nature, and intercourse has too much cultural meaning for it to be neutral in its consequences.

What are the facts? What does premarital intercourse do to the quality of the interrelationships of those involved? The facts are not clearly known, but during the past several years I have been seeking answers. I have conducted systematic interviews with college-level men seeking particularly information which would indicate how experience in premarital intercourse affected the quality of the relationships in which they were involved. This is, of course, a highly selected single-sex group.

I cannot set forth the data I have collected in detail. I will attempt only to outline some of the tentative insights which I have developed. These may be helpful in thinking through the issue of premarital sex standards, and in working with young people themselves.

1. *Every premarital intercourse experience is a unique experience.* No hard and fast statement about what will be the outcome of premarital coitus is possible. The personalities, levels of maturity, backgrounds, previous experiences, and motives of the participants differ. The circumstances under which intercourse occurs vary from couple to couple, and from time to time with the same couple. Only as we recognize this uniqueness can we think clearly about the innumerable meanings which premarital intercourse has for various persons.

2. *The quality of the couple's over-all relationship has much effect on the outcome of the sexual relationship.* When sexual relations occur with a prostitute or a casual pickup, obviously only the most tenuous over-all relationship exists. Whatever relationship there is, is motivated almost wholly by sexual purposes. There is little or no concern with personality values. Consequently there is practically no chance that intercourse (or copulation) will result in more trust and understanding or a greater capacity for cooperation. It seems almost certain to result in just the opposite.

On the other hand, a couple may have intercourse just before marriage. Here there is an over-all relationship based upon deep feelings and attitudes, and we are dealing with antenuptial intercourse. At this point the partners feel a real concern for each other's needs, and intercourse itself can provide (though it does not always do so) not merely physical pleasure, but a way of expressing their sense of unity and interrelationship.

Between these extremes are over-all relationships of varying degrees of closeness in which intercourse occurs—the casual summer friendship, good friends who are dating, steady daters, and the almost engaged. As we are able to differentiate degrees of affectional attachment, we find intercourse having different effects on the relationships of those involved, and probably on the subsequent relationships which the participants are able to establish with others.

3. *Circumstances beyond the control of either party may alter the quality of the relationship.* Even though attitudes are wholly altruistic and the relationship is openly and freely entered into by each, intercourse may still severely injure the relationship. An engaged couple, out of love, might freely agree to enter intercourse, yet be so immature and so unready to meet the situation that an unexpected pregnancy would alter the whole complexion of what had been for them, until then, a satisfactory relationship. Discovery, unexpected feelings of guilt or suspicion, or the strain of secrecy will sometimes produce the same results. A couple cannot be sure that because they have willingly, frankly, and honestly entered a sexual relationship that it will work out to their complete satisfaction. No human relationship is, of course, a fully safe and secure one. What we need in all relationships is help in knowing when we are taking undue risks.

4. Conflicting and self-centered motivations cause hurt, disillusionment, and disharmony among non-engaged couples experiencing premarital inter-course. Conflicting motivations eventually appeared more important than guilt feelings in causing trouble. Originally I had expected to find feelings of guilt much stressed by those whom I interviewed, and so was surprised at the small amount of guilt revealed. Much more guilt, I think, would have been voiced by a group of women. Women are taught to feel differently about premarital intercourse than are men. It was evident, however, that in relationship after relationship for the man the net effect of conflicting motivations was a sense of distrust, suspicion, and disrespect.

The boy might enter intercourse for physical pleasure, the girl to please him. A girl might invite intercourse because it seemed a way to attract a partner, or because it gave her a needed feeling of intimacy and closeness, the boy because it proved his masculinity, or his capacity for sex-ual functioning. In most cases these motives were not verbalized; sometimes they appeared to be unconscious motivations. Motive analysis is very com-plicated, especially when we realize the number and concealed nature of motives usually present in each situation.

Women are particularly likely to regard intercourse either as a move toward, or as a way of insuring a continuing, stable relationship. The man's interest is frequently mainly in securing emotional and physical satisfaction from intercourse. The result of this conflict in purpose is often hurt, dis-illusionment, and anger for both, and guilt, particularly for the girl.

When one participant has one purpose and the other a different one sooner or later the divergent motivations are exposed. The result is a growing sense of suspicion, distrust, the erection of barriers, and a feeling of being exploited. The relationship ultimately breaks with a feeling of hurt, bitterness, and a sense of having been used, which probably makes it more difficult for the persons to build good relationships with others later.

Similar motivations do not insure the development of a good relation-ship. The motives need to be other-centered rather than self-centered. An obvious illustration of like motives resulting in discord would be a situation in which each participant was expressing a personal rebellion against authority, but lacked any personal interest in his partner.

Divergent motivations may still exist in the engagement period. Two other factors are more likely to be present then, however, which tend to lessen the likelihood of divergent motivation. One is the increased capacity of the couple to communicate honestly with each other. The other is the increasing degree to which motivations are "other-centered." There is much less other-centeredness in the early dating relationship, and usually none in the strictly casual association.

5. An intercourse relationship which is accompanied by feelings of unity and acceptance appears to rest upon certain definite considerations. These considerations are a capacity for full and free communication between the partners, an ability to handle such unhoped for consequences as pregnancy, discovery, and parental disapproval, a genuine concern for each other's welfare, and upon the couple's paramount concern with the quality of their relationship, rather than sex itself. I have come across a number of intercourse relationships, all involving engaged couples, in which the partners have felt that while they were having intercourse their sense of intimacy and feelings of trust, confidence, and understanding also increased. This has resulted, I believe, from the presence of the factors indicated in the first sentence of this paragraph.

In the Burgess-Wallin study [1] of engaged couples, over 90% of those couples reporting premarital intercourse stated that they felt sexual relations had increased their sense of closeness. On the other hand, a number of engaged couples who have decided against having intercourse have reported to me their belief that their decision not to have intercourse has drawn them closer together. What does this mean? Probably that these couples have reached a point when they can talk with full frankness and trust, and a mutual respect which causes them to honor and respect each other. The experience of discussing so intimate a relationship with candor and respect increases their feelings of trust and regard, regardless of which way the decision goes.

For some couples already in love, intercourse has seemed to break down the final barriers to full and frank acceptance of each other, and so has increased their love for each other. Other engaged couples in spite of seemingly favorable circumstances have noted such divisive effects as these: "We began to make sex more and more the focus of our relationship," "Once we began to have intercourse, I (the man) seemed to lose interest in getting married," "Even though we loved each other the nagging fear of pregnancy spoiled the relationship for us" (the woman).

Much has been said about the Kinsey findings that approximately three-fourths of the women and most of the men who had had premarital intercourse expressed "no regret" over the experience. I am not satisfied to accept this as the only criterion for judging the quality of the relationship. Simply to voice "no regret" does not rule out the possibility of undesirable consequences for the speaker or his partner.

Both men and women frequently tell me they have no regrets over premarital intercourse, yet they relate in detail experiences which have obviously resulted in hurt feelings, recriminations, bitterness, distrust, and

---

[1] Burgess, Ernest W., and Wallin, Paul, *Engagement and Marriage:* Chicago: J. B. Lippincott Company, 1953, chapters 11 and 12.

suspicion. One "no regrets" man described how several of his paramours had tried to "trap" him, and how he managed to circumvent the desire of each for marriage while still keeping her in a mood to accept him as her partner in intercourse.

A number of persons clearly based their expression of "no regret" upon success in avoiding pregnancy or discovery. They seemed to have little awareness that the nature of their psychological experiences might affect attitudes toward the other sex, or ability to establish good relationships later.

While a feeling of guilt always disturbs an individual, it sometimes has the effect of cementing the relationship of a couple who bear affection for each other. For example, expressions of guilt sometimes lead to sympathetic efforts to understand and allay it. The result may be increased closeness.

In my judgment, practically all of the premarital coitus in the pre-engagement period, and an undetermined portion of intercourse in the engagement period, occurs under conditions which both then and eventually result in more suspicion, distrust, and less ability to set up good relationships. Couples who are relatively immature, who are unready to bear the responsibility of a permanent marriage relationship, who are over-eager for the sexual experience, who are unable to communicate with each other in a really trusting and confidential way will find it practically impossible in our culture to set up a sexual relationship which contributes to increased trust, confidence, and good will toward each other and toward people in general.

Up to this point discussion has centered on the implications of premarital intercourse for those who are most immediately involved. While I have only hinted at the broader ramifications the whole issue of the individual in his social and cultural relationships needs to have careful consideration by the counselor. What can adults working with young people do to help them think through the issues involved in premarital intercourse so as to achieve better personal interrelationships?

First, I return to my earlier suggestion that the central concern must be for improved personal interrelationships rather than with sex *per se*. This means a reorientation in thinking for many, but it is an approach which "makes sense" to young people in a way no other approach does. At the same time, it is in harmony with religious concepts. It is spelling out so far as sex behavior is concerned, the meaning of the injunction, "love thy neighbor as thyself," and of the Golden Rule. It answers positively the question, "am I my brother's keeper?" It puts sexual morality on a meaningful basis.

Focusing on a concern for interrelationships gives the minister and the counselor a framework within which to think, a point of view by which he may orient himself. The first reaction of some to this approach is that "all standards are being swept away." Actually the standards suggested are very real and positive. What is necessary is time for thinking through this point of view, and for recognizing how helpful it can be once understood.

Second, the minister in his role as counselor and teacher needs to remember that young persons cannot and ought not to be forced into any pattern of sexual behavior. No one, minister, parent, counselor, or teacher, can supervise young people so closely, or teach with such authority that they can insure no "stepping out of bounds" sexually. Their very success would result in inhibitions so severe as to destroy the whole spontaneity of life, and make the individual an emotional invalid. They can only give young people help in thinking through their problems, and hope that when they do have to make actual decisions they will be able to make them wisely. The problem is that young people today are called upon to make many decisions without guidance, adequate information, or insight.

We have hardly treated our young people fairly. Rigid taboos against premarital intercourse have long existed. Severe penalties have been assessed for their violation. But in the past, adults at least aided youth in their observance of the conventional code by strict chaperonage, taboos on sex discussion, and similar barriers to sex practices.

Today, we are trying to enforce about the same code, minus the barriers. In fact, young people are thrust headlong into situations where their only choice is to become sex-conscious. Newspapers, movies, and other media of communication make sex a daily conversation fare. The automobile, widely disseminated contraceptive information, and advertising all lend their force to awaken sex-consciousness and desire.

By the freedom which has been extended an engaged couple in our society we seem to have implied that, if after weighing the evidence conscientiously and sincerely they decide to enter intercourse, it is their own business. Having thus relaxed our sanctions, logically we should re-examine the basis of our judgments. They should be made in terms of the demonstrated effects which intercourse has upon the quality of interrelationships between the partners and the larger society, now and later.

We will be able to accept this view only as we are able to be less shocked and fearful of sex. Many young people have premarital intercourse and go on living successful and happy lives. Others, of course, meet with unhappy and even disastrous experiences. Our failure to discuss sex matters and issues freely as we do other issues of consequence has, however, left us unaware of the possibilities, outcomes, and problems involved in this area of conduct.

Third, we need to be realistic about the existing situation as it is related to sex standards. Young people themselves are fully aware of conditions.

Data from the Kinsey research have been printed in most of the widely circulated publications. Newspapers and magazines carry numerous articles on almost every aspect of sexual functioning. Sexual intercourse is a common topic of conversation at the high school level. Frequently, young people have referred to couples who were having intercourse, and later, I have found the information to be correct. Most couples hear rumors about acquaintances who have "gone the limit." A seventeen-year-old boy in a high school discussion group recently commented that few youth who dated actively completed high school without having to decide whether to engage in premarital sexual intercourse. His associates, both boys and girls, agreed with his statement. Many high school and college young men and women have known or know couples who are having premarital intercourse with no obvious untoward consequences. Contraceptive information of a kind is available to most high school youth, and about as frequently the contraceptives themselves.

Fourth, we need to build a different concept of the nature of sex and sex education. Young people ask for help on interrelationships. What they are given is either reproductive or physiological information or strictures against certain kinds of behavior without accompanying insight or understanding. They want help in understanding the emotional aspects of their sexual nature and that of the other sex, together with outcomes which can result from the various possible uses of sex in relationships with other persons.

An approach which simply "inveighs against" serves only to make matters worse. It produces neither understanding nor acceptance of one's impulses. It heightens guilt and fear, and makes the individual feel even more unworthy because of his inability to control or subdue his desires.

Sexual behavior and sex desires are regarded too largely as primarily physiological, and as motivated by desire for physical pleasure. These elements are doubtless components in all sexual behavior, and their intensity also varies from person to person and from time to time. We are far too little aware, though, of the extent to which psychological and emotional factors motivate sexual behavior, and of the subtleties of sexual motivations.

A rather common problem will illustrate the point. An engaged couple wants to avoid involvement in intercourse, yet they find their sexual urges building up in a manner which distresses them. They are in a more or less constant battle with sexual desires. A number of possible circumstances, all non-physical in nature, may explain the intensity of their feelings. They may feel guilty over having such impulses and so they fight them, and try to suppress them. This may and usually does intensify the problem. They may be persons who have felt starved for affection and intimacy. Their childhood and family life may have been marred by the feeling that they were unwanted and belonged nowhere. Now in their relationship each has found a responsive person, and in the joy of the new relationship the customary restraints are swept aside.

Here the problem is to help the couple understand themselves well enough so that they can make their decisions in regard to future conduct wisely, and in harmony with their concern for maintaining the quality of their interrelationships.

Sometimes one finds an engaged couple psychologically and emotionally ready for marriage. For some reason such as parental objection, lack of money and housing, or the fact that they plan for further education, this couple has had to postpone marriage indefinitely. Wanting to marry and knowing each other fully, they are denied this possibility because of circumstances which bear little or no relation to marriage readiness. A feeling of frustration and defeat builds up, and along with it a strong feeling of sexual need. When a couple in such a situation can plan, and hope that marriage can be achieved in the reasonably near future, their sexual tensions tend to subside to manageable proportions. Socially we need much more attention given to ways of making marriage possible when there is a sound readiness for it.

Sexual feelings will always be a part of the normal individual. A knowledge of his own motivations and needs, however, helps a great deal in living easily with sex. Individuals can order and direct their sexual impulses in much the same manner that they manage their other impulses. This capacity for direction is again influenced by psychological factors. The person who is more mature emotionally, is achieving normally in his educational and occupational pursuits, and who feels himself loved and appreciated has a greater capacity for self-direction of his sexual impulses. So in a very real sense, the greatest assistance we can give a person in achieving sexual morality is to help him toward maturity, give him a sense of individual worth and acceptance, and help him attain satisfying personal interrelationships.

CHAPTER 10:

Laws Regulating Marriage and Family Life

---

41 · Legal Regulation of Marriage *

RUTH SHONLE CAVAN

One of the problems of discussing the legal aspects of marriage in the United States is that laws pertaining to marriage and the family are state laws; therefore there are as many different sets of laws as there are states. Nevertheless, a general pattern runs through the laws due to the fact that almost without exception the basic laws have grown out of the English common law. This common root gives a similarity to the state laws but has not prevented deviations based on regional differences of thought and belief and on the difference in time of the passage of laws from the earliest laws of the Atlantic Seaboard to the relatively recent laws of some of the western states. This summary attempts only to give the general pattern, from which there are individual state deviations. In the reports available, the District of Columbia is included but not Alaska or Hawaii.

ALTHOUGH marriage is sometimes referred to as a civil contract, it differs greatly from other civil contracts. For instance, it often can be entered into at an earlier age than other contracts, and in this sense the marriage law is more liberal than that governing civil contracts. However, marriage cannot be terminated without appeal to the proper court, which may or may not grant the appeal; in this the law is more strict for marriage than for many

---

* A summary of some factual material in *The Legal Status of Women in the United States of America*, Women's Bureau Bulletin 157 (rev. 1956; Washington, D.C.: United States Department of Labor, 1956); supplemented from Harriet F. Pilpel and Theodora Zavin, *Your Marriage and the Law* (New York: Rinehart & Company, Inc., 1952); interpretation is the author's.
Biographical note on the author is given with article 6.

other kinds of contract. Legally, marriage is regarded as a relationship of supreme importance for the well-being of the whole society and for the careful rearing of children. The popular trend in the United States has been for marriage to be regarded more and more as the personal affair of husband and wife, to be entered or left at will, sometimes without much regard for the effect on children. The law takes another stand; marriage creates duties and obligations which the couple cannot neglect at will. Each state has numerous laws to regulate marriage.

Common Law and Written Law

The complexities of laws governing marriage are easier to understand when the distinction between common law and written law is made clear. Marriage is an old institution and the English common law still controls or influences some aspects of American marriage in the 1960's.

The basis for the laws of the various states lies in the English common law as it was at the time of the American Revolution and, in a few states settled by French or Spanish people, in French and Spanish civil codes. These early imported rules have been modified by constitutional provisions, colonial and state statutes or laws, and court decisions. The common law is known as unwritten law and the statutes and court decisions as written law. If no written law applies to a specific situation, the principles of the old English common law apply. The written law may simply repeat the common law or may change it or discard it altogether.

When the common law still operates in regulation of marriage, this fact will be pointed out. Often its continued use indicates that marriage laws are very much out of step with current social conditions. In other instances, the common law has only recently been replaced by more appropriate statutes, often after persistent efforts of determined women and their male supporters in the state legislatures.

Trend of Laws

In general, the trend of laws and court decisions has been in four directions.

First, laws have liberated married women from the subordinate status imposed by the feudal common law. According to this body of law, a woman's legal identity was destroyed by marriage. Her property and earnings belonged to her husband and her personal conduct was subject to his control. This concept was in keeping with the feudal hierarchy of control that placed strong leadership in the hands of men, who also carried heavy responsibilities. Gradually, laws in the United States have established economic and personal independence for married women. Many of the changes have come recently.

Second, although laws pertaining to marriage have not changed much in the past 75 years and in some respects have become stricter, court decisions have tended to interpret the laws leniently, especially those pertaining to divorce. Stricter regulation can be seen in laws requiring freedom from venereal disease or requiring a waiting or thinking-over period between application for the marriage license and its issuance.

Third, some old laws clearly out of step with the times and often now a means of exploitation are slowly, state by state, being discarded. Two examples are the right to bring breach of promise suits and recognition of common-law marriages.

Fourth, laws not thought of as marriage laws often indirectly affect the privileges or duties of marriage. Fathers are obligated to support their minor children; but laws granting aid to dependent children lighten the earlier obligations for ill or absent fathers. Old-age assistance (grants to old people in need) has lifted some of the burden of supporting old parents from their adult children who may be having a difficult time meeting the expenses of rearing a family. School attendance laws have relieved parents of the supervision of children for many hours during the week through most of the adolescent period; these laws also often increase the length of time during which parents must support their children.

With these various trends in mind, let us turn to specific areas of legal regulation.

Breach of Promise

Breach of promise refers to the breaking of an engagement. The engagement is regarded as a binding contract to marry, the breaking of which by one party may injure the other. Under common law, the injured party could sue in court the one who broke the engagement and claim money payment for damages. Gradually state laws have been passed abolishing this common-law right. By 1956, fifteen states had passed such laws.

Breach of promise suits usually are started by women. At an earlier period, the engagement was regarded in a sense as the beginning of marriage. If the man broke the engagement, the woman's reputation, and therefore her chances of future marriage to someone else, was often damaged. If the engagement was broken by mutual consent, neither man nor woman could bring suit.

At present an engagement is regarded by most young people as a private arrangement to permit them to test their compatibility for each other. It is a stronger relationship than steady or serious dating, but lacks legal connotations. Engagements, even after being publicly announced, are often broken. Regardless of feelings of frustration or rejection, neither man nor woman feels that either owes money to the other in payment of damages.

Breach of promise suits now are often abused. A wealthy man may be sued by an ex-fiancée who is perhaps more interested in acquiring a large sum of money than in remedying any actual damage to her reputation or previous financial status. The threat of a suit may force a man to make a money settlement to avoid unfavorable publicity. However, if the woman has invested money from which the man benefits or has given up some lucrative employment which she cannot regain, courts are inclined to require the man to reimburse her to the extent of actual money loss.

Who May Not Marry

The law does not compel anyone to marry, but it does regulate eligibility for marriage. Laws tend to rule out types of persons whom public opinion or the legislators have thought unsuitable for marriage. The laws do not set up positive standards which would tend to lift the quality of marriage. The laws set formal minimum standards for mate selection.

Age. In general, in the United States, children may not marry. According to the table of Marriage Laws, prepared by the Women's Bureau, which follows this article, in the majority of states the minimum age for a legal marriage, even with the consent of parents, is eighteen for males and sixteen for females. However, a number of states permit girls as young as fourteen and boys as young as fifteen to marry when the parents consent. Finally, in a few states laws have not been passed setting a minimum age. Then the old common-law rule of England still holds, and girls of twelve and boys of fourteen may marry with parental consent. As the table indicates, six states still permit these early marriages. In slightly less than half of the states, the minimum age may be set aside by a judge, usually when a girl is pregnant.

Without parental consent, the most usual minimum age is eighteen for girls and twenty-one for men. In actual practice, these ages are more nearly representative of the lower age of marriage than are the minimum ages with parental consent. In 1956 the median age for first marriages contracted by men was 23.1 years and for women 20.2 years. These figures mean that half of all men married when over 23.1 years and half of all women when over 20.2 years. Of course, half marry below these ages, but few reach down into the years when parental consent is required.

The old common-law rule placed the minimum age at about the age of puberty, at a time when educational attainments were also completed by about this same period. Present laws and customs allow not only for sexual maturity but for general bodily maturity, completion of secondary education, and some experience in economic independence.

When a person under the minimum age does marry, the marriage usually stands unless court action is taken to dissolve it. Thus young people may lie about their ages and marry. If no one (for example, parents) brings a suit in court to have the marriage annulled, the marriage stands.

Degree of Kinship. Members of an immediate family related by blood may not marry. The "marriage" or sexual relations between a parent and his or her child or between brother and sister is called incest. Public abhorrence as well as laws exact heavy penalties from adult offenders.

First cousins may not marry each other in more than half of the states and in a few states somewhat more remote relatives—sometimes including ones related by marriage—are forbidden to marry.

Prohibitions of marriages between close relatives are old and widespread. Almost the only exceptions are found in certain royal lines, where few people are of sufficient status to be able to marry a member of the royal family. An extreme example is the Ptolemies of Egypt who sometimes followed an Egyptian custom of brother-sister marriages.

Reasons for the prohibitions are not always clear. Some of them undoubtedly reduce tension and conflict in family and kinship groups. The prohibition of first-cousin marriages has certain implications for heredity, although it is obvious that this is not the primary reason, since such marriages are forbidden in groups which do not have a science of genetics. A defective family strain might be carried by both cousins and thus increase the probability that children of the marriage might inherit the defect. A favorable characteristic might similarly come to a child in double measure.

Whatever the reason for the origin of these laws, we now have ingrained attitudes of abhorrence against sexual relations, in or out of marriage, between closely related persons.

Interracial Marriages. There is a marked tendency in the United States for people to marry those similar to themselves, in occupational status, education, ethnic background, religion, and race. One's contacts tend to be with others like oneself. Public opinion and group pressures also tend to turn people toward their own groups when they court and marry. The only type of marriage between unlike people forbidden by law is marriage between certain races. Twenty-nine states prohibit marriages between Negroes and whites and in addition thirteen of these states forbid the marriage of whites and Orientals. In other states public opinion strongly opposes such marriages. As a consequence, few interracial marriages occur.

Other Prohibitions. Various states have selected certain physical grounds for prohibiting marriages, declaring them void if they occur. These conditions and the number of states using each as grounds for forbidding marriage are listed below:

Unsound mind	24 states
Epilepsy	14 states
Venereal disease in communicable stage	9 states
Habitual drunkenness	3 states
Tuberculosis in a communicable stage	1 state
Any communicable disease	1 state
Communicable disease if unknown to the other party	1 state
Drug addiction	1 state
Impotency	1 state

People with unfavorable behavior records may also be forbidden to marry. Three states have some type of prohibition of marriage by criminals. Two states forbid the marriage of a male who has been an inmate of a home for indigents unless he can show he is able to support a family.

Many of these prohibitions (all aimed at protecting the marriage partner or the children) are difficult to enforce, as it is not customary to require a certificate that these conditions do not exist and often the officer issuing the marriage license would have only the assertion of the applicant to guide him. True, many of the marriages are illegal or could be annulled—but often no one takes the step to bring about court action so that functionally the marriages may continue through the years and be accepted as legal.

Getting Married

Physical Examination. About four-fifths of the states require a physical examination whose purpose is to determine whether the person has a venereal disease (see table on Marriage Laws). A few states require a certificate of freedom from certain other diseases or physical defects. The nature of the examination is not always adequate; in fact, in a few states the applicants for a license to marry simply affirm that they are not infected. In different states, the examination must be taken within seven to forty days prior to the date of application for a license. The requirements are enforced by the refusal of the licensing officer to issue a license when a certificate is not presented. When the person who has had the disease later is able to present a certificate to show he no longer has it, he may secure a license. Most states provide for some exceptions, for instance, if the infected woman is pregnant. In a few such states the infected woman must undergo treatment after marriage. Since not all states require the certificate, a couple may evade the law in one state by traveling for their marriage to a state without the requirement.

When these laws were first passed, many people objected to the examination as a violation of their right of privacy in personal matters. However, the danger of one infected partner infecting the other is so great that public opinion has gradually moved to support the laws. Another danger is that a woman with venereal disease may infect her child before birth, in which case it requires special treatment for cure. Sometimes an infected child is born with some serious mental or physical defect. Venereal disease is not inherited. Its control lies in the hands of the man and woman who marry.

License. In most states, the couple desiring to marry must secure a license from a legally designated officer, usually the county clerk or a judge. The license becomes a matter of public record. Unless common-law marriages are permitted, a marriage ceremony must take place, with exchange of vows. In general, either a religious or a civil ceremony is sufficient; Maryland, West Virginia, and Delaware, however, require a religious ceremony.

Most states require witnesses to the marriage and also require that the marriage be recorded. The public record establishes the status of the man and woman as married people and is a later safeguard if husband or wife denies the marriage and disregards his or her obligations; it also protects the child against a charge of illegitimacy (unless the husband charges and proves that he is not the father). The license and the record of marriage remove marriage from the realm of purely personal and private relationships and make of it a socially responsible relationship.

Common-Law Marriage. Eighteen states recognize common-law marriages and enforce the rights and obligations of husband and wife in them. (See table of Marriage Laws.) Common-law marriages are ones in which a marriage ceremony has not been performed and usually in which a license has not been secured. They were not recognized in the common law of England but are a vestige from our own past when on the frontier judge and minister were often miles distant or passed through a given community perhaps once a year on their circuits. Meanwhile men and women fell in love, set up a home, and perhaps had a child. Sometimes they were married when the opportunity came; but often they indefinitely postponed the ceremony, although they performed all the obligations of a married couple and established a loving and protective home for their children.

Nowadays there seems little excuse not to have a marriage in compliance with the laws. A common-law marriage is a weak marriage. The man may desert, claiming he was never married. Many complications and possibilities for fraud can arise when one of the couple dies and someone, perhaps fraudulently, appears, claiming to be a common-law spouse and demanding rights of inheritance. Legitimacy and inheritance rights of children may also be questioned if the parents have not been legally married. Many states, therefore, have passed laws invalidating common-law marriages, sometimes continuing to recognize those contracted before a specified date.

In states that still recognize common-law marriages, the requirements stated above for a license and ceremony are merely directive and their disregard does not make marriage (common-law) invalid.

Waiting Period. More than half the states require a waiting period of one to five days, usually between the time of applying for a license and its issuance. A few states place the waiting period between issuance of the license and the time of the marriage.

The waiting period is aimed at the prevention of elopements, marriages on the spur of the moment, or marriages by people who are intoxicated. The waiting period gives the couple time for a second thought about their plans; it does not permanently prevent anyone from marrying.

Rights and Responsibilities of Husband and Wife

The laws outlining rights and responsibilities of husbands and wives to each other and to their children are minimum requirements. A marriage which did not rise above these laws would be a very meager relationship. Nevertheless, some marriages do not rise—in fact, sink below—and therefore laws are necessary to define the lowest limits of marriage.

Personal Relations. On the personal side, each partner has the right to live with the other, to have normal sexual relations, and to have the other's love, society, and assistance. The husband is obligated to support his wife in a manner appropriate to his income, even though she may have property or income of her own. The wife is obligated to make a home for her husband without demanding to be paid by the husband. If the husband does not support his wife when he is able to do so, she may sue him in court in most states, or often she may use nonsupport as the grounds for a legal separation or divorce. The husband has the right to choose where the couple will live, but the wife has the right to a home of her own, under her management. Thus there is a balancing of rights and obligations between husband and wife in establishing and maintaining a home.

Property Adjustment. On the property side, the trend has been to give women greater freedom in control of their property. The common law of England and older laws in the United States specified that, at marriage, all the personal property that a woman had at the time of marriage passed to her husband, who could also take over ownership of bonds and corporate stock and could control her real estate. She could not enter into contracts and all her earnings belonged to her husband.

Under statutes passed by the various states, the married woman now retains ownership of all property, both real estate and personal, belonging to

Consider, for example, these findings—which may be somewhat typical —from a recent study of senior high schools in California. Of the 205 schools studied, 90 per cent reported one or more student marriages during a one-year period. Nearly ten times as many girls had married as had boys, and most of those girls married out-of-school youths. Most of the marrying boys, however, had teamed up with girls still in school. The percentages of married students increased with each year in school. Among girls, 2.4 per cent of the sophomore class were married; 4.0 per cent of the junior class; and 5.7 per cent of the senior class. Nearly three fourths of the girls dropped out of school following their marriage as contrasted with very few of the married boys.

This high drop-out rate for girls may have been encouraged by the ill-defined and rather negative attitudes of some school officials toward student marriages. Many administrators have the fear (probably unfounded) that married students will talk about marital sexual experiences to unmarried students. Then, too, when a student wife becomes pregnant she is frequently requested or pressured to withdraw. If more schools offered effective courses in family life education, they could help prepare youngsters for the future and prevent some premature and usually ill-advised marriages. But too many of our high schools make only halfhearted efforts —or no attempts at all—in that direction.

It is natural for parents, teachers, school officials, and others to worry over today's wave of teen-age marriages. But is their worry well founded? The answer is *yes*—though, as will be shown, we need to move from the unproductive level of mere worry to that of seeking to understand and solve the problem.

Virtually all the research shows lower marital-happiness scores and higher divorce rates for those who marry quite young. Statistically speaking, the best time for marriage seems to be the early and middle twenties, not the late teens. There are at least three good reasons for this.

In Defense of Deferment

In the first place, teen-agers are not usually mature enough, in their emotions and judgment, for marriage. They are likely to choose their mates impetuously and to be nervous and unsure in their later adjustments. As a result they make very unstable husbands, wives, and parents. Moreover, pediatricians testify that the extremely young mother is most likely to be tense and anxious about motherhood and then to transfer this insecurity to the child.

Second, the younger a couple are at marriage, the shorter, generally speaking, has been their courtship—which means that there wasn't time to test the relationship and to prepare for the marriage. In other words, the relationship itself suffers from immaturity.

In the third place, it is likely that the circumstances may not be right. The boy and girl may not have finished school. He may still be facing his period of military service. Or the two of them may be unprepared in other ways to assume the social and economic responsibilities that marriage normally entails. These are reality factors outside the individual and outside the relationship. Because of them it seems likely that, given the same degree of maturity and involvement, success in marriage will be more probable at ages twenty-one to twenty-five than, say, at ages fourteen to eighteen.

Of course there are exceptions. Some couples who marry early do achieve real happiness, just as certain of those who wait longer do fail. Age in itself is not the primary consideration. But since many young people are, by virtue of their youth, immature, the chances of failure are greater in very youthful marriages.

It is probably no accident that the increasing divorce rate in the United States is paralleled by a decreasing age at marriage. The causes of divorce are many, to be sure, but marrying too young is definitely one of them.

Why the Rush into Matrimony?

Reasons for a trend toward youthful marriage seem to group themselves into three large clusters, which it may be worthwhile to examine.

There is the increasing *encouragement from contemporary culture*. Many of today's musical, literary, and dramatic presentations are designed to stimulate romantic and sexual interests. In consequence, marriage is made to appear as something glamorous, the answer to all problems. This unrealistic overvaluation gives rise to early and steady dating, which can lead to emotional and sexual involvement and eventually to premature marriage. Indeed growing-up has been so speeded up that in this modern day young people are permitted and even expected to do many things formerly reserved for adults. Going steady and getting married tend to fall in this category. They are avenues by which the youngster comes to feel that he can demonstrate his maturity and gain adult status. Finally, early dating, going steady, and marriage are "the style" today. Many teen-agers follow this course not because they particularly want to but because of social pressure—because it is "the thing to do."

Youthful marriages are, in part, a reflection of the *insecurities of our time*. The rapid tempo of living, the confusion arising from a complex and changing culture, the tensions of modern war—hot or cold—all tend to propel young people in the direction of steady dating and then marriage.

Having less to cling to in the culture they cling more to each other. Not far from central in all of this are the interruptions of military service and the almost constant threat of war.

Equally important is the growing number of unsettled and broken homes, which may leave children feeling rejected and "so alone." Also, along with the increasing divorce rate has come an increasing irresponsibility and laxness on the part of parents toward the care and guidance of their children. And parental rejection or abuse, real or imagined, tends to drive children out of the home. (It is the insecure and unhappy youngster who is most apt to turn to marriage as an escape.) Unfortunately this kind of marriage is often without a solid foundation, so that the same unfavorable conditions are passed on to the next generation.

No Need for a Nest Egg

Another reason for the rush into matrimony is that the *economic risk is smaller* today than it was in earlier generations. This country has enjoyed two full decades of prosperity, with a constantly rising standard of living, and most young people now find it easier to get jobs that pay well. More and more women are working, and the "two-job family" emerges as the norm, especially for the period immediately after marriage. Among many young couples it is customary for both husband and wife to work until they get established; hence lack of financial preparation is less of a deterrent to an early marriage.

Parents, too, often lessen the economic risk by their willingness to help support the young couple for a while after marriage, especially if the boy and girl are still in school. Along with this, social security under government sponsorship has reduced many of the economic risks inherent in marrying and rearing a family.

Related to these three social trends is the ever present and perhaps increasing phenomenon of premarital pregnancy. Some girls get married, or do so sooner than they otherwise would, because they find themselves pregnant. My own research has demonstrated that early marriages are associated with abnormally high rates of both premarital pregnancy and divorce.

The Path of Best Resistance

The $64,000 question, of course, is "What can be done about it all?" There is no easy answer. Perhaps part of the answer is for us to understand what is happening so that we can be tolerant and somewhat philosophic about the matter. There are fashions in dating and marriage as well as in dress, and these change from time to time. There is no point in taking a completely hostile position or in being continually miserable about what cannot be changed.

But this does not mean that we must be fatalistic and make no attempt to steer youth into a wiser course. With an understanding of the social currents of our times, parents, teachers, and others can do much to shape the features in the environment that influence behavior. As citizens they can work for such things as community betterment and world peace. As teachers they can impart the insight and impetus necessary for control. And as parents they can make their children feel secure, loved, and happy.

In the end it all boils down to the necessity for doing a better job of *family life education*—in the home largely by example and in the school largely by instruction. It must be an education that not only imparts facts but shapes attitudes, that builds values and provides incentives. And it must be an education that comes early enough to do some good, starting in elementary school and continuing through college.

If we are worrying about high school marriages, why not start by initiating good family life education at the high school level? This would have two desirable results: It would delay or prevent many of the early marriages now taking place; and to those few youthful marriages that are probably bound to occur in any event—human nature being what it is—it would give a better foundation.

44 · When Shall We Marry? *

RUTH HOEFLIN

This article reports the views of eight home economics students on the problem that confronts many students—whether to marry while still a college student and, if one does marry, how to handle the special situations that arise.

A HAPPY BRIDE who is almost eighteen, with a lawyer-to-be husband, a place to live near the campus, each with a part-time position and both enrolled in school autumn quarter—what could be better? Six weeks later—

---

* *Journal of Home Economics*, 47 (June, 1955), 416–418. Reprinted by permission of the publisher and the author.

The author, who holds the doctor's degree, is Associate Professor of child and family development in the School of Home Economics, Ohio State University. She has carried on research with the Ohio Agricultural Experiment Station.

disillusionment and fear had replaced their starry-eyed dream. Both husband and wife had been ill, and mother-in-law had to come to take care of them. They were evicted from their living quarters because their rooming house did not pass college inspection. She lost her job; money problems as well as housing problems loomed. Then the final straw—a sick grandmother needed constant care, and this young bride had to drop out of school. Besides, because of repeated absences, her grades had dropped.

The above illustration of the experience of a freshman started the search for facts and ideas among some of the married home economics girls on this subject of marriage and college. Was this a typical case? What were some of the problems of shouldering the responsibilities of marriage along with those of college study?

Talking It Over

We brought together a group of eight married home economics students and asked them to informally express their viewpoint on college marriages. Of course, opinions were colored by individual circumstances. The girls gave some good reasons for waiting until at least the junior or senior level, but those three who had married while either a freshman or sophomore admitted they would not have changed their plans. However, each of the three girls had left school for a while to earn money and then returned one to three years later. They had found that even a planned budget did not always cover emergencies. In a few cases these girls had followed their drafted husbands, wanting to make the most of every possible moment with them.

How had they managed the money problem? All agreed that the nest egg did not always last. Some of the girls were willing to accept money from their parents at least for their tuition fees. In one case the parents wanted so much for their daughter, Sally, to complete her schooling that they convinced the couple that they should accept financial help. Another couple was grateful that their parents had helped them over a few rough spots during this period of high living costs.

Two girls who had married with their "eyes wide open" did not own engagement rings, but felt that when a choice had to be made in expenditures, they preferred a wedding ring and some of the essentials for a home rather than a diamond.

Mary stated that she and her husband, both only children, had refused all offers of financial assistance. Since she was under age legally to marry, she had to obtain her parents' permission. Mary and her husband both agreed they were going to prove to their hovering parents that they could accept the responsibilities of marriage.

Most of our married students no longer have the benefit of G.I. assistance. When Dot, one of the group of eight, showed how well she and her husband were able to manage with his G.I. monthly check, the money they had saved from her two-year earning period, and his salary from the present part-time position, the other girls sighed.

The Time Problem

What are some of the specific problems besides money in these college marriages? (A budget of time as well as money seems to be essential.) Those duties or tasks which *have* to be done need to be listed or considered in planning. First things must be completed first. Some of the standards the girls would like to maintain are recognized as being out of reach in terms of time and energy and so decisions and choices have to be made. Sue raised this question: "I'm working almost full time, studying, and trying to keep up the house. I just can't seem to get everything done. Is it just me?" She seemed reassured to discover that all of the young wives felt somewhat the same way.

As a group, these wives admitted that some days were pretty bad, that grades versus fatigue were real concerns. On the whole, their grades had remained the same or in a few cases had even improved since marriage.

Most of these college wives felt that combining study with marriage was easier if their husbands were in school at the same time. Thus a study pattern could be worked out. Often the industriousness of one partner working on a school project inspired the other. With both in school, they also found they had something in common to discuss, especially when they could plan to take at least one similar course. In the case where the husband was out working and not in school, the wife occasionally felt some antagonism or resentment when he wanted to go out in the evening and she needed to study or clean house. In another case, when the husband was home from work because of a company strike, the wife found herself resenting his being able to read the newspaper while she came home from her day's work and still had to prepare the evening meal alone.

Phyllis found that many of her husband's friends couldn't understand why his wife was so determined to finish her education, especially since he had a good position. They had two small children; Phyllis had taken a quarter away from college during each pregnancy. She made an effort not to take too much school work home at night but to spend as much time with her family as she could. She said that she could never have managed without her husband's help and understanding. He took over the care of the children after the person hired for the day had departed. Sometimes she felt that she was "floating" in a separate world from her husband, just marking time until she was finished, she said. Yet she would not have postponed her marriage.

All of the girls felt that planned families were important, although they agreed that plans did not always work out. The two girls in the group who were expecting their babies just at graduation time in June admitted that these babies were coming sooner than expected.

Should a Mother Work?

One wife felt that a mother should be at home with her child and not work; a second felt that mothers should at least wait until the children are in school; while a third working mother felt that her child had developed a sense of responsibility since she was away from home and also developed a closer relationship with his father. All of the girls felt that the father had an important role to play in part-time care of their children.

Concerning this role of the husband, each girl felt that men are accepting more responsibility willingly when both husband and wife are in school or working. In fact, they felt that this shared homemaking is becoming a part of the current family pattern, at least among the college age group. One or two of the wives found that their husbands seemed to have unusually high standards of housekeeping and were a little too demanding at times.

Of course married life is not always rosy even without the dual responsibility of work and school. Quarrels or disagreements arise. Sally told of her parents' advice: "Never go to bed with an unsolved problem." The girls all seemed to agree that conflicts should be resolved before bedtime.

The girls as a whole agreed that being in home economics was a real asset. Many of their courses, they felt, were even more valuable now that they were married and could understand the purpose of them. They had learned to take from these courses what they could use and if, occasionally, some of the ideas or theories seemed unrealistic, this fact did not seem to disturb them. Their recommendation was that more courses should be made available to non-home-economics majors, some of whom seemed to be having more problems in such areas as management, meal preparation, children, and relationships. For the most part the girls also felt that their home economics teachers were interested in their marriage and their pregnancies, although occasionally they felt there was some disapproval or thought a few of their teachers felt they should have waited until graduation to marry or to start a family.

The one point these married girls continually stressed was how essential maturity is. They felt each of the partners needed to know what marriage involved beyond the first "rosy glow."

Two Viewpoints

In conferences with a group of juniors who have been part of a two-year research project, two viewpoints on marriage were found. One is to marry when the right person comes along but try to complete the education, at least that of the man. The other viewpoint, especially among the men, is to wait until they have finished their stint in military service before assuming the responsibility of marriage and rearing a family. A few of the men have expressed the idea that if their wives want to work and put them through college that is fine; but for the most part, the man seems to want his wife to be a homemaker and not attempt a dual job unless she too is finishing her education.

The girl feels differently. She is eager to complete her education but she also wants to marry; she is in a quandary. A few girls seem to feel that if they are not married or at least engaged by the senior year, something is wrong with them. In this research group (originally 400 men, 167 women in freshman class) the few girls who were married during the freshman year no longer are in school. Therefore it is difficult to say just what kind of an adjustment they have worked out in their marriages or whether they ever will be able to complete their education. Actually, this article does not take into account those students who after marriage abandon school and do not return because of the complications of combining both marriage and an education.

In all fairness, perhaps it should be pointed out that all girls do not feel the same way. One junior expressed her interest in a particular man but stated that they were waiting until he had finished his term of military service. Another engaged girl commented that both her mother and sister had left school after marriage. Now, because her mother still regretted her lack of education, this girl was determined to complete her last year and a half of home economics before marrying.

The group of married home economics girls in an informal meeting and the juniors in conferences have expressed the idea that both marriage and an education are important and that one should not or does not need to be sacrificed for the other. Now that graduation seems to be in sight, they are facing the future much more realistically than they did as freshmen.

45 · Married Undergraduates on the Campus: An Appraisal *

LESTER A. KIRKENDALL

This appraisal of college marriages is made, not by students as in the preceding article, but by a sociologist seasoned in counseling students and in studying marriage adjustment. Starting with the realistic statement that "campus marriages are here to stay," he reviews some of the possible disadvantages to husband or wife and then gives eight recommendations for avoiding handicaps and strengthening student marriages.

IN THE LATE 1940's a development of far-reaching consequence occurred in college and university education. The arrival of World War II veterans on campuses shattered almost overnight the tradition that an undergraduate college student body should be composed almost exclusively of unmarried students. Some of the veterans brought wives and children with them; others acquired them after their arrival. Students who were combining marriage and the pursuit of an education were found in practically every classroom.

Those concerned with higher education raised many questions about this development. Two common questions were:

1. Once the G.I. government-subsidized veteran group is graduated will campus marriages disappear?
2. Can marriage and securing an education (and often child rearing as well) be successfully combined? Can a family man or woman also do acceptable work as a student?

With time answers to these questions have emerged. We now know that campus marriages are here to stay. The presence of married students in a college does not depend entirely on financial subsidy from the government as some suggested. There are still married persons on most campuses who are receiving direct financial subsidy from the government, but they probably comprise a much smaller proportion of the total married student population than they did in the late 1940's. At the same time it is probable that

---

* *Coordinator*, 5 (December, 1956), 54–63. Reprinted by permission of the editor and the author.
The author's biographical sketch is given with article 40.

on most campuses the proportion of the entire student body which is married has grown.

An illustration of what is probably a typical situation is the enrollment figures from the University of Oregon found in Table 1. This table shows the proportion of married students in the student body from 1939 to the present.

TABLE 1: Percentage of Fall Quarter Enrollment Married, by Sex
University of Oregon, 1939–1956

	1939	1940	1941	1942	1943	1944	1945	1946	1947
Male	7.8	6.5	5.5	5.8	15.6	15.8	22.4	23.5	20.0
Female	3.5	4.1	2.2	3.5	4.0	4.3	4.9	7.9	9.0

	1948	1949	1950	1951	1952	1953	1954	1955	1956
Male	23.5	26.0	23.8	23.9	22.3	24.5	26.2	27.0	27.1
Female	9.2	8.7	7.6	7.7	9.2	9.3	9.3	12.0	10.9

In general, during the years between 1939 and 1956 the proportion of the University of Oregon men married has been at least two to three times larger than the proportion of women married. The proportion of men married has increased somewhat more than the proportion of women married.

Neither is there any longer any debate as to the possibility of completing a college education even though married. Too many persons have done it successfully to leave any doubt. (Not all who have tried it have been successful, but so many have and have been so outstandingly successful that all doubts about the possibility of successfully combining marriage and a college education have disappeared.)

Having settled these questions college faculties and administrators seemingly turned their attention to other problems. Married students were more or less left to shift for themselves except to the extent that they were provided with housing. With the increasing number of young people who wish to marry and continue their education, however, there now appears to be a renewed interest in married college students. At this time the points of concern are not sharply crystallized, nor has a body of factual information relative to married students and their problems been established through research. There seems only a growing awareness that when as large a proportion as one-fourth of the total student body is married some thought should be given to their needs and ways of providing for them.

What are some of the questions which are currently being raised about campus marriages?

Many persons working with college students are increasingly concerned with what has become a pretty standard arrangement for couples in a campus marriage, namely, the practice of the wife working full-time to support the couple or the family financially while the husband continues his education. One would infer this was quite a common plan to judge from the University of Oregon enrollment figures found in Table 1. This arrangement has enabled many a husband to finish school, but many wonder at what expense to the wife, the marriage, and the children, if there are any.

Under the above mentioned arrangement, the wife foregoes her education for the purpose of putting her husband through school. After that she expects ordinarily to become a full-time homemaker. Most couples feel that this will be the most profitable arrangement for them in the long run. Yet, it may ignore the fact that in the modern professional and business world more and more families are living on a standard which demands two incomes rather than one. After the couple leave the campus the wife may wish to work. One needs to add to this the number of wives who at some later time must become self-supporting, and the number who will require some kind of out-of-the-household work for personal satisfaction after the children are in school or have reached adolescence. The size of this group makes it readily apparent that many families may be working against their long-time best interests by accepting an arrangement which deprives the wife of her opportunity to get an education.

(Another problem arising from the arrangement in which the wife stops her education to work to put hubby through is that it may produce a vast chasm intellectually between husband and wife. A wife sometimes finds herself in a routine, dead-end job which may provide enough money for the husband to complete his college education, but which offers her no real opportunity for personal growth and development. At the same time the husband is pursuing an educational program which results in intellectual growth and the creation of interests which carry him beyond those of his wife. The educational gap between husband and wife is slowly and gradually increased. Sometimes at the end of the college educational program couples are already unhappily aware that the husband has outpaced his wife. They are in the sad plight of finding that the very sacrifices of the wife which made possible the husband's education have created a gulf between them and endangered their marriage. One wonders with how many other couples this same chasm shows up in later life, particularly in families where the business and professional success of the husband depends in part on the education, interests, and social competency of his wife.

The result mentioned above is not a necessary concomitant of the wife working while the husband goes to school. It is, however, a hazard of which a couple should be aware. Presumably it can be avoided by careful planning and the development of a sound companionship relationship between husband and wife.

Certain attitudes and practices in the college itself seem to encourage the pattern of wife-working-while-husband-goes-to-college. The encouragement may be overt or covert, but practices should be examined to note the underlying assumptions. For example, the common plan of granting the wives of married students the honorary degree, P.H.T. (Pushed Hubby Through), is a generous and good-hearted gesture. But does it at the same time encourage and establish the pattern under question to the detriment of both husband and wife?

Early in the history of campus marriages it was feared that the reversal of roles might be a source of conflict. That possibility was anticipated in situations in which the wife assumed the more-or-less traditional masculine activities of the family, while the husband continued school and took over some of the traditional feminine activities. The earlier concern of onlookers centered around a fear that men and women might feel ill-at-ease and uncertain as they engaged in tasks which were normally those allotted to members of the other sex. There is little evidence that this pattern of role reversal has been a very serious matter. The experiences of couples indicate rather that it has been healthy. From it each partner learned something of the problems and difficulties which confront the other as he performs his respective part in the maintenance of family life through carrying out the daily routines.

We may need, however, to be concerned with this problem at a deeper level. Counselors sometimes work with students in marital difficulty whose trouble seems to arise from certain feelings about role reversal. For example, some working wives harbor a resentment over the feeling that their husbands seem to be taking their efforts too casually. Some wives have expressed doubts that their husbands really wanted to assume the responsibilities and obligations of the head of the family.

A counselor sometimes finds the husband feeling dissatisfied with his role. He feels he is "cutting a pretty poor picture" as a man. Traditionally, he has assumed that upon marriage he would become the income-producer and head of the family. He finds instead that his wife has taken over those functions, and even though she makes no attempt to take advantage of the situation, her role as income-producer puts her in a dominant position. The husband finds that the planning has to be centered about what the wife can do, and his activities are necessarily dependent upon hers because she is providing the income.

In a number of these situations it appears that the conflict can be solved only after the husband is out of school, has a job in his own right, and is able to assume the role he feels he rightfully ought to play.

This situation illustrates the need for effective research on campus marriages. How seriously do these role reversals affect the adjustments of couples? How can they be met? How many such situations are there? Are there some quite beneficial results? We need to know answers to these questions more surely than we do now.

Another problem is that some couples, particularly those on very limited incomes, lead a more dreary and unrewarding existence than they ought to lead. This is particularly true when they have to, or do, forego so many rich and valuable social and cultural opportunities simply to maintain a minimum standard of living. Some couples marry very early in their college career and thus miss most of the social, extracurricular, and group experiences available to the unmarried undergraduate. Others, because of limited resources, find themselves carrying a burden of study and outside work which drags them to a low level of performance in many phases of life, both mentally and physically. Some find little time to give to the development of their marital relationship. How many married students face such circumstances is impossible to say. But one has only to discuss their situation with those who are in such circumstances to know that often the burden is heavy, that they are unhappy, and that the level of study and work efficiency is low.

Other problems could be mentioned. It seems better, however, to consider them in relation to some recommendations about campus marriages.

1. *Strong consideration should be given to arrangements for both husband and wife to continue their education.* When it is necessary to work to get through college perhaps both should plan to work. This kind of arrangement means that there is less chance of role-reversal of the damaging sort, and that the wives are not completely relinquishing their opportunities for securing an education. They have a better chance of growing and maturing along with their husbands. This is equally to the advantage of both.

This recommendation, of course, depends upon circumstances in both the college and the general community. It calls for arrangements which in some instances can be achieved only by coordinated planning on the part of the number of different persons and college agencies that would be involved.

2. *Marriage might better take place at the mid point or later in the college career.* If a couple enters marriage earlier than this they have a longer time in which financial scrimping will be necessary. Pregnancy is less likely to disrupt their plans. Sacrifices and hard work often strengthen a marriage, but continued and unrelieved strains can also weaken it. A couple might, therefore, be better advised to allot themselves a shorter time for enduring such strains as will be necessary to put themselves through school when their financial resources are limited.

3. The couple might well consider taking a longer than usual amount of time to complete their college educations. Traditionally college education takes four years of campus time. Many couples are still seeking to complete their education in four years and at the same time carry a part or a full-time job. They may get through college, but with a poorer quality education than is good. Or they may get through school, but at the expense of so much strain and tension upon them individually and upon their marriage that their relationship is damaged. Consideration should be given to various possible arrangements, e.g. full employment for both during the summer, a year's leave of absence from school to work, or year-around school attendance.

4. The couple might postpone the coming of children until the advent of children can be harmonized with the financial resources and the educational plans of the couple. This recommendation is less easily accomplished than some couples anticipate. Studies have indicated a relative lack of success in the attempt of campus married couples to control the activities of the stork. In one study made on the Michigan State college campus couples who had one or more children were interviewed to find whether they had planned for the child. The study indicated that a third of the parents had. Another third had not been planning for the child, but were not particularly disturbed over its advent. Another third had actually been seeking to avoid pregnancy for a time yet. In these circumstances many of the couples were disturbed over the arrival of a child before they were ready for it.

There are other aspects to this problem. For example, how can those who cannot conscientiously accept birth control harmonize their belief with the need for postponing the coming of children? How can a couple best arrange family routines with the advent of a child which is wanted, or which comes along by chance?

5. The couple might explore the possibility of borrowing money to complete their college education particularly if they are within a year or two of graduation. Many couples are very unwilling to graduate from college with any kind of debt. Yet they may work so hard to avoid borrowing that this interferes with their getting as good quality an education as they ought to have. It would seem desirable for a couple to explore the ways and means, times and circumstances for using credit in order to improve, and if necessary, to prolong a college education which promises to put them in a good position as far as earning power is concerned. At the same time they may put less strain on their marriage.

6. The college authorities should reevaluate their policies and plans in relation to the needs and circumstances of the married as well as the unmarried group. The traditional college atmosphere which developed from years of dealing with unmarried undergraduates changes slowly. Some glaring absurdities occasionally come to light as when the failure or low achievement of married students is reported to the parents of the student rather than to the student himself. The same incongruity is found at the high school level when, after a girl's marriage, she and her mother are called in to plan her program, while the husband is ignored. Could any better practice for causing in-law trouble be devised?

In the fall of 1956 for the first time University of Oregon student wives and husbands have been permitted to sit together "officially" at athletic games in the better sections of the stadium. Previously the undergraduate practice of putting the men and women into separate cheering groups prevailed.

Social and extra-curricular, and even curricular programs have developed around the needs and circumstances of unmarried students. What changes are needed? Is it not probable that married students may need quite a different type of program, and that undergraduate married students have needs which differ from married graduate students?

It might be profitable if an office or a service were established to give direct attention to advising, working with, and developing a program for married college students. Such services are provided for veterans, or foreign students when they make up less of the student body than do married students. The establishment of such a service might well be the subject of a study on various campuses.

7. *College authorities and married students both should study the possibilities which the college could offer married students for a rich positive marriage and family life on the campus.*

College faculties and authorities have never or have only vaguely realized that the married group offered the college any unique opportunities or challenges, educationally speaking. They have simply been students, married it is true, but still students to be put through exactly the same mill as students in the old days when all were unmarried. The students themselves usually seem ready to accept this approach. At any rate they go along with it without protest. The few who sense a lack are merely uneasy, and without any concrete ideas about what might be done.

Married students themselves contribute to the problem. They often regard their marriage as really beginning after they graduate from college. Instead of utilizing available social and educational experiences or participating actively in college activities they live a kind of inanimate existence, suspended in time and space. They are working hard to get through school so the husband, or the husband and wife, may get into their professional activities, get settled in some community, and begin to live. When this occurs, however, they may easily find themselves in a community much more poverty stricken in its opportunities for their growth and development than the college community. They are likely also to find the responsibilities of beginning professional life very exacting. Having established a pattern of postponing "living" during college days they can easily go in for another period of relatively sterile existence while they are getting ready to "really begin living." This, of course, can easily go on and on.

For a campus married couple to assume when they wed that their marriage and family life has begun in earnest would seem far wiser. The patterns for living they develop early in marriage now are likely to stay with them. Suppose they held this suggested attitude and utilized the college environment as actively and as fully as they could. They might easily find their early marital campus experience had helped them to establish an excellent basis for stimulating companionship and interaction in later years of their married life.

For the sake of putting across the idea, let us exaggerate the point. Is it not entirely possible that some progressive college of the future will seek to recruit married students by calling attention to the assets it can offer them? The college might advertise, "Begin your marriage on our campus. What better place to spend the early years of your marriage and to begin your family?" The authorities might point to the many cultural, intellectual, and social opportunities which offered special advantages to the young married couple. On the college campus they might have experiences which would help them build mutual interests and set up a pattern of active interaction between themselves and community activities. This in turn might very much enrich their married life.

The chance for couples to form lasting friendships with other young couples who are preparing for professional work in the same or parallel fields of activity might be stressed. On the campus they will meet other young men and women just beginning their family life and their professional careers in circumstances which will provide them opportunities to develop life-long friendships.

The college campus, it might be noted, is an excellent environment in which to begin family rearing. Courses on child development and family relations can provide an important source of help to young couples who are having or are expecting to have children. Nursery schools and child care facilities can make it possible for young parents to have above average facilities for the early care and education of their children, and opportunities for them to learn about the privileges and responsibilities of parenthood.

Parents, too, might be interested in seeing their children marry while in college realizing the value of this environment to a young married couple.

Is this too much to anticipate? I believe not, for the college environment, broadly envisioned and properly planned, could provide rich and stimulating experiences for young married couples during the early years of their marriage and family life. It could challenge them and help them build patterns of companionship and stimulating interaction. These in turn could serve as an excellent foundation for continuing happiness in their marriage. It could afford colleges a real opportunity to influence the family life of an important segment of the population.

8. *Careful study should be made of the problem of services for campus married couples.* Among these are housing, child care facilities, health services (including contraceptive information and obstetrics) and family counseling.

Clearly these are highly controversial areas. Whether or not the college should supply these services for families, whether a public agency such as a college could take a position on such an issue as contraception, and who should administer these services and how are questions which can easily raise blood pressure to be answered. Dodging them, however, does not alter the fact that they are issues.

9. *Research should be conducted on the problems and needs of campus marriages, and their long-run effects upon those who enter them.* Systematic studies should be conducted to answer the numerous questions centering on campus marriages. Admittedly some of the questions and issues raised in this article are speculative and controversial, but none of them are contrived. All represent concerns which have been raised by persons working with campus married couples themselves. They are concerns and issues which had better be dealt with now than later, for they will surely have to be dealt with. The college campus will never again be inhabited only by the unmarried.

46 · Why I Am Glad I Didn't Marry While in College *

MARION BUNTING

The author discusses the advantages that can come to a young woman who remains unmarried long enough to complete her education, taste of independence, develop her own interests, and follow her chosen career for a

* *Journal of Home Economics,* 47 (December, 1955), 757–758. Reprinted by permission of the publisher and the author.
The author graduated from the University of Idaho, marrying three years later.

period of time. She does not suggest never marrying, but feels that a girl gains maturity and personality growth through taking one thing at a time.

PERSONAL, professional, economic reasons all lead to one answer—I am glad I didn't marry while in college! In retrospect it seems one of my wisest decisions.

When I look back at my college experience I feel I gained immeasurably from a full social and academic life. My independent status allowed complete freedom to explore my interests. I enjoyed membership in social, academic, and political groups. I participated in extra class projects. Living and working in close contact with a large group of girls was an unscheduled course in human relations. If I had been married, many of these activities would have been necessarily curtailed. A married student must assume additional responsibilities that do not face the unmarried undergraduate: primarily the establishment and maintenance of a home and adjustment to married life in a college atmosphere. The axiom that "two can live as cheaply as one" often does not meet the test, and married students find they must seek outside work. The fortunate student may find work that relates to her college major. Usually, the job is just a source of income that requires time away from studies. A girl enters a college marriage realistically when she can see beyond mere physical attraction. Marriage in college requires a degree of maturity that many people do not attain at that age.

We all agree that college is not an end in itself. College is only a foundation towards a satisfying career and a purposeful life. In college we have the opportunity to develop and expand this foundation. The college atmosphere is primed for learning—book learning and, more important, learning about oneself. It is the one prolonged space in our lives when we are expected to explore our minds and personalities. There is time to find that individual known as self. I feel that in order to take advantage of all that may be attained in college a student benefits from freedom from the responsibilities of marriage.

A Career after College

If I had not followed my chosen field for a time after graduation, I would have felt cheated. It would have seemed unfair to my parents who sacrificed for my education, to my instructors who encouraged and inspired me, and to my alma mater which provided the facilities for my "apprenticeship."

The experiences obtained through leading a full and diversified college life proved the most helpful when I was working as a home economist. I had to rely on my own initiative, imagination, and judgment in many situations.

Most jobs today require more than book knowledge. Every employer seeks the person who can command himself and the many unexpected situations that arise on the job.

The Advantages

The store of personal and professional experiences obtained by pursuing my chosen career enriched and continued my self development; I met the public, worked with people of different ages whose opinions conflicted, worked with men as well as women—single and married. I was able to exchange ideas with veterans and newcomers in the professional world. Through radio work and public demonstrations before large groups of people I developed poise and confidence.

Unmarried, I was free to choose the job I wanted in a city I liked. When assignments needed extra work, I was able to stay overtime at the office. If a trip came up, I could leave on short notice. I believe that my promotions came more quickly because I was able to arrange my life as the job required.

As a career girl living within my own fixed income I learned to budget money. This financial independence later made management of family finances an easier task.

Although most of these experiences are eventually gained through marriage or can be acquired simultaneously with marriage, the opportunities for meeting such situations do not arise as often in married life. Also there is not the pressure that exists in business to meet the challenge and acquire the knowledge as quickly. After marriage the time necessary for complete professional advancement is usually not available.

After marriage when it seemed necessary to gain employment I found that the name I had established from my few years of professional work practically wrote the contract for a job. The jobs open to me were both professionally inspiring and financially rewarding.

Your Marriage Benefits

When one is weighing the merits of marriage over a career, one should realize that if the marriage in question is the right one it will wait. Mine did and I believe we are a happier couple.

Gaining confidence and maturity in the professional world have made me a more successful wife and mother. Family respect and admiration are always important in a satisfying family situation. My husband takes pride in my accomplishments. I also feel that I had fewer adjustments to make in marriage than had my friends who married while in college or immediately after college, perhaps because some of my personal and economic adjustments had already been made. These adjustments often turn that romantic so called "rosy glow" to grey depression.

The decision to marry while in college is a personal one. My independent college days better prepared me for a satisfying career and a happy marriage.

47 · Adjustments of Married Students *

JEAN MARCHAND AND LOUISE LANGFORD

This factual report gives the practical adjustments made by both husband and wife when both were attending college and when they had at least one child.

MARRIED war veterans may have charted a new course for the lives of young people aspiring to the professions. The long period of education necessary has in the past meant that a doctor was nearing thirty before marriage was considered feasible. But college enrollments in the past five years have included many men and women who were enjoying marriage and a family while getting an education.

The interview-questionnaire method for obtaining information formed the basis of a study made at Kansas State College of the adjustments of young families in which both husband and wife were attending college. Participating as subjects were 22 couples who were parents of at least one child under six years of age and 22 couples who did not have children.

The study was concerned with the effect of the married woman's attendance at school on her own and on her husband's activities. The objectives were: (1) to determine the effect of children on the home participation of mothers who are also students; (2) to determine the effect of children on the home participation of fathers who are also students; (3) to find the modifications of curriculum made by student women when they have children; (4) to find the modifications of curriculum made by student men

* *Journal of Home Economics,* 44 (February, 1952), 113–114. Reprinted by permission of the publisher and the senior author.

Louise Langford holds the degree of Master of Science from Kansas State University, where she is now Assistant Professor in the Department of Family and Child Development, School of Home Economics. She is author and coauthor of a number of articles in the field of child adjustment and family relations and has written the book, *Guiding the Young Child.*

Jean Marchand was a graduate student at Kansas State University at the time the article was written; she now holds the degree of Master of Science from this University.

when they have children; and (5) to find the arrangements made for care of children when both parents attend school.

The men of the study tended to share homemaking activities with their wives; men and women without children reported that they "always" or "usually" worked together at most tasks. Parents often worked together in caring for their children, but fathers less frequently than nonfathers assumed joint responsibility with their wives for other activities of homemaking. It seems probable that the time spent by fathers in caring for their children left them little time for other household tasks. Almost all of the fathers served as baby sitters at least part of the time that the mothers were in class. The "division of labor" between parents was less clear cut than that between husbands and wives in families without children. The latter checked that they "always" or "never" performed an activity, while parents more often indicated that " 'usually' I do it, but 'sometimes' he does it." This was again interpreted to be the influence of the unpredictable nature of children's needs.

Most men participated in homemaking because they enjoyed it and because they believed that husbands and wives should share these responsibilities. Furthermore, nearly all men said that their wives were too busy to do everything. Caring for their children was checked by the fathers as a pleasure more often than were the other activities of homemaking.

Effect of College Attendance on Happiness

Couples were asked to indicate their marriage happiness on a five-point rating scale which ranged from very unhappy to very happy. All but one couple rated their marriages as "happy" or "very happy." When asked how the situation would be affected if the wife were not attending school, some couples in each group thought that they would be more happy if the wife were not attending school; a smaller number of each group, less happy; while the largest number, one-half of each group, believed that their happiness would be unaffected. Some husbands and wives felt that they had no basis for an opinion on this point because they had been attending school all their married life. While some couples felt that they would have more time for leisure activities together if the wife were not going to school, others said, "I think we have more in common now while we are both going to school than we will have after graduation."

Being able to study at the same time was cited by both husband and wife as a reason for greater happiness when the wife was going to school. It was suggested that the wife's attendance at school made the husband happier because his wife did not demand so much of his time. Several couples asserted that their marriage was happier when the wife attended school because the wife was happier. One husband felt that it was a matter of principle; he said, "I don't think I should be the only one obtaining education. I think it would be unfair if I were the only one attending school."

One-half of the childless couples said that they had postponed children; the median length of marriage for this childless group was 1⅛ years, thus they had so far in their marriages not deviated greatly from the usual pattern of childbearing. Each of the five couples with children who indicated that they had postponed children were parents of one child born within the first 13 months of marriage, but they had postponed having a second child. Two couples had two children.

Living Quarters and Income

As living quarters, the college-operated apartments of the converted barracks type were usually preferred because of their efficient arrangement, their compactness, and their location near the college. These factors contributed to saving time and had the added advantage of relatively cheap rent which sometimes meant that money was available for college fees or for a baby sitter.

It is felt that the study should have included data on the source and amount of family income. It was known that nearly all of the men were attending school under the "GI Bill of Rights," but most families needed supplementary income. In case of this need in the childless families, the wife tended to provide part or all of it. When the need arose in the families with children, the wife's limited freedom away from home resulted in her sharing the financial burden to a lesser degree if at all. Hence, fathers were forced to assume a proportionately larger share of the load. Although several women planned to work for a few years until they furnished a home or until their husbands finished school, only three women out of the 44 said that they planned to combine a family and a career permanently.

Curriculum Adjustments

Most women in the study, particularly those who were mothers, did not attempt to carry the load of school activities which is ordinarily borne by the single college woman. When the time per week spent in laboratory and recitation classes was added to that devoted to study, a pronounced difference appeared between the women who had children and those who did not. Mothers averaged 28 hours per week for school work compared with 38 hours for nonmothers. This difference is explained by the fewer credit hours of enrollment for mothers; by the fact that they usually chose recitation classes in preference to laboratory classes because the latter required more time away from home; and by the finding that mothers averaged less time in study for each hour of credit than did nonmothers.

Several women reported that they had changed curricula because their interest had changed with the advent of a family. Mothers, in particular, frequently mentioned that they omitted some classes because they took too much time or because of the time of day at which the class was scheduled. Mothers often planned their classes after their husbands' schedules were arranged so that the fathers could care for the children during the mothers' absences.

Some men and nearly all women in the study indicated that they participated in fewer extracurricular activities because of their home responsibilities. This would seem to suggest the question: Has the married individual less need for such activities or do the usual college extra-class activities fail to meet the needs of the married man and woman?

Very few fathers indicated that they enrolled for fewer hours of school work because of their wives' school attendance. Some men from each group enrolled for courses offered at a particular time of day. Of interest was the statement by several men without children that they preferred to study in their homes rather than in the college library. Fathers, on the other hand, often studied in the library because it was quieter.

When the data were analyzed, the impression developed that these young people were fashioning a satisfying way of living for themselves and for their families. These couples seemed pleased with the co-operative approach to adjustments which they found necessary in combining school and family.

48 · *Housing for Married Students* *

LAWRENCE K. FRANK

If college students are to marry, they need housing other than the traditional dormitories or fraternity houses. The suggestions for adapting the physical

* *Journal of Home Economics,* 49 (May, 1957), 347–350. Reprinted by permission of the publisher and author.

The author, who graduated from Columbia University, is well known for his positions with various philanthropic foundations. From 1945–1951 he was director of the Caroline Zachry Institute of Human Development and since then has acted as consultant and lecturer at the Massachusetts Institute of Technology. He has been a national leader in the field of human development and parent education. Among his writings are *Society as the Patient, Nature and Human Nature, How to Be a Modern Leader, Your Adolescent at Home and in School,* and *How to Be a Woman.*

aspects of housing to the family needs of the occupants are also applicable to housing for people other than married college students.

THE INITIAL TASK, before any specific steps are taken in the way of design or specifications, is to recognize and delineate the kinds of living which graduate married students are seeking, noting especially the variety of perplexities and often acute conflicts they face which may be resolved to a considerable extent, or at least minimized, by more comprehensive planning.

It may be assumed that a university accepts some responsibility for providing this kind of housing because it recognizes that graduate students can and will be aided to cope with their professional tasks through more adequate housing. Such assistance, however, need not be limited to the provision of convenient, inexpensive apartments with the standard equipment. Indeed, the aim of student housing is, or should be, to provide for a way of living commensurate with the needs and the aspirations of students, incorporating in the housing whatever may be conducive to these purposes.

The goal, then, may be conceived, not as that of providing the minimum, but rather the economically optimum, of equipment, facilities, and services which will make married living and homemaking as feasible and rewarding as possible, specifically for students at the beginning of their marriage and family living, when of necessity their professional work makes heavy demands upon their time and energy and, be it noted, also places difficult burdens upon their wives.

It seems imperative, therefore, to inquire into the possibilities of providing what will enable these young couples, often with babies and young children, to cope with the many tasks of homemaking, during the two, three, or four years of their residence—years which may be crucial for the marriage and for the future development of their children.

If we attempt to inventory the situation confronting these young men and women, we may start with the more concrete circumstances and go on to the more subtle but often crucial phases of marriage and family life, which should be recognized and planned for as a basic contribution to the stabilization of marriage and family living, in this time of social confusion.

Initially we can note that graduate married students usually have but little income for living and limited funds for purchasing household equipment which at the end of their residence must be sold at a sacrifice or moved at considerable expense when they go elsewhere.

Likewise, we should realize that the wives of graduate students are often well-educated young women for whom housekeeping is both a novel and stimulating experience but also a demanding task, especially insofar as it requires hours of solitary activity in their own little apartment. If they are employed, as are many today who are helping to earn the family living, aiding their husbands through their professional training, they may have to carry the double or triple responsibilities of wage earner, housekeeper, and wife.

Further, these young people have babies in this early period of marriage, so that during their three or four years at the university they may have two or three children. The physical arrangements of space, equipment, and the presence or absence of facilities for families with young children may be largely absent, partially provided, or they may be made adequately available so that the housing genuinely conduces to child care and rearing and minimizes the many frustrations and strains encountered by families in much of our housing today. This calls for more than a nursery school or play space, however desirable they are as parts of a larger whole.

We can begin to see the many dimensions of this new family living and child care and rearing when we think of the 24-hour cycle of housekeeping with babies and young children, the continual conflict between the demands of the children and the requirements of housekeeping, conflicts which in the former large extended family were met by the presence of grandmothers, aunts and uncles, and older siblings, who provided additional hands, laps, time and energy, distracters and comforters. The young wife and husband today face all the persistent tasks and problems of family life in a small house or apartment, with none of these human "buffers" and reinforcers, and with limited opportunities for release from these incessant requirements. These internal domestic strains may in early marriage be intensified by the inexperience of the wife, her still strong desire for intellectual, scientific, stimulating interests which must be relinquished or subordinated to the immediate demands of house and children.

The father-student also may find it difficult to study in a small apartment with a baby or young children who make demands and are noisy. To leave wife and children at home while he goes out to study means not only all-day absence at classes but his continued absence at night.

Coping with these problems, learning to handle these complicated situations, developing the capacity for generosity, as against the self-centered demandingness of youth, is the way we mature as adults, learn to take our place as providers for, and protectors and comforters of, the next generation. But these tasks and this essential learning can be made less humanly costly and less disturbing for those students from whom we expect, indeed demand, ever higher achievement and concentrated study.

Kind of Housing Construction

What then can be imaginatively planned for family living, with an awareness of these needs and possibilities, starting with the basic space arrangements, equipment, and facilities designed for young married couples, with, and without, young children (we may assume the children will probably not exceed five years of age).

How far can equipment and facilities be planned to permit common use, to provide joint facilities and services and especially to make possible, *but not obligatory*, group or social performance of many basic tasks of housekeeping and child care within the buildings?

Desirable height—low buildings to facilitate ingress and outgoing by mothers with young children, and space for parking baby carriages should be one consideration.

If higher buildings are necessary, the upper stories can be planned for couples without children. Or the roofs could be designed and equipped as playgrounds with shelters, sand boxes, toilets, and other conveniences.

Interior construction and finishing should be designed to minimize cleaning and repairing of walls, floors, interior trim, and to provide maximum safety by installing such features as window guards, child-proof electrical outlets and switches, and safe gas connections. This calls for a critical scrutiny of all specifications in terms of potential hazards, vulnerability, and suitability for children, and minimization of the burdensome chores of housekeeping.

Provision of the maximum of built-ins will reduce the tenants' purchase of furniture and equipment, while allowing for individual decoration and personal utilization. This would include the basic utilities, stoves, refrigerators, and vacuum cleaner outlets requiring only a hose and its attachments.

Space should be arranged for flexible use so that cooking, eating, and living space are not rigidly separated but equipped with built-ins, folding tables, convenient cupboards and adequate storage space, bookshelves, lighting arrangements, and outlets. The criteria are convenience, economy, arrangements that facilitate co-ordination of housekeeping and child care and make possible the necessary reading and studying. Adequate soundproofing is essential to provide privacy and protection against the unavoidable noise of babies and children.

Sleeping rooms should include a room or rooms of suitable dimensions and equipment for a baby or children. It may be desirable to plan for transferring or moving a family from one apartment to another as its space requirements increase, providing specifically for one-child, two-child, and three-child families. Such moving could be scheduled for a "captive population" without hardship or indignity and would probably be more economical and effective than the conventional arrangements. Too much emphasis cannot be put on the opportunity to design housing specifically for a semi-permanent, identifiable population, as contrasted with the usual anonymous random population in urban housing, ordinarily viewed in terms of a few large classes—income, social-economic status, and varying demands for number of rooms.

Special Facilities

In terms of rentals to be charged, the amounts which these student families can pay as rent should be calculated, not merely in terms of space occupied and usual operating costs but what they can pay to obtain in addition to shelter a variety of equipment, facilities, services, and amenities which they would have to pay for in another way elsewhere, often at higher costs (including installment payments on furniture and equipment and losses due to sacrifice sale when leaving). A recalculation of rentals would permit more inclusive provision in the housing of these additional items, so that the allowable percentage of income paid as rental might be considerably enlarged but with genuine economic and other benefits to tenants.

In the housing development, either in each unit or allocated among other units, but accessible to all residents, there could be a variety of facilities, occupying space largely in basements, but at the same time, paying their way or earning their share of the rentable space by fees and subscriptions paid by the residents.

Thus, there might be rooms available for entertainment, hospitality, or parties too large for the individual apartments.

Rooms for transient visitors might be provided so that parents could be housed in the same or an adjacent building. These living quarters also could be managed co-operatively, and when not in use by student families or visitors could be used by other visitors to the university.

Space and equipment for laundry, ironing, and mending, with adjacent play areas for the children, would provide not only needed facilities but an opportunity for young women to get together to talk, drink coffee, smoke, or carry on the innumerable practices of women who have from time immemorial come together for water at the well or spring, at the river to wash clothes, at the markets for supplies and gossip. Likewise in each building there could be a well, but simply, equipped playroom for young children (also on the roof) with immediately adjacent comfortable space for the mothers to sew, talk together, and still be continually available to their children. Again, this would relieve the mothers of the often lonely isolation with a demanding child and no adult companionship from morning to evening.

There are distinctive masculine and feminine needs and concerns which can be met only in the company of males or females; these needs for like-sexed companionship may be intensified by marriage since the masculine-feminine relationship of necessity excludes these other interests. Thus, too often in our planning we have neglected the feminine needs, the fulfillment of which may strengthen family life and maintain feminine morale. Women's lives are oriented by and to interpersonal relations which to be satisfactory should embrace a wide range including husband, children, neighbors, and especially other contemporary women. To be able to talk with other women while the children play together is a much-needed facility in housing.

Obviously the nursery school itself should be provided with a variety of equipment and special facilities (floor heating, ultra-violet lights to offset the lack of sunshine in winter, small semi-isolation units for children with colds—especially important for mothers who work or go to school each day).

Since graduate students are working intensively during the day and often at night, family living may become episodic, with an occasional "spree" to relieve the tensions. It would be desirable to plan for a number of rooms, such as studios or workshops, in which together, or separately, husband and wife might find opportunity for creative work, doing what is individually fulfilling in the arts, or crafts, or other releasing activities, such as games, cards, folk or other dancing, or ping-pong. If these facilities were in the same building and the necessary wiring were installed during construction, it would be possible for parents to connect their own inexpensive intercom in the baby's or children's room to the recreation room and thus feel secure that the child was sleeping peacefully or his cries would be heard at once.

In adjoining buildings, if necessary to disperse facilities, there could be a variety of facilities, including space for dances, dramatizations, musical groups, presentations of moving pictures, television, or whatever the changing student group might prefer for leisure-time activities, including a social room for conversation and reading non-technical journals.

Indeed the provision of group or common facilities of a wide range should be considered as both conveniences and as offering occasions for genuine group or social relations. The principle is that of providing in housing, or in neighborhood planning, as many opportunities for shared use and enjoyment as feasible, on the theory that such shared use and active collaboration foster the kind of community spirit and belongingness we all desire in greater or less measure.

The common tasks, activities, needs and requirements of families, especially families of a special, identifiable group such as married students, offer possibilities for imaginative planning to provide a way of living that will be more conducive to an enhanced family living and child rearing than contemporary housing ordinarily is.

Services

In such planning the recurrent need for repairs, maintenance, servicing of equipment and gadgets could be foreseen and provided as an extension of the usual facilities. This would be covered by the rent, probably at less per family cost per annum or an annual subscription basis than the present high costs for extra-mural servicemen who are costly on a per house and per parts basis.

But here with such specialized tenants, much could be done to evoke a considerable group responsibility, a constant concern for the well-being of the houses and equipment as against the frequent irresponsibility and carelessness of rental tenants. Indeed the whole project would present an occasion for developing responsible living that is much more cogent and appealing than the usual didactic and exhortative teachings of civics and citizenship. Likewise, by helping young couples to discover ways of family living, providing facilities and services that are articulated and congruous with the family processes, a very real contribution may be made to stabilizing and enriching marriage and family living.

A "baby sitter" service, organized co-operatively, could be desirable, utilizing available students and residents, serving often on a reciprocal basis of helping each other (a baby-sitter bank) in play groups and nursery schools. Other common requirements of families might be met by arranging a linen rental supply, thus saving each family the investment, the storage of extras, and the chores of washing and ironing or sending to the laundry.

Cooked food, which could be ordered in the morning and picked up (or delivered) in the early evening offers another possible service. This same cooking equipment could be utilized for snack lunches for wives and for luncheons for children in the nursery school.

It is the aim of these suggestions also to indicate how far the requirements of health care and of mental health can be advanced by imaginative planning. This approach implies that care of physical health is essentially a part of the basic tasks and chores of housekeeping.

Likewise, mental health, as contrasted with diagnosis and treatment of disturbed personalities and neurotics, comes through the daily processes of family living, of cherishing baby care, of understanding, patient child rearing, in finding fulfillment of adult aspirations and needs for intimacy, affection, and reciprocal love. These, as well as physical health, can be advanced or obstructed by the kind of housing and facilities offered to families.

While housing developments cannot provide all that families need in the way of professional services, it is possible today to plan space and equipment so that prenatal and well-baby clinics can be scheduled in a housing development, thereby facilitating early and frequent attendance; that visiting nurse service can be available; that family counselors can be consulted on the innumerable perplexities and occasional serious problems which can often be resolved before they become critical, marital conflicts, parent-child conflicts and tensions, financial, legal, and other common difficulties that confront all families. Since these students are usually far from their own homes and families, they lack the usual sources of guidance and direction.

Again let it be said that these many services and facilities do not imply regimentation, interference, or coercion of families. Rather they suggest making many services more accessible, economically available, and more effectively articulated and co-ordinated than they are in the existing discrete agencies, private practitioners, and professional advisers. Many of these services could be provided to the tenants by arrangements with other professional institutions and agencies in the community.

To give the graduate students an experience in family living of this kind would be to develop a group of young professionals whose influence in their professions and as citizens might be of incalculable significance to the nation, wherever they go to work and live. Moreover, the university would be faced with a challenging opportunity to mobilize its varied professional knowledge and skills on a project in which the interrelation of architecture, planning, the humanities, and all the engineering skills can be worked out and exhibited overtly through a housing development that could set a new standard in family housing for the country.

CHAPTER 12:

Adjustment between Husband and Wife

---

49 · *Healthy Adult Personality* *

HENRY BOWMAN

One foundation stone to the building of a good marriage is the healthy personality of each partner. Personal "readiness for marriage" is a phrase often used to refer to the need for maturity and good balance of attitudes and emotions as the basis for adjustment in marriage. With warm understanding and simple vocabulary, Dr. Bowman discusses personality, the needs of the individual, and the attributes of the healthy adult personality.

MENTAL HEALTH may be defined as the ability to function effectively and happily as a person in one's expected role in a group. It is a condition of the whole personality and is not merely a condition of the "mind," as often supposed. It is an outgrowth of one's total life and is promoted or hindered by day by day experiences, not only by major crises as some assume.

Mental health should not be thought of only in terms of hospitals any more than physical health should be thought of only in such terms. Granted the importance of medical specialists, we still realize that a good part of an individual's physical health depends upon such day by day, in-the-home,

---

* "The Nature of Mental Health," *Clubwoman*, 37 (October, 1957), 16, 26, 28. Reprinted by permission of the author

The author, who received the degree of Doctor of Philosophy from Yale University, is Associate Professor of Sociology and Consultant in The Hogg Foundation for Mental Health, The University of Texas. He is nationally known as a leader in the development of education for marriage, through his earlier teaching at Stephens College, his textbook, *Marriage for Moderns*, and a series of films on marriage adjustment for classroom use. He has also contributed to many professional journals and is author of *A Christian Interpretation of Marriage*.

in-the-school, in-the-community experiences as eating, habits of personal hygiene, housing, and so on. This is as true of mental health.

Mental health is also a matter of degree. There is no hard and fast line between health and illness. It is not a simple matter to divide the population into two distinct groups, namely, those who should be hospitalized and those who should not. Many of us at one time or another exhibit traits and patterns of behavior which, if accentuated and continuous, would make us candidates for psychiatric care.

The Nature of Personality

Personality may be defined as the sum total of the individual, that cluster of traits and characteristics which make him a person. Each person is unique. Therefore, it is better to say that each individual *is* a personality rather than to say that he *has* a personality. There is no "he" that has a personality. He and his personality are one and the same.

Everyone has the same amount of personality. No one has any more or less than anyone else, just as climate may vary from state to state but no state has any more climate than any other. When we say, "He has a lot of personality," we are using the term in another sense and are referring to selected traits such as vivacity, enthusiasm, affability, friendliness.

An individual's personality is not all readily observable. It is like an iceberg only one-ninth of which shows above the surface of the water. The other eight-ninths are an integral part of the iceberg; but for the most part they are hidden from view except as the movement of waves reveals a little more here and there, now and then. In like manner, the ups and downs of life experiences may reveal more or less of an individual's personality. But there are certain deep-lying parts which never show above the surface. This is what psychologists have in mind when they refer to the conscious, the subconscious, and the unconscious.

Personality is an outgrowth of an individual's hereditary make-up and his experience within a given culture. Hence, it is a result of interaction among these factors; and it is in part socially determined. In the strict sense, then, personality is not hereditary, but some of its ingredients are inborn. Persons differ as to aptitudes, temperament, and so on. Yet as human beings we do have common drives, interests, and needs. In these there is variation in degree; but they are found to some degree in all persons.

The basic structure of personality is formed rather early in life. As one becomes older he tends to become less flexible, partly because his habit patterns tend to "set," and partly because each new experience constitutes a smaller proportion of his total experience in life. But his basic needs, interests, and drives go on. Some of these are discussed in what follows.

Security

The need for security is apparent even in infancy. It is a basic need all through life. Many persons feel insecure for one reason or another. But a feeling of insecurity is not necessarily the same as an inferiority complex, although many people confuse the two and use the latter term very loosely. A feeling of insecurity grows out of a situation in the light of which such a feeling is appropriate. An inferiority complex is a carry-over of a pattern of life formed in early years and exhibited in a situation in which it is apparently inappropriate. In a sense an individual with an inferiority complex reacts to an adult situation as if it were a childhood situation because his pattern of reaction was established in childhood.

Self-Preservation

Through his own interpretation of his experience each individual creates his own "world." In a very real sense this world is private and can be shared by others in a limited degree only. In one way, as we say, "no man is an island" because each person is a part of a web of social interrelationships. In another way, however, each of us "lives on a little island out in the middle of a foggy sea," as the song says. No two private worlds are exactly alike. The person's concept of himself is part of his private world. He will do what he feels is necessary to protect his *self* and his world. This protection sometimes takes such forms as rationalization, projection of blame onto others, retreat, boasting, and so on. In extreme cases it may take the form of neurotic or psychotic symptoms.

Love

Each person has a desire and a need to love and to be loved. If he does not seem to exhibit such a desire, it is because experience has "trained it out of him" or made him afraid to do so. This desire to love takes the form of concern for the other-than-self in a mature person.

It is unfortunate that in expressing affection within the family there is often a barrier placed between father and son. We assume that a child of either sex may express affection for the mother and the mother for the child. A girl may express her love for her father and her father for her. But shortly after babyhood in many homes a barrier is raised between father and son. There is an assumption that to become manly a boy should begin to put restrictions on his expressions of love. It is no wonder that so many men grow to adulthood with a certain hesitation in expressing affection and that so many wives complain that their husbands are not as demonstrative as the wives would like them to be.

In the rearing of girls, there has of necessity to be some training in self-protection, especially after puberty. A problem often arises when a girl learns the lesson of self-protection against exploitive, predatory men so well that she carries this same pattern and attitude into her marriage and continues to "protect" herself from her husband. Such a woman tries to be married and single at the same time.

Sense of Belonging

Each individual wants to be accepted by others. He wants to feel that he really belongs to the group of which he is a natural part. If he does not have this feeling in connection with his family or school group, he may seek a sense of belonging to some other group, in some cases an undesirable group.

This desire to belong is very prominent in the early teens. It often creates a problem for young people because belonging so often implies conformity. The pressure of the peer group is difficult to resist. A sense of belonging can best be achieved when the person also has a sense of responsibility for the group to which he belongs. How to achieve a balance between loyalty and conformity to the group on the one hand, and responsibility for the welfare of the group on the other, is one of the more pressing and complicated problems of youth.

Communication

Each individual has a desire and need to communicate with others. But in many families the doors of communication are closed, sometimes very early in a child's life. For example, when a child asks questions about "where babies come from" and is rebuffed by the parent. Sometimes when the doors are thus closed they can never be reopened. Parents often complain about this problem. They say something to the effect that they know the teenager is having problems but, "He won't talk them over with us." They may even be offended if the child turns to another person as a confidant. Such parents must, unfortunately, often be told that it is too late. The doors of communication between parent and child were closed so early and left closed so long that the lock and hinges have grown too rusty for the doors ever to open again.

Growth and Development

Each individual has a natural tendency to grow. Each one has his own distinctive rate and pattern of growth. In many cases injustice is done when a child is compared unfavorably with others relative to his growth or development. This is due in part to the not uncommon, erroneous assumption that every child should be at exactly the same point of growth at the same calendar age.

Maturity

The person's development may progress to maturity or it may stop at an immature level. If he does not become mature, there is likely to be conflict between what is expected of him and what he is able to achieve, between his personality and the role expected of him. The child in him and the adult in him are at odds.

The individual must learn to make choices. The immature person makes choices more on the basis of pleasure or pain. The mature person makes them more on the basis of value judgments or ethical principles. When an individual does not learn to make choices, there is likely to be conflict within his personality. Such conflict tends to tear a personality apart and prevent effective living.

Acceptance of Self

Each person needs to learn to live with and within his own limitations. A special problem in connection with acceptance of self is that, as a group, men tend to be more satisfied with the fact that they are men than women, as a group, are satisfied with the fact they are women. Some women continuously struggle against the fact that they are women. This tends to produce conflict, tension, rejection of the traditional feminine role of wife-homemaker-mother, ineffectiveness in living, and discontent. In the last analysis, no individual can fully accept his own sexual classification unless he also accepts the sexual classification of members of the opposite sex. Accepting both of these is necessary to becoming a whole person.

Sense of Achievement

The individual wants to have a sense of achievement. He wants to be recognized by others. If circumstances and experiences are not provided through which one can achieve success and recognition by desirable means, he may resort to the undesirable. One way to do the former is to adapt expectations to the child's interests and abilities. If this is not done, for example, when parents expect a child to prepare for a vocation for which he has no interest or aptitude, there are likely to be problems for all concerned.

Reaching Out

One of the peculiar characteristics of human beings as compared to other organisms is that humans have a tendency to reach out beyond their immediate experience. This is apparent in religion, in creative art, in human relations. Humans are not content with the world as they find it. They have a tendency to embellish and embroider experience. They have insatiable curiosity. Unfortunately many parents and teachers destroy this natural curiosity in children and youth. They thwart imagination. Some even go farther and at times confuse imagination with dishonesty to the great detriment of the child concerned.

The Healthy Adult Personality

Some wise person once said, "The biggest problem of childhood is to get over it before you're forty." By implication this suggests: first, the healthy adult personality has passed through and beyond the stage-typical behavior of the formative years; second, although such a personality may exhibit the results of beneficial learning experience, it does not carry into adulthood any part of childhood that has become fixed and crystallized in such a way that it is a permanent burden, such as, for example, an over-attachment to parents; third, the individual's development continues all through life. We might set up the following criteria:

1) On the one hand, he works for human betterment but, on the other hand, accepts most people and situations, especially minor situations, as he finds them; he does not always expect everybody and everything to be adapted to his comfort and convenience.

2) He feels himself a part of a group, especially of society as a whole, and derives his satisfactions in life more through the contributions he makes to others than through selfish, self-centered gain or pleasure. He has an honest feeling of usefulness.

3) He is aware of his relation to the universe. He is interested in religious values. To some reasonable degree his life is oriented toward ultimate reality.

4) He has a reasonable amount of self-confidence. This does not mean over-confidence. But he knows his own abilities and limitations and there-

fore can meet life successfully. He is not steeped in self pity. He does not feel the necessity of making alibis or altering facts to protect himself.

5) His personality is integrated. He is not torn by internal conflict—one part of him fighting against another part of him. He is characterized by a pattern of sound, consistent values. He is a whole person.

6) He approaches problems realistically and constructively. He does not evade problems and confuse his evasion with solution. Nor does he try to solve problems through worry, nagging, or complaint.

7) He has a forward look. He looks to the future not to the past. His life is not dull or empty or boring because he has live and growing interests. He does not rest on the oars of previous achievement. He does not miss opportunities in the present by gloating over the "good old days." Never for him the philosophy of "Make me a child again just for tonight." Rather he goes along with Robert Browning when the poet says, "Grow old along with me, the best is yet to be, the last of life for which the first was made."

50 · The Dynamics of the Marital Relationship *

ABRAHAM STONE AND LENA LEVINE

This discussion repeats the theme of the first article in this chapter—the need for personal maturity. The emphasis, however, is not on the individual but on the relationship between husband and wife, the ability to meet each other's needs, and the expansion of the marriage to include children in a family group. The dynamics of a happy, healthy, stable marriage consist of mature mutual love, sexual responsiveness, and sharing in parenthood. Adjustment in these areas may be complicated by personal physiological or emotional characteristics, by differences of religion, education, or other social factors, and by the vicissitudes of life. This article gives an understanding

* *Mental Hygiene*, 37 (October, 1953), 606–614. From a paper delivered before the Schilder Society. Reprinted by permission of the publisher and the authors.

Dr. Stone received the degree of Doctor of Medicine from New York University, and is now on the faculty of the College of Medicine at that University. He is also Director of the Margaret Sanger Research Bureau, New York. He was a special consultant on the Mission to India of the World Health Organization. His fields of interest include human fertility and infertility and their control. He has written widely, including (with Dr. Hannah M. Stone) A *Marriage Manual: A Practical Guidebook to Sex and Marriage.*

Lena Levine, M.D., is a gynecologist and psychiatrist. She is Assistant Medical Director of the Margaret Sanger Research Bureau. She also lectures and is the author of publications in various phases of marital relationships. With Dr. Stone, she is author of *The Dynamics of the Marital Relationship.*

of the dynamics of marriage and a constructive approach to their manipulation. The authors bring both professional training and years of experience in marriage counseling to this sympathetic analysis of marriage adjustment.

IN AN ANALYSIS of the dynamics of marriage, two factors need consideration: the persons and the marriage, the characteristics of the individuals involved and their interaction in the marriage.

Two unique personalities come to marriage. They have characteristics common to all human beings, but they also have individual characteristics due to their sex, their genetic inheritance, the ideas, feelings, and attitudes that they had acquired as a result of their development in a particular family, in a particular place in the family constellation, and in a particular social group. The kind of marriage the two will make will, to a considerable degree, therefore, depend upon the kind of people they are.

There is, however, also the other factor involved in marriage: the inter-relationship that results from the interaction of these two different personalities. In marriage the two individuals have to adjust themselves to each other as well as to many other new people and situations not of their own choice—the spouse's family, relatives, friends, and a new and different way of life. They have to be able and willing to give up much of their personal freedom, which they may have struggled long to achieve, in order to make a satisfactory adjustment to the new relationship. They must be able as well as willing to share the basic satisfactions that men and women seek in marriage—the security of love and companionship, sexual satisfaction, a home, and a family.

To make the many compromises and adjustments required for a satisfactory marriage, a person has to have a flexible and mature personality, he has to be physically and emotionally grown up. But emotional maturity alone is not enough. It may give the individual the potentiality for making the required adjustments, but it does not necessarily insure a good marriage. A person's own maturity will not inevitably guide him to choose a partner who is also mature; he may fall in love and marry a person who is not at all grown up, who has a character disturbance, or marked neurotic tendencies. Later, he may resent the mate's personality deficiencies and inability to grow and develop, and may not be willing to accept the fact that under such circumstances most of the adjustments have to be made by him.

The men and women we see in marriage consultation are of varying degrees of emotional development—some are adult and well-balanced, some are immature or with neurotic traits, and some are neurotic or psychotic. These people, the neurotic or even the psychotic, whom we see in our service, would not normally be seen in psychiatric offices, hospitals, or clinics because, as long as they are single, they manage to get along fairly well in life. When they marry, however, they become disturbed because their behavior is resented by their mates and because they are unable to make the required adjustments. They are found fault with and blamed for character traits that they themselves feel to be natural to them, and not subject to challenge or change. Seldom do they receive the type of acceptance that makes possible modifications of personality or even growth toward maturity.

Men and women seek love and emotional security in marriage. The need for emotional security, vital to the infant and the growing child, remains a need throughout the life of the adult as well. A mature love relationship between a man and a woman is a source of such security. Mature love differs from childish love in that it seeks not merely the satisfaction of self, but even more so the satisfaction of the beloved partner. It is also different from romantic love, which is a state of illusion in which the loved one is endowed with all the qualifications one would wish to find in him or her. Since our culture has placed a high value on romantic love, many men and women regard it as the basis for marriage. The realities of living, however, bring about a rapid disillusionment. Love of the kind to marry on is one in which the man or woman is fully aware not only of the assets, but also of the deficiencies of the partner. These are accepted as part of the individual, to be understood and lived with.

Mature love is normally expressed to the person loved with word and gesture, with signs of affection and tenderness. Yet American cultural values do not encourage the unrestrained expression of emotions. If it is manly not to show feelings, but to keep a stiff upper lip in the face of fear, grief, or anger, it is also not manly to be too emotional, demonstrative, or "womanlike" in feelings of affection and love. Lack of demonstrativeness, however, often becomes a source of irritation and resentment. "I know he loves me, but why doesn't he say so?" or, "Why doesn't he show his love in some way?" is a frequent complaint.

A husband is often perplexed at his wife's insistence upon a greater show of his love for her. He fails to understand that she has a far greater need for evidence of love and affection. This need is due to a fundamental difference in their emotional development. Both boy and girl start life with a greater dependence and attachment to the mother than to the father. In return, they give her the greatest share of their love. For the boy, this emotional relationship remains unchanged: as an adult, he again gives his love to a woman. The girl, however, must make a profound shift from mother love to father love if she is to be able to accept fully her husband's love. Hence, she seems to have a constant need for reassurance and support from her husband.

Mature love and an ability to express it and give it freely is an essential base for a good marriage. Not all people, however, possess the same degree of feeling or can demonstrate their feeling with equal facility. If we accept the fact that people have varying degrees of emotional capacity, then all one can expect is for the individual to express his feeling to the extent of his own capacity.

Another satisfaction men and women seek in marriage is a mutual response in their sex relations. A man and woman fully grown to maturity should normally bring a healthy heterosexual attitude to their marital relations. This will express itself in a mutually pleasurable response, with a culminating climax or orgasm for each. This good feeling extends to other areas in their relationship and facilitates the required adjustments.

But in the sexual sphere, also, many problems arise. The couple may be ignorant of the basic anatomical and psychological aspects of the sexual relationship, or they may be inhibited by cultural taboos and superstitions, by distorted attitudes, conscious or unconscious anxieties, and guilt feelings. Even though, intellectually, they may come to accept the normality of sex, they may yet be unable to free themselves from the emotional ties that bind them to their fears and inhibitions.

Constitutional variations in sexual capacity also have to be considered. First, there are the basic physical and biological differences between men and women. The male genitalia are external and superficial, while the vagina is internal and less subject to contact and stimulation. Erotic sensations in the male are usually felt chiefly in the sexual organs; in the female they are more diffused and they are rarely felt in the vagina before sexual intercourse has been experienced. In women, sexual desire is more cyclical and depends to a larger degree upon inner physiological and emotional stimuli than it does in the male. A woman, however, can accept the male at any time, even when she has no desire at all, while a man can function only when he has become stimulated and has erectile capacity.

Male arousal and response, in sex relations, furthermore is generally faster than that of the female. Many women have great difficulty in achieving orgasm, or can reach it only through clitoral stimulation and not at all through vaginal contact. Kinsey maintains that there is no difference between clitoral and vaginal orgasm, yet women who achieve orgasm both through clitoral and vaginal stimulation recognize a definite distinction. Many women are very much disturbed when they find that they can achieve orgasm only through manual clitoral stimulation and not through coitus. The reasons for this orgasm failure are still not clear. Is it due entirely to neurotic mechanisms? Is there possibly also an anatomical basis? Do the size of the clitoris, its distance from the vaginal orifice, the nerve distribution within the vaginal wall, the degree of genital development play a rôle? Certainly, until we learn more, we cannot eliminate the possibility that sexual maladjustments may be due to constitutional and anatomical, as well as to emotional, factors.

Since stimulation of sex desire is primarily psychic in origin, the type and strength of the stimulus required in a given instance is subject to many variations. With childbearing and age, a woman's body changes. She becomes less exciting and stimulating. The frequency and intensity of the sex urge may differ considerably between husband and wife. Sometimes he has more desire and she resents his frequent approaches; and at times her sexual desires may be greater or more frequent and the husband will find difficulty in meeting her needs. Her demands for prolonged lovemaking, which are frequently necessary for her physical and emotional satisfaction, may at times be irksome to him. If she takes the initiative and tries to arouse him, he may resent it, while she, in turn, may take his attitude as a sign of rejection or of his loss of feeling for her as a woman.

The ability to work out a mutually satisfactory sex relationship demonstrates an ability to consider not only one's own needs, but those of the mate as well. When the frequency of desire varies, as it so often does, working out a pattern satisfactory both to husband and to wife implies a willingness to change one's own rhythm or to give up some of one's own needs for the sake of the other. When the woman's response is slower, as it frequently is, the man's control of so powerful an impulse as the sex force shows evidence of thoughtfulness and consideration for the woman who is sharing this experience. Similarly, the wife who is willing to accept her husband and give him the satisfaction he seeks, even though she may have little desire at the time, shows the depth of her feelings for him—her pleasure in giving him something he needs and desires. The satisfactions of a mate's needs may be justifiable even when they are not necessarily mutual. The man should, however, be able to accept his wife in the sex relations without resentment, even if she does not have a complete response.

A third element in marriage is the desire to build a home and family. Most married couples want children, and only a small percentage remain voluntarily childless. There is a basic, powerful urge in women to conceive and to bear children. The use of scientific contraceptive methods merely makes possible the planning of parenthood. Planning and spacing children have become increasingly widespread among all social strata.

Yet this ability to plan has created new problems. It places the decision of whether and when to have a baby upon the parents themselves. Husband and wife do not always agree about the timing or the number of children. Nor do they always agree on the type of contraceptive to be used. The husband may wish the wife to take the necessary precautions, and she may want him to share the responsibility. Rejection of contraceptive methods or irregular use is sometimes a sign of unconscious conflicts regarding pregnancy and motherhood, or else an indication of a strong desire for a child.

Infertility can also become a difficult psychological problem in marriage. The lack of ability to procreate is a severe blow to self-esteem, and the knowledge of it leads to a marked feeling of inadequacy. Conversely, there may also exist deep-seated anxieties which contribute to the infertility. In any event, the resulting conflicts may lead to much marital dissatisfaction.

Mature mutual love, sexual responsiveness, and sharing in parenthood are the dynamics of a happy, healthy, stable marriage. Because of differences in personality, in physiological capacities, or in emotional needs, conflicts may arise in any of these areas. Other factors, too, may lead to marital disturbances. A married couple does not live in isolation. Cultural, religious, and educational differences, social and economic factors may be sufficiently acute to become a cause of serious difficulties in a marital relationship. Unemployment, illness, lack of adequate housing, and particularly in-law interference frequently cause anxieties and conflicts in a relationship that might otherwise have been very satisfactory.

Changing social, economic, and cultural conditions are modifying the structure and functions of marriage and the family. The social mobility that exists in the United States leads to the marriage of people from different social, educational, and religious groups, and this adds to the problems of adjustment. Technological advances, particularly the increasing participation of women in industrial and professional life, the progressive diminution of her economic dependence on her husband, labor-saving devices in the home—all of these are to-day affecting the character of marriage and family life.

The newer concepts of masculinity and femininity conflict with the stereotyped male and female rôles. The latter implied an aggressive, strong, dominant male and a submissive, weak, gentle female. A man went out of the home to earn the money to maintain the household and a woman remained in the home and limited her activities to being a wife, mother, and homemaker. In every culture the male has been the "provider" and the woman, the "preparer." To-day these rôles are being modified. A woman may be as capable in industry and earning capacity as a man is; she may even be able to earn more money than he does. When she works outside of the home, she expects him to participate in the household tasks. If she helps with "providing," then she would like him to help with the "preparing." This change in the previously well-defined rôles of men and women adds new stresses and strains to the adjustments in marriage. Many people are confused by these factors and are not ready or not equipped to recognize and accept them.

The gradual transition from an authoritarian, patriarchal family system to a democratic organization brings further problems. One of the many aspects of this newer concept of family life is the problem of mutuality. When women were submissive, they had few expectations, whether social or sexual. They were satisfied with their rôle of wife and homemaker. Now they expect to have mutual interests, mutual tastes, mutual attitudes to families and friends, and also mutual sexual gratifications. Since this is not always possible, one or the other or both may come to feel that there is something wrong with their relationship.

Formerly families were held together in spite of conflicts by external pressures of law, religion, and society. To-day these outer forces have begun to lose their effectiveness. Men and women can now separate without loss of status within the community or the family group. Marital stability depends, therefore, more on the cohesive power of an inner unity and harmony than on the adhesive forces of social pressure.

Infidelity is another threat to marriage. In the past, infidelity in husbands was tacitly accepted, and a wife, if she found out about it, merely had to wait until the affair blew over. But the women of to-day, now that the old fears of infection and conception no longer hold, may also be tempted by the adventure of an extramarital affair. This adds another difficulty to maintaining a stable, permanent family unit.

These changes in values and attitudes have come about relatively fast; they have not as yet infiltrated sufficiently into the pattern of family living. At present we are still in a stage of transition. Each new generation has to improvise its behavior instead of being able to lean on tested experiences. We have severed our moorings to the old and have not yet anchored to the new. This makes for much tossing about of family life.

Marriage is a dynamic relationship. It requires continual adjustments as the family begins, as it expands with the coming of children, and as it contracts when the children later leave to establish their own family units. Some of the dissatisfactions in marriage emerge in later life, among the older people, particularly when they have failed to make a satisfactory mutual adjustment earlier in their relationship and have remained together only because the children were at home.

These observations on the dynamics and the pathology of marriage are based on a psycho-bio-social orientation. They represent the viewpoint of the physician who treats the individual as a total person, as an integrated being with a body, a mind, and emotions, which interact and influence one another. This is the point of view of social medicine, which recognizes that man cannot be treated in isolation, but that he brings with him problems of his relationships with his family, his work, and his total social environment.

To summarize then:

1. Men and women marry to satisfy three basic needs—the need for love, sex, and parenthood; the need for the security of affection, for sexual satisfaction, and for the fulfillment of the desire for parenthood.

2. The numerous adjustments that are necessary in the marital relation result partly from constitutional biological differences and partly from the differences in the psychological and emotional equipment that men and women bring to marriage.

3. Cultural and social conditions and patterns of life influence materially both the biological and the psychological factors, and hence play an important rôle in marital adjustment.

4. Normal adjustments in marriage are made more difficult when there is pathology either in the biological or in the psychological make-up in one or the other mate, or in the social environment in which the couple lives.

51 · Don't Expect Too Much of Sex in Marriage *

PAUL H. LANDIS

Many writers both in the United States and from abroad have commented on the exaggerated interest that Americans have in sex. This interest probably results in part from our traditional prudery toward sex, and is expressed in and heightened by the scarcely concealed sexual suggestions of many popular songs, stories, and advertisements, and the revelations made by the Kinsey reports of the hidden prevalence of illicit sexual activities. As a consequence, many young people have come to view sexual activities as the most important part of marriage. Professor Landis takes a different point of view, calling for an understanding of sex expression as the symbol of deep ties between husband and wife that are often more important and permanent than the physical attraction of sex.

IN RECENT YEARS we have become so analytical about the sexual relationship in marriage that the true significance and beauty of physical love between husband and wife are too often lost.

* *Reader's Digest*, 65 (December, 1954), 25–28. Copyright 1954 by The Reader's Digest Association, Inc. Reprinted by permission of the publisher and the author.

The author combines an interest in rural sociology with an interest in youth and the family. With the degree of Doctor of Philosophy from the University of Minnesota, he is State Professor of Sociology, State College of Washington. He has served as officer in many sociological organizations. Among his books are *Social Control, Understanding Teen-Agers,* and *Making the Most of Marriage.*

We talk too much about sex. We read too much about it. Advertisements, magazine illustrations, television, movies, popular songs glorify sexual love on all sides of us. *This* kind of perfume will stimulate her passion, *that* brand of shaving soap will make him a real he-man. We overemphasize the erotic. We concentrate on physical satisfaction as the sole criterion of success in marriage. And, in doing so, we neglect the other vital dimensions of human love.

"What is sex," wrote D. H. Lawrence, "but the *symbol* of the relation of man to woman, woman to man? It consists of infinite different flows between the two beings, different, even apparently contrary. Chastity is part of the flow between man and woman, as to physical passion. And beyond these, an infinite range of subtle communication. At periods, sex desire itself departs completely. Yet the great flow of the relationship goes on, undying, and this is the flow of living sex, the relation between man and woman that lasts a lifetime, and of which sex desire is only one vivid manifestation."

To know that one is loved, and to love: these are the greatest satisfactions in life and they are not confined to physical relationships. The love of a wife or sweetheart has drawn men back from death, has ennobled many lives. A word spoken at the right moment may give more comfort and reassurance than any form of physical contact. The knowledge that another stands by and understands is, in critical moments of life, the ultimate value of love. If it were not for these deeper undercurrents marriage would long since have ceased to exist as an enduring human relationship.

It is the exceptional couple who are drawn to each other only because of physical attraction, and it is still more exceptional for two people to remain long together on such a basis. Two people meet, and their acquaintance grows to friendship because of mutual interests. They have common intellectual or recreational pursuits. They belong to, and work with, the same church groups or other organizations. They have a common past or share like aspirations. If these relationships are right, physical attraction usually comes as the culmination of their feelings, rather than having been the cause of them. Only as sex is supported by many other values does it remain important.

A young divorcée of my acquaintance still thinks back with tenderness upon a marriage that broke up because she and her husband had overestimated the importance of sexual response in their marriage.

"We would have been the happiest couple in the world, if, somehow, we could have forgotten all the stuff we ever heard or read on the subject of sex. My happiest moments were when we were together. I loved to feel his nearness and wanted nothing more than to satisfy his every wish. But he was sure that I should get the same excitement out of sex that he did.

We never relaxed and enjoyed the intimate life that could have been ours. Instead we searched for a kind of mutual ecstasy that was forever out of reach. Our sex life became a time of tension and awkward experimentation that left us more and more upset and dissatisfied. After a while I lost even the simple but deep happiness I had known in our intimate life, and from there on our marriage had little value or meaning to either of us."

Physical love *is* important to marriage. Granted. But we have gone to extremes in stressing its technical aspects. Many wives feel that there is something wrong with them—or their husbands—if they cannot achieve the kind of response they've read about. And many husbands feel that there is something wrong with them—or their wives—if the wife cannot achieve sexual climax. Some turn to the numerous books and pamphlets on married love. Others go to marriage counselors and doctors. Some run to divorce lawyers. But perhaps there is no real problem at all. *Perhaps they have only expected too much of sex in marriage.* Medical authorities believe that a third of married women rarely or never achieve sexual climax.

How physical love is expressed by a particular couple, and how often, is a highly individualized matter and it need not be standardized. Dr. Emil Novak of Johns Hopkins University, after 40 years of medical experience with women, says convincingly that there are many women who are physically and emotionally normal, who love their husbands devotedly, who have borne children, yet have never throughout their married lives experienced any great degree of physical gratification from the sex act. Nor do they feel frustrated or cheated.

It may be difficult for men to understand this. But with women, sex feeling is much more diffused throughout the body than with men. It is more closely related to affection and general emotional satisfaction.

"To large numbers of happily married wives," according to Dr. John Rock of the Free Hospital for Women at Brookline, Mass., "sexual expression is essentially a very rewarding *spiritual* experience with the man each cares for. She may derive real satisfaction from giving."

With many wives, also, the thought of possible motherhood is more important than anything else—the ultimate joy they feel in sexual intercourse stems from the realization that they may bear children. The emotion experienced may be tender and completely gratifying, without any need for physical climax. Physical love is never so meaningful to a couple, never brings them so close to a sense of oneness and of universal purpose as at those times when it is entered into with a definite intent to achieve conception. And fortunately, in nature's scheme, a woman's capacity to respond to sexual stimulation has no relation to her capacity to conceive.

Men, biologically, can often isolate sex from love feelings, and from its prime purpose of reproduction. Yet few men who have sought physical relief with another woman *without* love will deny that the true significance of the relationship is lacking. Physical release can be attained, but not the fulfillment and peace of mind that comes with love in marriage. Sex as physical release is one thing; as an expression of love it is quite another. The one is animal; the other sublimely human.

Furthermore, sexual desire varies widely in individuals, both men and women. The only criterion for weighing sex in marriage is whether the two people involved are happy in the relationship. If a wife is frustrated and unhappy in the sexual relationship, it may be wise to consult an understanding doctor or family counselor. For, to succeed, a marriage must have what each individual *needs* for sexual satisfaction.

But it must be remembered that sex may be a "sometime thing." For both husband and wife, it may change; be now intense, now delicate; now rapturous, now playful. There should be no set rules or regulations, no methodical techniques, no time schedules. Moods, conditions, circumstances are a part of every aspect of life, as well as of love and sex. "The happiest people in love do not *need* sensuality; they simply enjoy it when it occurs," wrote Prof. A. H. Maslow in *The Meaning of Love*.

More important than a specific organic reaction in the sexual relationship, a couple may find excitement and adventure as well as relief from tension, according to Dr. Nadina Kavinoky, past president of the National Council on Family Relations. "They can find also unity and spiritual oneness. And, in times of sorrow or trouble, even comfort and consolation."

Perhaps the doctor who said to me, when I asked him if he agreed that we were expecting too much from sex in marriage, gave the right answer: "No," he said, "we are expecting *too little*. Our emphasis has been too much directed toward physical satisfaction. But this is not enough. It is only momentary passion in the larger pattern."

Sex has a special, individual, meaning for every couple. If we love, and accept love, each in our own individual way, sex will fall into proper perspective.

CHAPTER 13:

Men as Earners

52 · Career as a Lifetime Choice *

B. KEITH DUFFIN

One of the concerns of young men as they approach marriage is how they can best fulfill their role as chief wage earners of their future families. Despite the fact that a high percentage of married women are employed, it is still true that the husband is the one who works steadily year in and year out and who earns the larger salary. Few wives work when children are young and in general their work is intermittent and less well paid than the work of men. The greatest burden of family support comes during the early years of marriage when children are young and the wife unemployed. Hence, a responsibility of the marriage-minded young man is to make a wise selection of a career which will engage his interest, give scope for his abilities and training, and adequately support a family. The first article, by a man with experience in counseling college students on career choices, sets forth some points to be considered in the choice of the first position.

A CAREER well chosen can last a lifetime. A lifetime in a rewarding, challenging career can be one filled with interest and happiness. A lifetime in an unsatisfying job can seem an eternity. Yet a large percentage of college graduates do not find career satisfaction and, to a large extent, only because they do very little to assure that they will.

Have you noticed that college students will often study long hours for

---

* "Making the Decision," *College Placement Annual* (1959), 13–14. Reprinted from the 1959 edition of the *College Placement Annual* by permission of the College Placement Council, Inc., the copyright holder, and the author.

The author received his bachelor's degree in Political Science from the University of Utah and studied law for two years at the same institution. He is Director of Placement at Brigham Young University and plays an active role in the Rocky Mountain College Placement Association, the Western College Placement Association, and the College Placement Council.

a single class, or with system and great concentration prepare for a test or search for information for a term paper? And they will repeat these activities semester after semester for four or more long years. But, finally, as graduation approaches, many will make almost no systematic or thorough study to meet the most important test of their college years—the finding of satisfying career opportunities. They simply do not prepare themselves to make wise choices as to kinds of jobs or companies to pursue or to make wise response to specific offers they may receive.

All people are faced with decisions to make from the earliest moment when, as children, they are given some free agency by their parents. Many of these decisions are made emotionally. Some are made logically as a result of accumulated experiences and thoughtful consideration of the problem at hand. Far too many, however, are made badly because they require maturity and study which are not brought to the problem.

A wise career decision requires a great deal of study not only of one's self, one's talents, training, and desires, but also of kinds of jobs and the companies, institutions, or organizations in which they can be found.

Starting with one's self, many questions should have been asked and answered long before graduation . . . [regarding one's interests, aptitudes, and attributes for success]. Certainly, as individuals take the step from school to work they can no longer postpone certain decisions they may have failed to make. Many must even decide whether to work for someone else or develop a business for themselves. Those choosing to work for someone else—and this is almost everyone—must decide between many alternatives, such as between the big company or the small company, between government or private industry, between urban or rural locations, between desk work or something more active. When these decisions are faced haphazardly, they are often made against bias rather than fact, or, perhaps, they are not made at all. And, unfortunately, when career decision making is done carelessly, many persons approach the finding and deciding upon a job as an end rather than as a beginning, and make selection primarily on the basis of the immediate job and the immediate compensation offered rather than upon the basis of long-term features of the opportunity.

For those persons planning to work for others, the selection of the company or organization to start with is of major importance. Certainly the job is important; however, the beginning job is not always the career job but often leads to it. Also, the same type beginning job may be found in many different companies or organizations but with unequal opportunity beyond that point.

A person facing career selection would be well served to develop a check list. Under company or organization, some of the items or questions which would appear, in one form or other, would be:

1. What is the age, stability, and growth pattern of this company?
2. What is the exact nature of the activity it is engaged in?
3. What kind of product is made or what service is given?
4. What is the opportunity for growth, if I am successful, in the kind of work I want to do?
5. What is the kind of ownership and what are the implications this has for my growth and also for the future of the company?
6. How and by whom is the company managed?
7. What is the size of the company?
8. Who are its competitors?
9. Where are the various offices and/or plants located?
10. What is the likelihood of transfer or travel?
11. What is the level of wages offered by this company in comparison with other favorable companies in the community?
12. What benefits beyond salary are offered? (While a decision would not hinge on these, they can be very important, particularly as a career advances toward retirement, and should not be overlooked when the beginning decision about a company is made.)
13. Could I respect this company and be proud working in it?
14. Are there special problems or virtues of importance not common to other companies?
15. Can I truly find in this company the kind of work which I would like to do over the many years of a career?

The answers to these questions should be carefully set and considered against the desires and goals of the person asking them.

In addition to the check list for companies, a similar check list for location is usually desirable because the worker spends more of his time in his home and community than at work, and his wife and family spend substantially all of their time there. For most people, flexibility as to location is desirable. However, both in connection with the place of the starting assignment as well as with the location of plants or offices to which an individual might expect to be transferred, he might well ask:

1. Are there favorable residential communities with good housing at reasonable cost fairly near the place of employment?
2. Are the schools favorably located? Are they adequately equipped and are they staffed with competent personnel?
3. What is the location of shopping areas in relation to housing?
4. Does the community provide ample and favorable opportunity for recreation, sports, entertainment, and for cultural participation and development?

5. What is the location of the nearest church which would satisfy one's desire for religious participation?
6. How far away are immediate family and other relatives?

The beginning job itself is of great importance and especially as an individual commences his assignment. There are many favorable companies and many pleasant communities. If a person selects a company which offers the kind of employment desirable to him and in a pleasant community, and succeeds in winning an opportunity with it, he should then turn his attention fully and energetically to the job at hand. He should recognize in advance that first jobs are often disappointing because much experience must be gained and much information about the company and its problems must be learned before significant responsibility can come.

The beginning job should be one which can flower into a satisfying career or provide an experience or a situation which will lead to such a career.

If the individual chooses wisely and performs in an effective manner, the jobs beyond the first will be increasingly interesting and challenging and monetarily rewarding.

So, prospective graduate, choose your career and company carefully. Then, having chosen carefully, determine to work with great energy, imagination, and loyalty for your company with the lifetime nature of your career in mind.

53 · The Importance of a College Education in Career Success *

PAUL C. GLICK AND HERMAN P. MILLER

The contemporary tendency toward marriage at an early age places many young men in the dilemma of trying to decide whether to postpone marriage

* "Educational Level and Potential Income," *American Sociological Review*, 21 (June, 1956), 307–312. Reprinted by permission of the American Sociological Society and the authors.

Paul C. Glick, Chief, Social Statistics Branch, Bureau of the Census, holds the degree of Doctor of Philosophy (sociology) from the University of Wisconsin. He combines an interest in the family with an interest in demography. He has written articles on the life cycle of the family and family disintegration, and is author of *American Families,* a statistical study.

Herman P. Miller received the degree of Doctor of Philosophy from American University and is a Statistician in the Bureau of the Census. He is author of *Income of the American People.*

until after graduation from college, marry and struggle on to graduation, or drop out of college and take the best job available for a partially trained man. The last choice may seem wise at the time: it permits marriage and the salary may be good. Doctors Glick and Miller point out, however, that the longer the period of preparation, the greater is the final income. A long-range view of marriage and of the needs of growing families calls for careful consideration of the amount of preparation needed to establish a permanently adequate standard of living.

IN OUR COMPLEX industrial society, educational attainment is one of the most important factors in determining the occupational and income levels to which a person can aspire. This fact assumes special significance in view of the rapid improvement in the educational level of American youth in the last two decades. Although half of the young people today complete a high school education, less than half of the high school graduates go on to college. These proportions might become larger if reliable information were disseminated widely about the potential rewards of completing successively higher levels of education. It is true, of course, that these proportions cannot grow beyond certain limits, inasmuch as some persons who have the capacity to acquire more than a modest degree of education do not have the motivation or the means to do so, and others lack the mental ability to pursue their education as far as they wish and can afford.

It seems reasonable to believe, however, that a majority of youths in this country who are willing and able to continue their schooling can justifiably expect to receive considerably higher incomes in the long run by completing their education through college instead of entering the labor market after finishing high school. This belief rests on the assumption that the American economy can make profitable use in the future of a much larger number of well-educated young people than it has in the past. Moreover, it refers only to material gains, whereas the prospects of achieving more subtle satisfactions from mastering a higher education are more compelling to many people than the prospects of greater financial success.

Average Annual Income by Educational Level

The first evidence in support of the foregoing thesis is presented in Figure 1. This chart is limited to men between the ages of 45 and 54 years because men in this age group are usually experiencing their peak earnings.[1] It is apparent from the chart that there is a progressive increase in the average amount of annual income associated with each increase in educa-

---

[1] This paper is confined to an analysis of data for men. Income figures cited refer to total income, including both earned and unearned income.

tion. The largest difference between any two successive groups is about $2,400; this is the amount by which the annual income of college graduates exceeds that of men who have attended college but have not graduated. Although the levels of the income figures may have already changed somewhat since the base year (1949) and will undoubtedly change in the future, the relationships between the figures will probably continue to show a similar pattern.

FIGURE 1 [converted into table form]: Average (Mean) Income for Men 45–54 Years Old by Amount of Education: 1949 *

Elementary	
None	$1,588
1–4 years	1,927
5–7 years	2,507
8 years	3,112
Average	3,556
High school	
1–3 years	3,588
4 years	4,519
College	
1–3 years	5,473
4 or more years	7,907

* Source: Derived from 1950 Census of Population, Vol. IV, Special Reports, PE, No. 5B, Education, Table 12.

The groupings of educational grades shown in Figure 1 are meaningful, but they contain different numbers of school years and hence do not make apparent the income differences associated with each additional year of schooling. Figure 2 tends to overcome this weakness. The increase in income for each successive education group has been divided by the average increase in the number of years of schooling from one grouping to the next higher one. The results show the increase in annual income associated with an increase of one year of schooling.

Figure 2 shows that each year invested in schooling can be associated with a monetary return. For example, men who had completed high school (but had not attended college) received, on the average, an annual income of $466 for each year of schooling above the level of those who had started but had not finished high school. This return tends to grow progressively as the higher educational levels through college graduation are reached. Furthermore, the statistics show that graduation at any level generally yields a bonus amounting to about twice the increment realized by the average man who starts a given type of school (elementary school, high school, or college) but does not finish. (Census data are not available to demonstrate the average monetary value of each year of post-graduate college training.)

FIGURE 2 [converted into table form]: Increase in Income per Year of Schooling, for Men 45–54 Years Old: 1949 *

Elementary	
None	
1–4 years	$136
5–7 years	165
8 years	303
High school	
1–3 years	238
4 years	466
College	
1–3 years	477
4 or more years	974

* Source: Derived from 1950 Census of Population, Vol. IV, Special Reports, PE, No. 5B, Education, Table 12.

Color Differences

The patterns pointed out in the foregoing discussion for all men 45 to 54 years old apply also to white men of the same age group, except that the values for the latter are somewhat higher. Among nonwhite men of similar ages, however, incomes are consistently lower and considerably less responsive to changes in educational attainment; the annual increase in income associated with an increase of one year in schooling is only about $100 at both the elementary and high school levels. Incomes of nonwhite college graduates are about $500 per year higher than those for nonwhite men with one to three years of college; this differential, however, is only about half as large as the corresponding one for white men.

Behind the dissimilar relationships between education and income among white and nonwhite men lie differences in vocational opportunities, among other things. To illustrate, the proportion of white men between 45 and 54 employed as service workers and laborers (two occupation groups with low average incomes) decreases significantly for each successively higher education group. Among nonwhite men in the same age group, on the other hand, the proportion employed as service workers or laborers decreases very little for successively higher education groups. Even a college education has not been a sufficient qualification to elevate a majority of the nonwhite men above the occupational level of service workers or laborers. Fairly rigid limitations to the utilization of the productive capacity of nonwhite men were evident in the 1950 Census statistics.

Life-Time Income by Educational Level

If education is regarded as a long-term investment, a consideration of life-time returns, as well as annual returns, on the investment should be enlightening. At best only rough approximations can be made in this case and these involve numerous calculations with the aid of life tables. In preparing the estimates which are shown in Figure 3, it was assumed that the

FIGURE 3 [converted into table form]: Estimated "Life-Time" Income for Men by Amount of Education *

Elementary	
None	$58,000
1–4 years	72,000
5–7 years	93,000
8 years	116,000
Average	133,000
High school	
1–3 years	135,000
4 years	165,000
College	
1–3 years	190,000
4 or more years	268,000

* Source: Derived from 1950 Census of Population, Vol. IV, Special Reports, PE, No. 5B, Education, Table 12.

survival rates for men 22 years old in each education class in 1950 would remain the same as those for white males in 1949, until they reached the age of 74 years or until death, if death occurred before the age of 74 years. It was also assumed that their incomes in future years would be the same as the averages in 1949 for successively older groups with similar amounts of education.[2]

The average man living under the conditions set forth would receive income amounting to a little over $130,000 during his economically most active years from 22 to 74. The figures range from close to half this amount for men with no education to about twice this amount for college graduates. Furthermore, the figures indicate that a man with a college degree

[2] The findings in Figure 3 first appeared in a paper by Paul C. Glick, "Educational Attainment and Occupational Advancement," *Transactions of the Second World Congress of Sociology*, Vol. II, London, 1954, pp. 183–193.

may receive approximately $100,000 more income during the economically most active years of his life than a man whose education stopped with high school graduation.

The fact deserves repetition that the "life-time" incomes presented are only estimates and are subject to the conditions assumed in preparing them. The income figures used reflect the extent of illness, disability, unemployment, wage and salary levels, inflation, etc., which prevailed in 1949. Changes in these conditions would naturally change the estimates. But since the average income figures used were all based on the experience for 1949, they have the advantage of representing constant dollar values for all periods of life. Again, it must be acknowledged that many men receive help from their families who thereby make it possible for them not only to gain a college education but also to become established in positions with more than average remuneration. Similarly, some men receive substantial amounts of income from inherited money and other unearned sources which are not related to their educational attainment. On the other hand, about one-third of the college students who are away from home come from families with less than average incomes and few of these students can therefore expect much financial assistance from their parents.

The Cost of a College Education

Although about nine-tenths of the young people attend public schools free of tuition at the elementary and high school levels, very few can attend college without incurring substantial expenses. Therefore, in assessing the monetary value of a college education, it is pertinent to take into account what a college education costs. In estimating this amount, two separate elements may be identified: (a) the direct costs of tuition, books, laboratory fees, and normal living expenses, and (b) the indirect cost, through loss of potential earnings during the period when the youth is engaged in his studies.

According to a recent study made by the U. S. Office of Education, a four-year college education requires, on the average, a direct (mean) outlay of about $7,000.[3] But since the average college graduate completes, in addition, about one-half year of post-graduate work, the total direct costs actually are close to $8,000. On the other hand, since the youth would incur normal living expenses whether he attended school or worked, the cost of subsistence may be deducted from the figures cited. An approximate figure for

---

[3] Ernest V. Hollis and Associates, "Costs of Attending College—A Study of Student Expenditures and Sources of Income," U. S. Office of Education, Bulletin 1956, No. 5, Department of Health, Education, and Welfare, Spring 1956. An important feature of this study is the light it throws on the rather wide range of costs of a college education.

the subsistence item is $600 per year; this is the amount permitted as a deduction from one's income for the support of a dependent person, according to tax regulations. Over a period of four and one-half years, the subsistence item on this basis would amount to $2,700. Subtracting this figure from $8,000 gives $5,300 as a more realistic estimate of the direct cost of a college education. (Of course, it is often the parents rather than the students who make most of this outlay.)

The indirect cost, namely, the partial loss of earnings for four and one-half years, may be estimated from census data. The average young man between 18 and 22 years of age who has graduated from high school but not attended college has an annual income of about $1,200, whereas the average college student earns only $400 per year. Thus, the college graduate probably loses about $800 income per year or a total of $3,600 during his college career.

Putting together the foregoing data yields an estimate of about $9,000 as the cost of a college education.

As already indicated, men with a college education should accumulate annual incomes over a life-time (from ages 22 to 74) amounting to about $100,000 more than those of high school graduates. If the $9,000 had been placed in a safe investment like U. S. Government bonds instead of a college education, the accumulated annual returns by the time he reached the age of 74 years would be only about $15,000 and the capital would still be only $9,000. Thus, the investment in bonds would have produced only about $24,000 in a life-time, or barely one-fourth the $100,000 advantage realized from college graduation. Even if it were assumed that the income from the bonds were reinvested annually (an assumption not made for the income of the college graduate), the investment would still have produced less than $45,000.

Conclusion

The evidence presented points to the conclusion that the completion of additional increments of education—and especially the completion of college—is associated, on the average, with increased earning power, but that this relationship is much less pronounced for nonwhite than for white men. Graduation provides a special bonus, whether it is from elementary school, high school, or college. Perhaps persistence in school until graduation reflects a complex of capabilities and motivational factors which are conducive to relatively successful performance in an occupation.

Like all other social phenomena, however, the incomes of college graduates have a range of variation. For example, the average income of college graduates during their first few years out of school is below that for men of the same age who quit school after finishing high school and acquired skills through experience. Even at the period of peak earnings, one-fourth of the college graduates make less than the average high school graduate of similar age who did not go on to college. Again, one out of every five high school graduates with no college training has a higher income during his peak years than the average college graduate of the same age.

Viewed in the light of all the facts, it seems safe to conclude that an investment in education generally increases the probability of financial success but does not guarantee its attainment.

Although the foregoing analysis offers answers to some questions, it leaves many others unanswered. For example, some factors, such as the person's intelligence quotient, his class rank at high school graduation, and the financial status of his parents, are no doubt related not only to college attendance but also to earnings in later life; to what extent are such factors independently associated with earning capacity? [4] Can it be established that differences in quality of school training at each educational level help to account for variations in subsequent earnings? Would the results of a longitudinal study based on earnings histories of persons with different educational backgrounds lead to essentially the same fundamental conclusions as those in the present study which are based on a cross-sectional analysis? These and many other worthwhile investigations that could be undertaken would probably require the collection of new data. Other investigations could be made, however, from the same source as the present study. These investigations could include analyses of the relationship between educational attainment and income level by age, sex, and color within broad regions of the United States.

54 · Executive Staff and Distaff: A Wives'-Eye View *

DUN AND BRADSTREET

A man's success in his chosen career is frequently much affected by the support given him by his wife and her ability to play the role expected of a wife

* Dun's Review and Modern Industry (February, 1957), pp. 70, 73–75. Copyright by Dun and Bradstreet Publications Corp. Reprinted by permission of the publisher.
[4] Earlier studies based on students in New York and Pennsylvania throw some light on this question. See Appendix by Elbridge Sibley, "The Relation Between College Attendance and Economic Status," in F. W. Reeves, A. D. Henderson, and P. A. Cowen, Matching Needs and Facilities in Higher Education, Albany: Williams Press, Inc., 1948; and Elbridge Sibley, "Some Demographic Clues to Stratification," American Sociological Review, 7 (June, 1942), pp. 322–330.

in his particular field of work. Employers, from college and church boards to industrialists, often wish to interview the wife of an applicant as well as the applicant himself. The relationship of the wife to her husband's success was highlighted by William H. Whyte, Jr., in several articles on wives of business executives published in *Fortune* and *Life* in 1951–1952. After considerable investigation he set forth that the wives of industrial executives viewed their role as involving stabilizing their tension-ridden husbands, mixing with the "right" people, and willingly shifting residence and social contacts as their husbands moved up the ladder of success. Their lives thus tended to be subordinate and supplementary to their husbands' business roles. These articles called forth protests from people who felt that the wife's opportunities for individual growth were being curtailed. Be that as it may, each occupation that a man enters carries expectations of the wife's role, unless husband and wife are to live more independently than is usually the case.

Whyte's findings may be considered a background for the article that follows, which consists of the rules for helping their husbands get ahead decided upon by a panel of six wives of young executives. The panel was held under the auspices of George Fry and Associates, a management consulting firm.

ONE EXECUTIVE's wife put it this way: "It's legalized bigamy. You marry the man and his job." Management looks searchingly at the home life of the young executive of promise, and the lady of the house is getting self-conscious about her key role in aiding or retarding her husband's advancement. There is an old motto to the effect that for every man who makes his way in the world there is a woman pushing from behind. She may be as conspicuous as a fussy little tug shoving an ocean liner against the tide, or as inconspicuous and quiet as the breeze puffing into the canvas of a schooner. In choosing its men, industry is making a pragmatic application of *cherchez la femme*, and the method gets more procedural and scientific every day. The ladies have become aware of their significance in the competitive effort for better executive jobs for the men.

Management has always looked on the woman of the house as an important, sometimes controlling, factor in a man's forward movement in a company. Many a big boss has once-overed the young wife at a social evening and examined her sphere of influence before giving the junior executive added responsibility. The only thing new is that the practice is now accepted as a routine part of the selection and development of promising high-level personnel.

At a recent management clinic conducted by George Fry & Associates, one subject was "Responsibilities of Mrs. Executive," with the wives of six young executives participating. Out of the discussion came the check-list of "characteristics of today's successful business wife" reproduced [at the end of this article]. Few of these apply to the career wife, who occupies a radically different status; they are the qualifications needed by the executive spouse who is called upon to shape her mind, attitude, temperament to her husband's forward movement in the company. If the wife of the executive plays second fiddle, she adds a vital note of harmony to the string ensemble of husband, boss, stockholder, and customer.

Among the most important questions under discussion at the clinic were these: How much should the executive's wife know about the company and her husband's job? How much of company policy should he tell her? When should a company secret be shared, if ever? How much can she advertise the company and its products to her friends and neighbors without getting involved in gossip about company policy and personnel?

There is the eternal tension between the female impulse to chat and the necessity of keeping names and incidents out of the idle chatter. The panel established the fact that it is necessary and desirable for the wife of the executive to know her husband's business, "its general organization, its key personnel, and the staff with whom he works."

The degree to which she enters her husband's business life often depends upon the nature of the business and his assignment. There may be a big difference in the activity of the research engineer's wife and that of the wife of the sales manager. One man may be away from home 10 per cent of the year, and the other 40 to 60 per cent as he jumps from branch to branch or market to market. All agree on one item: Hubby's office is out of bounds for the missus and her problems.

To what extent should the wife of the executive enter the social whirl of her husband's life, entertaining associates and customers? Some girls have more talent for public relations than others, and are gifted with a native tact in dealing with the brass. Some have the ability to buff the boss with an odd compliment without resorting to bold flattery. Others have this subtler gift: They can hand the brush-off to customers in their cups, and to the free-wheeling boys who don't know when they've worn out their welcome, without hurting anyone's feelings. The girls often develop a real skill in dealing with official guests, expected or unexpected, and making them feel at home.

One of the touchy subjects is "other women." Here is where current data, a lot of candor, and a little consideration are more desirable than envy, sulking, or grousing. For better or worse, "other women" are in business, and at various levels of authority. Many women executives think like men, but they also act like women at times, especially under the relaxing influence of a social atmosphere. The executive wife must be the understanding and trustful diplomat, and swallow her indignation when the inept remark is made or the embarrassing question is asked. She is most helpful, too, when she knows hubby's secretary, and coordinates the home and office schedule so that there is proper balance between private life and office life.

American business is a moving business, and executives are subject to change of location at short notice. It often means pulling up roots, severing pleasant social connections, taking children out of school, selling one home and buying another. The shifting about is a painful procedure. Women are usually rooted deeper in community life than their husbands. When the decision to move is made, the wife needs self-discipline more than any other time. She measures all phases of family welfare against the demands of the company that employs her husband. When the pluses outweigh the minuses, she takes the lead in making the decision to move. She pulls up stakes without recrimination. She looks hopefully for the new home, and cultivates new neighbors without nostalgia for the old friends and acquaintances.

One of the vexing questions is as personal as it is emotional: "Why were you passed by on the promotion list? How come Jack got the branch management job when you were in line for it?" Other questions she doesn't ask may often be on the tip of her tongue: "Are you losing interest in your work? Are you developing bad working habits? Are you getting in an emotional rut?" Here is where nagging is sandpaper on the sensitive tissue of a disturbed mind. A little praise and comfort would serve better.

If some men get in a rut and need a gentle or even vigorous push from the distaff side, there is on the other side the hard-driving executive who is a tough taskmaster for everyone, including himself. He expends his energies like a champing stallion until he is slowed down by ulcers or a coronary. No woman is encouraged by the vision of widow's weeds, but how can she slow down her man before he cracks up?

Here again she must be the diplomat rather than the whining sad-sack. She learns how to divert his interests to more serene pastures. She finds that he resents having the obit column flaunted in his face, and is much more amenable to the page which describes the Caribbean cruise. Sometimes she is successful in teaching him how to play with his children, or even his grandchildren, for a man of 50 is often beginning the joys of second parenthood even if he is far from second childhood.

Who makes the home decisions? Occasionally there is a home where the wife is too efficient and takes too many of the responsibilities away from the husband. She begins to wear the pants at home, figuratively and factually, and something happens to the male ego. No decision at the office is so burdensome to an executive that he can't carry also the weight of a "yes" or "no" about church, school, movies, or automobiles. The women of the management clinic panel were unanimous in stating that the man must wear the pants, and be made to exercise his authority just to keep his mace from getting rusty or dusty.

The perfect wife of the business executive doesn't exist except as an ideal, and the description of this lady of all qualities might make her sound like a bit of a prig and a bore. A good personality seems to require more than the copybook virtues. A lively wit in repartee often strikes fire, and even the boss can stand a joke at his expense once in a while. But pity the poor Milquetoast who shivers in terror when the lady of his house pinks the official hide of the visiting V. P. There are wives with the impulse of shrew, jay, and shrike, who speak their mind with or without provocation, and word gets back to the boss, and the husband never knows why he got the Siberian assignment. One magpie with the drumming bill of a wood-pecker hammered holes in the board of directors during a sponsored cruise, and hubby slid three rungs down the ladder in 30 days. But she seems to be the exception to a ragged rule of consistency.

The commercially perfect wife of a business executive has minor imper-fections, like the commercially perfect diamond that gets into the typical engagement ring. The bit of temper, petulance, evasiveness, and ambiguity are minor flaws that emphasize the humanity of the lady who really wants her man to get ahead, but doesn't want to be forgotten when the credits are shared.

One fact is obvious, to be sure. She can be a jewel of great treasure to her executive husband whether she is standing at his side or pushing from behind when his courage wanes. Yes, indeed, the executive wife is the hidden asset of many a well-managed enterprise.

The Responsibilities of MRS. EXECUTIVE

How well does your wife measure up to this prescription for the ideal executive spouse? You may wish to show her this set of rules drawn by energetic young executives' wives at clinic session—but be prepared for the consequences if she does not take kindly to the role of paragon!

1. *Personal qualities.* The successful business wife is, first of all, a good wife and mother. She is affectionate, well-adjusted, adaptable, and pos-sesses a sense of humor and a desire to grow and mature with her husband.

2. *Background.* Her background is similar to her husband's. Ideally, she is a college graduate and has had some business experience.

3. *Knowledge of her husband's business.* She has a knowledge of her

husband's business, its products or services, its general organization, its key peronnel, and the staff with whom he works.

4. *Her role in his work.* She is an intelligent listener and sounding board when her husband shares his business problems and experiences with her. When asked, she offers her counsel objectively.

5. *Attitude.* She encourages her husband in his work and understands its demands on his time and attention. She never nags or demands too much of him in his career.

6. *Confidences.* The successful business wife never commits the unpardonable sin of betraying a business confidence her husband has shared.

7. *The business wife and the office.* Except in emergency, her husband's office is a personal No-Man's Land for her problems or presence.

8. *Other women.* When her husband's position requires association or work with other women, the well-adjusted business wife is understanding and trusting. Her relationship with his secretary is cordial and one of mutual respect.

9. *Business and social life.* The successful business wife builds a happy social life for her family, but never permits it to influence business relationships or to interfere with her husband's business schedule. She maintains a joint business-social calendar with his secretary.

10. *Entertaining.* The best business wife is always a gracious, willing, and capable hostess to her husband's business guests—expected or unexpected!

11. *Community relationships.* Mrs. Good Business Wife is a good citizen too. She encourages her husband to take part in church and community activities and takes part herself.

12. *Her home: its appearance.* Mr. and Mrs. Businessman's home is attractive, neat, inviting, and reflects the pride, tastes, and needs of all the family.

13. *Her home: its atmosphere.* Her home is well-organized, relaxing, and as problem-free as possible.

14. *His health and relaxation.* She subtly cautions her husband when his pace is too rapid. She makes sure he finds time for the relaxation he enjoys and benefits from most.

15. *Joint projects.* The entire family spends some time each day or weekend working together on a home project or sharing recreation.

16. *In-laws.* The best business wife does her utmost, through personal contact and correspondence, to maintain a happy, understanding relationship for herself and her husband with his family.

17. *The budget.* Good business for the smart business wife is to see that the family lives within her husband's income.

18. *Moving.* When a transfer or job change is imminent, the successful

business wife shares in the decision. She takes the lead in establishing her family in the new community and adjusts herself and the children to their new life as happily and as quickly as possible.

19. *Their children.* She provides ample opportunities for her husband and the children to share happy relationships and activities. She does not abdicate all responsibility for discipline to him.

20. *Man and wife.* Fundamentally, the most successful business wife appreciates and maintains a home and family in which her husband is permanent chairman of the board!

CHAPTER 14:

Women's Roles, Old and New

55 · *Helping the College Woman Choose Her Role* *

CLARK E. VINCENT

Many articles on the contemporary married woman's choice of roles oppose homemaking to job holding, implying that the woman must choose between the two. Other articles suggest a series of roles, employment immediately after marriage, followed by childbearing and rearing, and a return to employment in middle age. Professor Vincent does not lay down any fixed rules in the matter. He probes into the background pressures on young women and explores the implications of different choices. He gives helpful suggestions for clarification of roles.

ALTHOUGH investigators may not agree as to the seriousness of the disclarity in the role of the college-educated woman of today, it has become a truism that her role is indecisive. The average library with its 25 to 50 references dealing with women's roles to every one reference concerned with men's roles, substantiates such a truism.

The threefold emphasis of this discussion is to indicate that, if we consider the social context of personality formation and individual behavior, (1) there are some very real pressures operating to make it extremely difficult for the contemporary college-educated female to clarify, and make decisive choices concerning, her own role; (2) the educational efforts to clarify her role are frequently misdirected, as evidenced by the failure

---

* Clark E. Vincent, "Role Clarification for the Contemporary College-educated Woman," *Journal of Home Economics,* 45 (October, 1953), 567–570. Reprinted by permission of the publisher and the author.

The author holds the degree of Doctor of Philosophy from the University of California where he also taught family sociology. He is now Associate Professor in the Department of Sociology and Anthropology at the University of Iowa. He is editor of *Readings in Marriage Counseling* and author of professional articles on unwed mothers, trends in infant care ideas, symptomatic frigidity, and psychosomatic illness.

to take into account the social sources of her role ambiguity; (3) some suggestions for role clarification are possible.

While the following may be applicable to other than college-educated females, the impressions were derived primarily from counseling sessions with college girls contemplating marriage and with college-educated mothers experiencing marital difficulties.

The Illusion of Three Alternatives

Theoretically, the dilemma of the college-educated female comprises the choice between a "homemaking career" and what we shall refer to as a "commercial career," or employment outside the home. Superficially, it would appear that such a decision would be relatively easy to make by either selecting one of the two alternatives or by combining both alternatives. However, such a choice is frequently an illusion for the college-educated female.

Suppose she chooses homemaking? A college girl cannot make this choice too explicit, for it assumes success in obtaining a husband, and there is the possibility that she may be the one woman out of every ten who will never marry. To her, emotionally, the risk is far greater than it appears statistically. Thus, in part for this reason, she may hesitate to major in home economics but select a major involving a higher male enrollment. But after four years of journalism, history, or home economics, the ideas expressed in textbooks as well as the emphasis upon scholastic achievement and the professional expectations of instructors may have indoctrinated her with goals in addition to or other than those associated with her original decision to be a homemaker.

If she successfully meets a husband during college, friends and instructors may actually reveal, or, she may interpret, verbal or facial hints of disappointment when she informs them that she is going to be a full-time homemaker after graduation. If she has not obtained a husband during her four years of college, she has little choice but to find employment—but not as a homemaker.

Suppose she decides initially to have a commercial career? She plans, dreams, studies, and after college spends a few years becoming established in her chosen career. But by the time she is prepared to receive professional recognition, the prospective husband—or the concern because there is no husband—intervenes. For, she lives in a society permeated with the values and the desirability of marriage and a family. However, there is also the realization that if she marries, marriage and especially children, if they are to arrive before she is "too old," are going to take her away from the competitive arena just at the time when her education and experience were going to bring her the long-sought recognition. What was once a clear-cut decision to have a commercial career becomes blurred.

What appears theoretically as a simple choice between two alternatives gives evidence upon closer scrutiny of being an illusion of a choice. *This is true not only prior to marriage but perhaps even more so after marriage.* The following are only some of the subtle pressures which cause the college-educated female constantly to rethink her decision and question her role regardless of her initial choice.

1. The average, middle-class husband desires a clean, well-kept home in which the children are reared in the latest scientific fashion. He expects his wife to be a perfect hostess and sensitive to the importance of "social status" for his professional advancement.[1] He assumes that she will continue to be an intelligent and witty conversationalist who is interested in and able to understand his business and professional transactions, despite the fact that she has been surrounded all day with the conversations of a six-year-old, a three-year-old, and an infant.

However, this husband also appreciates the income of a working wife, and he may imply quite innocently on occasion that his wife has little to do all day since he compares her with the neighbor who "manages her home" in addition to her outside occupation.

2. The woman who has mastered the "gospel" according to various women's magazines is instructed—frequently within a single issue—how to be the perfect hostess, an ideal wife and mother; how to be a frugal economist, a painter, plumber, mechanic, and practicing psychologist; how to be the model of civic participation, have a hobby, and work part or full time for "self-expression"; and how to remain eternally young.

Many of these articles imply that her life isn't complete as a homemaker and entice her with success stories of glamorous mothers who have careers in addition to homemaking. Still other articles tacitly assume that if she is only a career woman she is missing the greatest joys of womanhood.

3. There is currently an attempt to convince "housewives" that they are more than "just housewives." The homemaker is informed that she is involved in an art, a science, and the most worth-while profession. However, the average woman knows that domestic helpers are among the lowest paid workers and that they occupy one of the bottom rungs on the occupational prestige ladder.

---

[1] Whyte, W. H., Jr. The wives of management. *Fortune*, 44, No. 4 (Oct. 1951), pp. 86–88+; Whyte, W. H., Jr. The corporation and the wife. *Fortune*, 44, No. 5 (Nov. 1951), pp. 109–111+; and McLemore, E. W. Manifesto from a corporation wife. *Fortune*, 45, No. 3 (March 1952), pp. 83+.

She may be exhausted at the end of the day from giving "proper" psychological answers to the children's questions, repairing the electric mixer, making countless decisions on where and how much to buy, and encountering the hazards of traffic in shopping as well as in taking family members to and from work and school. However, she receives neither the prestige nor the status of the psychologist, the mechanic, the economist, or the taxi driver. Lacking such recognition, she repeatedly questions her homemaker's role and looks elsewhere for more rewarding roles. For she is made aware that for some reason filing letters and folding boxes bring more prestige than filing recipes and folding diapers.

4. If she works outside the home and leaves her children at a child-care center or nursery, she may be labeled as a delinquent mother by educators, ministers, and neighbors. However, if she remains home, psychiatrists may suggest that she is "too close" to her children and that such closeness is causally related to the fact that nearly 3,000,000 men were emotionally or mentally unfit for military service during World War II.[2]

5. She is told that motherhood is her responsibility, and she is reminded of her sacred duties and sacrifices as a mother. However, she is led to believe that she is incapable of motherhood and that she must rely on the child-rearing and infant-care "experts." This in spite of the fact that the "experts" have changed their opinions twice in three decades.[3]

Thus, although the college-educated female may have made an initial decision between the first two alternatives, *the implication is always present that a combination of both is the test* of a "successful woman." Many homemakers see a commercial career as the solution to their problems in the counseling situation, whereas many of the women employed outside the home have as their major goal to be able to "quit work and be with my family."

Suppose she chooses both a homemaking and a commercial career? It would appear that this is the decision reached by an increasing number of married women. The percentage of married women in the labor force increased 10 per cent—from 16.7 per cent to 26.7 per cent—between 1940 and April 1951, whereas "the labor force participation rate for single women and for widowed and divorced women has shown no significant change during recent years."[4] In April 1951 there were 10.2 million married women

---

[2] Strecker, E. A. *Their Mothers' Sons*. Philadelphia: J. B. Lippincott Co., 1946.

[3] Vincent, C. E. Trends in infant care ideas. *Child Devel.*, 22 (1951), pp. 199–209. [For a discussion of influence upon mothers of professional and technical advice, see "Emotional and cultural impacts on contemporary motherhood" by L. Kanner, *J. Child Psychiatry*, 2 (1951), pp. 168–175.]

[4] Marital status of women in the labor force: April 1951. U. S. Bur. Census, Current Population Repts., Ser. P-50, No. 37 (Dec. 26, 1951), p. 1.

in the labor force, which was 1.6 million more than the highest number during World War II.[5]

But if she does select this third alternative, she finds it a decision involving many difficulties. Census figures indicate a 10 to 15 per cent decrease in the number of domestic workers between 1940 and 1950; her husband may not be willing for her to work outside their home; she may not live in an area where both she and her husband can find their specialized fields of employment; she may not have the physical energy for both careers; and she may develop guilt feelings over neglect of the children. There is also the suggestion by some writers that the two roles are contradictory since one requires "drive, self-assertion, competitiveness, and assertion," while the other necessitates traits that are "protective or nurturing, passive and receptive." [6]

It may well be that in society's emphasis upon the third alternative for women, "female emancipation" becomes a misnomer. It is recognized that a part of the dilemma is related to the self-expectations which college-educated females have of themselves,[7] but these are not unrelated to the social context in which they are learned.

Misdirected Emphasis in Role Clarification

It is interesting that the books and articles concerning women's roles are frequently written for and to women, implying that it is the women who are to clarify their roles and that it is the female's role which needs clarifying. In reality it may be the male's role which needs clarification. Men still expect to work as they have always expected to work; and while their role has remained somewhat constant, their responsibilities may actually have decreased. Increasingly, we expect women to assist in breadwinning, politics, civic affairs, in the professions, in education, *and* we still expect them to be *the* homemakers.

Whether women should or should not work outside the home is beside the point in our present discussion. *The point is that if society continues to expect women to share many of the male's responsibilities, then society may need to expect men to share more of the female's responsibilities. The contemporary indecision in the college-educated female's role is as much related to overexpectation as it is to indecision between alternatives. To*

---

[5] Annual report on the labor force: 1951. U. S. Bur. Census, Current Population Repts., Ser. P-50, No. 40 (May 19, 1952), p. 1.

[6] Farnham, M. Battles won and lost. *Ann. Am. Acad. Pol. & Soc. Sci.*, 251 (1947), pp. 113–119.

[7] Rose, A. The adequacy of women's expectations for adult roles. *Soc. Forces*, 30, No. 1 (Oct. 1951), pp. 69–77.

clarify her role, we need to direct our educational emphasis toward those expecting so much of her and re-examine the role of the male in our society in relation to the added expectations we have of the female.

We may agree with Shakespeare that

> All the world's a stage,
> And all the men and women merely players:

but if we view personality formation and the learning process within the social context, we are made aware that we seldom write our own scripts. Contemporary women attempt to play the part or act the role being written for them by their husbands, ministers, women's magazines, and economic society, the rules of occupational competition, and professors' expectations. To clarify the contemporary woman's role our educational emphasis might more fruitfully be directed toward those writing her script.

Suggestions for Role Clarification

1. *Accept social reality.* Whether we believe that women should or should not work outside the home, the fact remains that almost 11 million married women are doing so and our economy could hardly withstand their withdrawal from the labor force even if it were desirable. The fact also remains that an increasing number of women who are receiving college educations and being trained in the same classrooms with men will want to work outside the home. If an increasing number of married women are to work outside the home, if available domestic help is decreasing, and if the standards for the successful wife, mother, and homemaker are continually raised, something or someone has to give.

2. *Conceive of homemaking as a "husband-wife" role, not as a "wife only" role.* This involves having home economics courses more applicable to male students. The sharing of homemaking frequently enables the husband to understand better the manual labor involved in the statement "the woman's place is in the home." We still retain an interesting concept of masculinity which regards sitting at an office desk all day as being more masculine than scrubbing floors, cleaning house, and disciplining youngsters. Conversely, the wife who works outside the home is frequently better able to appreciate the demands and strains in her husband's working world. Their area of interests-in-common is increased immeasurably when homemaking as well as breadwinning is shared.

It is to be recognized that males have lost some prestige in giving up their patriarchal throne and that some males experience a feeling of inadequacy in not being *the* breadwinner. Even though scrubbing floors and washing diapers may enable him to appreciate the lack of prestige associated with homemaking, it may also threaten his ego-security. However, the historical and social source of this ego-threat needs to be recognized. For when sharing breadwinning and homemaking roles is viewed as an ego-threat to the male, it usually implies the retention of the patriarchal conception of the husband-wife relationship as a dominant-submissive relationship.

With homemaking as a "we" role, it may be easier to appreciate that the wife who works outside the home also needs a psychological retreat from her work as does her husband, and that as a homemaker she needs a psychological retreat from *their* children. Some studies have indicated that the children having the best parent-child adjustment are those whose mothers are away from the home for from 10 to 30 hours a week.[8] If we view child-rearing as a mother *and* father role, then the 3,000,000 men rejected for World War II service were as much caused by an absent or disinterested father as by a too-close and too-interested mother.

3. *Appreciate the therapeutic nature of physical work.* At a time when the best-sellers are prescriptions on how to prevent worry and acquire peace of mind in the alleged stress and strain of modern living, too little attention is given to the therapeutic benefit of expending physical energy in homemaking tasks. Dirt may never be glamorous to the college-educated female, but *getting rid of it* may be therapeutic.

4. *Examine the self-image being given to college-educated females by their professors.* What kind of a script are college professors and especially home economics professors writing for their female students? Do they tend to assume that all their female students are interested in becoming a professional historian, sociologist, or home economist as the professor is? Are professors' self-images projected onto the female students through values which rate a commercial career higher than a homemaking career? Are courses offered which permit the female student to become a homemaker without being indoctrinated with professional data and methodology? Is there a recognition that homemaking courses are not necessarily "easier" or "softer" than other professional courses but are of a different kind and perhaps for that reason more difficult for the professionalized instructor to teach? Does the professor tend to increase the future homemaker's feeling of inadequacy by implying reliance upon the "experts" in child-rearing, husband-wife relationships, and homemaking skills?

5. *Examine whether women contribute to their own dilemma of "homemaking being just homemaking"* by continued low wages and servant relationships to their domestic help.

6. *Eliminate some of the role conflict for women by educating them*

---

[8] Nye, I. Adolescent-parent adjustment: age, sex, sibling number, broken homes, and employed mothers are variables. *Marriage & Family Living*, 14 (1952), pp. 327–332.

for both a homemaking and a commercial career. It appears realistic to do so since 90 per cent of them will at some time in their lives be homemakers and from 50 to 75 per cent will at some time be working outside the home.

7. *Enable the college-educated female to appreciate better the social sources of her self-image and role expectations.* With such an appreciation, it may be easier to redirect more fruitfully educational efforts in role clarification for both the college-educated female and male. With increased awareness of the social source of her role expectations, it may be easier for her to take greater confidence in her own ability as a wife, mother, and homemaker as well as in her ability to set her own individual limits on the demands society makes of her. With less incorporation of these "generalized others" of contemporary society, she need not be so confused in her role and so absorbed in the conforming, "participating, lubricating, integrating and communicating" struggle.[9]

56 · Should Mother Take a Job or Stay Home with the Kids? *

CHANGING TIMES, THE KIPLINGER MAGAZINE

This article gives a personalized view of choice of roles as a young woman might argue the pros and cons to herself in trying to reach a decision.

YOU MAY KNOW a woman like Jane R. She's the mother of two children—Jerry, five, and Anne, three. Jane is a college graduate and before she married Ralph, she had a good job as an assistant buyer in a department store.

She's been at home with her children for five and a half years now, and she's restless, bored and unhappy.

She wants to go back to work.

It isn't the money that appeals to her—Ralph is making enough to support his family in good style. Besides, she realizes that she wouldn't come out very many dollars ahead after she finished paying taxes and for a maid, nursery school, new clothes, transportation and lunches.

No, it isn't merely the money. It's just that she thinks she would be happier and therefore a better wife and mother, if she were working at a full-time job. Back in the business world, she thinks, she might recapture

---

* *Changing Times, The Kiplinger Magazine*, 7 (September, 1953), 22–24. Reprinted by permission of the publisher, The Kiplinger Washington Agency, Inc.
[9]Editor's note. *Fortune*, 44, No. 5 (Nov. 1951), p. 76.

some of the sparkle and vivacity which she feels has slipped away from her while she's been at home with the preschool set.

Well, would she? Is she right, or is she kidding herself?

Jane isn't the only woman who is asking these questions. About 15% of the women with children under six years of age are working. Although many of them must do it for the income, many don't have to. The doors of the business and professional world open wider every year to women. And the proportion of women who have had a college education or work experience, or both, has nearly doubled in the last ten years.

This change in the status of women has prompted many a husband and father to ask: Whatever became of the woman who wanted nothing more from life than a home, plenty of children and a dutiful husband?

The answer is that the young woman of today is the victim of a double cross. On the one hand, her college training or her work experience taught her to make a living, not to make a cake. So to one half of her being, success has come to mean just what it does to a man—success in a job.

But with the other half of herself, she wants to fulfil another set of aims and ambitions—marriage, children and a home. Those, too, symbolize success.

Whether she realizes it or not, Jane is about to come up against this dilemma, the double standard of success for women. Should she try to achieve success both places—at home and at work, too?

That's a tough question to answer. In order to answer it, Jane will have to do nothing less than decide what she wants out of life and what she owes to her family and to herself.

Six Sticky Questions

In the course of making the decision, she will bump into some awfully difficult questions—questions like these:

Am I up to doing two jobs? No matter who takes care of the children, Jane is still their mother. And that's a job. She may discover, if she goes back to the store, that she will work even harder at being a mother if she's not at home every day. Before work and after and on the week-ends, she'll try desperately to cram in the mothering that she isn't able to give during the weekdays.

Will this leave her enough energy to do her work at the store? Or will she find that both jobs suffer?

Can I hire a good substitute mother? It is on this thorny question that most mothers who would like to go back to work get stuck. When a mother hires someone to fill her shoes during the day, she wants more than an efficient housekeeper. What she really is looking for is a substitute mother. And such gems are rare.

As one young mother puts it, "It takes all the intelligence and energy I have to raise my kids the way I think they should be raised. And they are my children and I care about them. If I hire someone, I can't be sure she'll do a good job of raising them. No matter how faithful and conscientious she is, she can't possibly give as much to the job as I do."

But what if the children are in school? To be sure, during the time the children are in school the mother is free, and that's a good part of the day. Unfortunately, though, the school year and the work year run on different schedules. For nearly four months of the year, the children will be on spring, summer or Christmas vacations.

Then, too, children do get sick and stay out of school. In such emergencies, the mother must either stay at home and take care of them or make some hasty arrangement if she is to appear on the job at the proper hour.

A mother who once tried working described the day she quit this way: "Little Tommy woke up with a high fever, and Nancy had a headache. Neither of them could go to school. My husband was out of town on a business trip. Mary, our maid, didn't show up, and the furnace was out. I decided that morning that it wasn't worth it. I called up the office and told them I was quitting—right then and there."

How will my working affect my husband? When the wife and mother backs out of her household, something is bound to suffer. More responsibility will fall on the father's shoulders. And if he holds an important job that takes a lot of energy, he may find that his efficiency will be impaired and his progress impeded because he must pour an extra measure of his limited energy into those jobs which are normally done by his wife.

Will I lose a lot if I wait a few years? Caught up in the routine of housework, the mother in her late twenties becomes mesmerized—she thinks it will never end, that she will be spooning baby food into small faces and running that hateful vacuum cleaner for the rest of her days.

The truth of the matter is that the whole business will be over a lot sooner than she thinks. Certainly by the time she is in her late thirties or early forties, the children will be old enough to do without her constant attention and may actually be able to take over a good many of the chores around the house. And in a few years more she will have completely lost her job as mother. Then she will find that she has 20 to 30 active years ahead of her.

It is this stage of her life, not the active child-raising period—say the experts—that is most troublesome to women like Jane. And nearly all the psychologists who have studied women and their problems are agreed that Jane and others like her should make a serious effort to prepare themselves for this awkward stage by studying on the side, maintaining contacts, reading trade magazines, or doing volunteer or part-time work.

To be sure, Jane may have to start at the bottom again at 40 as she did at 20, when she was fresh out of college. But if she has ability, she will find that she can make up for the years spent in raising a family and satisfy her postponed ambitions.

This plan takes a lot less time and energy than the struggle to go back to work too soon.

What will I lose if I go back to work? Jane may see only the rosy side of that job at the store. She should step back for a moment to consider what she will be losing if she decides to go back to work.

Has she forgotten the unhappier side of the business world? The boss who tyrannized everyone in her department, the nights she had to work until her eyelids drooped, the ride on the crowded bus to and from the store, the office politics, and those days when the merchandising manager went on a rampage?

By contrast, does she see that she would be giving up being her own boss, some of her leisure, some of her outside activities, and some of the satisfaction she gets from homemaking and participating in community life through the P-TA, the church or the League of Women Voters?

And what about the summer afternoons at the swimming pool or out in the back yard with a good book? Admittedly, such moments are rare for most young mothers—but they just don't exist for the working mother.

Psychologically, too, Jane is bound to lose something. No matter how much she tries to overcome it, a young mother will have a feeling of shirking her responsibility if she voluntarily goes back to work. For some women, this guilty feeling actually develops into a feeling of defeat. They feel that they just don't have what it takes to be a wife and mother.

Why do I want to go back to work? That's the biggest question of all, and Jane must face it candidly and boldly.

Some women have excellent reasons. The necessity for increasing the family income, for example. And some women may feel that their talents or skills are so valuable that sacrifices must be made in order to enable them to work. A schoolteacher, for instance, may feel that the shortage of good teachers creates an obligation for her to go back to the classroom.

But many mothers who work take humdrum jobs which provide no real stimulation or satisfaction. Why do they do it?

Is it because going back to work is the easy way out? Is it because they haven't learned how to make a success of the career they chose for themselves when they said "I do"?

Raising children and running a pleasant home is a highly skilled and worth-while occupation. To do the job well takes intelligence, time and training. Frustrations occur, as they do in any job. And when they do, women may be tempted to throw in the towel—and duck out of the house and back to an office.

Jane must ask herself whether she has learned to cope with her children and with her housework, whether she takes a real interest in her home and her community. Has she, for example, explored the possibilities of getting outside of her housekeeping routine, with its periods of loneliness and boredom, without going back to work?

There's a mountain of outside work to be done and no one but mothers to do it. Sophisticates may smile at the myriad activities of housewives in community affairs, but the fact remains that if these women don't collect the money for the Red Cross, sit with the sick children in hospitals, serve on the library committee of the P-TA, lobby for a playground and volunteer for work in the local YWCA—then who will?

And will Jane, if she takes a job, be able to hold up her head among the other mothers who have given so much of themselves to the community while she has been off at work?

Neither Fish nor Fowl

On balance, the cards are stacked against Jane's chances of achieving success both at home and at work. In a unique study of college graduates, *They Went to College*, Ernest Havemann and Patricia Salter West concluded that "the working wife occupies a rather ambiguous twilight zone. By and large she does not combine the advantages of marriage with the advantages of a career—rather she seems to be in the unhappy position of being neither fish nor fowl, not quite a wife and not quite a career woman either. . . . On the basis of what we have measured, it appears that the average graduate who tries to be both wife and career woman is not fully successful either way."

57 · *Women as the Country's Major Labor Reserve* *

DRUZILLA C. KENT

Homemaking versus career is not debated in this article. Taking a long look ahead at the demands made on the production of this country by military and civilian needs, Dr. Kent points out that married women constitute the unused labor pool from which most of the expansion in workers of all types must come. She sees their entrance into employment less as a matter of choice than of necessity. She also emphasizes the responsibility of the community to ease the burden that increased employment will place on married women with children.

THE PEOPLE of this country face an "unprecedented" situation—unprecedented in regard to the amount of materials which must be produced in support of our program for defense, the size and composition of the labor force which will be required to maintain production schedules, and the length of time for which we can expect the situation to continue.

The future of the free world is dependent to a considerable degree upon the ability of the United States to produce the materials needed to meet the demands of a stepped-up military program, to maintain an adequate stockpile of essential goods and materials, and to aid other nations in their efforts to achieve economic recovery. These demands are based upon long-term objectives, and our very survival may be dependent upon our ability to achieve them. They cannot be achieved unless we can increase production. In addition to these demands, however, there are also the demands of our civilian population. We must make every effort to maintain and, if humanly possible, to improve the present standard of living of the people in this country. We are told that this situation may last 20 years or more— or the period of time covering a full generation.

* "Homemaking in the Defense Decades," *Journal of Home Economics*, 44 (January, 1952), 13–15. Reprinted by permission of the publisher and author.

The author, who holds a doctor's degree, is Professor of Home Economics Education at the University of Tennessee. The article reprinted here followed a special study of problems relating to the homemaker in the defense program made for the U.S. Office of Education.

Women Constitute Our Major Labor Reserve

It cannot be emphasized too strongly that the American economy cannot be sustained at its present level of efficiency and productivity, much less be expanded, without increasing the number of women in the labor force. Women now constitute 30 per cent of the American labor force. There is no replacement for the skills and training which women are contributing every day to American industry. In terms of sheer numbers alone, substitute manpower, in whom training might produce equivalent skills, is not available in the labor reserve, and, whether we like it or not, women with responsibilities for homemaking must be recruited and held in the labor force. Women today constitute the largest labor reserve in the nation, and four-fifths of the women included in this labor reserve are classified as homemakers.

For the first time in the history of this country, more married than single women are employed. Considerably more than one-half—indeed, probably as many as two-thirds of all women who are employed in full-time work today—can be assumed to be carrying the responsibility not only of adequate and satisfactory performance on a job but also of maintaining a home for themselves and other members of their families.

In 1949, almost half of the female labor force was composed of married women living with their husbands. Over four million of these women had children younger than 18 years of age and, of these, one and one-half million had children younger than school age, a situation which inevitably imposed additional responsibilities upon them over and above those which are involved in maintaining homes for themselves and other adults.

Families and Communities Face Adjustments

We must recognize that well over one-fifth of our families may have to make some very fundamental adjustments within the family. We should also face the fact that we may need to make some very fundamental adjustments in some of our other social institutions; we cannot make changes in any one of our basic social institutions without creating a need for changes in others closely associated with it.

The ability of a family to continue to function successfully when the wife and mother is employed full-time outside of the home seems to be due to one or more of a number of factors, some of which are more directly related to the family, others, to the community. Those which seem most influential from the standpoint of the family, itself, are: the managerial skill of the homemaker—her ability to organize the work of the home systematically; her knowledge regarding the essential factors relating to the well-being of the family—the values she considers important in making choices as to what to do or what to leave undone; the flexibility of the family—the extent to which family members are willing to make essential adjustments; their willingness to co-operate in the sharing of essential tasks; the ability of the family to secure a competent substitute to carry the responsibilities formerly carried by the homemaker; the kind of home in which the family lives—the extent to which it is (1) planned to eliminate the waste of time and energy and (2) equipped with modern, labor-saving equipment such as home-freezer units, automatic washers, modern stoves, and vacuum cleaners.

Those factors relating to the community which seem to be most influential in helping the family are: the attitudes of the community toward women with homemaking responsibilities working outside of the home; the attitudes of the community toward the division of responsibility within the family for tasks essential to their well-being; the willingness of the community to (1) make essential adjustments in the location and/or operation of existing services and (2) create new services needed by those families, such as child-care centers and youth recreation centers; the sensitivity of the community to the needs of these families and its aggressiveness in aiding them to solve problems which they cannot hope to solve as independent family units.

Women who may have been successful in operating their homes when they gave full time to their homes and families often find themselves in hopeless confusion when they attempt to carry, in addition, full-time employment outside of the home. The dual role demands an entire reorganization of the household schedule; it may demand, too, the use of short cuts in regard to various jobs, such as purchasing food once a week instead of going to the grocery store each day, learning new methods of food preparation, and the planning of meals which may differ materially from those to which the family has been accustomed.

Just as we cannot hope to escape making changes in other social institutions when we make a fundamental change in one, we cannot make a drastic change in the role of one member of the family group without making changes in the roles of other members. Many families will need help in making these adjustments and in exploring new roles for other members of the family. Division of responsibility will vary according to the particular family, but families must be helped to see that this division of responsibility within the home may be as important to production schedules in the plants as any improvement in practices within the plant. And they must be helped to see this within the framework of the whole social situation, for men, too, have been trained for a particular role in the family, and, to the extent that they feel a loss of prestige through no longer being "the providers" for their families and, in addition, find themselves having to do "woman's work" in the home, they may not only become less efficient in the plant where they work but may become a source of friction and discontent within the family group.

Planning Community Programs

The very existence of some of the problems interfering with the successful functioning of the employed homemaker may be inherent in the community. In addition to the attitudes toward the employment of homemakers, the organization of service agencies, the location, as well as the hours for opening and closing of schools, groceries, meat markets, department stores, shoe repair shops, laundries and dry-cleaning establishments, or shampoo parlors may be geared to a pattern of living which is no longer representative of those families who are least able to make adjustments to them.

There is no question but that the local community must assume a major responsibility for helping the family solve its problems. The future of the community is dependent upon the quality of family life in the homes of the community. If the millions of women at work are essential to our economy, we cannot permit them to work at the expense of their families.

Any community in which large groups of homemakers are entering full-time employment may render a distinct service to the community itself, to industry, and to the families of these women through developing a program designed to:

1. Maintain a continuous evaluation of their efficiency in relation to one or both of their dual roles
2. Locate those problems which seem to be interfering most seriously with their efficiency
3. Aid in bringing about changes which would seem most essential to an increase in their efficiency.

Home economists may be expected to take a leading part in helping communities study the development of production programs with special reference to the number of homemakers entering full-time employment outside of the home. They may need, too, to evaluate existing programs of homemaking education in order to determine their adequacy in terms of the needs of homemakers entering employment.

It may be necessary, in many communities, to develop a systematic program through some agency, such as the public school, to develop an appreciation of the significance of problems relating to the increased employment of married women with home responsibilities. For these problems are significant not only to the families of these women but to the entire community. Labor groups and the industries employing these women can be relied upon to participate in such a program, but efforts should be made to awaken the entire community to its responsibility in helping these families solve their problems. The way in which these problems will be solved in one community may not be the way which will work in another community, but they can be solved through intelligent effort and co-operation when the community realizes the issues.

No nation can afford to put the problems of the family into cold storage for a generation and especially those problems created by our efforts to save our way of life. Our way of life places a heavy responsibility upon the local community for dealing with those problems that directly affect the welfare of the individual and of the family. Directions which have been issued in regard to the National Plan for Civil Defense stress the role of the local community, the use of established agencies, and the importance of co-ordinating those agencies with any specific problem of defense.

As a people, we seem to realize how important it is for Rosie to have training which will enable her to operate the riveting machine efficiently. We must have airplanes, ships, and tanks which are carefully made in order that they may withstand the stresses and strains to which they will be subjected. It may be even more important, though, that Rosie have training which will enable her to operate her home with the same efficiency with which she operates the riveting machine. The family is being subjected to stresses and strains, and, in the long run, society may profit more by having strong, well-built families than by having produced strong, well-built mechanical equipment.

58 · *Young Women: Look before You Weep* *

ALICE NORMA DAVIS

Practical pointers are contained in this article for the young woman getting ready for her first full plunge into employment. The article differs from many others in that it discusses the employer's point of view toward women employees and gives some of the reasons why employers are sometimes reluctant to accept young women who apply.

* *College Placement Annual* (1959), pp. 27–29. Reprinted from the 1959 edition of the *College Placement Annual* by permission of the College Placement Council, Inc., the copyright holder, and the author.

The author, who has the Bachelor of Arts degree, is Director of the Vocational Office at Smith College.

THE EMPLOYMENT of women has become an important factor in the economy of the United States. We have progressed from a country in which teaching and nursing were considered about the only suitable careers for women to one in which nearly all fields are open to them. One hundred years ago, only one out of five women worked for a salary; now, four out of five women have some paid employment during their lifetimes. In 1890, women represented about one-sixth of the working group in this country; today, they make up almost one-third of the total labor force. That women are now more apt to return to work after they marry is evidenced by the fact that over half of all employed women are married. The average age of working women today is thirty-eight, despite the younger age at which college graduates marry.

So much for facts and statistics. Taken as a whole, they make it seem likely that, at some time during your life, you will be a working woman. That being so, it would seem to be a good idea for you to do some thinking and planning about it now, while you are still in college. Your placement office is a logical starting point. There you will find counselors to help you plan your course of action, literature on your particular areas of interest, directories of potential employers, and listings of specific job openings. In addition, many placement offices sponsor vocational conferences or lectures at which the opportunities open to you as a college graduate are described. Finally, the placement office arranges dates and interviewing schedules for employers who visit the campuses to recruit seniors for their respective organizations. Just about everything, in fact, which you will need to help you find the job you want. It will probably never be so easy again.

Taking any old job because it is a good way to kill time until you are married, or because it pays well and you and your husband need money, is one way of going at things—a fairly popular way. But it does seem a rather shortsighted approach if you realize that, by taking a few hours here and there during your four years at college to investigate the pros and cons of various jobs, you may be saving yourself from possible weeks or months of insecurity and unhappiness.

Whether you think your first job will be your last and will continue only for a brief premarital period or whether you see it as the beginning of a long and successful career, you should approach it with equal care and intelligence. There is certainly nothing to be lost by going at it in this way and, since Fate is an inscrutable creature, you may be very thankful that you did. By making a good beginning you will be laying the best foundation you can to help you cope with whatever turns your life may take.

Much has been written, and well-written, to help college seniors find their first permanent jobs. There are essays on the importance of self-analysis—knowing your likes and dislikes, your strengths, weaknesses, and limitations; evaluating your academic training in the light of the job you hope to have; realizing that, college graduate though you will be, an employer will justifiably consider you a greenhorn in the business world at first.

If you have held one or more summer jobs, you will be wise enough to avoid some of the more obvious pitfalls. You will, for example, know something about writing a good letter of application, or what to expect in an interview. You will also have an idea of the kind of job you want and more of an idea of those you do not want. But even with this important knowledge, it would be a good idea for you to do further research before taking your first permanent position. Careful preparation can help you avoid mistakes and false starts which can be costly for you and for the organization which employs you.

Up to this point, the employment picture for men and women is quite similar but from here on in, it is often different and in some ways more complicated for women. A college man goes to work and both he and his employer expect that he will continue in one job or another until he retires. He probably assumes that he will marry and have a family to support and that his wife will take care of their home and the children. He knows that his family will go with him wherever his work or inclination takes him. This is all comparatively straightforward and obviously oversimplified. But the corresponding employment picture—the one in which you are going to figure—may not even be capable of oversimplification.

The uncomplicated pictures exist. You may be going to fit into the time-honored pattern for women and you may—though in this age it is problematical—stay in it for the rest of your life. Or you may become a career woman and remain in your profession until you retire. But many of you are going to have to live your lives in and around a series of changes. You may be supporting your husband while he goes to business or professional school. You may then move to one or more different locations over the next few years. You will probably not work for a period of years while your children are small. You may want to, or have to, go back to work when your children are grown—or work part-time when they are in school. The combinations and complications are limitless.

Seeing into the future is not given to most of us. If we look at the fortune teller's crystal ball, we see a well-polished piece of quartz—nothing more. But it is possible for you to plan a course of action which will serve you in good stead whatever happens. The first step is finding the position which suits you and which you suit. Once you are actually working, you should bring to your job as much intelligence, concentration, and determination to succeed as though you were planning to make a career of it.

Employers are generally quick to recognize ability and effort in their employees and to reward them with increased responsibility or promotion. They are equally quick to see indifference and carelessness. If your job is nothing more than a source of income to you, your employer is quite likely to realize this and accept you on your own terms, letting you remain as long as you wish but probably right where you started. As for you, you may become increasingly bored and restless and dissatisfied and blame the company, the employer, the job, when actually you yourself are the cause of your trouble. Furthermore, making the best contribution you can to the organization which has employed you is your greatest insurance for the future. Good references from past employers can make the problems of shifting jobs or locations or of returning to work after a lapse of years much easier.

Another complicating factor with which you, as a woman in business, may have to cope is the initial attitude of the employer toward you. Because many women do not work more than one to five years after graduation, employers are dubious about investing time and money in training *any* woman. If you are engaged or married when you are interviewed for jobs, they are apt to be even more dubious. Some training programs are closed to all women; others, to engaged or married women. There is nothing to be gained by being resentful of these facts—you will most likely hurt no one but yourself. If you are able to accept these unpleasant realities and convince an employer that you are worth your salt, you will find that there are many jobs open to you and that among them is undoubtedly one which will please you and which you can do with satisfaction.

Even if you have to begin work under the cloud of your employer's conviction that your period of working for him will be brief, you will have a perfectly good opportunity to show him that, brief or not, your contribution is going to be valuable. You can make something of your job by giving it everything you have to give. There is satisfaction in doing a job well, particularly if you like what you are doing. Furthermore, promotion to a bigger job may be yours when you have displayed the qualities and the vision to handle it. And promotion is not the only way to a better job. Many people not only have made something of their jobs, but also have made something more of them. It has often happened that little, comparatively insignificant jobs have blossomed into big jobs through the efforts and ingenuity of the people who held them. Promotion to a ready-made, more important job is certainly gratifying; but knowing that your imagination, intelligence, and perseverance have created or developed a new and valuable area within your organization is an even greater source of satisfaction as well as a feather in your cap.

Something which is too often overlooked—and this applies to everyone alike, old and young, veterans of the working world and tyros—is the factor of enjoyment. For too many people it follows that: to work is to labor; to labor is to suffer; to suffer is to want to escape from work. This is an insidious attitude. It can result in your becoming the kind of person who lives the weekday mornings for the lunch hour and afternoons for closing time. It makes eight hours of each day a dreary bore. What's more, you are apt to find dissatisfaction with your job spreading into a general dissatisfaction with your life. This is obviously no answer to anything and it is entirely unnecessary. Work does not have to be unpleasant and onerous. If you can discover what you would best like to do and find the job which most nearly fits you (or will after you have served your apprenticeship), you are pretty sure to enjoy it. And if you enjoy your work, you are quite likely to find that your working hours go fast; that you have a general sense of well-being; that you are not tired out by five o'clock; that you are more fun and more interesting to your friends and family; and that the inevitable disappointments and frustrations which come to everyone are not shattering. You may, in fact, find that the more you enjoy your whole life—work and play —the closer you will come to that much talked of, sought after, and elusive ideal called happiness.

Practically any way you look at it, there is much to be gained and very little to be lost by spending some time and effort lining up your first job. Lao Tse has said: "The journey of a thousand miles begins with one step." You should want to make sure that your first step will be well taken.

CHAPTER 15:

Family Finances

59 · A New Look at the Family and Its Money *

FRANCES LOMAS FELDMAN

> Money is not only a medium of exchange; it may also have many symbolic meanings, for example, of security or status. It may be the means of asserting power or dominance or of giving rewards or punishment. Money is here considered not in terms of what it will buy but in its psycho-socioeconomic meanings and their effect on family life.

THE WORLD we live in is characterized by continual change. There are technological advances, increasing population with shifting urbanization and explosive suburbanization movements, economic depressions and recessions, wars, and changing fashions and standards of living. One pivotal factor, however, remains constantly important: money. But never before in the history of western civilization has the word "money" meant so much to so many. Money is the medium of exchange, a means for distributing the vast and increasing outpouring of the goods and services of our economic system. Money is a symbol of status and achievement, often the measure for human values and dignity. This is truly the age of the economic man.

Economists have tended to view money as having an objective reality, a life of its own, isolated from the emotional and intellectual life of the human beings whom it was designed to serve. They have applied complicated mechanistic concepts, frequently expressed in elaborate mathe-

* *Journal of Home Economics*, 49 (December, 1957), 767–772. Reprinted by permission of the publisher and the author.

The author is Associate Professor in the School of Social Work, University of Southern California. The article draws on research carried on under Mrs. Feldman's direction by the Money Management Project of the Welfare Planning Council of the Los Angeles Region. She is the author of *The Family in a Money World* and has contributed articles to journals and books.

matical formulas, to describe objectively the flow and use of money. Recently, however, there has been a mounting awareness and emphasis on the importance of the so-called subjective aspects of money, on the unique significance of psychosocial influences. There is increasing cognizance that an essential ingredient in skillful working with people is the understanding of the objective and subjective influences which affect, and are the effect of, money—the understanding of the dynamics of the interactions in the socioeconomic and cultural climate in which the individual grows and develops.

The universality of money as a causative or symptomatic component in a strikingly high proportion of the problems and preoccupations of human beings in our culture is evidenced almost daily in the headlined stories in the public press. One reads about the distraught husband who kills his wife because of "arguments over finances," about the parent who solves his inability to provide for his children by ending their lives or by armed robbery. One reads about the divorce suit in which "stinginess" is offered as one justification for the action, or about the divorced wife petitioning for increased child support from the ex-spouse who has remarried and has another family to support.

The ironic humor of the many current cartoons with a money theme provides another barometer of the feelings of people in our society about money.

Money Management Study

How truly these news reports and cartoons reflect the general, wide concern about people and money was brought into sharp focus several years ago in the process of a study conducted by the Research Department of the Welfare Planning Council, Los Angeles Region, in a large tract community occupied by young middle-class families with relatively good incomes. The purpose of this study was to gather in this community, typical of mushrooming housing developments, some basic data concerning the nature of the problems and pressures as well as the kinds of services required in such communities. The researchers were impressed by the spontaneous frequency with which group and individual interviews disclosed problems and tensions wherein money emerged either as a cause or symptom. They were further impressed with the dearth of social work literature dealing specifically either with money management counseling in social agencies or with the role of this element which touches *everybody* and so often is a source of confusion and anxiety. It was from this study experience that the idea was developed that there be brought together the content knowledge that might help social workers and others engaged in money counseling to carry out this function more effectively. The Beneficial Finance System made a money grant to the Welfare Planning Council, and thus the Money Management Project came into being.

An early and essential step of the Money Management Project was to ascertain the nature and range of problems coming to the attention of social workers and other counselors, in which money was a factor, and to learn particularly from social work practitioners what kinds of material they believed would be of practical use to them in understanding and dealing with such problems. The next step was to direct the questions and comments which had arisen to specialists from various fields that have some concern with human behavior and money. These specialists from psychiatry, law, economics, home economics, sociology, anthropology, and social work searched their own disciplines for relevant, current information, which then was used to provide the basis for *The Family in a Money World*, recently released by the Family Service Association of America.

Out of the many important points to be considered about the family in a money world, only a few can be selected for consideration here. Without making a judgment as to their relative priority or importance, I have chosen some which I think will be of particular interest. I propose that a new look at people and their money be taken from the panoramic point from which we can, first, view the new look of the world we live in—a money world; second, see the new look of the American family in this money world; third, take a new look at the meanings and use of money in the cycle of family life; and, finally, take a new look at some ways of working with families whose problems contain money factors.

The Money World

In all civilized nations, money constitutes legal tender for the payment of debt and for the obtainment of those things which, though essential to life, are nevertheless limited in supply. The very universality of money means that people like to have money; it is a source of satisfaction. It has come to have value not only for what it will buy but for itself, for it represents power to buy or possess. For many individuals the possession of money connotes more than a rational tool used by rational man; it symbolizes not only economic but social and emotional security as well. A combination of external and internal circumstances determines how the individual obtains his income and how he spends it.

Until the economic depression of the 1930's, the income of families in the United States came primarily from four sources. Wages (including commissions, fees, and payments for farm and other labor and services rendered) formed by far the largest. A considerably smaller, but nevertheless substantial, source was rents (including all payments that owners of fixed resources such as land and buildings receive for their use). The third source was interest payments, and the fourth source of income was profits or dividends from business investments.

As we moved from depression through war and into postwar periods, and as government in each period accepted increasing responsibility for economic security for individuals and groups, a fifth source of income to families, transfer payments, has assumed growing importance. Transfer payments—income for which no service is currently rendered (such as unemployment and old age insurance under the provisions of the Social Security Act, government life insurance benefits, military bonuses, public assistance)—in 1955 accounted for more than 5 per cent of the national income received by families, a close second to personal interest and dividends which constituted about 8 per cent of the income received by families! [1]

There has been not only a marked change in the source of national income received by families but a steady and perceptible change in amounts of personal income and attitudes about its use. There has been a startling growth of American middle-income and middle-rich classes. The number of consumer units (spending units) with incomes in excess of $4,000, after taxes, increased sharply between 1941 and 1956.[2] In 1929, fewer than 20 per cent of consumer units had annual incomes of $4,000 to $10,000. Now almost 50 per cent are in this range. Even if one adjusts for the changes in cost of living, there is an increase in the average real income of families and unattached adults of almost 47 per cent in 1955 over 1929. (Adjusted in terms of 1955 dollars, the average family personal income before taxes in 1929 was $3,760; in 1955, $5,520.)

In considering the rise in average income and the real increase in purchasing power of the dollar, however, it is essential to bear in mind the fact that, while experts disagree on the proportion, a sizable part of the current average income represents overtime earnings. Changes in production schedules or other economic factors can quickly result in an effective reduction of family income, income perhaps already committed to meet expenditures.

It should be noted that this increase in average income is family income, not individual income. It points to the growing numbers of family units containing two or more earners. It points to the fact that even though an unprecedented number of married women entered the labor market to meet wartime needs for increased labor forces, the number has continued steadily upward, and the prospect is that this trend will continue, for there

---

[1] *Survey of Current Business,* Biennial Edition, 1955, pp. 4, 197.
[2] 1956 Survey of Consumer Finances. *Federal Reserve Bulletin,* 42, No. 6 (June, 1956), pp. 559–567.

is strong evidence that our country's dynamic technology—although it may contribute to the obsolescence of certain skills—contributes to the creation of a market for more and *new* skills.

The increases have not been limited to average family income, number of household members employed, or number of married women in industry. The goods and services available per family in this country likewise have increased. The rise in levels of living is reflected in the shorter number of hours of work required each day in order to satisfy the basic needs and provide an increasing proportion of luxuries. It is mirrored in the increased amount of goods consumed and the changing buying habits of the American people. It is seen in the volume of sales of goods and services designed for leisure-time activities. It is evident in the improvement of housing conditions, in the fact that 55 per cent of all families now own their homes, in the rapidly expanding number of car owners, and in a myriad of other ways.

The last several decades have witnessed a new way of life for the average American. Through the use of consumer credit, durable goods have been accessible to those able to accumulate enough reserve for a down payment and who can budget their income for spending, facilitating an upward movement in living standards. This new way of life—buying today, paying later —marks some modification in attitudes toward the place of money in family living. It marks, too, some movement away from our New England heritage, namely, that the lower middle class gratifies its wants immediately, and that the middle class postpones gratification of its desires. It recognizes a changing relationship between people and government: a dependence on creation of controls when economic or social crises indicate the necessity for them. Here, then, is the climate of the money world in which we live.

New Look of the Family

Now let us glance briefly at the new look of the American family in this money world and highlight a very few of the meanings and uses of money in different phases of the cycle of family life. For as there is in the life of the individual a cycle of growth, development, maturation, and decline, so is there a cycle in the life of the family. It is a cycle marked by the stages of marriage, the birth of children, their emancipation, return of the parents to the childless state, and the death of each spouse.

Younger marriages in this country are much more frequent than they used to be, with a noticeable trend toward younger men marrying at an earlier age and marrying women whose ages are closer to theirs. Many factors may contribute to this trend: ease of obtaining employment both by men and by married women, imminence of conscription into military service, willingness of middle-class parents to continue financial support of young married people in college.

To the puzzlement of the demographers, the average size of the American family is expanding. This is a singularly significant fact when viewed with respect to a parallel and previously mentioned fact: the steadily increasing number of married women in industry. It may be conjectured that women with more children are able to care for their larger families and to work outside the home because of technological advances which facilitate household operation and supervision; or that the very size of the family necessitates the mother's employment to increase the family income; or that she prefers work in industry for monetary recognition to work in the home. Whatever the reason, this is a part of the new look of the American family.

Parents, at the time of the birth of their last child, are on the average much younger than was previously true. The children marry or otherwise leave the home when the parents are relatively young. And the period between the departure of the children and the further dissolution of the family because of the death of the parents has lengthened markedly. This now averages 20 years.

Money and Quality of Family Life

The presence or absence of financial resources in the various phases of the cycle of family life greatly influences the quality of the family's physical standards and well-being. The attitudes of the family members toward and about money, and the way they utilize it, has import for the quality of their relationships with each other and with the society in which we live.

The individuals entering into a new sharing experience as marital partners bring attitudes, impressions, and expectations created throughout years of separate existence in a money world. They also use money in a variety of ways in marital problems. Personal ingrained habits of spending are often used in instances of discordant marital relationships as a point of attack by the partner, or viewed as an attack, even though this is irrational. For example, a husband may be very controlling or dominating with regard to his wife, rigidly holding her to a tight budget or even doling out an "allowance" in small amounts. Actually, this may for him be a culturally determined role. He may come from a home in which the father, like others in his social circle, was the authoritative, thrifty provider, as responsible for the financial management of his home as for his business. On the other hand, this controlled disbursement of money may be a measure of the husband's recollections about a hungry youth in a period of economic depression and insecurity. To certain neurotic husbands, money may be an unconscious symbol of masculinity and power. The wife's retaliation against this kind of behavior by her husband, irrespective of the factors underlying his actions, may take several forms. She may spend money wastefully as an expression of hostility toward him, or even at an unconscious level to maintain a dominant role in her own right. She may handle the situation simply by making no effort to operate within the budget he has prescribed. To his use of limiting her funds as a way of keeping his mate in a dependent relation to him, the wife may respond by setting limits of her own. She may deny his basic psychological dependency needs—expressed, perhaps, through gambling or excessive use of money for alcohol—in charges of inadequate support and by refusal to feed him properly.

Considerable tension may be aroused because of the wife's working outside the home. Problems on this score are minimal if there are common goals understood and accepted by both marital partners and common handling of money. Many problems grow out of the environmental economic situation. There may be, for example, an unexpected or unpredictable loss of job, or a reduction in income, with neither of these related to the ability or capacity of the husband to perform at an adequate level in the job which he has, in fact, liked. Or the nature of the husband's work may involve considerable traveling. But if the marital partners have achieved a satisfactory joint ego ideal, are reasonably well-integrated personalities, they move together toward as effective an adjustment to this situation as is necessary. They may adopt measures for financial retrenchment until more income becomes available; they may utilize personal or other resources to tide them over; they may take steps to find other or more satisfactory jobs, or, if the latter is not practical, they adapt themselves to the reality limitations and work out acceptable compromises within these limitations.

The immature, hostile, or generally unhappy person confronted by these problems of environmental origin is hard pressed to work through a satisfactory solution or adjustment to the situation. If, further, the spouse is immature or demanding, their separate and combined feelings serve to exaggerate the negative aspects of their partnership and to build discord.

Attitudes Developed

It is in the beginning phase of the cycle of family life that the first tests of the quality of the partnership are made. The kind of relationship which the husband and wife establish, the nature of its strengths, the depths of its weaknesses will largely determine the quality of the family relationships which will follow. Marital harmony has many qualities. Marital discord takes many shapes. If they are not understood and alleviated or resolved in the beginning family phase before the addition of children obscures and complicates it, the entire family structure is placed in jeopardy.

The adjustments inherent in this new relationship of marriage become more complex with the arrival of children and the naturally attendant family expenses. As the family and the family needs expand, the availability of income and its use take on increasing meaning. Significantly, while the maximum size of the family (two or three children are under the age of 18) usually is reached when the father is between 35 and 45 years, the maximum family income generally is attained when the father is between 45 and 54 years old.[3]

Marriage, parenthood, and all relationships within the family are affected by the inescapable psycho-socioeconomic demands in a money world. Individual attitudes are developed within the framework of each one's own immediate family as he grows from infancy through childhood and adolescence and is graduated into an adult world with adult responsibilities. The child's experiences during his growing-up years, the economic and social position of his family, the attitudes and feelings of the family about money and social position, the way money is handled with the child, inevitably will color the formulation of his own complex attitudes.

For example, children are particularly sensitive to parental anxieties about money. They sense the tension which is created when the father brings home a smaller pay check or is laid off. They quickly become aware of dissension centered around money matters. Their own feelings are aroused when one parent depreciates the other in terms of the management of money. An aura of awe and mystery surrounds money; it has importance for the parents and involves the children's own feelings of happiness and unhappiness, security and insecurity.

Meanings and Use of Money

Money in our American culture is inevitably equated with security, love, deprivation, and achievement, and permeates the child's life very early. But some differentials exist within the culture. In the working-class group, he may know feelings of insecurity when the parents are worried about money, but he is also fairly clear about the fact that the insecurity is associated with money and not with his relationship to his parents. This reduces the confusion which otherwise arises, since the reality is one he can understand.

There is confusion of a different kind in the white collar, middle-income

---

[3] Paul C. Glick, The Life Cycle of the Family. *Marriage and Family Living*, 17 (February 1955), pp. 3–9.

group. Here money is used to show love, approval, punishment, and deprivation. Parents tend to conceal money difficulties from their children. Material acquisitions are seen by the parents as signs of achievement, success, status. The young dependent child translates this into money as a symbol of love or the denial of love. Parents may express their negative or rejecting feelings toward the child by material overindulgence as a means of handling guilt. This also is true in many situations where both parents are working, particularly if the mother is working to buy "nice things for the home." Guilt over this is often handled by over-giving, even to the very young child.

Because of their own personality constellation, parents sometimes are unable to meet the child's needs through their relationship to him. Money may then become the substitute for love and approval, the instrument for manipulation and control, the weapon for punishment. The use of money as a bargaining agent to secure the child's cooperation in doing his share of the family tasks is a false substitute for helping him achieve a sense of belonging and of his own importance as both a receiving and a contributing member of the family. Bribing the child with money to put forth more effort in his school work or to practice his music lessons sets up false stimuli for achievement and emphasizes the reward rather than his personal development and the increased satisfaction which comes with accomplishment. Depriving the child of money in order to enforce atonement for a misdeed or carelessness or for an injury to another is likewise inappropriate, since the payment of money cannot in fact compensate for such actions and may lead the perpetrator to believe that any kind of conduct is acceptable as long as he can pay for it.

The inappropriate use of money or its substitution for basic essentials in the parent-child relationship obscures the child's view of the value of money; the real relationship of money to life and living is clouded for the adult he becomes. This creates for him a real handicap in working out financial problems since very often the money problem is symptomatic of the deeper emotional problem which finds expression in the individual's use of money.

During the growing-up years of the children, the pressures are heavy to meet standards in the peer groups, both of the children and of the parents. Expenses tend to increase steadily through the stormy period of adolescence until the children have finished their education. After this, a plateau is reached where a respite is available from the cares and costs of child-rearing, and where the opportunity can be taken by parents to make provision for their retirement. The normal achievement of this plateau is by no means easy. The problems in its achievement may have been compounded by dependence on the family of maternal or paternal parents, by the breaking of the family with, perhaps, remarriage of either or both parents, and their establishment of new families.

The effectiveness of planning and managing in this new phase of the cycle of family life is a test of the quality of planning and managing that characterized earlier phases. It can be permeated with a sense of real satisfaction with many years of healthy living, of watching children grow into useful, contributing members of society, of a future still to be lived. Or it can be shot through with anxiety about the long years ahead, fear about using savings that cannot be replaced, conflict about being a burden on children who have their own growing families to support. Certainly these worries are not unrealistic even among many elderly couples who have been planful about their years of retirement. Not long ago the life expectancy of persons reaching their sixty-fifth year was three years—now it is thirteen. There have been concomitant rises in cost of living, and particularly medical and health costs, so that lifetime savings do not go as far as had been expected. Many understandable reasons may make it difficult for adult children to provide either funds or living space for elderly parents, even were this desired or desirable.

All too often, family roles are reversed when the older person or couple becomes partially dependent or totally so on younger members. This is very threatening to both. The older person's dependency conflicts are rearoused. He becomes demanding, hostile, or deprives himself rather than ask for help. He feels inferior, has lost his status as a parent and therefore as a person who has personal worth and integrity. The increased dependency and lowered self-esteem lead to guilt and depression; his behavior may seem decidedly childish.

Working with Families

Social workers and others who carry on money counseling with families have a responsibility for understanding the economic climate in which the American family lives and the psycho-socio-cultural factors which influence values and behavior. The counselor must have knowledge about the individual seeking help, for understanding whether, in our money economy, his patterns of spending and saving and his attitudes about money and its uses are rational or whether they are irrational and geared to meet neurotic rather than realistic needs. A concomitant to such understanding is the recognition by the counselor of his own attitudes and reactions to money. An example of the importance of this lies in the growing emphasis, either in regulation or legislation, upon ADC (Aid to Dependent Children) mothers' taking employment. Social workers and many public welfare administrators have expressed concern over this trend. Yet in light of the previously mentioned increasing pattern in our culture of mothers who are not dependent upon public assistance moving into industry, is it a part of the normal reality we desire for dependent families that—other factors being equal—ADC mothers accept responsibility for at least partial self-support? Or is this a normal reality from which they should be shielded because hard-earned tradition has stressed the unindividualized desirability of mothers' remaining in the home with their children?

The importance of individualization in the counseling process within the limits of the social agency, be it public or private, requires no emphasis; but some new consideration, for example, should be given to the place of money in the growth and development of the adolescent in the family dependent upon public assistance: the adult nature of the responsibility thrust upon the working adolescent to contribute his earnings to the maintenance of his family while financial planning with the family relegates him to the role of the child too young to participate in the planning.

Those who have responsibility for developing or adapting standard or other budgets must constantly be alert to changes in standards as the level of our economy rises. They must recognize, too, that employment of women also changes our attitudes about the importance of their simplifying their household tasks by purchasing automatic equipment usually on installment purchase plan. Installment buying is now a part of our culture and can be used creatively or destructively; it can no longer be viewed solely in terms either of poor personal management or excessive gratification of needs and desires.

Only a few of many ways have been touched upon here in which policy, practice, and concepts might be re-examined in light of the changing family in a changing economic system. Of paramount importance in this re-examination is the recognition and acceptance of a basic philosophic assumption that characterizes western civilization and our democracy: the positive identification of change and progress and adaptation to new conditions.

CHAPTER 16:

Interfaith Marriages

60 · Attitudes of College Students toward Inter-Faith Marriage *

ALFRED J. PRINCE

People tend to marry others with backgrounds like their own, of the same religious faith, race, and socioeconomic status. A minority of people, however, cross cultural and racial lines. When they do they may face special problems of adjustment of beliefs, customs, values, and attitudes in order to bring harmony into the marriage. The most frequent type of intermarriage in the United States occurs between people of markedly different religious faiths. This article gives the attitudes of more than a thousand students in one state university to dating and marrying persons of other religious faiths than their own, some of their experiences with interreligious dating, and their opinions as to how their parents would react if they married outside their faith.

THE PURPOSE of this study was to find out how young people of marriageable age—students attending the state university in Idaho, in particular—feel about inter-faith marriages. More specifically, the study was designed to seek answers to the following questions: (1) Are young people willing to marry outside their religious faith? (2) Will they do so only under certain conditions? If so, what are some of these conditions? (3) Are they willing to adopt the religion of their chosen mate, if by so doing, it will make marriage possible? (4) What are some of the reasons young people give why they do not want to marry outside their faith? (5) Is there any relationship between a person's expressed attitudes toward an inter-faith

* *Coordinator,* 5 (September, 1956), 11–23. This article is based on the author's unpublished master's thesis of the same title, completed at the University of Idaho in 1955. Reprinted by permission of the publisher and the author.
The biographical sketch of the author is given with article 39.

marriage and the attitudes he thinks his parents hold toward such a marriage? These are a few of the questions this paper hopes to throw light upon.

The data were obtained by pretested questionnaires from students living on the University of Idaho campus in January, 1955. Questionnaires were distributed to the students in their living groups following the evening meal. Questionnaires were completed by approximately two-thirds of the students, some 810 males and 483 females.

TABLE 1: Attitudes of College Students toward Dating, Going Steady, and Marrying outside Their Religious Faith *

Attitude	Male (N = 779)		Female (N = 475)		Total (N = 1252)	
	Yes Per Cent	No Per Cent	Yes Per Cent	No Per Cent	Yes Per Cent	No Per Cent
Would Date outside Religious Faith	97	3	97	3	97	3
Would "Go Steady" outside Religious Faith	80	20	72	28	77	23
Would Marry outside Religious Faith	62	37	52	48	59	41

* The 41 students in the study who stated that they had "no church affiliation" are not included in this table. With one exception, these 41 students would "date," "go steady with," and "marry" a Catholic, Protestant, or Jewish person, or a person with "no church affiliation." One student would date and go steady with a person in any of the aforesaid categories, but he would marry only a person with "no church affiliation."

As shown in Table 1, 97 per cent of the students reported a willingness to date outside their faith. Ninety-five per cent would also date a person who had no church affiliation.

Approximately one student in four would not "go steady" with someone of a religious faith different from his own. One student in eight would not "go steady" with a person who had no church affiliation. Girls were less willing to "go steady" outside their faith than were boys.

When it came to the question of marriage, 59 per cent of the students stated that they would cross religious lines and marry and 41 per cent would not. One student in four was opposed to marrying a person who had no church affiliation. Girls were also less willing to marry outside their faith than were boys.

One girl wrote:

My main objection to inter-faith marriages does not reflect any prejudice against either faith. It, to me, represents the possibility of an unstable family —not necessarily separation and divorce possibilities, but lack of an important spiritual bond. I feel that children are given an unfair chance even if I could bring my child up in my own faith. It could raise doubt and wonder when my husband and I went to separate churches. If the child wanted to go with one parent, then the other, he may end up indifferent to and/or confused by his own religion.

Another commented:

We have had two mixed marriages in our closely knit family circle—one, Jewish-Protestant, and the other, Protestant-Catholic—both have proven unsuccessful. Therefore, I could not enter such a relationship with much confidence, since both marriages failed because of religious differences. I am engaged to a Protestant; and if by chance he turned Catholic, our engagement would be broken. I have no confidence in the possible success of inter-faith marriages.

Another wrote:

I know that it is possible to have a happy and successful inter-faith marriage, but I think it depends on how strongly a person believes in his faith. Myself, I could never be happy with a man of a different faith from my own.

Another commented:

I can get along with people of faiths different from mine, but I could not build a successful marriage. Religion enters the picture too much.

When the data in Table 1 were related to the religious affiliation of the students, it was found that almost all Protestant and Catholic students would date someone of a religious faith different from their own. Only three per cent of the Protestant students and only one Catholic student would not date a person of a different faith.[1]

One Protestant student explained to the writer why she would date a Catholic but not a Jew as follows:

It is a result of the social pressures caused in my community. All Jewish friends of mine are banned from the clubs, etc. to which my parents and I

---

[1] The two Jewish students in the study would date, go steady with, and marry someone outside their faith. The eight students whose religious faith was classified as "other" (i. e., Greek Orthodox, etc.) were all willing to marry outside their faith.

belong. Therefore, it would cause embarrassment to both parties if it were not possible for us to attend dinner, etc. together.

More Catholic students than Protestants were willing to "go steady" with someone of a different faith. The percentages were 90 per cent and 75 per cent, respectively.

Catholic students were also more willing to marry across religious lines than were Protestant students. Only 29 per cent of the Catholic students reported that they would not marry outside their faith but more than 40 per cent of the Protestant students reported that they would not be a partner in an inter-faith marriage. It was also interesting to note that 70 per cent of the Catholic students were willing to marry a Protestant but only 54 per cent of the Protestant students were willing to marry a Catholic.

Thus, Catholic students were not only more willing to marry outside their faith than Protestant students were, but they were also more willing to marry a Protestant than Protestant students were willing to marry a Catholic. At the same time, however, more Catholic students wanted their mate to adopt their religion and/or to agree to have the children brought up in their faith than did Protestant students. A large percentage of Protestant and Catholic students—33 per cent of each group—stated that they would marry a Jewish person. Would similar results be obtained if this study is repeated at an eastern university having a larger percentage of Jewish students?

Students who attended church infrequently tended to be more willing to cross religious lines and marry than were students who attended church regularly. Of the 453 students who did not attend church or attended less than once a month, more than 75 per cent reported that they would marry outside their faith. On the other hand, of the 794 students who attended church once a month or more less than 50 per cent would marry a person of a different faith.

Table 2 summarizes the attitudes of the students toward inter-faith marriages. It will be seen that a slightly larger percentage of girls than the boys checked statements one and two. Both of these statements require a condition to marriage. On the other hand, but 17 per cent of the girls checked statement three which does not require a condition to marriage while 30 per cent of the boys checked the same statement. It appears, therefore, that girls were less willing to marry outside their faith unless the mate adopted their religion and/or agreed to have the children brought up in their faith than were boys.

In view of the foregoing statement, it is interesting to note in Table 2 that a somewhat higher percentage of girls were willing to adopt the re-

TABLE 2: Present Feelings of College Students toward Inter-Faith Marriage

Statement	Male	Female	Total Students Checking Statement
	Per Cent	Per Cent	Per Cent
1. I would marry outside of my religious faith if my mate were willing to change his (or her) faith to mine.	22	23	22
2. I would marry outside of my religious faith without requiring that my mate change his (or her) faith to mine, but he (or she) would have to be willing to bring up our children according to my faith.	25	28	26
3. I would marry outside of my religious faith without requiring that my mate change his (or her) faith to mine, and I would not object to our children being brought up in his (or her) faith.	30	17	26
4. In order to make marriage possible with my chosen mate, I would be willing to adopt his (or her) faith.	6	9	7
5. I would not marry outside of my religious faith.	17	23	19
Total	100	100	100

ligious faith of their mate than were boys. Baber [2] and Hoover [3] also found that girls are more opposed to inter-faith marriages than boys. Baber found that more boys were willing to adopt the spouse's faith than were girls.[4] Nine per cent of the men in his study were willing to adopt the mate's

---

[2] Ray Baber, *Marriage and the Family* (New York: McGraw-Hill Book Company, Inc., 1939), p. 149.

[3] Harry F. Hoover, *Attitudes of High School Students toward Mixed Marriage* (Washington, D.C.: Catholic University of America Press, 1950), p. 52.

[4] This tendency also appeared to be true for the remaining 51 students in the study who were not included in Table 3 and 4.

faith; but only five per cent of the women were willing to do so. In the present study, the percentages obtained were almost the reverse, with six per cent of the boys and nine per cent of the girls stating that they were willing to adopt their mate's religious faith.]

No significant differences were found in the responses of the lower and upper classmen to the statements in Table 2. However, students who attended church regularly tended to check statements one or two more often than did students who attended church infrequently.

As noted earlier, more Catholic than Protestant students reported a willingness to marry outside their faith. The question now arises: Are Catholic students also more likely to require the mate to adopt their faith than are Protestant students? Analysis of the data showed the answer to be yes. Seven out of ten Catholic students checked statements one or two. (See statements in Table 2.) Only four out of ten Protestant students checked these same statements. Furthermore, over 50 per cent of the Catholic students checked statement two, i. e., they would marry outside their faith if the mate agreed to have the children brought up in their religion but slightly less than 25 per cent of the Protestant students checked this same statement.

Although Catholic students appeared more willing to cross religious lines and marry than Protestant students did, Catholic students also expressed a desire for their spouses to adopt Catholicism and/or by insisting that the children be brought up in the Catholic faith. For example:

> Regarding whether I would marry outside my Catholic faith, my husband-to-be would have to consent to let the children be brought up in my faith and not interfere with my religious practices and beliefs. However, I would never insist that he alter his own ideas on religion should he be willing to agree to the above.

Another commented:

> I approve of inter-faith marriages; but in my case, I would want the party to be a Catholic or become a convert. However, I would still marry a non-Catholic providing the children were brought up in the Catholic religion.

Another wrote:

> I would marry a person of another faith if that person would change his faith to mine. I am going steady with a Protestant boy and we have discussed this problem and he has agreed to adopt my religion before we get married.

A Catholic male student wrote:

> A mixed marriage has two strikes against it from the start. Difference in religion is a spawning place for much friction. However, my marriage would

depend on the girl, not her religion, provided the children are brought up in my faith.

One male student who was seriously considering marrying a Catholic stated that he would not marry her unless he could first accept the teachings of the Catholic Church. He wrote:

> ✓ At present I, a Protestant, intend to marry a Catholic. I am studying the Catholic beliefs, but if I find that I can't accept them, I don't believe I'll marry her. She is a strong Catholic; and if I were to marry her without being able to believe in her religion, there would almost surely be undesirable results later in our marriage.

Another student commented:

> ✓ I was pinned to a boy who is Catholic and I am Protestant. For over a year, I went to church with him and tried to understand and accept the Catholic religion. I seemed to be unable to do so; thus, our relationship was broken.

To summarize briefly the data in Table 2, (1) slightly more than one-fourth of the students would cross religious lines and marry (apparently, without requiring any of the conditions specified in the statements in Table 2), (2) more than one student in five would consider an inter-faith marriage if the prospective mate would adopt the student's religion, (3) slightly more than one-fourth of the students would consider an inter-faith marriage if the children are brought up in their faith, (4) approximately one student in five would not marry outside his faith (even if the prospective mate were willing to adopt the student's faith or to allow the children to be brought up in the student's religion, and (5) seven per cent of the students were willing to adopt the religious faith of their mate, if by so doing, it would make marriage possible.

At this point, brief mention should be made of some of the reasons given by students as to why they do not want to marry outside their faith. Students were asked to check one or more of the following reasons: (1) Because of my religious conviction; (2) Because of parental objection; (3) Because I believe there is a probability that such a marriage would be unsuccessful; and (4) Other reasons (explain).

Briefly, it was found that 50 per cent of the students who were opposed to inter-faith marriages checked reason number three, i. e., "because I believe there is a probability that such a marriage would be unsuccessful." The other reasons, in order of frequency checked, were: one, two, and four. The majority of the students who checked category four wrote that they did not want to marry outside their faith because they foresaw difficulty arising over the religious training of the children. One student wrote:

The biggest objection to inter-faith marriage to me is the problem of raising the children in a religious faith. The parents often can agree which church each wishes to attend, but rarely can they agree on which church the children should attend.

Another commented:

I would not marry into the Catholic church because there would be the question of having to raise the children in the Catholic religion. Once they were Catholic, it would be almost impossible for them to choose freely any other religion.

One student whose parents are of different faiths wrote:

I, myself, don't believe in an inter-faith marriage particularly because of the case in my own family. I feel very strongly on this subject. It seems that when young people marry they only see themselves, and being in love, they don't seem to realize at the time how much religion may or can mean to their marriage in later years, and the trouble it may cause, especially when children arrive.

Another commented:

I am the result of a mixed marriage. It has worked out fairly well as my father belongs to no church and my mother had complete control of our

TABLE 3: Students Who Would Marry outside Their Faith and How They Think Their Parents Would Feel if They Attempted such a Marriage

Students Who Would Marry outside Faith	Both Parents Would Approve	Only One Parent Would Approve	Both Parents Would Disapprove	No Response	Total
	Per Cent	Per Cent	Per Cent	Per Cent	Per Cent
Protestant Students (N–1053)					
Would marry a Catholic person (N–565)	68	11	16	5	100
Would marry a Jewish person (N–359)	60	9	20	11	100
Would marry a person with no church affiliation (N–846)	82	6	5	7	100
Catholic Students (N–189)					
Would marry a Protestant person (N–133)	76	16	4	4	100
Would marry a Jewish person (N–57)	69	12	7	12	100
Would marry a person with no church affiliation (N–114)	70	9	11	10	100

education. Unless I change my view, I would not marry a person who is not a Catholic because I might be at a disadvantage in educating my children and because a major item like religion can cause undue friction.

This study examined the relationship between a person's expressed attitudes toward an inter-faith marriage and the attitudes he *thinks* his parents hold toward such a marriage. Students who would marry outside their faith felt also that their parents would approve an interfaith marriage. On the other hand, students who were opposed to an inter-faith marriage also felt that their parents would disapprove if they married outside their faith. As seen in Table 3, 68 per cent of the Protestant students who would marry a Catholic felt that both parents would approve the marriage, and 16 per cent felt that both their parents would disapprove. Similarly, 76 per cent of the Catholic students who would marry a Protestant felt that both their parents would approve the marriage, but only four per cent felt that both parents would disapprove.

In contrast, Table 4 shows that students who would not marry outside their faith also felt that their parents would *disapprove* an inter-faith marriage. Only a small percentage of them felt that their parents would approve such a marriage. It will be seen in Table 4 that 34 per cent of the Catholic students who would not marry a Protestant felt that both their

TABLE 4: Students Who Would Not Marry outside Their Faith and How They Think Their Parents Would Feel if They Attempted Such a Marriage

Students Who Would Marry outside Faith	Both Parents Would Approve	Only One Parent Would Approve	Both Parents Would Disapprove	No Response	Total
	Per Cent	Per Cent	Per Cent	Per Cent	Per Cent
Protestant Students (N–1053)					
Would not marry a Catholic person (N–482)	26	10	59	5	100
Would not marry a Jewish person (N–690)	17	7	69	7	100
Would not marry a person with no church affiliation (N–205)	28	11	55	6	100
Catholic Students (N–189)					
Would not marry a Protestant person (N–56)	43	16	34	7	100
Would not marry a Jewish person (N–131)	17	5	70	8	100
Would not marry a person with no church affiliation (N–75)	23	8	60	9	100

parents would disapprove the marriage; but 43 per cent of them felt that both parents would approve. Perhaps Catholic students are more apt to feel that as long as their mate is willing to adopt the Catholic faith and/or is willing to agree to have the children brought up in the Catholic religion, their parents will not disapprove if they marry outside their faith.

One should keep in mind, however, that the data in Tables 3 and 4 show only what the students *think* their parents' feelings are toward inter-faith marriages. Some students who answered the question, of course, knew their parents' attitudes toward inter-faith marriages. On the other hand, some, perhaps, had never heard their parents express any attitudes for or against inter-faith marriages but they assumed that their parents would disapprove of an inter-faith marriage for some reason or another. The point, however, is that there appears to be a relationship between a student's expressed attitudes toward an inter-faith marriage and the attitudes he *thinks* his parents hold toward such a marriage. And, in the final analysis, it is perhaps the attitude a person *thinks* his parents have toward a particular subject that more than likely will influence his own attitudes toward the same subject. Many students commented on their parents' attitudes toward interfaith marriages. One student wrote:

> I put that my parents would disapprove of my marrying outside my faith, but they would not forbid it. They would, however, discourage it.

Another commented:

> Both of my parents would disapprove of my marrying a Jewish person, not because of prejudice but because of little knowledge of the faith. My father would disapprove of a Catholic because he cannot agree with their philosophy of faith.

Another wrote:

> My parents would permit my marrying almost anyone with whom I was deeply in love, providing I retain my faith and the children are brought up in the Catholic faith.

A Catholic male student wrote:

> I have no doubt that my parents would have preferences, probably Catholic. But they would not disapprove of any other religion, as long as the children were brought up Catholic.

The final excerpt, written by a student in her junior year, shows the pressure some parents will exert on their children to prevent them from marrying someone of a different religious faith. She wrote:

> The past few years, I went with a Catholic boy. When I informed my parents that we were pinned, they refused to let me announce it, and insisted

that I return the pin immediately. Because of my parents' strong objections, we cancelled the announcement of the pinning, but because we were both very much in love, I secretly kept his pin. I kept on going out with the boy and for this reason my parents almost had me transferred to a private Protestant college in the East.

The fellow was willing to give up his religion and join my church. My own religious convictions would not allow for any other decision, but my parents still objected—saying that he would eventually return to the Catholic faith.

This problem caused much unhappiness for everyone concerned. In time, I developed an ulcer from worrying about it. I transferred schools, thinking that it would help me in thinking out matters more clearly—hoping I would forget the boy in time. I don't know whether this has helped or not, but I do know that I will never go through this same religious problem again. . . .

In conclusion, the findings in the present study show clearly that young people of marriageable age are well-aware of some of the problems that accompany inter-faith marriages. Although these students expressed a liberal view toward such marriages, they themselves would marry outside their faith only under certain conditions.

61 · *The Problem of Mixed Marriage—and the Solution* *

JAMES A. PIKE

After reviewing some of the barriers that mixed marriage presents to the growth of religious unity within a family, the author outlines point by point a way for the couple before marriage to examine the two religions in question and determine whether they can come to sincere agreement on religious beliefs. This procedure, as he points out elsewhere, depends upon the readiness of each person, regardless of his religious affiliation, to try to see both his own and the other's religion with some objectivity.

---

* James A. Pike, *If You Marry outside Your Faith* (New York: Harper & Brothers, 1954), pp. 102–112, omitting footnote, and 118–122. Copyright 1954 by Harper & Brothers. Reprinted by permission of the publisher.

The author holds the degree of Bachelor of Divinity from the Union Theological Seminary. He is active in many religious organizations and has written a number of books, among them *Beyond Anxiety* and the one from which this selection was chosen. At the time of writing *If You Marry outside Your Faith*, he was Dean of the Cathedral of St. John the Divine and a member of the faculty of Columbia University.

SUFFICIENT has been said to suggest the idea that a mixed marriage is not a good thing. Let us proceed briefly to summarize why:

1. A mixed marriage lacks a commonly held and articulated basis of ideas, purposes, and motivations.

2. A mixed marriage lacks the resources of marital health provided by common worship and common involvement in the most significant of all possible interests.

3. A mixed marriage robs the parents of a common relationship with their children on the deepest level, namely of spiritual life.

4. In a mixed marriage one of the parents—and sometimes both—are robbed of the opportunity of bringing to their children the best spiritual heritage that he or she knows, being barred from discharging this most important aspect of parental responsibility.

5. A mixed marriage (if one of the parties is a Roman Catholic) disenables one of the parties from following his conscience in regard to the planning of parenthood.

The "Common Ideals" Solution

As devastating as all of these factors—when marshaled—may look to an outsider, they may well not be strong enough to down the hopes of those whose love is strong and genuine. So there is generally a "last-ditch" improvisation designed to present a hopeful prospect. This particular improvisation is heard on the lips of "mixed" couples of all types.

Case 16. We have plenty of common ground under our feet: We have our love, we have our ideals; we know what we want out of life, we think that we can bring fine things to our children. And all this though we are of different religions.

Taking this doubtless sincere statement at its face value, what it really means is this: We have a common religion, the particular religious labels we bear are secondary to us. Though the couple might find difficulty in stating what these "ideals" are, difficulty in defining what the purposes of life are, if they really mean that Roman Catholicism, Presbyterianism, Judaism, or what not, is not to be the guiding norm of their lives nor the heritage given their children, then there are several important questions for them to consider: Is the new religion which they have invented ("our ideals," "our purposes," "fine things") really profound and meaningful, and will it abide not only during the sunny periods of life but during the crises? In adopting a view of life which is in effect a rejecting or subordination of their own religious heritages, do they have a really better way of life than these heritages represent? In what religious ceremony for their marriage and with what continuity of worship during their marriage (and with their children) will they appropriately express and deepen these convictions?

The True Solution

In most cases these questions cannot be answered satisfactorily. But nevertheless in the rebellion which this attitude expresses, and in their desire to do something new and creative in order to provide a common basis for the marriage, the couple is feeling after what is in fact the true solution, and it is the purpose of this chapter to present this solution.

Let us first begin by asking this question: Why are people what they are religiously? More often than not people are what they are because of what they were born. Now of all the reasons to hold to a particular religious faith this is the least convincing. Actually it would have been quite possible for the couple under consideration to have been born "totem-pole" worshipers: the fact that they were born such would not prove the validity of their position. The fact that one's parents are of a particular religious faith proves little also. One's parents can be wrong—and in fact most people of marriageable age have already decided that their parents are wrong in a number of particulars. So why not religiously? This is a good question to ask under any circumstances as a young person approaches adult life, but it is an especially good question to ask at the time of marriage. For now a new unit of society is being created and one which will be autonomous to a considerable degree. In the Bible which Roman Catholics and other Christians alike read is this word: "A man shall leave father or mother and cleave to his wife." Next to God and one's religious loyalty, loyalty to one's spouse is the first loyalty. Parents come second; and after the children are born, the children come second and the parents are third in the priority scale of allegiance. (Were this a general book on marriage counseling this point would be stressed for several pages.)

The solution, in a nutshell, is this: each of the parties, forgetting what he or she was born and forgetting what his parents are, should rethink his or her religious position in terms of what each really believes and what Church most nearly represents that actual belief. Naturally the religious allegiances in which the two are now actually involved should be given serious consideration in the study, but the search need not be limited to them. If it so happens that both parties can come to convictions which are represented by the same Church allegiance then there will be no mixed marriage. And that is the end of the problem.

It is important at the outset to state what the above paragraph does *not* mean. It does not mean that one should seek to persuade himself of the truth of the other's position or yield to it in order to simplify things. This is to make one of the parties into an adjective and leave the other a noun, and in fact to deify one of the two parties. This subjugation of the spirit of one to the other is bound to have difficult psychological consequences in all aspects of the marriage—beyond the question of religion proper. If, however, this honest reconsideration leads both to conviction as to a faith that happens to be already that of one of the two parties, both should have the humility to make possible the conversion of the heretofore outsider to this faith without any sense of having "yielded" to the other. In no case should one yield to the other; both should yield to the claims of truth as they have worked it out through honest study, soul searching and decision. Any other solution does violence to the integrity of one or the other of the parties. Too easy a victory here will be paid for in the end.

The problem for mixed marriages in which one of the parties is a Roman Catholic—to put it in the most painful but blunt manner—is this: If the non-Roman party declines to sign the antenuptial agreement and the marriage is performed by other than a Roman Catholic priest, the Roman Catholic is excommunicated and loses his religious *pou sto*. If the Protestant party does sign the promises he has ridden over his own religious allegiance roughshod, has committed a serious sin because of this decision not to exercise his primary responsibility toward his children, has put himself in the position of finding it very difficult to repent (and properly amend) his action. While his church may not "excommunicate" him in a formal sense, he should feel barred from communion with God—through the sacrament or otherwise—until he can work out some solution as to the matter of repentance for sin. So in essence both parties are in the same situation, or, to put it in another way, one of the parties is in a fix either way the matter is decided.

Though the problem is not so acute in the case of other types of mixed marriages, with different nomenclature much the same dilemma is presented.

At this point some people throw up their hands and utter such clichés as "A Catholic can never become a non-Catholic!" Such statements as this don't really hold water because they mean either "I don't care about the truth of it, I like the feel of it," or "My religion is right because I hold it." Furthermore it overlooks the obvious fact that all through history and at the present day many intelligent people have through conviction changed their religious allegiances: and no church can claim a one-way traffic in its direction.

Nothing but good can come from this approach to things. If as a result of careful study of his own tradition and of the principal alternatives a person decides to stay put, then it is obvious that he will henceforth have a much more mature faith and reasoned allegiance than he had before. On the other hand, if he decides to change his new allegiance such a change will be on the dignified basis of adult conviction, not on the basis which is so destructive of personal integrity: the yielding of one's loyalties because of the other partner or the marriage.

The Spirit of the Inquiry

Nothing could be more important than the spirit with which any such study is undertaken. If one party has entered it in good faith and the other has in mind only "to bring around" his partner, this attitude will become evident enough during the process and will have either the result of "putting off" the latter or of bullying him into submission. Naturally no one can be expected to be suspended religiously in mid-air in order to give objective consideration to all other possibilities; no one can be asked to forego his regular worship or his normal prayer life or the particular obligations imposed upon him by his own church while he examines the historical and theological foundations of his practices, and of their alternatives. If a family has decided to consider where in the community they would best like to live, life still goes on as usual in the old house, though the latter may be undergoing a more critical and systematic examination than would be customary.

Nor is there any thought that emotions should be ruled out. One's attraction to, antagonism toward, or intuitions about, particular religious teachings or practices are part of what eventually should be weighed in the balance. However, the human emotions are capable of great resiliency. We are capable of wider attractions than we realize; when we know the background and reason for a particular attitude or custom we often find that it is more attractive than we had imagined it could be. The same is true of the breadth of our antagonisms. When we allow what have often been suppressed resentments to come to the surface in the course of our survey of religious possibilities, we often find that we have not been as totally satisfied with our own tradition as we have claimed we have been.

> Case 17. When the subject of their religious differences came up, one of the first things Mary, a Roman Catholic, said to John, an Episcopalian, was: "I could never do without the Mass, and of course your church doesn't have that." But the first time she attended a choral celebration of the Holy Communion (the same service which the Roman Catholic Church calls "High Mass") in an Episcopal church she found in fact that she felt quite at home and as a matter of fact rejoiced at the fact that the service was in

her own language, commenting, "I had always wondered if it wouldn't be better if our service was in English; and I am frank to say that I like it that way better; I like the way the congregation all took part."

Case 18. A constant source of irritation to Bill had been the fact that his Roman Catholic friends had to get to Mass on Sunday come what may. Now in the course of his instructions from a Roman Catholic priest he is beginning to look at the thing "from the inside." He sees the point of such a rule and as a matter of fact finds himself highly critical of the laissez-faire attitude toward discipline of this sort which has been evidenced in his own Church.

Case 19. Of a strong Baptist background, Florence has never had any use for symbolism, vestments, or ceremony. But now that she has started to go to the Lutheran Church on alternate Sundays with Walter, who has carefully explained the various usages of his church, she finds these externals both beautiful and helpful to worship. She finds to her surprise that a fixed order of worship can make for more congregational participation, rather than less, as she had supposed.

Case 20. William, an agnostic of long standing, had always assumed that belief in the Divinity of Christ depended upon accepting the Virgin Birth— an idea to which he had a closed mind. Mary's minister explained to him that there were good grounds for accepting the Incarnation quite apart from the Virgin Birth, that many people who accepted the former did not regard the latter as essential, except as a mode of expressing the former. Thus this barrier to belief was removed. As he began to participate in worship, he found the phrase "conceived by the Holy Ghost, born of the Virgin Mary" quite appropriate to recite in the Creed as a way of expressing the Incarnation. Finally he came up with this idea one day: "It is such a good way to say it, maybe it was a good way for God to do it."

These illustrations should be sufficient to rebut the notion expressed in such statements as "but I could never . . ." or "I'll always . . ."

The Method of Inquiry

How shall a couple proceed to learn about the major alternatives? The tragedy of the education (high school or college) of most young people is that it has not included a systematic study of the major traditions in religion. To know these things is simply part of being an educated person, yet due to the secularization of public education and, until recently, of most higher education, most people approach adult life religiously illiterate. This means that the couple in question must now proceed to complete their own education. Customary educational methods are relevant in this connection.

First, it is important to talk to professionals devoted to the alternative positions. As we have seen, the Roman Catholic Church has already made provision for this aspect of the study. It generally requires of a non-Roman party instructions in the Roman Catholic faith. Normally the Roman Catholic party will attend also. Often the non-Roman party (and sometimes the Roman Catholic party) resents this rule. Actually it is a quite reasonable requirement. The difficulty is that it is usually not "fifty-fifty." To provide for this aspect of the study we need only to take what is now common practice as to the Roman Catholic side, and extend it to the other alternative: sessions should be arranged with a minister or other spokesman of that position also.

Meanwhile, the couple should be doing some reading together. Every religious tradition has provided some pamphlets and books which expound its attitudes and provide a rationale for its positions. The priest, minister, or other adviser may well be able to suggest these books and pamphlets.

. . . .

The third important element of the inquiry is actual experience in the worship of the several traditions under consideration. What is called for here is something halfway between a "balcony" attitude and the attitude of participation. One should make the responses called for in the particular liturgy, join in the prayers, sing the hymns and pray personally as one is being led in prayer by the clergyman. On the other hand, it is generally sensible for the visitor to be alert and observant as to what is going on and be critically related to it. In short it would be wrong to come to a service of worship with an attitude which can be summed up as "I dare you to convert me" or with a determination to try and like it regardless. To achieve the proper in-between attitude is, by the way, a very important test of maturity.

Case 21. Lydia, a Protestant, is attending her first Roman Catholic Mass with her friend, Joseph. He has handed her a missal with an English translation, but she is so fascinated with all that she sees around her that she takes refuge in the fact that practically all of the Roman Catholics present are not using missals but are saying the Rosary and reading devotional prayer books, and thus does not feel called upon to follow her missal. As a result she comes away with a feeling that the whole thing was a rather confusing experience. Actually it would have been fairer for her to have operated on the best level to which the Roman Catholic Church is seeking to bring its own people— namely, the use of a missal, which allows the worshiper to follow the service with the priest and choir.

Case 22. Helen, a former Roman Catholic who is now an agnostic, is attending an Episcopal service with Jim. Though the *Agnus Dei* is usually sung during the Communion at the Episcopal service, a hymn (which the Prayer Book permits) was used in this particular parish. "Where was the

Agnus Dei?" she whispers critically to Jim. Helen, away from the Roman Catholic Church for some years, still uses the Roman Catholic Mass, which is familiar to her, as the norm for all true worship. Actually she does not realize that the *Agnus Dei* was a quite late addition to the Latin Mass.

In selecting places of worship an opportunity should be given for the best of each tradition to present itself. It is not fair to compare a High Mass sung in a rural "carpenter's gothic" Roman Catholic church with a choral Eucharist in an Episcopal church with a large music budget, soaring arches and the finest stained glass; nor a small-town Congregational service with a Park Avenue Methodist church with a distinguished preacher. In any case a certain degree of generalization is called for. The couple should not be basing their judgment on the local church as such, but only on what the church or denomination as a whole represents. For what they will be giving their loyalty to is not a particular parish or congregation but to a world communion with a particular tradition.

Finally, discussion between the two parties is of great importance. The degree to which they can in this situation maintain objectivity, candor, and a sense of humor is a good test of the way they are apt to conduct their marriage. After an exceptionally poor sermon in the other party's church (*any* church—no denomination has a monopoly on this), the proper remark is not "Well, that's a point for my side, dear," but rather "I am sure *that* preaching is a purely local problem." In discussing points of doctrine or church history, the attitude should not be, how much can I rebut? but how much can I concede, with honesty? When a common ground is found on some things and differences on others, even then a deadlock is not to be declared. Some consideration should be given as to what other alternatives than those already considered offer affirmation of this common ground along with the particular other points which each of the parties feel should receive expression.

Case 23. Very important to Christopher, a Congregationalist, is a liberal attitude toward the Scriptures and certain Reformation principles such as the direct relationship of the individual to God and the place of the laity in the government of the Church. Very important to Marie, a Roman Catholic, is the Holy Communion and a traditional order of worship. Both agree on the basic essentials of the Christian faith. Their friends suggested that they look into the Episcopal Church. It so happened that there each felt he found what he was looking for, and the decision was not a compromise (as a sort of "middle" or "via media") but rather was the fulfillment of what each regarded as most important in religion, with ample room for what the other regarded as important. Three years later we find Marie especially gratified at the liberal attitude toward the Scriptures and the other Reformation principles which were dear to Christopher; and especially dear to Christopher is the Eucharist and an ordered liturgy.

In this chapter we have outlined the separate elements of the proper kind of consideration of alternative traditions. However, these particular methods need not fall strictly in this order. Consultation, reading, worship and discussion should all go ahead at once. Reading will lead to further consultation, as will worship. Discussion will lead to the need of further reading, etc. If the right spirit is present (along the lines we discussed above) and there is true respect between the parties, here we *can* affirm that "love will find a way." Negatively speaking, this much can be said: If in this most important realm of relationships, this kind of open dealing is impossible and if already we sense a dogmatic sense of rightness on one person's part and a "looking down the nose" at the other party's tradition, we can already sense the beginning of second-rate citizenship for one of the partners to the marriage—and the parties had better beware of the perils of the future.

CHAPTER 17:

Difficult Problems of Adjustment

62 · *Eight Reasons Why Marriages Go Wrong* *

JAMES H. S. BOSSARD

The high hopes of brides and grooms for happiness and permanence in marriage do not always materialize. Just as many engagements break up before marriage, so do many—although not as many—marriages end in separation or divorce. Other marriages are not terminated, but are rocked by constant or intermittent conflict and quarreling. If the basic causes for unsuccessful marriage can be identified, some progress may be made to avoid or compensate for them. In this article a sociologist who has devoted many years to the study of family life discusses eight reasons for marriage problems.

APPROXIMATELY 11 per cent of marriages in the United States take place in June. This month some 350,000 men and women will be united in holy matrimony. The distressing part of the story is that at least 80,000 of these people—40,000 couples—face the statistical certainty of divorce at some point in the years ahead.

Never has so large a proportion of our population been married. And the chances of a person getting married in the United States are greater than they are in other countries of the Western world. But the chances of these American marriages failing are also greater than chances of the same sort of failure in other nations. Currently, our annual toll of divorces and annulments approaches 400,000. In recent years, the number of divorces has ranged between one-fourth and one-third of total marriages. In selected cities, the divorce rate at times equals or exceeds one-half the marriage total.

---

* *New York Times Magazine* (June 24, 1956), pp. 5, 20–23. Reprinted by permission of the publisher and the author.

The author's biographical sketch is given with article 4.

Yet divorce is only one index of family disorganization. Almost 2,000,000 married persons are separated—temporarily or permanently—because of marital discord. And surveys reveal that one-fifth or one-sixth of all couples living together think of themselves as unhappy and that an equal number can report only "medium happiness."

For almost half a century, as a university teacher and student of family life, I have watched this situation develop and spread. From my studies and observations, I have come to think of the following factors as the chief hazards to matrimonial happiness for American youth.

I

Many people marry too young. The average age at which men and women marry for the first time has been dropping since 1890, and since 1940 has dropped sharply. It is now about 22 for men; about 20 for women.

Yet we know that readiness for marriage is more than a matter of years. Experts speak of a physiological age, a sexual age, a vocational age and the age at which a degree of emotional maturity is reached. Each of these stages of development has its own importance, but emotional maturity— the extent of a person's capacity to deal with life on a normal adult level— is perhaps the most important. Furthermore, adult behavior in marriage is possible only if paralleled by adult behavior in business and industry and citizenship. These qualities of maturity come as by-products of experiences in living, for which there is no substitute. Now, with the lowering of the marriage age, the extension of the required education period, and with so many more young people going on to college, it is evident that an increasing number of couples pass from the sheltered life of the schoolroom to the stark realities of a job and a wife or husband, and perhaps a child, with little or no intervening experience.

Consider how this works out. Yesterday *he* was a campus big wheel, living at the Epsilon Chi Omega house. *She* was one of the dating favorites at dear old Siwash. Now they are living in a two-room flat in a large city. It is hot. Today his boss was unreasonable, and the gadget in her kitchen wouldn't work. That night he muses: "If this dame hadn't chased me, I'd still be in clover." And she sulks herself to sleep with memories of last year's junior prom. It is a big transition for these two, on many fronts, in too short a time.

II

Modern patterns of courtship do not make for wise choices of matrimonial partners. The current premium is upon success in party-going, dancing, sports, petting and use of a patois which in my day was called "a good line." There is, in other words, an impersonality about present-day adolescent courtship similar to what one finds in more adult aspects of social life. We go to a cocktail party or reception, observe all the niceties, say the acceptable, innocuous things and by skillfully avoiding any controversial subject create the impression of being "nice," "adjustable," and having "a pleasant personality." All this, in courtship as in more mature social life, involves a kind of social maneuvering, little of which touches upon or reveals those qualities which matter so much if the couple is going to live happily together for the next forty or more years. When one thinks in terms of a lifelong union, being a good mixer and having a presentable pair of legs are somewhat less important than what one thinks about God, money and a crying baby.

III

Intermarriage between cultural groups can be a strain on both parties. This is the inevitable price we pay for the heterogeneity of our population and the diversity of our cultural strains. Among such marriages, the most important in their effect are those between members of different religious groups.

The number of interfaith marriages is large, and it is increasing. Recent studies show that half of marriages involving Roman Catholics are mixed marriages, valid or invalid, and that the percentage has been increasing steadily since 1910. A study made for the United Lutheran Church shows that 58 per cent of its members marry outside of their church and that there has been a marked increase in such marriages since 1936.

Mixed marriages are looked upon with disfavor by the leaders of all organized church bodies. The Central Conference of American Rabbis has declared that mixed marriages "are contrary to the tradition of the Jewish religion and should therefore be discouraged by the American rabbinate." The attitude of the Roman Catholic Church is definite and uncompromising; it considers invalid any marriage involving Catholics that is not solemnized in a religious ceremony under prescribed conditions. Within the last two decades, several Protestant denominations have been taking an increasingly firm stand on mixed marriages.

It is unfair to argue, as is sometimes done, that the concern of the church is purely one of self-interest, growing out of fear of losing members. It is true that persons contracting mixed marriages tend to drop away from their respective churches and are somewhat less concerned than usual with the religious rearing of their children. But there are other reasons for the attitude of the various churches. Their leaders, for example, have long known what recent sociological studies verify.

Three such studies (Landis, Bell and Weeks), covering a total of 24,184 families, show that there are approximately three times as many divorces or separations in Catholic-Protestant marriages as there are when the marital partners are of the same faith, and about four times as many when a Catholic father is married to a Protestant mother. And here again the story of marital unhappiness is far larger than divorce and separation statistics show.

Contemporary youth tends to be impatient with the verdict of experience concerning mixed marriages. "We are broad-minded," they say. "We are quite willing to respect each other's religious beliefs. Besides, religion is not as important as it used to be." What these young people overlook is the real nature of religion and its role in life. Religion is not merely a set of beliefs; it is a way of living and of thinking. Roman Catholicism is a culture pattern, as we sociologists put it; so is Judaism, or Methodism, or being an Episcopalian.

Each religion has its distinctive set of values, as well as its forms of worship, and these reach over and express themselves in the minutiae of the daily lives of their respective adherents. Eating fish on Friday is not a mere belief; it is a dietary institution. The observance of church holidays involves the organization of a family's leisure time.

Perhaps the real wonder is not that mixed marriages often fail, but rather that so many succeed. An old Chinese maxim has it that every boy should marry the girl who lives across the street from him. The meaning is still clear; people of the same background and circumstances are most likely to find marital happiness with each other.

IV

A marked emphasis on the romantic motif is hazardous in marriage. As currently interpreted, this means that a person marries solely for love, that marriage is the final realization of romantic attraction. It might be called the Hollywood concept of marriage, since the movies have done much to foster the lushness of its appeal.

To speak of emphasis upon romance as a pitfall to successful marriage is apt to cause misunderstanding. Surely, the critic will say, there is nothing new or unusual or alarming about love. And one must agree completely and wholeheartedly. Strong emotional attraction between persons of the opposite sex is as old as the human heartbeat and is one of the things that makes the world a brighter place in which to live.

The question that is raised here is the acceptance of romance as the primary, and often the sole, basis of marriage selection and maintenance. In the old days, marriages were arranged on the basis of more practical considerations, such as the judgment of parents and kinsfolk, the exchange of financial agreements, or the promotion of a career. In addition to these considerations, there was usually a long period of courtship during which the prospective mates and their respective families learned to know and test each other's mettle, for what people in other cultures know, and what we so largely ignore, is that marriage is not only the union of two individuals but also of two kinship groups.

I certainly do not advocate that romance as such should not be included in the ingredients of a happy marriage. My point is simply that romance alone is not enough.

In this respect, it should also be noted that sex in marriage means more than physical attraction or the sequence of romantic glow. Sex adjustment is a deep and pervasive achievement, often made slowly and on the basis of many factors. It involves a deep rapport between two people, the sort that can come only with mutual respect, reciprocal understanding and a sharing of common interests, and it is something quite different from the sentiment engendered by a trim ankle, a chic look or a conspicuous bosom.

V

A married person who seeks individual development of his or her personality is courting trouble. To these people a good marriage is one that contributes fully and freely to the personality development of each; a poor marriage is one that hinders such development. This sort of emphasis, of course, is but a phase of a much larger ideological pattern.

Many children encounter the pattern early in their school careers, when they are encouraged to "express themselves." Later on, they express what they have been taught in freedom of choice of their mates, often with complete disregard for the advice or admonition of parents, kinsfolk, pastor or priest. After marriage, this philosophy is maintained. Almost from the beginning, many husbands and wives organize their lives on an individualistic basis. The employment of married women, so widespread today, has enforced the trend.

One wonders if the advocates of individualism as a basis for marriage are aware of the logical consequence of such behavior. It is this: when one marries for personal happiness and fulfillment, then one must leave if his goal is not realized. If living with Jane Brown is essential to one's fullest personality development in 1956, what happens in 1957 when only Mary Smith can serve as the developing agent? If personality development is the sole base for marriage, than obviously when the base disappears the marriage is over.

VI

Parenthood is underestimated as a force in marriage. Less than five per cent of the space in current literature on family relations refers to the matter. Yet married people do have children—six out of every seven couples, in fact, and most of the others wish they could.

Our whole culture is guilty of this detour around the subject of parenthood. The family has historically been the moving force for the perpetuation not only of the race, but of civilization. Yet marriage clinics today deal only with the problems of husband-wife relations. American business, which has engulfed a liberal proportion of married women, considers parenthood an incident. Housing developments and rental offices often ignore children completely.

The lack of attention to the matter of parenthood in sociological writing is supplemented by instances of parents who themselves ignore their offspring. The children who get up and cook their own breakfast, or go without, while Papa and Mama sleep off a hangover brought on by the country club dance, are symbolic and not too exceptional. It is time, in fact, to remind young marrieds once again that the family is the connecting link between successive generations; that this indeed is the basic purpose of the family and that other functions relevant to it are secondary and incidental.

VII

Pressures to strive for higher social position strain family life. The popular democratic ideology about social classes in the United States today is strange and paradoxical. First, we are told that there are no social classes and that to recognize them or even speak of them is undemocratic. Second, as the *Fortune* magazine and other polls have shown, most people think of themselves as middle class. Third, most of us are breaking our necks, figuratively speaking, to rise in this "classless" society. Here is a weird mixture of fancy and fact which gives rise, among other things, to a mad scramble for status and advancement up the ladder.

From this scramble grow many problems bearing on family living. The show girl who marries the banana king's heir makes the news, but a whole host of less spectacular cases go unnoticed. In an open-class system, many ambitious parents nourish the hope that their children will "marry up." Others have done so, why not theirs? As a result, they develop the notion that no mate is quite good enough for their son or daughter. If only they had waited: tomorrow would have been better. Betty Smith's novel of a few years ago, "Tomorrow Will Be Better," poignantly pictures all this among lower-class folk.

Pressure by parents upon children to marry up is only part of a much larger story. Socially ambitious wives put their husbands on the griddle, forward-looking husbands do the same to their wives and many growing children give both parents the full treatment. This striving for status in our "classless" society is an individualizing process in which husband, wife and children tend to climb separately. Certainly nothing about the process fosters the development of familism.

VIII

There is far too little emphasis upon the family as a group. Perhaps no civilization in the world has ever formally educated so large a proportion of its young people in the area of family living as has ours—at the university as well as the secondary school level. But most of the emphasis has been upon how to get married rather than on how to stay married. Actually, a family is a project in group living. Its stability requires an emphasis upon group values rather than on the individualistic forces now so widely stressed.

Personally, I am convinced that there are techniques in group living whose nature can be identified, whose importance can be demonstrated, and whose use can be taught. For a number of years, Dr. Eleanor S. Boll, my research associate, and I have studied the relatively formal family procedures centering around holidays, natal days, vacations, family meals and the like. We have come to speak of these as family rituals, meaning prescribed family ways of doing things together which build up a feeling of rightness and happiness through participation.

By nature, ritual in family living is the same as ritual in religion, and the history of religions shows that those with the most elaborate and pervasive rituals are those that best retain the allegiance of their members. It is really very easy to understand this; all it means is that people can best be held together by doing things together.

There are no short or easy solutions to the marriage problems of the American people, no wonder drugs to cure our social ills. Success in family living is not assured by inheritance, legislative fiat, priestly blessing or parental strictures. As in other aspects of life, it must be earned through sound judgment, effective techniques and time-proven values. There are no other ways.

63 · *Why Marriages Fail: Infidelity* *

FAMILY SERVICE ASSOCIATION OF AMERICA

The ideal marriage relationship in the United States is lifetime fidelity between husband and wife. The ideal is often disregarded. The husband or wife who discovers that his mate has been unfaithful is very likely to be outraged or to feel that he has failed the mate, or both. Divorce may be the next step. However, many marriage counselors have pointed out that while the divorce ends the marriage and may soothe the outraged feelings of the faithful mate, it does not really solve anything. The infidelity is often a symptom of some underlying difficulty—the immaturity of one or both or some failure on the part of the faithful mate that has led the other to seek solace elsewhere.

In this article, the cases of two couples who had come to a family service association for counseling are analyzed as to causes and method of adjustment.

THE TWO COUPLES, the Kirks and the Foleys, lived in the same medium-sized city. They didn't happen to know each other, yet for a while last year they turned up separately, but at fairly regular intervals, in the same simply furnished office in a local family service agency. And for the same reason. Neither couple wanted a divorce. Yet all four individuals realized that without some kind of help their respective marriages were very apt to smash up. At the start they were all convinced that their unhappiness was due to only one factor, infidelity.

In the Kirks' case it was David who'd been unfaithful, chronically and almost from the start of their marriage three years before. It was an utterly unimportant type of infidelity, David informed the counselor airily, just casual encounters that didn't mean a thing as far as marriage was concerned. He happened to be "one of those guys who couldn't get along without a lot of women."

Betsey Kirk, who'd paid the initial visit to the agency, felt she was unhappy mostly because she couldn't make any sense out of her reactions to David's infidelity. She'd known about it from the start. It hadn't bothered

* Prepared in collaboration with Family Service Association of America, *McCall's Magazine*, 81 (January, 1954), 39, 52. Reprinted by permission of the publisher, McCall Corporation.

her deeply for a while, for she was an up-to-date girl who'd studied the statistics on the Kinsey report and had accepted (a bit regretfully) the light they seemed to cast on her own particular American male. She and David liked the same things and the same people—with some obvious exceptions—and since they got along just as well in bed as out of it she'd felt she had reason to hope he'd find other girls less interesting after a while.

Then one day a friend she was lunching with asked bluntly why she let David get away with so much. His affairs were engrossing the attention of the whole town. To her own surprise Betsey's up-to-date outlook turned into a horse-and-buggy, or even a Stone Age, one on the spot. She felt ill. She felt angry. And the next time David told her winsomely that sleeping around merely provided an outlet for his physiological tensions she even felt murderous.

From then on she didn't especially want to have intercourse with David. He sulked when she advised him to find his physiological outlets somewhere else. She raged at him when he took her advice.

"But I still keep wondering," Betsey told the counselor unhappily, "if a woman has any *right* to expect her husband to be faithful in this day and age." She looked greatly relieved when the counselor remarked temperately that any woman has a legitimate right to feel unsatisfied if she isn't getting what she really needs from her marriage.

The Foleys were ten years older than the Kirks—in their middle thirties —and a lot more prosperous. Ben Foley's business, which he'd built up from scratch, had done extremely well in recent years. Since Ben had been forced by circumstances to work his way through school and college, and later to support his mother until she died, he felt he was justified in being elated, even a bit smug, about his success. The only hitch, he told the counselor to whom he'd been sent by his family doctor, was that since he'd struck it rich he and Rae had gradually stopped being a couple and had turned into two people living uneasily alone in the same house.

Actually they were far from alone in that house. During the daytime there were the two kids, ages 8 and 10, rampaging around. Later an assortment of guests whom Ben described sadly as "those arty bums" turned up. The majority of these guests were masculine, and on at least one occasion, when Ben had stamped off to his office in the evening to put in what was actually some unnecessary overtime, he was pretty sure his wife had had intercourse with the bum who currently rated tops with Rae.

Rae Foley admitted to the counselor, some time later, that this was true. "But in this day and age an awful lot of women are unfaithful to their husbands," she said. "In my case it didn't mean a thing as far as our marriage is concerned. Ben and I just happen to have an entirely different set of intellectual interests."

Most people who commit adultery manage to convince themselves, as did David Kirk and Rae Foley, that their affairs aren't important as far as their marriages are concerned. And a great many victims of infidelity wonder, like Betsey Kirk, if they're not a little crazy to expect their partners to be faithful. Those who look at marriage from the outside—doctors, lawyers, sociologists—feel that both of these viewpoints are lopsided. Yet they point out that they're extremely easily arrived at "in this day and age."

Theoretically nobody at all is in favor of adultery. In this country, as in most others, people who get married are supposed to remain faithful to each other the rest of their lives. Our legal system backs up this theory to the hilt. Adultery is grounds for divorce in all forty-eight states, and all but four states provide for fines and/or imprisonment for the guilty party (but seldom invoke them except as a weapon against prostitution). Juries, reflecting popular opinion, rarely convict a man who has shot his wife's lover. No church condones adultery, and several of them demand excommunication for those found guilty of it. People in general feel so strongly about infidelity that the members of a family will hide any evidence of it after it has been discovered.

Yet in spite of this universal taboo infidelity is widespread in the United States, and most people know it, even without the assistance of a battery of tabulating machines. It has been pretty well established that more men are unfaithful to their mates than are women, although the exact number of either is still a matter of some debate.

Naturally enough, anybody who can qualify as an expert on almost anything has come forward with an explanation for this paradoxical state of affairs. Some commentators blame the widespread condoning of infidelity on "cultural attitudes," and especially on what they describe as an "upperclass outlook"—i.e., that adultery is all right as long as it's committed discreetly. Other theoreticians conclude, as David Kirk did, that most men, and maybe some women, just aren't naturally monogamous. Still others (among them a lot of fiction writers) go on the assumption that marriage begins to look drab to the majority of people after they've been married a while and they think a liaison will be the cure for this condition. Psychoanalysts for the most part are of the not too popular opinion that infidelity, especially when it reaches the point of promiscuity, may be closely related to homosexuality, in both men and women. Every sociological study of infidelity has shown it to be detrimental to marriage and almost always related to inadequacies and dissatisfactions of one or both partners. Practically any of these authorities might be right.

Until the time when someone comes up with the answers, the people most directly concerned with infidelity (their marriages are apparently cracking up because of it) have evolved some practical, rule-of-thumb conclusions. They've discovered that if a husband and wife want to stay married, and if they are willing to work together on the problem, a divorce growing out of infidelity can be avoided. They can't do this by ignoring infidelity when it exists. And the one who is unfaithful has to be willing to admit that something is wrong with himself or with his partner, rather than with this day and age, and he must undergo the experience of finding out just what this is.

At first glance David Kirk didn't seem like the kind of man who had to keep proving to himself that he was popular, that people wouldn't forget about him five minutes after he was out of their sight. He was good-looking, an amusing talker, and he had the kind of easygoing good manners which made men as well as women like him on first acquaintance.

David's family, who'd been well off, had sent him to a series of boarding schools and camps, where he'd always had a lot of friends. But, he realized now, he'd always shifted friendships as easily as he made them, had never been particularly close to anyone but Betsey. He was afraid, although it was hard to figure out why, that if he tried to be too close to a person he'd be "found out" and cast aside.

Maybe all those schools and camps had something to do with it. His parents hadn't sent him, as was the case with some boys, to get rid of him, but at times he'd wondered if this wasn't so. When he was home on vacations, he admitted, his mother had spoiled him outrageously. He supposed he'd been expecting Betsey to carry on this tradition, letting him do whatever he wanted. And he could see now that it wasn't fair to her, especially since she wasn't any too sure of herself. She'd grown up in the shadow of a sister who was a knockout, and Betsey underestimated her own attractiveness to an almost irritating degree.

Eventually David admitted, although a bit hesitantly, that he guessed all those affairs hadn't been a sign of extreme manliness, as he'd assumed, but exactly the reverse. And that he'd probably be a good deal more popular with himself, as well as with others, if he substituted one grown-up relationship for a number of very adolescent ones. Especially since he'd come to realize that he'd be lost if Betsey walked out on him.

Rae Foley reached about the same conclusion, in a far shorter time, quite possibly because she was willing to admit at the very start that she'd never really wanted those arty bums in her house and, on occasion, in her bed. Their appearance had coincided with a bad time in her life—when the kids first ceased being a constant care and went off to school, when Ben's business started booming and he no longer needed her to help him with the bookkeeping as she'd done at first, and when for no special reason she suddenly felt thoroughly unattractive and unwanted.

Ben, who bore down much too heavily on this business of being a self-made man and a rough diamond, seemed to think Rae was looking down her nose at him when she tried to get him interested in music or books.

Her new friends liked the same things she did. But they didn't, as she'd hoped, make Ben more interested in her. They didn't erase her doubts about her own attractiveness. And they didn't satisfy her sexually, as Ben had just been beginning to do when everything went wrong. In short, about all they did was to up the liquor bills and make the Foleys thoroughly unhappy—something, as Rae remarked, that any high-school girl ought to have been bright enough to figure out for herself.

"I guess I was just a little bit retarded," she said to the counselor. "And now that Ben has come around to the point where he admits that even a rough diamond can enjoy a good show once in a while, I'm pretty sure things will work out all right."

The counselor was pretty sure too. Less so when she thought of the Kirks. A card she received from them recently reported that they were having a rapturous second honeymoon in a little cabin on a lake in northern Wisconsin. But there aren't many temptations in northern Wisconsin, and she couldn't help wondering if when David returned he'd keep on remembering that he'd finally grown up.

64 · Alcoholism and the Family *

JOAN K. JACKSON

A personal and family problem now receiving intensive research is alcoholism. In this article Dr. Jackson, who has carried on extensive research in this

* *Annals of the American Academy of Political and Social Science*, 315 (January, 1958), 90–98. Reprinted by permission of the publisher. Several footnotes have been omitted.

The author is a sociologist who received the degree of Doctor of Philosophy from the University of Washington. She is Research Instructor, Department of Psychiatry, University of Washington School of Medicine and Consultant, Firland Sanatorium. The research here reported was supported in part by the National Institute of Mental Health, U.S. Public Health Service. Her findings have been reported in a number of professional journals in addition to the *Annals*, e.g., *Marriage and Family Living* and the *Quarterly Journal of Studies on Alcohol*.

field, discusses some alternative theories of the relation of the wife of an alcoholic to his alcoholism. She also treats the situation as a family crisis and shows the process that the family follows in attempting to adjust to the situation. The reader will find the discussion of how the crisis is handled useful also in connection with other kinds of critical disorganization.

UNTIL RECENTLY it was possible to think of alcoholism as if it involved the alcoholic only. Most of the alcoholics studied were inmates of publicly supported institutions: jails, mental hospitals, and public general hospitals. These ill people appeared to be homeless and tieless. As the public became more aware of the extent and nature of alcoholism and that treatment possibilities existed, alcoholics who were still integral parts of the community appeared at clinics. The definition of "the problems of alcoholism" has had to be broadened to include all those with whom the alcoholic is or has been in close and continuing contact.

At present we do not know how many nonalcoholics are affected directly by alcoholism. However, an estimate can be derived from the available statistics on the marital histories of alcoholics. The recurrently arrested alcoholic seems to affect the fewest nonalcoholics. Reports range from 19 per cent to 51 per cent who have never married—that is, from slightly more than the expected number of single men to three to four times the expected rate. The vast majority who had married are now separated from their families. Alcoholics who voluntarily seek treatment at clinics affect the lives of more people than jailed alcoholics. While the number of broken marriages is still excessive, approximately the expected number of voluntary patients have been married. Any estimate of nonalcoholics affected must take into consideration not only the present marital status of alcoholics, but also the past marital history. About one-third of the alcoholics have been married more than once. Jailed alcoholics had multiple marriages less frequently than clinic alcoholics.

There has been no enumeration of the children and other relatives influenced by alcoholism. From the author's studies it can be estimated that for each alcoholic there are at least two people in the immediate family who are affected. Approximately two-thirds of the married alcoholics have children, thus averaging two apiece. Family studies indicate that a minimum of one other relative is also directly involved. The importance of understanding the problems faced by the families of alcoholics is obvious from these figures. To date, little is known about the nature of the effects of living with or having lived with an alcoholic. However, there is considerable evidence that it has disturbing effects on the personalities of family members.

Once attention had been focussed on the families of alcoholics, it became obvious that the relationship between the alcoholic and his family is not a one-way relationship. The family also affects the alcoholic and his illness. The very existence of family ties appears to be related to recovery from alcoholism. Some families are successful in helping their alcoholic member to recognize his need for help and are supportive of treatment efforts. Yet other types of families may discourage the patient from seeking treatment and may actually encourage the persistence of alcoholism. It is now believed that the most successful treatment of alcoholism involves helping both the alcoholic and those members of his family who are directly involved in his drinking behavior.

The Alcoholic and His Children

The children are affected by living with an alcoholic more than any other family member. Personalities are formed in a social milieu which is markedly unstable, torn with dissension, culturally deviant, and socially disapproved. The children must model themselves on adults who play their roles in a distorted fashion. The alcoholic shows little adequate adult behavior. The nonalcoholic parent attempts to play the roles of both father and mother, often failing to do either well.

The child of an alcoholic is bound to have problems in learning who he is, what is expected of him, and what he can expect from others. Almost inevitably his parents behave inconsistently towards him. His self-conception evolves in a situation in which the way others act towards him has more to do with the current events in the family than with the child's nature. His alcoholic parent feels one way about him when he is sober, another when drunk, and yet another during the hangover stage.

What the child can expect from his parents will also depend on the phase of the drinking cycle as well as on where he stands in relation to each parent at any given time. Only too frequently he is used in the battle between them. The wives of alcoholics find themselves disliking, punishing, or depriving the children preferred by the father and those who resemble him. Similarly, the child who is preferred by, or resembles the mother is often hurt by the father. If the child tries to stay close to both parents he is caught in an impossible situation. Each parent resents the affection the other receives while demanding that the child show affection to both.

The children do not understand what is happening. The very young ones do not know that their families are different from other families. When they become aware of the differences, the children are torn between their own loyalty and the views of their parents that others hold. When neighbors ostracize them, the children are bewildered about what *they* did to bring about this result. Even those who are not ostracized become isolated. They hesitate to bring their friends to a home where their parent is likely to be drunk.

The behavior of the alcoholic parent is unpredictable and unintelligible to the child. The tendency of the child to look for the reasons in his own behavior very often is reinforced inadvertently by his mother. When father is leading up to a drinking episode, the children are put on their best behavior. When the drinking episode occurs, it is not surprising that the children feel that they have somehow done something to precipitate it.

Newell [1] states that the children of alcoholics are placed in a situation very similar to that of the experimental animals who are tempted towards rewards and then continually frustrated, whose environment changes constantly in a manner over which they have no control. Under such circumstances experimental animals have convulsions or "nervous breakdowns." Unfortunately, we still know very little about what happens to the children or about the duration of the effects.

Yet some of the children appear undisturbed. The personality damage appears to be least when the nonalcoholic parent is aware of the problems they face, gives them emotional support, keeps from using them against the alcoholic, tries to be consistent, and has insight into her own problems with the alcoholic. It also appears to mitigate some of the child's confusion if alcoholism is explained to him by a parent who accepts alcoholism as an illness.

The Alcoholic and His Wife

The wives of alcoholics have received considerably more attention than the children. The focus tends to be on how they affect the alcoholic and his alcoholism, rather than on how alcoholism and the alcoholic affect them. Most writers seem to feel that the wives of alcoholics are drawn from the ranks of emotionally disturbed women who seek out spouses who are not threatening to them, spouses who can be manipulated to meet their own personality needs. According to this theory, the wife has a vested interest in the persistence of the alcoholism of her spouse. Her own emotional stability depends upon it. Should the husband become sober, the wives are in danger of decompensating and showing marked neurotic disturbances.

A complementary theory suggests that prealcoholic or alcoholic males tend to select certain types of women as wives. The most commonly reported type is a dominating, maternal woman who uses her maternal role as a defense against inadequate femininity.

---

[1] N. Newell, "Alcoholism and the Father Image," *Quarterly Journal of Studies on Alcohol*, Vol. 11, March 1950, pp. 92–96.

Any attempt to assess the general applicability of this theory to *all* the wives of alcoholics runs into difficulties. First, the only wives who can be studied by researchers are those who have stayed with their husbands until alcoholism was well under way. The high divorce rate among alcoholics suggests that these wives are the exception rather than the rule. The majority of women who find themselves married to alcoholics appear to divorce them. Second, if a high rate of emotional disturbance is found among women still living with alcoholics, it is difficult to determine whether the personality difficulties antedated or postdated the alcoholism, whether they were partly causal or whether they emerged during the recurrent crises and the cumulative stresses of living with an alcoholic. Third, the wives who were studied were women who were actively blocking the treatment of their husbands, who had entered mental hospitals after their husbands' sobriety, who were themselves seeking psychiatric care, or who were in the process of manipulating social agencies to provide services. It is of interest that neither of the studies which deal with women who were taking an active part in their husbands' recovery process comment upon any similarities in the personality structures of the wives.

It is likely that the final test of the hypotheses about the role of the wives' personalities in their husbands' alcoholism will have to await the accumulation of considerably more information. No alcoholic personality type has been found on psychological tests; no tests have been given to the wives of alcoholics. Until we know more about the etiology of alcoholism and its remedy, the role of the wives' personalities in its onset, in its persistence, and in its alleviation will remain in the realm of speculation.

No one denies that the wives of active alcoholics are emotionally disturbed. In nonthreatening situations, the wives are the first to admit their own concerns about "their sanity." Of over one hundred women who attended a discussion group at one time or another during the past six years, there was not one who failed to talk about her concerns about her own emotional health. All of the women worry about the part which their attitudes and behavior play in the persistence of the drinking and in their families' disturbances. Although no uniform personality types are discernible, they do share feelings of confusion and anxiety. Most feel ambivalent about their husbands. However, this group is composed of women who are oriented towards changing themselves and the situation rather than escaping from it.

The Impact of Alcoholism on the Family

When two or more persons live together over a period of time, patterns of relating to one another evolve. In a family, a division of functions occurs and roles interlock. For the family to function smoothly, each person must play his roles in a predictable manner and according to the expectations of others in the family. When the family as a whole is functioning smoothly, individual members of the family also tend to function well. Everyone is aware of where he fits, what he is expected to do, and what he can expect from others in the family. When this organization is disrupted, repercussions are felt by each family member. A crisis is under way.

Family crises tend to follow a similar pattern, regardless of the nature of the precipitant. Usually there is an initial denial that a problem exists. The family tries to continue in its usual behavior patterns until it is obvious that these patterns are no longer effective. At this point there is a downward slump in organization. Roles are played with less enthusiasm and there is an increase in tensions and strained relationships. Finally an improvement occurs as some adjustive technique is successful. Family organization becomes stabilized at a new level. At each stage of the crisis there is a reshuffling of roles among family members, changes in status and prestige, changes in "self" and "other" images, shifts in family solidarity and self-sufficiency and in the visibility of the crisis to outsiders. In the process of the crisis, considerable mental conflict is engendered in all family members, and personality distortion occurs. These are the elements which are uniform regardless of the type of family crisis. The phases vary in length and intensity depending on the nature of the crisis and the nature of the individuals involved in it.

When one of the adults in a family becomes an alcoholic, the over-all pattern of the crisis takes a form similar to that of other family crises. However there are usually recurrent subsidiary crises which complicate the over-all situation and the attempts at its resolution. Shame, unemployment, impoverishment, desertion and return, nonsupport, infidelity, imprisonment, illness and progressive dissension also occur. For other types of family crises, there are cultural prescriptions for socially appropriate behavior and for procedures which will terminate the crisis. But this is not so in the case of alcoholism. The cultural view is that alcoholism is shameful and should not occur. Thus, when facing alcoholism, the family is in a socially unstructured situation and must find the techniques for handling the crisis through trial and error behavior and without social support. In many respects, there are marked similarities between the type of crisis precipitated by alcoholism and those precipitated by mental illness.

Attempts to Deny the Problem

Alcoholism rarely emerges full-blown overnight. It is usually heralded by widely spaced incidents of excessive drinking, each of which sets off a small family crisis. Both spouses try to account for the episode and then to avoid the family situations which appear to have caused the drinking. In their search for explanations, they try to define the situation as controllable, understandable, and "perfectly normal." Between drinking episodes, both feel guilty about their behavior and about their impact on each other. Each tries to be an "ideal spouse" to the other. Gradually not only the drinking problem, but also the other problems in the marriage are denied or sidestepped.

It takes some time before the wife realizes that the drinking is neither normal nor controllable behavior. It takes the alcoholic considerably longer to come to the same conclusion. The cultural view that alcoholics are Skid Row bums who are constantly inebriated also serves to keep the situation clouded. Friends compound the confusion. If the wife compares her husband with them, some show parallels to his behavior and others are in marked contrast. She wavers between defining his behavior as "normal" and "not normal." If she consults friends, they tend to discount her concern, thus facilitating her tendency to deny that a problem exists and adding to her guilt about thinking disloyal thoughts about her husband.

During this stage the family is very concerned about the social visibility of the drinking behavior. They feel that they would surely be ostracized if the extent of the drinking were known. To protect themselves against discovery, the family begins to cut down on their social activities and to withdraw into the home.

Attempts to Eliminate the Problem

The second stage begins when the family defines the alcoholic's drinking behavior as "not normal." At this point frantic efforts are made to eliminate the problem. Lacking clear-cut cultural prescriptions for what to do in a situation like this, the efforts are of the trial and error variety. In rapid succession, the wife threatens to leave the husband, babies him during hangovers, drinks with him, hides or empties his bottles, curtails money, tries to understand his problem, keeps his liquor handy for him, and nags at him. However, all efforts to change the situation fail. Gradually the family becomes so preoccupied with the problem of discovering how to keep father sober that all long-term family goals recede into the background.

At the same time isolation of the family reaches its peak intensity. The extreme isolation magnifies the importance of all intrafamily interactions and events. Almost all thought becomes drinking-centered. Drinking comes to symbolize all conflicts between the spouses, and even mother-child conflicts are regarded as indirect derivatives of the drinking behavior. Attempts to keep the social visibility of the behavior at the lowest possible level increase.

The husband-wife alienation also accelerates. Each feels resentful of the other. Each feels misunderstood and unable to understand. Both search frantically for the reasons for the drinking, believing that if the reason could be discovered, all family members could gear their behavior in a way to make the drinking unnecessary.

The wife feels increasingly inadequate as a wife, mother, woman, and person. She feels she has failed to make a happy and united home for her husband and children. Her husband's frequent comments to the effect that her behavior causes his drinking and her own concerns that this may be true intensified the process of self-devaluation.

Disorganization

This is a stage which could also be entitled "What's the use?" Nothing seems effective in stabilizing the alcoholic. Efforts to change the situation become, at best, sporadic. Behavior is geared to relieve tensions rather than to achieve goals. The family gives up trying to understand the alcoholic. They do not care if the neighbors know about the drinking. The children are told that their father is a drunk. They are no longer required to show him affection or respect. The myth that father still has an important status in the family is dropped when he no longer supports them, is imprisoned, caught in infidelity, or disappears for long periods of time. The family ceases to care about its self-sufficiency and begins to resort to public agencies for help, thereby losing self-respect.

The wife becomes very concerned about her sanity. She finds herself engaging in tension-relieving behavior which she knows is goalless. She is aware that she feels tense, anxious, and hostile. She regards her precrisis self as "the real me" and becomes very frightened at how she has changed.

Attempts to Reorganize in Spite of the Problem

When some major or minor subsidiary crisis occurs, the family is forced to take survival action. At this point many wives leave their husbands.

The major characteristic of this stage is that the wife takes over. The alcoholic is ignored or is assigned the status of the most recalcitrant child. When the wife's obligations to her husband conflict with those to her children, she decides in favor of the children. Family ranks are closed progressively and the father excluded.

As a result of the changed family organization, father's behavior constitutes less of a problem. Hostility towards him diminishes as the family no longer expects him to change. Feelings of pity, exasperation, and protectiveness arise.

The reorganization has a stabilizing effect on the children. They find their environment and their mother more consistent. Their relationship to their father is more clearly defined. Guilt and anxiety diminish as they come to accept their mother's view that drinking is not caused by any behavior of family members.

Long-term family goals and planning begin again. Help from public agencies is accepted as necessary and no longer impairs family self-respect. With the taking over of family control, the wife gradually regains her sense of worth. Her concerns about her emotional health decrease.

Despite the greater stabilization, subsidiary crises multiply. The alcoholic is violent or withdraws more often; income becomes more uncertain; imprisonments and hospitalizations occur more frequently. Each crisis is temporarily disruptive to the new family organization. The symbolization of these events as being caused by alcoholism, however, prevents the complete disruption of the family.

The most disruptive type of crisis occurs if the husband recognizes that he has a drinking problem and makes an effort to get help. Hope is mobilized. The family attempts to open its ranks again in order to give him the maximum chance for recovery. Roles are partially reshuffled and attempts at attitude change are made, only to be disrupted again if treatment is unsuccessful.

Efforts to Escape the Problem

The problems involved in separating from the alcoholic are similar to the problems involved in separation for any other reason. However, some of the problems are more intense. The wife, who could count on some support from her husband in earlier stages, even though it was a manipulative move on his part, can no longer be sure of any support. The mental conflict about deserting a sick man must be resolved as well as the wife's feelings of responsibility for his alcoholism. The family which has experienced violence from the alcoholic is concerned that separation may intensify the violence. When the decision is made to separate because of the drinking, the alcoholic often gives up drinking for a while, thereby removing what is apparently the major reason for the separation.

Some other events, however, have made separation possible. The wife has learned that the family can run smoothly without her husband. Taking over control has bolstered her self-confidence. Her orientation has shifted from inaction to action. The wife also has familiarity with public agencies which can provide help, and she has overcome her shame about using them.

Reorganization of the Family

Without the father, the family tends to reorganize rather smoothly. They have already closed ranks against him and now they feel free of the minor disruptions he still created in the family. Reorganization is impeded if the alcoholic continues to attempt reconciliation or feels he must "get even" with the family for deserting him.

The whole family becomes united when the husband achieves sobriety, whether or not separation has preceded. For the wife and husband facing a sober marriage after many years of an alcoholic marriage, the expectations for marriage without alcoholism are unrealistic and idealistic.

Many problems arise. The wife has managed the family for years. Now her husband wishes to be reinstated as head of the house. Usually the first role he re-establishes is that of bread-winner. With the resumption of this role, he feels that the family should reinstate him immediately in all his former roles. Difficulties inevitably follow. For example, the children are often unable to accept his resumption of the father role. Their mother has been mother and father to them for so long that it takes time to get used to consulting their father. Often the father tries to manage his change overnight, and the very pressure he puts on the children towards this end defeats him.

The wife, who finds it difficult to believe that her husband is sober permanently, is often unwilling to relinquish her control of family affairs even though she knows that this is necessary to her husband's sobriety. She remembers when his failures to handle responsibility were catastrophic to the family. Used to avoiding any issues which might upset him, the wife often has difficulty discussing problems openly. If she permits him to resume his father role, she often feels resentful of his intrusion into territory she has come to regard as her own. If he makes any decisions which are detrimental to the family, her former feelings of superiority may be mobilized and affect her relationship with him.

Gradually the difficulties related to alcoholism recede into the past and family adjustment at some level is achieved. The drinking problem shows up only sporadically—when the time comes for a decision about permitting the children to drink or when pressure is put on the husband to drink at a party.

Personality Disturbances in Family Members

Each stage in the crisis of alcoholism has distinctive characteristics. The type of problems faced, the extent to which the situation is structured, the amount of emotional support received by individual family members, and the rewards vary as to the stage of the crisis. Some stages "fit" the personalities of the individuals involved better than others.

Although each stage of the crisis appears to give rise to some similar patterns of response, there is considerable variation from family to family.

The wife whose original personality fits comfortably into denying the existence of the problem will probably take longer to get past this phase of the crisis than the wife who finds dominating more congenial. The latter will probably prolong the stage of attempting to eliminate the problem. Some families make an adjustment at one level of the crisis and never seem to go on to the next phase.

With the transition from one stage to another, there is the danger of marked personality disturbance in family members. Some become their most disturbed when drinking first becomes a problem; others become most disturbed when the alcoholic becomes sober. In the experience of the author, there has been little uniformity within families or between families in this respect. However, after two or three years of sobriety, the alcoholics' family members appear to resemble a cross section of people anywhere. Any uniformities which were obvious earlier seem to have disappeared.

Therapy and the Family

The major goal of the families of most alcoholics is to find some way of bringing about a change in father's drinking. When the alcoholic seeks treatment, the family members usually have very mixed feelings towards the treatment agency. Hope that father may recover is remobilized and if sobriety ensues for any length of time, they are grateful. At the same time, they often feel resentment that an outside agency can accomplish what they have tried to do for years. They may also resent the emotional support which the alcoholic receives from the treatment agency, while they are left to cope with still another change in their relationship to him without support.

Most families have little awareness of what treatment involves and are forced to rely on the alcoholic patient for their information. The patient frequently passes on a distorted picture in order to manipulate the family situation for his own ends. What information is given is perceived by the family against a background of their attitudes towards the alcoholic at that point in time. The actions they take are also influenced by their estimate of the probability that treatment will be successful. The result is often a family which works at cross purposes with therapy.

Recently there has been a growing recognition that the family of the alcoholic also requires help if the alcoholic is to be treated successfully. An experiment was tried at the Henry Phipps Psychiatric Clinic of Johns Hopkins Hospital. Alcoholics and their wives were treated in concurrent group therapy sessions. The Al-Anon Family Groups provide the same type of situation for the families of AA members and have the additional asset of helping the families of alcoholics who are still not interested in receiving help for themselves. Joint treatment of alcoholics and the members of their family aims at getting a better understanding of the underlying emotional disturbance, of the relationship between the alcoholic and the person who is most frequently the object and stimulus of the drinking behavior, and of the treatment process.[2]

Joint treatment of the alcoholic and his family has other assets, as Gliedman and his co-workers point out.[3] Joint theapy emphasizes the marriage. In addition, with both spouses coming for help, there is less likelihood that undertaking treatment will be construed as an admission of guilt or that therapy will be used as a weapon by one against the other. The wife's entrance into therapy is a tacit admission of her need to change too. It represents a hopeful attitude on the part of both the alcoholic and his wife that recovery is possible and creates an orientation towards working things out together as a family unit.

The members of an Al-Anon group with which the author is familiar receive understanding of their problems and their feelings from one another, emotional support which facilitates change in attitudes and behavior, basic information about solutions to common problems, and information about the treatment process and about the nature of alcoholism as an illness. Shame is alleviated and hope engendered. The nonalcoholic spouses gain perspective on what has happened in their families and on the possibilities of changing towards greater stability. Anxiety diminishes in an almost visible fashion. As they gain perspective on the situation, behavior tends to become more realistic and rewarding. By no means the least important effect derived from membership in the group is a structuring of what has seemed to be a completely unstructured situation and the feelings of security which this engenders.

---

[2] L. H. Gliedman, D. Rosenthal, J. Frank, H. T. Nash, "Group Therapy of Alcoholics with Concurrent Group Meetings of Their Wives," *Quarterly Journal of Studies on Alcohol*, Vol. 17, December 1956, pp. 655–70.

[3] *Ibid.*

65 · Casework with Parents of Children Born with Severe Brain Defects *

ADA KOZIER

Most children are born normal, but a few are born with serious handicaps or develop some permanent handicap early in life. How can parents best overcome the shock, learn to accept the child, and make the best preparations possible for its care? Miss Kozier, a skilled caseworker, reviews some cases and describes how the parents were helped to overcome their first emotional reactions and to plan for their defective children.

THERE HAVE ALWAYS BEEN children born with anomalies and malformations so severe that they could not develop sufficiently to fulfil a useful role in life. Societies have dealt with such children in various ways. Some earlier ones, such as Sparta, solved the problem entirely at the expense of the children by leaving them to die in the mountains. In other societies, some protection was provided for these unfortunate individuals and their families out of a respect for life based on religious conviction. Today, American society also has a reverence for life. The family with a defective child, however, is additionally burdened because our society is competitive and places great emphasis on individual achievement.

Medical advances in preventing congenital birth anomalies have thus far been limited. A beginning has been made, however, in understanding and treating the effects on the fetus of certain illnesses of the mother. Medical research is continuing to be done with the expectation that important new discoveries will be made.

In the field of public health, interest has been focused on the problems of infant mortality and prematurity. As a result, considerable progress has been made in the prevention of stillbirths and of fetal loss. Although this development has resulted in a large number of live births, it also has led to an increase in the number of children with

---

* *Social Casework*, 38 (April, 1957), 183–189. Reprinted by permission of the publisher and the author.
The author, now Case Supervisor of the New York Guild for the Jewish Blind, at the time of writing this article was Senior Caseworker for Mount Sinai Hospital Social Service, New York.

congenital anomalies [1] who survive. These anomalies include a wide range of malformations and widely varying degrees of impairment. One of the most serious congenital defects is an anomaly in the development of the brain itself. Although successful treatment is possible in some types of cerebral malformations, many babies born with congenital defects of the brain are beyond medical or surgical help.

Although the greatest part of this paper is applicable in some degree to children with other types of anomalies, my primary concern is with children born with severe, inoperable brain defects. Casework on behalf of children who are less severely handicapped often may be focused on enabling the parent and child to live together at home. When the handicap is severe, one may question the child's future adjustment in the community, and the possibility of institutionalization is often a major consideration in planning.

The Parents' Need for Help

In the past, cases involving children with severe brain defects were referred to the Social Service Department of our hospital chiefly for the purpose of obtaining help for the parents with the procedural aspects of institutionalization. Today, however, more and more physicians recognize the need for early referral to the social worker so that parents may also have help in clarifying their feelings in order to plan appropriately for themselves as well as for their child. With increasing frequency referrals are received not only from the clinics and wards but also from physicians who are serving semi-private and private patients. The cases to be discussed here are drawn from the experience of caseworkers in the Pediatric Neurology Clinic, the Pediatric Wards, and the Obstetric Nursery of the Mount Sinai Hospital.

Not only the parents but often physicians, nurses, and social workers as well react with severe shock to the birth of a baby with anomalies. During pregnancy some women have fears about giving birth to a "monster." Psychiatrists frequently attribute these fears to the woman's childhood fantasies. Perhaps such fears go back to earlier phases in the evolution of the human species. The well-known anthropologist, Margaret Mead, describes as "not fully human" a child who, "because of defect, neglect, or injury," is unable to participate in the process of continuing the great body of human inventions and experience.[2]

---

[1] Clemens E. Benda, M.D., *Developmental Disorders of Mentation and Cerebral Palsies*, Grune & Stratton, New York, 1952.

[2] Margaret Mead and Martha Wolfenstein (eds.), *Childhood in Contemporary Cultures*, University of Chicago Press, 1955, p. 6.

We know that many children with severe brain defect do not attain even minimal physical or intellectual functioning. Many cannot learn to sit, walk, or speak. Some, such as the children suffering from hydrocephalus, are truly terrifying in appearance.

In our culture, a parent makes a great emotional and material investment in the preparations for the birth of a baby. In many ways, a child represents to the parent an extension of his own self. When the baby is born, the mother's wish to be loved is partially transferred from her own person to that of the baby.[3] To the father, a normal child is often an affirmation, at least in part, of his own sense of success. The capacity to produce unimpaired offspring is psychologically and culturally important for the parents' sense of personal adequacy. In view of this emotional climate, parents who are faced with the birth of a baby with anomalies are subject to great suffering and disappointment. They are fearful of critical and rejecting community reactions to the child. Planning for the child is further complicated by the lack of adequate community facilities. Owing to these internal and external pressures, the parent's capacity to maintain his emotional balance is severely tested and his own functioning as well as the relationships within the family are subjected to strain.

Pearl S. Buck, in her book, *The Child Who Never Grew*,[4] tells of the many parents who wrote to her asking "first, what shall they do for their children, and second, how shall they bear the sorrow of having such a child." She describes her own deep suffering as she learned to conquer this potentially destructive experience. She believes that "endurance of inescapable sorrow is something which has to be learned alone." It is certainly true that every individual is always alone in the deepest part of this process of integrating harsh life experiences, but we recognize also the partial soothing of suffering that comes from the sympathy and understanding of family and friends. Today, there is growing acceptance of the fact that the individual whose capacity to function is threatened by difficult life experiences can derive help from a relationship with a professionally trained person.

When parents find it difficult to decide "what they shall do for their child," a social worker's skill can assist them in many ways. The stable, mature parent may make use of the social worker's knowledge of resources in his effort to meet as appropriately as possible the needs of his particular situation. Self-help groups of parents, established for mutual strengthening, employ social workers to interpret the need for

---

[3] Helene Deutsch, M.D., *The Psychology of Women*, Grune & Stratton, New York, 1945, Vol. II, p. 17.
[4] Pearl S. Buck, *The Child Who Never Grew*, John Day Co., New York, 1950, p. 5.

social action and to develop and mobilize support for it in the community.

Skilled casework counseling is called for when the parent's initial shock is so prolonged as to interfere with his functioning at home and in the community. The threat to him of having produced a child severely malformed may be so great that he may not be able to carry even the most urgent of parental responsibilities. He may try to leave his baby in the hospital indefinitely; he may deny the baby's need for special treatment; he may neglect the baby physically; or he may devote himself so exclusively to the child that he is cut off from other life experiences.

Accepting the Medical Diagnosis

At times when parents are overwhelmed by the medical diagnosis of their child's condition, they may continue to search for medical help beyond what appears to be reasonable. Certainly we respect a parent's need to explore every possible avenue for medical help. There is a subtle dividing line, however, between the rational search for help and aimless wandering from physician to physician in the search for advice. A parent may be primarily motivated not by love and concern for his child but by an inability to cope with his child's illness because of his exaggerated feelings of guilt, anxiety, and horror.

Mrs. R came to the Social Service Department on her own initiative. Her first baby, a daughter three weeks old, was on the semi-private floor of the hospital under the care of an eminent neurologist. He was the third physician the parents had consulted. The baby was suffering from hydrocephalus and had a lump protruding from the back of her head. The neurologist had advised that an operation to remove the lump could not be performed and that the baby's chances for survival beyond infancy were not good. He had suggested that the parents take the baby home.

Neither Mr. nor Mrs. R could think of taking the baby home and they asked that she be placed. They were too upset, however, to evaluate either plan. Mr. R deferred to his wife's wishes and said he wanted to do what would be best for her. Both looked to the social worker to take the problem off their hands.

Mr. and Mrs. R, now in their middle thirties, had waited seven years before planning to have the baby. They explained how they had lived in a small apartment, saving their money. Mrs. R had worked up to the date of delivery. It was evident from her own and her husband's reports that she had been overly careful not to make special demands on her husband during her pregnancy. The picture that emerged was one of a couple tense about parenthood, anxious for status and achievement, and intensely concerned about securing a financially comfortable environment for their child.

Mrs. R was sure she could not handle the baby's care at home and feared she might accidentally cause her death. Stumbling over her words, she said she "felt like a freak" when she looked at the child.

The caseworker helped Mrs. R to talk about her feelings of disappointment and frustration and also her feelings of guilt for having borne this defective child. Effort was focused on helping her to see herself and her baby as separate and different individuals, and to recognize also her responsibility for planning for the baby's care. Thus, more firmly oriented to reality, Mrs. R was enabled to move toward a beginning discussion of alternative plans.

Mrs. R could not consider a state institution; she felt she wanted to work to support her baby in a private nursing home. Taking the baby home remained a possibility.

Both parents visited a private nursing home to see how babies there were being cared for. Mrs. R could not bear the sight of babies under custodial care and was very upset when she returned to see the worker. As she discussed how she felt, she agreed that what she was looking for was a placement facility for healthy, normal children, and that she was not ready to accept her own baby as a hopelessly sick child who needed custodial care.

Mrs. R was defensive and stressed the fact that friends and relatives had encouraged her to seek additional medical advice. In her anxiety she pictured herself wandering with the baby from hospital to hospital in and out of New York indefinitely. Her right to seek further medical help was affirmed by the social worker and concrete suggestions were made on how to proceed. Mrs. R began to feel that while she was carrying on a search for surgery she would be able to care for the child at home. She was able to handle her inquiries rationally and to care for the baby at home until she found an out-of-town hospital willing to take the risk of surgery. After the growth was removed, Mrs. R was greatly relieved. She was aware that the baby's chances for survival continued to be poor.

This case illustrates the suffering to which parents of a child like this one are subjected and the difficulty they experience in making plans under the stress of unrelieved emotions. The parents could seek help only with the immediate and obvious part of the problem. Mrs. R was relieved of some of her feelings of horror and self-blame by being able to express them within the non-judgmental relationship that the worker provided. With the worker's realistic support she was enabled to explore possibilities and alternative plans for the baby's care and treatment. She gained a beginning awareness of her real problem in accepting the baby's condition and this helped her control her anxiety. A parent's way of handling himself in relation to having a severely damaged child reflects his basic personality structure and his already established patterns of behavior. Mr. and Mrs. R were able to make only a beginning in taking help. They may need a period of time in which to experience and integrate the correctness of the medical diagnosis before they can seek further assistance.

Planning for Institutional Care

I am not planning to discuss here the complicated arguments for and against the institutionalization of retarded and defective children since I am dealing only with a group of children for whom the prognosis is hopeless. In many cases it is possible, with the help of modern scientific advances in techniques of brain examination, to establish clearly that the child's potential for development is minimal. The physician is then in a position to make an early recommendation that the child be institutionalized, sometimes immediately after birth. At our clinic exacting procedures are followed to ensure accurate diagnosis before such a recommendation is made, and at that time parents are given a full explanation of the medical findings.

The hospital social worker helps a parent come to grips with the necessity of planning for his baby. A parent, owing to his feelings of helplessness, may endow the worker with power to resolve the problem for him and he may become angry when faced with the worker's limitations. The worker's understanding of the parent's personality and background, and knowledge of resources and reality factors will enable him to help the parent arrive at the most satisfactory plan.

Mrs. B had given birth to a premature baby who, at the age of forty-eight hours, suffered severe convulsions. Early in her contact with the worker, Mrs. B had revealed her deep anxiety and helplessness by saying that the family had suffered so much adversity recently that they had reached bottom—things could get no worse. She was convinced that the baby would get better.

The B family had suffered many upsetting economic setbacks. There had been serious marital problems just preceding conception; early in the pregnancy she and Mr. B had separated temporarily. Mrs. B had wanted the child but Mr. B had found the additional responsibility upsetting. Although they were now reunited and had made a superficial readjustment, there were still many underlying tensions in their relationship. A precarious balance had been established between Mrs. B's anxious need to control and Mr. B's immature fear of responsibility and initiative. Mrs. B, although able to share information with the worker and to seek sympathy and understanding, was anxiously concerned with keeping the status quo.

Mrs. B was deeply threatened by the baby's illness. She expressed fear that the baby would be retarded. She herself had been an honor student, and so was her older daughter. Her two sisters also were gifted and she had been quite competitive with them. She had always felt less loved than they were. Mrs. B also seemed threatened by the knowledge that her mother had been mentally ill during the later years of her life.

It was not surprising that Mrs. B, in the face of all these burdens and knowing that the prognosis was uncertain, found it very difficult to take the baby home from the Premature Ward. She tended to express resentment of medical procedures and needed help in recognizing that it was her fears of the future with which she was struggling rather than real questions about immediate medical care.

After the baby's discharge, Mrs. B heaped affection on her. The baby's continued convulsions and retarded development, however, kept Mrs. B in a constant state of tension.

The baby, attractive looking and dressed like a doll, was readmitted to the hospital at the age of one year. Further tests revealed that the cortex of the brain was not normally developed and that she was in all likelihood severely retarded; institutionalization was recommended.

Mrs. B reacted to this diagnosis and recommendation by wanting immediately to put away the baby's crib and give away her clothing. When she learned that permanent placement would not be possible immediately, Mrs. B tended to blame the worker. In response to her feeling of urgency she was offered a private placement plan on a temporary basis pending the baby's admission to the public institution. Neither Mr. nor Mrs. B could accept this plan and they decided to take the baby home temporarily.

Mrs. B had not wanted to know the name of the state institution to which the baby was to go for permanent placement. She was helped to face the fact that the baby would be part of her life, whether or not she knew her whereabouts.

At the worker's suggestion, the physician delayed discharge for a few days in order to give the parents more time to integrate their decision. For a while, Mrs. B had complained that her husband was reluctant even to talk about the baby and had left the whole decision to her. She was helped to take initiative in asking him to participate and the letter applying for the baby's placement in a state institution was based on a shared decision. Mr. B, in line with his previous pattern, was initially reluctant to be with his wife at the time of the baby's discharge. Supported by the worker, Mrs. B could tell him about her need for his presence at such a significant moment. Both parents, on the day of discharge, reacted with relief.

During the baby's hospitalization, Mrs. B spent a great deal of time in the hospital and this was discussed with her in terms of what it meant to her older child. She was able to visit less frequently as she made progress in resolving her conflict about plans for the baby. The older child, prompted by a neighbor, had asked whether the baby was dead and Mrs. B was helped to express some of her feelings about letting her daughter know of the baby's illness in more detail. She then prepared her daughter for the baby's return home and also for the possibility that eventually a permanent placement would be made.

Physical separation from the child frequently alleviates not only the problems posed by the child's need for continued nursing care but also the emotional pressures on the parents created by his physical presence in the home. Yet the decision to place the child is difficult for the parents to make and evokes their guilt and fear. Out of a need to remove the child from their lives without having to think and feel, parents sometimes seek to place the child hurriedly, disregarding realities. With these parents our goal is to help them separate from their child, not only physically, but emotionally as well.

When institutionalization is recommended and planned immediately after the child's birth, the question arises whether or not the parents should be encouraged to see their child before placement.

Mr. C, immediately after his baby's birth, demanded that it be placed, stating that "it" could not possibly be taken home. He said that he had been informed by the physician that the child was a Mongoloid and should be institutionalized immediately, without being seen by his parents. Mr. C expressed no desire to see the baby and said that his wife certainly should not do so.

Mr. and Mrs. C had told their friends that the baby was dying of leukemia. In view of this they felt that they had no alternative but to place him. Mr. C expressed guilt about the child's condition in indirect ways. He stressed how considerate he had been of his wife during pregnancy, sexually and otherwise. He said that his wife could not care for this child and expressed the fear that if she had to do so, the instability of her family background would emerge. He said that he did not even know what a Mongoloid child was or what it meant and wondered whether the worker could suggest any literature for him. Yet, when his questions were discussed, it developed that he had learned all the essential facts from the doctor.

Mr. C's eagerness to know as much as possible about his baby was in strange contrast to his decision not to see the child and his questions were evidence of his guilt and anxiety. Are such feelings relieved by a recommendation that the parent not see the baby? Dr. Alastair Beddie, who discusses this question in his article entitled "Mothers, Mongols and Mores," [5] warns against making recommendations which involve ethical decisions and which may be in conflict with the social mores. In our society the refusal of a parent ever to see his child is an act of extreme rejection. When a person in a highly respected and authoritative position recommends this extreme action, the parents' fantasies of the unseen baby's unbearably frightful appearance may be reinforced.

There may, of course, be cases in which the physical appearance of the child is such that seeing him may add to the parents' problems. Certainly, in these situations, parents have a right to decide whether or not to see the child. They should be helped to make the decision that is best for them on the basis of full knowledge of the facts.

In some cases we have found that the parents, although burdened with the hardship of caring for their child, cannot move toward separating from him. Despite their suffering, they seem to derive satisfaction from caring for the child at home. This reaction may be due in part to differing cultural patterns which are reinforced by the need for self-punishment, by problems in the marital relationship, or at times by the need to find justification for withdrawing from community living. Whether such reactions can be handled with the parent depends on the severity of his neurotic problems, his comfort or discomfort with earlier patterns, and his attitude toward seeking change. In these situations, the worker's self-discipline and professional integrity are often put to the test as it becomes necessary to remain identified with the medical diagnosis without putting pressure on the parent to comply with the recommendation for institutionalization.

The problem of parents who are faced with the question of institutionalizing the child who is suffering from a brain defect is often made even more difficult by the lack of adequate placement facilities, both temporary and permanent. This is a community problem that urgently needs to be solved.

Summary

In summary, parents whose newborn child is found to be suffering from severe brain defect are subject to great emotional strain which may

---

[5] Alastair Beddie, M.D., and Humphry Osmond, M.R.C.S.D.P.M., in *The Canadian Medical Association Journal*, July–December, 1955, pp. 167 ff.

affect their ability to plan appropriately for the baby and themselves. If not given proper help, they may make inappropriate decisions or their unresolved emotional tensions may constitute a continuing strain on their over-all social adjustment. Social work help should be offered at moments of disturbance and crisis, if parents want it and are able to use it. It should be directed toward helping them clarify their feelings sufficiently to see the child as a separate human being, and his handicap as an unfortunate accident of nature. Help with planning should be directed toward meeting the needs of the individual parent and child while at the same time the worker holds to the validity and importance of the medical diagnosis and recommendation.

CHAPTER 19:

External Stresses on the Family

69 · Unemployment: Crisis of the Common Man *

RUTH SHONLE CAVAN

Four kinds of external stresses that disturb family life are common in the United States: economic recessions and depressions, death of a family member, natural disasters, and wars. Other countries may have some or all of these and may have others. The United States has not suffered the effects of bombing, as some European and Asiatic countries have during recent wars; nor are we subject to famines as in some parts of Asia, nor to devastating plagues.

Recessions and depressions bring widespread unemployment, which not only affects the standard of living of a family but, perhaps more disastrous, disturbs the status of the husband relative to that of other members of the family and often calls for a new alignment of roles. Individual unemployment when there is no recession may have much the same effect. Such unemployment may result from chronic illness, the development of a handicap, removal of an industry to a new location, introduction of automation, or the difficulty of finding a satisfactory position immediately after graduation. Whatever the cause, unemployment often has the quality of a crisis—it is unexpected and the family is not adequately prepared to meet it. If it becomes permanent, drastic readjustment is necessary.

ANY PERIOD of widespread, prolonged unemployment raises the specter of possible family disorganization and even disintegration. The Great Depression of the 1930's led to a number of studies of family reactions to unemployment and lowered income. These studies can lay the founda-

* Marriage and Family Living, 21 (May, 1959), 139–146. Based on a paper read at the Groves Conference on Marriage and the Family, Washington, D.C., April 15, 1958. Reprinted by permission of the publisher and author.
A sketch of the author is given in connection with article 6.

tion for current studies and even for current methods of alleviation, with some consideration for the differences between the 1930's and the late 1950's.

In order to sharpen our view of the impact of unemployment on family life, this review of the depression studies is organized according to social class, so far as such a classification is possible in studies made before the concept of social class was well defined.[1]

The social classes discussed here are as follows:

1. The lower-lower class family:
   a. with long-term or permanent unemployment
   b. with regular repetitive unemployment
   c. usually employed, except in time of personal or economic emergency;
2. The family of the "common man," that is, upper-lower and lower-middle class, regularly employed except in time of great economic emergency;
3. The upper-middle class.

The family of the common man is discussed first, since the traumatic impact of unemployment seems most acute in this social class.

The Common Man, Upper-Lower and Lower-Middle Classes

The conditions imposed by unemployment and lowered income are most significant when seen against a backdrop of what the common man wants, expects, and has partially achieved. One of the chief values of the common man is to be self-supporting at all times, with a backlog of moderate savings. Often the family prides itself on "getting ahead," with a goal of upward mobility, if not for the parents, at least for their children. Wives may work regularly or intermittently and older children work, but the husband is the chief and most steady worker and makes the largest contribution to the family budget. Typically, his status is recognized as the highest in the family. The effort toward upward mobility is chiefly in the acquisition of rather expensive equipment, not always paid for, or in moving into a better neighborhood than the one in which the family originally lived. Culturally and socially, the family may not have established itself in the next higher class. Hence, considerable emphasis is placed on visible material possessions which are symbols of status.

---

[1] Family life according to social class is discussed in Ruth Shonle Cavan, *The American Family*, New York: Thomas Y. Crowell Company, 1953, Part II.

Four depression studies that concentrated on the common man are: [2]
Cavan and Ranck, whose study of one hundred Chicago families included sixty-eight of common-man status; Komarovsky who concentrated
on fifty-nine cases; Bakke, *The Unemployed Worker*, based on a number
of studies made between 1932 and 1939; and *Citizens without Work*, by
the same author, an eight year study of twenty-four families suffering
prolonged unemployment.

Reaction to Unemployment. A loss of or reduction in employment and
hence in income among these families poses a many-sided threat: loss
of the symbols of social class status; eventual probable application for
relief; disorganized personal reactions; disorganization and rearrangement
of roles within the family; downward social mobility.

First came the financial adjustment. At least at the beginning of the
depression, there was disbelief that the situation was anything except
a normal short lay-off. Men therefore were inclined to speak of deserving
a short vacation. When no recall came, they sought employment first in
their special skill, then in a less specialized and lower paid type of work,
finally in any work, and eventually at odd jobs. [Cavan and Ranck, Bakke
(2)] This devaluation of job status was a long-drawn out procedure. For
as long as six months, skilled workers held out for the old wages, but by
the end of twelve months, 85 per cent were willing, although often resentful, to take any kind of job. [Bakke (1), ch. 8]

If other members of the family found work, their employment eased
the financial strain, but often produced interpersonal strains.

As unemployment was prolonged, resources (symbols of status) were
used with the following order of frequency: credit, small savings, loans,
selling or pawning goods, and cashing of insurance policies. [Bakke (1),
ch. 8; Cavan and Ranck, p. 84] Expenses were reduced by having the
telephone removed, not taking summer vacations, dropping club mem-
berships, and the like. Some families moved to less expensive living
quarters; others moved in with relatives. As long as possible, invisible
reductions were made; but eventually it was not possible to conceal the
financial condition from neighbors. The final and most difficult financial
adjustment was in applying for relief. For these self-supporting and often
upwardly mobile families, relief was regarded as a personal disgrace. It

---

[2] Ruth Shonle Cavan and Katherine Howland Ranck, *The Family and the Depression*,
Chicago: University of Chicago Press, 1938; Mirra Komarovsky, *The Unemployed
Man and His Family*, New York: Dryden Press, 1940; E. Wight Bakke, *The Unem-
ployed Worker, A Study of the Task of Making a Living without a Job*, New Haven:
Yale University Press, 1940, No. 1; and Bakke, *Citizens without Work*, New Haven:
Yale University Press, 1940, No. 2. No. 1 and No. 2 are used in the text to distinguish
Bakke's two books.

was also the end of their hopes for upward mobility and often was preceded by definite downward mobility, partly because personal resources had to be reduced to a very low point before the family would be accepted by most relief agencies.

During this period of declining employment and exhaustion of resources, three types of reaction occurred.

1. Emotional reactions of husband and wife. The period preceding application for relief was a harrowing one as the family resisted the change in self-conception that relief made necessary. Worry, discouragement, and despondency were common emotional reactions. When forced to apply for relief, husband and wife cried at the agency. Definitely neurotic symptoms occurred in a minority of cases, as extreme insomnia, hysterical laughter, burning spots on the body, and suicide threats. However, out of the total of one hundred Chicago cases there were only two suicides, neither attributable solely to the depression. Husband and wife often shared equally in the emotional tension. In some families, one member, often the husband, became more disturbed than the others. A few drank heavily and several had "nervous breakdowns." [Cavan and Ranck, pp. 55–66; Komarovsky, pp. 36 ff., 66 ff.]

2. Changes in roles within the family. Although the husband is the chief earner in the family of the common man, it is accepted that the wife works when necessary, and that older children have an obligation to work part or full time as soon as they reach the legal age for employment. It was less true in the early 1930's than now that the wife works as a matter of choice and not simply from necessity. But even in the 1930's the employment of the wife was not taken as a threat to the husband's superior status, so long as it was conceded that the wife's employment was temporary.

The unemployment of the husband affected roles in three ways. First, when the husband could not find any work, his role suffered in the eyes of other members of the family. Wives sometimes lost their respect or accused their husbands of not trying to find work. Unless the husband could work out some role in the household (difficult to do), he really had no role to play. [Cavan and Ranck, Komarovsky, various items]

Second, when some members of the family usurped the role of the husband as chief wage earner, interpersonal relationships became strained. Apparently actual reduction in dollars earned was less devastating than change in roles; or, dire poverty was easier to bear than the husband's loss of status to some previously subordinate member. It seems to make little difference what members worked or how much or how little each earned, provided that the husband remained the largest contributor to the family purse. Tension was increased by the custom of children contributing their money to the family through the mother, who then often became the bursar for the family. [Cavan, Komarovsky, Bakke]

Third, when the family finally applied for relief and was accepted as a client further rearrangement of roles became necessary. The relief worker assumed a role superior to that of the husband. Since the relief worker was usually a woman, and dealt primarily with the wife, the husband now found himself subordinate both to his wife and to the woman relief worker. [Bakke (2)]

3. Change in social class status. In the hierarchy of social class levels, families on relief are relegated to lower-lower class status. Especially for upward mobile families, their descent to lower-lower class was embittering. When these families were forced to move, the search for lower rent sometimes brought many relief families into the same neighborhood. Bakke (1) speaks of entire neighborhoods of relief families.

As the depression progressed, certain cushions were devised. One of these was the Works Progress Administration (WPA), established in 1935, which provided work relief, At first, WPA workers were contrasted with persons still on relief; their self-respect increased and their social status was slightly improved. But in time, WPA workers were identified with relief cases and contrasted with persons privately employed. Their status and self-respect then again declined. [Bakke (1), ch. 12]

Another cushion was unemployment compensation, established in 1938, and by now a customary way to tide over short periods of unemployment. The implications of unemployment compensations are discussed later in this paper.

Readjustment of Family. Emotional disturbance usually continued until the family reached a level, however low, of stability. As soon as the family accepted this level as probably permanent, reorganization began as the family adjusted itself to its new level. As the depression decreased and various members of the family found work, upward mobility sometimes began again; however older members of the family often were unable to regain their former personal status, so that the family status might be organized around the older children as the chief earners.

Bakke (2) divides the readjustment process into experimental and permanent. He says that few families remained disorganized for a very long period of time. In experimental readjustment, the husband accepted his lowered status and a new hierarchy of statuses began to develop, with the wife granted the authority to manage finances and each child assigned a status relative to earning capacity. New interests and new plans for children developed, appropriate to the new social class status. The family drew together again with new roles that fitted together into an integrated pattern. Permanent readjustment came when the family stopped comparing the meager present with the more comfortable past, accepted rationalizations for the lowered status, and renewed a full round of family activities although of a different type than formerly.

In other families, the disarrangement of roles and lowering of statuses were less severe and consequently readjustment came more quickly. When the family did not have to make a residential move, loss of social status was less noticeable. Avoidance of relief through reduced expenses or help from relatives saved the family from the greatest humiliation. Activities and goals could be modified without great disorganization. [Cavan and Ranck, ch. 7]

Pre-unemployment Factors. Two studies, Cavan and Ranck, and Komarovsky, emphasized the previous family organization as a factor in the way in which families of the common man reacted to the depression.

Cavan and Ranck used the concept of well organized family, defined as a family with a high degree of unity and reciprocal functioning. Although well and poorly organized families varied in their reactions to unemployment, in general well organized families fared better than the poorly organized. They suffered emotionally as they approached the relief status, but also attempted to adjust realistically. The family group remained intact and as the lower status was accepted, family goals of a new type evolved. The family group worked together to overcome their problems.

Families disorganized prior to the depression tended to become more disorganized. Previous latent tensions between husband and wife or between parents and children came into the open under the increased tension of unemployment and low income. In a few cases the parents separated, adolescent children ran away from home, or the family broke into several small units. In some of these families, stability increased with the entrance of a relief agency whose worker helped to hold the family together by permitting the members to become dependent upon her. [Cavan and Ranck, ch. 7]

Komarovsky limited her research to a study of the relation between the husband's role as the economic provider of the family and his authority in the family. In forty-five out of fifty-nine cases, all on relief one or more years, the husband did not lose his authority in the family. In these families the authority of the husband was based either on love and respect, or on the traditional semi-patriarchal organization of the common-man family. Unemployment was not interpreted as a reflection on the husband.

When the authority of the husband was based on fear of the husband or was maintained for utilitarian purposes, his unemployment was followed by loss of respect and loss of authority. In some of these families, the wife did not respect her husband prior to the unemployment. When unemployment freed her from economic dependence upon him, the thin veneer of submission cracked. The husbands attempted to force respect from wife and children, psychologically or physically, or selected a few areas of dominance about which they would not yield; some sought compensation in alcohol or religion.

Summary of the Common Man and Unemployment. In general the upper-lower and lower-middle class families suffered greatly from prolonged unemployment which violated deeply revered values of the common man: relief substituted for self-support; transfer of the highest family status from the husband to some previously subordinate member of the family; and downward social mobility. The lengthy period of downgrading to relief status was the most difficult and was marked by severe emotional reactions. Readjustment came with acceptance of the condition of poverty and reorganization of the family in harmony with the reality of the situation. The well organized family with unity of purpose and reciprocal functioning of members in which the husband held his status on the basis of love and respect or tradition weathered the adjustment better than poorly organized families or those in which fear and utilitarian motives were at the basis of the hierarchy of statuses.

The Upper-Middle Class

The upper-middle class was less affected by the depression than the common man, and very few persons became relief clients.[3] Most upper-middle workers remained in their accustomed positions, sometimes at higher incomes than prior to the depression. The few whose businesses failed or who became unemployed tended to re-establish themselves by their own efforts.

However, one study concentrated on families, primarily upper-middle class, which had suffered a decrease of at least 25 per cent in their income, often accompanied by total or partial unemployment.[4] The reaction of these families was severe but was related chiefly to changes of personal status within the family. With a few exceptions, the families were able to remain in their homes and thus were saved one of the drastic steps in downward social mobility. They also managed to get along without applying for relief.

---

[3] W. Lloyd Warner and Paul S. Lunt, *Social Life of a Modern Community*, New Haven: Yale University Press, 1941, pp. 277-279; Winona L. Morgan, *The Family Meets the Depression*, Minneapolis: University of Minnesota Press, 1939.

[4] Robert Cooley Angell, *The Family Encounters the Depression*, New York: Charles Scribner's Sons, 1936.

Angell's main focus was on the effect of reduced income on interpersonal relationships among family members. The two elements of family life found most significant in type of adjustment were integration and adaptability. Angell applied these concepts to the way in which families accepted changes in relative status of family members, especially to lowered status of the husband. The most severe test came when the huband yielded his dominant status to someone else, for example, to the wife who became the chief wage earner. When the husband was able to retain his previous status or modified it only slightly, adjustment was easier. Successful adjustment to modified or markedly changed status called for a change of roles and acceptance of the change by all concerned.

Readjustment of roles without personal or familial disorganization was accomplished most readily by integrated, adaptable families. Unadaptable families, regardless of the degree of integration, experienced personal and/or family disorganization. Unintegrated families with a low degree of adaptability made unpredictable responses.

It was also found that adaptability increased with a non-materialistic philosophy of life, freedom from traditionalism, and responsibleness of the parents.

One may summarize Angell's study of upper-middle class families by saying that adaptability is more important than integration in adjusting to lowered income, but that the unstructured, unintegrated, and unadaptable family tends to increase in disintegration.

The Lower-Lower Class Family

Although lower-lower class families experience more unemployment than any other class, they are least affected by it. They may earlier have suffered from it, but in time they tend to accept unemployment as a normal way of life. These families contrast sharply with the unemployment families in the common man class and the upper-middle class.

Long Term or Permanent Unemployment. Permanently unemployed families are relief clients year in and year out, in prosperity as well as in depression; or they have found some unrespectable way to live without working. By the time unemployment is reached, there are usually physical and personality deficiencies, such as disease, vagrancy, petty thievery, alcoholism, unstable emotional reactions, or inability to work with others or to accept authority. Which of these conditions are causes and which effects of unemployment, it seems impossible to say. These deficiencies become a permanent part of the situation and often are used to manipulate relief agencies or the public into giving aid. They become assets rather than disintegrating elements in the family.

These families tend to accept their impoverished status and to stabilize family life at a dependency level. Some members may have been reared in similar families and thus have been socialized into this type of family from birth. Others, however, have slipped downward. With time, some kind of adjustment is made and the family develops rationalizations or a philosophy of life, appropriate family roles, and relationships with the outside world that enable it to function.

In his study, *The Beggar*, Gilmore describes a family in which begging set the mode of life through sixty years and five generations.[5] Beggars not reared in begging families sometimes reach this status after intermittent periods on relief. When all private resources have been exhausted and relief is unavailable or inadequate, these families turn to begging. Soon they have developed a philosophy that they cannot or should not work in ordinary occupations; they refer to begging as work. Even though all members of the family may not beg, the whole family shares the begging philosophy since the social status of the family is determined by even one begging member. Society places the beggar at one of the lowest social levels, but the beggar himself is protected from feeling debased by his philosophy.

Begging is a family project, which helps to unify the family. Whichever members of the family can make the greatest appeal for sympathy go out to beg, with the family as a whole sharing the proceeds. Parents who thus provide well for their children have family roles of authority and respect.

Studies of families permanently on relief also show how unemployment is accepted as a normal status. The function of the relief agency is important. The longitudinal study of one hundred Chicago families made in 1934–35 by Cavan and Ranck yielded twelve families that had been wholly or partially on relief prior to the depression. In time of high employment, they nevertheless lived in the social world of the permanently unemployed. Many of these families included at least one disorganized person, often the husband, whose disabilities gave justification for the relief status in the eyes of the family. The families held together, having adjusted family roles to the personalities of their members, sometimes in unorthodox ways. Important in the family organization was the relief agency, which often assumed functions typical of a husband.

---

[5] Harlan W. Gilmore, *The Beggar*, Chapel Hill: University of North Carolina Press, 1940, pp. 168–182; Chapter 5 on "Urban Beggardom" also is pertinent to family reactions.

The agency supplied money, sometimes managed the budgeting, helped the family plan, and in general gave stability and security in many areas other than financial.

A third report throws light on mobile unemployed families.[6] When the Atomic Energy Commission established a plant in southern Ohio, many mobile families were drawn into the area for employment. Social services were approached by six mobile families who were not seeking employment, but whose histories showed that their mode of life was constant migration back and forth across the country in battered automobiles, their means of support whatever they could get from relief agencies. The husbands as a rule were very infantile and dependent in personality type; the wives were docile. They wanted to be cared for by the agency. The family units were closely organized and void of conflict. The men maintained their family status through the skill with which they could manipulate the relief workers or community sentiment in their favor. Although the means were unconventional, the husband still held high status as the good provider. As with public begging, the technique of appeal was well developed. The man made the appeal for sympathy, playing up the needs of his family, and ingratiating himself with the relief worker or others in the community who might help him. As a rule, the men were at first successful in arousing interest and securing aid. As soon as efforts were made to provide employment, the family quietly disappeared, to turn up later in some other city. As with the dependent families in the Chicago study, already cited, the relief agency tended to assume many of the functions normally held by the husband.

It seems to be possible to conclude from studies of permanently unemployed people that permanent unemployment is not a traumatic, disorganizing experience. It is accepted as the customary way of life. The family devises ways to support itself without work and builds up a supporting philosophy and integrated family roles.

Regular, Repetitive Unemployment. The seasonal worker who follows a yearly routine of alternating periods of employment and unemployment typifies the above category. According to Hathaway's 1934 study of the migratory family, and other fragmentary sources, these families often are not rooted in any community and the standard of living tends to be low.[7] The families are not, however, disorganized. They have accepted

---

[6] Martha Bushfield Van Valen, "An Approach to Mobile Dependent Families," *Social Casework*, 37 (April, 1956), pp. 180–186.

[7] Studies of migrant workers usually are focused on conditions of work, health problems, and lack of education for the children. Few give very much information on family organization, roles, or reaction to unemployment. Some insight can be gleaned from

the mobile life and the rotation of employment and unemployment as normal for themselves. Often a regular route is followed year after year and the family knows in advance where it is likely to be throughout the working season. The off-season often finds each family in the same city every year. If the family has not been able to save sufficient money for the off-season, relief is sought. The whole yearly pattern can be foreseen. There is therefore no shock, no crisis, when seasonal unemployment comes; and there is a technique for handling the lack of funds.

The families are organized with the father as head. He makes the arrangements for work for the family as a unit. He therefore has authority and respect. Once the family has accepted migrancy as a way of life, the husband fulfills his role if he makes good contacts for work during the working seasons; he is not considered a failure if the family must apply for relief in the off-season.

The seasonal working family, like the permanently dependent family, illustrates adjustment to unemployment, the maintenance of roles within the family, and as a consequence little personal or family disorganization as a result of unemployment. Since both types of family tend to be at a bare subsistence level with or without relief, there is no question of downward social mobility. These two types of unemployment are cited to illustrate that unemployment is not necessarily disorganizing, when it is part of the customary way of life, when roles are integrated, and when the family has developed techniques acceptable to itself for securing maintenance when there is no earned income.

One or More Members Usually Employed. These families are marginal between self-support and dependence on relief agencies—between the common man and the permanently unemployed.

They are usually able to meet their own expenses, but any emergency that either throws the chief wage earner out of work or increases expenses leads the family to some source of temporary help. These temporary lapses from financial self-sufficiency are recognized as emergencies beyond personal control. They do not cause the family to change its conception of itself as self-supporting, nor do family roles change, although one member of the family may temporarily carry out the functions of another member.

A few such families appeared among the one hundred Chicago families studied by Cavan and Ranck. The long-continued unemployment of the depression came as a crisis with which the families could not cope.

Marion Hathaway, *The Migratory Worker and Family Life*, Chicago: University of Chicago Press, 1934. *The American Child*, published bi-monthly, November to May by the National Child Labor Committee, contains numerous articles regarding the handicaps of migratory life for children.

They could not understand the cause of the depression unemployment, as they had been able to understand previous short periods of distress. They were forced to apply for relief for an indefinite period of time. They were also compelled to change their conception of themselves as self-supporting, and to adjust roles and sometimes class status to conform to their relief status. The reactions of these families were similar to the reactions of common man families who had never been on relief prior to the depression.

Conclusions

Briefly, one may conclude that the following reactions to prolonged unemployment may be expected:

1. The common man struggles to maintain personal status, family integration, and social class status.
2. The upper-middle class family (when affected at all) struggles to maintain personal roles, especially of the father, within the family.
3. The permanently or seasonally unemployed accept their position as normal, adjust personal statuses and roles, and integrate relief agencies or public donors into the family.
4. Even when family disorganization is marked, the family tends to reorganize once the downward decline in personal and class status reaches a stable point.
5. Characteristics facilitating good adjustment are a well organized family prior to unemployment, adaptability, responsibleness, and a non-materialistic and non-traditional philosophy of life.

Applicability of the 1930 Research to the 1950 Family

A higher percentage of married women work now than in the early 1930's, a situation that gives more economic security. We assume that the family is more equalitarian in its functioning. Do these two facts, taken together, mean that the unemployed husband could yield the dominant role (which he still retains) more gracefully to his wife than he could in the early 1930's? If so, his emotional disturbance should be less.

The great number of cars, summer homes, electrical household equipment, suburban homes, and college educations that have been bought since World War II suggest increased upward mobility, or at least the collection of material symbols of upward mobility. Many of these are being bought on the installment plan and therefore are insecurely owned. Would prolonged unemployment bring a great downward movement in social class status? Snch a movement would increase bitterness and disappointment.

Do families of the common man category have the same aversion to relief that they had in the 1930's? To anything called "relief," probably they have. But the nation-wide forms of relief instituted by the federal government in the 1930's operate under sugar-coated names such as pension, aid, insurance, and compensation. The fact that employees pay into Old Age and Survivor's Insurance has created a wide-spread idea that they also pay into other forms of aid, such as Old Age Assistance or Pensions and Unemployment Compensation. Actually, they have not done so, but their belief that they have makes it easier for them to apply. The eligibility rules for public assistance programs have been widely publicized and people are urged to apply when eligible; they are not urged to be strong, independent, and self-sufficient. Nor does the public agency probe into family relationships or violate the feeling of privacy of the family. When eligibility rules have been met, the applicant receives a check which he may spend as he chooses. It seems probable, therefore, that the unemployed person today accepts Unemployment Compensation as his due and not as charity.

Unemployment Compensation is designed to tide a family or worker over a short period of unemployment. It is much less than the person's wages and it runs for only a few months. If the person becomes re-employed soon, he does not lose social class status and probably family roles are not disturbed. However, if he has no other income, he must reduce expenses and if he has private resources he must dip into them. With long term unemployment, the Unemployment Compensation runs out along with the private resources. At this point, the person is in the same position that the 1930 unemployed person was when he had exhausted his resources; Unemployment Compensation has simply postponed or prolonged the decline to relief status.

It seems probable that the socio-psychological trends and adjustments of the 1930's would be found in the 1950's, but that the conditions under which these trends and adjustments would work themselves out have changed.

70 · Adjusting to the Death of a Loved One *

THOMAS D. ELIOT

One of the inevitable experiences that people face is death of members of the family. The better health and prolonged length of life of the present period reduce the probability of death of husband, wife, or children in the early years of marriage. Nevertheless, even these first years sometimes bring death, if not in the immediate family, then of parents, other close relatives, or friends. As the years of marriage increase, the probability of death does also. Many people shrink from the thought of death and dislike facing the types of adjustments that must be made when a death occurs.

Dr. Eliot, who began to study bereavement some thirty years ago, here traces the series of reactions that typically follow a death and also gives some suggestions for adjustment.

BEREAVED families experience a sequence of fairly distinguishable stages, according to objective studies. These include: cognizance of the actual approach of actual death, immediate reactions to actual death, pre-funeral period, funeral and disposal, mourning period, and recovery or stabilization period. These "stages" overlap, or blend to some extent. There are infinite variations within the range of the non-pathological or "normal."

Cognizance of the Approach of Death

Death itself usually occurs so quietly that it is not necessarily recognized until a physician declares it. Probably death itself, for most of those dying, is not a difficult experience. If the patient is in pain, death is relief, and not the cause of pain. If the patient is unconscious or unaware of approaching death, he is spared the fears of the unknown or of extinction. Such fears are presumed to have a biological basis in

---

* Abstracted and adapted from parts of "Facing Instantaneous Wholesale Abolition and Bereavement," a paper delivered at the 1958 Annual Meeting of the Groves Conference on Marriage and the Family. By permission of the author.

The author is Professor Emeritus of Sociology at Northwestern University. His degree of Doctor of Philosophy in social economics is from Columbia University. He has written extensively in the family field, the latest production being a study with Arthur Hillman of families in the Norwegian culture, carried on while on a Fulbright research professorship in Norway.

survival-value, but are characteristic of humans as beings of conscious observation, and such fears are sometimes complicated by certain theological beliefs and guilts.

Immediate Reactions

The writer once listed various observed or reported immediate effects of bereavement as follows: (1) denial or rejection of the facts, a natural but only temporary defense, including dissociation of emotion, sense of unreality, or "feeling no grief"; (2) preternatural or detached calm; (3) shock, in a physiological sense; (4) exaltation or preternatural cheerfulness; (5) self-injury or suicidal impulses; (6) blame of self or others, revenge; (7) suppression of grief; (8) intense longing; (9) abandoned weeping. One should add (10) sense of relief and (11) rationalization— whether naive or intelligent. Some of these, of course, can be noted in sequence or combination.

The impulse to die, with or instead of the deceased, whether in order to save the deceased, to join the deceased, or to escape unbearable grief, is occasionally reported, with or without overt expression. It may have a guilt component, or an element of faith in future reunion.

Despite sincere love and sorrow, the circumstances of many deaths, especially of some incurable and of the aged, are a relief to the survivors as well as to the deceased. Such attitudes need not be guiltily suppressed: others can understand them. They are often rationalized: God had mercy on her suffering; it was better so; it is in the course of nature; Death is sometimes a friend.

The Pre-Funeral Period

Usually, following the immediate reactions at the instant of bereavement, there are more or less quick readjustments, often stimulated by recognition that there are "things to be done." If the bereaved do not do them the bereaved are worked upon by those who are less involved or better controlled. Fulcomer recognized five types of responses in the post-immediate stage, in which he includes the funeral episode.[1]

(1) The acquiescent type: behavior being as nearly usual as circumstances permit. The facts are recognized and at least intellectually accepted. The conventions are fulfilled or tolerated. There is self-direction and responsibility. There is a touch of the stoic.

---

[1] David M. Fulcomer, *The Adjustive Behavior of Some Recently Bereaved Spouses: A Psycho-Sociological Study,* unpublished Ph.D. dissertation, Northwestern University, 1942.

(2) The excited type: characterized by over stimulation, talkativeness, an urge to constant activity, active interest in the formalities, and restlessness. The self-control and cheer seem artificial, perhaps a matter of pride or of defense against the inner pain, or of admirable courage fostered by some code or standard.

(3) The protestive or blaming response: characterized by violent crying, moaning, and/or weeping, the "Why?" pattern—the "why" of cause, of purpose, or of resented injustice. The tendency is to blame self, others, fate, God. These persons are self-centered, not sharing in the arrangements. They show no self-control at funeral or grave.

(4) The detached type: displaying little weeping, but impassive or apparently indifferent. These persons take no active role in necessary arrangements but do some unimportant or irrelevant acts. Habitual routines are gone through in some sort of daze, as are the funeral rites. There is lack of direction and almost lack of orientation, or partial dissociation.

(5) The despondent type: depression rather than active weeping occurs. There is self-centered suffering, wish to be alone, lack of energy, compliance with ritual but minimum participation, and a loss of appetite and sleep.

Fulcomer notes that while the predominant behavior is usually of one of these five types, there may also be episodes in which one or more of the other type-behaviors emerge. He notes also that acquiescent and despondent responses are more frequent among men; protestive responses are more frequent among women.

Other patterns of behavior frequently reported in the post-immediate period are: dependence on others, consoling others, praising the deceased (possibly from over-compensatory guilt), active efforts to deny the fact of death, revulsion against funeral conventions and theological doctrines, a feeling that the world has stopped, and numerous others. A grieved person is especially helpless when it is precisely the deceased who would normally be the confidant consoling the bereaved.

During this period the bereaved's attention is turned inward because of the struggle between the actualities of the outer world forced into his consciousness, and the organized, more or less unconscious resistance of his wishes and habits against the acceptance of the outer facts.

There may be a continuity or consistency between the types of response shown in the immediate and post-immediate stages, as, for example, from stoicism to acquiescence, weeping to despondency, or dazedness to detachment. On the other hand, there may be (especially for cyclothymic temperament) a sharp shift of mood as from dazed to excited, or from lacrimose to revengeful. Many of the behaviors and feelings noted in this whole section recur or continue into the later "stages" of mourning and recovery.

We have no way of measuring depths of grief, but there is tentative evidence that the more the status, role, and affectional habits of the bereaved have depended upon and been organized around the role of the deceased, the greater is the disturbance and disequilibrium to be readjusted. In general, parents may grieve more painfully over the loss of their children than *vice versa*. Loss of spouse tends to be worse than loss of parents, especially if the child has been "weaned" of his early dependence.

One may trace these types of response to bereavement back to corresponding and recognizable types of emotional habits and temperament which probably would appear in the person's total response to other kinds of family crises.

Funerals as a Family Service

The funeral is an ordeal for the family, and many deplore its elaboration for mere security of status or competitive display. Yet there are social-psychological values and functions which funerals serve. Family pride may be traditionally and symbolically represented and satisfied. The death which is thus publicly recognized, is made more real. It begins to be accepted as actual and to that extent is adjusted to by the bereaved.

Mourning, Grief-Work, and Readjustments

In the period after the funeral, difficult transitions to new, socially durable roles are made, for better or for worse. Responsibilities have to be assumed or rearranged. Properties are to be redisposed. Decisions are to be made, or the family drifts. For some, there is a definite turning-point stage between the funeral and stable readjustment. The behavior of the bereaved, however, often is experimental: several types of distraction, defense, compensation, or projection may be attempted before the life situation process is gradually repatterned or channelized again. The moody person especially may start out on a depressed, despondent level (insomnia, no appetite, inactivity, silence) but be drawn by habit or necessity into the participation of a job. It is during this period that family contacts and guidance are most influential.

Our culture gives to men more than to women opportunities or necessities for return to normal roles and duties. Women often receive ego-satisfaction from receiving attention rather than through action. A person who has always been a seeker of attention, and who has suddenly found satisfaction in being noticed because of bereavement may crave such attention or fear to give it up. Friends are flooded with talk about the deceased and the misery of the bereaved. Without verbalizing such a purpose, the bereaved seeks to make others weep for and with her.

The process of mourning is paralleled by the process of recovery. During mourning, the bereaved person recalls the loved one: but, for episode after episode, he comes to realize that the reality is no longer the same. Gradually, emotions and energies, habitually attached to the deceased, are free to be dispersed or transferred to other objects. As the late Williard Waller pointed out, memories of the deceased will recur until all significant events of the relationship have been recalled. If these memories are repressed, they will tend to obsess the personality. But if they are permitted to come into conscious memory and are reviewed and revalued, they can be placed among other memories of one's past and tensions will relax. The working over of memories and reorientation of roles during the mourning stage have been called the "grief-work" by Rogers. These processes are necessary for adjustment.

The period of mourning also permits the relaxing or releasing of any resentments the bereaved may have felt toward the deceased (however sincerely loved), and the expiation, self-punishment, or other accommodation or assimilation, of any guilts felt on account of previous grudges or spites. Hate and love are often ambivalent attitudes. The bereaved, in order to avoid or offset a feeling of guilt, may constantly need to demonstrate to himself and to others his role as mourner.

In the period of mourning there may be a strong wish to be alone. This is at least natural, if the situation is confusing or jarring, or has been exhausting in activity and details. One needs rest and time to reorient. But if social withdrawal, seclusion, despondency or silence threaten to become a habit, crippling to the usefulness or happiness of the bereaved, then family or friends should create situations which make it easy for them to outgrow the desire for seclusion and to re-enter accustomed or new social roles. On the other hand, lonesomeness may be feared and avoided by the bereaved.

The wish for reunion with the loved one may, of course, find expression in beliefs in immortality. Such beliefs (whether unquestioned or accepted as a last resort against intolerable despair and grief) are of course an important element in the attitudes of many bereaved persons.

All the reaction-patterns of grief-work are compensatory, that is, they are the organism's efforts to restore equilibrium. They should be tolerated as such by friends, counselors, and by the bereaved themselves. Only if the reactions threaten to become habitual, repressive, or over-compensatory do they need to be re-corrected by advice or self-guidance.

Recovery and Stabilization

In the later readjustment period, we normally get the relaxation of personal tensions, fixations, and obsessions, along with the habituation of whatever shifts of role were precipitated by the event. Fulcomer, classifies the types of stabilized adjustments during this period into five types:

(1) Transfer or displacement of attachments from the deceased to some other person, who may be another member of the family or a new member acquired through "adoption."

(2) Participation in organizations and causes, whereby the grief is sublimated through some type of activity, perhaps of a welfare nature.

(3) Identification with the deceased by means of assumptions of the roles of the dead, fulfilling the wishes of the dead, carrying on his life values, or living up to his expectations.

(4) Memory phantasy of the deceased. Memories may become a fixation, with a regressive effort to relive or to glorify the dead person's life.

(5) Repressive-seclusive. After preliminary responses on dazed, protestive, and attention-seeking levels, Fulcomer's Case 8, refusing to move from a large home, resisted help, and indulged in memories by elaborate settings, reminders, and fantasies. But she withdrew from all her social clubs and was cold or resistant, despite friendly warnings. She was childless. The typical repatterning is deliberate holding aloof from normal interaction; solitary living; fixation on painful private mementoes as a satisfying symbol of continuity; resistance to others' efforts to modify the pattern or the attitude. Such persons are masochistic voluptuaries of grief.

Suggestions for Adjusting to Bereavement

In summarizing the foregoing discussion, some suggestions may be drawn out to aid in adjustment.

1. Adjustment can be expected to be a long, slow process. The first reactions can be expected to change several times before final adjustment is reached. It is of little use to try to hurry the process. It is therefore of little use to try to fill time completely full of activity; this may simply result in repressing or delaying the normal process of adjustment.

2. First reactions may be expected to be intense, although one cannot predict what form they will take.

3. The funeral often has a beneficial effect: it forces the bereaved

person to face the fact of the death, gives opportunity to pay honor to the deceased, and provides activity. Friends and relatives gather and the general spirit is one of cooperation and consolation.

4. A more difficult phase of adjustment comes after the funeral when the normal responsibilities and tasks of everyday living must be resumed. Among the adjustments usually necessary, are modifications in the roles played, changes in sources of emotional satisfaction, and often the restructuring of finances. Although the person should not try to crowd out his normal feeling of grief, these necessary adjustments should be made as soon as feasible and a new pattern of living established.

5. Although the roles, personal relationships, and emotional responses of living will never be quite the same after bereavement as before, since one person of the constellation has been removed, new roles, new personal relationships, and new emotional responses will develop. They should be allowed and encouraged to develop. The deceased one becomes part of a welcome memory, but life must be lived in the active present.

CHAPTER 20:

Questions of Heredity

71 · The New Baby *

AMRAM SCHEINFELD

How does heredity work? The stream of heredity carried by the genes from generation to generation is the theme of this article. How does each child receive his peculiar combination of genes? To what extent does the mother influence her baby before it is born? These and other questions are answered clearly and simply.

Life Begins

The conception of a new baby takes place the instant a sperm from the father enters and fertilizes an egg waiting in the mother. Usually one egg every four weeks is produced by a woman (although sometimes two or more are produced, which may give rise to twins, triplets, etc.). The egg comes out of either of the two ovaries and moves down into one of the two fallopian tubes. Here the egg is ready to be fertilized.

Fertilization. In the act of intercourse the husband propels into the wife's vagina many millions of sperms (from 50,000,000 to 500,000,000 in an average single ejaculation). These sperms are so small millions could be packed into a pinhead. Like the tiniest imaginable tadpoles, they swim first in the stream of seminal fluid, then in the secretions of the vagina and womb. Only a small proportion get into the womb, and fewer still into the tubes. But should any sperms reach the egg, the moment a single one enters there is an instantaneous toughening of the covering of the egg which shuts

* *The Human Heredity Handbook* by Amram Scheinfeld, Chapter 2 with minor deletions. Copyright 1956 by Amram Scheinfeld. Published by J. B. Lippincott Company.
    The author is a well-known nontechnical writer in the field of human heredity. He is the author of *You and Heredity* (and *The New You and Heredity*), *Women and Men,* and *The Human Heredity Handbook.*

out all other sperms. Thus, of all the millions of sperms entering the race, only a single one can win out and fertilize the egg.

The Heredity Elements

If we could look through a powerful microscope and follow the process of conception, we would see this: As the sperm enters the egg, leaving its tail outside, the sperm-head opens and out comes a batch of twenty-four tiny little worm-like bits of living substance. At the same time a little globule inside the egg (the *nucleus*) also opens up, and out comes another batch of twenty-four of the same tiny little worm-like things. These little things in both the sperm and the egg are called *"chromosomes."* They carry *every thing a child inherits* from the parents. . . .

The chromosomes. As we examine them more closely, we find that among the chromosomes in each set—whether the twenty-four from the father or the twenty-four from the mother—one may differ from another in shape and size. But there is a more remarkable fact. Every chromosome from the father finds an exactly matching type, of its same shape and size, among the chromosomes waiting in the mother's egg.* . . .

The genes. Most often, when chromosomes are seen under a microscope, they are in a compressed form (which gives them their worm-like appearance). But at certain stages they stretch out, and then we find that each chromosome actually consists of hundreds of clear, jelly-like particles, strung together like beads. These beads are called *"genes"* (pronounced "jeans"). And it is these genes which act like wonderful little chemical workers to carry out the processes of heredity. Every gene differs from the others in some way, and has some special job to do in the fashioning and developing of a baby, from conception to birth. But even after birth, and throughout life, the genes continue their work.

The Stream of Heredity

"Acquired Characteristics." One of the most important aspects of heredity is this: The genes as they pass along from generation to generation *are not changed in their workings* by any changes parents make in their own traits,

---

* [*Editor's note.* Scheinfeld points out the one exception in Chapter 4. Every man and every woman has 24 pairs of chromosomes. One of each pair is transmitted to their child, giving the child 24 pairs. In the mother the two so-called sex chromosomes are identical and are called X chromosomes. In the father, the paired sex chromosomes differ, being called X and Y. The new child always receives an X chromosome from the mother —that is all she has to contribute. From the father it may receive (apparently by chance) either an X or a Y chromosome. If it receives from the parents an XX combination, it will be a girl; if an XY combination, it will be a boy].

or that are made in their traits by environment. Establishment of this fact has upset the old theory of the *inheritance of acquired characteristics*—that traits acquired by persons during their lifetimes, or environmental changes made in them, could indeed be transmitted to their offspring. The theory has been disproved by many experiments. Even before the science of genetics came into being, skeptical scientists had taken note of the fact that generations of binding of feet among Chinese, circumcision among Jews, mutilations among primitive peoples (enlarging lips, scarring faces, tattooing, etc.), had in no way produced any corresponding changes in their newborn offspring. Leaving no further doubts, scientists have since made countless experiments with lower animals—altering parts of their bodies, feeding them different diets and chemicals, training them in various ways for many generations—without in any way changing hereditary traits. . . . How and why the genes retain their identity can now be best understood by looking into the processes through which eggs and sperms are formed.

Human egg production. When a little girl baby is born, she already has in her tiny ovaries all the eggs—in rudimentary form—which will take mature shape and emerge after she achieves puberty. And within each rudimentary egg there already are present exact replicas of all the chromosomes and genes which the girl baby received from her parents at conception, and from which will be drawn all the chromosomes her own children will receive. An immediate question, then, is this: In what possible way could the genes so tightly enclosed in the eggs (whether rudimentary or mature) suddenly be made to change in conformity with anything or everything happening to the female in whose ovaries they are? It is obviously ridiculous to think that if a dark-haired girl bleached her hair blond, that would make her "dark-hair" genes suddenly turn into "blond" genes. Or if she got her straight hair permanently waved, that would cause her "straight-hair" genes to change suddenly so that her baby would be born with wavy hair. But it is no less ridiculous to assume that whenever a mother, or future mother, makes a change in any other trait of her body, mind or character (or any such change is made in her), the results will immediately cause the genes concerned with that trait to change their workings in conformity with the new requirements.

.   .   .   .

Human sperm production. As with a little girl baby, a boy baby, too, when he is born already has set aside within him all the "germ cells" from which will some day come his contributions to his children's heredity. A difference between the sexes is that while in the female the eggs themselves are already present at birth, in the male the sperms do not begin to be fashioned by the germ cells until he achieves puberty. Another difference is that while the eggs of the female are limited in number (because she will usually produce no more than one a month for a period of about thirty years), the sperm production of the male, once it begins, goes on into the billions and billions, often throughout his lifetime. But except for the difference in numbers, the sperms of a male are the same as the eggs of a female with respect to the nature of their genes. In the male, too, all the genes carried in his sperms are exact replicas of those which he received from his parents at conception, and cannot be changed in their workings by any changes that are made in his own traits. . . .

Mother and Child

Although a child's genes can in no way be changed by the parents' acts, habits or experiences, this hardly means that a child's *traits* will not be affected by these influences. Obviously, parents can affect their child environmentally in a great many ways, from birth onward; and in the mother's case, her influences on the child's body and mind may begin from the moment of conception. However, there has been much confusion regarding the extent to which the mother's condition is responsible for various traits appearing in babies. Often conditions which are blamed on prenatal factors are due to heredity, and at other times the reverse is true.

Prenatal relationships. The developing baby is in no sense ever a part of the mother's body. Though growing within her, the baby is always a distinct individual (as courts have ruled). Biologically there is a wall—the *placenta*—between the mother and baby. The mother's blood, which carries the nourishment, stops on one side of the wall and the blood elements are broken down and strained through it. There is therefore no more *direct blood* tie between a mother and child than between a father and child. The baby manufactures its own blood according to the formula prescribed by its "blood" genes. In fact, the baby's blood may be so different chemically from the mother's—for instance, with respect to the "Rh factor"—that an interchange of blood substances may sometimes cause serious damage. . . . Other hazards to the unborn baby: *Germs*, if the mother has any germ disease; *alcohol*, if the mother is a heavy drinker; *drugs*, if the mother is an addict; abnormal *hormonal or chemical states* in the mother; *dietary deficiencies*. Any of these factors—which, fortunately, occur in only a minority of the cases—may disturb the normal development of a baby, and produce various congenital diseases, defects or abnormalities which may be mistakenly regarded as hereditary. . . .

Prenatal "impressions." The basis of many popular myths has been the belief that what goes on in the mother's mind can have profound effects on the baby she is carrying: That marks or deformities could develop in a baby in resemblance to something which strongly impressed or frightened the mother during pregnancy; that by her listening to good music her child would be more musical; or by her reading elevating books the child would be brainier, etc. Actually there is no nerve connection between the mother and the baby, and no way her thoughts could reach the child—and certainly no way that her thinking could affect the child's genes. All that might happen is that her mental and nervous state, if good, might benefit her physical state, and therefore help the child; or, contrariwise, if she is badly upset during pregnancy, the nourishment and environment for the child might be worsened.

The mother's age. While the genes the mother transmits to her baby are exactly the same whatever her age (since her eggs with their quotas of genes were formed before her own birth), the prenatal environment she provides may change as she grows older. For one thing, aging is apt to bring more diseases, internal upsets and disorders. Thus, with older mothers (mostly those beyond the late thirties), the risk of defects and abnormalities in babies may increase. . . . However, if the mother is healthy and fit in all ways, her age by itself may affect the child very little.

Father's Influence on Child

Once a father has made his contribution to the child's heredity at conception, by way of the sperm, his influence on the child's traits can be only those exerted after it is born. But as in the mother's case, the "like father, like son" theory often confuses environmental influences with hereditary effects. If a father's (or mother's) alcoholism, criminality, degeneracy or other bad traits are repeated in children, this need not at all mean that heredity is responsible. Nor can the repetition of good traits of behavior and temperament be necessarily credited to heredity. In every case the home environment and the hereditary histories of *both* parents must be weighed together.

The father's age. Unlike the situation with the mother, the age of the father has nothing to do with the prenatal condition or development of a child. This follows from the fact that the *genes* in the father's sperms are in no way changed by his aging. So long as a man can go on producing fertile sperms (and some men have done so into their nineties), these sperms will be exactly the same in the quality and workings of their genes, and the traits they can produce in children, as the sperms of the man when he was young and robust. (The statement may be no surprise to livestock experts, who know that thoroughbred stallions and blooded bulls can be mated into their relatively old ages, without any deterioration in the quality of offspring.) Nor will the fact that a man has been seriously disabled in a war or an accident, or has acquired a serious disease, affect the *heredity* of his children.

72 · *How Much Like You Will He Be?* *

HERBERT YAHRAES

Most people are curious about how much they have inherited from their parents and how much of themselves they will pass on to their children. For fifty-two characteristics, the author shows in a table whether the characteristic is inherited, probably or possibly inherited, or definitely not inherited. He also explains the intertwining of hereditary and environmental influences in a number of characteristics that a growing child displays.

You REACH down, pick up your young son and swing him high in the air. He looks at you wonderingly. And suddenly you find yourself wondering, too.

What lies ahead for the little guy? What kind of man will he grow up to be? How smart? What likes and dislikes will he have? What skills?

He seems to have inherited his mother's eyes. Has he inherited her musical ability, too, and her amiable disposition? He seems to have his father's hair. Then will he have your bent for mechanics, your way with a football?

Or doesn't heredity count in things like that? Is the important point not what he was born with but how you help him to grow up from now on?

Geneticists have learned a great deal about the inheritance of such characteristics as the curliness of people's hair, the color of their eyes, and their predisposition to certain ailments. They know less about how and whether you pass along intelligence, aptitudes, and personality.

But they do have evidence now that almost everything a person is—his mental and emotional makeup as well as his physical—can be attributed in some part to heredity.

Heredity is a great gamble. Your genes, numbering perhaps 20 or 30 thousand, are represented twice in each of your body cells. They are part-

---

* *Popular Science Monthly*, 171 (November, 1957), 163–166, 260, 262. Reprinted by permission of the publisher and the author.

The author is a graduate of Lafayette College and was a Nieman Fellow at Harvard University. After wide experience in newspaper reporting and editing he turned to magazine writing, specializing in medical and scientific articles; he has also written a number of pamphlets for the Public Affairs Committee. He has received several citations including, with his wife, the Lasker Award for medical writing in magazines.

ners, one member of a pair occupying a certain spot on a chromosome and the other occupying the same spot on a duplicate chromosome. They work together to influence a trait, by controlling chemical reactions.

When a new individual is formed, he gets one partner of each pair from his father—*which* partner is a gamble—and the other from his mother.

Given enough information about you and your family, geneticists can quote you odds on some other heredity propositions—for example, against your child's being born with clubfoot, or with Rh-negative blood, or with a tendency to diabetes. Many such traits are controlled largely by one gene in a partnership.

As for personality and behavior, though, no such control has been found. In fact, if it weren't for a special case—identical twins—scientists would still be doubting that the genes had anything at all to do with it.

What We Can and Cannot Inherit

Some characteristics listed here, notably blood type, are entirely determined by heredity. But for most of them heredity plays only a part. A person might inherit genes that make him susceptible to an ailment or give him a capacity for a particular talent. But he'll never develop ulcers or become a great musician unless everyday life moves him toward that pattern. It's not certain, either, whether he will pass these particular genes on to his first, second, or any subsequent child.

Characteristic	Yes	Probably	Possibly	No	Remarks
Aggressiveness			x		
Alcoholism				x	
Arthritis	x				
Artistic talent		x			
Blood pressure		x			
Blood type	x				Exclusively
Cancer susceptibility			x		Yes, for some rare forms
Color blindness	x				Almost exclusively
Courage			x		
Crossed eyes	x				Almost exclusively
Curly hair	x				
Diabetes	x				
Dimples	x				
Emotional stability		x			In part
Eye color	x				Almost exclusively
Finger length	x				
Food, tastes in				x	
Gestures				x	
Hairiness	x				

What We Can and Cannot Inherit (*continued*)

Characteristic	Yes	Probably	Possibly	No	Remarks
Hay-fever susceptibility		x			
Head shape	x				
Heart-disease suscepti-bility		x			Certain types
Height	x				Also affected by diet, etc.
Intelligence	x				Influenced by en-vironment, too
Longevity	x				
Math talent	x				
Mechanical knack				x	
Mental deficiency		x			Some types
Money		x			
Musical talent		x			
Near- or far-sightedness		x			
Nose shape		x			
Obesity		x			To some extent
Pain sensitivity				x	
Personality				x	To some extent
Polio susceptibility				x	
Rheumatic-fever suscepti-bility		x			
Schizophrenia			x		Evidence not clear
Scientific talent			x		
Self-confidence				x	
Sex drive				x	
Shyness				x	
Sociability				x	
Sports talent			x		
Sunburn susceptibility		x			
Teeth, shape of		x			
Teeth, susceptibility to decay				x	Early diet, care important
Temper				x	
Tuberculosis susceptibil-ity		x			
Twins, tendency to have		x			
Ulcer susceptibility				x	Evidence not clear
Writing talent			x		

Why *identical* twins? Because they've developed from the same fertilized egg, so they have the same inheritance. *Fraternal* twins, on the other hand, have developed from two separate eggs fertilized by two separate sperm, so their inheritance is no more alike than if they had arrived years apart.

When fraternal twins, or ordinary brothers and sisters, differ in some trait, there's no telling why; but if identical twins differ, the answer must lie in environment, either pre- or post-natal: Their circumstances in the months before birth may not have been exactly the same. Or possibly there has been some difference—scarcely noticeable—in the way they've been brought up.

Fortunately for the science of genetics, every once in a while a pair of identical twins is separated early in life.

Some years ago, for example, two identical twin boys were adopted by different families shortly after their birth and were brought up in quite different circumstances. One lived steadily in Salt Lake City and went through high school. He had a sister. The other wandered around the country with his foster parents and eventually landed in New York City. He went only a while to high school. There were no other children.

Yet when the two met as young men they showed remarkable similarities. In two I.Q. tests the high-school graduate scored 104 and 101; the other 97 and 98. Both were weak in math. In many cases they missed the same questions.

They got almost identical scores on a test measuring such personality traits as speed of decisions, self-confidence, and interest in detail.

One boy was particularly fond of music; the other, of drawing. They both liked sports. Amazingly, both had boxed in public and won championships.

Geneticists and psychologists have studied many other such cases. They have also observed identical twins who have been brought up together, and they have studied what happens when foster children of one intelligence level live with families of a different level.

You do inherit intelligence, they have found. Identical twins usually show only very small differences on I.Q. tests except when there has been a great difference in the twins' schooling. For instance, a girl who had been brought up on a farm and gone only through eighth grade scored 89, while her identical twin, who had lived in a small town and gone through high school, scored 106. In conversation, though, the country girl seemed just as intelligent as her twin. Besides, the difference of 17 points was no greater than you yourself might show if you were tested at two different ages.

In almost every case like this, the twin who has gone to school longer shows a higher I.Q. So, although you do inherit your brain power, your ability to use it to get a high score on a formal test depends partly on your education.

Orphans demonstrate what can happen. When they're adopted into good homes, studies show that not only their personality blossoms out, but their intelligence too. Children of apparently mediocre intelligence will close about half the gap between themselves and their foster parents. For instance, if a child's I.Q. is 80 while that of his new parents is 120, another test within a few years will probably show him at 100. We can't change our heredity, but we can do a lot about how we use what we've inherited.

If you and your wife are both bright, your children are likely to be bright, too. Some may have higher I.Q.'s than you, some lower—and there's no way of predicting how smart any given child will be—but the average intelligence of all of them will usually be about the average of you two.

There's an exception. Parents with a very high average may have children averaging not quite so high. As Dr. Gordon Allen, a geneticist with the National Institute of Health, explains it, this may be because the high intelligence of the parents was determined in part by their environment, which they probably cannot duplicate for their children. For example, the circumstances that forced you to take a job in order to finish your schooling may have been more advantageous—as far as pushing up your I.Q. goes—than the circumstances that will permit your son to take things easier.

This works the other way, too. Parents with an I.Q. below average may have been held down by a lack of opportunity rather than by an inherent weakness in intelligence. They could have children whose I.Q.'s are average or above.

Because heredity *is* such a magnificent gamble, you may have a musical, artistic, mathematical, or other type of genius among your children even if you and your wife are not so gifted.

Geneticists theorize that a genius arises when all the necessary genes —perhaps dozens are involved—have come together in one person quite by lucky chance, and when this person also has the urge and the opportunity to develop in accord with his capabilities. You may have inherited some of these genes and your wife others but, lacking the whole set, neither of you sets the world afire. It just could be that your little guy got them all.

Genius seems to spring up spontaneously but *talent* often runs in families —shaped in part by the genes but more by family atmosphere and family traditions.

Your boy will get his love of nature from his old man, all right, but he'll get it in large part because the old man will take him on walks and camping trips and point out some of the fascinating aspects of nature.

And if your boy turns out to have a talent for cabinetmaking, as you have, he'll have got that from you, too—but mainly because you've let him work alongside you without driving him or setting impossible standards.

So far as is known now, musical talent has a stronger heredity basis than most others. That's because some of the qualifications of a musician—a sense of pitch, for example, and the ability to recognize tones—are closely linked to physical characteristics, the kind most directly influenced by heredity.

If you've been an exceptionally good sprinter—or swimmer, tennis player, boxer, or ball player—your boy is much more likely than the youngster next door, whose parents never showed any aptitude for athletics, to be good here, too.

But the capacity for being outstanding in any line is not enough. Neither is interest or drive. Both are needed.

Suppose that the little guy complains after school some day that he just can't "get" French. Your wife recalls that she was never very good at French herself. Has he inherited his difficulty?

If he's of average intelligence, probably not. "Brightness" in a particular subject seems to depend largely on interest. While intelligence in general is inherited, the youngster who "can't get" or "just hates" a certain subject may well have been influenced mostly by remarks at home or the attitude of his pals. Or maybe the teaching's at fault.

Mathematics seems to be different. Identical twins—unlike ordinary brothers and sisters—generally have the same aptitude for mathematics, even when they've been raised apart.

Our children inherit at least some of their personality traits, too, the study of twins indicates. Virtually all research so far has been on the gloomier side. For example, a British geneticist, James Shields, studying a group of London youngsters, was interested in such problems as moodiness, over-shyness, fears, hysteria, delinquency.

In the few cases where one twin had got into actual trouble with the law for stealing or some other delinquency, the other twin had, too. This was so whether the twins were identical or fraternal—suggesting that environment had been a stronger influence than heredity.

But in other cases, both members of a pair of identical twins turned out to be much more likely to have the same personality maladjustment than both members of a pair of fraternal twins. Identical twins were affected the same way by a bad family situation; fraternal twins were not. Heredity, the investigator concluded, had strongly influenced the youngsters' personalities.

Dr. Franz J. Kallman, principal research scientist at the New York State Psychiatric Institute, has indicated the influence of heredity in the mental illness, schizophrenia, by finding that when one identical twin had it, in most cases the other twin had it, too. But with fraternal twins, in most cases, the second twin did not. It seems hereditary, then. On the other hand: some medical analysts say they have traced cases of "split personality" to childhood experiences.

Animal studies, too, are throwing light on whether our youngsters inherit parts of their personality. For example, Dr. J. L. Fuller, of the Jackson Memorial Laboratory, Bar Harbor, Maine, reports that some strains of rats make many errors in a maze; others, only a few. Some strains under laboratory observation run only a few feet a day; some run several miles. There are strains of mice that have convulsions when a door bell rings, and strains that don't. Terriers and basenjis will fight harder for a bone than will such dogs as beagles and cocker spaniels.

Working with guinea pigs, other investigators have reported that even the sex drive—high, low, or medium—is inherited.

There's a danger, though, in applying these findings to man because human behavior, unlike animal, is powerfully stimulated by learning and custom and conscience.

Your child hasn't inherited any fully developed traits. He has inherited combinations of genes that will make the development of certain traits possible if the circumstances are right.

Luckily for you—and him—some of the most important of these circumstances are under your control.

73 · Will Yours Be a Normal Baby? *

JACK HARRISON POLLACK

One of the secret worries of many prospective parents is whether their child will be born a normal baby. According to Mr. Pollack's article, about one baby in every hundred is born with some malformation. Much needless worry arises from lack of understanding of what causes defects when they do occur, and especially about the way heredity works. A recent development of counseling in heredity opens the way for parents who have some reason to be concerned to secure a scientific opinion on the probability that their chil-

* *Today's Health* (published by the American Medical Association), 36 (March, 1958), 16–21, 52. Reprinted by permission of the publisher and the author.
The author, after graduation from the University of Pennsylvania, turned to writing as a profession. He now writes articles on health, education, psychology, children, family relations, politics, and business, based on careful investigation, which are published in a wide variety of nationally known magazines. He has won two awards for public service stories.

dren will or will not inherit certain defects from them. This article not only discusses heredity counseling—what it is and what it does—but gives the odds that a baby may inherit some defect known to have occurred in a parent or his relatives.

TODAY the brightest heredity news is that the chances of children inheriting certain physical and mental defects can often be predicted. In recent years, over 15 little-known "heredity counseling" clinics connected with medical centers or universities have quietly sprung up in the U.S. and Canada. At these clinics, the counseling is done by geneticists—scientists trained in studying human heredity.

What's more, this new type of medical social service is usually free. Your family doctor can refer you to a heredity clinic if he believes it can help you.

Parents generally visit a heredity clinic *after* the birth of a defective child. There, a heredity counselor—who deals in facts not fears—estimates the risks of a couple's future babies being born abnormal. It isn't wild, hit-or-miss guesswork. Before any predictions are made, a family tree is carefully investigated. Advice-seekers often receive complete physical examinations themselves, including x-rays, electro-encephalograms, blood, vision, psychological, and other tests. A heredity counselor may also probe hospital records, search old family Bibles, and church records, and, occasionally, even drive hundreds of miles to interview distant relatives.

After evaluating all these facts, a heredity counselor often calmly tells you the mathematical probability—the odds—of your children inheriting certain abnormalities. Naturally, no mere mortal can predict nature's handiwork with absolute certainty. Yet risks for malformation recurrences in families can frequently be estimated, even when an inheritance pattern is unclear.

For example, if one parent and one child already have harelip and cleft palate, the risk of the next child inheriting them is about 10 percent. But if only one parent is affected, the odds drop to two percent.

Even after hearing the approximate odds many couples still ask: "Doctor, should we have another child?" But heredity counselors scrupulously refrain from advising you whether or not to have children. Guiding instead of deciding, they merely try to clarify *your* thinking by giving you, wherever possible, the scientific likelihood of specific traits appearing in your unborn child—so that you and your mate can make *your own* intelligent decision about having children.

"What is an acceptable risk for one family may not be for another," explains Dr. Sheldon Reed, a leading heredity counselor, who directs the University of Minnesota's Dight Institute. "Many factors must be considered such as religious principles, guilt feelings, and whether the parents already have normal children. If a heredity counselor tries to *sell* advice, he may get rebuffed."

Another outstanding heredity counselor, Dr. C. Nash Herndon, professor of medical genetics at North Carolina's Bowman Gray School of Medicine, adds: "The risks vary from a high of 50 percent down to practically zero. But risk figures are usually much less than parents had feared."

Once risks are clearly understood, though, parents can accept the birth of an abnormal child with far less shock than if they hadn't been warned.

About one in every 100 babies is born with some malformation. These malformations tend to run in families. If a woman bears a malformed baby who dies, she runs a 5 to 11 percent risk that her next child will also be defective. If she has borne two malformed children, the risk jumps to 15 to 25 percent, studies by the University of Pennsylvania's Dr. Douglas Murphy show.

Heredity clinics are not birth control clinics. On the contrary, heredity clinics encourage reproduction in numerous families by putting imaginary fears to rest.

Take the young couple whose first baby was born with congenital heart disease. Told by a heredity counselor that the odds of their later children inheriting it were merely one in 50, they went ahead and produced two other children who were normal. "We took a chance when we heard that the risk was a lot less than we had thought," reveals the happy mother.

Another worried couple, whose first child, a boy, was born with a club-foot, was informed by a heredity counselor that their future children would run a 3 to 8 percent risk of having the same defect. The wife wanted a daughter badly enough to risk another pregnancy—and she gave birth to a healthy girl. Clubfoot—which occurs about once in 1000 births—affects boys more often than girls.

Many married and about-to-be married persons have exaggerated fears about a "family disease." Epilepsy, for instance, often worries people disproportionately perhaps because of its ancient social stigma. Actually, the medical odds are more favorable toward it than is popularly believed. There is about one chance in 20 to 40 that an epileptic parent will have a child with the disease. And the odds are only one in 70 that the seizures will become chronic. Moreover, epilepsy isn't contagious; many drugs now successfully control it, and the type which develops after age 30 doesn't tend to run in families.

But one young couple refrained from reproducing because the husband's brother had convulsive seizures. Luckily, six years ago this couple visited a heredity clinic and had an electro-encephalogram taken. Though the wife's brain potential appeared normal, her husband's E.E.G. indicated *petit mal* seizures. The heredity counselor explained, "At worst, not more than one in eight of your children could be expected to develop seizures." Recently when the heredity counselor saw this couple, he was pleased—but not too surprised—to learn that they now had four healthy normal children.

Heredity counselors neither sugar-coat nor minimize the facts. Dr. Lee Dice, who founded the first U.S. heredity clinic at the University of Michigan in 1939, once told a healthy couple with a defective child:

"If you are prepared to risk the emotional shock of another such child, then by all means, try again. You have far more than the average couple to offer the normal child you will probably have."

Several years ago a young Minnesota mother gave birth to a Mongoloid boy and then to a normal girl. Both pregnancies were uneventful. Their doctor referred them to a heredity clinic. The couple was told that there was a small but real risk that they might have another Mongoloid child. Prepared for the worst, the couple accepted the gamble and produced two normal children.

Many parents feel ashamed when they have an abnormal child. A husband frequently blames his wife, and many a mother wonders if she did something during pregnancy to injure her baby.

A tormented Eastern father whose child was born a dwarf felt guilty because of youthful indiscretions. His anxiety was relieved when he was shown that the deformity stemmed from a mutation in his recessive genes—something over which he had no control.

A troubled Southern couple, whose child was born with a hip dislocation, worried that the defect resulted from their bitter quarreling during the wife's pregnancy. But this couple was reassured when told that it stemmed from hereditary factors.

People are likewise shown that an abnormality can result from factors other than heredity. A woman who refused to have any children insisted, "There is a mental disease in my family and I'm stuck with it." But when the heredity counselor studied her genetic history, he learned that her brother's brain had been damaged when the mother was given excessive radiation during pregnancy.

At many heredity clinics, people learn that mere chance—instead of heredity—can be the villain.

Consider the couple whose son died from a circulatory defect. Later, their infant daughter died a week after birth from a defective windpipe. When the woman considered becoming pregnant for the third time, she asked a heredity counselor whether she or her husband inherited a defect

which would doom all of their children. The heredity expert found nothing genetic to account for the first two tragedies. And the woman cheer-
fully went ahead and had her third baby—who was born normal.

Another couple had two normal children, but their third baby was born
hydrocephalic—with an enlarged head—and had to be delivered by Cae-
sarian section. The couple wanted to have another child and were seriously
considering artificial insemination until they heard about the Dight Institute. Here, a capable heredity counselor learned that the mother had
influenza during her early pregnancy and suspected that the hydrocephaly
might have resulted from meningitis and was not hereditary. Even if it
had a genetic basis, the chance of a hydrocephaly repetition was only about
3 percent. Betting on these 97 out of 100 odds, the couple decided to skip
the artificial insemination and try having a normal child—which they did.

All sorts of questions are asked at heredity clinics. A common one is:
"Should first cousins marry?" In approximately half of the states, it is illegal
for them to do so. Congenital diseases are four times more common among
first cousins than among children born of parents who were not blood
relations, a Swedish study recently showed. At heredity clinics, people are
often told: "If you have one or more abnormal genes, the chance are 1 to
8 that a similar gene will also be present in your first cousin (compared to
1 in 500 to 1000 in the general population). In second cousins, marriage
is less dangerous—merely 1 in 32 of their genes are the same. For third
cousins, only 1 in 128 genes are identical, making the risk still smaller.

Hair color is another popular question. For example, if both you and
your mate have red hair, all of your children will probably be redheaded.
But if one of your redheaded children marries someone with blonde hair,
then *their* youngsters will probably not be redheaded.

Skin and eye color are also frequently asked about. Many parents wonder
whether a light-skinned mulatto married to a white person can produce a
dark baby. Heredity counselors explain "no" because a child cannot be
darker than the two parents. Two mulattos, though, can produce children
somewhat darker than either parent.

"What are the chances of my having twins?" is another common question. It is about one in every 85 births. Triplets? One in 7000. Quadruplets?
About one in 50 million. Quintuplets? About one in 57 million.

Though nearly everyone welcomes this scientific information, a few
refuse to face the stubborn genetic facts. One couple, for instance, wanted
to be told that their albino child was just an exaggerated Scandinavian.

Medieval myths are likewise scotched at heredity clinics, such as the old
wives' tale that harelip results from a mother having looked at a rabbit
during her pregnancy! Other superstitious mothers are assured that listening
to good music will *not* make their unborn children more talented! And

that being in the "right" mood during conception has absolutely no effect upon traits which a child inherits. Counselors also remind other misinformed persons that alcoholism and drug addiction are *not* inherited; that the tendency to develop diabetes is definitely known to be inherited. Syphilis is not inherited, but if the mother has syphilis the child probably will get it *in utero*. That's why there is so much emphasis on pre-marital examinations for syphilis and treatment of the syphilitic expectant mother.

Heredity clinics also inform people about diseases like diabetes, rheumatic fever, and schizophrenia where only a *susceptibility* is inherited. "How can I keep my child from getting this disease?" many parents ask. Fortunately, not everyone who inherits a *tendency* toward a disease actually develops it. Environment and preventive measures play a large part because today treatment is constantly improving for the "susceptibility" diseases. For example, thanks to diet and insulin, many of the million U.S. diabetics are now known to be reproducing in greater numbers. University of Michigan heredity counselor Dr. James V. Neel says: "Nearly every hereditary trait can be altered by environment." It even applies to schizophrenia where a child whose parent has this severe mental disease has a one in six chance of developing it, according to New York geneticist Dr. Franz J. Kallmann.

Because a condition is hereditary, it doesn't mean that it is hopeless, as is often mistakenly assumed. Many inherited defects can be corrected, such as crossed eyes in babies. Today a harelip and cleft palate can be repaired by plastic surgeons. And a clubfoot can often be straightened with a promptly applied plaster cast. Similarly, congenital heart defects can be cured through skillful surgery.

Heredity clinics even occasionally help solve knotty paternity disputes. Though no conclusive method exists of proving who is the father of a child, blood tests can show who is *not*. More than one heredity counselor has proved to a suspicious husband that a rival couldn't possibly have been the father of his wife's child—and thus prevented a divorce.

If you believe that you have a heredity problem, perhaps your family doctor can refer you to a heredity clinic. Geneticists prefer to work through your doctor because he knows your medical and family history—often since childhood. Family doctors are the first to spot possible defects whether it is in a baby's delivery or a developing eye cataract. This reliable medical information is invaluable to a heredity counselor in evaluating your problem.

Heredity counselors *cannot* advise you by mail. There are no canned, mail-order answers to heredity questions. No two cases are alike. "Each case must be evaluated individually," reminds Dr. F. Clarke Fraser, one of Canada's foremost heredity counselors.

Ideally, a heredity clinic should have both an M.D. and a Ph.D. geneticist as directors. It also should have laboratory assistants, field researchers, statisticians, and others working as a team. The best location for a heredity clinic is in association with a well-equipped teaching hospital.

Today's overworked heredity counselors give thousands of hours freely each year. Minnesota's Dr. Sheldon Reed believes that the U.S. should have at least 100 heredity clinics—one in every large city and at least one in every state. "We ought to spend at least as much time studying the heredity of human beings as we do of Guernsey cattle," he reasons.

Some day heredity counseling will probably be a routine pre-marital service. If couples about to marry are shown that they carry abnormal genes, they could then decide whether to marry and adopt normal children.

To illustrate how heredity counseling can help an unmarried person, several years ago an intelligent, 28-year-old girl refused to marry a man who had proposed to her. "We're incompatible," was all she would enigmatically say. When she visited a heredity clinic, she admitted her fears that if she married, her children might inherit her uncle's mental disease. Shown that her risk was minimal she got married—and today has two healthy, normal children.

A sad footnote to this story is the case of the 54-year-old spinster aunt who accompanied her to the clinic that day. Years earlier, the aunt had needlessly refrained from marrying because of the same fear of "bad family blood." Told that the same hopeful odds would have applied to her, the unhappy aunt swallowed hard but closed her eyes and silently thanked God for the heredity clinic which had helped her niece.

Genetics is still a young science, dating from the 1866 findings of an Austrian monk named Gregor Mendel. "Many persons think of genetics as just a study of people with six fingers or two heads. It's much more than that," says Dr. Charles F. Wilkinson, Jr., chairman of New York University Postgraduate School of Medicine. Though the mystery of the genes is far from solved—and probably never will be completely—geneticists are continually learning more about hereditary defects. Even though these authorities must sometimes frankly answer, "We don't know—yet," they can estimate many risks. "We are emotional rather than objective about our ancestors," reminds Dr. Reed. "People accept heredity traits which they admire, and reject those which they deplore.

Every parent deeply wishes to produce "perfect" offspring because one of the heaviest burdens on earth is having a defective child. "Is my baby all right?" is still the first question a mother asks after giving birth. If the answer is "no" or evaded, her next question to herself is an agonizing, "Why?"

Abnormalities used to be considered punishments for sin or crosses to be borne stoically. Thanks to today's heredity clinics, much of the mystery and folklore is being taken out of childbirth. Helpful modern knowledge has been substituted for ancient superstition.

In recent years, great strides have been made in preventative medicine, especially in immunization, and in battling communicable diseases. Perhaps one of medicine's next major advances will be in preventing and controlling inherited diseases.

74 · The Rh Factor *

G. S. PULFORD

The Rh factor puzzles many prospective parents, often unnecessarily when they do not understand what it is all about. In this authoritative but reassuring statement an explanation is given of the meaning of the Rh factor, why it develops in certain people, the conditions under which a baby will have it, and what can be done about it.

SINCE the Rh factor was first described 11 years ago [in 1940], it has attracted widespread popular interest and scientific investigation. The general interest is understandable because so many families are potentially affected by it although the number of babies actually made ill or killed by Rh incompatibilities is much less. Scientifically the Rh factor is interesting because it is essentially the only substance found normally in blood that causes disease.

The nature of the disturbance is described scientifically as an antigen-antibody reaction. This is like the usual response when a person is given an immunization. When one is immunized, say to diphtheria, his body reacts by building up substances called antibodies to fight the diphtheria germs. Following this, whenever he is again exposed to diphtheria, those antibodies are mobilized to defend his body and destroy the diphtheria germs. Remember the word antibody and how it is used, for it will recur often in this discussion. Antibodies are agents produced when a foreign substance enters the body. They act to destroy the foreign substance.

The case of the Rh factor is similar. Rh is the name given to a protein substance normally present in the blood cells of approximately 85 per cent of all people. When one possesses this blood cell protein, he is termed Rh positive. The 15 per cent who do not have that factor are termed Rh negative. Normally, blood cells do not pass between an unborn infant and his mother. Usually, however, toward the end of pregnancy a few infant red

* Today's Health (published by the American Medical Association), 29 (November, 1951), 27–28. Reprinted by permission of the publisher.

The author, who received his medical education at the University of Michigan, is a practicing pediatrician in Palo Alto, California.

blood cells may pass from the infant's circulation to the mother's blood stream. If the infant's cells possess the Rh protein (that is, he is Rh positive) and the mother does not (she is Rh negative) then she may build up antibodies to this foreign protein of the infant. The antibodies are much smaller than a blood cell and pass readily between the mother and infant. Similar antibody transmission is the way the mother will pass on to the baby temporary immunity to certain diseases she had as a child, such as chicken pox. When the Rh antibodies enter the baby's blood stream, they cause destruction of the baby's blood cells and produce a disease known as erythroblastosis. The name erythroblastosis is taken from the special type of cells found in the blood of these babies.

A baby with erythroblastosis may have anemia because of the rapid rate of blood destruction. His liver and spleen may become enlarged because they work overtime to help remove the destroyed blood cells from the body. After the period of rapid blood destruction these two organs return to normal. Jaundice, a yellow discoloration of the skin and eyes, is prominent usually shortly following birth because the immature liver of a newborn baby is not yet capable of efficiently removing all the pigment liberated when the red blood cells are destroyed.

Kernicterus, or yellow discoloration and injury to the brain, is a rare complication that occurs in 12 per cent of the live-born babies afflicted with erythroblastosis. Two-thirds of these babies die within one week despite treatment. The remainder will have residual damage in the form of either spasticity or impaired mentality or some degree of both. This may be great or slight. Within one week it can usually be determined from the behavior of the baby whether this complication exists. It is seen more frequently in small babies weighing less than five and one-half pounds and occurs twice as often in boys. It is not necessarily seen in those babies with severe anemia or other forms of the disease, but there is a family incidence of kernicterus. Following a baby with kernicterus in a family, any subsequent child affected by Rh incompatibility is very likely also to suffer this complication.

A cold statistical analysis of the implications of Rh reactions is comforting:

a. One pregnancy in every seven has the proper setup for Rh difficulties. This means a mother who is Rh negative and a father who is Rh positive.

b. In only one pregnancy in every 450 is the child affected with erythroblastosis. This is only one in every 65 who potentially could have trouble.

c. Only one pregnancy in every 5600 will result in a child who will live with any residual defects from erythroblastosis or kernicterus such as spasticity or mental retardation. This gives pretty good odds for avoiding difficulty, even though Rh incompatibility exists.

The reason so few infants are actually made ill compared to the relatively large number who potentially could be made ill is that several safety factors are at work to prevent affliction. First, many Rh negative women fail to produce antibodies even when they are exposed to Rh positive cells. They may have two or three Rh positive babies before developing antibodies. The greater the number of pregnancies required to sensitize the mother, the better the prognosis for the infant because the mother is capable of forming only few or weak antibodies. It is not rare for a mother to have four or five healthy Rh positive babies before an afflicted child is born.

Secondly, many fathers termed Rh positive are actually half Rh negative so that half of the babies would be Rh negative. The mother then is not exposed to the foreign protein. This may be determined by some complicated tests on the father's blood or by testing the infant's blood after birth. If the infant is also Rh negative, then the mother was not sensitized or made immune by that pregnancy.

Thirdly, there is a growing trend toward smaller families. The baby born of a first pregnancy is never afflicted unless the mother was previously sensitized by transfusion with Rh positive blood. The first Rh positive baby born to a mother after she has been sensitized by a previous pregnancy has a 30 per cent chance of having no difficulties whatsoever. Eighty per cent of this group born alive will live. That leaves one in five from second pregnancies who will die after birth even though he receives treatment.

After the first afflicted baby there is a 40 per cent chance that any future pregnancies will end in abortion or stillbirth. If, however, the child is born alive, there is still a 75 per cent chance that he will recover completely.

Usually, after one baby has been born with erythroblastosis, any subsequent Rh positive child will suffer the same disease. That does not necessarily have to occur in every case, however, because there is individual variation of response to maternal sensitization, and occasionally an Rh positive child will be born with either no disease or very mild disease after a previous child was severely affected. This variation permits us always to be hopeful despite the fact that a mother has already had a number of afflicted children.

The treatment of erythroblastosis has varied in the last ten years as our knowledge of the illness has increased. It is now generally felt that affected babies should receive transfusions with blood that does not contain the Rh protein (and is thus Rh negative) so that antibodies from the mother cannot react with the transfused blood and destroy it. In many cases three or four small transfusions of this sort are all that is necessary. In some instances it is felt advisable to do what is called an exchange transfusion shortly after birth. One or two quarts of blood are put into the baby as an equal volume is removed. This results in nearly complete replacement of all the baby's blood with Rh negative blood that cannot be destroyed by the antibodies produced by the mother. The use of blood from a non-pregnant Rh negative woman for transfusion purposes is currently being investigated. Baby girls with erythroblastosis generally have a milder form of the disease than do boys, and it has been suggested that the use of female Rh negative blood for transfusion to affected infants results in a greater survival rate. That theory requires further investigation. The hope of future research is a substance called a haptene that is capable of reacting with the maternal antibody to neutralize it when given either to the mother during pregnancy or to the infant after birth. Such haptenes have been used so far only in a few experimental studies.

In a general way it can be stated that early treatment will help to prevent serious illness or death. However, despite all treatment now available a certain number of affected babies will not survive. But from the statistics previously reviewed, it can be seen that that number is small compared to all of the completely normal children born to families with Rh incompatibility. These parents should be encouraged to have children, if they so desire, at least until one child is afflicted. Since the first child affected will usually be only moderately ill, this program is relatively safe. With an intensely sensitized woman and a husband who is completely Rh positive, adoption may be considered. After the first affected child, any discussion regarding future children must be made on an individual basis after consultation with the family physician.

75 · Two for One *

JOHN LENTZ

An exciting thought to prospective parents is that they might have twins. This article tells what the chances are that any given birth will produce twins—or quintuplets, for that matter. The difference between fraternal and identical twins is explained, and also the degree to which identical twins are exactly alike. The author also asks, "Are twins worth all the trouble?" The article will help the reader answer this question for himself.

* *Today's Health* (published by the American Medical Association), 36 (September, 1958), 26–27, 69. Reprinted by permission of the publisher.

The author, who holds the Bachelor of Science and the Master of Science degrees in the biological sciences, is a copywriter for Young and Rubicam, Inc., where he specializes in writing health advertisements for one of the large insurance companies. He is a member of the National Association of Science Writers, a former contributing editor of the *American Journal of Public Health*, and the author of many articles and booklets dealing with medicine and public health.

"SURE YOU aren't having twins?"

There's hardly a prospective mother who isn't asked this question during her latter and more obvious prenatal days.

"Twins!" the mother-to-be usually exclaims in a tone of desperation. "How would I ever manage?"

Doctors say, however, that expectant mothers usually glow with added pride and joy when told that twins are *really* on the way. And why not? To give life to two new human beings at the same time is a wondrous thing. Then, too, twins are infinitely fascinating and appealing. Indeed, most of us would agree with Dr. H. M. Parshley, the famous biologist, who said: "Twins, by their very likeness, add charming variety to the lives of all of us."

In some remote sections of the world, however, twins are feared as omens of evil. Mothers who bear them may be cast into exile until they are "purified" for having committed the sin of mating with a witch-man. One twin may be permitted to live because he represents good; the other may be put to death because he represents evil.

In contrast, other primitive people hail twins as divine beings possessed of miraculous powers. They are believed to have the ability to forecast the weather, to control fire and flood, and to cure diseases. Because of these remarkable virtues, mothers of twins are held in great esteem.

While we share no such mystical or superstitious beliefs, we do regard twins with a certain awe. And as any mother of twins will testify, opinions on the subject are generally a peculiar mixture of fact and fallacy. So let us consider some frequently-asked questions about twins—and answer them with information based on medical research.

How often do twins occur? In 1954, the latest year for which complete figures exist, the National Office of Vital Statistics reported that 43,220 sets of twins were born. The number has probably gone up since, in keeping with the booming birth rate.

As for other multiple birth, 398 sets of triplets were reported in 1954. Quadruplets and quintuplets are, of course, very rare. A lavish gift of babies, like the celebrated Dionne quintuplets, has been reported only 60 times in the last 500 years. Twins are born once in every 85 births; triplets, one in 7000; quadruplets, one in 50 million; and quintuplets, one in 57 million births.

What are the different types of twins and how does medical science explain their origin? Twins are of two types—*identical* and *fraternal*. About one-third of all sets of twins are identical, and the other two-thirds are fraternal.

Identical twins always develop from one egg, or ovum, fertilized by a single male cell, or sperm. At some more or less early stage of development, the single fertilized egg splits in half to form two individuals. They are always of the same sex and they have exactly the same heredity. In other words, they are precisely the same individual in duplicate or "single individuals split in twain."

By contrast, *fraternal* twins come from two separate eggs fertilized by two separate male cells. Hence, they are two entirely different individuals who, through exceptional circumstances, were born together. Fraternal twins may be of the same or of different sex. Since they differ in their hereditary make-up, fraternal twins may bear no resemblance to each other. In fact, they may be as unlike as any other two children of the same family.

What factors seem to favor the birth of twins? Statistical studies show that twinning is favored by a cold climate, rural location of the parents, and the age of the mother. The older the mother, the better the chance for twins. Even mothers between the ages of 45 and 50 average more twins than do young mothers between 15 and 20. The father's age appears to be unimportant.

Causes advanced for twinning have ranged from works of the devil to plain evidence of improper behavior on someone's part. It is definitely known, however, that an inherited tendency for twins runs in certain families. A couple who have had twins are likely to do so again. And twins are themselves very likely to produce two-at-a-time babies.

Are twin births hazardous? Obstetrical problems may attend twin births if the cords by which the babies are attached to the placenta become twisted together or if the babies are large. Fortunately, the first condition seldom occurs, and large twins are rare—on an average, they weigh little more than five pounds when born. The birth of twins is handled far more skillfully and safely now than in the past. Possible complications can be anticipated and prepared for well ahead of delivery, as twins can be detected by x-ray studies, usually around the sixth month of pregnancy.

What about the physical and mental disadvantages of twins as compared to children born singly? It is true that twins may start life with some disadvantage. They are generally born prematurely—or about two weeks earlier than babies born singly. A study made in New York State some 10 years ago showed that mortality of twins during the first month of life was three times that of babies from single births.

But here again the outlook is brighter, owing to vast improvements for the care of premature babies. After overcoming the disadvantage of prematurity, twins develop at the same pace as that of other infants. Despite a popular theory that twins, one or both, usually commence life with a mental handicap, the I.Q. of twins is practically the same as that of the general population.

Which is the more important factor in the lives of twins—heredity or environment? Volumes have been written on this question, but no absolute conclusions have been drawn. One of the most exhaustive studies ever made (on 100 pairs of twins) revealed that "physical characteristics are least affected by environment, intelligence is affected more, educational achievement still more; and personality or temperament the most." The heredity-versus-environment argument might be settled if a large enough group of identical twins could be reared apart under different circumstances. This type of study will, of course, be hard to come by.

Are identical twins really identical in all respects? No, identical twins are never truly identical in all respects. This is because even before birth they do not have identical environments as shown by the fact that one identical twin may be born alive, the other dead. Moreover, one may develop a little faster than the other and throughout life may be slightly heavier and more vigorous. Yet identical twins usually have such remarkable similarities that it is often impossible to distinguish them in the absence of some very noticeable telltale sign.

As a rule, identical twins are so much alike that scientists can identify them—not only by obvious outward resemblances—but also by similar physiological and structural characteristics. For example, blood pressure, pulse rate, hair texture, palm, sole, freckle, and finger patterns of one-egg twins are so closely correlated that the likenesses can only be attributed to identical heredity.

Twins are also much alike in their character traits, tastes, preferences, and interests. This is probably due to the environment which they share. Invariably they are treated, dressed, and schooled alike; and they may share all they have from toys to maternal affection. Though it may be nothing but morbid coincidence, identical twins have attempted suicide within a few hours of each other, separate and unknown to each other, and at practically the same spot.

What are the facts about the attachment of twins for each other? The attachment of identical twins is generally extraordinarily close and lasting, especially in childhood. It is typical of them that they are very hard to separate even for a day. They are so accustomed to eating, sleeping, bathing, and playing together that separation throws their schedule out of kilter.

On the other hand, the feeling of attachment among fraternal twins is not so strongly developed. They can be separated without difficulty. Indifference, enmity, and competition are just as frequent among them as among regular brothers and sisters.

Do identical twins write alike? Though identical twins may be almost exactly alike in all other respects, their handwriting exhibits almost no similarity. Each twin has his own characteristic writing speed, word spacing, and letter formation. For instance, the penmanship of the Hilton Sisters (Siamese twins) varied greatly. Daisy wrote a distinctly "feminine" script, while Violet's penmanship was of the "manly" variety. In drawing, however, twins may use similar techniques.

What is the explanation for Siamese twins? In the early stages of development, two bodies may fuse and form Siamese twins. This connection may occur anywhere—sides, backs, fronts, or heads, and is purely an accidental event. They can be separated if the fusion has not resulted in sharing of a common important organ, such as the liver. Siamese twins happen once in five million births.

Are twins worth "all the trouble"? Despite double work—feedings, baths, and mountains of diapers—mothers of twins take it all in their stride. Perhaps that's because twins provoke twice as much mother love as one child. Then too, dads respond magnificently to the demands of twins. As Dr. Benjamin Spock has observed: "You never realize how important a father can be in child rearing until you've seen a father of twins in action."

What medical advances may come from studies of identical twins? Studies of identical twins may reveal ways by which vital organs can be transplanted from one person to another. In some operations, pieces of bone have been successfully transplanted, forming a temporary bridge over which new bone growths occur. But in attempting to transfer kidneys, adrenal glands, livers, and other complicated organs, surgeons usually cannot make the grafted organs "take" permanently.

The trouble is that the body rejects or refuses to accept tissues taken from other human beings, even close relatives. This hostility toward donated organs—an allergic-like reaction—is due to differences in the protein content of the organs of all individuals—*except those of identical twins*. Since the make-up of their tissues is precisely the same, no biological or chemical barrier exists to interfere with organ transplants.

For instance, kidney transplants in identical twins have been successful. At Boston's Peter Bent Brigham Hospital last November [1957] a 14-year-old boy donated one of his kidneys to his identical twin, who was suffering from a chronic kidney disease. The operation was the sixth such transplant performed at the hospital.

Physicians hope to find ways to make patients into "temporary identical twins" long enough to permit transplants of vital organs. The obstacles are great. But think of the lives that could be saved by replacing diseased organs with healthy ones!

CHAPTER 21:

The First Baby

76 · How Many Children Do Young People Want? *

CHARLES E. BOWERMAN

The ups and downs of the birthrate are of interest not only to the population specialists, but to school people, manufacturers of children's supplies, and prospective parents. As this article points out, the birthrate increased after World War II and has tended to remain at a higher level than was anticipated. One way to gain some insight into future rates of birth is to ask young people how many children they want. This article gives some interesting responses.

ONE OF THE MOST interesting and significant trends to occur in the United States in recent years is the change in the rate at which children are being born. The general facts about this trend are well known. During the 1930's the birth rate had reached such a low level that an actual decline in our population was anticipated within a relatively few years. Suddenly, during World War II, the number of new babies increased at a surprising rate, but this was generally thought of as a result of the increase in the rate of new marriages and a reaction to the economic prosperity of the war period. It was expected that once men were back from the war a year or two and the marriage rate had leveled out, we would resume the pre-war birth rates. This decline did not occur, however, and it is now generally believed by scholars that the birth rate will remain at a high level for some time to come.

* "Attitude Norms about Optimum Size of Family," *Coordinator*, 4 (March, 1956), 8–12. Reprinted by permission of the publisher and the author.

The author holds the degree of Doctor of Philosophy from the University of Chicago. He is Professor of Sociology and Research Professor in the Institute for Research in Social Science at the University of North Carolina. He is especially interested in research on marital adjustment and adolescent-parent relationships. He has published a number of research articles in professional journals.

Recent trends can be summarized briefly as follows. There has been a significant decrease in the percent of families without children. At 1940 rates, about one woman in five was going through the child-bearing period without having children. It now appears that this rate will be cut approximately in half for the present generation of mothers. There is also a big decline in the percent of women having only one child. On the other hand, there appears to be a continuing decrease in the number of families having more than five children. Rates at which fifth children are being born are remaining fairly stable, but rates for births of second, third, and fourth children have increased steadily since the beginning of the war. These facts indicate a significant change in our birth folkways. There is also considerable evidence that the differentials in birth rates between rural and urban areas and between socio-economic classes are being reduced. In fact, it is possible that the negative relationship between birth rate and economic status may disappear or even be reversed, with people having children in accord with their financial ability to pay the costs.

The implications of these trends, if they can be regarded as somewhat permanent, are of great importance. The effects on our school system are quite apparent. It is also believed that our present period of economic prosperity is in part based on the belief that we will have an increasing population for a considerable time to come, and therefore an expanding economy requiring investment in capital goods and plant. The implications for the family system are not too clear, as yet. It appears, however, that the size of family is becoming more standardized, with a decrease in childless and one-child families as well as a decrease in the large family with six or more children. Families with two, three, or four children will be the mode. Possibly some of the variations in family patterns and organization are a function of varying size, and with the stabilization of size there may develop more institutionalized forms of organization within the family. It is also possible that the somewhat negative orientation to the problem of having children, which accompanied the popularization of birth control methods, has given way to a widely-accepted value system in which a moderate number of children are considered highly desirable.

The exact reasons for this change in our birth rate are not known. Our continued high level of economic prosperity and rising standard of living have often been cited as primarily responsible. This at least must be viewed as a condition which has made it possible for many families to have children in excess of what they would otherwise plan for. However, with fairly widespread knowledge of the means of controlling numbers, one can only conclude that there has been a fairly significant change in attitude toward the having of children and the numbers desired. These attitudes may be partly a result of conditions existing in a particular family, such as financial condition, employment of the wife, health factors, and the adjustment of the marriage. It is the thesis of this paper, however, that this kind of attitude fluctuates within a fairly narrow limit set by more generalized social attitudes and norms about the number of children there "ought" to be in a family. Furthermore, it is believed that this generalized attitude has become much more crystallized in the last decade or so around the new norms that are developing, and that it is a potent force in determining the number of children any particular family will desire.

To get some indication of existing attitudes, a year ago we gave a short questionnaire to 330 high school seniors, in Seattle, in which they were asked how many children they would like to have when they got married. We were rather surprised to find that only 5 percent said they wanted no children or only one child, and just 2 percent wanted five or more. Forty-six percent said they thought two was the right number, 30 percent said three, and 17 percent wanted four. Boys and girls did not differ at the extremes, but girls were a little more likely than boys to want three rather than two. These findings indicate a fairly positive attitude, openly recognized and expressed, toward having a moderate number of children. The attitudes expressed are much closer to current rates than to those of a generation ago, where it is likely that somewhat different views would have been expressed by a high school group. The question can be raised, of course, about the relationship between attitudes expressed while in high school and later performance. It is probably more important to consider such responses as the reflection of the normative values held in the society. As to the permanency of such attitudes, the only available evidence is from the study of Burgess and Wallin in which they report a slight increase, in the number of children desired, between the time of engagement and three years after marriage.[1]

To get additional evidence on existing attitudes, a brief study was conducted at the University of Washington to see if another sample would express the same normative attitudes, and to see what was the range of acceptable family size around the optimum. Furthermore, we wanted to see if there was any relationship between desired number of children and several background factors. The sample was restricted to male students, as those thought to be least likely to express normative values and more likely to react to personal considerations. A brief questionnaire was given to a random sample of 239 of the 550 students living in the men's dormitory. The forms were filled out anonymously and placed in a sealed box. The students were interested and cooperative and seemed to be sincere in their responses.[2]

---

[1] E. W. Burgess and Paul Wallin, 1953. *Engagement and Marriage*, J. B. Lippincott, New York, page 705.

[2] Appreciation is expressed to Mr. Warren M. Russell for assistance in collecting and tabulating the data for this study.

In response to the question, "Anticipating future marriage, how many children would you like to have?", only three of the 239 students said they wanted none, and two said they wanted one child. At the other extreme, eight students named 5 as the optimum number, and five wanted six or more children. Thirty-eight percent wanted two children, 36 percent three, and 18 percent indicated four as the number they would like to have.

To get an idea of the range in numbers that would be acceptable, the question on optimum number was followed by a question, "I believe I would not want to have more than _____ children, or fewer than _____ children." The students who gave zero or one child as optimum were adamant in sticking to this number, only one of the five saying he would consider one more than the best number as acceptable. These five can therefore be considered as having personal norms lying outside the general norms, and it is significant that they are so few in number.

Of those naming two as the best number, 76 percent were willing to have three or four, while only 7 per cent thought it would be all right to have no children, and 53 percent would not want less than two. Of those naming either three or four as the desired number, 30 percent wanted to limit themselves to this number, but 70 percent were willing to have either one or two additional children. At the lower limits, 74 percent of those wanting three or four children said two was the smallest number they would like, and only 9 percent would be satisfied with less than two. These figures would tend to verify the existence of fairly strong norms at two to four children, with less freedom of varying from the norms at the lower level than at the upper level.

The number of children desired was cross-tabulated against several background items to see if there was any relationship. There was slight difference by religious preference, with Catholic and Jewish students wanting a slightly higher number, on the average, than Protestants (3.0, 3.2, and 2.8, in order named). With respect to age, there was no difference in the average number named for students over 18, but those 18 and under gave a slightly lower average than those who were older. Economic status of parental family, as indicated by father's income, was very slightly negatively correlated with number of children desired.

It was interesting that those students who were closest to marriage (engaged) had the highest average number of children desired. On the other hand, those who were not even dating wanted as many as those who were dating, and almost as many as those going steady.

The highest relationships were for those factors indicating differences in early family relationships, number of siblings and happiness of parents' marriage. The average number desired for only children was just 2.6, while the average of those with one to three siblings was 2.8, and for those with four or more siblings the average was 3.6, which although higher than that for the other students was in almost all cases fewer than in their parental family. In relating number of children desired to happiness of parents' marriage, it was found that those who rated the marriage as very unhappy wanted an average of only 2.5 children, whereas those who rated the marriage as very happy gave an average of 3.1, with in-between marriage ratings giving an average of 2.9. Even here, however, this factor did not seem to make students depart from the norms, but just to vary within the limits of those norms.

In conclusion, these results would seem to be in accord with the following two hypotheses: (a) Current social norms reflect a positive attitude toward having children and these norms are sufficiently incorporated into the attitudes of the individual to strongly affect his decision as to the number of children he desires. These norms are for two to four children, with a slightly higher number being acceptable but not strongly desired by most people, whereas it is becoming less acceptable to have fewer than two children, and (b) Variations within these norms are thought of as an area of personal freedom of decision, but the factors influencing this decision are decreasingly those of categorical factors such as occupation and economic status, rural-urban residence, religion, etc., and decisions are increasingly made on the basis of attitudes toward children and the kind of family relationship desired, resulting partly from the nature of the experience in one's early family.

77 · Should You Have a Baby the First Year? *

DAVID R. MACE

Opinion on when to have the first baby is divided into several factions. One group supports the widely held opinion that husband and wife should take a year or two to become adjusted to each other before the wife becomes

* *Woman's Home Companion*, 76 (December, 1949), 38, 93. Reprinted by permission of the author. This material also appears in David R. Mace, *Marriage: The Art of Lasting Love* (New York: Doubleday & Company, Inc., 1952).

The author, born in Scotland, was educated at London, Cambridge, and Manchester Universities. He helped lay the foundation for the marriage guidance movement in England, before coming to the United States in 1939. He is Associate Professor, Family Study Department, Psychiatry, Medical School, University of Pennsylvania. He is the author of many articles, both professional and for the general public, and of a number of books including *Marriage: The Art of Lasting Love*, and *Success in Marriage*.

pregnant. Another group, opposed to contraceptives, accepts the attitude that nothing should be done to control the spacing of babies. Yet a third group, not opposed to contraceptives, or approving the controlled spacing of children, advocates having the first baby relatively soon after marriage before husband and wife become set in a pattern of activities and expenses that almost excludes a baby.

Dr. Mace presents the arguments pro and con for a baby during the first year of marriage and makes clear that his own position is on the pro side.

For Hilda's grandmother marriage meant beginning an entirely new life. It meant leaving the home where she had always lived and becoming overnight the mistress of a new establishment of her own. It meant a break with her former associates and activities. Most important of all it meant the very real possibility, within a year, of being a mother. In fact the quaint faded photograph of Hilda's grandmother taken on her first wedding anniversary shows her with her first-born on her knees.

But when Hilda became engaged to George two years ago, marriage was no longer something you took in one tremendous leap. You assimilated it by easy stages. Hilda and George, for example, couldn't afford a place of their own so they were going to settle at first with Hilda's people. Thus Hilda's bridal chamber would be the familiar room she had slept in nearly all her life. Since there was no new establishment over which she could preside, Hilda planned to continue with her job. That would be better than idling about at home; and what she earned would help build up the savings she and George needed to start a family.

There was just the slightest shake in Hilda's voice as she outlined her plans. Of course they were going to be very very happy. But somehow this marriage wasn't the tremendous step she had always imagined. Apart from the fact that she and George would be together as man and wife, everything would be pretty much as before.

The truth of the matter was that she was frankly envious of Grandmother —especially over that baby.

The new pattern of marriage today is not of course altogether of our choosing. It has been partly thrust upon us. Changing economic circumstances have forced many young people to regard getting married, setting up a home and starting a family as three separate successive stages in their pilgrimage toward the goal of a full and happy family life.

But if we could clear away the obvious economic obstacles to achieving that goal the first year, would Hilda and George really want to start their family right away as Grandmother and Grandfather did? Is it advisable that they should?

Young people are often perplexed. So many couples postpone parenthood because the conditions under which they marry appear to offer no reasonable alternative that it is difficult to know how they would act if they were free to have their first baby any time they liked. I suspect that a great many of them would not follow Grandmother's example.

One school of thought strongly advocates a period of mutual adjustment for every couple before they embark upon the responsibility of having a child. Husband and wife, it is said, must have some time alone together in order to achieve emotional rapport before they can work efficiently as a team in the service of their offspring. Above all, they must make a satisfactory sex adjustment before the issue becomes confused by the exacting demands a baby makes upon their time and energy—and focus of attention.

These are cogent and weighty arguments. In proper circumstances I have been convinced by them myself and have presented them to young people who have come to me for advice. I would still do so. But I am becoming more and more conscious that we haven't given enough attention to the other side of the case. That tremulous quiver in Hilda's voice, that momentary mistiness in her eyes—have we perhaps underestimated their importance?

Let's look at the arguments again. First, there's the one about getting a good home ready. Of course we want a good home for every child. But are we perhaps oversolicitous about material comforts and conveniences? Presidents of the United States have been born in log cabins; pioneers of this great nation have first opened their eyes upon covered wagons which soon after their birth were jolting westward again. What we call physical hardship today would in the past have seemed luxury. Hang it all, babies are not fragile pieces of Dresden china—though we sometimes treat them as if they were. They are tough little fellows with quite remarkable powers of endurance. Some babies even survived concentration camps. In the light of that, you can't convince me that having a child before the home is all you'd like it to be is going to do Junior any harm worth mentioning. Let's recognize that this is a fifth-rate argument not worth bothering about if other considerations are favorable toward embarking upon parenthood.

Secondly, there's the question of emotional adjustment of husband and wife (leaving out for the moment the specifically sexual factor). Two people who are going to be parents, it is argued, should have grown accustomed to each other and learned to cooperate harmoniously. A child may be physically tough but he's terribly susceptible to emotional tension. It would be unwise to let him make his appearance in the midst of it. So let's first give the couple a year or two for their mutual adaptation.

This is a more important argument. Indeed if it were entirely sound it might settle the question. But the facts don't quite back it up. Two people who get married are not, if they have any sense at all, at the beginning of the task of mutual adjustment. They have been seeing a great deal of each other during their courtship, which ought to have lasted at least a year. If they have not just spent this time in light lovemaking, they should have come to marriage with pretty full knowledge of each other and plenty of experience in cooperation and teamwork. The truth, I suspect, is that many modern couples want to delay parenthood because they have scamped the premarital adjustment assignment and are obliged to use the early days of marriage to catch up.

Of course there are personal adjustments to be made in marriage which cannot be compassed during courtship. The very closeness and intimacy of married life decides that. But what sort of adjustments are they? Fundamentally they aim to bring about the smooth achievement of the shared life. Learning and growing by doing together is the keynote of early marriage. And what is more appropriate than to fulfill each other creatively by producing a child, their joint possession and their joint responsibility? In the profoundly significant activity of caring for this child they will make more satisfactory adjustments in a day than they could accomplish in a month discussing books or planning a garden.

The pregnancy, however, may be emotionally disturbing to Hilda. And isn't this dangerous when she and George are making their first ventures in shared living? Quite possibly. But George is much more likely to be patient and tolerant if this upheaval takes place in the rapturous early days of marriage—when he is bursting with the joy and pride of having Hilda as his very own—than after a year or so when the newness has worn off.

Then comes the question of the crisis which the first child brings to marriage. But I believe that it strengthens rather than weakens the case for early parenthood. Almost all the possible dangers of this time grow in intensity as parenthood is delayed and the couple settles down to a marriage which includes no bassinet. The crisis arises largely because the coming of the baby breaks up the established pattern of married living and compels the couple to shape a new regime including the child's needs. Later parenthood substantially adds to the number of changes that must be made.

Thirdly, let us turn to the question of sex adjustment. This, to the exponents of the delayed parenthood theory, is generally the central argument. Until full mutual satisfaction has been achieved in sexual union, it is said, the marriage bears at its heart insecurity and tension. If Hilda has a child before she becomes fully responsive to George's love-making the new and exciting fulfillment of becoming a mother may crowd out her half-hearted interest in the sex life and precipitate a crisis.

All this is profoundly true. Every experienced marriage counselor knows that it is hard to exaggerate the importance of mutual sex fulfillment. In the early years of marriage in particular it is often decisive in the achievement of settled mutuality in the whole relationship. In normal marriages nothing else can be completely right if this adjustment is not right. If it could be proved that willingness to have a child soon after marriage is likely to interfere with satisfactory sex adjustment, I would pursue this theme no further.

But *has* that been proved? I think not. The achievement of a satisfying relationship by the wife (and that, in nine cases out of ten, is the real hindrance to satisfactory adjustment) is not essentially a matter of time but rather a question of proper understanding, and above all of right atmosphere. If it is not established during the first year of marriage, my experience as a counselor would suggest that there is no more likelihood of its being established in the second year than in the third or the fourth.

My point is that under normal conditions there is every opportunity for a couple to achieve sexual harmony without postponing parenthood. Medical investigations based on the testimony of married people who made no attempt to delay parenthood indicate that on the average a newly married wife doesn't conceive for six months or so. Since it is perfectly safe to continue sexual union for at least the first six months of pregnancy, that gives the average couple a year to achieve mutual satisfaction.

Despite the possibility of pregnancy and its complications. I believe the general atmosphere under these conditions is more favorable to achieving adjustment than where conception is deliberately put off. The artificiality created by the need to take precautions is absent. Husband and wife can feel entirely free and unfettered. The wife has no nagging dread of pregnancy as she has wholeheartedly accepted the possibility of motherhood. I believe that many wives can never be free and spontaneous in sexual union until they have accepted its full implications without mental reservation. I believe also that many newly married girls consciously or unconsciously shrink from making use of contraception. Moreover, it is just these particularly sensitive women who often have most difficulty making a satisfactory sex adjustment.

I am not here raising any personal objection to planned families. What I am doing is to question seriously the modern custom of beginning married life with the use of contraceptives. I know the custom is based on widely current attitudes about marriage and parenthood—attitudes I have in some measure shared. But I am now seriously asking whether these attitudes are in the best interests of successful marriage. I believe the whole question deserves to be re-examined.

Further than that I am not prepared to go. Hilda and George must make up their own minds on what is a peculiarly personal matter. They may well feel that in the light of their circumstances the course they have chosen is right—that they are justified in delaying parenthood. But I hope they will agree with me that, in the interests of happy marriage, parenthood ought not to be delayed without very good reason. Perhaps the doubt in Hilda's mind which prompted her to come and talk things over with me in the first place represents something which it is not altogether wise to suppress.

In short, wasn't Grandmother right after all?

78 · *Crusading in Child Care* *

BENJAMIN SPOCK

From time to time some new theory or practice in child care comes to public attention and, becoming a fad, may be used in inappropriate ways. Understood, these theories and practices may contribute to the well-being of mother and child. Dr. Spock examines four "new" practices in child care, explaining what is involved in each, its limitations and its values.

I WANT to discuss some of the values and also some of the limitations of crusading in child care. I'm thinking of natural childbirth, rooming in, breast feeding, self-demand schedules. None of these practices is new. In fact, they all go back to the beginnings of the human race. But they have all received new emphasis—and some of them new names—in the past dozen years as a result of the increasing awareness of the importance of emotional factors and the realization of how far we had got away from nature owing to our rapid technical progress.

The best known advocate of a more natural childbirth is Dr. Grantly Dick Read, an English physician who wrote Natural Childbirth in 1933, and then Childbirth Without Fear in 1944. There have, of course, been many other obstetricians who have strongly advocated keeping childbirth as natural as possible, reducing the use of anesthetics and instruments to a minimum. But the problem has always been the woman's pain or fear of

* "Dr. Spock Talks with Mothers," Ladies Home Journal, 73 (January, 1956), 50, 124, copyright 1955 by The Curtis Publishing Company. Reprinted by permission of the publisher and the author.
The author received the degree of Doctor of Medicine from Columbia University. He is Professor of Child Development at Western Reserve University. Interested in the emotional development of children and in preventive psychiatry, he is best known publicly for his book Common Sense Book of Baby and Child Care. He is coauthor of A Baby's First Year and Feeding your Baby and Child. He is also author of the series of articles, "Dr. Spock Talks with Mothers," from which this selection was chosen.

pain, and the doctor's wish to spare her this. Doctor Read, as a result of years of practice, observing the differences between those women who had painful labor and those who didn't, became convinced that the main cause of pain was improper functioning of the nerves and muscles of the uterus during labor, and that this in turn was brought about by the woman's own tenseness and fear. In other words, fear of pain was indirectly the cause of pain. He gradually developed a training program for pregnant women which, first of all, reduced their anxiety by teaching them what goes on during pregnancy and delivery and reassuring them that labor need not be very painful. He also taught them by words, charts and exercises how to co-operate with nature by relaxing mentally and physically during those times in labor when relaxation is helpful and by making the right physical effort when that is valuable.

He found that these training methods made it possible for a great majority of his patients to have their babies without much pain and without the need for anesthetics. (Anesthesia was always available whenever a woman might wish to use it, but very few wanted it.) He felt that just as important as the lack of pain for the mother, and the lack of any danger to the baby from the anesthetic, is the tremendous sense of achievement and joy the mother feels in this act of creation if she is wide awake, knows she has carried it out through her own efforts, sees, hears, takes into her arms and perhaps puts to breast the baby she had just brought forth.

(There are two confessions that new mothers often make, at least to themselves: they don't feel for the first few days the maternalness toward the baby that they expected to feel, and they can't help wondering whether the baby whom the nurse brings in from the nursery is really theirs. I suspect that these bothersome feelings would be much less likely in "natural childbirth" than in deliveries in which the mother is under general anesthetic.)

Doctor Read's ideas, as you can imagine, were originally met with great skepticism on the part of physicians and on the part of mothers (who naturally felt that they knew better than any man what labor was really like). But as the years have gone by, more and more doctors and mothers who have had experience with the method have been convinced too.

"Rooming in" is the name given to a lying-in arrangement in which newborn babies, instead of being kept together in a nursery, cared for by nurses and brought to their mothers only for certain feedings, are instead kept close to their mothers and mainly cared for by them throughout the hospital stay. Nurses are very much on hand, but their principal job is to teach and help the mothers in baby care rather than do it all themselves.

In this system mothers, particularly new mothers, have the opportunity to hear about and actually to practice baby care while they are surrounded by experienced professional people to whom they can turn whenever they have a question or a worry. This is much more comfortable than having to take over for the first time when they are all by themselves at home, have no definite idea what this young stranger's habits, moods, movements are like, and have never perhaps bathed him, changed him or carried him about.

A particular advantage of rooming in is that the mother can put her baby to breast at the times when he himself wakes up and is hungry, instead of having to conform to a strict time schedule. This favors the success of breast feeding. The breasts produce no milk for the first two or three days, but this is usually no hardship for babies because they tend to be sleepy and unhungry those days. Then, in response to glandular changes, the mother's milk comes in. But nature counts on the baby's hunger to stimulate the breasts—by the frequency and completeness with which he empties them—to increase the supply to meet his increasing needs.

Typically, it is just when the milk comes in that most babies become much more wakeful and hungry. In fact, most of them have what are called "frequency days" in the latter part of the first week, when they may want to nurse (at least briefly) as often as ten or twelve times in the twenty-four hours for a couple of days. Then, as the milk supply becomes established and the baby gets enough each time really to satisfy him, the number of times he wants to nurse drops off to about six or seven. I think you can see how rooming in with its great flexibility provides for the matching of the milk supply to the baby's needs, with an efficiency that a regular schedule can't possibly provide.

Another advantage of rooming in, as usually practiced, is that the father is allowed to visit the mother *and* the baby. He can even take the baby in his arms or change a diaper. This may not seem important to some women, but every father who has felt like a rank outsider (allowed to see his baby only through a nursery window) can imagine what a difference it would make to be allowed to be part of the family right after the baby was born. I always knew this in a secondhand, theoretical kind of way. But I really felt it when my second son was born, while I was in the Navy, in the very hospital with which I had been connected as a civilian. I rushed up to the nursery, where I had always been welcome as a pediatrician come to examine new babies, in order to make friends with my own baby. But the head nurse blocked the door firmly and reminded me that fathers were not permitted in there. I have never felt so unwanted and unworthy.

Rooming in is nothing new. Throughout the world and throughout the ages most babies have been born at home and just naturally "roomed in." For a long while after hospitals began to be used for childbirth in Europe and America, babies were kept with their mothers, and this arrangement has never changed in some parts of Europe. In other words, the system under which babies are kept together in a nursery, apart from their mothers, is really the exception and the "new" procedure. It was adopted because it seemed like an efficient way to provide nursing care for babies and seemed likely to protect them from the germs of the large number of patients, visitors and staff people in any hospital. (Recent experience suggests that the rooming-in unit, with two to four mothers, is actually a safer place for babies than the large nursery.) The nursery system was also reasonably well adapted to bottle feeding, which was becoming so common. Since it was efficient from the point of view of hospital administration and since its psychological disadvantages for mothers and fathers were hardly noticed at the time, it became universal in America in a few decades. It has taken real pioneering on the part of a few doctors who had a special interest in the psychological side of the lying-in period—John Montgomery, Preston McLendon, John Parks, Edith Jackson—to set up the first rooming-in experiments. Those who have been close to rooming in are convinced of its value for mothers (especially new mothers, since experienced mothers know the ropes and have already gained their self-confidence), for fathers, for babies and for breast feeding. However, it requires significant changes in nursing administration, nursing practice, nursing philosophy, hospital administration, hospital architecture, doctor philosophy, patient attitude. You can see why it takes a long time and lots of enthusiasm on the part of somebody even to introduce a small experimental rooming-in unit into any hospital, and much longer still before it gains wide acceptance.

Two things seem almost unbelievable now about the "self-demand" feeding schedule for babies: that it struck us as so revolutionary when the first experimental case was written up in a medical journal in 1942 by Doctor McLendon, a pediatrician, and Mrs. Simsarian, the mother of the baby; and that the method has been so widely adopted in so few years. When people complain that change comes about too slowly, they should think of this example and gasp.

Here again there was nothing basically new in "self-demand" except the name. Up until the end of the nineteenth century almost all the babies who had ever been born anywhere were fed when they cried for it, and even in the twentieth century it was really only the babies born into "Western civilization" who were fed by the clock. But in these areas strict scheduling had been accepted so thoroughly that it seemed as if there had never been any other way.

Self-regulated scheduling hasn't benefited just the minority of babies who would have been miserable without it. I believe it has made a fundamental change in the attitude toward feeding—in fact, toward child care generally—of the young mothers of the past ten years. When mothers of the earlier period were instructed by conscientious doctors to feed certain amounts of formula at certain times of day and at no other times (on the assumption that this was the way to avoid intestinal upsets and spoiling), it made feeding sound like a technical, somewhat hazardous, slightly grim business. It encouraged a mother, in a sense, to mistrust her own natural feelings (of wanting to feed her baby when he seemed to want it) and to mistrust her baby's feelings too. It encouraged her to be arbitrary and bossy, whether she had any such inclination or not. It certainly made it hard for her to think of feeding as something that is natural and even fun.

The attitudes that were developed in the mother in regard to feeding had a tendency to persist and to carry over into other aspects of child rearing, such as toilet training and obedience training (don't expect the child to conform, make him!). Though I have no statistics, I think that the frequency of feeding problems has decreased tremendously in the past decade and that the ease with which mothers have got along with their children has increased noticeably.

Breast feeding didn't have to be rediscovered because it never disappeared completely from the American scene. (It became pretty rare in many areas, though. I remember about fifteen years ago getting off the elevator on the maternity floor of a large hospital in New York and having one of the nurses say in tones of amazement, "Aren't you the doctor who's taking care of the breast-fed baby?" She made me feel as queer as if I had driven up in a buggy.) I think that there has been some increase in breast feeding in recent years, but it certainly can't be said to be sweeping the country— which is too bad. When it goes well, it is so easy. It's a real pleasure for the mother spiritually and physically, as well as a source of great pride. It expedites the warm, strong bond between mother and baby (though I'll be the first to admit that they can get along fine together on bottle feeding too). From my own experience I don't think it need have any deleterious effect on the mother's figure if she controls overweight and if she uses a well-supporting brassière during pregnancy and lactation. (What we need in order to popularize breast feeding is not so much the urging of doctors as the testimonials of a few gorgeous movie actresses.)

So far I have listed rather briefly some of the values of four recent trends in infant care. Now I ought to explain what I mean by the limitations. I used the word "crusading" in the beginning of the discussion because for certain people it is crusading. These trends may have started as scientific inquiries, but the importance of the activities themselves (childbirth and infant feeding), the dramaticness of the conclusions reached (e.g., that childbirth need not be agony, that an infant can schedule himself), the fact that these conclusions were in harmony with a growing wave of impatience with mechanical concepts and a longing to get back to basic human fundamentals, immediately inspired the strong enthusiasm and allegiance of a number of professional and lay people. They had felt for a long time there must be a better way to do these things—they only needed to have the way shown.

I am one of those who are enthusiastic about these trends and I hope they become universally accepted. The limitations I am thinking about concern not the procedures themselves but the effect they have on some parents during this transitional period we are living in. I have known of young women who have become convinced of the values of natural childbirth—from having learned about it in a college course or simply from reading—but who found by the time they were pregnant that there was no physician in town who used these principles. So they either made arrangements for their prenatal care and delivery in another city (which is quite inconvenient, but otherwise all right if it can be managed) or they felt disappointed and pessimistic about having to begin child rearing under such unfavorable circumstances.

I have received letters from women who discovered that rooming in was not available in any lying-in hospital they could reach and who became convinced this would impose a handicap on themselves in their new career and on their babies' good adjustment to life.

I have talked with a number of mothers who assumed that a completely self-demand schedule was so much the law of infant care that nothing should be allowed to interfere with it—certainly not their own convenience. They would not wake the baby, for instance, just before going to bed themselves, but would expect to be wakened by him an hour or two later. They would still be providing meals at very irregular and unhandy hours for a big, husky six-month-old or even going back to regular night bottles for a one-year-old who had become a restless sleeper.

You have probably known women who set their hearts on breast feeding, went through a very difficult period in the hospital, and on returning home failed to make a go of it, and felt that they had shown their inadequacy as mothers and had deprived the baby of a vital experience.

To me, these all seem examples of parents' becoming overconcerned with procedures, each of which has real value but none of which is so vital that its absence would be seriously detrimental. Millions and millions of American babies were born and brought up in the first half of this century without natural childbirth, rooming in, self-demand or breast feeding, and of course most of them have turned out quite well.

I'm not making this point for the purpose of minimizing the advantage of these newer methods. What I'm concerned about is the fact that some of these conscientious new parents lose their sense of balance and forget all the other good things they are providing. They forget some of the other things that all babies need, such as a parental sense of humor, or firm parental guidance when the infant gets the foolish idea that he doesn't want to go to bed at bedtime. Other parents unwittingly dig a sort of trap for themselves into which they fall if the natural childbirth and rooming in can't be secured or if the supply of breast milk proves inadequate. The emotional reaction, especially to lack of success in breast feeding, is occasionally quite severe. This is unnecessarily hard on the parents and deprives the baby of the parental serenity which—I think anyway—he would enjoy even more than the procedures.

Maybe I'm taking myself too seriously in thinking I can keep young mothers and fathers from getting themselves in a jam through too crusading a spirit, just by my Polonius type of advice. After all, it's the nature of good young people to be crusaders, to be impatient with senseless traditions, to want to enlist in a fine cause and push it hard. That's how a lot of the world's progress has been brought about. In part, crusading is an expression of a stage of one's growing up in which one unconsciously proves that he is not only as smart as his old parents, but even smarter—and not one whit less idealistic. It also comes from quite realistic awareness that people who are less young have a tendency to cling to outworn and even undesirable customs simply because of habit. I don't want young people to stop being crusaders. I guess I only want them not to do their most earnest crusading in the field of child care, which should be relaxed and enjoyable.

79 · If You Want to Adopt a Baby *

CHANGING TIMES, THE KIPLINGER MAGAZINE

Adoption is by no means a rare thing. Nevertheless, many childless couples who would like to adopt shrink from doing so: they do not know how to go about it or they have heard tales of an adopted baby who developed into a child unsuitable for his particular home. Among couples who have decided to adopt, some go through the slow process of securing a baby through an approved adoption agency; others, impatient, secure a baby from the mother directly or through a doctor, nurse, or lawyer without the careful

* Changing Times, The Kiplinger Magazine, 8 (January, 1953), 29–31. Reprinted by permission of the publisher, The Kiplinger Magazine Agency, Inc.

study and checking of background given by the agency. This article goes into detail on the procedures to follow and explains why the adoption should be made through an authorized agency.

WITH SOME 250,000 children lacking responsible parents and about three times that many couples looking for babies to adopt, you would think it a simple matter to get the homeless children and the childless adults together. But it isn't.

Adoption is, in fact, a complicated and many-sided business. It is complicated, first, by the very fact that it involves the awful responsibility of deciding the whole future of a helpless child. Too, it involves difficult emotional problems on the part of both natural and foster parents. And, finally, the whole process must be done within the framework of laws that seek to protect everyone in on the adventure.

So if you want to adopt a baby, be prepared to work at it. Nothing about it will be either fast or easy, and considering that it is a lifetime proposition, it probably shouldn't be.

But if you are successful as an adoptive parent, you will find the experience of taking someone else's baby into your home satisfying and heartwarming.

To make an adoption work takes a lot of planning and a lot of knowledge. Here are some of the questions you will come up against as you go about finding your baby, plus some answers produced by people who have spent their lives helping parents like you.

Most natural parents give less thought to their own worth than people about to adopt a child do. The latter, facing a drawn-out inquisition by adoption agencies and maybe by a judge, are likely to agonize over their suitability and resources.

Don't worry too much, though. Adopted children, like all children, must take their chances on facing every adversity.

What the agency people are looking for, on the material side, are a few simple and obvious qualifications. As a would-be parent you must, of course, have some degree of economic security to offer the child, and be normally healthy and reasonably intelligent. There must be room in your home for the child to sleep and play comfortably.

They naturally prefer couples to single women, though widows and spinsters are not totally barred from adopting children. As to age, a rule of thumb is a maximum of 40 for the wife and 45 for the husband, but often older couples can adopt children.

On the less tangible side, the placement people want assurance that there is love and respect on both sides of the household, that husband and wife are united in their desire for a child, and that the desire comes from an unselfish motive.

Incidentally, look to your own motive. The only sound one is the sincere desire to have a child to bring up as your own. Any other involves selfishness and a risk for the baby.

Where Do You Go?

Once you have finally made up your mind that you want a baby and for the right reason, you have a choice of courses. You can take the slow but safe way through your state department of public welfare, or you can take a risky short cut. It's up to you, of course, but compare the relative safety of the methods.

One thing you shouldn't do is buy a baby. In the black market, babies are sold for up to $2,000. Don't touch them.

Then there is something which its critics call the "gray market." There is nothing evil here, and no profit is involved. Using this source may speed your search for a child, but it is the risky way to proceed.

The usual procedure is for a well-intentioned middleman, generally a doctor or a lawyer, to arrange an adoption in a friendly way. Usually, of course, the child belongs to an unmarried mother. The doctor or lawyer knows about her and also knows that you want a baby. What's simpler than giving you the infant straight out of the hospital with practically no red tape?

In many, many instances these adoptions work out beautifully, but here are the dangers:

The mother has decided to give up her child in a time of great stress and physical weakness. What if she changes her mind?

Since you take the child as a very young baby, there is no chance for it to be adequately tested for physical and mental disabilities. (Six months is about the minimum age at which tests can be made successfully.) Seldom do you learn the baby's full inheritance. Was there, for instance hemophilia in the family tree, which the necessarily cursory investigation by the friendly go-between failed to turn up?

Your other approach to adoption is through an authorized agency. Here you will find the red tape seemingly endless, the waiting sometimes unbearably long. But at the end you can be sure there will be no hitch.

Every state has a department responsible for dependent and neglected children, their care and their placement for adoption. It is usually called the department of public welfare or the department of public assistance.

Such departments maintain offices in the larger cities and, in addition, authorize certain charitable institutions to become placement centers. You can find out the names and locations of those in your state by writing to the state welfare board or inquiring at local social service agencies.

Why Must You Wait and Wait?

Everyone knows that it takes many months, often years, for anxiously waiting couples to find children through the agencies. Why?

Well, here's a statistical picture. It is true that some 250,000 children are being cared for in institutions and boarding homes, but many of these are what the agencies call "unadoptable." That means that they have parents who are unwilling to relinquish their rights, or that the child has a serious mental or physical defect.

The result is that only about 75,000 children are actually adopted each year. And 10 times that number of would-be foster parents are impatiently waiting.

Another factor in the time lag is the slow, careful way the agencies work. Take a look at the process of handling dependent babies and their mothers and you'll see why.

The basic idea behind the agencies' work is that the baby comes first, but natural parents also have airtight legal and moral rights. That's why unmarried mothers are never hurried into a decision to give up their children, and why families are given every help in repairing the falling walls of their homes.

And while the parents see whether they can straighten out their lives, the child must be cared for by the state.

During this time the child is tested for mental and physical disabilities and his family history is carefully studied. Sometimes at this stage the child lives in a foster boarding home instead of an institution. This gives him home life and mother care rather than the impersonal atmosphere of an orphan's home.

The agencies have been severely criticized recently for rather rigid standards as to what is an adoptable baby and for keeping children in temporary care overlong while they attempt to make "too perfect" matches between child and foster parents. Most agencies are now trying to move more rapidly, but there is still a considerable time lapse.

Once a child is ready for adoption, the agency combs its list of applicants in the difficult job of determining which baby for which family. They no longer insist that the color of the eyes is so important, but they do try to match parent to baby on these points:

Racial and Religious Background. Matching in these particulars is the law in many states. And this as a rule takes care of the problem of similarity in general appearance between parent and child.

Age. It is believed that parents should adopt a child of about the age of one they might have had. Thus, young couples are more likely to be given infants, and middle-aged people, older children.

Inherited Abilities. The child of a ditch-digger plumped into the home of a professor may run into trouble about the time his father wants to send him to law school and he wants to go to work as a mechanic. Heredity isn't everything, of course, but placement agencies prefer not to chance a mixture of radically conflicting inheritances.

What Do You Go Through?

The steps in adoption are not so difficult as you might think, even though there is a tangle of law to wade through. The legal fine points vary from state to state, but here in general is what you will face.

The Application. When you first call on the agency to announce your big decision to adopt a child, you will fill out a long and quite inquisitive form. Don't demur; it's necessary.

Then there will be a talk with one of the agency workers about just what you want in the way of a child. This is where you may be able to cut your waiting time if you can bring yourself to be at least as unchoosy as natural parents must be.

The vast majority of adopters want baby girls under a year in age with normal health and intelligence. Most expect to be captivated by a winning smile or golden curls. Unfortunately, there just aren't enough little girls of that description to fill the demand.

So try to be as flexible as you can in your mental image of the child you seek. If you are willing to take an older child, especially a boy, your order will be easier to fill.

Inspection. Some time—maybe a month or more—will pass without anything happening, but eventually an agency worker will call at your home. She is not going to look for dust on the doorframe or peer into the cluttered hall closet. All she wants to know is whether the home looks comfortable and happy and whether there is room for a new occupant.

The First View. An interminable period later, when you are about to give up hope, you will be invited down to the agency to see a real, live baby. You will be told everything about the child's history except the names of his parents. None of his drawbacks will be kept from you, nor any of his good points, either. Don't feel you have to take the first baby offered you. It's a big decision, and no one will hold it against you if you refuse the child.

But suppose you fall in love with a dimple or something and feel suddenly and deeply that THIS is the baby for you. Then you can probably take the baby home very soon, but you have not finished.

Making it legal. First comes your petition to the court, in which you request permission to adopt this particular child. The agency will help you, but you'll need a lawyer, too.

The court also must have documents showing the consent of the child's parents. The agency will furnish these.

Next there will be a private and confidential hearing before a judge. If you have used an agency, the hearing should be brief and routine. If not, the judge might ask that an investigation be made of the circumstances surrounding the adoption.

If all goes well, however, you will be granted the child for a probationary period, usually from six months to a year. During that time you will be visited by agency workers. (Their advice can be very helpful in the first trying days.) At the end of the period, the court will issue a final decree, and in most states it will issue a new birth certificate with the baby's new name.

Is the Child Really Yours?

Breathe easy. No one can take him away now. He is yours—by choice, by love and by law. There may be difficult days ahead, but the difficulties probably won't be so much different from those of any parent with any child.

A last reminder, though. To be successful, an adoption should be as nearly like a normal family relationship as possible, but always remember it is not quite the same. It must be planned a little better, and worked at just a bit more.

CHAPTER 22

Children and Parents

80 · Some Principles of Positive Parent-Child Relationships *

GERTRUDE K. POLLAK

American families tend to revolve around their children, and the development of well-balanced children is regarded as one of the highest values of family life. This goal does not imply that the parents should dominate their children; they should help them develop their own personal qualities within socially acceptable boundaries. Mrs. Pollak, who has had wide experience with parents' groups, suggests nine principles that may guide parents.

A NUMBER of principles of positive parent-child relationships emerge from our experience with parent groups and can be identified as follows:

1. *The role of the parent is to help the child develop socially acceptable behavior which will at the same time satisfy, in so far as possible, the child's healthy needs and drives.* In order to fulfil his role, the parent must be able both to set limits to a child's behavior and to provide as much opportunity as possible for the gratification of his wishes and the fulfilment of his needs and desires. Since it is necessary to accept and conform to societal demands and mores, the child must develop socially acceptable behavior. He is best helped to do this in the sheltered and protected setting of his family. On the other hand, conformity to societal demands should not be achieved at the price of crushing the child's individuality. Conformity is not the ultimate goal of child rearing and even if the child does conform it does not

* "Principles of Positive Parent-Child Relationships in Family Life Education," *Social Casework*, 37 (March, 1956), selection from pages 133–135. Reprinted by permission of the publisher and the author.

The author holds the master's degree from the Graduate Department of Social Work and Social Research, Bryn Mawr College. She is Director of Family Life Education of the Family Service of Philadelphia. Her publications include six articles published in journals for clinicians and social workers.
492

necessarily mean that child rearing has been successful. The child's individuality must have latitude to find expression and to develop, within the *broad* limits of society's demands and mores and the general framework and code for acceptable behavior. Many a parent is confused by his own concept of what constitutes acceptable behavior for a little girl or little boy and rejects behavior on the child's part which does not "conform" to the feminine or masculine role in its strictest interpretation. Such an attitude is rooted, in most instances, in the parent's own feelings about femininity or masculinity. The concepts of socially acceptable behavior and of conformity must be applied and interpreted with flexibility, in a broad and non-restrictive way.

2. *In evaluating the child's behavior and setting standards for him, parents should keep in mind the concept of "age-adequate maturity."* What is acceptable behavior at the age of three is not acceptable at the age of six. On the other hand, behavior that can be expected at the age of six should not be expected at the age of three; examples: not masturbating in the living room; sharing toys with other children; and so on.

3. *Parents should "give" to a child according to his particular needs.* This applies to such widely different areas of giving as demonstration of affection, the granting of privileges and the assignment of responsibilities, the giving of material things such as bicycles and toys, and so on. Parents often state proudly that they "treat all their children alike." This is obviously not the answer to each child's needs and wishes, nor is it the best way to offer him those opportunities for personality development which will be most helpful to him.

4. *The child's confidence and trust in him is the parent's strongest ally in coping with the difficult problems of growing up; parental actions should never threaten or undermine this confidence.* This means, among other things, that the parent should always tell a child the truth, although the amount of information given to the child will differ at various stages of the child's development, since the amount should be related to the child's capacity to absorb such information. This principle applies especially to such important areas of parent-child relationships as how to explain death and how to give information on body functions and the origin of life.

5. *Parental example and parental behavior will do more to influence the child's behavior, standards and values, and his concept of the world around him, than the parents' spoken words—their advice, exhortation, warnings, scoldings, or threats.* "Do as I do" has deep meaning in terms of parent-child relationships and in terms of identification and superego formation. There are few life situations in which the saying "Do as I say, not as I do!" is more inappropriate as well as more ineffective.

6. *Parents should recognize as much as possible not only their children's*

feelings and needs, but also their own feelings, needs, emotions, and con-scious as well as some of their unconscious motivations. Parental anxiety, hostility, disapproval, aggression, or rejection, as well as such positive emotions as approval, support, pride, and love, strike a responsive chord in their children, whose reactions tend to be in direct response to these emotions. In many instances, what the parent expresses verbally is at considerable variance with his real feelings and his emotional reactions. Children have an uncanny ability, however, to spot the parent's true feelings and to react to the underlying emotion rather than to the camouflage of the spoken word.

7. *Parents should realize that they do not carry the total and exclusive responsibility for the child's development.* A variety of other factors, such as constitution, cultural and racial factors, conditions of the environment in which the family lives and over which it has no control, and the experiences of the child outside of the home, will contribute to his development. These factors affect the child positively and negatively; they either support parental goals and influences or thwart and undermine them, depending on the nature of the specific factors at work in the child's life situation. Parents are not omnipotent. How forceful, for example, is the impact of the subgroup to which a teenager belongs, with its code for acceptable clothing, language, and dating habits! A more realistic evaluation of the parental role and of parental responsibility will do much to alleviate the confusion, undue anxiety, and insecurity which trouble many parents and which often affect negatively the discharge of the specific parental function with which they are so concerned.

8. *A balance of needs and satisfactions should be maintained within the family.* The wishes and needs of one member of the family should not be satisfied to such a degree that the needs and wishes of other members of the family remain unmet. It is necessary, therefore, when planning for the satisfaction of specific needs, to look at the family as a unit, as well as to look at the needs of each family member.

9. *In attempting to meet the needs of individual members of the family, the changing character of these needs and satisfactions should be kept in mind.* The content and quality of the parent-child relationship which meet a child's needs at one point will not be adequate at a later stage of development. Family relationships must be dynamic in character. In the happy home, family relationships are characterized by their flexibility. In passing, it may be pointed out that some of these principles, especially the principle of flexibility, apply also to marital relationships; the parent-child relationship is not the only family relationship that requires adaptability. More important, an adaptable, flexible, and harmonious marriage relationship is a prerequisite for harmonious parent-child relationships within the home.

This does not mean, however, that no friction should exist within the marriage relationship. It means, in the main, only that the forces of the positive feelings that bind the partners together are predominant in the marriage relationship.

The specific questions that parents in discussion groups are inclined to ask can easily be related, either directly or indirectly, to these principles. For instance, the problems of aggression and discipline, which we have found to be of concern to all parent groups, can be seen in a broader perspective if two concepts are used: that of helping the child to behavior that will satisfy his needs but will also be socially acceptable, and that of "age-adequate maturity" for evaluating his behavior. The realization that it is necessary to modify the parental role and the content of the parent-child relationship at various age levels is most helpful to parents who are coping with the problem of the child's developing independence. The parent's role with the young child will be quite different from his role with the adolescent. With the latter, the parent is puzzled by the characteristic problems of dating, of hours to be kept, and of the adolescent's need to merge into the peer group.

81 · Parenthood as Crisis *

E. E. LE MASTERS

Many preparations can be made ahead of time for the birth of a baby— equipment can be bought, books on baby care read, and finances put in order; but the full impact of the baby as a new, helpless, demanding member of the family about which family organization and activities must revolve at least for a time does not come until after the baby is brought home from the hospital. Professor LeMasters likens the experience to a crisis, that is, a situation for which the husband and wife do not have an adequate set of attitudes and habits to make adjustment easy. In fact, they may become somewhat disorganized before they adapt themselves to being parents.

* *Marriage and Family Living*, 19 (November, 1957), 352–355. Reprinted by permission of the publisher and author.

The author holds the degree of Master of Science in Social Work from Western Reserve University and of Doctor of Philosophy (sociology) from Ohio State University. He is Professor of Sociology at Beloit College. He has carried through many small research projects and writes for various professional journals. He is author of a college textbook, *Modern Courtship and Marriage*.

Introduction

In recent decades the impact of various crises on the American family has been subjected to intensive analysis. Eliot,[1] Waller,[2] Angell,[3] Komarovsky,[4] Cavan and Ranck,[5] Koos,[6] Hill,[7] and Goode[8] have published what is perhaps the most solid block of empirical research in the field of family sociology.

In all of these studies of how the modern family reacts to crisis, it appears that the shock is related to the fact that the crisis event forces a reorganization of the family as a social system. Roles have to be reassigned, status positions shifted, values reoriented, and needs met through new channels.

These studies have shown that crises may originate either from within the family itself or from the outside. It has also been demonstrated that the total impact of the crisis will depend upon a number of variables: (1) the nature of the crisis event; (2) the state of organization or disorganization of the family at the point of impact; (3) the resources of the family; and (4) its previous experience with crisis.[9]

These studies report a sequence of events somewhat as follows: level of organization before the crisis, point of impact, period of disorganization, recovery, and subsequent level of reorganization.

This study was conceived and designed within the conceptual framework of the above research.

The Present Study

In the study being described in this report, the main hypothesis was derived through the following line of analysis:

A. If the family is conceptualized as a small social system, would it not

---

[1] See Thomas D. Eliot, "Bereavement: Inevitable but Not Insurmountable," in *Family, Marriage, and Parenthood*, edited by Howard Becker and Reuben Hill, Boston: D. C. Heath and Company, Second Edition, 1955.

[2] Willard Waller, *The Old Love and the New*, New York: Liveright, 1930.

[3] Robert C. Angell, *The Family Encounters the Depression*, New York: Charles Scribner's Sons, 1936.

[4] Mirra Komarovsky, *The Unemployed Man and His Family*, New York: Dryden Press, 1940.

[5] Ruth Cavan and Katherine Ranck, *The Family and the Depression*, Chicago: University of Chicago Press, 1938.

[6] E. L. Koos, *Families in Trouble*, New York: King's Crown Press, 1946.

[7] Reuben Hill, *Families Under Stress*, New York: Harper and Brothers, 1949.

[8] William J. Goode, *After Divorce*, Glencoe: The Free Press, 1956.

[9] See Hill, *op. cit.*, for an excellent review of this research.

follow that the *adding* of a new member to the system could force a re-organization of the system as drastic (or nearly so) as does the *removal* of a member?

B. If the above were correct, would it not follow that the arrival of the *first* child could be construed as a "crisis" or critical event? [10]

To test this hypothesis, a group of young parents were interviewed, using a relatively unstructured interviewing technique. In order to control socio-economic variables, couples had to possess the following characteristics to be included in the study: (1) unbroken marriage; (2) urban or suburban residence; (3) between twenty-five and thirty-five years of age at the time of study; (4) husband college graduate; (5) husband's occupation middle class; (6) wife not employed after birth of first child; (7) must have had their first child within five years of the date interviewed. Race and religion were not controlled.

Using these criteria, forty-eight couples were located by the device of asking various persons in the community for names. As a precaution, the exact nature of the study was not stated in soliciting names for the sample —the project was described as a study of "modern young parents."

Once a name was obtained that met the specifications, every effort was made to secure an interview. No refusals were encountered, but two couples left the community before they could participate, leaving forty-six couples for the final study group. The couples, then, were not volunteers. All of the interviewing was done by the writer during the years 1953–1956. Both the husband and wife were interviewed.

Typical occupations represented include minister, social worker, high school teacher, college professor, bank teller, accountant, athletic coach, and small business owner.

Various definitions of "crisis" are available to the worker in this area. Webster, for example, states that the term means a "decisive" or "crucial" period, a "turning point." [11] Koos specifies that crises are situations "which block the usual patterns of action and call for new ones." [12] Hill defines as a crisis "any sharp or decisive change for which old patterns are inade-quate." [13] This is the definition used in this analysis.

A five point scale was used in coding the interview data: (1) no crisis; (2) slight crisis; (3) moderate crisis; (4) extensive crisis; (5) severe crisis.

---

[10] To some extent, the original idea for this study was derived from Hill's discussion. See *op. cit.*, ch. 2.

[11] *Webster's Collegiate Dictionary*, Springfield: G. and C. Merriam Co., Second Edition, 1944, p. 240.

[12] Koos, *op. cit.*, p. 9.

[13] Hill, *op. cit.*, p. 51. See also his review of definitions in ch. 2.

The Findings

The essential findings of this exploratory study are as follows:

1. Thirty-eight of the forty-six couples (83 per cent) reported "extensive" or "severe" crisis in adjusting to the first child. This rating was arrived at jointly by the interviewer and the parents.

In several cases there was some difference of opinion between the husband and wife as to what their response should be. In all but two cases, however, the difference was reconciled by further discussion between the interviewer and the couple. In the two cases, the wife's rating was recorded, on the theory that the mother makes the major adjustment to children in our culture.

For this sample, therefore, the evidence is quite strong in support of the hypothesis. The eight couples (17 per cent) who reported relatively mild crisis (values 1-2-3 in the above scale) must be considered the deviants in this sample.

Stated theoretically, this study supports the idea that adding the first child to the urban middle class married couple constitutes a crisis event.

2. In this study there was strong evidence that this crisis reaction was *not* the result of not wanting children. On the contrary, thirty-five of the thirty-eight pregnancies in the crisis group were either "planned" or "desired."

3. The data support the belief that the crisis pattern occurs whether the marriage is "good" or "poor"—for example: thirty-four of the thirty-eight in the crisis group (89 per cent) rated their marriages as "good" or better. With only three exceptions, these ratings were confirmed by close friends. By any reasonable standards, these marriages must be considered adequate.

4. There is considerable evidence that the crisis pattern in the thirty-eight cases was not the result of "neurosis" or other psychiatric disability on the part of these parents. Judging by their personal histories, their marriages, and the ratings of friends, it seemed clear that the vast bulk of the husbands and wives in the crisis group were average or above in personality adjustment.

5. The thirty-eight couples in the crisis group appear to have almost completely romanticized parenthood. They felt that they had had very little, if any, effective preparation for parental roles. As one mother said: "We knew where babies came from, but we didn't *know* what they were like."

The mothers reported the following feelings or experiences in adjusting to the first child: loss of sleep (especially during the early months); chronic "tiredness" or exhaustion; extensive confinement to the home and the resulting curtailment of their social contacts; giving up the satisfactions and the income of outside employment; additional washing and ironing; guilt at not being a "better" mother; the long hours and seven day (and night) week necessary in caring for an infant; decline in their housekeeping standards; worry over their appearance (increased weight after pregnancy, et cetera).

The fathers echoed most of the above adjustments but also added a few of their own: decline in sexual response of wife; economic pressure resulting from wife's retirement plus additional expenditures necessary for child; interference with social life; worry about a second pregnancy in the near future; and a general disenchantment with the parental role.

6. The mothers with professional training and extensive professional work experience (eight cases) suffered "extensive" or "severe" crisis in every case.

In analyzing these cases, it was apparent that these women were really involved in two major adjustments simultaneously: (1) they were giving up an occupation which had deep significance for them; and (2) they were assuming the role of mother for the first time.

Interpretation of the Findings

There are, of course, various ways of interpreting the findings in this study. It may be, for example, that the couples obtained for the sample are not typical of urban middle class parents. It might also be true that the interviewing, the design of the study, or both, may have been inadequate. If we assume, for the present, that the findings are reliable and valid for this social group, how are we to interpret such reactions to parenthood? It is suggested that the following conceptual tools may be helpful.

1. That parenthood (and not marriage) is the real "romantic complex" in our culture. This view, as a matter of fact, was expressed by many of the couples in the study.

In a brilliant article some years ago, Arnold Green [14] suggested as much —that urban middle class couples often find their parental roles in conflict with their other socio-economic commitments. If this is true, one would expect to find the reconciliation of these conflicts most acute at the point of entering parenthood, with the first child. Our findings support this expectation.

---

[14] Arnold W. Green, "The Middle-Class Male Child and Neurosis," *American Sociological Review*, 11 (February, 1946), pp. 31–41.

2. Ruth Benedict has pointed out that young people in our society are often the victims of "discontinuity in cultural conditioning." [15] By this she means that we often have to "unlearn" previous training before we can move on to the next set of roles. Sex conditioning is perhaps the clearest illustration of this.

Using this concept, one can see that these couples were not training for parenthood, that practically nothing in school, or out of school, got them ready to be fathers and mothers—*husbands* and *wives*, yes, but not *parents*. This helps explain why some of the mothers interviewed were actually "bitter" about their high school and college training.

3. One can also interpret these findings by resorting to what is known about small groups. Wilson and Ryland, for example, in their standard text on group work make this comment about the two-person group: "This combination seems to be the most satisfactory of human relationships." [16] They then proceed to pass this judgment on the three-person group: "Upon analysis this pattern falls into a combination of a pair and an isolate. . . . This plurality pattern is the most volatile of all human relationships." [17] This, of course, supports an earlier analysis by von Wiese and Becker.[18]

Viewed in this conceptual system, married couples find the transition to parenthood painful because the arrival of the first child destroys the two-person or pair pattern of group interaction and forces a rapid reorganization of their life into a three-person or triangle group system. Due to the fact that their courtship and pre-parenthood pair relationship has persisted over a period of years, they find it difficult to give it up as a way of life.

In addition, however, they find that living as a trio is more complicated than living as a pair. The husband, for example, no longer ranks first in claims upon his wife but must accept the child's right to priority. In some cases, the husband may feel that he is the semi-isolate, the third party in the trio. In other cases, the wife may feel that her husband is more interested in the baby than in her. If they preserve their pair relationship and continue their previous way of life, relatives and friends may regard them as poor parents. In any event, their pattern of living has to be radically altered.

Since babies do not usually appear to married couples completely by surprise, it might be argued that this event is not really a crisis—"well adjusted" couples should be "prepared for it." The answer seems to be that

---

[15] Ruth Benedict, "Continuities and Discontinuities in Cultural Conditioning," *Psychiatry*, 1 (May, 1939), pp. 161–67.

[16] Gertrude Wilson and Gladys Ryland, *Social Group Work Practice*, Boston: Houghton Mifflin Company, 1949, p. 49.

[17] *Ibid.*

[18] Leopold von Wiese, *Systematic Sociology*, adapted and amplified by Howard Becker, New York: Wiley, 1932.

children and parenthood have been so romanticized in our society that most middle class couples are caught unprepared, even though they have planned and waited for this event for years. The fact that parenthood is "normal" does not eliminate crisis. Death is also "normal" but continues to be a crisis event for most families.

4. One can also interpret the findings of this study by postulating that parenthood (not marriage) marks the final transition to maturity and adult responsibility in our culture.[19] Thus the arrival of the first child forces young married couples to take the last painful step into the adult world. This point, as a matter of fact, was stated or implied by most of the couples in the crisis group.

5. Finally, the cases in this sample confirm what the previous studies in this area have shown: that the event itself is only one factor determining the extent and severity of the crisis on any given family. Their resources, their previous experience with crisis, the pattern of role organization before the crisis—these factors are equally important in determining the total reaction to the event.

Conclusion

In this study, it was hypothesized that the addition of the first child would constitute a crisis event, forcing the married couple to move from an adult-centered pair type of organization into child-centered triad group system. Of the forty-six middle class couples located for this study, thirty-eight (83 per cent) confirmed the hypothesis.

In all fairness to this group of parents, it should be reported that all but a few of them eventually made what seems to be a successful adjustment to parenthood. This does not alter the fact, however, that most of them found the transition difficult. Listening to them describe their experiences, it seemed that one could compare these young parents to veterans of military service—they had been through a rough experience, but it was worth it. As one father said: "I wouldn't have missed it for the world."

It is unfortunate that the number of parents in this sample who did not report crisis is so small (eight couples) that no general statements can be made about them. Somehow, however, they seem to have been better prepared for parenthood than was the crisis group. It is felt that future work on this problem might well include a more extensive analysis of couples who have made the transition to parenthood with relative ease.

---

[19] This is essentially the point of view in Robert J. Havighurst's analysis, *Human Development and Education*, New York: Longmans, Green, 1953.

If the basic findings of this study are confirmed by other workers, it would appear that family life educators could make a significant contribution by helping young people prepare more adequately for parenthood.

82 · A Study of Interviews with Husbands in a Prenatal and Child Health Program *

ROSE BERNSTEIN AND FLORENCE E. CYR

Apparently the role of father does not come easily and naturally to all men. How do young men, some out of college but not well established occupationally, some still in debt for furniture and the like, usually anticipating an unplanned baby, face their first experience of fatherhood? This is the question for which an answer was sought in the study reported here. The article points out also how the information gained was used by caseworkers in aiding husbands and wives to attain better adjustment. This discussion may suggest ways in which couples might themselves surmount some of the problems occasioned by the introduction of a baby into a family not fully prepared to receive him.

THE ROLE of the father in the emotional development of his child has been receiving increasing attention from social workers. With this increased attention has come a corresponding recognition that early in his wife's pregnancy the responses of the husband as a prospective father can have implications for his later functioning in actual fatherhood.

Until recently, interest in the prospective father has been focused primarily on helping him to accept the emotional and physiological changes that may be taking place in his wife during pregnancy—changes such as increased irritability and moodiness, passivity and dependence, fatigue and diminished sexual interest. A more precise appraisal of what happens to the father in relation to his child, his wife, and himself seems imperative if we are to begin to understand him in his role in the mother-father-child unit which constitutes the basic family pattern in most areas of American society. Both the helping person and the father need to understand what re-

* Social Casework, 38 (November, 1957), 473–480. Reprinted with permission of the publisher, of the Department of Maternal and Child Health of the School of Public Health of Harvard University, and of the authors.

The authors are members of the staff of the Department of Maternal and Child Health, School of Public Health, Harvard University, which sponsored the research upon which the report is based.

sponses are set in motion from the moment of his first realization, joyous or apprehensive, that a new life, for which he must henceforth share a major responsibility, is on the way.

The following report is based on a study of social work interviews with men whose wives, pregnant for the first time, were participating in a special clinic program, designated as a Family Health Clinic.[1] This clinic was established in 1950 under the auspices of the Harvard School of Public Health in affiliation with the Boston Lying-In Hospital and the Children's Medical Center, with a multidiscipline staff in obstetrics, pediatrics, nutrition, social work, public health nursing, and psychiatry.

The focus of the clinic's service was essentially preventive, based on the assumption that although pregnancy is a normal experience, a first pregnancy is a radically new experience for the woman and carries potentials for stress. Treatment was directed toward the future mother-child relationship. However, the husband, as an essential influence in her environment, was encouraged to accompany his wife to the prenatal and well-baby clinics and to participate in discussions with various staff members as fully as was feasible.

Characteristics of the Group

This study of social work interviews with husbands was undertaken in an attempt to assess the possible usefulness of such contact; to learn the meaning of the experience of approaching fatherhood to the man; to ascertain what worries and what strengths the newly emerging role evoked in him; to assess the extent to which the information gained from these interviews illuminated the wife's problems; and to evaluate the influence of this additional understanding on the caseworker's treatment plan.

Of the sixty-nine cases which will comprise the comprehensive social study, thirty-one contained recorded interviews with husbands who had been seen at least once prior to the birth of the baby. In these husbands no outstanding features in regard to race, religion, national origin, or occupational distribution were noted, although certain features in regard to age, educational level, and income were noteworthy.

This was a group of rather young men, who, with few exceptions, had taken on the responsibilities of marriage early in adult life; almost two-fifths of them were scarcely out of their adolescent years. They were approaching fatherhood at a correspondingly early age.

---

[1] This program was made possible by a grant from the Association for the Aid of Crippled Children, New York. A description of the program is given in "Social Work in a Preventive Program of Maternal and Child Health," by Florence E. Cyr and Shirley H. Wattenberg, *Social Work*, Vol. II, No. 3 (1957), pp. 32–39.

They were predominantly in the low-income bracket, were paying rentals out of proportion to their incomes, frequently for apartments that would not be suitable for a family with a baby. Half the couples were in debt for furniture, clothing, or a car. The plans for payment of these items were being interrupted inasmuch as the plans had been based on the wife's continued working. All but three of the wives had continued working until the pregnancy was well advanced; in at least half the cases the loss of the wife's earnings threatened serious hardship for the family.

An unusually large number of these husbands were college-educated men, several of them still studying. A number of the men were in the process of advancing from low-paying or unsuitable jobs, so that there was a measure of occupational mobility in the group.

In the vast majority of the cases the pregnancy was unplanned.

The couples coming to this clinic, especially organized with a multidiscipline team, may not be representative of our young adult population. The research aspect of the project may have had some appeal for the husband with advanced education. Also, the special services offered in the project may have attracted the participation of some who might still be in the early period of marital adjustment, of others who had yet to complete their education or training, or were still trying to find themselves vocationally. On the other hand, these factors may have no relation to motivation in attendance at a special clinic but may be indicative of recent trends toward early marriage and parenthood today, with their attendant problems.

The husbands were not uniformly enthusiastic about coming to the clinic so that the climate and productivity of the interviews with them varied. However, it was possible to place the subjects discussed in the interviews in four major categories: (1) general information about pregnancy, the function of the clinic, and hospital procedures; (2) environmental subjects —including finances, housing, study and work schedules, and post-partum care for mother and baby; (3) feelings related to parenthood, to himself and his wife as persons, to their capacity for fatherhood and motherhood, and to the stability of the marriage; (4) past personal history and family relationships of the husband.

Discussions about pregnancy far outnumbered each of the other three categories, which in turn had a fairly equal distribution. In spite of changing personnel and some shifts in focus in the development of the clinic program, there was a measure of consistency in the subjects discussed with the husbands. This was probably a reflection of the setting, the program, and the special nature of the husband's experience at the time he came to the clinic.

It is perhaps worth noting here some of the information that emerged from the social histories. About half of the men reported having been separated from mother, father, or both, by death, divorce, or desertion before the age of fourteen. Substitute care had been provided by stepparents, relatives, boarding schools, or institutions. Others mentioned severe alcoholism or cruelty in their own fathers, domineering mothers, or general recollections of childhood unhappiness. One-third reported predominantly positive memories of early family relationships. This again suggests the possibility that early emotional deprivation may have influenced the motivation of many of these men in attending the clinic and seeing the social worker.

Problems Seen by the Husbands

Despite the consistency in the subjects discussed in the interviews, there was considerable variation in the extent to which the husbands saw these same subjects as problems in their present situation. Most of the men made specific mention of being either currently worried about certain aspects of their situation or feeling that these would become troublesome after the birth of the baby. Matters that were troubling them varied from concern about the appropriateness of their living arrangements for a new baby, a need to revamp work and study schedules, and questions about changes in their wives during pregnancy, to a rather fundamental and thoroughgoing questioning about themselves and their fitness for fatherhood. This last concern not infrequently included questioning about the wives' readiness for motherhood.

Personal problems (concerning self, wife, marital relationships, or relations with their own families) were mentioned more than twice as frequently as were environmental ones (about finances, housing, work or study arrangements, post-partum plans, and so on).

It is recognized, of course, that the area in which the husband professed to see the problem may not always have been the primary source of the difficulty. Fairly typical of the kinds of pressures felt by the husbands was the bewilderment of one who already had a heavy load of college courses and thirty hours of work a week, and felt he would not be able to meet his wife's increased demands for attention, particularly since he would be pressed to earn more after the birth of the baby. Another husband saw himself as unable to relate to people except on an intellectual basis, and feared he might have a child of less than superior intelligence.

For a number of men, prospects of fatherhood rekindled thoughts of childhood unhappiness and emotional deprivation in relation to their own parents. Frequently accompanying these recollections was the determination to avoid similar unhappiness for their own children even though they questioned their ability to provide the climate that they considered essential for happy childhood.

Age, education, race, and whether or not the pregnancy had been planned, did not seem to have any bearing on whether they expressed concern about problems, or in what areas they saw them, except for some relation between income and financial problems. However, one important factor seemed to be whether the husband was seen alone or in the company of his wife. The separate interview tended to produce a freer discussion of problems and a greater emphasis on personal, as compared with environmental, problems than did the joint interview.

This does not deny the usefulness of the joint interview. In fact, when used purposefully, it had diagnostic and treatment value. A striking, albeit unusual, use of the joint interview occurred in a situation in which one husband used the worker to communicate to his wife doubts and uncertainties about their situation which he had been unable to confide to her directly.

Feelings about Prospective Fatherhood

Whether seen alone or with their wives, when the husbands were able to speak relatively freely, they revealed the range of feelings that can be experienced by a man in this kind of situation. Two-fifths of the men responded with open delight to the thought of their wives' being pregnant. An equal number were frankly unhappy about it—for the most part, they thought, because of the unfortunate timing. The others accepted the inevitable with resignation.

Yet the men's responses to their wives' being pregnant did not parallel the degree of confidence they expressed regarding their adequacy as fathers. Among those who seemed most pleased at the thought of having a child were some who expressed profound doubts about their readiness for fatherhood. Conversely, some who were frankly dismayed at the thought professed to feel themselves quite adequate to the task of fatherhood, although in some of these cases the worker sensed deep anxiety under the self-assurance expressed.

Neither the way in which the men accepted the fact that their wives were pregnant, nor their concept of themselves as fathers, showed any relation to age, education, income, nationality, or racial background. Some of the younger and less secure financially were most confident; some of the older, more comfortable economically, were most questioning. However, most of those who spoke of their problems in terms of personality adjustment and relationships seemed also to be grappling with the question of their readiness for fatherhood. These insecurities were recognized by the staff as potential hazards in the later functioning of the newly forming family unit.

Reactions to Birth of Baby

An attempt was made to see whether the husband's feelings about the pregnancy and his readiness for fatherhood were reflected in his immediate reaction to the birth of the baby and the extent of his participation in its care at home. Although there was a good deal of variation in the extent of the fathers' activity in the care of the baby, as a group they seemed to be participating more fully than might have been anticipated if some of the prenatal indications were used as a guide. All but a few of the mothers reported their husbands to be participating on a moderately satisfactory or high level. As in previous aspects of the study, background factors such as age or education of the fathers did not seem to have any bearing on the extent to which they participated in the care of the baby. There were a few situations in which cultural factors seemed to be in evidence, where the father felt the physical care of the baby was exclusively the mother's responsibility. However, the group in which cultural factors might be operating was too small and too diverse to permit any general interpretation.

Actually the reactions of the fathers seemed to develop in stages. The immediate response to the birth of the baby seemed to be uniformly positive. The mothers reported the fathers "delighted" and "struck with the miracle of it." Earlier expressed sex preferences seemed to have been forgotten, and whether boy or girl, the baby seemed to be what each had hoped for all along. This response was true also of the fathers who had previously seemed most indifferent or fearful.

Up to six weeks after the birth, most of the mothers were still referring to their husbands' positive interest in the baby, their playing with him, feeding him, dressing him, and being generally helpful. Although there was no fixed time at which changes began to occur, it was usually about two months after the birth of the baby that the mothers began to report a drop in the level of participation of some of the husbands. Whether this was actually a change in the father's performance, whether the mother was increasing her expectations of him, or whether it was some of each could not be judged from the available material.

It is interesting to note that some of the fathers showed a particular aptitude in what might be referred to as the feminine aspects of parenthood. When they accompanied the mothers to the clinic, they seemed to the case-worker and other staff members more comfortable and competent in the handling of the baby, gentler and more maternal than the mothers. In fact, the mothers themselves were quick to recognize this, and "he's a better mother than I am" was a not infrequent comment from them. In a few cases this superior competence became somewhat of a problem, in that it presented an immediate standard of achievement which some mothers were slow in meeting, and toward attainment of which they needed support and encouragement. In none of these situations, however, did the staff members feel that the father was using this attitude to belittle the mother.

The pattern of the fathers' initial reactions to the birth of their babies and their participation in infant care suggested that even the least enthusiastic had internal resources for responding positively, for a time at least, to the reality of the living child whom they had had a share in bringing into being. From this study the question can be raised as to the nature of the changes that took place in the fathers' attitudes toward the babies during infancy and what these changes meant to the mothers. These are questions of concern to those interested in promoting a favorable climate for the developing child.

The Caseworker's Use of the Interview with the Husband

The caseworker's interview with the husband was examined in relation to the content of the interviews with the wife, the worker's evaluation of the troublesome aspects of the situation, and the extent to which the worker's efforts were influenced or changed as a result of the contact with the husband.

Most of the records showed that these interviews gave the worker a deeper understanding of the wife's situation; puzzling features were clarified, uncertain impressions were confirmed, even when conflicting but nonetheless helpful information resulted. In the case of an insecure, rather dependent young girl, her apparent unreadiness for motherhood was a cause of some concern to the worker. However, the husband showed himself to be a person of unusual warmth and stability, with a capacity for accepting his wife's slower development toward maturity, and with no discernible need to exploit this dependency, so that the worker was reassured about the wife's ultimate ability to move into the maternal role without the intensive kind of help that seemed indicated prior to the contact with the husband. In another situation the wife's repeated protestations about her husband's delight at the thought of a family seemed "too much." When the husband was seen he poured out a story of doubt, uncertainty about himself, his wife, and their general circumstances which confirmed the worker's questions about the basis for the wife's too eager acceptance of their new situation. In still another case, mentioned earlier, the husband, in a joint interview with his wife, was able to use the worker to communicate to his somewhat astonished wife his annoyance with her excessive demands for attention and her failure to recognize the pressures of his work schedule, and some basic questions about their readiness for parenthood, thus illuminating the situation in a way the wife was not able to do.

The use the worker made of her contact with the husband depended upon how she interpreted the problems he presented. For the most part she tended to identify the problems as primarily emotional rather than environmental twice as frequently as did the husband. When she recognized environmental problems, she dealt with them directly at the time of the interview: (1) by appropriate reassurance and universalizing regarding some of the perplexing changes occurring in the wife; (2) by anticipatory guidance—discussion of future aspects of the pregnancy and ways of making the experience more gratifying for him and his wife; (3) through suggestions directed toward easing environmental pressures, such as budget advice, suggestions for employment or housing.

In general, when the worker identified the problem as primarily an emotional one, the change in casework plan was directed toward the wife. The following situations indicate the way in which work with the wife was refocused in terms of a problem revealed by the husband. In one case the worker felt that the relationship between husband and wife was being disturbed by the wife's strong tie to her mother, who was playing an important role in plans that should have been the exclusive concern of husband and wife. The husband, himself an insecure and self-doubting person, was unable to assert himself as the head of his newly developing family, and was giving vent to his frustrations in moodiness and temper outbursts. Counting on the wife's essentially understanding nature and on her recognition of her husband's devotion to her, the worker directed her efforts toward encouraging the wife in loosening the ties to her own family and in bolstering her husband in his new role. In another situation, where the husband seemed unable to supply the extra attention and "mothering" that the wife needed, the clinic personnel attempted to assume this role temporarily during this trying period in an effort to alleviate the wife's demands on her husband, at the same time satisfying some of the wife's dependency needs, and in some measure reducing the tensions between them.

Whether the worker felt that the source of the difficulty was largely in the husband, in the wife, or in both, the wife remained the primary focus of treatment as the worker attempted to relieve tensions in the family situation. Although in practically every case the worker suggested the possibility of a second interview with the husband, the initiative for this was left with him.

Post-partum Interviews

Fifteen fathers were seen within a year after the birth of the baby. Although no common element could be found among them that would explain why these particular fathers were being seen, most of them seemed eager for the interview and talked fairly freely with the worker. Most of the interviews were held jointly with the mothers and took place under less than optimum circumstances, in the clinic, where continuity of discussion was sometimes impossible because of the baby's restlessness; the interviews had to be brief because of the pressure of the father's work or class schedules. When there actually was some opportunity for leisurely discussion, the problems brought up by the fathers paralleled those that they had presented in the prenatal interviews: housing, the burden of heavy study and work schedules, and financial problems. Added to these were difficulties more specifically related to the presence of a young baby in the home: disturbed sleep, lack of quiet or privacy for study, growing irritability on the part of the mother at being left alone so much—particularly when the father's schedule necessitated his being away from home a good deal—and concern about his seeing so little of the baby. Insufficient recreation for the husband and wife together was a problem in several situations, due either to lack of funds for hiring a baby sitter or lack of time on the husband's part. In a few cases, it was related to the father's fearfulness about leaving the baby with a stranger.

In a few cases in which the father was seen alone he again referred to previously expressed doubts about his or his wife's readiness for parenthood. On the whole these concerns seemed less pressing at this time than at the prenatal interview. Some of the husbands who were not seen until several months after the birth of the baby referred to the "nightmare" of the early weeks of the baby's life, the constant crying, the tenseness of the parents, their fatigue and discouragement. Nevertheless, the general approach to their situation of most of the fifteen husbands seemed more relaxed than it had been in the prenatal interview. And in spite of the undercurrent of worry and responsibility, most of the fathers seen after the birth of the baby indicated pleasure in the baby and a feeling of importance in the role of paterfamilias.

The pattern of help offered by the caseworker paralleled to some extent that found in the prenatal interviews with the husbands. Help given directly to the father was limited to the interview situation and consisted of anticipatory guidance, reassurance, and generalization about the normal growth problems and changing habits of infants as well as encouragement of his participation in the care of the baby. This help was designed primarily to alleviate the father's anxiety, to help him allow for the baby's developing individuality, and to enlist his co-operation in carrying out the recommendations of other clinic personnel, mainly the nutritionist and pediatrician. As indicated previously, when the father's problems seemed excessive, efforts were made to alleviate his difficulties through strengthening the wife.

It is not known to what extent special factors may have influenced the selection of fathers who were seen after the birth of the baby, and findings relating to this group cannot be considered typical. However, the interviews with the fathers who were seen during this period seem to substantiate the idea that the early days of parenthood can present severe problems to the new father as well as to the mother. Although many of these problems can no doubt be considered "normal" and eventually self-adjusting, and are frequently mitigated by deep feelings of satisfaction in parenthood, the arrival of a baby can nevertheless set tensions in motion in the mother and father, separately or in relation to each other, which can have serious consequences for the new family.

Summary

The major aims of the study were to find out: how men whose wives were pregnant for the first time were reacting to their new status as prospective fathers; what problems they saw as most pressing in relation to the new situation; the extent of their participation in the care of the baby; the caseworker's use of the interviews with the husbands and the influence of these contacts on the treatment plans. These men were taking on the responsibilities of a family at a relatively young age, following unplanned conceptions. Although of better than average education, they had not yet reached occupational stability. They were in precarious financial circumstances and were somewhat dependent on their own or their wives' parents for help. Their childhood experiences were characterized to a large extent by loss or deprivation in basic parental relationships.

The nature of the setting in which the interviews took place and the special character of the experience the husbands were undergoing at the time were reflected in the subjects discussed in the interviews. These included general information about pregnancy, clinic and hospital routines; environmental considerations, such as finances, housing, work and study plans, and post-partum care. Feelings about themselves, their wives, and prospective parenthood figured prominently also, as did personal history and family relations. Worries about environmental matters included insufficient finances, inadequate housing, heavy work and study schedules which were not allowing them enough time with their wives. Emotional problems centered around anxiety about their wives' immaturity and dependence, their own feelings of insecurity as people or of inadequacy as fathers, and with some, indifference or aversion to the thought of fatherhood.

It is recognized that in some respects this group may not be representative because of certain unusual background factors. They may reflect the problems resulting from a trend toward earlier marriages.

In view of the problems anticipated by many of the husbands, their reactions to the birth of the baby and their later participation in its care were more positive than had been expected. As fathers they were uniformly delighted for a period following the birth of the child and participated actively in the care of the infant for about two months. Well over half continued to participate in the care of the baby beyond that time. Several of the fathers showed greater skill and assurance in the handling and in the care of the child than did their wives.

The use the caseworker made of the prenatal interview with the husband was influenced by the function of the clinic, by the special character of the husband's experience at the time, and by the extent to which the interview increased the worker's understanding of the total situation. Anticipatory guidance and reassurance about changes in the wife were calculated to allay his anxiety and to help him accept these changes. In most cases the worker's understanding of the situation was increased as a result of her interview with the husband. However, the worker's interpretation of the difficulties frequently differed from his in that she tended to see problems related to emotional rather than environmental stresses more frequently than he did. Whenever she recognized environmental stress, help for this was offered directly to the husband in the interview. In general, the husband's emotional stresses were dealt with through the wife.

Despite the circumscribed scope of the study and the limited applicability of its findings, there are indications pointing toward the need for a continued search for understanding of this subject. There is apparently a strong capacity in men for responding to the birth of their children. We need to know why, in some men, this initial response is not sustained, the extent to which personal or situational factors are at work, and the possible influence of cultural trends on our patterns of living and our concept of the role of the father in the family today. This increased understanding is necessary if we are to try to help parents provide the kind of climate in which their children can develop healthy identifications.

83 · The Psychological Role of the Father in the Family *

O. SPURGEON ENGLISH

The role of the mother in the family has long been the subject of both poetry and research. It is only recently, however, that much attention has been given to the role of the father, other than to his function as financial mainstay and head of the family. Dr. English, a psychiatrist, gives a concise, comprehensive review of the various roles that the father should play in order to create the atmosphere in which his wife can function best as mother and to bring his children the love and guidance that will aid them in personality development.

THE PSYCHOLOGICAL role of the father in our society has been hard to grasp. Just as his social role has been continuously changing, so his psychological role assumes new forms as customs, beliefs, thoughts, and knowledge change.

Traditionally, Father has been looked upon as the breadwinner. In times past, so much of his time and energy was used in this role that at home he was thought of as taciturn and stern, albeit kind. He was respected but feared by his children who never learned to know him very well. He accepted the fact that he earned the money and Mother cared for the home and raised the children. A stereotype of the Victorian days was the father who was supposed to be very busy and very successful, indulging his children in many things in order to compensate for the fact that he really was not very interested in them at all and preferred the company of older people.

The more modern picture of Father is that of the enthusiastic young man barely out of his teens, interested in his wife and children, who likes his home and likes to work around it. He enjoys helping his wife with household duties and with the routine care of the children. He even likes to take care of them for an evening if his wife needs or wants to go out by herself!

* *Social Casework*, 35 (October, 1954), 323–329. Reprinted by permission of the publisher and the author.

The author, a psychiatrist, is Professor and Head of the Department of Psychiatry, Temple University School of Medicine and Hospital. Among his publications are numerous articles in journals and books; he is coauthor of *The Emotional Problems of Living* and of *Fathers Are People Too*.

We should like to believe that fathers like this are replacing the older types. But facts seem to show that modern fathers do not really understand their role much better than their predecessors did. The purpose of this paper is to indicate why Father has such an important role to play in the life of his growing young boy or girl and to emphasize that his role in the family has many facets—he must be husband, father, member of the workaday world, teacher, mentor, and hero. The how, when, and where of his activities will make themselves evident if the importance of these roles is made clear.

The Changing Culture

A great change has occurred in this country in the direction of urbanization. According to statistics compiled in 1951, "In 1790, 19 out of every 20 Americans were rural residents; the United States was largely a nation of farmers. At present, only seven out of every 20 Americans live in rural areas, and, of those, less than half are farm residents. Instead of one out of 20, now 13 out of every 20 Americans are city folk. About half of them live in communities of at least 100,000 inhabitants, and the rest in places with populations ranging from 2,500 to 100,000." [1]

These figures carry with them many implications as far as the role of the father in the family is concerned. In the past, not only were many of these rural families farm families, where the children worked much of the time beside their parents, but in many instances Father lived near his work, was home for the mid-day meal and did not spend an hour or more each morning and evening in traveling to and from his work. These circumstances made Father more of a tangible, living entity in the home. At least he had more time to be with his children and they to be with him. He did not have to plan to be with his family; he was just always there. He may not have been actually aware of the "acting out" of his parental role, but his children saw him at his work and even helped him with it. They saw him with his friends, his neighbors, and business acquaintances. He communicated his philosophy and opinions of life in the ordinary course of living. They saw male friendliness, kindness, and justice in actual operation. They formed a definite image of how a father should behave. Moreover, in the rural areas of twenty-five or more years ago, entertainment was scarce and what there was of it was likely to be of the "home-made" type in which the child was more often a participant than merely an onlooker. The church, the schoolhouse, and the grange hall were centers that encouraged cohesive

[1] Louis I. Dublin and Mortimer Spiegelman, *The Facts of Life: From Birth to Death*, Macmillan Company, New York, 1951.

relationships. Leisure-time activities were a group affair with Father serving as leader. He was a positive (even though stern) influence in shaping his children's personalities. He knew his family as people, as individuals with their limitations, accomplishments, needs, and abilities.

Modern urban life has changed this. Today members of a family may sit together in front of a television set or at an outdoor movie but they are not actively communicating with each other. They are not getting close to each other; instead, they are losing touch. They are communicating with an image on the screen rather than with someone real—and there is a great difference in what results. What a child shares with his father could be more conducive to security and to sound, practical knowledge of people than all that cinema and television combined can give. E. E. Cummings says it this way: "Why (you ask) should anyone want to be here, when (simply by pressing a button) anyone can be in fifty places at once? How could anyone want to be now, when anyone can go whening all over creation at the twist of a knob? . . . As for being yourself—why on earth should you be yourself; when instead of being yourself you can be a hundred, or a thousand, or a hundred thousand, other people? The very thought of being one's self in an epoch of interchangeable selves must appear supremely ridiculous." [2]

It would seem then that our changing culture has tended to fragment family life. An increasing number of diversions for both adults and children cuts down the time a family spends together. Movies, adult classes, an educational trip, television—each has its inherent value in developing personality, yet each tends to isolate and divide the individuals within the family.

These cultural changes and this fragmentation of family life, coupled with modern knowledge of the personality needs of growing children, should indicate quite clearly that parents of today must compensate for some of these social changes by an enhanced quality and quantity of interest in their children. And Father, who for one reason or another has defaulted in his role as parent, must enter the picture again to give his children help with the many emotional and psychological problems of growth.

This means more intensive parental participation in order to neutralize the effects of these influences; this means also that Father must work more intensively and cooperatively with his family. Not only must he replace some of this impersonal kind of entertainment which has diverted the child from participating in the "business of living" that characterized family life in the past, but he must augment and strengthen the pattern of family life as a whole.

---

[2] *i, six non-lectures,* Harvard University Press, Cambridge, Mass., 1953.

Father as a Husband

One might well ask at this point—"But what is unique in the role of Father in the family? What does he do that is over and above complementing or supplementing Mother's role? He can provide an extra pair of hands but would not any good maid be of far more practical value?"

Life and personality development are composed of more than kind treatment, a full stomach, and diversion, important though these things may be. There are some facets of personality that grow and develop only in a home where there is a father playing his various roles in a mature way. When he is a genial participant in family life, he serves to introduce these elements more surely into the life of the growing child.

We live in a world of two sexes, with the man and woman performing certain unique functions, some of which are mutually complementary and others mutually exclusive. The mature mother, for instance, is warm, tender, affectionate, and attuned to the basic needs of her infant. She understands his rhythms of eating, sleeping, playing, and eliminating, as well as his emotional needs for touch, fondling, and companionship. It is probably within the potentialities of male psychology to perform these functions also, just as it has been possible for woman to enter the realm of man's activities. But the fact that anatomically and physiologically man does not function in such a way as to bring him into close contact with the infant has prevented him from even having been tested out in these areas. Moreover, it seems unlikely that he ever will perform these womanly duties in rearing the young. Just as the mother is anatomically and physiologically adapted to coming into close contact with the young from birth—and before— so it is logical that she have the psychological equipment to use her talents for giving loving, tender care in the difficult human task of getting the physiological rhythm of the infant's body regulated. Freud's contribution in this area has been invaluable, and it is quite generally accepted that a warm, friendly, accepting psychological climate is necessary in order to promote physiological health and freedom from psychosomatic illness. It is not so well understood that this climate is necessary for a healthy emotional feeling tone which will lay a firm foundation in the infant for happiness, a sense of well-being, and confidence or "mind strength."

In order for the mother to accomplish these things properly and consistently there are certain contributions that a father should make. In this role he may not seem to be directly "fathering" his children—yet actually he is doing so. His strength and power are passing through the mother to the child or children. He is keeping her in the mood for her job by consistently providing material comfort for her through his labor. He gives her security and freedom from anxiety about food, clothing, and shelter. Further, he shows an interest in her activity, her creativeness, her work, and her needs, both emotional and physical. He "loves" her in that he satisfies her, stimulates her, comforts her, and assists her in the realization of her personality. This he does uniquely, as a male, in the fulfilment of his role in society. A maid, a sister, a friend, or a mother can perform these duties only partially, and it is neither socially acceptable nor biologically consistent for them to be done by a person other than the father of her child.

Since the pattern of society is heterosexual, a woman, if she is normal, can accomplish a more complete emotional fulfilment and wholesome personality growth through the father of her child than from any other source. A woman is so dependent upon "psychological sets" in her personality that even if persons other than her husband could fulfil as much as 90 per cent of her needs, she would reject them as inappropriate sources.

Father as a Parent

So much for the father's psychological role as it functions through the mother toward the infant in the early days and weeks of life. Father must, in addition, play his own psychological role with his child. He should prepare himself to teach, mold, influence, inspire, and develop his child so that the child may become a mentally healthy, good citizen who will be able to love and be loved, to enjoy life and be creative. By showing interest early in the life of the infant he awakens a corresponding interest in the infant toward him. In the beginning this may be only a small awareness, but it is an important one. Boys and girls develop their earliest and most decisive ideas about masculinity from their fathers. It is Father who evokes a process in his child which might be called "animating the mind" toward the male sex. If he delays showing enthusiasm and interest in his child too long, it becomes harder to create a "depth" of relationship with him which will make it easy for the child to grow in a healthy and happy manner.

As the child moves out of infancy it is essential for Father to continue to show interest and thereby make his boy or girl feel important. It is not enough for Mother alone to try to create this feeling of importance; Father needs to join her in this. One of the commonest lacks in the human personality is a feeling of worth, of what might be called confidence or self-respect. Scarcely any child develops enough of this commodity and both Mother and Father should do more to ensure its presence. Just as Mother helps, Father, too, can help with his child's small problems. Dressing and undressing, helping with toys, teaching adeptness with objects around the home or in the yard are pertinent examples.

Let it be clearly emphasized that it is most important for Father to play the same role in the life of his daughter that he does in the life of his son. In some families there seems to be an unwritten agreement that Father shall avoid the domain of the females. The tacit assumption seems to be that the girls belong to Mother and that if Father has any time at all he will give it to the boys; nothing need be expected of him in relation to his daughter or daughters. Few adult women feel real closeness and comfort and understanding in their relations with men. One of the reasons for this is that an opportunity to develop these feelings was just not given to them early enough in life. Consequently, it is important to remember that the emotional development of girls calls for just as much interest, attention, and concern on the part of the fathers as is given to boys.

All children between the ages of 3 and 7 have the problems of learning the difference between masculine and feminine traits and patterns, and of incorporating them into their own personalities. It is in this phase of development that the oedipus complex is usually solved. Although many people question its validity, astute observers notice that a real problem exists here in learning to love and learning to relate oneself to the parent of the opposite sex. Until this phase arrives, a boy, for instance, has usually received a great deal of attention from his mother and many of his needs have been met by her. He now begins to view his father as a rival for his mother's affection. He shows this in a variety of ways such as being fretful, antagonistic, moody, unhappy, critical of his father, or, perhaps, unusually aloof. Father needs to understand the conflict the child is going through and must exercise patience. He should foster his son's identification with himself in a friendly manner and try to draw him into masculine interests both within the home and without. The solution of the oedipus complex for the boy is a gradual "giving up" of his mother and an acceptance and desire to be like his father. This is made easier when the father becomes someone that his son would like to emulate. To misunderstand, to scold, or to criticize the child tends to slow up or interfere with the normal psychological growth processes.

By the same token a girl can learn to understand the pattern of life and can see that the attention of men brings with it prestige and pleasure. She, too, during the oedipal phase, has a sense of rivalry, this time with her mother, which makes her vie for her father's attention, wanting him exclusively for her own. She feels jealous of her mother and often acts in an antagonistic and hostile fashion toward her. She will talk about marrying her father when she grows up. To some this sounds like accidental childish prattle, but to others it has considerable psychological significance. We believe that solving the oedipus complex is an important and profound psychological experience which requires wisdom, tact, and understanding on the part of fathers as well as mothers, in order to have it run a satisfactory course. The oedipus complex is, of course, not a new phenomenon. For centuries, friendly and intuitive parents have seen it in action, have understood it and have helped their children through it without giving it any name or thinking about it in an unusual way except as a normal growth process.

It is important to emphasize again that children learn to love when quite young. Mature love and social harmony develop only if both sexes are taught how to love. Consequently, Father, as well as Mother, must be a participant in the child's development. If he does not understand his role or retreats from it, he then makes development all the more difficult or forces some kind of repression and immaturity. He should permit his son to love his mother but want the youngster to join him in masculine interests as well. He should help his daughter to know and enjoy men, setting himself as the first example.

Father as Counselor

Father can be of great help with the grade school child during the time when the child, whether boy or girl, feels unsure of himself, and when he must, to a large extent, be under the direction of women. A child can easily develop resentment at the imposed learning process when he is surrounded by women almost to the exclusion of men. What with Mother at home and the female teacher at school—both eager for him to learn and progress—it is easy to see how he can feel smothered by women. Boys in the lower grades are afraid of being "sissy" and any innate lack of grace or docility is often implemented by an inhibition or even refusal to accept the female orientation of the teacher as to what constitutes acceptable behavior or performance. Here Father can help, explain, encourage, approve, teach various skills, and share in a host of activities that will help popularize the learning process which the female teacher is trying to accomplish. He can attend Cub Scout meetings. He can help with the chauffeuring of the children to school events if this is the customary way of transportation. He can take an interest in his child's friends and share some experiences with them. He can approve educational activities. He can help to see that work gets done. He can set little tasks about the home and make sure they are completed. He can inquire whether homework is done—listen to reading and spelling if necessary and give approval and at times a reward when diligence brings results. This interest helps to make work a pleasure rather than a drudgery and makes co-operative effort easier for the child all his life.

Fathers are often less well acquainted with educational procedures than mothers. In line with the dictum that people are generally critical of the things they do not know about, the uninformed father, rather than admit his ignorance, is often negative in his attitudes toward modern education. Think of the father, for example, who utters disapproval of classes in art, dancing, or dramatics without first trying to understand their value; and think of how a child is handicapped in participating by his father's attitude that these things are for sissies and are based on women's whims. It has been suggested that the increased number of boys in special classes for retarded children is due in large measure to such conflicts in the young male.

Grade school children have a good deal of free-floating aggression and their sense of justice and fair play is in a somewhat rudimentary form and needs direction and strengthening. Father should talk to the child of this age about future plans and grown-up activities in order to bring to him an awareness of the various activities, values, and drama of the world outside the home.

Somewhere in the growing-up process, Father can and should help his child get acquainted with his sexual self. Father carries equal responsibility with Mother in answering questions or giving information. It is not suggested that there is a specific time for Father to take an interest in this subject of sex. Sexual activity begins in infancy and questions play a continuous part in the child's growth. Sex should be discussed freely and questions answered when and as often as a child asks them. It is important to remember that the term "psychosexual development" implies that sexuality runs through all of a child's development. The time to be aware of it and to help the child with it is all the time.

During puberty and adolescence the growing child of both sexes is beset with insecurity, uncertainty, inadequate self-esteem, questions about his life around him, problems of ethics, as well as thoughts for the future. Father should be ready to give counsel about choice of a vocation and to stimulate as many interests in the outside world as the youngster can comprehend and make use of. Too much stress cannot be laid upon the fact that the growing male child needs plenty of opportunity (provided by his father) to identify with a male. Life is long and hard and full of decisions, and it is important for a young man to feel confidence in himself—a confidence that he gains through the continuous, friendly, interested contact with his father. A girl, if she has a good relation with her mother, will of course tend to identify with her—and needs to do so. Father, however, can, through his interest in her, make it easier for her to be at ease with members of the opposite sex and to learn co-operation with them. Father will need to have had a good relation with his daughter during puberty and adolescence to be able to relinquish her to her male contemporaries—a psychological role, incidentally, which fathers have not handled too well in the past. The doting father is prone to feel that no boy is good enough for his daughter. The father who has never enjoyed his daughter's companionship may resent anyone else's doing so and, unless he has been close to and had a friendly and trusting relationship with her, he may be over-strict and prevent her from having the wholesome experiences of adolescence which lead to maturation.

A father can further guide his children during adolescence in vocational choice, and he can make them aware that responsibilities await them in a world for which they need to be well prepared with a strong personality, as well as with whatever special training will be required for the fulfilment of their vocational aims.

So, it can be seen that personality development is a complicated affair into which elements from both sexes must enter in order to give the greatest strength and greatest understanding, the most wisdom and versatility. The world is demanding more and more of people. Since it is a world that is socially and biologically dependent upon the two sexes, both sexes must play their roles in accordance with both traditional and modern demands in order that the growing child may see how this is done. He must get the feel of it from the home, in which the mother is made free by the father to play her role and where the father demonstrates a clear picture of the best in masculine traits. Father's ways of loving his children and helping them to grow may not seem so very different from those of the mother. For instance, Mother cooks things the child likes to eat, darns his socks, and nurses him when ill. Father, too, shows his love by working for the family, fixing a broken toy, or bringing home to the dinner table an interesting story from the outside world. They both teach such things as fair play and responsibility. Yet, the father does have his own role to play; it differs in many ways from that of the mother. And while he plays his role he dresses differently, his voice sounds different, his body contour is different, and his ways of looking at things are different.

It would be unfair to say he is a "symbol" in one sense of the word. He is not merely symbolic since he is very human and real. Nevertheless, he does play a unique part in nature's plan for reproducing the young and helping them to grow up. The American father cannot afford to be a non-entity in the family. He cannot leave child rearing so much to the women of our nation. Such a division of labor is likely to produce lopsided personalities.

Variants of the Father's Role

Because Father's role in the family now seems to be pointed toward a more co-operative, socially integrated pattern it is hard to formulate. We still lack the proper terms to define our acceptance of what seems to be his more passive, flexible role. It is all right for Father to enjoy more tender feelings toward his children, but how do we express this? How do we compensate for our old ideas of masculine ruggedness and aggressiveness and substitute new concepts of tenderness which will not be considered feminine or oversoft? Perhaps we just lack the names for these changed relationships. Or perhaps there are too few words that can convey the meaning of these new roles. We are almost tempted to say that Father is not doing a better job in child rearing because we lack the ability to formulate his significance specifically. When we can realize and define the importance of his role we shall soon have concepts and words for the needs of the child and for the feelings of the father who responds to them. If we were to try we might suggest the following as being variants of the father's role:

1. Companion and inspiration for the mother;
2. Awakener of the emotional potentials of his child;
3. Beloved friend and teacher to his child;
4. Ego ideal for masculine love, ethics, and morality;
5. Model for social and vocational behavior;
6. Stabilizing influence for solution of oedipus complex;
7. Protector, mentor, and hero for grade school child;
8. Counselor and friend for the adolescent.

This effort to define the psychological role of the father brings up certain questions for future investigation. So far in the study of the psychodynamics of mental disease we have described the pathological factors under the name of environment, family, and parents and we have talked of rejecting mothers and stern fathers. Little effort has been made to *quantitate* the role of the father psychologically as follows:

1. How much of the psychopathology in a given case has been due to the absence of the father?
2. How much of the psychopathology in a given case has been due to the indifference of the father to the mother even though he was devoted to the child?
3. How much of the psychopathology has been due to the favoritism of the father for a certain child in the family?
4. How much of the psychopathology of a delinquent child can be shown to be due to the indifference or unwise management by the father of the child himself?

Since the mother plays such a large role during feeding and toilet training, she undoubtedly is a crucial factor in producing some of the health or psychopathology of that period. But, as we hope we have shown, the father's influence is definitely not absent even then, and he plays an increasing role as time goes on. If a mother, for instance, is sufficiently orally depriving to produce alcoholism or schizophrenia in her progeny, could the father, if he knew enough, prevent this catastrophe, or could he mitigate its severity, and if so how would he go about it? These areas of family living need some good research work, utilizing the psychiatrist, social worker, and psychologist. Such quantitation of the father's role in abetting the production of illness may indicate how much more seriously the American father must take his role in family life.

Much has been said about the role of the mother in producing greatness in the human personality but very little has been said about the role of the father. The men of this nation have made excellent use of the natural resources of their country. They have taken the coal, the oil, the metal, the wood and have accomplished amazing things. They have paid less attention to human resources. The time has long since arrived when they should take more interest in their offspring and participate more actively in their personality development. Father is a definite entity psychologically as well as in reality. He should be more conscious of what his role is and play it with greater pleasure and distinction.

84 · *How to Hold a Family Council* *

ALMA H. JONES

Emphasis is now placed on development of children's personalities, cooperation, increasing independence, and parental guidance. How does the parent strike the middle ground between authoritarianism on the one hand and abdication of all control on the other? In this article a woman with years of experience in the field of child development offers ten suggestions for making family decisions a cooperative affair among older children and their parents.

* *Family Life*, 13 (January, 1953), 1–2. Reprinted by permission of the Publisher, The American Institute of Family Relations.

The author received the degree of Master of Science in Nutrition and Child Development from Columbia University. After thirty years on the faculty of Iowa State College, she was retired and then served on the staff of The American Institute of Family Relations. She is the author of more than three hundred publications of various kinds in her field.

EVERY FAMILY needs to talk over their daily affairs, their future plans, and to iron out their problems together. In this way they'll understand each other's viewpoints better and find better solutions to their problems.

Especially, in the case of families of older children and youth, we think of the family meeting, or council, as a necessity for handling weightier problems, for growth of well-rounded personalities of children, and for keeping family relations on an even keel. In fact, some of the so-called "upheavals" of youth, often attributed to the "stress and strain of the difficult years" frequently are no more than an expression of youth's need to have their ideas and contributions considered by the family.

In following the plan of pooling the ideas of each person for the greatest good of the group, you may be surprised at the really good ideas that children offer; and, often, at their willingness, and even eagerness, to follow the plans laid down. Everyone is more willing to do their part in carrying out plans when they have a "say," as it is commonly expressed.

Example of problems that meetings or family councils can decide might include: Who will do certain household tasks or chores; how family possessions will be used, as the car, radio and TV, and money; and what plans are best for family or community recreation? Now, the question comes, what are some ways of making a family council work for smoother functioning of families and better training in living?

1. In the beginning, plan a meeting to take care of something simple, pleasurable, and, in which all can have a part. A convenient example to consider might be a family outing to a suitable point of interest.

2. Pick a time when the family is naturally together, with some leisure, as after the evening meal.

3. Give each person a chance to offer his ideas. In the case of fairly young children, the parents may suggest only a part of a plan for all to consider, or set some limits to start with, so that the problem won't be complicated.

4. Listen to each person's ideas and respect their confidences in expressing themselves freely and honestly. Be careful not to "pooh-pooh" or, allow the child to be "shouted down" by brothers and sisters. Show children that their choices matter, and that each must try to make choices that will be fair to others.

5. Get all the facts. In the case of the family outing, the best route to take might have to be decided by the older children's study of maps; or the things to do could be settled by referring to a travel guide, or by asking others who know from experience what to see and do for the most fun.

6. The group should make the decision with the real facts and everybody's interest in mind. The final decision on plans will need to be made on the basis of what will bring the most happiness for all concerned. Such problems as how every one can share the work to get ready for the outing,

the need of some one to caress and fondle him and help him with his troubles, he will adjust quite readily to his stepmother.

The younger a child is, the more helpless he is, and the more he craves affection and mothering. He cannot live happily without such attention; it is a necessary part of his growth and development. If he receives the affection he craves, he is willing to accept a substitute parent with fewer reservations than an older child. An older child has too many memories, and if they are pleasant ones of a mother or father who has departed, he is still attached to them, and he cannot too easily forsake them. He will be more apt to consider the stepparent as an unwelcome intruder into the family circle. He will be resentful, distrustful, and suspicious.

The stepparent's lot is not a happy one. Very often a stepmother finds a child of five or six rather difficult to manage. If he has been pampered by an overindulgent aunt or grandmother, he may have developed habits that can be changed only with great difficulty. Here youthfulness will not always assure a successful adjustment to a stepparent. There are quite a few other factors that enter into the situation. These are previous upbringing and physical, mental, and emotional health.

As the child grows older, the difficulties of adjusting to a new situation increase. This is particularly true when a stepparent enters the picture. The child has already made adjustments to his own parent and has arrived at a more or less satisfactory situation; he is set in his ways and he has succeeded in adjusting himself to his family situation. With the arrival of a stepparent, he has to rearrange his ways of living to suit this new parent, and the older the child is, the more difficult it is for him to do this.

When children are striving to attain status of individuality and independence, it is particularly difficult to accept the added burden of the new family tie. A stepmother may earnestly desire to make a good home for her stepchildren, but, try as she may, she will find that in many ways her ideas and standards will differ from those to which the children have become accustomed. Rarely has she had anything to do with the upbringing and training of the children, and she has not had an opportunity to become familiar with their habits, ways of thinking, personalities, and physical peculiarities. Had she been with the children from the time they were born, they could have grown up together gradually and things would certainly be easier.

In addition, some stepmothers have had little experience in dealing with children. Even the most carefully thought-out plans may become disrupted when one of them acquires an adolescent stepchild, particularly if he has been overprotected and overindulged by some relative. She will have a very difficult time trying to undo the damage that has already been done. No matter how skillful and patient she may be, she is already under a disadvantage because she is a stepmother and as such all her actions are suspect. Every move she makes is regarded with suspicion by the stepchild, and the situation becomes very difficult.

It is not at all surprising that a child reveres and idealizes his departed parent, for even though there are, without the least doubt, many good and worthy stepparents, he feels rather dubious about the chance of having a second home as good as the first. The first of everything seems better and more desirable. If the mother has died and there are several children, a caretaker is undoubtedly required. A new factor has now entered into the picture. The father has a more restricted range of choice than before the first marriage. There are many women who will not want to take care of and bring up some other woman's children. The father may make a good choice or a bad one. No one actually knows until the stepmother has entered into the family circle and begins to function as a substitute parent. She may have the intelligence and personality to be a good stepmother, or she may not. In some cases, there may be a poor beginning with subsequent improvement of the situation.

One of the most pressing problems a stepparent, especially a stepmother, must face is that of finding satisfactory rôles for her stepchildren. If the children are no longer infants or very young, they have become accustomed to certain rôles, and these cannot be disturbed with impunity. If a stepmother comes into a home and, in her desire to institute a coöperative household, assigns the task of washing dishes to an overgrown boy, athletically inclined, who regards such a task as a "sissy" one, she will get into difficulties. If she is wise and understanding, she will study the personalities of her stepchildren, their desires and inclinations, and assign to each a task that he or she would like to do. A little common sense will go a long way in a situation of this kind.

The child's emotions are of the greatest importance in the family situation. Insecurity very often manifests itself in rivalry for affection. When a child feels uncertain and insecure, he may make a strong effort to get his full share, and quite often more, of affection. He will endeavor to keep for himself as much as possible the attention of his real parent and resent bitterly sharing any of it with one who is a newcomer into the family circle. Quite often a stepchild feels that, instead of having got a mother for him, his father has got a wife with whom the child must share his father. Often, when there is a very close relationship between the child and the real parent, the child resents the coming of a stepparent and uses every endeavor to crowd out the newcomer.

When a child feels that he is being crowded out of the affection of the real parent, by the stepmother, it makes little difference how good she is; he will turn against her. In this instance, jealousy is a very important factor. The child is jealous of his father's affection and does not want to share it with any one. Jealousy is also manifested when the father begins to show affection for the stepmother with apparent disregard for the child. Jealousy may then become mingled first with envy and later with resentment.

There may be times when a child is rejected by the stepparent and then gradually is rejected by the real parent. In order to hold the new mate, the real parent will pay increasing attention to the stepparent and thus crowd the child out. Affection is withdrawn from the child and concentrated exclusively on the stepparent. This will intensify any feelings of jealousy and envy, which may have existed only in slight degree before.

Quite a few children have complained that the stepparent becomes the dominant and central person in the home and exerts undue influence on the real parent. When this is the case, the child is almost entirely left out of the family picture and he comes to feel that he is unwanted.

The status of a stepchild is never a very happy one at the outset. If a parent in a well-integrated family dies, the child loses a companion, a sympathetic friend, a guide, and a counselor, to whom he has been closely attached, and this quite often has a disastrous effect on him. The orderly pattern of life in the home is often changed with rather unnerving abruptness, and the child is left adrift emotionally. He has the uncomfortable feeling that he no longer has a haven of security to which he may return with confidence after buffetings in the outside world.

The stepchild is often plagued with feelings of insecurity because of his situation. A feeling of insecurity may come about in one of several ways. When a child considers that he is treated differently from others, he feels insecure. He does not know how to respond to an unpatterned situation, nor does he know how to adjust to it. When the stepparent treats the child differently from the way he has been treated by his real parent, he becomes bewildered. He feels that he is being singled out for special treatment not to his liking or understanding. He feels somewhat stigmatized, somewhat different. This leads to insecurity, intermingled with feelings of inferiority and jealousy.

Sibling rivalry, particularly when favoritism is shown to a brother or sister, very often leads to feelings of insecurity and frustration. Quite often this may be serious in an unbroken home, but in a home that has a stepparent, it may become a very significant problem. When a child is born to the second union, it demands the greater portion of the mother's affection and attention, and the father also gives some of his time to the new arrival. Because this new child has two real parents while the stepchild in the family has only one, the baby usually has certain advantages that tend to make the older child feel less important and for that reason less secure.

Quite often children apologize for the difference and even tell lies to conceal the fact that they have a stepparent. Because of the traditional attitude toward stepparents, and particularly toward the stepmother, the stepchild often develops a sense of inferiority because he, unlike other children, has a substitute parent. Because of this, many children who acquire stepparents in infancy are not told about it. However, when they learn the true facts later on, they experience some emotional shock and disappointment.

The stepchild has special problems of his own to face and solve. He cannot do this alone, without help from the adults in his family. But quite often just a little common sense and ordinary consideration will go a long way toward making his life a happier one.

CHAPTER 24:

In-laws and Grandparents

88 · *Marriage Makes In-laws* *

EVELYN MILLIS DUVALL

A marriage is never really limited to the relationship between husband and wife. Even if they are both orphans or live across the continent from their parents, the influence of early family experiences stays with them. Religious beliefs, basic values, unconscious emotional likes and dislikes, fears and enthusiasms often are based upon childhood training or early informal experiences. Most couples are not orphans and many live in or near the community where their parents or other close relatives live. In-laws cannot be disregarded; they are part of the family group, through the effect they have had in molding the personality of husband and wife and often as frequent visitors.

In-laws are often referred to as a problem. But need they be? Dr. Duvall's book, *In-laws, Pro and Con*, is based upon an intensive study of information contributed by over five thousand men and women in individual and group interviews and in letters written in response to a network radio contest soliciting letters on "Why I Think Mothers-in-Law Are Wonderful People." Her book goes beyond mothers-in-law and covers the entire situation. The brief selections that follow analyze the in-law situation and give a general framework for understanding specific in-law experiences.

HE WAS STATIONED at Great Lakes. She was living with the children at her parents' home in Michigan. Their separation was not easy for either of them, and he called home every week to talk with her—just to hear the sound of her voice, he said. One night her voice was heavy with tears as she begged:

---

* Evelyn Millis Duvall, *In-laws, Pro and Con* (New York: Association Press, 1954), selections from pages 276–280 and 293–296. Reprinted by permission of the publisher. The author's biographical sketch is given in connection with article 6.

"Try to find a place near you for the children and me. I can't stand this living with in-laws any more!"

Touched and baffled, he replied:

"What in-laws are you talking about? You're living with your own folks, aren't you?"

Her response was a poignant—

"Everybody's in-laws when you're married."

That young wife put her finger on a sore point in the relationships of the married couple and either set of parents. Once a man and woman marry, they are faced with the challenge of identifying with each other. This means making new loyalties in which they both come first in each other's eyes. It necessarily involves breaking away from both sets of parents. Old identifications with the members of both families now must undergo a change to the place where "everybody is an in-law when you are married."

But old loyalties and responsibilities carry on in the lives of both the husband and the wife. They still are adult children of the parents who knew them when. . . . They still are and want to be part of the families they came from and married into. At the same time, their own new family unit must and should come first.

.   .   .   .

When a man marries, he may try to tell himself that he is not marrying her family, he is marrying the girl. But let the first holiday come along, or the first baby, and he will find out whom he married. As will his wife. The marriage of the two people unites the two families from which they both have come, as inexorably as it binds the couple.

Every married couple belongs to three families. They belong first of all to themselves. They are the WE of the new family they are founding together. But, at the same time they also belong to *his* family, and to *hers*. If they are to establish a strong family unit of their own, they must inevitably realign their loyalties to the place where *our* family comes before either *yours* or *mine*.

This is the elemental triangle of married living. Unless the cohesive force in the new family unit is stronger than that which ties either of the couple to the parental home, the founding family is threatened, as we see in the figures.

In Figure 1a, "YOU" have in-law trouble because "MY" family is too close. It may be because I am still immature and not ready to emancipate myself from my parental home. It may be that one or more members of my family is possessive and finds it difficult to let me go. It may be that circumstances within my family require from me more loyalty and attention than I can comfortably give at the time that I am involved in building my own home and marriage. Whatever the reason, if the forces pulling me/us toward loyalties to "MY" home are too strong, the development of "OUR" common sense of identity is delayed or weakened.

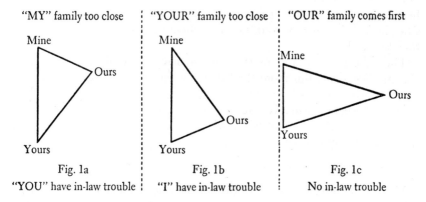

"MY" family too close	"YOUR" family too close	"OUR" family comes first
Fig. 1a	Fig. 1b	Fig. 1c
"YOU" have in-law trouble	"I" have in-law trouble	No in-law trouble

In Figure 1b, "YOUR" family is too close, and so "I" have in-law trouble. Because "YOU" are bound so tightly to "YOUR" family, I am pulled away from mine, and "WE" make little progress in establishing "OURS."

In Figure 1c, "OUR" family unit comes first in our joint loyalties. We are threatened neither by the ties that bind us to "YOUR" family, nor by the bonds that unite us to "MINE." We are able to make progress as a new family because the force of our common identification pulls us out and away together into a home of our own. Now we can share in the common heritage of both your family and mine because we are not threatened by the pull from either. Only thus are WE free to enjoy being members of the entire extended family, without the stress of in-law strains.

The basic task in the early years of marriage is to cement the marriage bonds to the place where the two feel, behave, and fundamentally *want to be* ONE. This is the explicit commitment of the marriage ceremony in which the man and wife promise, "Forsaking all others, keep Ye only to him/her as long as Ye both shall live."

Any intrusion or threat from either his family or hers may be considered an in-law problem. The autonomy of the married pair is so imperative for the solidity of the union that there is a peculiar sensitivity to any conflicting force emanating from either parental home. For this reason, anything that a member of his family or hers does that imperils the independence of the pair may be construed as an in-law difficulty.

Identifications Shift at Marriage

For twenty years, more or less, a girl is identified with her childhood family. She is known as their girl. She carries their name. She thinks of herself as a member of that family. Her loyalties are to them. Her sense of who she is, is in terms of who they are, where they live, what they do, how they look at life.

Then she marries, and must evolve a new set of identifications. She changes her name. But more than that, she changes her sense of who she is and to whom she belongs. She is no longer her parents' little girl. She is now her husband's wife. Where once her loyalties were to her father and mother and to their way of life, now her loyalties must shift to center in those held in common with her husband.

.   .   .   .

Marriage adjustment involves the sorting out of older loyalties and developing new patterns of identification. These consist not only of practices and ways of living, but most basically of concepts of self. As we marry, we must re-examine our sense of self, and rediscover what it means to be a wife, a mother, a husband, a father. These concepts have been in the process of building throughout our early experience with ourselves and with others.

By the time we marry we have a vast miscellany of concepts and pictures in our heads of the way things should be and how we should conceive of ourselves. The more powerful of these conceptions of role have come out of former identifications with those important to us—father, mother, siblings, and the other special people of childhood and youth. Some of these ways of life, picked up in our association and identification with those close to us, carry over unchallenged through the rest of life, as do language patterns and personal hygiene and table manners for most of us. But some of these earlier identifications must undergo extreme shifts as the new sense of self as husband or wife develops.

The implications of shifting identifications from the childhood home to the extended family that comes into being at marriage are many. . . . At the moment, one more question is pertinent.

In-laws by definition are those relatives that one gains in marriage. The question is: How can we feel the same love and acceptance for the mate's family that we have for our own flesh and blood? Through two decades, more or less, we develop tender, special love feelings for our own primary family group and the people in it. Then, with the pronouncement as man and wife, we are expected to love the other's people as our own. Granted that warm acceptance is a strong unifying factor in in-law relationships, how is it attained?

The simplest answer seems to be that to the extent to which we have learned to love in our childhood homes, we have developed the capacities of affection and acceptance in ever widening relationships. This is therefore a matter of relative maturity, a factor of great importance in the business of living with others.

89 · How to Get Along with In-laws *

PEGGY MARCUS

This article describes an interesting questionnaire study in which an index of good adjustment of young wives to in-laws was first established and then factors found to be associated with good adjustment were selected by proper statistical methods. Nine factors and four "feeling tones" were found. Since most of the factors existed prior to the marriage, they may be thought of as indicative of future good in-law adjustment.

"AND THEY married and lived happily ever after." . . . So go the fairy tales.

With one out of every five marriages ending in divorce, however, the reliability of these storybook endings is in question. The present high divorce rate has increased public concern as to the causes of domestic discord and brought about a renewed interest in means for its prevention and treatment.

In recent years, marriage counseling services have been set up under many different auspices to give aid not only to ailing marriages but to young couples contemplating marriage. Terman [1] has said:

Genuine research on the causes of marital unhappiness has barely begun. It was only in 1924 that the pioneer studies of Davis and Hamilton were launched and only in 1929 that their results were published. The importance

* "In-law Relationship Adjustment of Couples Married between Two and Eleven Years," *Journal of Home Economics*, 43 (January, 1951), 35-37. Reprinted by permission of the publisher.

The author was a graduate teaching assistant in the department of child development and family relationships in the New York State College of Home Economics at Cornell University when she wrote this article. The basis for the article was research for her Master of Science degree.

[1] Terman, L. M. *Psychological Factors in Marital Happiness.* New York: McGraw-Hill Book Co., Inc., 1938, p. 377.

of the problem and the success thus far attained call for the continuance and intensification of such research. The attack should proceed from many angles, for every methodological technique has its peculiar limitations.

A frequently cited cause of marital disharmony is relationships with in-laws, but a review of the research on marriage adjustment has brought to light very little information on the factors associated with successful or unsuccessful adjustment to in-laws. It was the purpose of this study to ascertain what factors present before and after marriage are associated with in-law adjustment.

A list of items from source materials on marriage and family relationships, class discussions, and traditional armchair speculations, which had some relevance to in-law relations, was compiled and organized into the questionnaire form. To simplify the study, the schedule was directed to the wife only. Consequently, the findings are a reflection of *her impressions* about the relationships she and her husband have with their respective in-laws. Burgess and Cottrell [2] found the ratings of husband and wife to be reliable and stable when comparisons were made between independent ratings by husbands and wives of their own marriage and of their parents' marriage. Thus it was assumed that the wife's ratings for her husband would be valid. Inasmuch as previous studies have shown that most in-law problems are between women, it seemed more important to get the wife's point of view.

One hundred and forty-six questionnaires were mailed to home economics graduates of the classes 1939 and 1940 who had been married at least one year.

The questionnaire was accompanied by a letter explaining the purpose of the study, assuring anonymity, and soliciting co-operation. Seventy-nine schedules were returned completely answered.

The respondents ranged in length of time married from two to eleven years, with a mean length of 6.4 years.

A good relationship, as defined for the purposes of this study, is one in which the patterns of behavior of the persons involved are mutually satisfying. It was almost impossible to measure this relationship directly, but it was possible to make some estimate of how well or how poorly people are adjusted on the basis of certain indications of their feelings toward each other. On this assumption, an index of the degree of adjustment of the husband or wife to their respective in-laws was constructed.

With the aid of my committee, it was decided that the items chosen for the index should meet the following criteria: (1) be reliable indicators of

---

[2] Burgess, E. W., and Cottrell, L. S., Jr. *Predicting Success or Failure in Marriage.* New York: Prentice-Hall, Inc., 1939, p. 43.

feelings and attitudes; (2) be able to be answered by all of the respondents; (3) apply to the present relationship.

After careful examination of schedules, eight items were selected:

1. Feeling of acceptance by in-laws
2. Feeling about visits to in-laws
3. Nature of correspondence with parental homes
4. Mode of address to in-laws
5. Unasked advice given by parents-in-law
6. What parents have done for the couple
7. What the couple has done for the parents
8. Rating of in-laws' personality traits

After many hours of discussion and separate ratings by two members of my committee and myself, a measurement of in-law adjustment, sufficiently precise and discriminating for this investigation, was established.

Since the answers to the questions in the schedule were not all short, objective answers and could not be scored by precise numerical designations, it was decided that a subjective rating of good, fair, or poor would be given by the judge for each of the items.

The parents were considered as a couple. If the parents were divorced and both parents had remarried, a composite adjustment of all four was made. When one parent was deceased and the remaining parent had not remarried, adjustment to the one parent was considered in the same way as adjustment to both.

To determine the reliability and validity of the index, the following procedure was employed.

The two committee members and I agreed to make independent estimates of the same 10 questionnaires picked at random. Agreement on each individual item and the final estimates was reached with 100 per cent unanimity. Another attempt to test the consistency of adjustment ratings was made as follows: When I had completed the ratings for the remaining 69 schedules, my committee members judged the last 5 I did to determine whether my judgments were the same as when we did the first 10. Here again, complete agreement was found. The consistency of the ratings was accepted with a reasonable amount of confidence.

After all the schedules were rated according to the criteria set up, every factor that I believed might contribute to the total adjustment was measured against the ratings. By employing the Chi-square formula, I was able to get a measure of the significance of each factor.

All items were considered separately for the husband's and wife's adjustment with their in-laws.

In-law interaction did not appear to be the difficult problem popular belief has led us to expect. For both the husband and wife, there was a tendency for good adjustment with their in-laws. Examination of the table will reveal the striking skewness in the distribution of adjustment ratings that occurred in this study.

The factors most significantly related to good in-law adjustment for both husband and wife were:

1. *Approval of couple's marriage by the parents.* Our national mores may sanction individualism and free choice of mate, but parents still have some power of veto. At least, it might be said they are interested in the marital future of their children and usually give expression to their approval or disapproval. In the total sampling, there was no schedule in which this question regarding the attitude of the parents toward the marriage of the couple was not checked. Parents are used to guiding their children and, in a decision that is so important to their child and themselves, they cannot help wanting their vote to count. If the couple marries in spite of the parents' opposition, there is likely to be some hostility, making adjustment more difficult to achieve.

Distribution of Total Adjustment Ratings

Rating	Wife's Adjustment to Husband's Parents	Husband's Adjustment to Wife's Adjustment
	Per Cent	Per Cent
Good adjustment	58	68
Fair adjustment	36	24
Poor adjustment	6	8

The findings of this investigation strongly supported this hypothesis, with a less than 1 per cent significance, for both husband's and wife's adjustment.

2. *Meeting the prospective partner's family before marriage.* Books on marriage, written for young people, strongly advise getting into each other's home and meeting the prospective partner's families. In light of this emphasis, it was interesting to note that adjustment was far more favorable for those husbands and wives who met their in-laws before they were married and particularly before they were engaged. The relations of in-law adjustment to the time the husband met his wife's parents, and the wife met her husband's parents, was of less than 1 per cent significance. This seems related to the importance of the parents' approval of the marriage. If they met their child's future spouse, they would feel that their role of consultant and adviser was not neglected.

3. *Friendliness of parental families toward each other when they met.* Even though it is important for the new spouse to know his partner's family

before marriage, it did not appear to matter greatly whether the parental families knew each other before the couple's marriage. However, if and when they did meet, their feelings toward each other appeared to be an influence upon the young couple's adjustment with their respective in-laws.

4. *A separate household for each couple and their children, free from the presence of other relatives.* Findings of the present study substantiate the popular impression of the undesirability of living with relatives. In addition to a rating scale that pointed to the unsatisfactory arrangement of double living, all but nine respondents who gave information on this point made one or more comments such as "Need to be alone" and "We are much better friends now that we have our own homes."

5. *Happy marriage of the parents and of the couple.* The nature of this association may be explained by the fact that, if the parents are happily married, they have less need for overattachment to their children. The explanation for the relation between the couple's marriage happiness and in-law adjustment may well be that the problem is a basic lack of maturity on the part of one or both of the spouses.

6. *Marriage between persons of the same religion.* For the couples in this study, this factor was significantly related to in-law adjustment.

7. *Wife's education for marriage.* A question, directed to the wife only, asked if she had taken a course in marriage. A less than 5 per cent value was found for the wife's adjustment with her in-laws with definite likelihood of good adjustment if she had taken a marriage course at Cornell or some other institution, and a 2 per cent level of probability for the husband's adjustment if his wife took the marriage course.

8. *Happy relationship between the parents and grandchildren.* The amount of time the older couple spent with their grandchildren was not so important as the feeling tone that existed between the grandparents and grandchildren. When the adjustment to in-laws was good, the relationship with the children was more often a happy one; or perhaps, restated, if the relationship lacked interest or was annoying, poor adjustment resulted.

9. *Similarities in the pattern of social activity.* Two factors related to the wife's adjustment to her in-laws were: (a) The couple and the husband's parents were alike in the pattern of their organizational activity, and (b) the couple was married more than seven years.

Only one factor was statistically significant for the husband's adjustment with his in-laws which was unrelated to the wife's adjustment. That factor was his having the same education as his wife or more.

In addition to the above statistical findings, the feeling tone that seemed to stand out most clearly between those with a good adjustment and a poor adjustment indicated:

1. That those young couples with a good adjustment seemed to be

working as a unit, accepting both families as their own and regarding all problems as a common task. (Those with a poor adjustment, on the other hand, showed the tendency to blame the spouse's family for friction in all areas.)

2. That an intimate title of address to in-laws, such as Mother and Dad, was almost always found among those with a good adjustment.

3. That in-law adjustment is a mutual process as implied by many of the respondents. (In answering the question "What did you or your husband do to make an adjustment with your parental families?" those with good adjustment stated, "None was necessary," implying complete acceptance of each other from the beginning. Others did not find the adjustment so easy at first but made sincere efforts to understand their in-laws. The responses of the poorly adjusted seemed to imply easy defeat or lack of acceptance of the fact that adjustment with in-laws was part of their responsibility.)

4. That the young couple needs the security of the parents behind them but not interference or control. (When the respondents were asked "In what ways have your parents and your parents-in-law helped you and your husband?" there was almost complete unanimity of response from those with a good adjustment and such statements as "They have never interfered, but they have always given us the security that they would give us help when we needed it," and "We can always talk things over with them, but they don't meddle." The poorly adjusted registered many complaints about the "too free and frequent advice" and, when they were asked to list any conflicts that existed between the couple and the parental families, almost all implied lack of freedom for the couple to lead their own lives in their own way.)

The purpose of this study was to ascertain what factors present before and after marriage are associated with successful or unsuccessful in-law adjustment. The sample on which the study was based was limited to 79 home economics college alumnae and their husbands. This is small and not representative of the general population, but it is my hope that the findings may throw some further light on the subject of in-law adjustment.

90 · What Grandmothers Are For *

EDITH G. NEISSER

In time parents-in-law become grandparents. With the birth of a child, relationships between a young couple and their parents change and new roles are in order all the way around. This sympathetic article presents the valuable contributions that grandparents can make to their grandchildren, which are in addition to what parents give their children.

"WILL YOU accept a collect call from Mr. Stephen Clark in Elmtown? All right, Elmtown, go ahead with Springfield."

"Hi, Dad. You've got a brand-new grandson. Born half an hour ago. Marian's fine. Sure, everything's O.K. But the young man was two weeks ahead of schedule and we have a problem. You know Marian's mother was coming to look after Betsy if things had gone as we'd planned. Now she can't get off. It's registration week at the school, and she's the dean's secretary and I guess his right hand. My vacation is all set for early next month, so I can give Marian a hand then and look out for Betsy. But I can't switch dates on such short notice, so right now . . ."

"Hello, Stevie. Congratulations. This is Mother. I grabbed the phone. Would you like me to come and take care of you and Betsy? Fine. I'll leave on the eight-o'clock train in the morning. Of course it'll be all right with Dad. See you tomorrow. Love to Marian. Good-by, dear."

This call and many similar ones come to grandparents over and over again. Probably most of us, when asked "What are grandparents for?" would answer "To meet emergencies." The definition of an emergency varies with the distance and the flexibility of the grandparents involved.

Steve and Marian Clark, who lived a good hundred miles from Marian's working mother and three times as far in the opposite direction from Steve's parents, knew their parents could be counted on in a pinch. But it had to be a tight pinch before they would ask either grandmother to drop everything and come to their rescue. Acute or prolonged illness, new babies, per-

* *National Parent-Teacher*, 51 (January, 1957), 20–22.
The author, who has the Bachelor of Arts degree from Vassar College, formerly was child guidance editor of *Childcraft*. She is active in various civic and family education groups and has written widely in the field of family relations. Among her publications are *The Eldest Child, Brothers and Sisters*, and several pamphlets for the Public Affairs Committee including *How to Be a Good Mother-in-Law and Grandmother*.

haps a carefully timed vacation for the younger Clark couple—such situations might justify a request that one of the grandmothers come and take over. Except when faced with special circumstances like these, Steve and Marian were wary about asking for help. As Marian said, "If we cry 'Wolf!' too often, we'll kill the goose that lays the golden eggs." Marian was more poetic than accurate in her speech, but her mixed metaphor did convey their point of view.

The Clarks' friends, the Hillstroms, could put an "Emergency" label on packages of experience quite different in size and content. The small Hillstrom children were richly endowed with four available grandparents and a great-grandmother. To young Nell Hillstrom an emergency might be unexpected guests, having the house torn up with painters, a sniffle that kept one of the youngsters housed for a few days, or just the feeling that if she couldn't get an hour of peace and quiet she would simply collapse. At the drop of a hat she could pack the two-year-old and the four-year-old off to whichever grandmother was free for a few hours or for the day, and everyone would be pleased with the arrangement. If one of the youngsters was kept indoors with a minor complaint or if Nell had a dentist's appointment, Granny, who was an active seventy-five, would be on hand as a sitter.

Widening the Circle of Security

Some of the other contributions grandparents make to their children's children are less obvious but equally vital. The extra measure of affection they can give the children is a strong bulwark, stronger than we sometimes realize, in reinforcing the emotional well-being of these small persons. To love and to be loved by several adults is a bracing tonic to the spirits of the young, and as a rule grandparents have an ample supply of this tonic.

Grandparents often, all unawares, serve as a means of widening their grandchildren's horizons. A small child feels safe and at ease when his mother is around, but for many one- and two-year-olds the dark rim of outer space begins just beyond the sound of Mother's voice. Even three- and four-year-olds are not sure that anyone but Mother (and maybe Father) really knows how to make them comfortable.

The first time four-year-old Lucy was to go on a day's excursion with her grandfather, she seemed troubled. Her mother explained that Grandpa and Lucy would drive to a farm where Lucy had visited earlier in the summer with her mother and father. They would see the cows, feed the chickens, watch the ducks, and then maybe have a boat ride on the lake and lunch on the way home.

"How'll Gramps know what I like to eat? Does he know I don't want a high chair like babies? Does Gramps know where the farm is? If I have to go to the bathroom can I ask Gramps to take me? Does he know where bathrooms are?" she asked her mother while she was getting dressed.

In spite of Lucy's misgivings, however, the expedition was a huge success. When she came home she announced, "Gramps is almost as good as Daddy. He knows lots of 'portant things."

To have discovered that "lots of 'portant things" are generally known outside your own home is indeed the beginning of wisdom.

Grandparents are the ideal persons to give a small child the feeling that contentment is to be found with someone other than Mother and Father. Grandparents, in what they say and do, are likely to be sufficiently similar to the youngster's own parents to bridge the gap between the familiar, which involves a minimum of risk, and the unaccustomed, which is dubious. Two-, three-, and four-year-olds are dyed-in-the-wool conservatives!

Because Grandmother's ways are similar but yet not identical to Mother's, the preschool child absorbs another big lesson as he spends time with the older generation. He finds out that there is more than one good way to eat your supper, get ready for an outing, or close a door. He gets the idea that variations on a well-known theme, such as the day's routine, are not hazardous but perhaps even pleasant. From casual incidents he may arrive at the philosophy that when in Rome you can, without serious inconvenience, do as the Romans do. That attitude can be better preparation for the first days at school than knowing how to read a few words or add a few numbers.

Home Ways Are Not the Only Ways

When Chester's father deposited him at Grandfather's ranch for a week-long visit, the three-and-a-half-year-old had some illuminating experiences. Breakfast in Chester's home was a catch-as-catch-can affair. His father left for work at six-thirty every morning. When Chester heard him in the kitchen, he would get up and join him for ten precious minutes and a pre-breakfast piece of toast and jelly. Then Chester would go back to his room and play quietly until his mother called him. By this time his brother and sisters were clamoring that the school bus would be there any minute and they couldn't wait for eggs and bacon.

Their mother, with that clairvoyance vouchsafed to mothers of four children between half-past-seven and half-past-eight in the morning, located pencils, mittens, books, and sweaters while she stirred the oatmeal. Chester meandered around in the midst of this cheerful confusion, a banana in one hand and a sock in the other.

Breakfast at Grandfather's was a far cry from this hurly-burly. Grandpa and Uncle Joe came in from the orange grove ready for a big, leisurely meal. Grandma did not press sausage and buckwheat cakes on Chester, for she remembered well that three-year-old appetites are not usually at their heartiest early in the morning. But she did not allow him to wander around the breakfast porch half dressed. "Everybody sits at the table, and you'll miss a lot of fun if you aren't here," she announced. After the first two days Chester fitted into the orderly pattern of what he called "Grandma's sitting-down buckfust."

What about the charge that grandparents are overly indulgent, that they counteract the discipline of mothers and fathers, and that (oh, horrid thought!) they spoil their grandchildren? Some grandparents—and probably all at times—are less firm in certain matters than are a child's parents. Yet as long as Grandma makes it clear that "you may do this here with me, but at home with your mommy you do it her way," she is not undermining a mother's regulations. She is not apt to be spoiling anybody or anything either.

Children, Too, Need Relief from Pressure

Everyone needs some place "to get away from it all." What better refuge could there be than Grandmother's or Grandfather's house? If a grandparent lives under the same roof with the grandchildren, his or her room may offer almost as much change in emotional temperature as does a separate dwelling.

More than ever today, when the three- or four-year-old is likely to have one or two younger brothers or sisters, or perhaps several older ones, does he need once in a while to have an affectionate adult all to himself. Today's homes are often crowded, mothers are necessarily hurried, and the preschool boy or girl lives under more pressure than we realize.

For the eldest in the family, a chance to be with Grandmother or Grandfather may mean an opportunity to get some of the babying that he may have missed because a younger brother or sister crowded so quickly on his heels. "Don't have to be big here! Don't want to be big," a two-and-a-half-year-old veteran of two new arrivals in the family muttered as his grandmother carried him into bed. Backsliding? Yes, it was, but backsliding within reasonable limits may sometimes have curative powers.

To the youngster who is always scrambling to keep up with several older brothers and sisters, who feels the older ones look down on him as a baby, being with Grandmother may be a distinct release from the strain of proving himself in every activity. After a few hours or a few days, he can return home refreshed.

That Lovely Thing Called Leisure

Grandparents have a most precious gift to present to children—time. They have time to answer questions and to listen. They will let a small person look at all the cars as a long freight train goes by or inspect every spoon in the drawer without saying, "Hurry up, your sister is waiting for us on the corner" or "Give that back to me right away. I've got to feed the baby; he's so hungry he can't wait another minute." (The patience of a grandparent may be born of the knowledge that at the end of the day or the end of the week he can retreat into his adult world, but its part-time nature is the virtue of the office.) To a youngster in a large family, an unhurried day now and then is balm to the spirit. Most grandparents feel that one grandchild at a time as a guest or companion is the happiest arrangement— a plan that would get the vote of the small children, too.

One four-year-old put her problem in a nutshell. After Grandpa had finished the second reading of her favorite book, she cuddled up to him and said, "I like you 'cause you read it all. You don't say, 'No more time' like Mommy." She was thoughtful for a minute. Then she added, "You got plenty of time?" When he assured her that he had, she said contentedly, "I like plenty of time. When I'm a big lady I'm going to have plenty of time like you and Gramma." It is a happy child who feels that a grownup has plenty of time for him.

Grandparents make still another contribution. They serve as a link with the past and give a child a feeling of having roots. Gone are the dim attics of a grandmother's house where a youngster could find old family portraits and lovely, if somewhat battered, keepsakes. Yet even in those streamlined, functional apartments where grandparents are likely to be found these days, some photograph, some trinket, or some well-worn utensil in the kitchen will catch an observant three- or four-year-old's eye and draw forth the question, "Where dis from?" or "What's that for?" or "Who's that funny lady?" As Grandpa or Grandma talks about the fact that the old blue bowl came from far across the ocean long ago, or that the funny lady in the picture was his mother or her grandmother, a small child's world expands. He may not understand the explanation the first time, but he will undoubtedly return to the same line of inquiry later. "Tell me about Daddy when he was a little boy" or "Tell me about when your grandfather kept a horse in the back yard" are requests that bespeak a healthy curiosity and a vaguely stirring desire to establish a connection with far-off times and places.

What are grandparents for? To answer that question we may borrow the syntax of Ruth Krauss' *A Hole Is to Dig* and reply that "grandparents are to accept"—in all that the word *accept* implies—the many calls that come to them. And in accepting, as it were, the collect calls, they also collect rich rewards of their own.

91 · What's Wrong with This Family? *

FAMILY SERVICE ASSOCIATION OF AMERICA

This brief account of a family outing is analyzed to show why the grandmother and her son bicker, whereas her daughter-in-law is able to maintain her composure.

"WHY DID WE have to pick out this place? We could at least have some shade," Grandma Russell complains. Actually it's a grand day, and the whole Russell family is pepped up for a picnic, except Grandma, who finds something wrong—as usual.

"The way you let those children run wild, one of them is sure to get hurt." Grandma is centering her criticism on her daughter-in-law. She also complains because the eggs are not boiled enough and because they are going to eat off paper plates.

"I told you this would happen," says Grandma. Jane has stumbled and cut her leg. John Russell can't keep quiet any longer. "Look, Mother, you can pick on me, but lay off Mary." He adds, "We ought to be able to raise our kids without your butting in."

"Why don't you talk back to her?" John asks after they've taken Grandma home. But Mary answers: "I don't like family fights. Anyhow, it's better to give in to her once in a while." Who has the right slant—John or Mary?

What's Right:

It was a good idea for the Russells to include Grandma in the family picnic, even though it didn't work out. Children need grandparents and aunts and uncles as part of their "bigger" family, not only for the extra affection and feeling of belonging, but also so they can learn to adjust to a wider number of people. Older people, too, need the affection and stimulation of the younger generation and a feeling of being part of the family.

* Prepared in cooperation with the Family Service Association of America, *Better Homes and Gardens*, 29 (July, 1951), 14–15, 95. Copyright 1951. Meredith Publishing Company, Des Moines, Iowa. Reprinted by permission of the publisher.

What's Wrong:

John sees his mother's behavior simply as a matter of "butting in." This is understandable because: (1) She is still his mother whose control he has spent a good part of his life breaking away from; (2) John feels responsibility to *both* his mother and his wife, and he is angered because he feels forced to defend the latter against the former.

Grandma Russell ought to see things a little more clearly. Chances are she was enjoying herself more than she let on.

If John hadn't felt so personally involved, he might have understood what was happening to his mother—and kept his temper. For many years she had had her own family—*depending* on her. Like a doctor in retirement, she found it hard to really give up "practicing."

Unlike her husband, Mary Russell is not as involved emotionally with Grandma; therefore she finds it easier to be tolerant. She is able to see that she and John will lose little of their own independence if occasionally they take what Grandma Russell says without fussing about it. In fact, Mary realizes that accepting *some* of it gracefully and without quarreling may reassure Grandma that she is still a valued member of the family. And this may make it less necessary for her to be a complainer. Even if Grandma continues to throw out barbs of criticism, Mary will feel that as long as she and John are sure of each other and of their way of bringing up the children, Grandma's fussing needn't bother them.

But it will help, too, if grandparents can recall that in their younger years, they, too, wanted to be independent and free to raise *their* children the way they wanted.

CHAPTER 25:

Forestalling and Solving Problems

92 · *The Discussion Group* *

GERTRUDE K. POLLAK

Three widely used ways have been developed to aid the unmarried or married person work out a successful choice of mate and marriage adjustment. One is the college course or short informal course that young people enroll in prior to marriage, usually referred to as a course in preparation for marriage. Since many of the readers are probably familiar with such courses, they are not discussed further.

The second approach is the discussion group, often of young married people coping for the first time with problems of parenthood. These may be called parent-study groups or mother-study groups if they are limited to mothers. Typically, they are led by a person trained in family-life education, family casework, or child development. They make a wide appeal to parents who are not sure they are using the best methods of child rearing or who wonder whether their children are worse than other children.

The third approach is through individual counseling, preferably carried on with both husband and wife, separately or jointly. Marriage counseling is carried on by family service and other case work agencies, marriage counseling centers, mental health clinics, and psychologists and psychiatrists in private practice. Usually the relationship between husband and wife has become so strained that it is unbearable to one or both.

The first article, written by the Director of Family Life Education in a family service agency, deals with the discussion group composed of parents. It explains the influence that the group itself has on each member as he

* "Principles of Positive Parent-Child Relationships in Family Life Education," *Social Casework*, 37 (March, 1956), selections from pages 135–138. Reprinted by permission of the publisher and the author.
A biographical sketch of the author is given with article 80.

reveals his anxieties and perplexities, the role of the professionally trained group leader, and the way in which discussion subjects are chosen. An important point made is that family life education is education and not therapy, but it is education of emotions as well as of intellect.

IN THE family life education discussion group, three major factors are responsible for the development of better understanding of family relationships on the part of the participants, and a better understanding of themselves and their children in their mutual interaction.

The Influence of the Group

The first factor is the group itself. Group members give suggestions, support, and criticism. Their contributions immensely enrich the individual parent's necessarily narrower point of view, and add to his understanding of the specific situation with which he is faced. New possibilities for coping with problems and for dealing with particular situations in the home come to the attention of the parents who participate in the group discussions. The parent also realizes that he is not the only one who has to deal with this problem. Other parents have faced or are facing this same problem or very closely related ones and, what is more, they have solved it, or have attempted to solve it. This realization relieves much of the anxiety that one witnesses in parents. It also helps to answer some of the questions and concerns of many parents, particularly young parents or parents of only children, which can best be expressed in the question that is often voiced, incidentally, in these very words: "Is my child normal?" (Although some parents do present, consciously or unconsciously, a picture of a parent-child relationship or of a child's personality which is deviant from the norm, they are not the majority in family life education groups. With such a parent an individual contact is made in order to suggest the use of resources for therapeutic help.) It is this writer's experience that many of the anxieties and concerns of parents in parent groups about the normality of their child are not justified, and the alleviation of such unjustified anxiety is in itself a therapeutic experience for the parent. This experience is one of the helpful by-products of participation in a family life education discussion series, and is often mentioned by participants in their evaluation of the group experience.

Role of the Group Leader

The second main factor in the parents' use of the discussion group is their relationship with the discussion leader. The latter is a person of experience and professional knowledge who, at the same time, accepts, understands, and is positively motivated toward the individual group members. Particularly when the parent has had a negative experience with his own father or mother, the experience of being related to an accepting and understanding parental figure provides an opportunity for him to have a corrective emotional experience. Through it, he can get some emotional release, a feeling of worthiness, a reduction of anxiety or of aggressiveness—depending on his own personality structure and needs. In turn his relationship with his own child is thereby benefited. Since parent-child relationships are so apt to be colored by the parent's own experience as a child and within his own family, the relationship of the group members to the discussion leader—which of course varies in intensity and has different transference phenomena according to the personality of the parent and of the discussion leader—is one of the most important factors in helping the parents grow and mature through the use of the discussion group.

The fact that the leader is a person with professional knowledge and experience is a second important facet of the group leadership role—and one that social workers tend to underestimate. He brings to the group his professional competence and his specific knowledge in the area of ". . . family interrelationships and their effects on behavior and social functioning . . . the role of the family in furthering optimal development of its members, by providing both emotional security and suitable growth experiences for its members." [1] This is the broad area in which parents need help and can use the knowledge that the discussion leader from the family service field brings to the group.

It is one of the most important, and often one of the most difficult, tasks of the discussion leader to help the group members develop the kind of relationships with himself and with each other which will be of the greatest help to them in working toward their goals of a better understanding of family relationships and of parenthood; at the same time he must keep in mind the purpose of the group. Family life education is primarily education, not therapy. As education, it addresses itself to the egos of the group members and uses their ego strength.[2] Learning is the tool of education; learning how to be a better parent is the goal of such a group experience. The necessary knowledge and skills in the area of parenthood cannot be acquired, however, through a learning process that involves only the person's intellectual capacity.

---

[1] *Scope and Methods of the Family Service Agency*, Family Service Association of America, New York, 1953, p. 4.

[2] Peter B. Neubauer, M.D., "The Techniques of Parent Group Education: Some Basic Concepts," in *Parent Group Education and Leadership Training*, Child Study Association of America, New York, 1952, p. 12.

Parent-child relationships are inevitably charged with emotions. For many parents they are anxiety provoking since they tend to arouse memories of the parents' own early life experiences. The ghosts of old fears, old rivalries, and old loves haunt the present. The intellect alone cannot cope with such powerful dynamic forces. How can the leader of a discussion group help to channel these powerful forces in such a manner that the educational goals of the group as a whole, and of the majority of its members, are furthered?

Group members inevitably develop both positive and negative transference reactions to the leader as the group experience progresses. It is equally inevitable that the leader will have certain countertransference reactions which may be positive or negative. It is important, however, for positive reactions toward the group leader to be dominant, since one of the conditions of learning in the area of parent-child relationships is a positive relationship to the discussion leader. Identification with the leader is one of the channels through which learning is achieved, and careful control of negative relationships and of negative transference and countertransference phenomena is essential. Such control applies chiefly to the mode of their expression and to the degree to which they are acted out in the group setting. Understanding of transference and countertransference reactions and alertness to their manifestations are essential attributes of a good discussion leader. Although he needs to be watchful for evidences of *too* positive transference or countertransference, this is not potentially as threatening to the learning goal as its negative counterpart.

The role that the discussion leader assumes and the use of his professional self are the most important contributing factors to group learning. The group's reactions will reflect the quality of the leadership and will differ in accordance with the nature of the leadership. From our experience with family life education groups it would appear that the permissive and passive leader will stimulate the revelation of personal experiences, anxiety-provoking material, and perhaps even unconscious material. The discussion leader who is authoritarian and "in full command" of the group, on the other hand, while preventing some of this too personal revelation, will also prevent the group from full participation. With him, the interest of the group members flags and the group may disintegrate. Such leadership inhibits the establishment of a positive relationship to the leader through which identification and learning achievement could occur.

Although some limits are necessary, so that the group will in the main seek the goal it set up for the discussions, the paths the group takes in its pursuit of this goal are of its own choosing. No two groups of parents discuss the same problems or topics in exactly the same fashion or in the same order, and it is the group and not the leader who makes the selection. To provide a constructive experience for parent groups, leadership must be clear and directive as to the end goal of the group experience—a better understanding of family relationships of whatever type that group selected for its meetings—but permissive as to the special areas of family relationships which the group wishes to explore in order to achieve the goal.

Such leadership does not prevent the group members from discussing their own experiences as children or from expressing their conscious feelings about their own parents and their childhood fears, frustrations, anxieties, or pleasures. Discussing these things frees parents to understand better their children's similar experiences and emotions. It also frees them to cope with the present with less distortion created by feelings that belong in the past.

Choice of Content

A third important factor, which is closely related to the question of the role of the discussion leader and to the nature of the learning experience of the group, is the choice of the questions to be discussed. By and large, the questions chosen should be those that are likely to be of interest to all or to the majority of the group members. Furthermore, the particular aspects of each question that is to be discussed must be carefully selected and evaluated in terms of the educational goal. For example, one group chose—and very rightly so—to spend considerable time on the problem of children's fears. What are children afraid of? What can the parent do to help the child who is afraid? Are all fears unrealistic and damaging to the child's personality? Although all these questions were discussed in the group, what was not considered suitable for group discussion was the dynamic meaning of fear in children. For example, no interpretation was given as to the dynamics at work when children are afraid of animals that bite, are afraid of being cut, of being mutilated, and so on.

Summary and Conclusions

Family life education programs offered by the family service agency use casework knowledge and casework skills. In the group setting, the specific questions asked by the parents are discussed and are used to develop with each parent group those principles of positive parent-child relationships which have meaning for the particular group. A number of principles that are useful for parents in their efforts to deal more constructively with their children have been identified. An increased understanding of these principles cannot be developed through an intellectual process only. A prerequisite for its development is the emotional experience provided by the interaction of group members as well as by the group's relationship to the discussion leader as an accepting, understanding, professionally trained person who is willing to share with the group his knowledge of and experience concerning family relationships. Another prerequisite is the relief of anxiety, which comes from the realization that other parents deal or have dealt with the same or similar problems and often have dealt with them successfully. Simultaneously, the parents' horizons are broadened as new ways of coping with the problems of everyday living are suggested and discussed by group members and the leader.

Certain safeguards, such as the specific ways in which the discussion leader consciously uses himself in the group situation, or his selection of specific questions for discussion by the group, help the members steer a middle course between too much self-revelation, with its resulting anxiety, and too little involvement in the discussion. The combined impact of the relief of anxiety, the emotional experience of being accepted and understood by group members and leader, the realization that one is not alone in facing problems, and the opportunity to learn new ways of coping with problems, strengthens parents and frees them for better parenthood.

93 · *Marriage Counseling* *

LORNA C. BRANGWIN

Written from the point of view of the counselor, this article nevertheless gives a clear idea of what the client may expect from counseling and what the objectives of the counselor are. The article is well illustrated with cases which show the way in which a diagnosis of the individual case is made and the type of interaction that goes on between counselor and client.

To EVERYONE interested in the well-being of people, the widespread evidence of malcontent, disharmony, and disruption in family living in our culture is a matter of deep concern. These threats to family life seem to endanger the very foundation of our social structure, since the family is its basic social unit. Actually, in spite of tremendous changes in modes of living in recent years, brought about in part by the impact of world events,

---

* "Marriage Counseling—The Viewpoint of the Caseworker," *Social Casework*, 36 (April, 1955), 155–162. Reprinted by permission of the publisher and the author.

The author, who holds the degree of Master of Social Welfare from the University of California, is a caseworker with the Family Service Bureau, Oakland, California. In addition to the article reprinted here, she is coauthor of two other professional articles published in *Social Casework*.

happy, healthy family life still exists. The family may change but it still survives. Every culture, from the most primitive to the highly civilized, has followed in some form this pattern of human living. The philosopher Santayana [1] has described the family as one of nature's masterpieces, in that it is so nicely adjusted to harmonize the natural interests, and thus to meet the needs, of those who compose it. Most of us would agree that, in the sense of the ideal, this is so. We are troubled, however, because marriage, the relationship on which the family is founded, so often fails to achieve enough mutual satisfaction for the partners. Consequently, the climate for happiness and stability in family life is all too often unfavorable.

Because of this widely prevalent concern, ways and means of alleviating unhappiness in marriage are being sought everywhere. From these efforts have emerged a great number of services that proffer "marriage counseling." They represent many different points of view and are offered by persons with varied experience and training—ministers, physicians, psychologists, sociologists, social workers, and others.

Family agencies traditionally have shared the general concern about breakdown in marriage. They have offered to troubled married people a service that has come to be designated as "marriage counseling." They have considered this kind of service as an integral part of their efforts to fortify and uphold the values in family living. They are diligent in their endeavors to develop an increasingly scientific approach to marital, as well as to other interpersonal and environmental, problems. Excellent articles have been written on the subject by leaders in the social casework field, and valuable knowledge has been contributed by specialists in related disciplines. Many aspects of the diagnosis and treatment of marital problems have been discussed, so that little that is new, in the light of our present knowledge, can be added. I should like to review, however, some of the characteristics of the casework approach to these problems, to discuss the process entailed, and to delineate, in a measure at least, the contribution of the family agency.

The Principle of Self-Direction

The philosophy of social casework is based on the idea of respect for the individual as he is, whatever his attributes or limitations. It assumes his right, within certain boundaries set by his own capacities and by the needs of others, to determine how he shall conduct his own life and to make his own decisions. Other concepts emerge naturally from this basic idea of personal worth and responsibility. Each individual is entitled to warm

---

[1] Paraphrased from George Santayana, *The Life of Reason*, Charles Scribner's Sons, New York, 1954 (first published in 1905–06).

understanding and response, without being judged for his mistakes and failures, or condemned for attitudes that may deviate from those of the person whom he consults. He has the right also to self-direction, to encouragement, and to engage in activity, within his capacities, in his own behalf. No one can assume the burdens or solve the conflicts of another human being; to attempt to do so can only undermine the individual's faith in his own competence, and increase his dependency and his feeling of helplessness. Help of any kind is most effective if it enlists the recipient's participation.

As I work with clients and supervise other caseworkers who are in the process of developing their professional competence, I am constantly impressed with the responsibility entailed in meeting requests for guidance. This is a responsibility that involves not only the individual who makes the request, but also his family and, in a broader sense, the social group to which he belongs. Such responsibility cannot be assumed lightly. When a person requests help with marital problems, there is likely to be a sense of urgency and desperation in the request; it has, in all likelihood, been precipitated by a crisis or by a building of tension that has grown beyond the bounds of tolerance. The need for help may seem to be an admission of failure, and the client often tells us that he has "tried everything," and that this request is a last resort. To such a person marriage is not usually a relationship entered into lightly, and the danger of its possible breakdown is a serious threat. He has found that his own methods of coping with the difficulties are not working, and he looks to someone else who is equipped with wisdom greater than his own. He may hope to incorporate some wider, more objective knowledge into his own thinking and feeling. It follows, then, that he has the right to expect the utmost wisdom that it is possible to extend to him. To offer casual advice would be seriously to misuse the role in which we are placed. On the contrary, he is entitled to all the knowledge and skill at our command, and to the human compassion that gives them meaning and substance.

The Counseling Process

In view of the importance of the principle of self-direction, "marriage counseling" may be a misnomer. Do family agencies offer counseling as the term is generally understood? The most familiar definition of counseling is "advising" or "admonishing." Furthermore, many people have come to associate any effort toward alleviation of marital stress with "advice" from someone in authority. This definition, with the connotations emerging from its broad use, does not apply accurately to family agency services.

Unfortunately, caseworkers have been less than explicit in defining the process by which they seek to relieve some of the strain and tension in marriage. The contradiction implied in the use of the term might be resolved if more thought were given to the specific processes by which sound diagnosis and appropriate treatment goals are reached. The casework profession, after all, is a relatively new one, which has achieved its present status by adding to its own concepts and philosophy the knowledge of other professions. Casework has been able to stand, as it were, on the shoulders of such disciplines as psychiatry, sociology, and anthropology. It is still in the process of development, and we must constantly keep in mind the need to re-examine casework practice and redefine its methods.

How, then, do we proceed in our endeavor? If we look only at the disturbance in the marriage, we are merely considering a symptom. If ways and means are prescribed to alleviate the symptom, without understanding the dynamic forces which have caused it and which operate in its current manifestations, then nothing of lasting value can be accomplished.

A systematic study process, which has come to be known in casework as psychosocial diagnosis, is essential if the nature of the disturbance is to be comprehended and sound measures initiated for dealing with it. This process involves the understanding of each individual in terms of his present functioning, and as he is influenced by a combination of forces—his inner drives and needs, and external tension and pressure. The inner forces have been determined by his life experiences. His endowment of physical health, intellect, and energy; the degree of satisfaction or deprivation in affectional relationships during his early years; the quality of his methods of fortifying himself against anxiety, fear, anger, and helplessness—all these have bearing on his attitudes toward others and on his ability to view his situation and react to it in terms of what seems to be its reality. He is, of course, affected by other personalities and by some circumstances beyond his control. His success or failure in coping with them will depend largely on whether internal tensions lead him to make situations difficult for himself and to conceive of his situation only in accordance with his own needs. In other words, the potent, largely unconscious drives that derive from past experience are carried over into the current situation and are a vital part of the conflict in which he is enmeshed.

The extent to which this complex interaction of forces operates is almost always obscure to the person himself, but he will reveal it in many ways. Occasionally he will describe his dilemma lucidly, although unaware of its essential meaning, and will portray the extent to which the adult relationship of marriage is colored by the unresolved frustrations and disappointments of childhood. This was true when a client, after bitterly complaining of her husband's dependence on her, cried, "I'm tired of this. I don't want to be his mother—I want him to be my father!"

There is a repetitive quality in every relationship, a tendency for the individual to seek compensation for earlier needs that have not previously been met. Because marriage is unique in its intimacy and personal meaning, the tendency is strikingly evident in that relationship. Furthermore, each partner seeks, and usually finds, with almost uncanny precision, a mate whose needs mesh with his own. Much of the psychic energy of both may be expended in the attempt to resolve old conflicts; often the very conflict itself seems to give satisfaction, as though the continuation of old battles were the only pattern that seems familiar and comfortable. Many such marriages are adequately satisfying to the partners as long as a kind of balance can be maintained in the mutual gratification of emotional needs. Thus Santayana's concept of the adjustment of "natural interests" often applies even when a marriage seems to rest precariously on a neurotic foundation.

An indispensable preliminary process, no matter how limited the scope of subsequent treatment, is the evaluation of the partners in marriage in terms of their total personalities, the symptomatology they display, their adaptive capacities, and their individual motivation toward change and growth. It is only as each individual's role in the marriage is understood and the nature of the problem, as both contribute to it, is clarified, that we can undertake a treatment plan of a professionally responsible nature.

It is understandable that people who are experiencing inner discomfort and pain should want a quick remedy, a magic formula that will bring relief and comfort. Although we cannot give this kind of relief, we can certainly understand the desire for it. The unhappy married person may not be sufficiently ready to involve himself in exploration of the factors in his situation because he feels that the pain he is experiencing is being imposed on him entirely by external forces—usually by the unacceptable behavior of his partner. He can only demand that something be done to change the other person. When this is so, there is little we can do to help him. To illustrate, I refer to Mrs. D.

Mrs. D, angry and unhappy, wanted the caseworker to talk to her husband and "straighten him out." He had always done a good deal of gambling; Mrs. D had known this before their marriage but had been confident that family responsibility would change him. He had settled down for a while, but after the birth of their first child he went back to his old ways. The second child had not been planned and Mr. D seemed to resent the added responsibility. He began staying away from home for days at a time, and often gambled away his entire pay check. He was usually contrite afterward, and promised his wife repeatedly that he would change. Mrs. D forgave him each time and had managed to supplement their income with part-time domestic work. Now, however, the baby had become ill and needed her constant care. Debts had accumulated, and Mr. D was ignoring them completely. Mrs. D desperately demanded that her husband be forced by someone else to relieve her of these overwhelming burdens. Is it surprising that she asked us to perform magic? It might be a temptation, in such a situation, to advise Mrs. D to divorce her husband. The caseworker knew that there was little likelihood that a man like Mr. D would change. This was a familiar story, and the knowledge of the dynamics underlying such behavior made the caseworker very pessimistic about Mr. D. It was possible, however, only to recognize Mrs. D's feeling of desperation and to test her ability to consider the alternatives. When it was clear that she was not ready to contemplate any change on her own part, she was helped to understand as best she could that change could not be forced on her husband. Suggestions of practical resources were offered to Mrs. D, but her conviction was strong that "just the right person" could do what she asked, and she rejected any alternative to her own plan.

Modification through Counseling

A number of factors may combine to prevent a client's meaningful use of our help, so that our most careful thought and effort can only verify his need to perpetuate the situation that causes him distress. Many clients, however, are ready to participate with us in appraisal of their difficulties and of the means by which change can be brought about. The N case will illustrate the procedure by which modification may be brought about in an unhappy marriage. As often occurs, only one partner, Mrs. N, was sufficiently motivated to enter into a continued relationship with a caseworker. Although Mr. N came to the agency a few times, he did so only at his wife's insistence.

Mrs. N applied for help from the family agency on the recommendation of her doctor. She was experiencing increased severity of physical symptoms, a recurrent involuntary twitching in her neck and shoulders, which were the result of neurological damage due to birth injury. The symptoms had been controlled to some extent through physiotherapy during her childhood and adolescence. They had flared up during the past year, and this exacerbation was ascribed to emotional tension.

Mrs. N was an attractive, well-groomed woman of 29. Her handicap, while noticeable, did not detract from her good appearance or her poise. The N's had been married for six years and had one child, Danny, aged two. Mrs. N had worked during the early part of her marriage while Mr. N completed his studies in geology. When he became established in teaching, she resigned from her job with a publishing firm. She had always dreamed of having a family and home of her own. However, because of financial pressure they had moved to her mother's home shortly after Danny's birth. Although Mrs. N was very unhappy with the arrangement, her husband seemed quite content to remain there. She felt that her marriage was deteriorating rapidly. Mr. N spent a great deal of time and money on his hobby of photography, and was so absorbed in his own interests that he had almost no time for family life. He had become sarcastic and critical, seldom discussed anything with her, and was quite uninterested in sex relations. All this made Mrs. N feel depressed, and she wondered if he were staying with her only out of pity. She was becoming irritable with Danny, and found his care a physical and emotional strain. She had lost her former ease in social situations, and was feeling, all in all, that she was worthless and a failure.

Mrs. N indicated that all her life she had been affected by her handicap. She felt different from her siblings, two older brothers and a sister, and never had anything in common with them. They seemed, from her descriptions, which might have been colored by her feeling, to be dramatic, quite unstable people. Throughout our contact with Mrs. N the picture of her mother remained unclear, but it seemed that she was a very self-absorbed woman, incapable of giving Mrs. N the affection and understanding she needed.

Her father, who had died shortly after Mrs. N's marriage, played the more important role in Mrs. N's life. He was described as cold and remote, absorbed in interests outside the home. When he was angry he would not speak for hours. He was sarcastic, and often turned his sarcasm on Mrs. N. She was afraid of him when she was young, but in adolescence she came to "worship" him. She admired him as a man of purpose, and also realized that he was concerned about her and loved her, even though he could not be demonstrative.

It was through her father that Mrs. N met her husband. Mr. N studied geology with the father, and shared Mrs. N's admiration of him. She thought the main reason she had married Mr. N was to prove to her father that she could be sexually attractive; he had often told her that she must develop her mind, because this was the only way she could appeal to men.

Mr. N, in his interviews, appeared to be a very passive man, who gave an impression of detachment in all his relationships. He seemed to find his main satisfaction in the area of his work, but even here removed himself from people. Although he expressed sympathy for Mrs. N because of her handicap, he seemed to have little understanding of its meaning to her. He did express genuine feeling for his son, of whom he seemed very proud.

The relationship of husband and wife seemed much like that of siblings, based to a great extent on their individual identifications with Mrs. N's father. It was clear that this relationship was strongly influenced by the unfulfilled emotional needs of each of the partners. Since Mr. N appeared inaccessible, the relationship could be modified only through helping his wife. Even then, in view of the somewhat doubtful satisfactions for Mrs. N in the relationship, it appeared not unlikely that if she did benefit from treatment she might decide not to remain in the marriage.

Appraisal of Mrs. N's personality and evaluation of her capacities were necessarily influenced by consideration of the possible effects of her handicap. In view of such a limitation, it was a temptation to overestimate her strength and potentialities. She was intelligent and had accomplished a good deal in education and professional development. She had made a rather good adjustment in recreational activity and in the forming of social relationships outside the family. She had managed to hold a job, to marry, and to have a child, all of which seemed remarkable in view of a lifelong handicap. It was necessary to look beyond the constitutional strength and adaptive capacities that these attainments indicated to the elements in her basic character structure. The evidence of emotional deprivation in familial relationships, the quality and nature of her defenses, when assessed in terms of her present functioning, indicated that her essential strength was fragmentary. Her ideas of life and people were somewhat distorted, and her capacity to make relationships impaired. Her defenses had been effective in the relatively impersonal area of professional achievement, but they were not working well in the intimate relationships involved in being a wife and mother.

In view of the tentative diagnosis, it seemed that supportive treatment, geared toward helping Mrs. N to become re-stabilized and to function as she had previously, would be appropriate. On the other hand, Mrs. N had shown an extra potential in terms of her capacity to adjust and to master limitations. Also, some flexibility and limited capacity for insight were observed. These factors indicated that the goal of treatment might later be extended beyond re-stabilization to include some greater degree of understanding and insight on Mrs. N's part so that she could feel more comfortable with herself and give more to her family. This could take place only if the earlier part of the treatment were effective.

A supportive relationship, with predominantly positive feeling for the caseworker, had developed during the initial period of study. Mrs. N was not sure of her own goals, but she had demonstrated a real desire to be more comfortable and self-confident. The primary aim in treatment was to strengthen her sense of reality and to help her gain satisfying achievements.

The plan was carried out through a long period of interviews. An important part of treatment during the early months was the caseworker's participation in and support of Mrs. N's plan to acquire a job. The discussion around this area was on a simple, realistic level, and served, because of the positive casework relationship, to give strength to Mrs. N's effort to proceed with the difficult task. When it was finally accomplished, and a satisfactory child-care plan made, Mrs. N's symptoms diminished, and the generalized anxiety she had been feeling gradually subsided. She gained confidence with success in her work and she began to think more realistically about her marriage. At the same time, greater acceptance of her feminine role was indicated by a new, genuinely warm feeling about Danny.

As the early, limited goal was approached, a second evaluation of Mrs. N's personality was made. She had shown capacity for insight from the first, but testing of this was avoided when it appeared that she had all she could cope with in handling her everyday life problems. The goal shifted to some extent, in that insight into the meaning of her marriage was encouraged, still to a limited degree. She responded by thinking of the positive and negative aspects of the marriage. She recognized that because of her aversion to being pitied, she had often been oversensitive to any sign of rejection from her husband. This bit of understanding made it possible for her to reach out to him a little more spontaneously, and to share some of her feelings with him. Mr. N's response to the change in his wife and to the relief from financial pressure was gradual, but in the course of time he emerged a little from absorption in his own interests and participated to a greater extent in family activity. When he finally agreed that they should move to a home of their own and gave every indication of willingness to assume a part of the responsibility involved, Mrs. N felt that they were on their way toward a happier adjustment. There were still many frustrations for her in their daily living, but somehow she found it possible to cope with them more appropriately, with less feeling of being a kind of unappreciated Cinderella.

Brief Counseling Service

It is not always necessary to enter into a long-continued treatment plan with our clients. Occasionally, in the course of the study process itself, even before diagnostic impressions can be fully substantiated, we find that we have helped the client to find solutions of his own, to modify his situation to the point that harmony is restored.

Mr. S was a mild-mannered, pleasant young man. He conveyed, by his physical appearance and by his manner of presenting himself, a kind of sturdy self-reliance and stability. It was he who arranged interviews for himself and his wife after he had heard from a friend about the agency.

He told the caseworker that a week previously he had left home because it seemed to him that it was useless to continue the marriage. His wife had become very critical, nagged him about little things, and repeatedly reminded him of past grievances to the point that he could not believe that she cared for him. However, they both had been most unhappy during the separation, and he returned home within a few days. He said earnestly that he really loved his wife. They had been quite happy during the first two years of their marriage. Even now, when she was not angry and upset, he could not ask for a more satisfying companion. Although he voiced a good many complaints about what he considered his wife's unjustified criticism of him, it was significant that he said he wanted to "understand himself," to find out what he could do to improve the situation.

Mrs. S's attitude was strikingly different from her husband's. She could only complain of his deficiencies as she saw them, and proved quite unable to examine her own part in their troubles. She thought Mr. S spent too much time away from home. His recent activity in helping his father remodel a house seemed to her a deliberate expression of lack of concern for her, even though he was earning extra money. She had felt deserted when Mr. S was sent overseas during his enlistment in the Marine Corps active reserve. It became quite clear, also, that the recent temporary separation had been a terrifying threat to her. Her willingness to come to the agency seemed to be an attempt to ally the caseworker with her in the hope that her husband would be influenced to remain with her and to comply with her demands.

Mrs. S gave information about her background which shed light on her great need to be cared for and to maintain control. Her mother was never well after Mrs. S, the oldest in the family, was born, and she died after the birth of a third child, when Mrs. S was still quite young. The father could not keep his family together, and the children were shifted from one relative to another. It was not until Mrs. S married that she again felt some measure of security. The danger of losing her husband seemed to her to be a threat of wilful desertion, for which she could not possibly be responsible. It was evident, as Mrs. S revealed her current feelings in the light of the extreme early deprivation she had experienced, that she had a serious personality disorder. This was emphasized by the fact that she had gone through a psychotic episode after the birth of her first child. She told about this with marked blandness, and, as if she needed to deny the meaning it had had for her, she stressed the normalcy of her second pregnancy and delivery.

Mrs. S's overwhelming dependency, her need to blind herself to serious disturbances in her life experience and in herself, and her tendency to place unreasonable blame for the marital difficulty on her husband, made the possibility of modification in her attitudes remote. Had Mr. S demonstrated interlocking needs which prevented an appreciable measure of gratification for either him or Mrs. S, there could have been little hope for the marriage. As it was, Mr. S proved to have a personality that enabled him to fit his own needs to hers in a manner that was satisfying to both of them. He displayed unusual capacity for caring for others, and found considerable satisfaction in his wife's dependency. He took pride in his ability to provide for his family, and felt responsibility and concern for his children. He said that, as the oldest in a family of three, he had been given recognition and praise for the care he gave his younger siblings, so that caring for his own family seemed to be natural.

After the first satisfying period in the marriage, Mr. S had been quite unprepared for his wife's mental illness and the subsequent change he sensed in her. He was able to admit that he was haunted by the fear that she might become ill again, so he avoided argument, which might upset her, simply by walking out of the house when she started to scold. All his savings had been used to provide private care for Mrs. S when she was ill, and he had found it necessary to work on extra jobs to make up for the financial loss. He had joined the active reserve of the Marine Corps, with which he had previously served, only because he could make extra money. He had enlisted with Mrs. S's consent, so that her resentment when he was sent overseas in the Korean emergency seemed to him quite unjustified. According to Mr. S, his wife had acted as if he had been on a pleasure trip, leaving her to assume full responsibility for the family.

In the course of only four interviews, Mr. S found a remarkable measure of relief, and finally reported that he and his wife were getting along so much better that he did not feel it was necessary to continue. He explained that, in trying to understand his own feelings as they were involved in the conflict with his wife, he had come to understand her better also. He saw that she needed a great deal of protection and assurance of his affection. Although her criticisms and demands were excessive when she felt rejected, she responded to his efforts to please her by trying in turn to please him. He recognized also that his attempts to avoid upsetting her had only made matters worse. He was finding that letting her have her way in decisions that were important to her, but standing firm on those about which he had conviction, seemed to make things go much more smoothly. He groped for words to account for the change that had taken place, and came to the conclusion that his feelings and thoughts had been "shadowy." Talking them through, looking at his own and his wife's contributions to their differences, had somehow put everything into perspective so that he could see more clearly what he could do to bring contentment to their lives.

Conclusion

In conclusion I should like to reiterate that satisfying marriage and resultant happy family life still flourish and form the basis of our social structure. Happiness in marriage is achieved most readily by those who are free, through combinations of fortuitous circumstances, to attain harmony of their "natural interests" through family living. For these people, the frustrations and disappointments that are an inevitable part of living are more than balanced by the satisfactions of common interests and shared goals, and by mutual love and respect. To those who, for a variety of reasons, have failed to find a sufficient degree of satisfaction in marriage, the family agency offers its services.

It is the conviction of family agency caseworkers that these services can be of lasting benefit and meaning to clients if they are based on scientific appraisal of the individual personalities involved and of the complex interaction between marital partners and among all members of the family group. It is only as caseworkers bring to bear the utmost of their diagnostic skill and knowledge, tempered always by genuine concern for the individual, that they can fulfil responsibly their share of the task assigned to the family agency in helping people achieve happier family life.

Correlation of This Book
with Marriage and Family Texts

1950 OR LATER

Correlation of This Book with Marriage and Family Texts
Published or Revised in 1950 or Later

(The reader should use the index to locate short discussions of any specific subject.)

Text chs.	Baber: Marriage and the Family. McGraw-Hill, 1953	Becker and Hill: Family, Marriage and Parenthood. Heath, 1955	Bee: Marriage and Family Relations. Harper, 1959	Blood: Anticipating Your Marriage. Free Press, 1959	Bowman: Marriage for Moderns. McGraw-Hill, 1960
	Related Articles in *Marriage and Family in the Modern World: A Book of Readings*				
1	1–8, 11, 14, 16, 17	1, 12–17	7, 8, 11–17	5, 26–28, 34	3, 6, 7, 8, 11, 23–25
2	12, 13	3, 18–22	49	60, 61	1, 4, 5, 12–17, 55
3	41, 42		35	29–33	25, 34–37
4	18–22, 29, 30, 43, 60, 61		39	25, 35–38	30, 43, 49
5	26–28, 31–33, 44–48	12, 13	49	39, 40	18–22, 26–28, 31–33
6	6, 23–25, 35–38, 49, 62–65	34, 35, 49, 50	25, 35–38	41–48	39, 40
7	50, 51, 88–91	25–28, 34–38	5, 26–28, 34, 39, 40	31–33	29, 30
8	71–75, 78, 80–82	5, 29, 30, 34, 60, 61	29, 30		29, 60, 61
9	83, 84	18–22, 31–33, 39, 40, 43, 44, 46	39, 40	49, 54, 55	2, 41, 42, 50
10	56–58	49, 74	30, 60, 61	62–65	24, 50, 62–64, 70, 88, 89
11	54, 55	2, 4, 25, 37, 45, 47, 50, 51, 55, 56, 88, 89	31–33, 41, 42	62, 66–68, 85–87, 92, 93	23, 37, 51
12	9, 10, 15, 52, 53, 59, 69	51, 61–65, 93	2–4, 6, 50, 51, 63	25, 37, 50, 51	9, 52–59, 69
13	42, 66, 67	9, 52–59, 69	88–89	9, 52, 53, 56–59, 69	71–75

14	68, 70, 85–87	71–75	71–84	2, 6, 24, 25, 88–91	6, 10, 65, 76–84, 90, 91
15	76, 77	78	62–65	71–77, 79	43–48
16	39, 40	80, 84	50, 83	78	41, 42, 66–68, 85–87, 92, 93
17	39, 40, 79	6, 10, 15, 16, 48	41, 42, 66–68, 85–87	80–84	
18	92, 93	16, 53	1, 92, 93		
19		41, 42, 67, 79, 86			
20		60, 61		2, 6–11	
21		63–70, 85–87			
22		7, 8, 11, 23, 68, 70			
23		41, 42, 66, 67, 86			
24					
25					
26		84, 90–93			

Correlation of This Book with Marriage and Family Texts
Published or Revised in 1950 or Later (Continued)

(The reader should use the index to locate short discussions of any specific subject.)

Text chs.	Burgess and Locke: The Family. American Book, 1950	Butterfield: Planning for Marriage. Van Nostrand, 1956	Cavan: The American Family. Crowell, 1953	Cavan: American Marriage. Crowell, 1959	Christensen: Marriage Analysis. Ronald, 1958
		Related Articles in Marriage and Family in the Modern World: A Book of Readings			
1	2, 3, 7, 8, 11–13	1–4, 7, 8, 11	1–5	1–5	1–5
2	22	5, 34	12	7, 8, 11, 12–17	6–11, 14, 16, 17
3	12	26–28, 39, 40		35, 49	7, 8, 11, 12, 13
4	13–16	18–22, 29, 30, 35–38, 60, 61, 68	12–17	6, 18–22, 26–28	71–75
5		31–33		5, 34	35
6	18–21	62	69	25, 36–38	36, 49
7	17	17, 23–25, 30, 43–47, 49, 50, 55	69	29, 30	23–25, 52–58
8	49, 80, 83, 84	9, 52, 53, 56–59, 69		60, 61	
9	54–56	10, 15, 16, 48		31–33	39, 40
10		6–8, 11, 41, 42, 51	60, 61	39, 40	26–28, 36–38
11	2, 6, 54–58	50, 51, 88–91	6–11, 49	41–48	18–22, 41, 42
12	25, 26–28, 31–33, 35–38	71–79	26–28	2, 24, 25, 50	29, 30, 60, 61
13	29, 30, 60, 61	80–84	18–22, 29–34, 41–48	25, 37, 51	39, 43–48
14	4, 24, 25, 50, 51, 88	16	39, 40	9, 10, 15, 16, 59, 69	31–33, 41, 42
15	9, 59		25, 35–38		2, 50

16	14–16, 39, 40, 48, 51	62–70, 85–87, 92, 93	24, 25, 37, 50–59	52–58	9, 51–59, 88–91
17		5, 34	62–68	23, 62–64, 66–70, 85–87, 93	10, 15, 48, 62–67, 69, 85–87, 92, 93
18	62, 63, 65, 81, 82		71–87	88–91	76–79
19	64, 69		69	71–77, 79, 81, 82, 90, 91	80–84
20	23, 66–68, 70, 85–87		7, 8, 11, 23, 70, 88–91	71–78	88–91
21			14, 16, 17, 92, 93	65, 76, 80, 83, 84	5, 23, 34, 68, 70
22	1, 10, 15, 48, 92, 93			92, 93	92, 93

Correlation of This Book with Marriage and Family Texts
Published or Revised in 1950 or Later (Continued)

(The reader should use the index to locate short discussions of any specific subject.)

Text chs.	Clemens: Marriage and the Family . . . for Catholics. Prentice-Hall, 1957	Duvall: Family Development. Lippincott, 1957	Duvall and Hill: When You Marry. Heath, 1953	Fishbein and Kennedy: Modern Marriage and Family Living. Oxford, 1957	Himes and Taylor: Your Marriage. Rinehart, 1955
		Related Articles in *Marriage and Family in the Modern World: A Book of Readings*			
1	1-4, 6-11	1-4, 6-11	3; 35, 49	1	
2		12-22	25, 35-38	12-14, 16-22	18-22, 26-28
3	1-4		26-30		35-38
4	25, 35-38	69	18-22	60-61	5, 25, 34, 39, 40
5	5, 34, 52, 53, 55-58	6, 41, 42	31-33, 41, 42		
6	18-22, 26-28, 39, 40	23-25, 37, 41-51, 88, 89			29, 30, 49, 60, 61
7	29, 30, 60, 61	71-79	39, 40	41, 42, 66-68, 85-87	31-33, 39, 40
8	31-33, 41-48	80-83, 90, 91	5, 29, 30, 34, 43-48, 60, 61, 68	29, 30	88-91
9	6-8, 11, 23-25, 49-51	35		35-38	43-48
10	2, 88-91	9, 10, 59, 85-87	2, 4, 6-8, 11, 25, 37, 50, 51	26-28, 31-33	41, 42
11	60, 61	26-28, 84	9, 10, 15, 16, 52-59, 69	39, 40	2-4, 6-8, 11, 50, 63
12	25, 37, 51	29-33, 36-40, 43-49, 52-58, 60, 61, 88, 89	24, 62, 88, 89, 92, 93		29, 50

13	71–79	88–91	23, 63–65, 69, 70	6, 7, 8, 11, 41–48	25, 37, 51
14	80–84, 87	7, 8, 11, 23, 70, 90, 91	66–68, 85–87, 92, 93	3	10, 15, 16, 48
15	83	62–69, 92, 93	4, 5, 35–37		9, 53, 59, 69
16			71–75	25, 37, 51, 93	
17	9, 52, 53, 59, 69		76–79, 90, 91	2, 24, 25, 49, 50	
18	62–65, 92, 93		80–84	54, 55	52–58
19			60, 61	56–58	71–78
20			1, 12–17, 52, 83	9, 10, 15, 48, 52, 53, 59, 69	
21			1, 92, 93	63	
22					79
23					80–84
24				71–75	1, 92
25					41, 42, 62–68, 85–87
26				76–78, 81, 82	93
27					
28					
29					
30				35, 65, 80, 83, 84	
31				79	
32				68, 85–87	
33					
34					
35					
36					
37				84, 92	

Correlation of This Book with Marriage and Family Texts
Published or Revised in 1950 or Later (*Continued*)

(*The reader should use the index to locate short discussions of any specific subject.*)

Text chs.	Hirning and Hirning: Marriage. American Book, 1956	Kane: Marriage and the Family: A Catholic Approach. Dryden, 1952	Kirkpatrick: The Family, as Process and Institution. Ronald, 1955	Koos: Marriage. Holt, 1957	Judson T. and Mary C. Landis: Building a Successful Marriage. Prentice-Hall, 1958
	Related Articles in *Marriage and Family in the Modern World: A Book of Readings*				
1	1, 12–17	1–5, 7–8, 11	1, 7, 8, 11	1–5, 12–17	1–8, 11–14, 17
2	3, 4, 9, 41, 42, 52, 53, 59	18–22	3, 23–25, 36, 37	41, 42	23–25, 55
3		14–17	18–22		52–54, 56–58
4	23–25	12–13		35, 49, 50	26–28
5	4	26–28, 31–33, 35–40, 93		29, 30, 60, 61, 69	18–22
6	35–38	3–5, 29, 30, 43–48, 60, 61	12–17, 57	18–22, 26–30, 39, 40	5, 34
7	29, 30, 49, 60, 61	29, 30, 60, 61	55	25, 34–38	29, 30
8	92		6, 17	31–33	49
9	26–28, 39, 40	24, 25, 35, 49, 50	35, 71–79, 81, 82	6–11, 43–48	35–38
10	18–22, 39, 40	6, 9, 10, 12, 13, 52–59, 69	83	24, 25, 50, 51, 54–58	43–48, 68
11	31–33	62–65, 81, 82, 88, 89	43–49	62–65	39, 40
12	6–8, 11, 41–48	23, 41, 42, 66–68, 70, 85–87	26–28, 36–38	37, 51	60, 61
13	2	51, 71–79	29–33	9, 52–54, 59, 69	31–33

14	2	80, 83, 84	39, 40	60, 61	41, 42
15	24, 25, 37, 50	1, 12–17, 41, 42, 92, 93	2	88–91	50, 62–64, 66, 67, 92, 93
16	25, 37, 51		3–5, 41, 42	71–82, 90	25, 37, 51
17	71–79, 81, 82		52–58		23, 70, 88, 89
18	62–65, 88, 89		50, 51, 59, 60, 61, 88–91		60
19	41, 42, 66–68, 85–87		71–84	66–68, 85–87	9, 52, 53, 57–59, 69
20	10, 15, 16, 55–58, 80, 83, 84, 88–91		62–65, 69, 70, 88–91	7, 8, 11, 23, 70, 88–91	10, 15, 16
21			41, 42, 66, 67	92, 93	71–75, 78
22			68, 85–87		76, 77
23			92, 93		79
24					65, 80–82, 90, 91
25					83–87
26					

Correlation of This Book with Marriage and Family Texts
Published or Revised in 1950 or Later (*Continued*)

(The reader should use the index to locate short discussions of any specific subject.)

Text chs.	Paul H. Landis: Making the Most of Marriage. Appleton-Century-Crofts, 1960	LeMasters: Modern Courtship and Marriage. Macmillan, 1957	Magoun: Love and Marriage. Harper, 1956	Merrill: Courtship and Marriage. Holt, 1959	Mihanovich, Schnepp and Thomas: Marriage and the Family. Bruce, 1952
	Related Articles in Marriage and Family in the Modern World: A Book of Readings				
1	3, 4, 5, 12–14, 17, 35	1–5, 14, 17	25, 35–38		1–5, 12–14, 17
2		12, 13	1–11		18–22, 24, 25–33, 41–49
3	3		35	25, 29, 36–38	39, 40, 51, 71–75, 92, 93
4	23–25	18–22	49	38, 54	35–38, 50, 88–91
5	24, 25	26–28	39, 40	12–17	9, 10, 15, 16, 52, 53, 55–59, 69
6	54–58		29, 30, 43–48, 60, 61	26	60, 61
7	52, 53		18–22, 26–28, 36, 37	27, 28	
8			31–33	18–22	41, 42
9	18–22, 35–37	31–33	41, 42	29, 30, 60, 61, 68	2, 6, 50, 51
10	38	39, 40	25, 37, 51	29, 35–37, 88, 89	71–84
11	26–28	41–48, 50, 92, 93	9, 24, 25, 49, 50, 52–59, 69, 88, 89	31–33, 39, 40	23, 69, 70
12	39, 40	25, 29, 35–38, 49	71–84	6–8, 11, 41, 42, 50	41, 42, 62–68, 85–87

13			41, 42, 62–68, 85–87, 92, 93	25, 37, 51	
14	29, 30	54, 69	60, 61	24, 25	12–14
15	60, 61	88–91		9, 54–56, 59	7, 8, 11
16	30, 68	60, 61		52, 53, 57, 58	
17	5, 34, 43–49	25, 37, 51		76, 77, 81	
18		63		78, 81, 82	
19	31–33	9, 52, 53, 59, 69		65, 79, 80, 83, 84, 90, 91	
20	39, 40	10, 15, 16, 48		62–64	
21	1, 2, 6, 41, 42, 88, 89	55–58		29, 49	
22	50	23–25		41, 42, 66, 67, 85, 86	
23		54–56		11, 23, 70	
24	24, 25, 37, 51, 63	71–79, 81, 82		68, 87	
25	24, 25, 51	65, 80, 83–87		92, 93	
26	9, 52–59	41, 42, 62–64, 66–68			
27	10, 15, 16, 48, 69	6–8, 10, 11, 90, 91			
28	71–75, 78				
29	65, 76, 77, 79, 81, 82				
30	80, 83				
31	84				
32	5, 34				
33	6–8, 11, 23, 70, 90, 91				
34	41, 42, 62–64, 66–68, 85–87, 93				
35	92, 93				

Correlation of This Book with Marriage and Family Texts
Published or Revised in 1950 or Later (Continued)

(The reader should use the index to locate short discussions of any specific subject.)

Related Articles in Marriage and Family in the Modern World: A Book of Readings

Text chs.	Peterson: Education for Marriage. Scribner's, 1956	Skidmore and Cannon: Building Your Marriage. Harper, 1958	Truxal and Merrill: Marriage and the Family in American Culture. Prentice-Hall, 1953	Waller and Hill: The Family: A Dynamic Interpretation. Dryden, 1951	Winch: The Modern Family. Holt, 1952
1	1–5, 12–17	1–5, 7, 8, 11–17, 57	1	1, 6, 12–17, 24, 25	1, 2, 12–17, 41, 42
2	6, 71–75		12–22	2, 3	18–22
3	80, 83, 90, 91	35, 49			9, 52, 53, 57, 59
4	49, 84	35–38		49	69
5	18–22, 26–28, 39, 40	26–28			
6	29			18–22	35
7	7, 8, 11, 23–25, 29, 30, 43–48, 60, 61	18–22, 60, 61	35–38	25, 35–38	6–11, 71–79
8	9, 52–59, 69	29, 30, 68	5, 26–28, 34, 39, 40	26–28	80–82
9		60, 61	29–33		55, 56, 83
10	25, 31–33, 35–38	3, 41, 42, 71–75	9, 50, 52–58, 69, 88, 89		49, 84
11	41, 42, 93	88–91	2, 51	5, 29, 30, 34, 43–48, 60, 61	23–25, 55, 88–91
12	30, 43–48	30, 43–48	3	31–33, 41, 42	35–37
13	24, 25, 37, 50, 51, 88, 89	31–33	24, 25	4, 6–8, 11, 50	25, 37–40

14	71–79, 81, 82	39, 40	6, 9, 15, 16, 41–48	51, 55, 59, 69, 88, 89	38
15	78	6, 51	7, 8, 11	62, 64	29, 60, 61
16	25, 37, 51	2, 25, 37, 50, 51		36, 37, 39, 40, 54	2–5, 25–28, 31–34, 37, 50, 51
17		24, 25, 35–38	6		62–68, 85–87, 92, 93
18	9, 55–59	9, 10, 15, 16, 48, 52–59, 69		6, 9, 10, 71–79, 81, 82	
19		62–64	49	56, 80, 83, 84	
20	62–68, 84–87, 92, 93	41, 42, 66–68, 85–87	76–84, 90, 91	90, 91	
21		76–79	62–65	64, 65, 69, 88, 89, 91	
22		65, 80–84	60, 61	23, 68, 70	
23		23, 70, 90, 91	23, 66, 70	41, 42, 63, 66, 67	
24		1, 92, 93	41, 42, 66–68, 85–87	68, 85–87	
25			92, 93	92, 93	
26					

Index

603